Understanding the *
Volume II

The Pot Plot: Marijuana, Hip Hop and the Scientific Assault on Black America

Wesley Muhammad, Ph.D.

A-Team Publishing
Atlanta

A-TEAM PUBLISHING
PO Box 551036
Atlanta GA, 30355
www.ateampublishing.com

Contents

Part II:

Nixon's War

Part III:

Scientific Genocide

VII. THC and Female Sexual Behavior – in Males
Excursus: White Scientists and Black Zombies

Part V:

The Weaponization of Hip Hop

Part VI:

The Queering of Hip Hop

Part I

The Testosterone Conspiracy And the Estrogen Assault

Chapter One:

The Government Declares War on Black Masculinity

I.   *The Motive*

Depending on what defining criteria are used, there were between 750 and 820 urban rebellions or riots across hundreds of U.S. cities in the eight years between 1964 and 1971 (and approximately one thousand over the course of the decade, 1960-1971, according to some reports), resulting in at least 228 deaths, 12,741 people injured, 69,099 arrests, with 15,835 incidents of arson. 1967-1968 were the zenith years, with more than 160 disorders occurring in 128 cities in

the first nine months of 1967 alone.[1] This "convulsive wave of mob violence" with "black ghettos explode[ing]...in a cataclysm of frustration and rage" was trivialized by a number of white sociologists (such as the influential Seymour Spilerman) as "instances of substantial racial violence" rooted in "Negro aggression."[2] "Negro aggression" is a key phrase here that will take on great significance as we proceed.

The Detroit Rebellion in the summer of 1967 was one of the biggest urban rebellions in the history of the United States. Over five days in July 43 persons died (33 African Americans

---

[1] John F. McDonald, "The Great Society and the Urban Riots" in idem., *Postwar Urban America: Demography, Economics, and Social Politics* (New York: Routledge, 2015) 127-135; Virginia Postrel, "The Consequences of the 1960's Race Riots Come Into View," *The New York Times* December 30, 2004; Seymour Spilerman, "The Causes of Racial Disturbances: A Comparison of Alternative Explanation," *American Sociological Disturbances* 35 (1970): 627-649.
[2] Spilerman, "Causes of Racial Disturbances," 630.

and 10 Whites), 1200 were injured, more than 7000 were arrested, and an estimated $50 million in property damage was caused. Governor George Romney ordered the Michigan Army National Guard in and, at first, President Johnson refused to send in federal troops due to the stipulation of the Insurrection Act of 1807 restricting the government from deploying military troops within the U.S. until state or local authorities declared a state of insurrection in their area. This Governor Romney did and on July 24 President Johnson sent in the 82nd and the 101st Airborn Division, "which meant that the people of Detroit were to be considered a rebelling enemy force."[3] The 17,000 officers and military personnel that occupied the streets thus "gave the appearance that the city was a warzone," which it literally was after July 24.

The Detroit rebellion was "a cultural hinge point, after which nothing was the same,"[4] according to Michael Hodges of **The Detroit News**. Its significance was not restricted to the city or even to the U.S., but had global implications, according to University of Washington Bothell professor Scott Kurashige:

> The Detroit uprising...marked a dramatic turn in the battle over alternative futures, and it was *central* to an overall pattern of social rebellions, anticolonial revolts, and global uprisings of the oppressed in 1967-68 (emphasis added-WM).[5]

As we shall see below, the U.S. government also recognized what was *really* going on in its cities – the apparent beginnings of a revolution.

Somehow, this cataclysmic convulsion abruptly fizzled out during the Nixon administration, never to truly percolate or erupt again (until 1992).

> The period of 1964 to 1971 was a period of widespread urban rioting that is unique in U.S. history. The nation has experienced a small number of large-scale urban riots since 1971, such as Miami in 1980

---

[3] Carvell Wallace, "After Michigan's governor declared a full 'insurrection,' the president sent tanks to fire on Detroit," **Timeline** July 23.
[4] Michael Hodges, "Rebellion or riot: three books examine Detroit 1967," **The Detroit News** July 19, 2017.
[5] Scott Kurashige, "1967 Detroit riots, 'resistance,' then and now," **Al Jazeera** July 23, 2017.

and Los Angeles in 1992, but there has been no repeat of the riots of the 1960s.[6]

How was this fizzling out affected? The subsequent Nixon Administration's chief domestic policy, it appears, was: actively pursuing the quieting of this "cataclysm of frustration and rage," but not by urban reconstruction or economic relief for the poor. Rather, through an intense covert war on Black America, a war directed in particular against the Black male's body, mind, and masculinity-a carceral and *chemical* war.

II.   *The Government Prepares for Revolution and War*

Detroit in particular compelled President Johnson to respond to the rebellions in two ways that are critical here (in addition to treating it legally as an insurrection).

First: President Johnson established the National Advisory Commission on Civil Disorders to investigate the cause of the riots. President Johnson put attorney David Ginsburg, former counsel to the Jewish Agency in Washington,[7] in charge as executive director. On November 22, 1967 the first draft of the Commission's report was delivered to Ginsburg by Robert Shallow, the Commission's deputy director of research. Entitled "The Harvest of American Racism: The Political Meaning of Violence in the Summer of 1967," this first draft was blistering. The 120 social scientists who worked on the report collected data damning to Johnson's Great Society programs, "tokens" that, the report said, failed to tamper with the "white power structure" enough to have a real impact. It was not "Negro aggression" that lay at the root of the riots, but white racism reinforced by the white power structure. The 176-page report observed: "A truly *revolutionary* spirit has begun to take hold, an unwillingness to compromise or wait any longer, to risk death rather than have their people continue in a subordinate status (emphasis added)."

Revolution – even *violent* revolution - was in the air among Black people in 1967, and the careful observers saw it. "The Harvest" likened the urban rebels to Colonial

---

[6] McDonald, "The Great Society and the Urban Riots" 131.

[7] William Grimes, "David Ginsburg, Longtime Washington Insider, Dies at 98," *The New York Times* May 25, 2010.

revolutionaries of America's early beginnings. In a provocative chapter entitled, "America on the Brink: White Racism and Black Rebellion," the authors argue that "whites must change." The draft concluded that these "revolutionary" uprisings could only be dealt with via a major investment in and transformation of the Black communities. But this damning indictment of President Johnson, the Great Society, and American White Supremacy never saw the light of day, except as a battered manuscript that managed to escape the destruction that was ordered for it and now grows dusty in a presidential library.[8] When Ginsburg and his deputy Victor Palmieri read the draft report, the former lost his cool, cursed and screamed while the latter threw the manuscript against the wall. After all, Deputy Executive Director Palmieri had described the process of the Commission's staff recruitment as "a war strategy."[9] *War* was the underlying objective, not relief for the inner-cities. Thus, what happened next was predictable: "The executive staff of lawyers concluded that a new report would need to be written. *Ginsburg fired all 120 social scientists who had worked on the draft*."[10] Fired too was Shellow, who happened to have also been Assistant Director of Research at the National Institutes of Health! According to one researcher, the White House sent an appointee to the Commission with instructions to "re-work Harvest into an acceptable form."[11]

The "acceptable" report, released on February 29, 1968 and now known as the official Kerner Report, is much milder than "Harvest" in its language and indictments, but it is still

---

[8] A creased and battered manuscript today lies in the archives of the Kerner Commission at the Lyndon B. Johnson Presidential Library in Austin, Texas. It still has the hastily scrawled letters "DesTRoy" across the front page. See Malcolm McLaughlin, "Harvest of American Racism," in **The Long Hot Summer of 1967: Urban Rebellions in America** (New York: Palgrave MacMillan, 2014) 43-60.

[9] Michael Lipsky and David J. Olson, **Commission Politics: The Processing of Racial Crisis in America** (Transactions Books, 1971) 161.

[10] Julian E. Zelizer, "Fifty Years Ago, the Government Said Black Lives Matter," **Boston Review** May 5, 2016.

[11] See Kevin Mumford, "Harvesting the Crisis: The Newark Uprising, the Kerner Commission, and Writings on Riots," in **African American Urban History Since World War II**, ed. Kenneth L. Kusmer and Joe W. Trotter (Chicago and London: The University of Chicago, 2009) 209-210.

hard-hitting enough in its analysis to provoke anger by President Johnson and even backlash by President Nixon (viz. his collusion with Attorney General John Mitchell to railroad and set up for prosecution and conviction Otto Kerner, who chaired the Commission, because of the controversial findings of the Report[12]). The Report ultimately blamed white racism and economic inequality for producing the conditions that provoked the riots. The riots involved mostly young Black men who were acting against oppressive White society, authority and property, the Report argued. Unless the prevailing conditions were corrected, large-scale and continuing violence could result, followed by White retaliation. This prediction of continuing violence from young Black males of America's cities was taken to heart.

Second: The same month that the Kerner Report was published, February 1968, a governmental blueprint for suppressing domestic civil disturbances – a counterinsurgency plan - was officially constituted as the federal contingency plan for handling the revolution seen coming. The Department of Defense Civil Disturbance Plan 55-2, codenamed Operation Garden Plot, was a joint Justice Department-Pentagon program for the imposition of martial law in the event of civil disorders. The principal components of Operation Garden Plot were the following:

** A Domestic War Room was established in the basement of the Pentagon to serve as a command center for the deployment of 25,000 specially trained airborne troops stationed at Fort Campbell, Ky. and Fort Bragg, N.C. This War Room was fitted with detailed blueprints for military occupations of every prominent U.S. city that had experienced urban unrest or was profiled as a potential center of such disorders.
** The Justice Department's Interdepartmental Intelligence Unit (IDIU) was established as a massive computer dossier bank drawing in profile information on millions of American citizens gleaned from every federal and state agency maintaining computerized records. The IDIU conception was not to build a static bank of "dirty laundry," but to maintain an ongoing "tracking capability"... On the basis of the "tracking" and as one feature's of Garden Plot, a list was compiled by the Justice Department (under the name ADEX) of individuals

---

[12] According to released Nixon Oval Office Tapes, May 28, 1971 NARA 506-13.

7

targeted for immediate detention at the first activation of civil disorders.

** Corollary training programs for civilian and local and state police officials were conducted in every region of the country to bring local government agencies directly into the Garden Plot umbrella and to facilitate the transition from civilian to martial rule. These training programs were also designed as profiling and recruiting vehicles for establishing networks in every major city through which to implement counterinsurgency policies against the local populations.[13]

The Nixon Administration will inherit Operation Garden Plot and make use of it in the War that it waged on Black America.

III. *Pathologizing and Criminalizing Black Masculinity: Project Ferdinand*

In the wake of the black urban uprisings of the late 1960s, America became preoccupied with the threatening figure of the young black male as well as the overall danger of rebellion and social chaos. Led by [the National Institute of Mental Health] and the Justice Department, the federal government began to develop an overall program for biomedical control of violence...It...was inspired by fear of violence in the inner-city and aimed at control of young black males. Peter R. Breggin and Ginger Ross Breggin, "a biomedical program for urban violence control in the US: the dangers of psychiatric social

---

[13] "Carter Administration Revives 'Operation Garden Plot,'" ***Executive Intelligence Review*** 4 (April 5, 1977): 1-4, 2-3. On Operation Garden Plot see further Peter Dale Scott, ***The American Deep State: Big Money, Big Oil, and The Struggle for U.S. Democracy*** (Lanham: Rowman & Littelfield, 2017) 148-149; Donald Goldberg and Indy Badhwar, "Blueprint for Tyranny," ***Penthouse Magazine*** August 1985, p. 72; Frank Morales, "U.S. Military Civil Disturbance Planning: The War At Home," ***CovertAction Quarterly*** 69 (Spring/Summer 2000); James W. Button, ***Black Violence: Political Impact of the 1960s Riots*** (Princeton: Princeton University Press, 1978) 133: "Better known as the domestic war room, the Directorate had 150 officials to carry out around-the-clock monitoring of civil disorders, as well as to oversee federal troop deployments when necessary. At the cost of $2.7 million, this massive directorate also developed policy advise for the secretary of the Army on all disturbances and maintained intelligence packets on all major U.S. cities."

control," ***Change: An International Journal of Psychology and Psychotherapy*** 11 (March 1993).

Ferdinand The Bull was a gentle and kind natured fighting bull who, while the largest and strongest bull among his peers and capable of great ferocity, persistently refused to do any fighting. All he wanted to do was sit around all day enjoying the beautiful smell of flowers, that herb. Nothing the matador could do to Ferdinand would make him want to fight his tormentor. That's the Black Man in America. But we were deliberately *made that way* scientifically in a documented operation I call Project Ferdinand.[14]

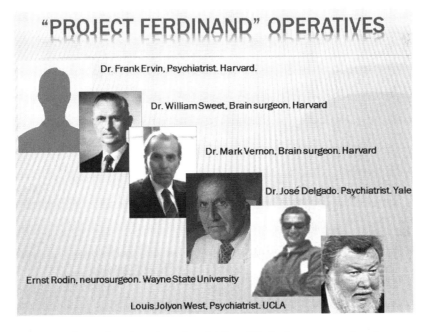

"PROJECT FERDINAND" OPERATIVES

Dr. Frank Ervin, Psychiatrist. Harvard.

Dr. William Sweet, Brain surgeon. Harvard

Dr. Mark Vernon, Brain surgeon. Harvard

Dr. José Delgado. Psychiatrist. Yale

Ernst Rodin, neurosurgeon. Wayne State University

Louis Jolyon West, Psychiatrist. UCLA

The scientists involved identified the aggressive inner-city males as "Fighting Black Bulls," like that black Aurochs bull in this 19th century painting below fighting off a pack of pale wolves. That was once the Black Man, the strongest and most fearless of all mega beasts of the Old World, but Project Ferdinand used psychochemical weapons to chemically castrate

---

[14] On Project Ferdinand see Wesley Muhammad, ***Understanding The Assault of the Black Man, Black Manhood and Black Masculinity***, **Volume I** (Atlanta: A-Team Publishing, 2017) 153-168.

us and make us fearful and docile towards the pale wolves surrounding us here in America. The Pot Plot grew out of Project Ferdinand.

The Detroit Rebellion motivated the Project Ferdinand operatives. The letter by the Boston doctors Vernon Mark, Frank Ervin and William Sweet to the *Journal of the American Medical Association* published in September 1967, "Role of Brain Disease in Riots and Urban Violence,"[15] was stimulated by the Detroit uprising. They claimed that this uprising was a display of "pathologic aggression"; that the young Black males at the root of the rebellion suffered from mental illness: "mild epilepsy" caused by a damaged or malfunctioning **amygdala** (an almond-shape set of neurons located deep in the brain's medial temporal lobe). This diseased amygdala was "causally related to poor impulse control and violent behavior." This mental illness was not limited to rioters though: the social protestors and their leaders were motivated by this "psychomotor epilepsy" as well.[16] Ultimately, "chemical lobotomy" or "psychopharmacological intervention" would be the method used to subdue the "black masculinized hostility" seething in America's inner-cities.

As Dr. Jonathan Metzl, Frederick B. Rentschler II Professor of Sociology and Psychiatry and Director of the Center for Medicine, Health and Society at Vanderbilt University documents: "psychiatric definitions of insanity...police racial hierarchies, tensions, and unspoken codes...Mainstream culture ... defines threats to this racial order as a form of madness that is...overwhelmingly located in the minds and bodies of black men."[17] Some psychiatrists classified this specifically black male psychosis as a form of epilepsy; some as a form of schizophrenia. As a consequence of the urban rebellions of the '60s, the latter term especially came to be used to pathologize not only   radical protest against the racial order

---

[15] Frank Ervin, Vernon Mark and William Sweet, "Role of Brain Disease in Riots and Urban Violence," *Journal of the American Medical Association* 201 (September 11, 1967): 895.
[16] Vernon Mark and Frank Ervin, "Is There a Need to Evaluate the Individuals Producing Human Violence?" *Psychiatric Opinion* 32 (1968): 5; David Bird, "More Stress Urged on Cause of Civil Disorders," *New York Times* Aug 14, 1968: 19; Vernon H. Mark,
[17] Jonathan M. Metzl, *The Protest Psychosis: How Schizophrenia Became A Black Disease* (Boston: Beacon Press, 2009) ix.

and dominance hierarchy, but to pathologize *angry black masculinity*: "mainstream white newspapers in the 1960s and 1970s describe schizophrenia as a condition of angry black masculinity,"[18] Metzl writes. A symptom of this racialized disease is a "social belligerence that requires chemical management" via "psychochemical technologies of control." An example of these is the antipsychotic drug Haldol first released in 1967 (See **Picture 3)**. Metzl observes:

> Nowhere was this racialized resonance between emerging definitions of schizophrenia and emerging anxieties about black protest seen more clearly than in pharmaceutical advertisements for new antipsychotic medications that appeared in the pages of leading American psychiatric journals...[A]n advertisement for the major tranquilizer Haldol from the **Archives of General Psychiatry** showing an angry, hostile African American man with a clenched, inverted Black Power fist. This James Brown-like figure literally shakes his fist at the assumed physician viewer, while the orange, burning, urban setting appears to directly reference civil unrest in cities such as Los Angeles, Detroit, and Newark...(T)he ad compels psychiatrists to diagnose *masculinized black anger* and unrest as explicit threats not to patients, but to the social order represented by "white" doctors. The ad gives phantasmagoric illustration to [...the...] contention that black anger corporeally threatens white authority. Indeed, the high-profile ad works by asking doctors to identify with their own projected fears – it asks its assumed white viewers to be scared. The ad goes a step further by suggesting that a doctor's racial anxiety could be assuaged by *chemically subduing threats represented by unruly black men.*[19]

> The Haldol ad ...suggests that the politicized figure...will assault the assumed viewer of the image if not given Haldol immediately...[T]he ad troublingly posits Haldol as a clinical treatment for a social, political, economic, and of course racial "problem."[20]

---

[18] Metzl, **Protest Psychosis**, xv.
[19] Jonathan M. Metzl, **The Protest Psychosis: How Schizophrenia Became A Black Disease** (Boston: Beacon Press, 2009) 102 -103.
[20] Jonathan Metzl, MD, PhD, "Images of Healing and Learning: Mainstream Anxieties about Race in Antipsychotic Drug Ads," **Virtual Mentor: American Medical Association Journal of Ethics** 14 (2012): 494-502 (496, 497).

Chemically subduing the threat to white society posed by angry Black masculinity became the objective not only of the pharmaceutical companies but of federal and state government as well.

When you go from over 1000 uprisings in a decade (1960-1971) to 4 or 5 or even 10 significant uprisings over 3 decades, something happened, and it wasn't economic advancement or social improvement. What happened to make the Black Man so peacefully accepting of his wretched lot in racist America? What happened was Government-funded psychiatrists and white social scientists diagnosed the problem of the urban uprisings as a problem of the Black male mind, a disease in his brain that manifests as a pathological "black masculinized hostility," i.e. black masculinity that is hostile to white oppression and abuse. After the uprisings of the 1960s Black male masculinity was literally defined as a social illness rooted in a brain sickness. And if Black masculinity is the *diseased condition* of the Black Male in society, what is the socially *heathy condition* of the Black male in society? Answer: if aggressive Black *masculinity* is the medical *problem*, then docile Black *femininity* is the medical *solution*.

How exactly did the government transform a fearless fighting bull into a fearful, docile ox? By chemically targeting 2 things: our amygdala and our testosterone. By damaging our amygdala, which was the aim of Project Ferdinand scientists, and/or by diminishing testosterone to a level too low to act on the amygdala, a number of catastrophic results occur:

1. No threat can even be perceived and therefore no appropriate physical and psychological response to the threat can be mounted. [Thus, Black Americans sit surrounded by a pack of pale wolves and don't even perceive them as *the* threat to our very existence that they are. The "Negro" still wants integrated equality with his natural predator. The White Man is not the natural predator of the Black Man. He is the natural predator of the Negro. There is a difference.]

2. The person with a damaged or inactivated amygdala can be made "docile, subdued, and easy to manage" by an enemy because such damage mutes the instinct to fight, like Ferdinand.

3. Depending on which part of the amygdala is damaged, even an apex predator can be made to fear its easy prey – like a cat terrified by a mouse; or the prey can be made to fail to perceive and respond to the threat posed by his natural, long time enemy - like a mouse that continues to sniff around casually as a hissing snake approaches, or like a cat who continues to clean its fur unbothered by the barking dog approaching. This is how the Negro is in the presence of his 400-year tormentor.

How did we go from over 1000 urban uprisings between 1960 and 1971 to only a handful or so since then? Because the Black man's amygdala and testosterone were successfully targeted during the 1970's up until this very day. How did this happen? The process by which you turn a strong, fearless fighting Bull of the inner-city into a Ferdinand, a tame, castrated ox is to interfere with his amygdala, lower his testosterone and raise his estrogen, thereby biochemically feminizing him. Weed is a part of this process. As we shall demonstrate, the weed being smoked lowers testosterone in men and raises estrogen levels. In addition, the THC significantly reduces amygdala reactivity to signals of threat.[21] It interferes with the amygdala's ability to perceive threats in our environment. Thus, with our lowered testosterone and our

---

[21] See below.

13

unresponsive amygdala, we don't even perceive the threat posed by our Enemies. In addition to our lack of threat perception we don't have the biochemical fuel – testosterone - necessary to propel us to seek power by rising up against our tyrannical 400 year-long oppressor. We don't have "the juice."

IV.   *The Black Muslim Problem*

But there is more. This "mental disorder" referred to as "back masculine hostility" was said at this time to be caused by...Islam. In 1968 two Jewish[22] psychiatrists from New York, Walter Bromberg and Franck Simon, published an article claiming that the cause of this "racialized" schizophrenia, which they describe as a "protest psychosis," was caused by the Islam of the Most Honorable Elijah Muhammad and the Nation of Islam[23]: "Bromberg and Simon argued that themes of Africa and Islam, so central to the ideologies of Elijah Muhammad, Malcom X, and other leaders, were the causal agents in the path to insanity."[24]   They claimed that the psychotic hostility evidenced in the urban rioters or Civil Rights protesters "emerged because black men listened to the words of Malcom X, joined the Black Power Movement, or 'espoused African or Islamic ideologies." This caused a "reactive psychosis" in Black men, the psychiatrists claimed.

> influenced by social pressures (the Civil Rights Movement), dips into religious doctrine (the Black Musslim [sic] Group), is guided in content by African subcultural ideologies and is colored by a denial of Caucasian values and hostility thereto. This protest psychosis among prisoners is virtually a repudiation of "white civilization."

> The religious ideas are Moslem in character, either directly from Mohammedan practice or improvised: they uniformly are

---

[22] Walter Bromberg, is definitely Jewish, having "grew up in a Jewish environment in New York City": ***Discovering the History of Psychiatry***, ed. Mark S. Micale and Roy Porter (New York: Oxford University Press, 1994) 71. While I could find no confirmation on the ethnicity of Franck Simon, "Simon" is an Askenazi Jewish surname, but not exclusively so. It is said to come from the Hebrew Šim'ôn, "listen."

[23] Walter Bromberg and Franck Simon, "The 'Protest Psychosis': A Special Type of Reactive Psychosis," ***Arch Gen Psychiat*** 19 (1968): 155-160.

[24] Metzl, ***Protest Psychosis***, 101.

14

overdetermined and point towards the eventual (and current?) supremacy of the black race over the whites. The psychotic productions merge into utterances of those Moslems (in the USA) who advocate no less than dethronement of the traditional evaluation of white supremacy in religion and culture.[25]

Thus, these scientists are persuading America that the mental health problem attributed to the urban rebels is caused by listening to the Black Muslims and joining the Nation of Islam or the Black Power Movement: "Schizophrenia was a particularly complex term for Black Power, Black Nationalism, Nation of Islam, and other movements advocating nonpassive resistance or armed self-defense."[26] And if the Black Muslims/Nation of Islam are a problem, they are a problem *to be solved.* We will be this idea again.

America became preoccupied with the threatening figure of the inner-city Black male (especially those influenced and the Nation of Islam) and the US Government consciously decided to "mind-fix" him first through a program of psychosurgery - sticking needles in our brain to damage particular areas[27] - and secondly to chemically subdue the threat posed by "Black masculinized hostility" by shooting us up with a whole medicine cabinet of drugs - psychochemical agents - intended to medicate and thus cure us of our aggressive Black masculinity. This is what the Most Honorable Elijah Muhammad called "the assault by chemico-biological scientists." And marijuana was one of those medications, as we shall see. It's medicinal indeed: it medicates the Black male's manhood.

---

[25] Walter Bromberg and Franck Simon, "The 'Protest' Psychosis," *Arch Gen Psychiat* 19 (1968): 155-160 (156).
[26] Metzl, *Protest Psychosis*, 121.
[27] See Wesley Muhammad, *Understanding The Assault on the Assault on the Black Man, Black Manhood, and Black Masculinity* (Atlanta: A-Team Publishing, 2016) 154-159.

Chapter Two:

Testosterone: The Power Hormone

I.　　*What is Testosterone?*

Testosterone is a steroid hormone. Hormones are the chemical messengers of the endocrine system (ES), which is a collection of various glands in the body that secrete these chemical messengers (hormones) directly into the blood stream. A steroid is a chemical derived from 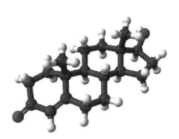 cholesterol. In the male testes are enzymes which progressively shape the cholesterol molecule by chopping off bits or adding atoms, thereby sculpting the cholesterol base into any one of the desired steroid hormones. Testosterone is one such steroid hormone belonging to the family of hormones called *androgens*, which are the male or *masculinizing* hormones in vertebrates (from the Greek *andros* meaning male human being). The female or feminizing steroid hormones are called *estrogens* because they produce the state of "estrus" where the female animal is in heat. The term derives from the Greek *oistros*, meaning "frenzy."

Women have testosterone too but only 1/10 of what men have. The average man has 300 to 1000 nanograms of testosterone in a deciliter of blood plasma. The average woman has 40 to 60 nanograms per deciliter. Testosterone is produced in the testes of men and ovaries of women and an amount is also produced in the outer layer of the adrenal glands in both sexes.

While a man's testosterone is produced in his testes the complex process that regulates the amount and timing of this production actually begins in his brain. The hypothalamus, which is an area at the base of the brain that regulates much hormone activity, sends a signal to the pituitary gland. This signal is in the form of the release to the pituitary of a substance called gonadotropin releasing hormone (GnRH). GnRH then produces two other hormones: follicle stimulating hormone (FSH) and luteinizing hormone (LH), which together are known as gonadotropins. LH then is released into the blood and travels to the testes where it stimulates the production of testosterone by Leydig cells. When FSH is released into the blood and travels to the testes it is involved in the production of sperm.

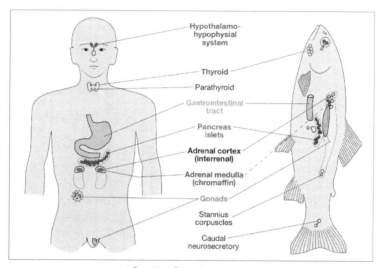

The Endocrine System

Testosterone and other androgens have their effect only by binding to a large complex protein called an Androgen Receptor (AR) located in the cytoplasm of the cell which then (after binding) travels to the cell nucleus and activates or deactivates certain genes.

II.   *The "He" Hormone: Gender Difference and Sexual Orientation*

Testosterone "is at the root of what we call 'masculinty'," in the words of Dr. Joe Herbert, Emeritus Professor of Neuroscience at the Univesity of Cambridge.[28] ***The New York Times*** writer Andrew Sullivan calls it "The He Hormone,"[29] citing an important embryological fact: "You need testosterone to turn a fetus with a Y chromosome into a real boy, to

---

[28] Joe Herbert, ***Testosterone: Sex, Power,*** **a**nd the Will to Win (Oxford: Oxford University Press, 2015) 33.
[29] Andrew Sullivan, "The He Hormone," ***The New York Times Magazine*** April 2, 2000.

masculinize his brain and body." The male brain is organized in a sex-specific manner by a surge of testosterone during the prenatal period. Testes begin secreting testosterone at around the eigth week of gestation. This testosterone surge – two actually[30] - is most important for the development of gender identity as it masculimizes the body *and the brain* of the fetus.[31] As Allan Mazur and Alan Booth describe:

> [Testosterone] and other testicular secretions cause the external genitalia to form into penis and scrotum rather than clitoris and labia, and internal ducts take the male form. The central nervous system is masculinized in rats and probably in humans, too. The general rule, somewhat simplified, is that early exposure to greater amounts of T will produce more male characteristics (masculinization) and fewer female characteristics (defeminization), whereas *less exposure* to [testosterone] will produce the reverse. Perinatal manipulation of animal subjects, and developmental abnormalities among humans, show convincingly that even genetic females will show male forms if dosed early enough with T, and *genetic males will show female forms if deprived of the hormone* (emphasis added).[32]

Gender identity develops as a result of an interaction between the developing brain and the sex hormones.[33] The latter act as a

---

[30] Dick Swaab and Alicia Garcia-Falgueras. "Sexual differentiation of the human brain in relation to gender identity and sexual orientation." Functional Neurology 24 (2009): 17-28 (18): "The early development of boys shows two periods during which testosterone levels are known to be high. The first surge occurs during mid-pregnancy: testosterone levels peak in the fetal serum between weeks 12 and 18 of pregnancy (18) and in weeks 34-41 of pregnancy the testosterone levels of boys are ten times higher than those of girls."

[31] D.F. Swaab, "Sexual differentiation of the human brain: relevance for gender identity, transsexualism and sexual orientation." Gyecol Endocrinol 19 (2004): 301-312 (301, 302): "it is the prenatal testosterone surge that is most important for the development of gender identity"; "for the development of human male gender identity and male heterosexuality, direct androgen action on the brain seems to be of crucial importance."

[32] Allan Mazur and Alan Booth, "Testosterone and dominance in men," Behavioral and Brain Sciences 21 (1998): 353-397 (355).

[33] Olaf Hiort, "The differential role of androgens in early human sex development," BMC Medicine 11 (2013): 1-7 (1): "the main aspects of

"fetal programing mechanism" imprinting gender identity as well as sexual orientation and behavior in the fetal brain.[34] Dick Swaab and Alicia Garcia-Falgueras point out regarding the fetal brain:

> During the intrauterine period the fetal brain develops in the male direction through a direct action of testosterone on the developing nerve cells, *or in the female direction through the absence of this hormone surge.* In this way, our gender identity (the conviction of belonging to the male or female gender) and sexual orientation are programmed into our brain structures when we are still in the womb. However, since sexual differentiation of the genitals takes place in the first two months of pregnancy and sexual differentiation of the brain starts in the second half of pregnancy, these two processes can be influenced independently, *which may result in transsexuality* (emphasis added).[35]

Androgens (testosterone and DHT) therefore make the fetus a somatic "He." But the process is complex and unfolds in a stringent and time- and dose-dependant manner.[36] In other words, the fetus must be exposed to the *right amount* of testosterone (and its metabolites) at the *right times* in order for the fetus to be fully androgenized or masculinized. Otherwise, the XY fetus will *feminize* to one degree or another by default. The female form is *not* the original or first form that a fetus takes in the womb – that's an outdated proposition – but it *is* the default form when there is an androgen shortage.[37] This can set up a conflict between a person's chromosomal sex (e.g. XY) and either gonadal/somatic sex (*soma* = "body") or neurological

---

gender development arise from the endocrine induced differentiation of sexual organs including the brain."

[34] Michael V. Lombardo et al. "Fetal Programming Effects of Testosterone on the Reward System and Behavioral Approach Tendencies in Humans," Biol Psychiatry 72 (2012): 839-847.

[35] Dick Swaab and Alicia Garcia-Falgueras. "Sexual differentiation of the human brain in relation to gender identity and sexual orientation." Functional Neurology 24 (2009): 17-28 (18). See further D.F. Swaab, "Sexual differentiation of the human brain: relevance for gender identity, transsexualism and sexual orientation." Gyecol Endocrinol 19 (2004): 301-312.

[36] Olaf Hiort, "The differential role of androgens in early human sex development," BMC Medicine 11 (2013): 1-7.

[37] See below.

sex. That is to say: an XY fetus can grow up to be a male physically (somatically) and a female neurologically or vice versa. The brain is sexually dimporphic. This means the male brain and the female brain have many differences[38] and many of these differences are the result of the impact or lackthereof of testosterone.[39] So a male brain that is impacted by an insufficient amount of testosterone at the proper times could develop femal brain features and thus female behavioral features later in life.[40]

III.   *Did Life Start as Female?*

It is a common misconception that a fetus starts existence in the womb as a female and then differentiates as a

---

[38] Swaab and Garcia-Falgueras. "Sexual differentiation of the human brain," 19: "A sex difference in brain weight is already present in children from the age of 2 years and sex differences can thus be expected throughout the brain from early in development. In the adult human brain structural sex differences can be found from the macroscopic level down to the ultramicroscopic level. Functionally, too, a large number of sex differences in different brain regions have recently been described. Sexual differentiation of the human brain is also expressed in behavioral differences, including sexual orientation (homo-, bi- and heterosexuality) and gender identity, and in differences at the level of brain physiology and in the prevalence of neurological and psychiatric disorders." See further M.A. Hoffman and D.F. Swaab, "Sexual Dimorphism of the Human Brain: Myth and Reality." Exp. Clin. Endocrinol. 98 (1991): 161-170; Nancy G. Forger, "Epigenetic mechanisms in sexual differentiation of the brain and behaviour." Phil. Trans. R. Soc. B. 371: 20150114; Kl. Matsuda, H. Mori and M. Kawata. "Epigenetic mechanisms are involved in sexual differentiation of the brain." Rev Endocr Metab Discord 13 (2012): 163-171; Margaret M. McCarthy, "Sex Differences in the Brain," The Scientist October 1, 2015; Zhou, Jiang-Ning et al., "A sex difference in the human brain and its relation to transsexuality." Nature 378 (1995): 68-70.
[39] See also Hilleke E. Hulshoff Pol et al. "Changing your sex changes your brain: influences of testosterone and estrogen on adult human brain structure." European Journal of Endocrinology 155 (2006): S107-S114.
[40] On "female structures in male brains and vice versa" caused by hormone manipulations see D.F. Swaab, "Sexual differentiation of the human brain: relevance for gender identity, transsexualism and sexual orientation." Gyecol Endocrinol 19 (2004): 301-312 (306).

male via the action of the SRY gene. See for example Andrew Sullivan, who is a gay white male from *The New York Times*:

At conception, every embryo is female and unless hormonally altered will remain so. You need testosterone to turn a fetus with a Y chromosome into a real boy, to masculinize his brain and body... Without testosterone, humans would always revert to the default sex, which is female. The Book of Genesis is therefore exactly wrong. It isn't women who are made out of men. It is men who are made out of women. Testosterone, to stretch the metaphor, is Eve's rib.[41]

Sullivan's remarks are a garbled mix of fact, fiction, and outdated and disproved embryological presumption. As Claire Ainsworth points out in *Nature*:

That the two sexes are physically different is obvious, but at the start of life, it is not. Five weeks into development, a human embryo has the potential to form *both* male and female anatomy. Next to the developing kidneys, two bulges known as the gonadal ridges emerge alongside two pairs of ducts, one of which can form the uterus and Fallopian tubes, and the other the male internal genital plumbing: the epididymis, vas deferentia and seminal vesicles. At six weeks, the gonad switches on the developmental pathway to become an ovary or a testis. If a testis develops, it secretes testosterone, which supports the development of the male ducts. It also makes other hormones that force the presumptive uterus and Fallopian tubes to shrink away. If the gonad becomes an ovary, it makes oestrogen, *and the lack of testosterone causes the male plumbing to wither.* The sex hormones also dictate the development of the external genitalia, and they come into play once more at puberty, triggering the development of secondary sexual characteristics such as breasts or facial hair...

For many years, scientists believed that female development was the default programme, and that male development was actively switched on by the presence of a particular gene on the Y chromosome. In 1990, researchers made headlines when they uncovered the identity of this gene, which they called SRY. Just by itself, this gene can switch the gonad from ovarian to testicular development. For example, XX individuals who carry

---

[41] Andrew Sullivan, "The He Hormone," *The New York Times Magazines* April 2, 2000.

a fragment of the Y chromosome that contains SRY develop as males...

By the turn of the millennium, however, *the idea of femaleness being a **passive** default option had been toppled by the discovery* of genes that actively promote ovarian development and suppress the testicular programme — such as one called WNT4. XY individuals with extra copies of this gene can develop atypical genitals and gonads, and a rudimentary uterus and Fallopian tubes. In 2011, researchers showed that if another key ovarian gene, RSPO1, is not working normally, it causes XX people to develop an ovotestis — a gonad with areas of both ovarian and testicular development. These discoveries have pointed to a complex process of sex determination, in which the identity of the gonad emerges from a contest between two opposing networks of gene activity.[42]

A fetus starts life as gonadally and anatomically *neutral* or "bipotential," *not* as female. While the fetus will have chromosomal sex, XY or XX, both of these start off with the same equipment: Wolffian ducts and Müllerian ducts, which will later become the male and the female reproductive systems, respectively. For the first 5-6 weeks of gestation the fetus possesses *both* sets of ducts, regardless to whether it is an XY or XX fetus.

The female fetus begins her process of sexual differentiation when the bipotential embryonic gonad begins to develop oocytes—between 11 and 12 weeks of gestation. In the absence of gonadal T production, the wolffian duct structures regress, and, lacking AMH (anti-müllerian hormone), the müllerian ducts differentiate into the fallopian tubes, the uterus, and the upper third of the vagina. Because T levels are low, the 5-reductase, type 2 (enzyme) at the genital ridge lacks the substrate to form DHT. Therefore, there is no "zipping up" of the labioscrotal folds, resulting in formation of open labia, a perineal vaginal orifice, and a perineal urethra. The regression of the wolffian duct structures, the differentiation of the müllerian duct structures, and the maintenance of open labioscrotal folds along normal female lines does not require a gonad, nor does it require the fetus to be a genetic female. XX or XY fetuses with dysgenetic or streak gonads also exhibit development of the internal and external genitalia along female lines. XY fetuses with complete androgen insensitivity resulting from mutations in the androgen receptor gene (complete

[42] Claire Ainsworth, "Sex redefined." **Nature** February 18, 2015.

testicular feminization) have functional testes that produce T and AMH. However, as a result of the inability of T or DHT to act and the presence of AMH, the fetus does not develop wolffian or müllerian duct structures, respectively, and the external genitalia develop along female lines.[43]

We Did NOT Start As Female

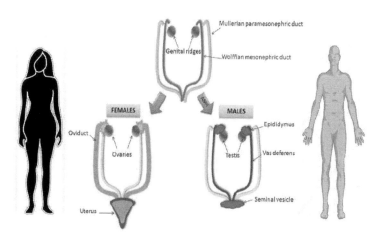

During this time, the Y chromosome is inactive, but so is one of the X chromosomes; only one X expresses itself at this time. This may have something to do with the fact that the Y chromosome, while so much smaller than the X chromosome, is so much more powerful than the X whether it (the X) is single, double, or more. As Dr. Joe Herbert remarks:

> Very occasionally, babies are born with additional X chromosomes together with a Y (e.g. XXY, XXXY ect.) Remarkably, despite any number of (larger) X chromosomes, the presence of even one (tiny) Y ensures that they are male.[44]

---

[43] T. Keta Hodgson and Glenn D. Braunstein, "Physiological Effects of Androgens in Women," in *Contemporary Endocrinology: Androgen Excess Disorders in Women: Polycystic Ovary Syndrome and Other Disorders, Second Edition*, ed. R. Azziz et al. (Totowa, NJ: Humana Press, Inc., 2006) 49-62 (49).
[44] Herbert, *Testosterone*, 36-37.

Even a fragment of the already tiny Y chromosome can cause an XX baby to develop as a male.[45] The extra X chromosomes (XXY, XXXY, etc.) do have feminizing effects. The resulting condition is called hypergonadotropic hypogonadism, which is a failure of the testes to produce sufficient quantities of testosterone and as part of the feedback response the pituitary gland is stimulated to produce higher levels of luteinizing hormone (LH) and follicle-stimulating hormone (FSH). One resulting disorder, Klinefelter's syndrome, is characterized by gynecomastia (man-boobs), azoospermia (semen containing no sperm) and testicular atrophy (shrinkage of the testicles).[46] There is feminization, but secondary feminization of a *male*.

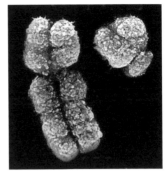

X (left) and Y (right) Chromosomes

The Y chromosome starts expressing itself at around 6-8 weeks, at which time the SRY gene located on the Y chromosome initiates the process that turns the neutral gonads into the male testes. In those testes testosterone is produced, which masculinizes the embryo. Also in the testes another hormone is produced, anti-Müllerian hormone, which causes the female Müllerian ducts to disintegrate and disappear while the testosterone makes the Wolffian ducts develop into the male reproductive system.

Life in the womb therefore begins *not* as a female that secondarily morphs into a male. It starts as either a *chromosomal male* or *chromosomal female* while the gonads are neutral - *not* feminine - and the reproductive machinery is bi-potential: both sets of ducts are present. The female phenotype is thus *not* the primary embryonic phenotype. Far from it.

Nor does the penis start life as a clitoris, as is often falsely claimed. Before there is either a penis or a clitoris there

45 Claire Ainsworth, "Sex redefined." **Nature** February 18, 2015.

46 Andrea L Gropman and Carole Samango-Sprouse, "Neurocognitive variance and neurological underpinnings of the X and Y chromosomal variations," **American Journal of Medical Genetics Part C (Seminars in Medical Genetics)** 163C (2013):35–43.

is the undifferentiated *genital tubercle*, which is a body of tissue present during the bi-potential stage that forms at around 4 weeks of gestation. This is neither a clitoris nor a penis (though it looks more like a proto-penis). It requires the action of testosterone's stronger form, DHT, to convert the neutral genital tubercle into a penis by elongating it. In the absence of testosterone, the "nub" (as the genital tubercle is called) will still undergo change and growth. But because the tools (androgens) necessary to fully develop it are not present, the nub only experiences minimal growth becoming the female clitoris instead. The claim that the penis started life as a clitoris is therefore erroneous. The clitoris didn't even start life as a clitoris. It is closer to the truth to say that the clitoris started life as a proto-phallus. However, the most accurate and scientific statement is that both the penis and the clitoris started as an undifferentiated body of tissue, the genital tubercle, which, under the influence of androgens became the male organ or due to a lack of androgens became the female form.[47] Along with this bipotential genital tubercle, the early embryo has bipotential genital folds as well that will fuse under the influence of DHT and become the testicular scrotum of a male child or, absent any androgens, will not fuse and instead become the lips of the vulva of a female.

On the other hand, the female phenotype *is* the default form, but not a *passive* default form. That is to say: if the tools (androgen hormones) necessary to fully masculinize the body and the brain of the embryo are not present, the embryo will by default feminize. As Dick Swaab and Alicia Garcia-Falgueras point out:

> During the intrauterine period the fetal brain develops in the male direction through a direct action of testosterone on the developing nerve cells, *or in the female direction through the absence of this hormone surge...*The production of testosterone by a boy's testes is necessary for sexual differentiation of the sexual organs between weeks 6 and 12 of pregnancy. The peripheral conversion of testosterone into dihydrotestosterone (DHT) is essential for the formation of a boy's penis, prostate and scrotum. Instead, the development of the female sexual

---

[47] Gerald R. Cunha and Laurence Baskin, "Development of Penile Urethra," in **Hypospadias and Genital Development**, ed. L. Baskin (New York: Kluwer Academic/Plenum Publishers, 2004) 87-102.

organs in the womb is based *primarily on the absence of androgens* (emphasis added).[48]

It is the *absence* or *dearth* of the masculinizing hormones testosterone and DHT that produces the female phenotype by default. This is also evidenced by the "Androgen Insensitivity Syndrome." If a male has sufficient testosterone but it cannot be activated because the androgen receptors are insensitive to it, the male phenotype cannot form and a female phenotype will form instead - by default.

> If we needed an even more dramatic example of the central importance of the androgen receptor then here is one. There are rare mutations of the androgen receptor that make it unable to bind to testosterone or DHT, and thus enter the nucleus and influence DNA. If the failure to bind is complete (this will depend on the exact nature of the mutation), then the individual, though genetically a male with a Y chromosome, testes, and testosterone just like any other male, is completely unaware of his own testosterone and will grow up to look like, feel like, and be like a female- though one without a uterus or ovaries. This condition is called 'androgen insensitivity syndrome' (AIS) and it is a glaring demonstration that testosterone is at the root of what we call 'masculinity'.[49]

The all-important androgen receptor (AR), so critical to the masculinizing program (AR-regulated gene expression is responsible for male sexual differentiation in utero and male pubertal changes), comes from a gene that is actually located on the X chromosome (Xq11.2-q12), not the Y.[50] Women have an abundance of ARs which are distributed across most female reproductive tissues, but theirs is inactive because women don't possess the sufficient amount of testosterone or DHT to activate these androgen receptors.[51] When women want to change sex,

---

[48] Dick Swaab and Alicia Garcia-Falgueras. "Sexual differentiation of the human brain in relation to gender identity and sexual orientation." *Functional Neurology* 24 (2009): 17-28 (17).

[49] Herbert, *Testosterone*, 32-33.

[50] Wenqing Gao, Casey E. Bohl and James T. Dalton, "Chemistry and Structural Biology of Androgen Receptor," *Chem. Rev.* 105 (2005): 3352-3370.

[51] Kamil Zaręba and Iwona Sidorkiewicz, "Recent Highlights of Research on Androgen Receptors in Women," *Developmental Period Medicine* 21 (2017): 7-12; Chawnshang Chang et al.,

however, they can get testosterone injections which will activate the ARs. A "female-like pattern (of AR activity) was found in men with low testosterone levels".[52]

So the female form *is* in fact the default form: it is (partly) created by default in the absence of the requisite amount of masculinizing androgens, especially T and DHT. The XX fetus is initially feminized *not* principally by the action of estrogens (that's later) but by the natural *absence* or dearth of androgens; and the XY fetus is also feminized by an *androgen deficiency* or androgen receptor insensitivity. However, the full female phenotype is not strictly the *passive* default option. The feminization of the XX (female) embryo also requires the *active suppression* of the male phenotype through such genes as WNT4 and through the *active promotion* of the female phenotype through activation of such genes as RSPO1. This makes sense, given that the original (Black) women was first produced *by* and *from* the original (Black) man, according to the Most Honorable Elijah Muhammad. The scientific data is consistent with this.

ADAM'S "RIB"

He (Allah) wanted a different human being than Himself, so He studied Himself. He made a woman by studying Himself. He made a woman secondly so this solved His problem of a search for another man;[53] It's the woman who is the 2nd self.

"Androgen Receptor (AR) Physiological Roles in Male and Female Reproductive Systems: Lessons Learned from AR-Knockout Mice Lacking AR in Selective Cells," **Biology of Reproduction** 89 (2013): 1-16; Abdulmaged M. Traish et al., "Role of androgens in female genital sexual arousal: receptor expression, structure, and function," **Fertility and Sterility** 77 (2002): S11-S18.

[52] D.F. Swaab, "Sexual differentiation of the human brain: relevance for gender identity, transsexualism and sexual orientation." **Gyecol Endocrinol** 19 (2004): 301-312 (303).

[53] The Honorable Elijah Muhammad, **The Divine Sayings of The Honorable Elijah Muhammad, Messenger of Allah.** Volumes 1,2 & 3 (Secretarious Publications, 2002) I:5-6.

Man is the 1st self;[54] The Black Woman was made by the God who made Himself.[55] – The Most Honorable Elijah Muhammad

It isn't women who are made out of men. It is men who are made out of women. Testosterone, to stretch the metaphor, is Eve's rib. – Andrew Sullivan

Andrew Sullivan's above claim certainly cannot be sustained. He did, however, look to the right place for clarity and identity of the biblical "rib" from which Eve came: biochemistry. Androgens control male sexual development, the primary sexual characteristics (reproductive system) as well as the adult male phenotype or secondary male sexual characteristics (for example body hair, taller stature, heavier skull and bone structure, larger larynx and deeper voice, etc.). Estrogens control the development of female secondary sexual characteristics (for example breast enlargement, lower waist to hip ratio, longer upper arms, etc.).

What needs to be understood is: "the difference between 'maleness' and 'femaleness' is not an absolute one, but instead is governed by a subtle balance of the ratios of estrogenic vs. androgenic actions."[56] Indeed, and what most don't realize is this: "Androgens are the most abundant of the sex hormones in women; while their concentrations are measured in nanomoles, estrogens are measured in mere picomoles."[57] Quantitatively, women secrete greater amounts of androgen than of estrogen.[58] The major androgens in women, listed in descending order of serum concentration, include dehydroepiandrosterone sulphate (DHEAS), de-hydroepiandrosterone (DHEA),

---

[54] Elijah Muhammad, "The Position of Men and Women," December 1967. Found at http://muhammadspeaks.com/home/the-nation/muslim-men/the-position-of-men-and-women/. Accessed June 10, 2014.

[55] Muhammad, *Theology of Time*, 152.

[56] Evan R. Simpson, "Aromatization of androgens in women: current concepts and findings," *Fertility and Sterility* (2002): S6-S10 (S8).

[57] T. Keta Hodgson and Glenn D. Braunstein, "Physiological Effects of Androgens in Women," in *Contemporary Endocrinology: Androgen Excess Disorders in Women: Polycystic Ovary Syndrome and Other Disorders, Second Edition*, ed. R. Azziz et al. (Totowa, NJ: Humana Press, Inc., 2006) 49-62 (49).

[58] Henry G. Burger, "Androgen production in women," *Fertility and Sterility* 77 (2002): S3-S5 (S3).

androstenedione (A), testosterone (T), and dihydrotestosterone (DHT).[59] "Men do have higher circulating levels of T than woman; however, quantitatively, T is the most abundant active sex steroid in women throughout the female lifespan."[60] The normal ovary produces relatively larger amounts of androgen compared with estrogens,[61] and in women androgens modulate the physiological function of many reproductive and sexual organs, including the ovaries, uterus, vagina, oviducts, clitoris, and mammary gland.[62] The "T-E_2 ratio...is normally maintained at relatively high levels throughout a woman's lifespan" and "androgen activity is normally quite abundant in healthy women throughout the entire life cycle."[63]

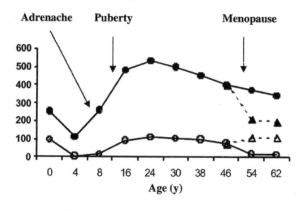

Average E_2 and T levels across the female lifespan, with dashed lines predicting changes in hormone levels resulting from pharmacological E therapy beginning at menopause. —●— T (pg/ml), —○— E_2 (pg/ml), --▲-- T/ERT, --△-- E/ERT.

Dimitrakakis. Androgens and the mammary gland. Fertil Steril 2002.

[59] Burger, "Androgen production in women," S3.
[60] Rebecca Glaser and Constantine Dimitrakakis, "Testosterone therapy in women: Myths and misconceptions," **Maturitas** 74 (2013): 230-234 (231).
[61] Constantine Dimitrakakis, Jian Zhou, and Carolyn A. Bondy, "Androgens and mammary growth and neoplasia," **Fertility and Sterility** 77 (2002): S26-S32 (S26).
[62] Abdulmaged M. Traish et al. "Role of androgens in female genital sexual arousal: receptor expression, structure, and function," **Fertility and Sterility** 77 (2002): S11-S18 (S11).
[63] Dimitrakakis, Zhou, and Bondy, "Androgens and mammary growth," S30, S31.

An additional critically important fact for our discussion is this: "Testosterone and androstenedione are the necessary precursors to the formation of estradiol and estrone."[64] Androgens are the obligate precursors for the synthesis of all estrogens in the female body, and "T is the major substrate for E2"[65] DHEA, DHEAS, A4, and T serve as the prohormones for the production of estrogens in the ovaries, adrenals, and a variety of peripheral tissues. How are estrogens made from androgens?

Steroids can be divided into different groups of parent compounds, based on the number of carbons that they contain: Pregnanes are C21 steroids because they contain 21 carbons; Androstanes are C19 steroids with 19 carbons and Estranges are C18 steroids with 18 carbons.[66] From pregnanes come the hormone progesterone (P), named for its progestational role in maintaining pregnancy. P is thus traditionally regarded as a "female hormone." This is a misnomer, however. While P's role in female-typical behaviors has been well-documented, it is only relatively recently that the role of progesterone as a modulator of the male endocrine system has become more and more

[64] Abdulmaged M. Traish et al., "Role of Androgens in Female Genitourinary Tissue Structure and Function: Implications in the Genitourinary Syndrome of Menopause," **Sexual Medicine Reviews** 6 (2018): 558-571 (560).

[65] T. Keta Hodgson and Glenn D. Braunstein, "Physiological Effects of Androgens in Women," in **Contemporary Endocrinology: Androgen Excess Disorders in Women: Polycystic Ovary Syndrome and Other Disorders, Second Edition**, ed. R. Azziz et al. (Totowa, NJ: Humana Press, Inc., 2006) 49-62 (49); James Woods and Elizabeth Warner, "The History of Estrogen," @ https://www.urmc.rochester.edu/ob-gyn/ur-medicine-menopause-and-womens-health/menopause-blog/february-2016/the-history-of-estrogen.aspx; Rebecca Glaser and Constantine Dimitrakakis, "Testosterone therapy in women: Myths and misconceptions," **Maturitas** 74 (2013): 230-234 (231); Dimitrakakis, Zhou, and Bondy, "Androgens and mammary growth," S29.

[66] Frank Z. Stanczyk, "Production, Clearance, and Measurement of Steroid Hormones," in idem, *Glob. libr. women's med., (ISSN: 1756-2228)* 2009; DOI 10.3843/GLOWM.10278.

evident.[67]   P has "many faces" and in fact exerts an equally important influence on the brain and behavior of males.[68]

P is synthesized in women in the ovaries and in men in the Leydig cells of the testicles as well as in the adrenals of both. Progesterone modulates the male endocrine system and male sexual behavior in biphasic (dose-dependent) manner.[69] At normal, physiological levels, P has *androgenic* effects in males; P synthesizes with and facilitates testosterone action. In castrated rats P has be shown to fully restore male sexual behavior, even in the absence of testosterone.[70] At higher than normal levels, however, P has *anti-androgenic* effects. It inhibits the effects of testosterone and *feminizes* male neurology, physiology and behavior. However, higher than normal levels of P in a female can *masculinize* female neurology, physiology and behavior.[71]

While P is involved with the female menstrual cycle, pregnancy, and embryogenesis, it is also involved in the capacitation of male sperm and biosynthesis of T in Leydig cells. The process of capacitation renders the sperm capable of interacting with the oocyte and of engaging acrosome reaction. Some studies suggest that the absence of P actions on sperm can result in male infertility.[72] This all suggests that progesterone is neither a "female hormone" nor a "pregnancy" hormone, but a gender-neutral *reproductive* hormone, as well as a gender-neutral neurosteroid, offering neuroprotection. P balances against overactivity of androgens and of estrogens. It is the case that reproductive age women have more progesterone than do men (normal range: men =< 1ng/mL; women = 1ng/mL – 90ng.mL), and this makes sense given the more sophisticated "reproductive equipment" in the female. As pointed out by Christine K. Wagner:

---

[67] M. Oettel and A.K. Mukhopadhyay, "Progesterone: the forgotten hormone in men?" *Aging Male* 7 (2004): 236-57.

[68] Christine K. Wagner, "The many faces of progesterone: A role in adult and developing male brain," *Frontiers in Neuroendocrinology* 27 (2006): 340-359 (355).

[69] Diane Mitt, Larry J. Young, and David Crews, "Progesterone and Sexual Behavior in Males," *Psychoneuroendocrinology* 19 (1994): 553-562.

[70] Wagner, "The many faces of progesterone," 343.

[71] Wagner, "The many faces of progesterone."

[72] Oettel and Mukhopadhyay, "Progesterone: the forgotten hormone in men?" 240-241.

P is much more than a 'progestational" hormone and indeed, much more than simply a "female" hormone. P can facilitate, inhibit or mimic the actions of testosterone in male-typical behaviors in species ranging from lizards to humans.[73]

The bipotential progesterone steroid has 21 carbon atoms. Cleavage of the side chain results in the loss of 2 carbons and the production of the androstane series of C19 steroids, which are the androgens containing 19 carbons. The aromatase enzyme cleaves the C10-C19 carbon-carbon bond of the androgen, resulting in the loss of the 19-methyl group. This produces the 18-carbon estrane steroids, including the estrogens.[74]

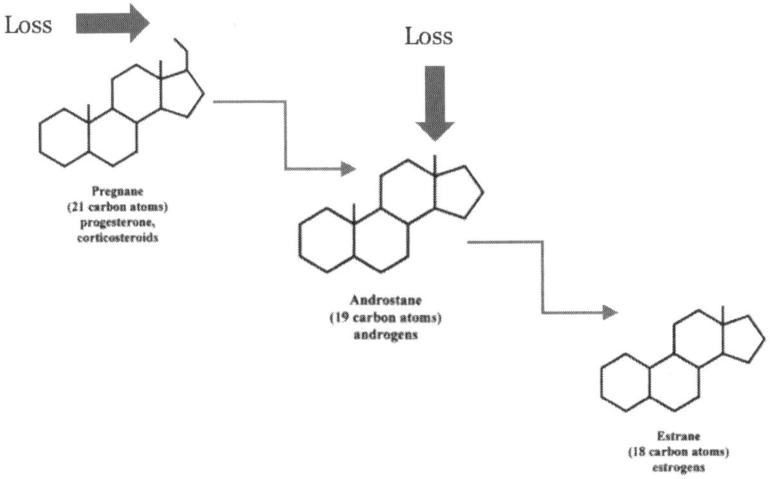

Loss

Loss

Pregnane
(21 carbon atoms)
progesterone,
corticosteroids

Androstane
(19 carbon atoms)
androgens

Estrane
(18 carbon atoms)
estrogens

Testosterone can be regarded as a circulating pro-hormone, which is converted in target cells on the one hand to 5α-

---

[73] Christine K. Wagner, "The many faces of progesterone: A role in adult and developing male brain," *Frontiers in Neuroendocrinology* 27 (2006): 340-359 (355).

[74] Francis K. Yoshimoto and F. Peter Guengerich, "Mechanism of the Third Oxidative Step in the Conversion of Androgens to Estrogens by Cytochrome P450 19A1 Steroid Aromatase," *Journal of the American Chemical Society* 136 (2014): 15016-15025 (15016); Tommaso Falcone and William W. Hurd, *Clinical Reproductive Medicine and Surgery* (Philadelphia, PA: Mosby, 2007) 18.

dihydrotesterone (DHT), and on the other hand to estradiol... Testosterone circulates at concentrations which are an order of magnitude greater than those of estradiol in the blood of postmenopausal women.[75]

The important point for our discussion is this: the feminizing hormones (estrogen) all derive from the masculinizing hormones (androgen). As T. Keta and Glenn Braunstein observe: "the physiological effects of estrogens in women indirectly reflect a role for androgens, for if there were no androgens, there would be no estrogens."[76] This biochemical femininity therefore derives from biochemical masculinity. The "rib" of Adam from which Eve the "female" emerged would thus be the androgens. It should also be pointed out that "Although testosterone can be converted to estradiol, the reverse does not happen."[77] Estrogens generally cannot convert back to androgens. The androgen-to-estrogen process is unidirectional. Most females don't develop male characteristics because testosterone and other androgens act differently in their bodies, being quickly converted to estrogen by aromatase.

IV.   *The Power Hormone*

As Austrian political analyst Karin Kneissl argues in her 2012 German-language work, ***Testosteron Macht Politik*** ("Testosterone Makes Politics"), male testosterone is much more than a libido hormone: it is a driver of world revolutions. Male testosterone, she points out, is the thread uniting the European revolutions of 1848 to the uprisings of the Arab Spring. Testosterone motivates men to seek power by overthrowing (violently or otherwise) oppressive overlords. Thus, testosterone is, as ***Time Magazine*** declares, The Power Hormone.

---

75 Evan R. Simpson, "Aromatization of androgens in women: current concepts and findings," ***Fertility and Sterility*** (2002): S6-S10 (S6).
76 Keta Hodgson and Braunstein, "Physiological Effects of Androgens in Women," 59.
77 "Testosterone in Women," ***American Scientist*** 103 (March-April 2015), 83; Traish et al., "Role of Androgens," 560.

BEHAVIOR

Testosterone, the Power Hormone

Biology meets history in a new book on revolution, riot and the sex hormone testosterone. Author Karin Kneissl explains

By Laura Blue   July 27, 2012

What do the Arab Spring, religious Crusades and Europe's revolutions of 1848 have in common? All were fueled by a surplus of hapless young men, according to Karin Kneissl — an Austrian academic, author, and political analyst. In her new German-language book, *Testosteron macht Politik* (crude translation: "Testosterone Makes Politics"), Kneissl lays out her case for the primary male sex hormone as a driver of world affairs.

- Roger Kirby, "Testosterone and the struggle for higher social status," *Trends in Urology & Men's Health* January/February 2014: 11-14:

  There is now a mounting body of evidence about the effects of testosterone on social interactions in animals and humans, as well as an understanding of the basic neurobiological mechanisms that underlie these effects. Based on these recent findings, it would appear that the role of testosterone in human social behaviour might be best understood in terms of the struggle for, and maintenance of, higher social and economic status.

  the role of testosterone in social interaction in humans might be best conceptualized as a motivator for elevated social status.

- David Terburg and Jack von Honk, "Approach-Avoidance versus Dominance-Submissiveness: A Multilevel Neural Framework on How Testosterone Promotes Social Status," *Emotion Review* 5 (2013): 296-302:

  testosterone shifts reflexive as well as deliberate behaviors towards dominance and promotion of social status. Testosterone inhibits acute fear at the level of the basolateral amygdala and hypothalamus and promotes reactive dominance through upregulation of vasopressin gene expression in the central-medial amygdala...All these effects of testosterone...serve to increase and maintain social status.

- David Terburg, Henk Aarts and Jack van Honk, "Testosterone Affects Gaze Aversion From Angry Faces Outside of Conscious Awareness," *Psychological Science* 23 (2012): 459-463:

  testosterone motivates social dominance in humans in much the same ways that it does in other vertebrates: involuntarily, automatically, and unconsciously.

  testosterone has been identified as a driving force for engaging and prevailing in confrontations for social dominance (...), which underlie the formation of social hierarchies (...).

- Christopher Eisenegger, Johannes Haushofer and Ernst Fehr, "The role of testosterone in social interaction," *Trends in Cognitive Sciences* 15 (2011): 263-271: Several recent studies suggest that testosterone facilitates particular social emotional mechanisms that tend to enhance the ability of an individual to achieve and maintain a high social status.

  it appears that testosterone promotes status-seeking and social dominance motives, and thus plays an important role in social status hierarchies.

- Allan Mazur and Alan Booth, "Testosterone and dominance in men," *Behavioral and Brain Sciences* 21 (1998): 353-397:

  In men, high levels of endogenous testosterone (T) seem to encourage behavior intended to dominate – to enhance one's status over – other people.

Testosterone implicitly – automatically and unconsciously – predisposes the individual for reactive social aggression and dominance, it is believed; it prepares the individual for reactive-reflexive defense of social status and promotes instinctive dominance behavior.[78] Dominance behavior is activity motivated by the desire to achieve dominance or high social status.

V.   *Testosterone Medicates Fear*

It is believed that testosterone (T) produces its effect on dominance seeking through decreasing fear and encouraging risk taking. T promotes threat vigilance, enabling one to detect potential challenges and to act to defend status.

In humans, single acute doses of testosterone have been shown to reduce subconscious fear (...) and fear potentiated startle (...). Together, these results suggest that testosterone takes its effect on status seeking through decreasing fear...[T]estosterone seems to act at different neurobiological nodes that are important contributors to status-seeking and status maintenance behaviors. Studies in animals suggest that testosterone has anxiety-reducing properties...Testosterone administration studies confirm that the hormone also has fear-reducing properties in humans. A further important function of testosterone is its role in motivation; animal models have shown a tight link with the dopaminergic system within striatal areas. Thus, together with the ability to reduce fear and buffer stress responses, testosterone might have a pivotal role in

---

[78] Sina Radke et al. "Testosterone biases the amygdala toward social threat approach," Sci. Adv. (2015): 1-6; David Terburg and Jack von Honk, "Approach-Avoidance versus Dominance-Submissiveness: A Multilevel Neural Framework on How Testosterone Promotes Social Status," Emotion Review 5 (2013): 296-302.

promoting upward movement in a status hierarchy by facilitating the engagement in a competition for status. By contrast, testosterone can promote threat vigilance, which enables an individual to not only detect potential status challenges, but also, as a consequence of, and facilitated through the mechanisms detailed above, act accordingly to defend its high status position. These effects might be mediated by the amygdala...[79]

Ample evidence from animal research indicates that the gonadal steroid hormone testosterone has fear reducing properties...[T]estosterone administration [to humans] resulted in reduced fear potentiated startle, without affecting baseline startle.[80]

Jack van Honk and colleagues document it most convincingly in their 2005 study:

The destructive value of excess fear has been emphasized in both animal and human models of psychopathology (...). Overgeneralized, exaggerated behavioral and autonomic responses to threat and novelty are observed when pathological fear sets in (...). This happens when fear circuits of the brain have become hyperexcitable, the core of abnormality in most disorders of fear and anxiety (...). A neurobiological mechanism argued to be importantly involved in these hyperexcitable fear circuits is the endocrine-neuroendocrine amygdala cascade. Heightened levels of the steroid hormone cortisol exaggerate and sustain fearfulness by facilitating corticotropin-releasing hormone (CRH) gene expression at the amygdala (...).

Contrariwise, one of the most replicated findings in research on the relationship between steroid hormones and emotional behavior involves reductions in fear after treatment with the steroid hormone testosterone. This phenomenon has been demonstrated in a large variety of species using an excessive range of behavioral assessment paradigms...The androgenic steroid...possesses dual-sided, aggression-increasing and fear-reducing, motivational properties.[81]

---

[79] Christopher Eisenegger, Johannes Haushofer and Ernst Fehr, "The role of testosterone in social interaction," Trends in Cognitive Sciences 15 (2011): 269.

[80] Erno J. Hermans et al., "A single administration of testosterone reduces fear-potentiated startle in humans," Biological Psychiatry 59 (2006): 872-874.

[81] Jack van Honk, Jiska S. Peper, and Dennis J.L.G. Schutter, "Testosterone Reduces Unconscious Fear but Not Consciously

Testosterone is thus believed to confer high motivational drive, low fearfulness, and high stress resilience. In this way T promotes the acquisition of dominance in society. "Testosterone lies at the core of social approach and dominance-seeking behavior across species."[82] And a very small, walnut-sized portion of the brain is the command center of this activity.

VI.   *The Amygdala*

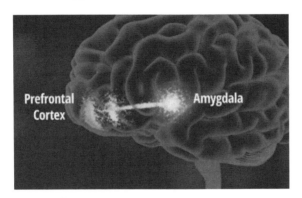

Approach and avoidance are two different behavioral responses to environmental stimuli that make people tend to approach positive situations and avoid negative situations. Approach motivation refers to behavior *toward* desirable stimuli and sensitivity for *reward* cues; avoidance motivation is characterized by behavior *away* from aversive or negative stimuli and by sensitivity for *punishment* cues. These behavioral responses are considered to be vital for survival, especially as reactions to social threat. Approach-Avoidance behavior is another way to describe the "Fight-Flight" responses to danger or threat.

The natural tendency for many people is to avoid threatening situations in order to protect themselves from harm or to escape negative repercussions. Such behavior is motivated in part by a high sensitivity to punishment potential and the consequent fear. However, others might approach aversive or

---

Experienced Anxiety: Implications for the Disorders of Fear and Anxiety," Biological Psychiatry 58 (2005): 218-225.

[82] Sina Radke et al. "Testosterone biases the amygdala toward social threat approach," Sci. Adv. (2015): 1-6 (1).

threatening stimuli in the environment in search of a *reward* outcome.

Some people are motivated to *approach* social threats in pursuit of a rewarding outcome (such as dominance acquisition) while others are motivated to *avoid* them out of fear of the negative repercussions (such as injury or death). Scientists now know that these two options have a neurological and biochemical basis, rooted in the amygdala.

The amygdala is an almond-shaped nerve center in the forebrain that is our threat-processing center responsible for detecting and responding to threats in our environment. When a threat is consciously or subconsciously detected a signal is sent alerting the rest of the body to prepare for fight or flight. Circuits responsible for stimulating defensive responses to predators involve the amygdala. When the amygdala is damaged, previously threatening stimuli like predators (e.g. a snake to a mouse) come to be treated as benign or harmless, because the threat is not perceived.

The amygdala modulates threat approach and threat avoidance, and these two responses have different outcomes in terms of social hierarchy. As Sina Radke et al. inform us:

> Threat vigilance can prime divergent motivational reactions, namely, threat approach, but also threat avoidance. Threat approach has been theoretically and empirically linked to social dominance, whereas threat avoidance is a clear sign of social submissiveness.[83]

Whether the amygdala signals towards treat approach or threat avoidance is determined to a large degree by which of two contrasting hormones activates it: testosterone or cortisol. Radke and colleagues have provided "evidence for a neuroendocrine mechanism in which testosterone biases the organism toward threat approach and away from threat avoidance by modulating amygdala responses... (T)estosterone primes the individual for defense of its status in social challenges."[84] David Terburg and Jack von Honk have also reported findings that suggest that "the mechanism by which testosterone implicitly predisposes the individual for reactive social aggression and dominance is through the upregulation of

---

[83] Radke et al. "Testosterone biases the amygdala," 1.
[84] Radke et al. "Testosterone biases the amygdala," 2.

vasopressin gene expression in the [central-medial amygdala]."[85]

Testosterone, which is a product of the HPG Axis,[86] induces hyperactivity or signaling of the amygdala. This increases threat perception and promotes aggressive response to a threat once perceived by reducing sensitivity for punishment and inhibiting fear and stress.[87] On the other hand cortisol, a product of the HPA Axis[88] which is heavily involved in fear and stress, has the diametrically opposite effect on the amygdala than testosterone. Cortisol dampens amygdala reactivity and thus desensitizes it toward threat and danger. And "heightened cortisol predisposes one to fear."

> The mutually antagonistic properties of the hormones cortisol and testosterone have been observed not only on the psychobiological but also on the neurobiological level. This starts off with the mutually inhibitory functional connection between the hypothalamic-pituitary-adrenal (HPA) and hypothalamic-pituitary gonadal (HPG) axes (...). Cortisol suppresses the activity of the HPG axis at all its levels, diminishes the production of testosterone, and inhibits the action of testosterone at the target tissues (...). Testosterone, in its turn, inhibits the stress-induced activation of the HPA axis at the level of the hypothalamus (...). Crucially, in one of their core action mechanisms, these steroid hormones bind to amygdala-centered, steroid-responsive neuronal networks (...) that regulate and facilitate neuropeptide gene expression. On the behavioral level, animal data show that testosterone

---

[85] David Terburg and Jack von Honk, "Approach-Avoidance versus Dominance-Submissiveness: A Multilevel Neural Framework on How Testosterone Promotes Social Status," Emotion Review 5 (2013): 296-302 (297).

[86] The Hypothalamic-Pituitary-Gonadal Axis, which is a reference to those three endocrine system glands as if they were a single entity because (when) they act in concert to regulate the reproductive system.

[87] Stefan M.M. Goetz et al., "Testosterone Rapidly Increases Neural Reactivity to Threat in Healthy Men: A Novel Two-Step Pharmacological Challenge Paradigm," Biol Psychiatry 76 (2014): 324-331; Sina Radke et al. "Testosterone biases the amygdala toward social threat approach," Sci. Adv. (2015): 1-6 ; David Terburg and Jack von Honk, "Approach-Avoidance versus Dominance-Submissiveness: A Multilevel Neural Framework on How Testosterone Promotes Social Status," Emotion Review 5 (2013): 296-302.

[88] The Hypothalamic-Pituitary-Adrenal Axis.

elevates vasopressin gene expression at the amygdala, thereby increasing the likelihood for *behavioral approach* (...). Cortisol, on the other hand, increases amygdaloid CRH [corticotropin-releasing hormone] gene expression, which promotes *behavioral withdrawal* (...).[89]

High testosterone together with low cortisol acts on the amygdala to facilitate a fight response when confronted by a social threat. Testosterone reduces fear and induces aggressive approach. High cortisol however inhibits testosterone, increases the states of fear, punishment sensitivity, and behavioral inhibition, and thus induces fearful withdrawal from a threat. High testosterone predisposes one to dominance acquisition while high cortisol predisposes one to social submissiveness.

---

[89] Jack van Honk, Jiska S. Peper, and Dennis J.L.G. Schutter, "Testosterone Reduces Unconscious Fear but Not Consciously Experienced Anxiety: Implications for the Disorders of Fear and Anxiety," Biological Psychiatry 58 (2005): 218-225 (223).

HPG Axis
GnRH = Gonadotrophin releasing hormone
LH = Leutinizing hormone
FSH = Follicle stimulating hormone

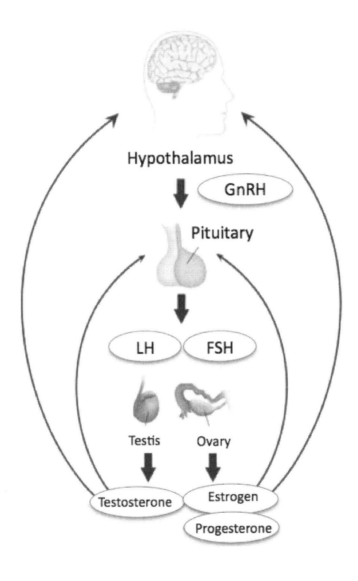

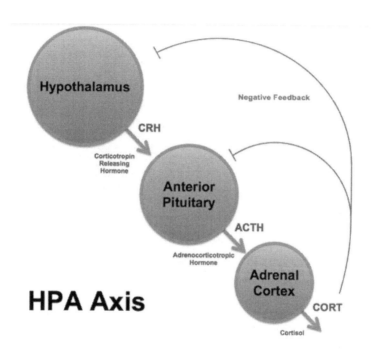

Chapter Three

The Black Man: From Mr. T to Mr. E

I.   *Different "Racial" Endowments*

Richard Lynn, professor emeritus of psychology at the University of Ulster and a controversial race theorist, is nonetheless correct when he affirms that "There is direct evidence for higher testosterone levels in Negroids than in Caucasoids..."[90] African and African-descended populations are widely attested to have higher T levels as well as more numerous and more sensitive androgen receptors (see below) than Europeans and Asians. The most thorough study to date (2011, with 2005-2006 data) has shown that African-Caribbean men do indeed have significantly higher T and dihydrotestosterone (DHT) levels than European men.[91] This makes sense because vitamin D increases the biosynthesis of testosterone and African peoples have the most optimal vitamin D status.[92]

Vitamin D status is directly associated with T levels in men. The more vitamin D synthesized in the body, the more T that can be synthesized and low vitamin D is associated with low T levels.[93] The principal source of vitamin D for humans is

---

[90] R. Lynn, "Testosterone and gonadotropin levels and r/K reproductive strategies," Psychol Rep 67 (1990): 1203-6.

[91] Frank Giton et al., "Serum sex steroids measured in middle-aged European and African-Caribbean men by gas chromatography-mass spectrometry," European Journal of Endocrinology 165 (2011): 917-924.

[92] "there is something about testosterone synthesis that needs vitamin D," suggests Dr. Mary Ann McLaughlin from Mount Sinai Hospital in New York City and lead author of the study: Rupa Lyengar et al., "Association Between Testosterone, Vitamin D and Cardiovascular Risk," The Journal of Urology 193 (2015 Supplement): e621.

[93] L M. Wentz et al., " Vitamin D Correlation with Testosterone Concentration in Male US Soldiers and Veterans," Journal of Military and Veterans' Health 24 (2016): 17-23; L M. Wentz et al., " Vitamin D Correlation with Testosterone Concentration in Male US Soldiers and Veterans," Journal of Military and Veterans' Health 24 (2016): 17-23; Ningjian Wang et al., "Vitamin D is associated with testosterone and hypogonadism in Chinese men: Results from a cross-sectional SPECT-

ultraviolet B (UVB) radiation from the sun. Solar irradiation converts 7-dihydrocholesterol to the biologically active form of vitamin D, 1,25-dihydroxyvitamin D, which is synthesized in the epidermal layer of skin when sunlight strikes it. This is why Africans, especially equatorial Africans, have the most optimal vitamin D status.[94] African populations whose home experiences abundant sun-light year-round synthesize the most vitamin D and are protected from both UVB toxicity as well as vitamin D toxicity (= too much vitamin D) by the skin pigment melanin which absorbs just enough UVB to produce optimal vitamin D levels while screening out the dangerous excess. And because African peoples have the most optimal vitamin D levels, African males biosynthesize the most testosterone.

African and African-descended males not only have more T than white males, they also produce more of the most potent androgen, 5α-dihydrotestosterone (DHT), which is 4 x's more potent than T. Around 10% of a male's T is converted to DHT via an enzyme called 5α-reductase Type II. DHT is more potent than T because it more easily binds with the androgen attachment site or androgen receptor (AR) than does T and it stays bound longer. DHT is responsible for the sexual differentiation of male genitalia during embryogenesis, the maturation of the penis and scrotum at puberty, sebum production, the growth of facial and body hair, and the development and maintenance of the prostate gland and seminal vesicles. If "testosterone is at the root of what we call 'masculinity'," as argued by Dr. Joe Herbert, Emeritus Professor of Neuroscience at the University of Cambridge,[95] it is T's

---

China study," Reproductive Biology and Endocrinology 13 (2015): 1-7; Camille E. Powe et al., "Vitamin D-Binding Protein and Vitamin D Status of Black Americans and White Americans," The New England Journal of Medicine 369 (2013): 1991-2000; David M. Less et al., "Association of hypogonadism with vitamin D status: the European Male Ageing Study," European Journal of Endocrinology 166 (2012): 77-85; S. Pilz et al., "Effect pf vitamin D supplementation on testosterone levels in men," Hormone and Metabolic Research 43 (2011): 223-5.

[94] Martine F. Luxwolda et al. "Traditionally living populations in East Africa have a mean serum 25-hydroxyvitamin D concentration of 115 nmol/l," British Journal of Nutrition 108 (2012): 1557-1561.

[95] Joe Herbert, Testosterone: Sex, Power, and the Will to Win (Oxford: Oxford University Press, 2015).

metabolite DHT that is most responsible for *somatic* or physical masculinity.

African and African-descended populations have higher DHT production. Litman et al. documented in 2009 that "Black men (of the U.S.) had higher DHT levels and DHT to testosterone ratios than white and Hispanic men."[96]

> Blacks had significantly higher DHT levels, compared with Hispanics (P=0.034) and whites (P = 0.031); DHT levels for Hispanics and whites did not differ (P = 0.829). Based on the multivariate model, the mean DHT level of a 40-yr-old black whose blood was drawn 2 [hours] from awakening with BMI [body mass index] less than 25 kg/m2 would be approximately 51.2 ng/dl (1.78 nmol/liter), whereas the level for a white would be 46.7 ng/dl (1.62 nmol/liter) and a Hispanic 46.2 ng/dl (1.60 nmol/liter)... Men who describe themselves as blacks have the highest DHT levels and DHT to testosterone ratios, compared with those who describe themselves as Hispanics or whites.[97]

The enzyme that converts T to DHT, 5α-reductase Type II, is encoded by the *SRD5A2* gene. There are certain variants of this gene that are exclusive to Black men and which correlate to elevated 5α-reductase activity and higher T-to-DHT conversion rate in Black men than white men.[98]

> Thymine-Adenine (TA) dinucleotide repeat and A49T variants of the SRD5A2 gene, which encodes a type II 5-α-reductase, are prevalent in [African American] men. In addition, these two polymorphisms were shown to correlate with the elevated 5-α-reductase activity and higher conversion rate of testosterone to dihydrotestosterone (DHT), respectively, in AA patients.[99]

---

[96] Heather J. Litman et al., "Serum Androgen Levels in Black, Hispanic, and White Men," The Journal of Clinical Endocrinology & Metabolism 91 (2006): 4326-4334 (4326).

[97] Litman et al., "Serum Androgen Levels," 4329, 4330.

[98] RK Ross wt al., "5-alpha-reductase activity and risk of prostate cancer among Japanese and US white and black males," Lancet 339 (1992): 887-9; Juergen K.V. Reichardt et al., "Genetic Variability of Human SRD5A2 Gene: Implications for prostate Cancer," Cancer Research 55 (1995): 3973-3975.

[99] Bi-Dar Wang et al., "Androgen Receptor-Target Genes in African American Prostate Cancer Disparities," Prostate Cancer Volume 2013: 1-13 (1-2).

Not only do African and African-descended males produce the most T, but their T is also more accessible to them than other groups because African and African-descended males have more androgen receptors. The androgen receptor (AR) is a protein that is activated by binding to androgen hormones (e.g. testosterone and dihydrotestosterone) and in turn activates the hormone. As long as testosterone is "free," i.e. unbound, it is inactive and thus unable to do what T is supposed to do to the body and the mind. Only when T binds with the AR is it activated and thus effective. The more ARs there are in a body, the more T that can be activated and utilized.

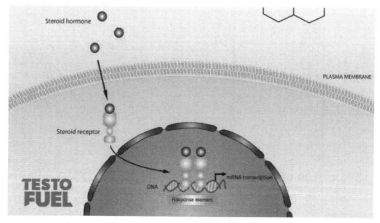

Operation of Testosterone on Androgen Receptor and on DNA

But that is only half of the story. The AR itself has to have the required level of "sensitivity" to the hormone in order for it (the AR) to be activated by the testosterone or DHT and thus to activate them. Physiologically, functional ARs are responsible for male sexual differentiation in utero and for male pubertal change.[100] In the case of "androgen insensitivity," the ARs don't adequately respond to the androgens (T or DHT) and the consequence is that a genetic male (XY) will be born with the physical and neurological traits of a female (such as

---

[100] Wenqing Gao, Casey E. Bohl and James T. Dalton, "Chemistry and Structural Biology of Androgen Receptor," Chem. Rev. 105 (2005): 3352-3370.

gynecomastia or "man boobs" and testicular atrophy or shrinkage) because the T and DHT were incapable of sufficiently binding to and activating the AR.[101] Women have ARs but theirs are inactive due to insufficient activating T and a "female-like pattern (of AR activity) was found in men with low testosterone levels".[102] When women want to change sex they can get testosterone injections which will activate the ARs.

DNA is made up of a long chain of four molecules – A (adenine), T (thymidine), C (cytosine), and G (guanine). These are like four different kinds or colors of beads on a long necklace. Like the beads on a necklace the four molecules can occur in any order. The genetic code is a long stream of three of these molecules, called DNA triplets (e.g. ATT, CGA, etc.), that are translated into proteins through RNA. When these DNA triplets are repeated (e.g. ATTATTATTATT) the number of repeats is crucial as it can determine the effectiveness of the protein. This is the case with the AR protein. The AR has a particular DNA triplet, CAG, that can have an average sequence of about 10 to about 30 repeats in different men. The sensitivity of the AR is inversely related to the number of CAG repeats.[103] That is to say: the fewer the number of repeats (and thus shorter the chain), the more sensitive (and thus effective) the AR, and therefore the greater the masculinization. On the other hand, the greater the number of repeats the less sensitive and effective the AR. The length of these CAG repeats impacts the degree of "maleness" or androgenicity that is produced. There are degrees or gradations of androgenicity and the lower the sensitivity of the AR, i.e. the longer the CAG chain, the lower the degree of "maleness" or androgenicity.[104] One study found that there is a

---

[101] Michael Zitmann and Eberhard Nieschlag, "The CAG repeat polymorphism within the androgen receptor gene and maleness," International Journal of Andrology 26 (2003): 76-83.

[102] D.F. Swaab, "Sexual differentiation of the human brain: relevance for gender identity, transsexualism and sexual orientation." Gyecol Endocrinol 19 (2004): 301-312 (303).

[103] See Joe Herbert, Testosterone: Sex, Power, and the Will to Win (Oxford: Oxford University Press, 2015) 31-33.

[104] Michael Zitmann and Eberhard Nieschlag, "The CAG repeat polymorphism within the androgen receptor gene and maleness," International Journal of Andrology 26 (2003): 76-83.

1.7% decrease in AR activity for each additional CAG repeat.[105] Complete insensitivity of the AR leads to a female phenotype.

There are ethnic differences in the length and thus the sensitivity and activity of the AR. African males have the shortest CAG_n repeat polymorphism and thus the highest grade of "androgenicity" or maleness: 6-20 repeats (Africans) vs. 21-22 (Caucasians) and 22-23 (Asians).[106] In an AR study covering Africa, Asia and North America the "results reveal that populations of African descent possess significantly shorter alleles for the two loci than non-African populations (P<0.0001)."[107] In a study of Afro-Caribbean and Caucasian subjects, Afro-Caribbeans were shown to have the shortest repeat lengths and greatest predicted AR activity.[108]

_____

[105] Grant Buchanan et al., "Structural and functional consequences of glutamine tract variation in the androgen receptor," Human Molecular Genetics 13 (2004): 1677-1692 (1682-1683).

[106] Grant Buchanan et al., "Structural and functional consequences of glutamine tract variation in the androgen receptor," Human Molecular Genetics 13 (2004): 1677-1692 (1679): "The normal distribution of the AR-CAG microsatellite has been reported as 6-39 repeats, with a median of 19-20 in African American, 21-22 in White Caucasians, 22-23 in Asian and 23 in Hispanic populations." See further: Michael Zitmann and Eberhard Nieschlag, "The CAG repeat polymorphism within the androgen receptor gene and maleness," International Journal of Andrology 26 (2003): 76-83; R.A. Kittles et al., "Extent of linkage disequilibrium between the androgen receptor gene CAG and GGC repeats in human populations: implications for prostate cancer risk," Hum Genet 109 (2001): 253-61.

[107] R.A. Kittles et al., "Extent of linkage disequilibrium between the androgen receptor gene CAG and GGC repeats in human populations: implications for prostate cancer risk," Hum Genet 109 (2001): 253-61.

[108] Christine M. Ackerman et al. "Ethnic Variation in Allele Distribution of the Androgen Receptor (AR) $(CAG)_n$ Repeat," J Androl 33 (2012): 1-11: "The range of alleles differed among ethnicities, with the Thais and Caucasians having the largest range (6–40 repeats, 32 alleles total) and the Afro-Caribbeans having the smallest range (9–37 repeats, 24 alleles total). The Caucasians, our largest group (7786 individuals, 13 822 chromosomes), had the highest number of rare alleles (frequency <.01 , n = 18), and the Afro-Caribbeans, our second smallest group (2261 individuals, 3933 chromosomes), had the fewest rare alleles (n = 6). A20 through A23 were common to all ethnicities (frequency >.05). The most common CAG repeats were A18 in Afro-Caribbeans (.17), A21 in Caucasians (.19), A23 in Hispanics (.15), and A22 in Thais (.21). The mean CAG repeat lengths were Afro-Caribbean

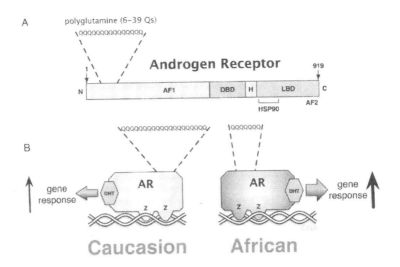

A

polyglutamine (6–39 Qs)

Androgen Receptor

N | AF1 | DBD | H | LBD | C

AF2

HSP90

B

Caucasion   African

gene response   gene response

The AR gene structure characteristic of Caucasian males shows 20 CAG repeats, each repeat shown here as a "Q." In contrast, the AR gene structure characteristic of African males shows 7 CAG repeats or "Q's". The difference is profound. Photo from Assumpta C. Nwaneri, Lucien McBeth and Terry D. Hinds Jr., "Prostate Cancer in African American Men: The Effect of Androgens and microRNAs on Epidermal Growth Factor Signaling," *Horm Cancer* 7 (2016): 296-304.

This is true for the Black male in America as well:

studies have shown that AA men have significantly shorter CAG repeats in comparison to CA men...[109]

The mean and median CAG repeat length in blacks were statistically significantly shorter than in whites. Black men were twice as likely as whites to have fewer than 20 CAG repeats (56.9 % versus 28.5%, P=6,0001).[110]

19.6 ± 3.2, Caucasian 21.9 ± 2.9, Hispanic 22.6 ± 3.1, and Thai 23.1 ± 3.3."

[109] Assumpta C. Nwaneri, Lucien McBeth and Terry D. Hinds Jr., "Prostate Cancer in African American Men: The Effect of Androgens and microRNAs on Epidermal Growth Factor Signaling," Horm Cancer 7 (2016): 296-304.

[110] O. Sartor, Q. Zhen and J.A. Eastham, "Androgen receptor gene CAG repeat length varies in a race-speficif fashion in men without prostate cancer," Urology 53 (1999): 378-80.

And this means that among all races the African male is the quintessential "He-Man," because he has the most "He-Hormone," i. e. testosterone; he has the most ARs to accommodate all of the testosterone; and he has the most sensitive ARs to effectuate the testosterone. This is why Africans and African-descended populations are naturally more physically robust than non-Africans. They outclass Europeans for weight, chest size, arm girth, leg girth, muscle fiber properties, bone density, and general masculinization.[111] The Black Man is the world's Mr. T (Testosterone).

And the Caucasian is his opposite: a near She-Man. The longer CAG repeat chains characteristic of the European results not only in reduced AR action but also in elevated estrogen levels and action. Ilpo T. Huhtaniemi et al. demonstrated in a study of 3000 men from eight European countries that the longer CAG repeats of Caucasians are associated with heightened estradiol (E2) production and action in men. This combination of decreased AR action and increased E2 production and action can produce a phenotype that "resembles mild forms of androgen insensitivity syndrome," i.e. a feminized phenotype.

We present here the largest dataset to date of *AR* CAG repeat measurements from a group of 2878 European men aged 40–79 yr. The mean repeat length measured, 22.1 +/- 3.1 (SD), is in agreement with previous data on Caucasian populations ... The *AR* CAG repeat length correlated directly with all measures (total, bioavailable, free) of serum T and E2, and there was a strong positive correlation between circulating levels of T and E2. Because the transcriptional activity of AR decreases with increasing CAG repeat length, a parallel increase in molar concentrations of E2 and T levels implies *a concomitant increase in the ratio of estrogen/androgen bioactivity...* We found that the T and E2 concentrations were highly correlated, and hence the E2/T ratio remained constant as the CAG repeat length increased. In this sense, *the long CAG repeat with increased E2 production resembles mild forms of androgen*

---

[111] P.F.M. Ama et al., "Skeletal muscle characteristics in sedentary Black and Caucasian males," Journal of Applied Physiology 61 (1986): 1758-61; Bruce Ettinger et al., "Racial Differences in Bone Density between Young Adult Black and White Subjects Persist after Adjustment for Anthropometric, Lifestyle, and Biochemical Differences," The Journal of Clinical Endocrinology & Metabolism 82 (1997): 429-434.

insensitivity syndrome. Because androgen action is relatively impaired but estrogen action is maintained, when the CAG repeats become longer, the effective bioactive estrogen/androgen ratio must increase... Estrogens have direct inhibitory effects on testicular Leydig cell function and spermatogenesis, which may explain why men with longer CAG repeats have higher frequency of idiopathic infertility (emphasis added).[112]

The Black male and the white male are thus biochemically very different, and this fact undergirds the differences in PCa incidence among Black and white men.

II.   *America's So-Called Negro*

After over 400 years of suffering under American White Supremacy, the American Black male is a shell of his old self. Nevertheless, despite having been biochemically assaulted for so long he still has the highest T levels in America. As **The New York Times** writer Andrew Sullivan notes:

Studies have shown that inner-city youths, often exposed to danger in high-crime neighborhoods, may generate higher testosterone levels than unthreatened, secluded suburbanites... Even more unsettling is the racial gap in testosterone. Several solid studies, published in publications like Journal of the National Cancer Institute, show that black men have on average 3 to 19 percent more testosterone than white men.[113]

Inner city Black males indeed have higher T levels.[114] In 1986 Black college age males in Los Angeles were shown to have serum testosterone levels 19% (mean) and 21% (free) higher than white males, and after adjustment 15% and 13% higher,

---

[112] Ilpo T. Huhtaniemi, "Increased Estrogen Rather Than Decreased Androgen Action Is Associated with Longer Androgen Receptor CAG Repeats," J Clin Endocrinol Metab 94 (2009):277–284.

[113] Andrew Sullivan, "The He Hormone," The New York Times Magazine April 2, 2000.

[114] Allan Mazur, "The age-testosterone relationship in black, white, and Mexican-American men, and reasons for ethnic differences," Aging Male 12 (2009): 66-76; "Testosterone Is High among Young Black Men with Little Education," Frontiers in Sociology 1 (2016): 1-5.

respectively.[115] In 1992 Ellis and Nyborg studied a different age group – middle aged men – and still found that "compared with non-Hispanic white men, black men had significantly higher levels of serum testosterone. Hispanic and Native American men had mean values similar to white men."[116] This fact was often stated in studies:

Significantly higher serum levels of total testosterone (P<.1) and SHBG[117] (P<.02) were found in the (young adult) African American than in the Caucasian men in both the morning and evening, whereas free testosterone levels were similar in both groups.[118]

Serum testosterone concentration appears to be higher in black men than white men, especially at young ages...After adjustment for age and [body mass index], total testosterone was higher in blacks (0.21 ng/ml; P = 0.028) than whites, an approximately 3% difference.[119]

Young adult African-American males have higher circulating levels of testosterone than Whites.[120]

In studies of men in their 20s and 30s, higher plasma testosterone concentrations have been observed [in African-Americans].[121]

---

[115] R. Ross et al, "Serum testosterone levels in healthy young black and white men," Journal of the National Cancer Institute 76 (1986): 45-8.
[116] Lee Ellis and Helmuth Nyborg, "Racial/ethnic variations in male testosterone levels: a probable contributor to group differences in health," Steroids 57 (1992): 72-75 (73). They found a 3.3 % higher T level in Black men compared to white men.
[117] SHBG = Sex Hormone Binding Globulin
[118] S.J. Winters et al. "Testosterone, sex hormone-binding globulin, and body composition in young adult African American and Caucasian men," Metabolism 50 (2001): 1242-7.
[119] Susan M. Gapstur, "Serum Androgen Concentrations in Young Men: A Longitudinal Analysis of Associations with Age, Obesity, and Race. The CARDIA Male Hormone Study," Cancer Epidemiology, Biomarkers & Prevention 11 (2002): 1041-1047.
[120] Nancy Potischman et al., "Pregnancy Hormone Concentrations Across Ethnic Groups: Implications for Later Cancer Risk," Cancer Epidemiology, Biomarkers & Prevention 14 (2005): 1514-1520 (1518).
[121] Sabine Rohrmann et al., "Racial Variation in Sex Steroid Hormones and the Insulin-Like Growth Factor Axis in Umbilical Cord Blood of

Testosterone and SHBG are not notably different in white and Mexican-American (MA) males. In the age range 20-69 years, black men (during the years 1988-1991) average 0.39 ng/ml higher testosterone than white and MA men (p < 0.001).[122]

A meta-analysis conducted in 2014 found:

After age adjustment, free testosterone levels were significantly higher in black than in white men ([weighted mean difference] = 4.07 pg/ml, 95% CI 1.26, 6.88). Depending on the free testosterone concentration in white men, this WMD translates into a racial difference ranging from 2.5 to 4.9%.[123]

Hui Hu et al. also reported in 2015, with an important caveat:

Black males had higher concentrations of total, free, and bioavailable testosterone compared to white males...We also found that *black males experienced a more dramatic age-related change in testosterone levels than white males.* These results suggest that testosterone levels more frequently *fall below the necessary threshold in black males, which may eventually lead to the development of PCa* and help explain racial disparities in PCa. However, this hypothesis warrants further investigation.[124]

Why do Black males suffer such a drastic decline in T levels as compared to white men? We believe that we can demonstrate that this fall in testosterone is no accident. The American Black male's testosterone has been targeted and deliberately diminished.

Male Neonates," Cancer Epidemiol Biomarkers Prev 18 (2009): 1484-1491 (1487).

[122] Allan Mazur, "The age-testosterone relationship in black, white, and Mexican-American men, and reasons for ethnic differences," Aging Male 12 (2009): 66-76.

[123] A. Richard et al., "Racial variation in sex steroid hormone concentration in black and white men: a meta-analysis," Andrology 2 (2014): 428-435.

[124] Hui Hu et al., "Racial Differences in Age-Related Variations of Testosterone Levels Among US Males: Potential Implications for Prostate Cancer and Personalized Medication," J. Racial and Ethnic Health Disparities 2 (2015): 69-76 (71).

III. *Superior From Birth*

"Black men are exposed to higher levels of circulating androgens from birth to approximately age 35 years,"[125] affirms Curtis Pettaway writing in the ***Journal of the National Medical Association***. Indeed, the Black male in Africa and in the diaspora has the highest level of testosterone and the most effective androgen profile. While in the womb his Black mother predisposes the Black male fetus to a very masculine profile, more so than does the white mother for her son. Pregnant Black mothers bathe their sons in much higher levels of androgens (and estrogens) than pregnant white mothers do their sons.[126] As Nancy Potischman et al. reported in 2005:

> Caucasian women had statistically significantly lower levels of androstenedione, testosterone, estrone (an estrogen), and prolactin compared with Hispanic women. The mean levels in Caucasian women were 10%, 16%, 24%, and 29% lower, respectively, than levels in Hispanic women. Levels for these hormones were similarly lower in comparisons of Caucasian with African-American women, although not statistically significant for estrone. The mean levels were 31%, 69%, and 29% lower among Caucasian compared with African-American women for androstenedione, testosterone, and prolactin, respectively. Although not statistically significant ($P < 0.10$), estradiol was 10% and 12% lower among Caucasian women compared with Hispanic and African-American women, respectively. Androgens were notably higher among the African-American sample compared with either Hispanics or Caucasians. Progesterone was modestly elevated among the African-American women compared with Hispanic ($P < 0.05$) and Caucasian women ($P < 0.10$). There were no differences in

---

[125] Curtis Pettaway, "Racial Differences in the Androgen/Androgen Receptor Pathway in Prostrate Cancer," Journal of the National Association 91 (1999): 653-660.

[126] Sabine Rohrmann et al., "Racial Variation in Sex Steroid Hormones and the Insulin-Like Growth Factor Axis in Umbilical Cord Blood of Male Neonates," Cancer Epidemiol Biomarkers Prev 18 (2009): 1484-1491; Tanya Agurs-Collins et al., "Racial variation in umbilical cord blood sex steroid hormones and the insulin-like growth factor axis in African-American and white female neonates," Cancer Causes Control 23 (2012): 445-454.

the concentrations of DHEAS and SHBG across the three groups.[127]

The *natural* greater amount of endogenous estrogen in the Black woman's uterine environment vs. the white woman's is no threat to the developing male fetus. This is because the fetal brain is protected against the effects of the mother's circulating estrogen by the protein α-fetoprotein, which is produced by the fetus and binds to the estrogen, inactivating it and thus nullifying the potential effects.[128] This is why, despite the higher circulating estrogen in the Black woman's uterine environment during gestation as compared to the white woman's, Black male neonates showed no higher exposure to estrogen than did white male neonates according to studies of umbilical cord blood concentrations (which provide an estimate of prenatal exposure).[129] The mother's high circulating T, on the other hand, is not bound by α-fetoprotein and is in fact *protective* to the male fetus against cancers. Something will happen, however, and things will change. That "something" is an estrogen assault against the Black man and woman in America.

---

[127] Nancy Potischman et al., "Pregnancy Hormone Concentrations Across Ethnic Groups: Implications for Later Cancer Risk," Cancer Epidemiology, Biomarkers & Prevention 14 (2005): 1514-1520, 1516.

[128] Dick Swaab and Alicia Garcia-Falgueras. "Sexual differentiation of the human brain in relation to gender identity and sexual orientation." Functional Neurology 24 (2009): 17-28 (17): "The fetal brain is protected against the effect of circulating estrogens from the mother by the protein α-fetoprotein, which is produced by the fetus and binds strongly to estrogens but not to testosterone." Also John A. McLachlan and Retha R. Newbold, "Estrogens and Development," Environmental Heath Perspectives 75 (1987): 25-27.

[129] In a 2009 study of cord blood concentrations of sex steroids of 75 Black and 38 white male neonates born at Prince George's Hospital Center in Cheverly, MD and the Johns Hopkins Hospital in Baltimore, MD, Rohrmann et al. found that, while the molar ratio of T to sex hormone binding globulin was higher in Black vs. white male neonates, "Cord blood estradiol concentrations did not differ by race." Rohrmann et al., "Racial Variation in Sex Steroid Hormones," 1487.

IV.   *From Mr. T to Mr. E (Estrogen)*

While Ross et al. found in 1986 that college age Black males of Los Angeles had around 12-21% higher T than white males of the same background, at the same time (1986) S.R. Srinivasan et al. studied a different population of Black and white males in Bogalusa, Louisiana and made an equally important discovery. They studied the steroid hormone levels of adolescent boys (11-17 years of age) enrolled in the Bogalusa Heart Study in 1981-1982 in the small biracial Louisiana town (64% white, 36% Black). 509 boys were examined (258 Black, 251 white). Unlike what Ross et al. found among the young adult population of Black males in Los Angeles, the adolescent Black boys of Bogalusa had testosterone levels that were no higher than that of the white adolescents. But this is no shocker necessarily. Testosterone levels peak - and thus diverge the most between races - during young adult years. However, what was shocking about the Black boys of this small Southern community was: "Black boys had significantly higher levels of estradiol...than white boys." They go on: "Black boys consistently had higher estradiol and lower levels of androstenedione levels than white boys, while the levels of testosterone, DHEA-S, and progesterone were similar in the races."[130] Lowered T and elevated E levels are often directly connected because estradiol and estrone feed back to the hypothalamus and the pituitary and inhibit T production.

How did the world's Mr. T become in this small Louisiana community Mr. E? A clue to the answer may lie in the fish found in the city's water source, Pearl River. In 2003 Ann Oliver Cheek and colleagues reported endocrine disruption in a wild population of longear sunfish (*Lepomis megalotis*). The Pearl River at Bogalusa receives industrial discharge from the community's longstanding paper mill, the Bogalusa Paper Mill, operating there since the 1930s. The mill produces unbleached kraft paper, which is paperboard (cardboard) produced from

---

[130] [S.R. Srinivasan et al., "Racial (black-white) comparisons of the relationship of levels of endogenous sex hormones to serum lipoproteins during male adolescence: the Bogalusa Heart Study," Circulation 74 (1986): 1226-1234; R.J. Richards et al., "Steroid hormones during puberty: racial (black-white) differences in androstenedione and estradiol—the Bogalusa Heart Study," The Journal of Clinical Endocrinology & Metabolism 75 (1992): 624-631].

58

chemical pulp in the kraft process, the process of converting wood into wood pulp using sodium sulfide. Wastewater from the mill spills into the river carrying unbleached kraft effluent and recycled pulp mill effluent with it. Cheek et al. discovered that male longear fish downstream from the mill had significantly lowered 11-ketotestosterone (the main androgen in male fish) and elevated estradiol. Thus, they report:

> Males downstream of the outfall have slightly lower T levels and slightly higher estradiol levels than males upstream and the ratio of T to estradiol is significantly lower in downstream males, indicating that exposure to mill effluent has a slightly demasculinizing effect on males. [131]

In 2003 also Maria S. Sepulveda et al. studied the endocrine effects of bleached and unbleached kraft mill effluent on Florida largemouth bass (Micropterus salmoides). They note that pulp and paper mill effluent can stimulate reduction in gonad size, delay of sexual maturation, and reduce production of sex steroids or hormones. Georgia Pacific's Florida kraft mill is the Palatka plant which discharges effluent into Rice Creek. Sepulveda and colleagues found that the kraft effluent masculinized female fish by lowering estradiol as well as vitellogenin (VTG), the precursor protein of egg yolk found only in the blood of females, while also demasculinizing male bass by raising estradiol levels and lowering 11-ketotestosterone levels.[132]

The hormonal profile of male fish exposed to kraft mill effluent resembles that of adolescent Black boys of Bogalusa, who are also exposed to kraft mill effluent. This cannot be mere coincidence. Rather, we will document in great detail in an upcoming writing that such environmental contamination has been weaponized against the masculinity of Black males. This tiny town of Bogalusa, LA is just the tip of the iceberg. There has

---

[131] A.O. Cheek et al., "Models and Murkiness: Evaluating Fish Endocrine Disruption in the Laboratory and the Field," in Proceedings of the 3rd International Conference on Pharmaceuticals and Endocrine Disrupting Chemicals in Water, March 19-21, 2003, Minneapolis, MN (Mississippi-Alabama Sea Grant Consortium, 2003) 1-12 (3).
[132] Maria S. Sepulveda et al., "Effects of Pulp and Paper Mill Effluents on Reproductive Success of Largemouth Bass," Environmental Toxicology and Chemistry 22 (2003): 205-213.

been a deliberate effort to diminish the testosterone levels of Black males and raise their estrogen levels, thereby biochemically feminizing them *and causing cancers.*

In 2007 Sabine Rohrmann and colleagues published a very important study: "Serum Estrogen, But Not Testosterone, Levels Differ between Black and White Men in a Nationally Representative Sample of American's."[133] What they discovered showed that Bogalusa was not a local, isolated occurrence but representative of a national phenomenon. Rohrmann et al. studied the hormone levels of 1413 men aged 20 to 90 years. Data was collected from the Third National Health and Nutrition Examination Survey (NHANES III), which was a cross-sectional study of the U.S. civilian non-institutionalized population conducted between 1988-1994. Rohrmann et al. analyzed the stored serum of 1470 men from across the country: 674 non-Hispanic white, 363 non-Hispanic Black, and 376 Mexican American males, with 57 "others."

They made an astounding discovery: "Contrary to the postulated racial difference, testosterone concentrations did not differ notably between black and white men. However, blacks had higher estradiol levels."[134] It is not that Rohrmann et al. did not find higher T among this national sample of Black men than white men. They did, just not "significantly higher," meaning the difference between Black and white T levels did not reach p = 0.05. However, Allan Mazur reanalyzed the data used by Rohrmann et al. using more refined methods and came to a different conclusion: those Black males *did* have significantly higher T levels than whites and Hispanics, an average of 0.39 ng/mL (nanogram per milliliter).[135] Nevertheless, this margin is small compared to the natural margin between Black and white T levels, so we *are* in fact witnessing the incredibly diminishing T levels of Black men in America, the results (we shall show) of

---

[133] Sabin Rohrmann et al. "Serum Estrogen, But Not Testosterone, Levels Differ between Black and White Men in a Nationally Representative Sample of American's," The Journal of Clinical Endocrinology & Metabolism 92 (2007): 2519-2525.

[134] Rohrmann et al. "Serum Estrogen, But Not Testosterone, Levels Differ," 2519.

[135] Allan Mazur, "The age-related relationship in black, white, and Mexican-American men, and reasons for ethnic differences," *The Aging Male* 12 (2009): 66-76.

a scientific assault that began in earnest during the Nixon Administration (1969-1974).

This data also revealed the incredibly elevated estrogen levels among Black men: "At all ages, non-Hispanic black men had higher estradiol concentrations than non-Hispanic whites and Mexican Americans; this difference was significant in the young and middle-aged groups."[136] The Black men in this national sample averaged an estradiol level of 40.80 pg/mL (picograms per milliliter of blood) compared to 35.46 pg/mL (white men) and 34.46 pg/mL (Mexican Americans).

Rohrmann et al. followed up this study in 2013, this time focusing on 12-19 year olds of NHANES III instead of the adult men of the 2007 study. In contrast to the first findings with the latter group (20-90 year olds), "Estradiol concentration was *lower* in non-Hispanic blacks and Mexican American compared with white Americans (emphasis added)." They say further:

> In 12-15 year olds, none of the hormones were statistically significantly different between any of the racial/ethnic groups, although several patterns were present. Total and free testosterone concentrations were lower in non-Hispanic blacks than non-Hispanic whites...Total estradiol concentrations were similar between non-Hispanic blacks and Mexican Americans, but possibly higher in non-Hispanic whites. For free estradiol, concentrations were highest in non-Hispanic whites, intermediate in Mexican Americans, and lowest in non-Hispanic blacks...In the 16-19 year olds...[t]otal and free estradiol and SHBG concentrations appeared to be higher in non-Hispanic blacks compared to the other two groups.[137]

Thus, they conclude: "Unlike what we previously observed in adults, estradiol levels were not highest in non-Hispanic blacks after multivariable adjustment."

This is a quite important observation. While in the adult sample, Black men were found to have higher estradiol levels than white men, this was not the case with adolescent Black and white boys. Both T and E2 levels were pretty congruent among the adolescents (12-15), which is consistent with what we know from other studies. In particular, Hui Hu et al., working with a

---

[136] 2521
[137] David S. Lopez et al., "Racial/ethnic differences in serum sex steroid hormone concentrations in US adolescent males," **Cancer Causes Control** 24 (2013): 1-17.

nationally representative sample of 1,554 Black, white, and Hispanic men from the 1999-2004 NHANES, documented the important *age-related variations* in T levels.[138] That is to say, between the ages of 12 and 15 Black males may actually have *lower* T than white males. However, in Black males T levels rapidly increase with age, peaking higher than white males and peaking earlier than white males at 20-30 years of age. From 20-39 Black males had considerably higher levels of total, free and bioavailable testosterone than white males. This seems to be the natural rhythm of the Black male's vs. the white male's testosterone journey: higher T in utero, lower (or equal) T during adolescence, T peaking earlier by 20-30 years old and higher, and then T maintaining its superiority through around 39 years old. But then something dramatic occurs: By middle age Black males in America suffer a rapid drop in T that is not witnessed in his white counterparts to the same degree. Environmental forces no doubt contribute to this otherwise inexplicably rapid decline in T levels that for Black males occurs much earlier than white males and to a far greater magnitude. We are documenting that this is a result of this society's deliberate assault on Black male testosterone levels.

There is also the evidence of umbilical cord blood (UCB). UCB is the current method of assessing fetal hormone levels during a typical pregnancy. UCB is normally collected after delivery near term, thus serum hormone concentrations are believed to reflect fetal levels rather than maternal levels at late stage gestation. Through this means we can speculate on hormonal "endowments" of babies of different ethnicities or, how Black and white males hormonally "start" the race in the morning of life. In a joint Howard University and Johns Hopkins University 2009 study Rohrmann et al. analyzed steroid hormone levels in the cord blood of male neonates, 75 Black and 38 white and found that, after adjusting for maternal and birth factors (birth weight, placental weight, mother's age and parity, and time of day of birth) Black neonates had higher cord blood concentration of T than white neonates as well as a lower concentration of Sex Hormone Binding Globulin

---

[138] [Hui Hu et al. "Racial differences in Age-Related Variations of Testosterone Levels Among US Males: Potential Implications for Prostate Cancer and Personalized Medication," *Journal of Racial and Ethnic Health Disparities* 2 (2015): 69-76].

(SHBG).[139] SHBG is the glycoprotein that tightly binds to T making it biologically unavailable and inactive. The less SHBG one has in his blood, the more T that is biologically available to activate receptors. The more SHBG, the less T available. Rohrmann et al. found here that Black neonates had a higher molar ratio of T-to-SHBG, which means Black neonates started life with more T available to them than white male neonates who had higher SHBG which bound up their already less testosterone. Rohrmann et al. also found that Black neonates were *not* born with elevated estradiol levels compared with white male neonates. So the phenomenon of the Black Man as Mr. E is not a natural phenomenon but an environmentally induced one in later stages of life.

So Rohrmann et al.'s 2013 findings that Black males and white males had similar T levels at 12-15 is consistent with what we already know. Nor are Black males' estrogen levels noteworthy in this 2013 study. They have no more estradiol than white adolescents (though this is notable as well). However, by 16-19 the impact of environmental estrogens begins displaying itself, as Black males of that age group are reported here to show higher estradiol levels. This trend will continue. As the environments that most Black males tend to live in have been deliberately made estrogenically toxic (see below), we are bombarded daily with sources of excess estrogen all while our environment is also made to diminish our T levels. This is how the world's Mr. T became the world's Mr. E, I believe.

The *world's* Mr. E? Yes, the world's. In 2010 a major study of serum sex steroid levels in 5003 men 65 years and older from five different countries, racial and geographical variation (US, Japan, Hong Kong, Sweden, Tobago) was conducted. Orwell et al. found that:

Black men (from the United states and Tobago, West Africa) had higher estrogen levels than Caucasians or Asians. Total and free estradiol levels were 10-16% higher and estrone levels were 27-39% higher in Black men after age and (body mass index) adjustments. Moreover, in Blacks the ratio of total estradiol:

---

[139] Sabine Rohrmann et al. "Racial variation in sex steroid hormones and the insulin-like growth factor axis in umbilical cord blood of male neonates," **Cancer Epidemiol Biomarkers Prev** 18 (2009): 1484-1491.

total testosterone and estrone:androstenedione (4-dione) were increased compared with other groups.[140]

Wow. With few exceptions, by old age Black men in America had accumulated much more estrogen in our blood than any other people on the earth, it appears (and the few exceptions are Black men, but from other isolated areas[141]). How does this occur? Not naturally. Orwell et al. give an extremely important clue by noting:

> We demonstrate not only that Black men in the United States and Tobago have higher mean estradiol levels than populations of Caucasians and Asians but also provide evidence (higher estrone levels and reduced precursor/product ratios) that implicates increased aromatase activity as the likely explanation.

Aromatase is the enzyme in the body that naturally converts testosterone into estrogen, a process called aromatization. Aromatization helps maintain the critical testosterone-to-estrogen ratio in men and the estrogen-to-testosterone ratio in women. For men who need much more T than E, only about 1/10 of a male's T is naturally aromatized into E. The opposite is true of women: they require a lot of E and little T, so aromatization occurs much more frequently in females, resulting in less T and more E. Higher estrogen levels means lower testosterone levels also because estradiol and estrone feedback to the hypothalamus and pituitary and shuts off T production. If men experience excessive aromatization, causing more than normal amounts of T to be converted to E, the effect is lower T (by both processes: conversion to E and inhibited production) and elevated E ratios, which can produce a whole host of problems - from prostate cancer to

---

[140] Eric S. Orwoll et al. "Evidence for Geographical and Racial Variation in Serum Sex Steroid Levels in Older Men," *The Journal of Clinical Endocrinology & Metabolism* 95 (2010): E151–E160.
[141] See e.g. Frank Giton et al. "Serum Sex Steroids measured in middle-aged European and African-Caribbean men by gas chromatography-mass spectrometry," *European Journal of Endocrinology* 165 (2011): 917-924.

feminization.[142] Black men in America are suffering from *hyperaromatization*, a likely main cause of the rapid decline in testosterone in adult Black men and the excessively high levels of estrogen.

What might cause this hyperaromatization in American Black men? Among other things: the endocrine disrupting pesticides that have disproportionately concentrated use in inner cities - including aromatase promoter Atrazine - and have targeted Black and Brown children, as well as the heavy alcohol use among Black males in America (among other life style choices and factors). These and other factors make Black males particularly susceptible to overstimulation of the aromatase enzyme. But in reality, he is under an Estrogen Assault.

V. *The Estrogen Assault*

Theo Colborn and Kristina Thayer reported in 2000:

Sixteen top predator species in the Laurentian Great Lakes have exhibited reproductive problems or population decline since the 1950s (...). This list includes nine bird species (Bald Eagle, Black-crowned Night Heron, Caspian Tern, Common Tern, Double-crested Cormorant, Forster's Tern, Herring Gull, Osprey, and Ring-billed Gull); three mammals (Beluga whale, mink, and otter); two native fishes (lake trout and sauger); and one reptile (snapping turtle). The tissues of all the troubled animals held relatively high concentrations of organochlorine pesticides and industrial chemicals...Most often the adult animals appeared healthy and only the offspring expressed health problems (...). A systematic review of these health problems revealed a suite of developmental and functional effects that reflected disturbance of the endocrine system (...). These included: thyroid dysfunction in birds and fish; decreased fertility in birds, fish, and mammals; decreased hatching success in birds, fish, and turtles; gross birth deformities in birds, fish, and turtles; metabolic abnormalities in birds; behavioral abnormalities in birds; *demasculinization and feminization of male fish and birds; defeminization and*

---

[142] Stuart J. Ellem and Gail P. Rusbridger, "Aromatase and regulating the estrogen:androgen ratio in the prostate gland," ***Journal of Steroid Biochemistry and Molecular Biology*** 118 (2010): 246-251; David L. Hemsell et al. "Massive Extraglandular Aromatization of Plasma Androstenedione Resulting in Feminization of a Prepubertal Boy," ***The Journal of Clinical Investigation*** 60 (1977): 455-464.

masculinization of female fish and birds; and compromised immune systems in birds and mammals (emphasis added).[143]

Endocrine disruption is the interference with the proper functioning of the endocrine system, especially the activities of the various steroid hormones. Endocrine disruption is often caused by a certain class of chemicals called *endocrine disrupting chemicals* (EDCs). These are natural or synthetic compounds, such as the organochlorine pesticides and industrial chemicals mentioned above, that alter the hormonal and homeostatic systems.[144] EDCs settle into the receptors (androgen receptors and estrogen receptors) intended for hormones and garble the signals, thereby disrupting the body's chemical communication. These compounds are at the root of a global, multi-species phenomenon of demasculinized males. "A large body of scientific data built up over many decades indicates a cause-effect link between exposure to a complex cocktail of chemicals and the feminization and demasculinization of wildlife species, particularly those living in or around the aquatic environment," Susan Jobling and Richard Owen informs us.[145]

Many of these EDCs are *estrogenic*, meaning they mimic the action and effects of the feminizing estrogen hormones. They are called "xeno-estrogens." These estrogen-mimicing chemicals are now said to "flood the environment."[146] The three most common natural estrogens are called estrone (E1), estradiol (E2) and estriol (E3). Estrogen plays an essential role in the growth and maintenance of female secondary sexual characteristics (such as breasts and pubic and armpit hair) and

---

[143]Theo Colborn and Kristina Thayer, "Aquatic Ecosystems: Harbingers of Endocrine Disruption," Ecological Applications 10 (2000): 949-957, 949.

[144] Evanthia Diamanti-Kandarakis et al., "Endocrine-Disrupting Chemicals: An Endocrine Society Scientific Statement," Endocr Rev. 30 (2009): 293-342. (IV.E.2.); Andrea C. Gore et al., "EDC-2: The Endocrine Society's Second Scientific Statement on Endocrine-Disrupting Chemicals," Endocr Rev. 36 (2015): E1–E150.

[145] Susan Jobling and Richard Owen, "Ethinyl oestradiol in the aquatic environment," in European Environment Agency, Late lessons from early warnings: science, precaution, innovation (Copenhagen, Denmark: European Environment Agency, 2013) 279-307.

[146] Paul D. Thacker, "Livestock flood the environment with estrogen," **Environmental Science & Technology** July 1, 2004.

influences the structural differences between female and male bodies: the female's smaller and shorter bones, broader pelvis, narrower shoulders, curved and contoured body due to estrogen increase of fat storage around the hips and thighs, smaller voice box, shorter vocal cords and thus a high-pitched voice, etc. Importantly, estrogen also activates the female hypothalamus to promote female-typical behavior such as lordosis (position of acceptance of male mating attempts). Males have estrogen but only a small amount compared to females. Estrogenic compounds that raise estrogen levels to unnaturally high levels can therefore feminize males, especially male embryos. As Deborah Cadbury notes in her important book, *Altering Eden: The Feminization of Nature*:

> the extraordinary intricate process by which the fetus develops into a male...involves a series of carefully orchestrated hormonal cues where timing was critical, involving male and female hormones. There was the follicle-stimulating hormone released by the pituitary, which in turn drives estrogen production by the Sertoli cells and the formation of Müllerian-inhibiting substance, a hormone which makes the female ducts regress and disappear. At the same time, testosterone, the male hormone, is released by the developing testes and drives masculinization of the reproductive tract...there was one common factor that could disrupt the whole process: excessive exposure to the female hormone estrogen during development...Estrogens, it appeared, could throw the entire delicate system out of balance and mess up development permanently.[147]

And this is in fact a widespread phenomenon, as reported by Gwynne Lyons.

> Feminization of the males of numerous vertebrate species is now a widespread occurrence, with many males of egg laying vertebrate found to be abnormally producing the egg yolk precursor protein, vitellogenin. Vitellogenin (VTG) is synthesized by the liver of nonmammalian vertebrates and induced in response to oestrogen. A decrease in male sex hormone, or in the ratio of the male:female sex hormones can lead to weak male secondary sex characteristics including intersex reproductive organs (part female ovary, part male

---

[147] Deborah Cadbury, Altering Eden: The Feminization of Nature (New York: St. Martin's Press, 1997) 18.

testis), small penis, ineffective mating behaviour, and possibly low fertility.[148]

Male white sucker fish in the Boulder Creek in Boulder, Colorado have turned into females due to the estrogenic concentrations (from birth control residue, etc.) in the effluent discharged from the Wastewater Treatment Plant upstream: "The males have bumps on the forehead and often attack each other. The fish exposed to the effluent water lost their bumps and acted like girls."[149] But the problem of widespread estrogen-induced aquatic transsexuality or even intersexuality was first noted in the waterways of the United Kingdom in 1978 when wild male roach (*Rutilus rutilus*) were found having developed eggs in the testes.[150]

In males xeno-estrogens can contribute to atrophy of the testes, reduced sperm counts, small penises, as well as cancer of the prostate and testes.[151] These synthetic estrogens can feminize a male organism even at a molecular level. Exposure can imprint female genes into the male reproductive tract in such a way that they could become active, or switched on, later in life, producing "molecular pseudohermaphroditism." As Cadbury explains:

> exposure to a potent synthetic estrogen during development could cause three major changes. Firstly, there were structural changes obvious to the naked eye at birth: the reproductive abnormalities such as male and female reproductive systems developed side by side. Secondly, there were the delayed effects, visible under the microscope: changes that were consistent with vaginal or prostate cancers. Thirdly...estrogens, at an even more fundamental level, had altered the way genetic material in the

---

[148] Gwynne Lyons, Effects of Pollutants on the Reproductive Health of Male Vertebrate Wildlife – Males Under Threat (UK: CHEM Trust, n.d.) 1-2.

[149] See David O. Norris et al., "Demasculinization of male fish by wastewater treatment plant effluent," Aquatic Toxicology 103 (2011): 213-221.

[150] Susan Jobling et al., "Widespread Sexual Disruption in Wild Fish," Environ. Sci. Technol. 32 (1998): 2498-2506; "'Troubled Waters': The Impact of water-polluting chemicals on fish populations," Paper read November 2013 at Leeds, UK.

[151] Sherrill Sellman, The Hormone Heresy: What Women Must Know About Their Hormones (Honolulu: GetWell International, 1998) 38-39.

cells expressed itself. Messages were now scrambled, so that males could express female proteins.[152]

We are in the process of documenting that the Black community is under a deliberate *Estrogen Assault.* Our neighborhoods are targeted for estrogenic contamination through our food, water, air and environment. And we believe the evidence strongly points to this fact as the context of Black America's various health crises, including our Cancer Crisis.

---

[152] Cadbury, Altering Eden, 56-57.

Chapter Four

If Black Masculinity is the Disease Black Feminization is the Cure

I.   *Scientific Roots*

On November 30, 1910 the New York *Evening World* published a social commentary by renown cartoonist Maurice Ketten (real name Prosper Fiorini) entitled "Man and Woman: As they Were, As they Are, As They Will Be." This cartoon commentary drew from the writings of American painter John White Alexander. In three panels the past, present and future of biological and cultural gender are represented. The first panel,

"As They Were," depicts "Man" with a robust masculinity – physically and culturally – and "Woman" as the "delicate sex." In Panel Two, "As They Are," Man and Woman of Ketten's and Alexander's day mirror each other physically and culturally: the huge man and dainty woman of Panel One now have physical parity and both look as though they dressed from the same closet. In the future depicted in the third panel, the Man is a dainty effeminate, completely feminized physically and culturally. On the other hand, the future female towers over him with a robust musculature, now a "manly woman," "a sexless substitute for man" that is "so manlike in figure that she will look ridiculous in woman's attire."[153]   This, Ketten and Alexander warn us, is the future of gender in America.

What is of utmost importance is that, in the very year this prediction was made – 1910 - the science necessary to make this prediction a reality emerged. The scientist responsible for this science was Dr. Eugen Steinach, Director of the Biological Institute of the Academy of Sciences in Vienna and one of the leading endocrine researchers of the early 20th century. "Eugen Steinach was born in 1861 to prominent Jewish parents in the city of Hohenems, in the Austrian province of Vorarlberg."[154] Steinach is arguably the Grandfather of The Testosterone Conspiracy and The Estrogen Assault (TCEA). With his student, closest colleague and fellow Jew Heinrich Kun, these two are the "Batman and Robin" of the research and experimentation phase of the TCEA. Steinach's endocrinological work between 1910 and 1930 showed that gender and sexuality were

Eugen Steinach

Heinrich Kun

---

[153] John White Alexander, "Woman Developing Mannish Figure While Man is Becoming Effeminate," New York *Evening World* November 23, 1010.
[154] Per Södersten et al., "Eugen Steinach: The First Neuroendocrinologist," *Endocrinology* 155 (2014): 688-702 (689).

chemically manipulatable.[155] During these two decades of sophisticated laboratory investigation of sex gland function, Steinach's experiments challenged fundamental ideas about masculinity and femininity indicating that, although biological sex might be *determined* by genetic factors, the characteristics of sex – anatomical and behavioral – could always be *modified* by manipulating the hormone levels. "The results of these experiments were published in 1910, and justly caused a revolution in the views held by scientists in regard to the relation between the sex glands and secondary sex characteristics."[156]

Steinach established that growth into a sexually active male depended on chemicals secreted from the testicles (what we now know as testosterone) and he established that it is Black males who possess the greatest amount of this testicular chemical or "juice of the testicles."[157] Steinach further pioneered the surgical procedure of castrating an infant male guinea pig and transplanting ovaries into it and removing the ovaries (ovarectomy) of female guinea pigs while transplanting testes. This produced revolutionary results: the successful reversal of the sex of these experimental animals. When Steinach transferred ovaries and testes in guinea pigs a few days old he found that through these glands the character of each sex underwent a "slow but radical transformation over toward the

---

[155] Cheryle A. Logan, "Overheated Rats, Race, and the Double Gland: Paul Kammerer, Endocrinology and the Problem of Somatic Induction," *Journal of the History of Biology* 40 (2007): 683-725: "But from 1910 to 1930, it was Steinach who had amassed the most convincing evidence showing that the interstitial cells made up a distinct gland that controlled sexual development. They produced the hormones, then termed "incretions," and it was their products that regulated the onset of puberty, the development of male and female sexual characteristics, and the intensity of the sex drive."

[156] Van Buren Thorne, "Dr. Steinach and Rejuvenation," *The New York Times* June 26, 1921, p. 42; "What Determines the Development of the Secondary Sexual characters?" *JAMA* Vol. 58, February 17, 1912, p. 484; "The Modification pf Secondary Sexual Characters," *JAMA* Vol. 60, February 21, 1941, pp. 618-619.

[157] Cheryle A. Logan, "Overheated Rats, Race, and the Double Gland: Paul Kammerer, Endocrinology and the Problem of Somatic Induction," *Journal of the History of Biology* 40 (2007): 683-725 (692ff).

other," causing experimental hermaphroditism.[158] What Steinach discovered was the role that hormones played in *controlling* the development of secondary sexual characteristics and how much control that gives scientists to manipulate gender and sexuality. And of course, "the main scientific aim of these researches on animals was...to gain insight into the corresponding conditions in human beings."[159]

Experiments in which infant males were castrated (thus denied testosterone) and given ovaries (thus being exposed to estrogen) and ovarectomized infant females (denied estrogen) were given testes (thus exposed to testosterone), showed that males developed female accessory sexual morphology (e.g. functioning milk glands) and behaved like females as adults, while females developed morphological characteristics of males and behaved like males as adults. These striking results established Steinach as a pioneer in mammalian reproductive endocrinology and sexual development...Steinach had demonstrated that [sexuality] was flexible...In the early years, his most striking demonstration of the developmental flexibility of sexuality was the creation of experimental hermaphrodites in mammals...Changes in hormones could produce varying blends of masculinity and femininity *in the same individual*.[160]

Steinach's 1910 work offers perhaps the most precise early experimental evidence that hormones shape the development of brain and behavior in frogs and mammals.[161]

---

[158] Eugen Steinach, "Geschlechtstrieb und echt sekundäre Geschlechtsmerkmale als Folge der Innersekretorischen Funktion der Keimdrüsen," ***Zentralblatt für Physiologie*** 24 (1910): 551-566.
[159] Ernest Harms, "Forty-Four Years of Correspondence Between Eugen Steinach and Harry Benjamin," ***Bull. N.Y. Acad. Med.*** 45 (1969): 761-766 (763-764).
[160] Cheryle A. Logan, "Overheated Rats, Race, and the Double Gland: Paul Kammerer, Endocrinology and the Problem of Somatic Induction," ***Journal of the History of Biology*** 40 (2007): 683-725 (689).
[161] Per Södersten et al., "Eugen Steinach: The First Neuroendocrinologist," ***Endocrinology*** 155 (2014): 688-702.

Guinea pigs from Steinach's series of feminization experiments. From left to right: normal brother, feminized brother, normal sister and castrated brother.

In addition to pioneering the laboratory production of hermaphrodites or transgenders, it is said that Steinach also "solved the riddle of homosexuality."[162]

Steinach, characteristically, was not concerned solely with the somatic sexual characters but also with sexual behavior. When his 'feminized' animals reached puberty, they did not display characteristically male mating behavior and showed no interest in females in heat. Instead, they behaved exactly like females, showing the characteristic defense-reflex of females: the raising of a hind foot and sharp backward strike to prevent being clasped by an unwelcome male. Intriguingly, these feminized males were often more feminine in certain ways than average females of their kind. The feminized male, for instance, was even smaller in stature than the usual female, and 'his' breasts were comparable to the breasts of a pregnant female, rather than a young female of 'his' age. The feminized males even lactated; infants of the species recognized them as females and followed them around for milk. The experimental animals obliged by suckling them in what Steinach considered to be the typically feminine way. For Steinach, lactation and maternal care of the young constituted the highest expression of femininity. In 'masculinized' females – females whose ovaries had been removed in infancy and replaced with testicular grafts – the nipples, mammary glands, and uterus remained uninfluenced. The 'indifferent' characters such as build and fur

[162] Chandak Sengoopta, "Glandular Politics: Experimental Biology, Clinical Medicine, and Homosexual Emancipation in Fin-de-Siecle Central Europe," *Isis* 89 (1998): 445-473 (464).

were transformed however, to typically masculine forms. The sexual behavior was masculine: the experimental animals pursued females in heat, fought with other males over possession of females, and clasped them in the typically male way.[163]

What Steinach and colleagues discovered was the role of estrogen in the development of female secondary sexual characteristics *and sexual behavior* and he discovered that estrogen induces female sexual behavior *in males* exposed at an early age. They discovered and demonstrated that by diminishing a male's testosterone and exposing that male to excess estrogen, bisexual and homosexual behavior can be induced in the male; Steinach therefore established the hormonal basis of homosexual and bisexual behavior. Steinach's student Heinrich Kun in 1934 reported that castrated male rats were feminized with a single injection of estradiol benzoate, inducing lordosis (=position assumed by some female mammals during mating).[164]

> In the 1930s, Eugen Steinach's group found that estradiol induces lordosis in castrated rats and reduces the threshold dose of testosterone that is necessary for the induction of ejaculation, and that estradiol-treated intact rats display lordosis as well as mounting and ejaculation. *The bisexual, estrogen-sensitive male had been demonstrated* (Emphasis added).[165]

Steinach therefore proved the hormonal basis of transgenderism and homosexuality and his research laid the foundation for later sex change operations. "All of his experimental findings, Steinach asserted, *were clearly*

---

[163] Chandak Sengoopta, " 'Dr Steinach coming to make old young!': sex glands, vasectomy and the quest for rejuvenation in the roaring twenties," *Endeavour* 27 (2003): 122-126 (124).

[164] Heinrich Kun, "Weibliches Sexualhormon und psychische Brunst des Weibchens. *Anzeiger Akad Wsch Wien* 8 (1934):75-77.

[165] Per Södersten, "Steinach and Young, Discoverers of the Effects of Estrogen on Male Sexual Behavior and the 'Male Brain'," *eNeuro* 2 (November/December 2015): 1-11; Per Södersten et al., "Eugen Steinach: The First Neuroendocrinologist," *Endocrinology* 155 (2014): 688-702.

applicable to humans,"[166] writes Chandak Sengoopta. He says further: "This dream of controlling sexual characteristics and behaviour drew Steinach out of the laboratory into the clinic."[167] It is thus no surprise that the world's first male-to-female sex change surgery was performed on Lili Elbe in 1930 in Dresden, Germany by some of Steinach's own followers.[168]

These researches excited the medical fields. Steinach presented his feminized guinea pigs to the physiological congress in Vienna in 1913 to the surprise of his scientific colleagues.[169] Steinach was nominated for the Nobel Prize 11 times, from 1921 to 1928, for his pioneering and revolutionizing endocrinological work.[170] The burning question from the findings of the "Steinach Revolution" was asked by the magazine ***Physical Culture*** in January of 1937: "Can Sex in Humans Be Changed?" Just some of the article reads:

ALL the old landmarks are going, nothing is static, everything flows. Old dreams and old nightmares become realities. Life is created in the laboratory. Sex is no longer immutable. Recently the astonishing news made the rounds that science had actually succeeded in changing the gender of two female athletes. The miracle was accomplished by surgery and duly acknowledged by law...

While sex is determined in the chromosomes, it nevertheless requires the proper male or female sex hormones to develop naturally. If an endocrine disturbance exists, a faulty sex development may take place. This faulty development, being of an endocrine nature, may be amenable to endocrine treatment.

---

[166] Chandak Sengoopta, "Glandular Politics: Experimental Biology, Clinical Medicine, and Homosexual Emancipation in Fin-de-Siecle Central Europe," ***Isis*** 89 (1998): 445-473 (459, 464).

[167] Chandak Sengoopta, " 'Dr Steinach coming to make old young!': sex glands, vasectomy and the quest for rejuvenation in the roaring twenties," ***Endeavour*** 27 (2003): 122-126 (123).

[168] Ilia Stambler, "The Unexpected Outcomes of Anti-Aging, Rejuvenation, and Life Extension Studies: An Origin of Modern Therapies," ***Rejuvenation Research*** 17 (2014): 297-305 (300).

[169] Van Buren Thorne, "Dr. Steinach and Rejuvenation," ***The New York Times*** June 26, 1921, p. 42

[170] Ilia Stambler, "The Unexpected Outcomes of Anti-Aging, Rejuvenation, and Life Extension Studies: An Origin of Modern Therapies," ***Rejuvenation Research*** 17 (2014): 297-305 (300).

CAN SEX IN HUMANS

BE CHANGED?

By Donald Furthman Wickets

ALL the old landmarks are going, nothing is static, everything flows. Old dreams and old nightmares become realities. Life is created in the laboratory. Sex is no longer immutable. Recently the astonishing news made the rounds that

The medals awarded to him were won in good faith. Equally sensational is Case No. Two. A native of Czecho-Slovakia, Zdenek Koubkov (née Zdeneka Koubkova) reaped athletic honors as a woman. In 1932 he won the hundred-meter championship at the Women's

Courtesy of Mr. Samuel J. Slate and the New York Athletic Club

Was Chevalier d'Eon de Beaumont man or woman? This is the famous Assaut d'armes between d'Eon and Saint George at Carlton House, London, April, 1787, before the Prince of Wales

science had actually succeeded in changing the gender of two female athletes. The miracle was accomplished by surgery and duly acknowledged by law.

Mary Weston, who held (and still holds) the shotput record for women in Great Britain, is Case No. One. In 1926 Mary won the British javelin championship of her sex. "She" also, at one time or another, represented her country's womanhood at the Olympic Games. Today, Mary Weston, now known as Mark Weston, is a young man legally and is happily married to a normal young woman. Dr. L. R. Broster, a London surgeon, certifies: "that Mark Weston, who has always been brought up as a female, is a male and should continue to live as such." Discussing his athletic records before his transformation, Weston insists that he believed at the time that he was a woman.

Olympics. Sports writers called him "the fastest woman on legs." For twenty-three years Zdenek lived as a woman—at one time as a corset fitter—an occupation which, as his nascent masculinity asserted itself, he found at times decidedly embarrassing. No one, except himself, doubted his femininity. However, in 1935, while he was wearing his running togs, suspicion as to his true sex arose. An investigation ensued. Shortly afterward (according to his story related to Gordon Kahn in the *New York Daily Mirror*), Professor Milosh Kileka, head of a surgical institute in Podol, decided to emphasize Zdenek's masculinity by means of an operation. The operation was so successful that the Czecho-Slovakian government officially sanctioned Zdenek's transfer from the female to the male classification.

16

The investigations of Professor Eugen Steinach and other students of biology have shown that our so-called secondary sexual characteristics are largely influenced by our hormones. Various differences in bodily structure, some patent, some elusive, are controlled by the glands of internal secretion.

Steinach has reversed the sex of animals by transplanting a female gland upon a male, or a male gland upon a female.

He has also, by similar methods, created animals having the sex equipment and the characteristics of both sexes... Steinach's experiments reveal that the hormones have a two-fold purpose! One, to strengthen the specific sex characteristics of the individual. Two, to inhibit the development of the characteristics of the opposite sex. For man is a bisexual animal fundamentally and when the dominant gland ceases its vigilance, the characteristics of the suppressed sex assert themselves...

Every male produces certain female hormones, and every female certain male hormones. By increasing the supply of female hormones in the male beyond the normal percentage, the secondary sexual characteristics are profoundly affected.

SIMILARLY, by increasing the male hormones in the female beyond the amount needed for her endocrine balance, a parallel change is wrought in the female. These effects have been illustrated most strikingly in rats, guinea pigs, mice and monkeys. In human beings, experiments of this type are not feasible. It is, moreover, far more difficult to affect the constitution of men, because it is infinitely more complex than that of the lower animals...

The man or the woman who receives a balanced sexual constitution when the male and female element first join together, whose glands secrete the requisite hormones and who achieves sex maturity without being sidetracked from the path of evolution by some psychic or nervous disturbance, will be normal in his or her sexual behavior.

All human beings pass through a stage where sex is more or less undifferentiated, where they are attracted almost equally by either sex. But in 95 out of a 100 cases the bisexual or homosexual components, present in all, sink to the bottom of the stream of consciousness, not to be dislodged except by some emotional or physiological explosion, or by the analyst delving in the deeps of the unconscious.

HOWEVER, any stage in the threefold development outlined may be interrupted or impeded; the slightest variation, the slightest derangement, may, consciously or unconsciously, anatomically or psychically, affect the direction of the sex instinct and constitution. Even within the compass of the "normal" there are infinite variations. My friend, the late Dr. Magnus Hirschfeld, of the Institut fur Sexualwissenschaft in Berlin (suppressed by the Nazis), calculated that the number of different sexual types equals 46,046,721, or three raised to the sixteenth power...

WE are now in the position to revert to our original query. Is it possible to change the sex of human beings? We cannot reply categorically. Our answer must be a conditional "yes" or a conditional "no." It is possible to correct certain errors of nature, but it is impossible, with the present limits of medical science, to change the sex of a mature, normally developed human being. It is possible, at least theoretically, to induce lactation in a male by stimulating the mammillary gland, if he subjects himself to the experiment before puberty. It is possible, under similar circumstances, to accentuate the growth of rudimentary male organs in the female. Science can, age may, and accident will, bring about marked changes in the secondary sexual characteristics, even of a mature individual. But it is not possible to turn a full-fledged male into a female, or a full-fledged female into a male. The surgeon's knife can dissolve (with certain qualifications) the marriage between Salmacis and Hermaphroditus. The endocrinologist can enhance the male or the female characteristics of the pseudo-hermaphrodite; the plastic surgeon can eradicate some malformations. But complete transformation of sex is not accomplished even in animals; Steinach's laboratory males and females are incapable of reproduction. [171]

II.   The "Steinach Revolution" Comes To
       America: Harry Benjamin

Steinach's most famous disciple of twenty years and his main American representative was Harry Benjamin. "Born into a bourgeois German-Jewish family in Berlin, Harry Benjamin (1885-1986)...is known as 'the father of transsexualism.'"[172] Benjamin was fascinated with Steinach's sex-changing experiments on guinea pigs and became Steinach's American disciple in clinical endocrinology as applied "to the hormones of sex reversal in transsexualism."[173]

---

[171] Donald Furthman Wickets, "Can Sex in Humans Be Changed?" **Physical Culture** (January 1937): 16-17, 83-85 (17).
[172] Friedemann Pfäfflin, "Benjamin, Harry (1885-1986)," **The Encyclopedia of Human Sexuality**, First Edition. Edited by Patricia Whelehan and Anne Bolin (John Wiley & Sons, Inc., 2015) 1-2. His father was Julius Benjamin and his mother was Bertha Hoffman Benjamin. See further Ernest Harms, "Forty-Four Years of Correspondence Between Eugen Steinach and Harry Benjamin," **Bull. N.Y. Acad. Med.** 45 (1969): 761-766; Harry Benjamin, "The Steinach Operation: Report of 22 Cases with Endocrine Interpretation," **Endocrinology** 6 (1922): 776-786.
[173] Richard Ekins, "Science, Politics and Clinical Intervention: Harry Benjamin, Transsexualism and the Problem of Heteronormativity,"

Harry Benjamin, Endocrinologist

NOW!
THE FIRST
COMPLETE REPORT
AND REVIEW OF

THE TRANSSEXUAL PHENOMENON

ALL THE FACTS
ABOUT THE CHANGING
OF SEX THROUGH
HORMONES AND SURGERY

HARRY BENJAMIN, M.D.

Including:
Case histories,
detailed description of surgery
plus
24 pages of photographs,
some previously available
only to physicians.

In America, Benjamin "took the revolutionary step of seeking to secure 'sex change' surgery for suitable applicants."[174] Understanding the neuroendocrine origins of transgenderism, Benjamin was one of the pioneer appliers of Steinach's discovery of the feminizing effects of estrogen exposure in males: "the much desired gynecomastia, the shifting of body fat to the hips, loss of body hair with heavier growth on the scalp, and improvement of skin texture and occasional cure of acne."[175] Thus, Benjamin is now known as the "founding father of contemporary western transsexualism,"[176] and his 1966 publication, *The Transsexual Phenomenon*, is known as the "Transsexual Bible."[177] The following is no overstatement: "He was an extraordinarily brave pioneer who, with hindsight, may be seen as playing a major role in enabling contemporary manifestations of transgender diversity to flourish."[178] The precise role he played in today's transgender phenomenon - specifically today's *Black* transgender phenomenon - will elaborated below.

Sexualities 8 (2005): 306-328; Charles L. Ihlenfeld, "Memorial for Harry Benjamin," *Archives of Sexual Behavior* 17 (1988): 1-31 (16).

[174] Ekins, "Science, Politics and Clinical Intervention," 309.

[175] Harry Benjamin, "Transvestism and Transsexualism in the Male and Female," *The Journal of Sex Research* 3 (1967): 107-127.

[176] Ekins, "Science, Politics and Clinical Intervention," 315.

[177] Ekins, "Science, Politics and Clinical Intervention," 315.

[178] Ekins, "Science, Politics and Clinical Intervention," 319.

III.   *The Secret History of Black Transgenderism as Social Change*

Between 1964 and 1967 Harry Benjamin headed a research group which studied transsexualism. During these meetings the idea was raised of applying sex-change surgery on transsexuals. One member of that group was John Money, a psychologist and sexologist from Johns Hopkins University who attended the monthly meetings in New York. The research undertaken by that group was integral to the official establishment of the Johns Hopkins Gender Identity Clinic in 1965, and John Money was the driving force.[179] Money did a Harvard dissertation in 1952 entitled, "Hermaphroditism: An Inquiry into the Nature of a Human Paradox."

In 1966 the Gender Identity Clinic began a secret experimental program of sex change surgery. ***The New York Times*** was the first to report the news after stumbling upon it: "The Johns Hopkins Hospital has quietly begun performing sex change surgery...Johns Hopkins is the first American hospital to give it official support."[180] The most prestigious medical center in the world thus became the first academic institution to give transgender surgery official support. The Male-to-Female (M-to-F) surgery involved removal of the external genitals and creation of a vaginal passage: "Female hormone treatments before and after surgery gradually reduce secondary male sexual characteristics such as body hair and enhance feminine appearance through breast development and the widening of hips."[181]

Through John Money and the Gender Identity Clinic the dream of Eugen Steinach to change human sex became officially operationalized in America. As Money relates:

> Harry Benjamin...became my living-person link with early 20th century psychoendocrinolgy. He was my exemplar of the continuity of scholarly history-and of the dependence of my own scholarship on that of my professional forebears...Harry

[179] Lisa Downing, Jain Morland, Nikki Sullivan, "Pervert or sexual libertarian?: Meet John Money, 'the father of f***ology'," ***Salon*** January 4, 2015.
[180] Thomas Bubkley, "A Changing of Sex By Surgery Begun At Johns Hopkins," ***The New York Times*** November 21, 1966.
[181] Thomas Bubkley, "A Changing of Sex By Surgery Begun At Johns Hopkins," ***The New York Times*** November 21, 1966.

Benjamin knew Eugen Steinach in his youth and had been influenced by his investigations into the endocrinology of rejuvenation...and into the prenatal endocrinology of sex-reversal in guinea pigs...It was Harry Benjamin's destiny to become Steinach's most famous disciple ...Without the evidence of Harry Benjamin's pioneering success in the hormonal and the surgical sex reassignment of transsexuals, there would have been no program set up for the treatment and rehabilitation of transsexuals at Johns Hopkins...The Johns Hopkins transsexual program was a source of immense satisfaction to Harry Benjamin, for it vindicated and authenticated his otherwise lonely advocacy of a group of patients generally despised and ridiculed by the medical establishment.[182]

It was Harry Benjamin who provided the secret experimental program of sex-change surgery at Johns Hopkins with its "inaugural patient"; a Black Man, Avon Wilson. Avon was quietly converted into a pseudo-Black Woman, Phyllis Wilson, who then pranced around the night clubs of New York being shown off (*New York Daily* October 4, 1966).

One psychiatrist associated with the Gender Identity Clinic confessed: "I think transsexualism was viewed by some *as a cause* as opposed to a medical condition."[183] What *cause* was behind and was served by this secret program of transgender surgery, the inaugural patient of which was a Black Man? This transgender surgery had a social agenda called in the press "social-reform-through-sex-change-surgery."[184] The Gender Identity Clinic explored the idea of sex reassignment surgery as the means to transform into more law-abiding citizens patients who had "inadequate social and moral judgement and a long history of petty and sometimes major criminal offenses."[185] That means, for example, that so-called anti-social behavior and petty criminality – such as the civil disobedience of the Civil Rights agitators and the rioting of the inner city Black young males – can be corrected through sex-change surgery, by chemically and surgically turning men into women or pseudo-women.

---

[182] Charles L. Ihlenfeld, "Memorial for Harry Benjamin," *Archives of Sexual Behavior* 17 (1988): 1-31 (16).
[183] Laura Wexler, "Identity Crisis," *Baltimore Style Magazine* Jan/Feb 2007.
[184] Wexler, "Identity Crisis."
[185] Wexler, "Identity Crisis."

There was an arrangement in some cases where, instead of sentencing someone to jail a judge would sentence them to sex-change surgery. In January 1965 a judge (James K. Cullen) in the Criminal Court of Baltimore signed a court order for a 17-year old (white) boy – a former patient of John Money who had a hand in this remarkable legal proceeding – to undergo sex reassignment at Johns Hopkins as a girl in lieu of incarceration for burglary.[186] The boy, who was a transvestite but did not want to be a *transgender* (he reportedly expressly rejected the idea of a sex change: "there would be no point to this since he would not enjoy sex if his genitals were removed"), fled the psychiatric unit that he was held in, never to return.

Plastic surgeon John Hoopes, head of the Gender Identity Clinic at the time, admitted: "The program, including the surgery, is investigational. The most important result of our efforts will be to determine precisely what constitutes a transsexual and what makes him remain that way (1966)." This was an *experimental* program. Later Hoopes confessed:

> Prior to the surgery, these patients were at least male or female but after the surgery the males converted to females weren't really females and the females converted to males weren't really males...*you've created a new breed. You've created something you don't know what to do with*...I never saw a successful patient. For the most part they remained misfits.[187]

It was Money who pioneered the use of progestin drugs, specifically medroxyprogesterone acetate (MPA) – better known as Depo Provera – as a chemical castrater. The first clinical use of MPA/Depo Provera as an androgen-depleting agent was by John Money and colleagues in 1966, though the drug was not yet approved for such usage at the time.[188]

> Depo-Provera is a synthetic progesterone approved by the FDA for use in women as a contraceptive. When used in men, it works to reduce sex drive by inhibiting the release of follicle-

---

[186] For details of this case see Julian Gill-Peterson, "Queer Theory is Kid Stuff: A Genealogy of the Gay and Transgender Child," doctoral dissertation, Rutgers University, New Jersey, 2015. Pp. 120f, 170ff.
[187] Wexler, "Identity Crisis."
[188] John Money, "Discussion on hormonal inhibition of libido in male sex offenders," **Endocrinology and Human Behavior** (London: Oxford University Press, 1968).

stimulating and luteinizing hormones from the anterior pituitary gland.' Limiting the release of these two hormones reduces the amount of testosterone produced by the testicles. The net effect is a reduction of both the amount of testosterone in the bloodstream *and the aggression that it produces*. Depo-Provera also increases the metabolism of testosterone by the body, accordingly lowering its presence in the body. In effect, then, Depo-Provera "burns the candle from both ends" by simultaneously limiting the production of testosterone and decreasing its prevalence in the bloodstream.[189]

Money and colleagues pioneered the use of MPA/Depo for sex-offenders but also as a medication for "impulsive aggression," "uncontrollable paroxysmal rage," "nonsexual anti-social behavior (for example robbery, destructiveness, threats, etc.)," and "severe angry-aggression behavior disorder."[190]   Also, "black masculine hostility."

MPA/Depo was capable of feminizing male fetuses and masculinizing female fetuses, as well as *homosexualizing* both after they become adults. In 1967 Money reported on "Progestin-Induced Hermaphroditism," i.e. cases of woman given progestin drugs like MPA during pregnancy resulting in the fetal masculinization of their female infants with abnormality of sex differentiation.[191] In addition, a 2017 study

---

[189] Raymond A. Lombardo, "California's Unconstitutional Punishment for Heinous Crimes: Chemical Castration of Sexual Offenders," *Fordham Law Review* 65 (1997): 2611-2646 (2613); Gary Gordon et al., "Effect of Medroxyprogesterone Acetate (Provera) on the Metabolism and Biological Activity of Testosterone," *J Clin Endocr* 30 (1970): 449-456;

[190] John Money, "Use of an Androgen-Depleting Hormone in the Treatment of Male Sex Offenders," *The Journal of Sex Research* 6 (1970): 165-172; John Money et al., "47,XYY and 46,XY males with antisocial and/or sex-offending behavior: Antiandrogen therapy plus counseling," *Psychoneuroendocr.* 1 (1975): 165-78; Claus Wiedeking, John Money and Paul Walker, "Follow-up of 11 XYY males with impulsive and/or sex-offending behaviour," *Psychology Medicine* 9 (1979):287-292; John Money and Richard G. Bennett, "Post Adolescent Paraphilic Sex Offenders: Antiandrogenic and Counseling Therapy Follow-Up," *International Journal of Mental Health* 10 (1981): 122-133.

[191] Anke A. Ehrhardt and John Money, "Progestin-Induced Hermaphroditism: IQ and Psychosexual Identity in a Study of Ten Girls," *The Journal of Sex Research* 3 (1967): 83-100.

showed that bisexuality was common among men and woman whose mothers were exposed to progestins while pregnant and that treating a woman with a progestin during pregnancy appears to be linked to the child's sexuality later in life.[192] And *this* drug will be designated by the U.S. government as the chemical means of calming the Black Rage in inner city Black males.

---

[192] J.M. Reinisch et al., "Prenatal Exposure to Progesterone Affects Sexual Orientation in Humans," **Arch Sex Behav** 46 (2017): 1239-1249; Hannah Osborne, "Progesterone during pregnancy appears to influence child's sexuality," **International Business Times** April 4, 2017.

Chapter Five:

White Male Fragility and
The Assault on Black Masculinity

I.   *The Crisis of White Masculinity*

American White masculinity has suffered a perpetual crisis from the 1830s to the present. The American Civil War was the major turning point for middle-class attitudes toward masculinity. In the South, White manhood was defeated, humiliated, and forced to retreat into defensive, violent, racialized fantasies. Black men became "the antihero in a sadomasochistic (homosexual but heterosexualized) reenactment of [White Southerners'] own subjectively experienced 'crisis' as 'men'."[193] Southern White men were the sons of the defeated Confederacy and as such their manhood and masculinity were denied. The Confederacy is feminized in the propaganda of the time and Jefferson Davis, the President of the Confederate States, was frequently depicted in the Northern press cross-dressed as the "President in Petticoats," wearing his wife's clothing while fleeing Union soldiers "in feminine fear."[194]

Fortunes changed for the better for White masculinity after World War II. The male insecurities produced by the Depression of the 1930s was followed by a post-war economic boom of the 1950s. The period 1946-1963 saw the renegotiation of hegemonic masculinity. The new white-collar, college educated, corporate, suburbanized man in his trademark grey flannel suit replaced the "marketplace manhood" of 19th century America personified by the small merchant, self-made man with emphasis on individuality and control.[195] However, "almost

---

[193] Peter Lang, "The 'Crisis' of White Masculinity," **Counterpoints** 163 (2001): 321-416 (331).
[194] Lang, "'Crisis' of White Masculinity," 345.
[195] Thomas Andrew Joyce, "A Nation of Employees: The Rise of Corporations and the Perceived Crisis of Masculinity in the 1950s," **Graduate History Review** 3 (2011): 24-48.

from its inception, the new white masculinity of the post-World War II era was in crisis."[196]

Depiction of Jefferson Davis, President of the Confederate States, as "The President in Petticoats"

The 1960s produced new White male anxieties as a consequence of the many social agitations and *rebellions* against the recovered White masculine authority: civil rights, feminism, gay rights, and urban rebellions or riots. People whom the American WASP (White Anglo-Saxon Protestant) saw as his inferior were now challenging his hegemony. As Steven M. Gillon writes:

> Until the 1960s, white men sat unchallenged atop the United States' cultural and economic pyramid. They did not have to compete against women or African Americans in the workplace, and they benefited from laws and customs that sustained their privileged position. They not only ruled the workplace, they

---

[196] Douglas Taylor, "Three Lean Cats in a Hall of Mirrors: James Baldwin, Norman Muiler, and Eldridge Cleaver on Race and Masculinity," **Texas Studies in Literature and Language** 52 (2010): 70-101 (72).

dominated American politics and exercised virtually unchallenged power at home...And then their world exploded.[197]

This challenge to White male authority will produce a vicious backlash, the worst of which was directed at and felt by Black males in the inner-city.

II.   *American "Homophobia"*

Sociologist Michael Kimmel argues that American manhood and masculinity are animated and defined by the White male's fear of other men. Kimmel refers to this fear as *homophobia*, not in the socially repurposed sense of "hatred toward gay people," but in the literal sense of "fear (*phobia*) of other men(*homo*)." In particular, White males "fear that other men will unmask us, emasculate us, reveal to us and to the world that we do not measure up, that we are not real men,"[198] says Kimmel. Indeed, "The fear of being seen as a sissy dominates the cultural definitions of manhood" in America. Relevant here is no doubt the phenomenon of straight White men engaging in gay sex as an integral part of their *masculinity*. Jane Ward, Associate Professor of Women's Studies at the University of California, Riverside, has documented that "straight men-specifically white men-are having sex with other men to affirm just how straight they are, because to be straight and still be able to perform 'gay sex'-while always remaining uninterested-is the height of white masculinity."[199] Ward argues that homosexuality is a "vital ingredient," "a constitutive element," of White heterosexual masculinity and that "homosexual contact is a ubiquitous feature of the culture of straight white men"

> white straight-identified men manufacture opportunities for sexual contact with other men in a remarkably wide range of settings, and...these activities appear to *thrive* in hyper-

---

197 Steven M. Gillon, "Why are so many white men so angry?" **The Washington Post** August 29, 2017.

198 Micheal Kimmel, "Masculinity and Homophobia: Fear, Shame, and Silence in the Construction of Gender Identity," in **Theorizing Masculinities**, ed. Harry Brod and Michael Kaufman (London: Sage Publications, 1994) 213-219 (214).

199 Jane Ward, **Not Gay: Sex Between Straight White Men** (New York and London: New York University Press, 2015.

heterosexual environments, such as universities, where access to sex with women is anything but constrained.[200]

Because the "homosexual ingredient" of White heterosexual masculinity is more often than not kept invisible, White masculinity is constantly under the threat of exposure. As a defensive paradigm constructed to prevent being unmasked, this "homophobia" sources much of American racism. "Being seen as unmanly is a fear that propels American men to deny manhood to others, as a way of proving the unprovable – that one is fully manly."[201] In order for the White male to protect his own sense of manhood, everyone else must be seen and presented as *unreal men*: Native Americans, Japanese, but especially Black men. Thus, the birth of the myth of "The Negro as The Lady of The Races" is rooted in this innate "Crisis of White Masculinity."[202]

III.   *The Bohemian Grove and Racist, Murderous Homosexual Culture in High Places*

the Bohemian Club [is] one of America's most elite organizations. Every Republican president since Calvin Coolidge along with America's top CEOs and media moguls has been a member of the all-male fraternity, which meets once a year for a secretive two-week bacchanal in the California redwoods. **Playboy** *March 2004.*

Founded in 1872 in San Francisco, the all-male Bohemian Club consists of "2,500 of America's richest, most conservative men".[203] These men do not represent the powerful but the "ultra-powerful."[204] These 2,500 - "Mostly, the members are old white guys"[205] – represent America's military-political-

---

[200] Ward, **Not Gay**, 5, 7.
[201] Kimmel, "Masculinity and Homophobia," 217.
[202] On the Myth of The Negro as The Lady of the Races see Wesley Muhammad, **Understanding The Assault on the Black Man, Black Manhood, and Black Masculinity** (Atlanta: A-Team Publishing, 2016) 93-95.
[203] Julian Sancton, "A Guide to the Bohemian Grove," **Vanity Fair** May 2009.
[204] Adair Lara, "The Chosen Few: S.F.'s exclusive clubs carry on traditions of fellowship, culture – and discrimination," **SFGate** July 18, 2004.
[205] Lara, "The Chosen Few."

industrial high command.[206] Every year for two weeks in July these super rich and ultra-powerful men gather at Bohemian Grove, a 2,700 acre campground in Monte Rio, California. They gather for "super-secret talks" and a deeply racist (among other things, members have been known to dress in blackface[207]) and homosexualized form of "druid worship."[208]

Future U.S. presidents Ronald Reagan and Richard Nixon together with Harvey Hancock (standing) and others at Bohemian Grove in the summer of 1967.

On the business side, the Bohemians gather and make decisions that impact the world. J. Robert Oppenheim, "the father of the atomic bomb," Edward Teller and other members of the Manhattan Project mapped out the atomic bomb at Bohemian Grove in the autumn of 1942 and there they decided to drop the bomb, "resulting in the bombing of Hiroshima and Nagasaki three summers later."[209] Richard Nixon, who had

---

[206] See also Cecil Adams, "Behind the Bohemian Grove," *Washington City Paper* April 2, 2010; Alexander Cockburn, "Meet the men Who Rule the World," *The Nation* June 14, 2001; "Power Camps," *Time* June 24, 2001.

[207] Lara, "The Chosen Few."

[208] Elizabeth Flock, "Bohemian Grove: Where the rich and powerful go to misbehave," *The Washington Post* June 15, 2011.

[209] Andrew Chamings, "The Most Secretive Club in America," *The Bold Italic* February 4, 2019; Adair Lara, "The Chosen Few: S.F.'s

been a Bohemian Club member since 1953, launched his successful 1968 election campaign from Bohemian Grove. The leader of the most powerful nation on the planet is often determined at this yearly gathering.

Bohemian Grove Owl

The Bohemian Grove's central feature is a man-made lake, watched over by the club's totem, a towering 40-foot owl shrine with a creepy "slightly diabolical vibe."[210] At this site the two-week bacchanal is opened with a cultic ceremony "with Druidic, Masonic, Ku Klux Kan, and Aryan forest-worship overtones"[211] and called the Cremation of Care ceremony. Led by a high priest, these ultra-powerful old white men dressed in red robes and sharp-pointed, KKK-like hoods perform a mock-sacrifice before the owl of a human effigy of a child made of black muslin and called "Dull Care." This black-colored human

exclusive clubs carry on traditions of fellowship, culture – and discrimination," *SFGate* July 18, 2004; Elizabeth Flock, "Bohemian Grove: Where the rich and powerful go to misbehave," *The Washington Post* June 15, 2011; Nick Schou, "Bohemian Grove Exposes Itself," *OC Weekly* August 31, 2006.

[210] Alex Shoumatoff, "Bohemian Tragedy," *Vanity Fair* May 2009.

[211] Shoumatoff, "Bohemian Tragedy."

effigy represents their "archenemy" (as the "archenemy of Beauty," which they allegedly represent).[212] The effigy is then placed in a little boat with a carved skull on its tip and its prow, set on fire, and sent across the lake.[213]

There is very disconcerting evidence that what is now a black-colored child effigy used in a mock sacrifice was originally a living Black young male that was ritually murdered. On archive.org there is a trove of old photos reportedly from Bohemian Grove. The Bay Area online culture magazine *The Bold Italic* published two such photos, one of a 1909 Bohemian Grove ceremony showing a young Black male tied to a table and surrounded by a crowd of old white males (and a few females), and another photo from that year of a lynching.[214]

[212] G. William Domhoff and U.C. Santa Cruz, "Social Cohesion & the Bohemian Grove," from *WhoRulesAmerica.net* @ https://whorulesamerica.ucsc.edu/power/bohemian_grove.html.
[213] Shoumatoff, "Bohemian Tragedy"; G. William Domhoff and U.C. Santa Cruz, "Social Cohesion & the Bohemian Grove," from *WhoRulesAmerica.net* @ https://whorulesamerica.ucsc.edu/power/bohemian_grove.html.
[214] Andrew Chamings, "The Most Secretive Club in America," *The Bold Italic* February 4, 2019.

1909 photo 1 from archive.org which, according to *The Bold Italic*, is a Bohemian Grove gathering.

1909 photo 2 from archive.org which, according to *The Bold Italic*, is a Bohemian Grove gathering.

On an indirectly related note, castrated bull testicles are a delicacy at Bohemian Grove. Every year a cattle baron from central California brings to the camp a large supply of bulls' balls from his newly castrated herds: "No one goes away hungry," observes Domhoff, "bulls' balls are said to be quite a treat."[215] Readers of our **Volume I** recall our demonstration of the "Black Bull" as a symbol and metaphor of the Black Man/Black God and of the cultic, ritual killing of the Black Bull in secret white (supremacist) societies in antiquity and more recently.[216]

This leads us to the second feature that characterizes the men and culture of Bohemian Grove: homosexuality. President Nixon himself said in 1971: "The Bohemian Grove, which I attend from time to time – is the most *faggy goddamned thing you could ever imagine*, with that San Francisco crowd. I can't shake hands with anybody from San Francisco."[217] Transvestism is a hallmark of the yearly bacchanal, as these ultra-powerful men host and engage in elaborate drag shows.[218]

Photo of Bohemian Grove drag show according to *The Bold Italic*.

[216] Wesley Muhammad, ***Understanding The Assault of the Black Man, Black Manhood and Black Masculinity***, **Volume I** (Atlanta: A-Team Publishing, 2017) 102 and Part Three.
[217] Adair Lara, "The Chosen Few: S.F.'s exclusive clubs carry on traditions of fellowship, culture – and discrimination," **SFGate** July 18, 2004.
[218] Elizabeth Flock, "Bohemian Grove: Where the rich and powerful go to misbehave," **The Washington Post** June 15, 2011; Andrew Chamings, "The Most Secretive Club in America," **The Bold Italic** February 4, 2019.

As journalist Philp Weiss writes: "The girls were all played by men, and every time they appeared – their chunky legs and flashed buttocks highly visible through tight support hose – the crowd went wild."[219] Homoeroticism or homosexual undertones "suffused this spectacle, as they do much of ritualized life in the Grove."[220] These ultra-powerful old white men go naked underneath their kilts: "it's a guys-only affair, and, historically, there's always been talk of buggery in the dappled shadows under the redwoods."[221] *Buggery* is anal intercourse. As one member remarked, when it comes to women, "It's not excluding, *it's getting away from.*"[222] During the yearly Bohemian Grove mid-July gathering famous gay male porn stars have been hired as "waiters" and "valets," to serve food and drink and "attend to every need" of the campers.[223] *This* is what is meant when the summer camp is descried as "The Greatest Men's Party on Earth" – White men - "merely a playground for the powerful and their entertainers."[224] There have been credible witness reports of children reported missing being sexually abused and murdered at Bohemian Grove.[225]

This Bohemian Grove homosexuality and pedophilia gives greater context to White House homosexuality and pedophilia. One such case of a GOP male homosexual prostitution and pedophile ring connected to Reagan and George H.W. Bush Administration officials and media figures was revealed in 1989 by **The Washington Times.**

---

[219] Philp Weiss, "Masters of the Universe Go to Camp: Inside the Bohemian Grove," **Spy Magazine** November 1989: 59-76.

[220] Philp Weiss, "Masters of the Universe Go to Camp: Inside the Bohemian Grove," **Spy Magazine** November 1989: 59-76; Alex Shoumatoff, "Bohemian Tragedy," **Vanity Fair** May 2009.

[221] Alex Shoumatoff, "Bohemian Tragedy," **Vanity Fair** May 2009.

[222] Lara, "The Chosen Few."

[223] Richard Johnson with Paula Froelich and Chris Wilson," "Gay Porn Star Serves Moguls," **New York Post** July 22, 2004 (Page Six).

[224] G. William Domhoff and U.C. Santa Cruz, "Social Cohesion & the Bohemian Grove," from **WhoRulesAmerica.net** @ https://whorulesamerica.ucsc.edu/power/bohemian_grove.html.

[225] "Eye Witness to Murder at Bohemian Grove," **Media Monarchy** August 27, 2012.

Paul M. Rodriquez and George Archibald of **The Washington Times** revealed that "A homosexual prostitution ring is under investigation by federal and District authorities and includes among its clients key officials of the Reagan and Bush administrations, military officers, congressional aides and U.S. and foreign businessmen with close social ties to Washington's political elite".[226] Members of major news organizations procured gay male prostitutes as well.

Military and intelligence authorities reportedly were aware of "a nest of homosexuals at high levels of the Reagan administration."[227] The central figure in this homosexual prostitution ring reportedly was Craig Spence, a conservative lobbyist and political operative during the Reagan-Bush years, whom **The New York Times** described as "Washington's ultimate power broker." We are told that Spence ran a gay prostitution ring which serviced White House officials and employed adolescent boys. He threw "parties" at his D.C. home well attended by the powerful and connected of D.C. and beyond. Children from Boys Town and other orphanages in Nebraska (the Franklin Child Abuse ring from Omaha) as well as from China were reportedly flown to Washington to be

---

[226] Paul M. Rodriquez and George Archibald, "Homosexual prostitution inquiry ensnares VIPS with Reagan, Bush," **The Washington Times** June 29, 1989.
[227] Paul M. Rodriquez and George Archibald, "Homosexual prostitution inquiry ensnares VIPS with Reagan, Bush," **The Washington Times** June 29, 1989.

exploited and abused by Republican politicians and others at Spence's parties.

Friends were led to believe that Spence carried out homosexual blackmail operations for the CIA. He "often intimated that he worked for the CIA".[228] According to the *Times* Spence electronically bugged his dinner parties attended by White House officials, media celebrities and high-ranking military officers to obtain potential blackmail material.[229] Spence had so much clout he was able to organize one o'clock in the morning tours of the Reagan White House for male prostitutes. Ultimately this would be Spence's undoing.

Those male prostitutes that "toured" the White House during booty-call hours belonged to the escort service of the "D.C. Madam" Henry Vinson, who ran the gay escort service patronized by Spence for his elite party guests. Spence reportedly would spend $20k per month on male prostitutes for his White House and other upper echelon patrons. Vinson says among his customers were CIA Director William Casey, Congressman Barney Frank and Donald Gregg, National Security Advisor to Vice President George H. W. Bush (1982–1989) and US Ambassador to South Korea during the Bush Presidency. Vinson, who was slapped with a 43-count RICO indictment and spent five years in prison because of this scandal, claims that these men (Casey, Frank, and Cregg) liked "18-year-old (male) escorts with minimal body hair and a slender swimmer's physique."[230] Vinson says,

> I ran the largest gay escort service that's ever been exposed in Washington, D.C. and my ultimate downfall was precipitated by the fact that I provided escorts to a CIA asset named Craig spence. He used my escorts to blackmail politicians and other

---

[228] John Mintz, Martha Sherrill and Elsa Walsh, "The Shadow of Craig Spence," *The Washington Post* July 27, 1989.
[229] Jerry Seper and Michael Hedges, "Spence was targeted before raid on ring," *The Washington Times* July 10, 1989. See also Cliff Kincaid, "D.C. Homosexual Prostitution Rig is Big Global Story, But Not in U.S.," *New York City Tribune* July 3, 1989
[230] Henry Vinson with Nick Bryant, *Confessions of a D.C. Madam: The Politics of Sex, Lies, and Blackmail* (Walterville, Oregon: Trine Day, LLC, 2014); idem, "CIA Director William Casey and the Boys," @ http://blog.confessionsofadcmadam.com/?paged=2&tag=dc-madam.

power brokers and I ultimately became the fall guy for a sprawling conspiracy whose coverup was engineered at the pinnacle of the Bush one administration."[231]

Vinson claims that Spence disclosed to him that it was *the CIA* who bugged his home for audio-visual blackmail. While Vinson served time in prison, Spence himself was "suicided." Later, in 2005, a pal of President George W. Bush who ran a gay prostitute service, James D. Guckert (he used the online name Jeff Gannon) was given a White House press pass and access to classified CIA documents.[232] Like father, like son.

Connected to this D.C. scandal was also a horrific military-Church of Satan child abuse case based in San Francisco, California but involved fifteen Army-run day cares and elementary schools, including West Point. At the Presidio of San Francisco, headquarters of the Sixth Army, the U.S. Army ran a preschool and day care program. There, at least 60 children were allegedly ritualistically abused sexually in a horrifying manner, being infected with AIDS and other diseases such as Chlamydia. This pedophile operation was reportedly led by Lt. Col. Michael Aquino, a high-ranking Army officer with security clearance. He is an Aryanist (neo-Nazi) and a Satanist with a "Temple of Set" right behind the Military Intelligence Building at the Presidio.[233] According to victim testimony Aquino dressed as a woman during the ritualized sexual abuse. In 1990 following an investigation for satanic ritual child abuse Aquino was processed out of the Army.[234] The Craig Spence homosexual ring, the Franklin Child Abuse case and cover-up, and the U.S. Army/Lt. Col. Aquino alleged satanic ritual child abuse cases were each and all connected with the Iran-Contra Affair.

[231] Henry Vinson Interview with Jason Hartman, **Holistic Survival Show** @ https://www.holisticsurvival.com/hs264/.
[232] Helen Kennedy, "Bush Press Pal Quits Over Gay Prostie Link," **New York Daily News** February 10, 2005.
[233] Linda Goldston, "Army of the Night," **San Jose Mercury News** July 24, 1988.
[234] "The Case Against Highest Ranking Lt Colonel Michael Aquino – Satanic Pedophile," **The Event Chronicle** October 2, 2014.

Chapter Six:

Prison Experiments
And The Homosexuality Project

I.   *White Male Fragility and the Rise of Black Male Mass Incarceration*

The Black "explosions" in the urban cities – or "ghetto mutinies" - during the decade of the 60s was most troubling to White male authority, explosions whose cause was attributed by some sociologists to a pathological Black masculinity inspired by the Islam teachings of the Honorable Elijah Muhammad. The response from this bruised and fragile White masculinity was the carceral explosion and the phenomenon of mass incarceration of young Black males, a phenomenon that began under President Richard Nixon.[235] As French sociologist Loïc Wacquant documents, mass incarceration – or what he prefers to call *hyper*incarceration – was "a delayed reaction to the civil rights movement and the ghetto riots of the mid-1960s".[236]

> But the ethnic transformation of America's prison has been at once more dramatic and more puzzling than generally recognized. To start, the ethnoracial makeup of convicts has completely *flip-flopped* in four decades, turning over from 70 percent white and 30 percent "others" at the close of World War II to 70 percent African American and Latino versus 30 percent white by century's end. This inversion, which accelerated after the mid-1970s, is all the more stunning when the criminal population has both shrunk and become whiter during that

---

[235] Brandon M. Terry, "Race and the Mass Incarceration Society," **The Harvard Crimson** December 13, 2004: "These urban rebellions set the stage for the new method of social control-the mass incarceration society"; Walker Newell, "The Legacy of Nixon, Reagan, and Horton: How the tough On Crime Movement Enabled A New Regime of Race-Influenced Employment Discrimination," **Berkeley Journal of African-American Law & Policy** 15 (2013): 3ff: "the growth of American prisons has been the direct result of a backlash against the Civil Rights Movement." The early-1970s were the first years of prison expansion, under President Nixon.
[236] Loïc Wacquant, "Class, race & hyperincarceration in revanchist America," **Dædalus** 139 (2010): 74-90 (74).

period: the share of African Americans among individuals arrested by the police for the four most serious violent offenses (murder, rape, robbery, and aggravated assault) dropped from 51 percent in 1973 to 43 percent in 1996, and it continued to decline steadily for each of those four crimes until at least 2006. Next, the rapid "blackening" of the prison population even as serious crime "whitened" is due exclusively to the astronomical increase in the incarceration rates of lower-class African Americans (emphasis original).[237]

The "Big House" of the first half of the twentieth century was predominantly white, repressive, and relatively safe. The post-1965 prison is violent, unstable, and largely Black and Brown.[238] The Big House aimed at rehabilitating the convict, but "today's prison has for its sole purpose to *neutralize* offenders";[239] "By entombing poor blacks in the concrete walls of the prison...the penal state has effectively smothered and silenced subproletarian revolt."[240]

What goes on in the prisons yesterday and today, especially the human experimentation, is relevant to every Black person because, as a result of this deliberate mass incarceration of Black men, the constant human traffic between the prison and the urban Black community meant and means that much prison culture has bled into – actually is hemorrhaging into – the larger Black community making these two spheres – prison society and urban Black America – homologous in many ways. Homologous means two things are similar in structure suggesting a common ancestry. We will show that this was done deliberately. Wacquant refers to the *ghettoization* of American prisons and the *prisonization* of American ghettos.

---

[237] Wacquant, "Class, race & hyperincarceration," 79.
[238] John Irwin, "The Decline of the 'Big House' Prison: What Can Be Done to End the War Behind the Walls?" **The Washington Post** December 15, 1977.
[239] Loïc Wacquant, "Deadly Symbiosis: When ghetto and prison meet and mesh," **Punishment & Society** 31 (2001): 95-133 (112).
[240] Wacquant, "Deadly Symbiosis," 119.

II. *Prison Experimentation in Behavioral Control*

In April of 1961 a very important symposium took place in Washington D.C. entitled, "The Power to Change Behavior Symposium Presented by the U.S. Bureau of Prisons."[241] This symposium, organized by the National Institute of Mental Health, brought together prison wardens and their staff, behavioral scientists and social scientists. The aim of the symposium was to discuss and develop behavior modification techniques that could be tested on the thousands of captive US prisoners and then applied to society at large. At this time, the jails and prisons were being impacted by Black people as a result of the non-violent civil disobedience tactics of the Civil Rights Movement beginning in 1954, the Freedom Riders and such.

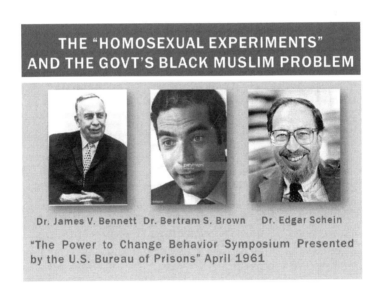

THE "HOMOSEXUAL EXPERIMENTS" AND THE GOVT'S BLACK MUSLIM PROBLEM

Dr. James V. Bennett   Dr. Bertram S. Brown   Dr. Edgar Schein

"The Power to Change Behavior Symposium Presented by the U.S. Bureau of Prisons" April 1961

The symposium was chaired by Dr. James Bennett, Director of the U.S. Bureau of Prisons, and co-chaired by Dr. Bertram Brown, at that time a staff psychiatrist at the National Institute of Mental Health (NIMH) and Special Assistant to President John F. Kennedy. The keynote speaker was Dr. Edgar

---

[241] Symposium proceedings published in **Corrective Psychiatry and Journal of Social Therapy** 8 (1962): 91ff.

Schein,[242] associate professor of psychology at Massachusetts Institute of Technology and, before that, Chief of the Social Psychology Section at the Walter Reed Army Institute of Research where he studied, with CIA funding, the brainwashing techniques used by the Chinese during the Korean War. [243] Schein in fact was a consultant to the CIA's Human Ecology Fund and knowingly received CIA funding for his research.[244] Dr. Schein was the son of a Hungarian Jewish experimental physicist who married a "very German blonde woman" in order, Schein believed, to "pass" as non-Jewish.[245] Schein learned something during this research that the U.S. Government would seize upon and use to great effect against the Black Man and Woman. He learned that brainwashing is the ability to deliberately change the behavior and the attitudes a captive population by a group of men who have relatively complete control of *the environment in which that population is confined*, be it a prison, a concentration camp or a ghetto. In other words, to successfully control a group's behavior and modify it to meet your desires, you don't have to have control of the person's body, you need only have control of *his environment* and by manipulating that environment you can manipulate his behavior and "coersively persuade" him to adopt a culture that he otherwise would have resisted. Dr. Schein called this technique "coersive persuasion."[246] At this symposium Dr. Schein outlined 24 Methods of physical, psychological and chemical control to be tested on inmate populations and later used to "make society safe."

After his talk, the training director encouraged the wardens to apply Schein's techniques in their prisons. The director Bennett assured the gathered prison staff that bureau headquarters in Washington "are anxious to have you

---

[242] Edgar H. Schein, "Man Against Man: Brainwashing," **Corrective Psychiatry and Journal of Social Change** 8 (1962): 92.
[243] William A. Reuben and Carlos Norman, "Brainwashing in America? The Women of Lexington Prison," **The Nation** June 27, 1987, pp. 881-883 (883).
[244] Patricia Greenfield, "CIA's Behavior Caper," **APA Monitor** December 1977, pp. 1, 10-11.
[245] Edgar Schein Oral History Interviews, Indiana University @ https://tobiascenter.iu.edu/research/oral-history/audio-transcripts/schein-edgar.html.
[246] Jessica Mitford, "The Torture Cure," **Communicator** (Springhill, Novia Scotia) October 1974, pp. 6-14 (7).

undertake some of these things".[247] And as expected, "Schein's advice to the conference about brainwashing techniques and the director's encouragement were followed, not surprisingly, by formal introduction of new behavior modification programs in federal prisons."[248] Schein's presentation has an "overwhelming influence on the prison systems of today."[249]

III. *Black Muslim Masculinity as a Problem For Prisons*

Muslims, do you know that we are the only thing that stands in between their wicked plan of the demasculinization of Black men? The ONLY thing that stands between that is the Nation of Islam! - The Honorable Brother Minister Farrakhan, Watergate Hotel Press Conference, November 16, 2017

At this 1961 symposium there were two main focuses: 1.) Behavior Modification techniques to be tested on inmates and then applied to society and 2.) a persistent *problem* that prison personnel around the country were confronted with and which needed urgent resolution in order for them to be successful in their endeavor. What was that persistent problem? "A persistent subject during the symposium was the 'problem of Black Muslims' within the nation's prisons during this period," reported Brett Story.[250] The Bureau of Prisons, like the rest of the "White Power" structure, was confronted with a Black Muslim Problem. At the symposium the question was urgently raised: "How shall we manage the Muslims?"[251] Mitford reports:

> Much attention was focused on what to do about the Black Muslims: "not so much whether you take action against the Muslims as a group," as one speaker put it, "but how can you counteract the effects of the kinds of techniques they use to recruit members and cause general mischief in the prison

---

[247] Greenfield, "CIA's Behavior Caper."
[248] Stephan L. Chorover, **From Genesis to Genocide: The Meaning of Human Nature and the Power of Behavior Control** (Cambridge: The MIT Press, 1979) 200-201.
[249] Lisa Morgan and Little Rock Reed, "Editors' Introduction," **Journal of Prisoners on Prisons** 4 (1993): 2,
[250] Brett Story, "The Prison Inside: A Genealogy of Solitary Confinement as Counter-Resistance," in Karem M. Morin and Dominique Moran (edd.), **Historical Geographies of Prisons. Unlocking the Usable Carceral Post** (Routledge, 2015).
[251] Mitford, "The Torture Cure," 7.

system?" To which Dr. Lowry responded, "We found that many of these Negro Muslims were highly intelligent...here again, we have to apply techniques which we heard about in terms of appreciating what the goal of the Muslims is, or of any other group, and then doing some analytic study of the methods that they are using so that we can try to dissipate the forces that are going in the direction that we regard as destructive." "On ways of dealing with the unruly," a panelist offered this: "To some extent where we formerly had isolation as a controlling technique, we now have drugs, so that drugs in a sense become a new kind of restraint. The restraint, therefore, is biochemical, but it is a restraint nevertheless."[252]

Elijah Muhammad and his "highly intelligent" Black Muslim men are a problem to and for White Supremacy in society and in prison. What exactly was the general mischief that Elijah Muhammad's highly intelligent Black Muslims were creating in the prisons? By changing the pattern of race relations, specifically challenging the racial hierarchy of the prisons and of society, the Black Muslims were considered a seriously "disruptive force" that caused a "crisis in corrections."[253] As Cornell University Law School Assistant Professor James Jacobs wrote: "Prison officials saw the Muslims not only as a threat to prison authority but also a broader revolutionary challenge to American society."[254] Also, "To many whites (in 1968), the revolutionary posturing of groups such as the Black Panthers and the Nation of Islam gave rise to fears 'that the Mau Mau [were] coming to the suburbs at night.'"[255] Indeed, "Official investigations into prison temples reveal the wider fear that the

---

[252] The Report is presented in **Corrective Psychiatry & Journal of Social Change** Second Quarter 1962, as described in Jessica Mitford, "The Torture Cure," **Communicator** (Springhill, Novia Scotia) October 1974, pp. 6-14 (7).

[253] Eric Cummins, **The Rise and Fall of California's Radical Prison Movement** (Stanford, California: Stanford University Press, 1994) Chapter 4: "Taking The Yard, Freeing The Mind: The Black Muslims."

[254] James B. Jacobs, "Race Relations and the Prisoner Subculture," **Crime and Justice** 1 (1979): 1-27 (6).

[255] Walker Newell, "The Legacy of Nixon, Reagan, and Horton: How the tough On Crime Movement Enabled A New Regime of Race-Influenced Employment Discrimination," **Berkeley Journal of African-American Law & Policy** 15 (2013): 13.

organization was covertly planning a violent assault upon white America."[256]

There were two primary ways that the Muslims made themselves such a headache to the U.S. Bureau of Prisons. The first: The 1871 Virginia Commonwealth definition of inmates as "slaves of the state" was operative throughout the prison system and was used to deny inmates basic constitutional rights. The 13th Amendment did not totally abolish slavery. The so-called Punishment Clause stipulated that slavery was abolished except "as a punishment for crime whereof the party shall have been duly convicted." So inmates were deemed slaves and denied many constitutional rights but it was the Muslims, the most organized group ever to reside in American prisons, who fiercely challenged the 1871 definition by, on their own, battling legally and successfully in court the denial of inmate rights. With no professional help these highly intelligent Black Muslim followers of The Most Honorable Elijah Muhammad prepared legal cases by using the prison libraries to educate themselves in case law and preparing briefs. It was these Muslims who primarily gained judicial recognition of the constitutional rights of prison inmates. This vexed prison officials because they didn't want to see the "Negro" as anything other than a legal slave and the Muslims weren't having that, even in prison.[257]

The second crime that the Muslims committed against the racial order of prison society and society in general was inspire a restored masculine identity among the Black prisoners. As Zoe Colley writes, "in a world where African American men felt emasculated by poverty and white racism, conversion to the Nation of Islam offered prisoners a renewed sense of masculinity."[258] In contrast to the subdued masculinity created by the prison environment and it's resultant reaction, a contrived and violent "hyper-masculinity," the Black Muslims offered an alternative Black masculinity: disciplined, respectful

---

[256] Zoe Colley, "'All America Is a Prison': The Nation of Islam and to. he Politicization of African American Prisoners, 1955-1965," *Journal of American Studies* 48 (2014): 393-415 (396).
[257] Livia Gershom and Christopher E. Smith, "What the Prisoners' Rights Movement Owes to the Black Muslims of the 1960s," *JSTOR Daily* January 22, 2018; idem, "Black Muslims and the Development of Prisoners' Rights," *Journal of Black Studies* 24 (1993): 131-146; James B. Jacobs, "Stratification and Conflict among Prison Inmates," *Journal of Criminal Law and Criminology* 66 (1976): 476-482.
[258] Colley, "'All America Is a Prison'," 408.

of authority, hygienic, intellectual, fearless, and unified.[259] As one writer put it: "What distinguished the Muslim men in the prison from the general inmate population is not their religious identification, rather, it is their performance of masculinity, which could only be achieved through practice of [their] Islamic faith."[260] When then the Bureau of Prisons declares their intent to analyze the goal of the Muslims in order to counter the methods used to achieve that goal, what is the goal of the Black Muslims? The goal is to transform the so-called Negro in America into a Nation of Gods by restoring manhood to the Black Man and virtuous womanhood to the Black Woman. This goal presented and presents a clear and present danger to the racial order of America, inside the prisons and out.

The goals of the two civilizations – Islam vs White/Jewish – are in conflict, especially as it relates to how the Black male population (in society and in prison) will be influenced. The Black Muslims are a destructive force to White Supremacy's goal for Black men and this destructive force must be "dissipated." And so Dr. Bertram Brown said at the Symposium:

> How should we manage the Muslims? How can we counteract the effects of the kinds of techniques they use to recruit members, etc. and cause general mischief in the prison system?

With Dr. Brown's encouragement Dr. Bennett issued a national directive to target the Black Muslims across the country with behavior modification techniques, assuring the gathered prison staff that bureau headquarters in Washington "are anxious to have you undertake some of these things: do things perhaps on your own-undertake a little experiment of what you can do with the Muslims, what you can do with some of the psychopath individuals."[261] "The result," according to Alan Eladio Gómez, "was a national directive to experiment with these techniques,

---

259 Susan Van Baalen, "From 'Black Muslim' to Global Islam: A Study of the Evolution of the Practice of Islam by Incarcerated Black Americans, 1957-2007," Ph.D. dissertation, Georgetown University, Washington D.C., 2011. 68.
260 Antoinette Marie Kane, "Islamic Conversion Confined: A Look at Why Black Men Convert to Islam While Incarcerated and the Effects Conversion has on their Processes of Reentry," Senior Project, Bard College, Annandale-on-Hudson, New York, 2016, p. 73.
261 Greenfield, "CIA's Behavior Caper."

originally used against American POWs in Korea, on the Black Muslim prison population." [262] In order for the government to achieve its goal for the so-called Negro the government must target and neutralize the *Black Muslim Problem*. Richard L. Aynes thus wrote in 1975:

> Recently the American public has become quite sensitive to the charges that the Soviet Union has used its mental institutions as caretakers for its political and intellectual nonconformists... Yet similar activities are being conducted in the United States and little if any outcry has arisen... The obvious political motivation of [behavior modification advocates] may be seen in their attitude and action toward the Black Muslims. The Muslims enforce a type of discipline and morality upon the adherents of their sect which results in an organized, nonviolent, noncriminal life. By their religious belief the Muslim's have demonstrated an ability to make the exact type of "conversion" in an inmate's behavior which [behavior modification advocates] claim they are trying to make. But, instead of being warmly received as contributors to the reduction in crime and recidivism, the Muslims are considered prime for behavior modification programs.[263]

IV. *How Prisons Became "Breeding Dens for Homosexuality"*

Something of the quality of the research...can be inferred from the stream of monographs, research reviews, and reports that flow out of the prisons. [The convict's] captors having arranged life for the prisoner so that he becomes enraged, perhaps goes mad, and (no matter what his original sexual preferences) turns homosexual, they (his captors) invite researchers to put him under their microscope and study the result. - Jessica Mitford, "The Torture Cure" (1974).

---

[262] According to Marion warden Ralph Aron. See Alan Eladio Gómez, "Resisting Living Death at Marion Federal Penitentiary, 1972," **Radical History Review** 96 (Fall 2006): 58-86 (60).
[263] Richard L. Aynes, "Behavior Modification: Winners in the Game of Life," **Cleveland State University** 24 (1975): 422-462 (458-459).

The Most Honorable Elijah Muhammad said in 1973: "the jails, prisons, and the federal penitentiaries are all *breeding dens* of homosexuals."[264] Edwin Johnson described also in 1971:

> That prison shall have a homosexual environment is determined by the State. The male prisoners are deprived of all normal sexual intercourse for a median period of three years (or up to life). The male prisoner is forced to sleep in the same cell with another male adult. He is forced to bathe with males and defecate with them publicly. He may be stripped in front of his peers at any time and searched in a humiliating and degrading ritual. For the rest of his prison life, except for rare visits from family, his whole life is predicated on homosexualized group contact. Is it any wonder, then, that prisons are breeding grounds for homosexual membership?[265]

In this regard we should recall the observation of Professor Ward:

> white straight-identified men manufacture opportunities for sexual contact with other men in a remarkably wide range of settings, and that these activities appear to *thrive* in hyper-heterosexual environments, such as universities, where access to sex with women is anything but constrained.[266]

And...in prison. I have said that, if you scratch the surface of a "masculine" heterosexual White man you will find a homosexual there.[267] George Chauncy documented that in pre-World War II New York, for example, "conventionally masculine men living in sex-segregated immigrant communities (such as Italians)...[engaged] in extensive sexual activity with other men without risking stigmatization and the loss of their status as 'normal men,'" so long as he was the "on top" actor and/or the other man was an effeminate, because the idea that straight men could engage in casual sex with other men, boys, or "fairies" "predominated in working-class culture"

---

264 Elijah Muhammad, **The Fall of America** (Chicago: Muhmmad's Temple of Islam No. 2, 1973) 90.
265 Edwin Johnson, "The Homosexual In Prison," **Social Theory and Practice** 1 (Fall 1971): 83-95 (85).
266 Ward, **Not Gay**, 5, 7.
267 See Wesley Muhammad, **Understanding The Assault on the Black Man, Black Manhood, and Black Masculinity** (Atlanta: A-Team Publishing, 2016) 77-100.

of New York.[268]   So when it is said that "The hallmark of masculinity in prison is the penetration of another male, the 'premier act of domination.,"[269] this is the hallmark of *White masculinity*.

Because gays commit crimes just like straight people, there has been for a long-time homosexuality and even a "Queens Row" where gays are segregated in prison. But the *predatory environment* that is now characteristic of American prisons *is orchestrated from on high* and is a break from the past. Prison staff today condone and legitimize the sexual abuse of inmates and institutional governance practices foster prison rape.[270] And as SpearIt reports, "according to the data, guards not only...ignore such (sexual) attacks, *they even orchestrate them*."[271] Indeed, "Correctional officers, administrators, mental health staff, support staff, teachers have all been identified as violating inmates sexually."[272] Guards orchestrate attacks on inmates by other inmates and they arrange rape rooms for "booty bandits" – known rapists - to have access to inmates. Such "booty bandits" are used regularly to punish insubordinate inmates. Staff also force inmates to have sex with each other.[273] Prison staff use sex and rape as tools to control or manage inmates.

But this prison environment of orchestrated high violence and homosexuality is a relatively *new* prison phenomenon, and it coincided with the "blackening" of the

---

[268] George Chauncy, **Gay New York: Gender, Urban Culture, and the Making of the Gay Male World, 1890-1940** (New York: Basic Books, 1994) 65.

[269] SpearIt, "Gender Violence in Prison & Hyper-masculinities in the 'Hood: Cycles of Destructive Masculinity," **Washington University Journal of Law & Policy** 37 (2011): 89-147 (111).

[270] Kim Shayo Buchanan, "Our Prisons, Ourselves: Race, Gender and the Rule of Law," **Yale Law & Policy Review** 29 (2010): 1-82 (4-5).

[271] SpearIt, "Gender Violence in Prison & Hyper-masculinities in the 'Hood: Cycles of Destructive Masculinity," **Washington University Journal of Law & Policy** 37 (2011): 89-147 (119).

[272] Robert W. Dumond, "The Impact of Prisoner Sexual Violence: Challenges of Implementing Public Law 108-79-The Prison Rape Elimination Act of 2003," **Notre Dame J.L. & Legis.** 32 (2006): 152.

[273] SpearIt, "Gender Violence in Prison," 123.

prison population during the politically turbulent 1950s and 1960s. As **The Washington Post** describes:

> In the "big house" (of the 1950s and prior) the prisoners – mostly white – lived according to the "convict code" (basically prisoner solidarity)...Prisoner leaders – "right guys" – taught and enforced the code. A few prisoners carried on illegal activities like making "pruno" – a nasty tasting prison brew – and got involved in prison sex, a peculiar sexual world with "jockers" -the masculine partners, "punks" – prison-made homosexuals, and "queens" -self-admitted homosexuals. But most prisoners stayed close to a few prison friends, worked at their job assignments, took up hobbies, played sports, read, and tried to stay out of trouble...By and large the big house was a mean and monotonous place, but peaceful....Today's prisons, in contrast, are torn by violence...[274]

Both the repressive "Big House" whose main characteristics were isolation, routine, and monotony, as well as its successor the more relaxed "correctional institution" were mainly white and relatively *peaceful*. African Americans and other ethnic minorities were there, but they were Jim Crowed into their own sections, sometimes maybe buried in "Black Bottom" areas within the prison.[275] But because the Africans Americans accepted their subhuman status even within the prison system, a relative peace reigned in these institutions during the 1940s and early 1950s. Then "the peace was shattered" by the introduction into the system in the late 1950s and 1960s of *a new Black mentality*. The arrest in large numbers of the more militant civil rights agitators, urban insurrections and, most importantly, the growth of the Black Muslims within the prisons made the Black inmates more assertive and less accepting of their Jim Crow-prescribe position: "when black prisoners became more assertive and finally militant, racial hostilities intensified and set off an era of extreme racial violence, which disrupted the patterns of order" that existed previously.[276] This was the beginning of the changes that produced the penal system environment that

---

[274] Irwin, "The Decline of the 'Big House'."
[275] Johnson, Dobrzanska and Palla, "The American Prison," 32.
[276] John Irwin, **Prisons in Turmoil** (Boston, 1980).

prevails today. This is because prison and societal authorities set out to *neutralize* the Black militant/Muslim threat within the prisons and without, which meant *viciously assaulting the Black masculinity* of the new militant Black men, actually turning it own its head.

Edgar Schein's brainwashing and behavioral modification techniques were being piloted at, for example, Marion Federal Prison in Illinois by 1968.[277] Marion became a behavior modification laboratory specifically for the "control (of) revolutionary attitudes in the prison system and in the society at large."[278] Other prisons sent their "trouble makers" to Marion – militants, political agitators, prison lawyers, and especially Black Muslims – on whom the new techniques would be tried. One of the techniques used at Marion and other institutions was/is *chemotherapy* or

> the use of drugs (some still in the experimental stage) as 'behavior modifiers,' including antitestosterone hormones, which have the effect of chemically castrating the subject, and Prolixin, a form of tranquilizer with unpleasant and often dangerous side effects.[279]

According to a report from former prisoner Eddie Griffin:

> Chemotherapy is administered four times daily at Marion. The loudspeaker announces: 'Control medication in the hospital...pill line'. Valium, librium, thorazine and other 'chemical billy-clubs' are handed out like gumdrops. Sometimes the drugs mysteriously make their way into the food.[280]

"Control medication." In some cases in a number of prisons dosages of female hormones were used to counteract "super masculinity."[281] Such female hormones given out to prisoners in

---

[277] Jessica Mitford, "The Torture Cure," **Communicator** (Springhill, Novia Scotia) October 1974, pp. 6-14 (7).

[278] According to Marion warden Ralph Aron. See Alan Eladio Gómez, "Resisting Living Death at Marion Federal Pwnitentiary, 1972," **Radical History Review** 96 (Fall 2006): 58-86 (58).

[279] Mitford, "The Torture Cure," 9.

[280] Eddie Griffin, "'Breaking men's Minds: Behavior Control and Human Experimentation at the Federal Prison in Marion," **Journal of Prisoners on Prisons** 4 (1993): 1-8 (6).

[281] Phil Stanford, "A model, clockwork-orange prison," **The New York Times** September 17, 1972.

the Illinois prison system also produced breasts in male inmates.[282] Pornography was also used as a tool in behavior modification.[283]

What is the aim of the use of these female hormones and anti-testosterone chemicals given to the inmates, and what role does pornography play as a tool in this process? What is the nature of the "behavior modification" that is desired? Jessica Mitford revealed in 1974:

> The theme of prison as a happy hunting ground for the researcher is very big in current penological literature. ... James V. Bennet (director of the U.S. Bureau of Prisons) poses the question, "What will prisons of A.D. 2000 be like?" And answers it: "In my judgement the prison system will be increasingly valued, and used, as *a laboratory and workshop for social change*"...Something of the quality of the research...can be inferred from the stream of monographs, research reviews, and reports that flow out of the prisons. [The convict's] captors having arranged life for the prisoner so that he becomes enraged, perhaps goes mad, and (no matter what his original sexual preferences) *turns homosexual*, they (his captors) invite researchers to put him under their microscope and study the result [such as] A forty-eight page monograph titled "Homosexuality in Prisons," published in February 1972 by the *Law Enforcement Assistance Administration*...(emphasis added).[284]

Whoa. So the prison has become a "laboratory and workshop" for *social change* and one of the experiments was the artificial induction of a homosexual culture by turning men *into* homosexuals. Then, various researchers are invited into the prison to see and to study what was accomplished. How are captives of the prison experimentally turned homosexual like lab rats? Prison conditions were scientifically engineered with

---

[282] John Money and Carol Bohmer, "Prison Sexology: Two Personal Accounts of Masturbation, Homosexuality, and Rape," *The Journal of Sex Research* 16 (1980): 258-266 (260).

[283] According to Marion warden Ralph Aron. See Alan Eladio Gómez, "Resisting Living Death at Marion Federal Penitentiary, 1972," *Radical History Review* 96 (Fall 2006): 58-86 (59).

[284] Mitford, "The Torture Cure," 9. See also idem., "Experiments Behind Bars: Doctors, drug companies, and prisoners," *The Atlantic* January 1973, pp. 64-73; Silja J.A. Talvi, "The Prison as Laboratory," *In These Times* December 7, 2001.

control mechanisms, behavior modification laboratories, status degrading ceremonies, and chemical feminizers.

V.   *How the Philadelphia Prison System Scientifically Created a Homosexual Culture and Exported It Into the Black Community*

There is no better illustration of this process than the homosexual "project" that was undertaken at Philadelphia's largest prison. Between 1951 and 1974 the University of Pennsylvania, in collaboration   with the CIA, the US Army Chemical Corps and various commercial companies such as Dow Chemical, used primarily Black inmates at the Holmesburg Prison in Philadelphia as human guinea pigs and subjected them to a series of horrific scientific experiments. Inmates were deliberately injected with herpes, vaccinia, syphilis, gonorrhea, malaria and dioxin (the toxic contaminant of the U.S. military's infamous Agent Orange).[285] Holmesburg became a "huge Kmart of human-research opportunities." Between 1962 and 1966, 33 pharmaceutical companies tested 153 experimental drugs at the prison.[286]

The architect of this University of Pennsylvania (U of P) Research Project was Dr. Albert Kligman, a dermatologist and a Jew, the son of Jewish immigrants from England and the Ukraine. Dr. Kligman shared the Holmesburg prison experimentation program with Dr. Milton Cahn and his brother Dr. Burt Cahn, Jews. So too Dr. Edgar Schein, who helped develop the brainwashing and behavior modification techniques that targeted primarily Black inmates- he was a self-

---

[285] Allen M. Hornblum, **Acres of Skin: Human Experiments at Holmesburg Prison** (New York and London: Routledge, 1998); idem, "They were cheap and available: prisoners as research subjects in twentieth century America," **BMJ** 315 (1997): 1437-1441; idem, "Subjected To Medical Experimentation: Pennsylvania's Contribution To Science' in Prisons," **Pennsylvania History** 67 (2000): 415-426.

[286] Allen M. Hornblum, "How Black Prison Inmates in Philadelphia Were Turned Into Human Guinea Pigs: A Memoir," **Tablet Magazine**   February   26,   2018   @ https://www.tabletmag.com/jewish-news-and-politics/256001/black-prison-inmates-experiments; Lawrence O. Gostin, JD, "Biomedical Research Involving Prisoners," **JAMA** 297 (2007): 737-740.

confessed Jew. Why do I emphasize the Jewish heritage of these key figures? It is because we are exposing another chapter in the history of the secret relationship between Blacks and Jews, a chapter in history we are calling "The Secret Relationship Between the White Jew and the Black Homosexual." The plot to demasculinize the Black Male in America is a collaborative effort between the US Government and the Synagogue of Satan. We don't say that Jews were the primary conspirators, but Jews were and are key players in the conspiracy, not a conspiracy theory but a demonstrable conspiracy fact.

THE UNIVERSITY OF PENNSYLVANIA RESEARCH PROJECT

Dr. Albert Kligman and Solomon McBride

As part of his experimental work on these overwhelmingly Black prisoners of Holmesburg Dr. Kligman did extensive work on chemical and biological warfare agents for the US military and the CIA.[287] In fact, in 1964 Holmesburg Prison became a secret military and CIA testing site. In that year the U.S. Army Chemical Corps installed three trailers with padded cells inside the heavy walls of Holmesburg. The Army trailers had the U of P insignia on them and between 1964 and

---

[287] Hornblum, *Acres of Skin*, 124ff; Bill Richards, "Memos Show Humans Used in Cia Drug Tests," *The Washington Post* January 5, 1979.

1968 "the Army and the University were turning 320 prisoners into human guinea pigs in secret warfare experiments."[288]

By the 1960s prisoners were the guinea pigs of choice for a cross section of corporations and government researchers. They were "cheaper than buying a chimpanzee and the results were better," it was said.[289] Also, "Prisoners were used because they were cheap and *nobody gave a damn what happened to them.*" [290] By that time (the 1960s) Pennsylvania became a hotbed and even the hub of unethical experimentation on inmates in the country, and Holmesburg was the epicenter of that research.[291]

The key to the two decades of successful running of the human experimentation project in the Pennsylvania prison system was to have a ready supply of cheap and *willing* test subjects. But how was the project able to secure so many human guinea pigs for these unethical and *dangerous* experiments for so long? One word: Money. Another word: desperation. Most inmates were in desperate need of money because "The majority of inmates in the Philadelphia prison system in the late 1960s and early 1970s were unsentenced prisoners awaiting trial. Money to hire an attorney or make bail before a forthcoming trial was a constant preoccupation among these inmates."[292] Three-quarters of the inmate population were involved with the project because 84.4% of the inmates were *detentioners*: untried defendants made to wait an average of nine months for their day in court. Former inmate Allen Lawson, testifying before the Senate in 1973 (the Subcommittee on Health of the Committee on Labor and Public Welfare), explained:

> You need (money) especially when you are first arrested. You have to take care of your basic necessities. You have to get an attorney. You have to try to get money together for your family. Usually when poor guys are locked up, they are snatched off the street. If they own anything, they are going to lose it. You have

---

[288] Aaron Epstein, "At Holmesburg Prison, 320 human guinea pigs," *Philadelphia Inquirer* November 25, 1979.
[289] Quoted in Hornblum, *Acres of Skin*, 24.
[290] Quoted in Hornblum, *Acres of Skin*, 31.
[291] Hornblum, *Acres of Skin*, 31,71; idem, "They were cheap and available"; idem, "Subject To Medial Experimentation."
[292] Hornblum, *Acres of Skin*, 24.

117

to have money to protect your own belongings. The guys in prison don't have the money to make bail...[293]

Prison workers received meager wages of 15 cents to at most 50 cents per day to make shoes, knit socks and shirts, sew trousers, and work in the plumbing shop. But these jobs were reserved for sentenced inmates. For the majority who were at this time untried detentioners largely "snatched off the street" and desperate to regain their freedom, the tests or dangerous experiments were *deliberately* made their only way to make money. One could receive $5 for a blood study or a biopsy. In 1961 the total inmate income was significant: "prisoners were paid $160,000 by (U of) Penn for acting as guinea pigs in various tests."[294] Twenty percent of this inmate income, however, kicked-back to the prison. By participating in as many tests as possible and surrendering their bodies to cruel experimentation, inmates try to raise the ten percent bail bond required for their freedom.

Cash greased the wheels of the university research program. As Fred Foxworth, a retired deputy warden says, 'They never had a problem getting volunteers. The inmates needed the money.[295]

This fabricated situation of desperation coupled with this sole opportunity for untried detentioners to make the much need money, combined to create a *totally controlled environment and population*. Kligman described the prison as "an anthropoid colony, mainly healthy', under *perfect control conditions*". He boasted that the inmates were an "experimental population I could control."

We know where they are, what they're doing, what they're eating; and if they're given pills six times a day, we know they are taken.[296]

---

[293] Hornblum, **Acres of Skin**, 194-195; "Senate Panel told of Guinea Pig Tests on Cons Here," **Philadelphia Daily News** Thursday, March 8, 1973, p. 3, 45.
[294] Hornblum, **Acres of Skin**, 47.
[295] Hornblum, **Acres of Skin**, 23.
[296] Hornblum, **Acres of Skin**, 38.

the guys will knock their brains out to please you. If the experiment does not pan out, they get depressed. They become emotionally involved in the project...I feel almost like a scoundrel-like Machiavelli-*because of what I can do to them.*[297]

Col. James Ketchum who oversaw the psychochemical weapons research of the U.S. Army Chemical Corps at Holmesburg recounts the total control Kligman had over his "anthropoid colony."

> Holmesburg is a large, maximal security prison. When first I passed through its massive gates and entered its gray interior, I felt a moment of apprehension. I had never been in an OZ-like prison before, where men who had committed serious crimes were allowed to wander around outside their cells. Some were physically close enough to throw a punch, which kept me on high alert. I was surprised to find, however, that we were never harassed with catcalls, funny looks or hostile gestures, much less physical assault. I soon learned why these dangerous men moved aside respectfully as we passed among them. Although Kligman paid only small sums for skin testing, the prisoners considered him to be a walking ATM. (Not surprising, considering that prisons pay almost nothing for a days work.) It was understandable that when "the Man" walked by, he and his guests were granted friendly deference.[298]

Kligman reassured Ketchum: "We don't have any problem with the men we test. A little money can buy a lot of cooperation." This total control of this Black male population in Holmesburg Prison is vitally important to understanding the *Homosexual Project* that was a part of this larger U of P Project. The scientifically induced homosexuality among convicts that was mentioned in the report on the 1961 symposium was operationalized at Holmesburg Prison.

Holmesburg Prison administrations were historically known as "the cruelest sadists who ever lived," in the words of Pennsylvania governor George Earle (1935-1939).[299] In the 1920s Holmesburg Prison authorities would welcome new inmates in a particular way: they would reward a group of Black inmates with "small favors" and those Black inmates would go

---

[297] Hornblum, ***Acres of Skin***, 39.
[298] James S. Ketchum, M.D. ***Chemical Warfare: Secrets Almost Forgotten*** (Santa Rosa, California: ChemBooks Inc., 2006) 165.
[299] Hornblum, ***Acres of Skin***, 31.

into the cells of new inmates and, as initiation into life at Holmesburg, beat them up.[300] By the 1960s, when the prisons of America were starting to swell with Civil Rights demonstrators and urban insurrectionists or what they call rioters, the Holmesburg "welcome" policy had changed: Black men were still given "small favors" to welcome new detainees – in this case the small favors were U of P research dollars. But unlike the 1920s where the unfortunate newby was jumped by a gang of Black men, in the 1960s under the auspices of the U of P and prison authorities, certain Black men received research money for *homosexually gang raping new inmates.* Homosexual rapes were a means of social control, behavior modification, and the calculated unmanning of the Black males that were being herded into the system.

Many of the gross details of this Homosexual Project were revealed in an explosive 1968 report by Alan Davis, Chief Assistant District Attorney of Philadelphia who conducted a three-month investigation of the Philadelphia prison system (the Detention Center, Holmesburg Prison, and the House of Correction).[301] It is clear that the homosexual rape culture that is a signature of today's prisons' predatory environment was new at that time. When in the summer of 1968 two separate defendants told the Court of Common Pleas No. 8 in Philadelphia County that they had been gang raped while being transported in a sheriff's van, two independent investigations were launched to investigate such allegations: Judge Alexander F. Barbieri appointed Chief Assistant District Attorney Davis to conduct the investigation while Police Commissioner Frank L. Rizzo launched a parallel investigation. These two investigations were eventually merged.

---

[300] Hornblum, *Acres of Skin*, 31.
[301] Alan J. Davis, "Sexual Assaults in the Philadelphia Prison System," *Trans-Action* 6 (December 1968): 8-17.

Philadelphia Sheriff's Van where gang rapes occurred while police drivers
"roll merrily on their way"

The (joint) investigation found that "sexual assaults in
the Philadelphia prison system are epidemic" *and* that this
homosexual culture was green-lighted (actively or tacitly) by the
prison authorities and funded by the University of Pennsylvania
Research Program. Within minutes of admission simply for pre-
sentence evaluation young men were raped. Rapes even
occurred in the Sheriff's Vans that transported detentioners
from the three facilities to City Hall. Designed to accommodate
fifteen passengers, 40 inmates were crammed inside and, with
no windows, the vans were often used to inflict punishment on
an inmate or "send a message." For example, a witness would
be thrown in the same van with the people he is set to testify
against. Davis discovered that in these vans during the rides to
and from City Hall gang rapes and other sexual assaults
occured, all while "The van drivers roll merrily on their way".[302]
It is simply not believable that these sheriff department drivers
were "blissfully unaware of what is taking place."

---

[302] Davis, "Sexual Assaults in the Philadelphia Prison System," 12.

Davis' 3-month long investigation covered the time period of June 1966 through July 1968. Davis documented 156 sexual assaults during that two-year period with 176 perpetrators. This is astounding. Not only is the number of victims remarkable, but how in this short period are *176 men persuaded to engage in homosexual rape?!* But these 156 assaults and 176 assaulters were but the "tip of the iceberg," Davis affirms, as evidence suggests there were *at least 1880 sexual assaults across the three facilities*. A guard from the Detention Center affirmed there were 250 sexual assaults there in a single year. [303] The number of perpetrators across the three prisons therefore must have been greater than 1880. Again, how are *so many men* convinced to engage in homosexual rape, all under the watchful eye of the prison administration *and the U.S. Army who was on the grounds*? Again, two words: money and desperation. As Davis reports:

> We learned of repeated instances where homosexual "security" cells were left unguarded by a staff that was too small or too indifferent, or who turned their backs so that certain favored inmates could have sexual relations. Many of these male prostitutes were created not only by force and the threat of force, but by bribery."[304]

Bribery was used to sexually subvert these economically and legally desperate men: "economic advantage" played "an important role...in the creation of homosexuality," reports Davis.[305] An illustrative case cited in Davis' report is that of Stanley Randle, a 38-year old con man serving 4-11 years. Randle was employed in the U of P Project as a research assistant in laboratory cell 806, a cell that was disbursed $10-$20,000 a year which Randle used to financially entice new inmates needing money into homosexual activity. Randle was granted the power to decide which inmates "got on the tests" and which tests they got on. With the assistance of prison guards Randle had his selection of which new inmates were diverted to his cell. He then turned those inmates out by "sexually subverting these men,"[306] all with the money provided by the University of Pennsylvania Project and under the careful

---

[303] Davis, "Sexual Assaults in the Philadelphia Prison System," 13.
[304] Davis, "Sexual Assaults in the Philadelphia Prison System," 13.
[305] Davis, "Sexual Assaults in the Philadelphia Prison System," 13.
[306] Davis, "Sexual Assaults in the Philadelphia Prison System," 13-14.

eye of the U.S. Army who was on site. Thus, while all of this was taking place in the open view of the guards and other staff, Davis was informed by a guard that "higher ups" instructed the guards "not to interfere in the affairs of the inmates working for the U. of P."[307] The end result: the U of P project "contributed to homosexuality in the prison," Davis concludes.[308] That is certainly an understatement.

A federal report four years later identified these sexual assaults as "a series of degradation ceremonies visited upon the newly imprisoned,"[309] the purpose of which to control the behavior of the inmate. This is a vital admission. It was sociologist Harold Garfinkle who coined the term and concept, "status degradation ceremony."[310] This is a public ritual of humiliation often involving *punishment practices* designed to expel a person from a group or strip him/her of their *identity* as a group member, thereby *degrading his status.* An important aspect of a status degradation ceremony is the irony between what the person *appeared to be* or *presented himself to be* previously and what, after his humiliation, he now stands *revealed to actually be.* And these "Before" and "After" identities are usually dialectical opposites, such as "a man" vs. "a woman." In fact, the aim of the ceremony is the ritual destruction or *obliteration* of the original persona and *transformation* or *reconstitution* of the person *into its dialectical opposite identity*; for example, via these prison degradation ceremonies the perceived Mr. Aggressive Masculinity is reconstituted as Mr. Docile Femininity. The public denouncement of the ritually degraded person thus is: "I call on all men to bear witness that *he is not* as he appears *but is otherwise* and in essence of a lower species."[311]

This is very consistent with what we read in Davis's report:

[307] Davis, "Sexual Assaults in the Philadelphia Prison System," 14.

[308] Davis, "Sexual Assaults in the Philadelphia Prison System," 14.

[309] Peter G. Buffum for the National Institute of Law Enforcement and Criminal Justice, **Homosexuality in Prisons** (Honolulu, Hawaii: University Press of the Pacific, 1972) 5.

[310] Harold Garfinkel, "Conditions of Successful Degradation Ceremonies," **American Journal of Sociology** 61 (1956): 420-424.

[311] Garfinkel, "Conditions of Successful Degradation Ceremonies."

We were struck by the fact that the typical sexual aggressor does not consider himself to be a homosexual, or even to have engaged in homosexual acts. This seems to be based upon his startling primitive view of sexual relationships, one that defines as male whichever partner is aggressive and homosexual whichever partner is passive...A primary goal of the sexual aggressor, it is clear, is the conquest and degradation of his victim. We repeatedly found that aggressors used such language "Fight or fuck," "We're going to take your manhood," "You'll have to give up some face," and "We're gonna make a girl out of you." Some of the assaults were reminiscent of the custom in some ancient societies of castrating or buggering a defeated enemy.[312]

During the period of Black social assertiveness, political agitation, and the urban rebellion of "Black masculine hostility," these Black men entering the Philadelphia prison system were subject to a horrific *status degradation ceremonies* involving homosexual rape, the aim of which was clearly to "expose" these Black men to be *the opposite* of assertive men. Underneath this systematic and systemic degradation ceremony in the Philadelphia prison system was the determination to show "the Negro as the Lady of the Races."

This system of homosexual rape was not only experimental, it was also *punitive*. As Davis wrote:

This, then, is the sexual system that exists in the Philadelphia prisons. It is a system that imposes a punishment that is not, and could not be, included in the sentence of the court. Indeed, it is a system under which the least hardened criminals, and many men later found innocent, suffer the most.[313]

Punishment for what? Punishment for Black masculine hostility toward White Supremacy and its racist abuses. Again, this horrendous system *was green-lighted* by the prison administration. As Davis concludes:

Why has this situation been allowed to continue for so long, despite the fact that it was brought to the attention of public officials at least two years ago? The answer is simple: The responsible city officials have blatantly neglected their duty.[314]

---

[312] Davis, "Sexual Assaults in the Philadelphia Prison System," 16.
[313] Davis, "Sexual Assaults in the Philadelphia Prison System," 9.
[314] Davis, "Sexual Assaults in the Philadelphia Prison System," 13

Superintendent Hendrick "throughout his lengthy career...allowed the medical experiments on prisoners," even showing up and *observing* some of the experiments.[315] The Superintendent and the three wardens (of the three facilities) admitted knowledge of the fact that "virtually every slightly built young man committed by the court is sexually approached within a day or two after his admission to the prison."[316] And they *let it happen*.

This system was exported to other prisons around the country. In 1980 John Money and Carol Bohmer published a study confirming that the male prison is "an environment that breeds sex offending."[317] They report on a unit the prison administration satirically called "Safekeeping," which was probably the most dangerous housing a man could have. The cellhouse clerk sold the young inmates as they came in for $25 to $100. That inmate was then told they have to submit to the homosexual abuse or die (some did commit suicide). "The administration is aware of such transactions and knows details-dates, prices paid, the clerks involved. Nothing is done."[318] This orchestrated, licensed and funded culture of homosexual rape helped spawn a subculture of consensual homosexuality. If a targeted man wanted to avoid the violence and trauma of gang rape, he would have two basic options open to him. The first option was to enter "voluntarily" into a homosexual relationship for protection.

This artificially induced culture of homosexual rape was a part of an experiment in and *for social change* and the homosexual culture created was in fact *designed* to bleed into and shape the Black community outside the prison walls. Davis confirmed this when he says: "Holmesburg Prison is nothing but a factory of crime, where inmates are programmed to commit rape and robbery in preparation of the day they are released."[319] "Criminologists have long maintained that men

---

[315] Hornblum, **Acres of Skin**, Photo insert 6.
[316] Davis, "Sexual Assaults in the Philadelphia Prison System," 9.
[317] John Money and Carol Bohmer, "Prison Sexology: Two Personal Accounts of Masturbation, Homosexuality, and Rape," **The Journal of Sex Research** 16 (1980): 258-266.
[318] Money and Bohmer, "Prison Sexology," 261.
[319] Gayle Ronan Sims, "Prominent city attorney, negotiator Alan Davis dies," **Philadelphia Inquirer** May 10, 2007.

who are victimized by sexual assault in prison often leave prison far more violent and anti-social than when they went inside,"[320] reports McGuire. Researchers have studied it and found that, in many cases the victim of the homosexual rape will become a part of the homosexual community once released, while the homosexual aggressor on the outside lives a public life of heterosexuality with a wife and children, but still having those homosexual tendencies.[321] This prison programing and orchestrated homosexual rape is, I am suggesting, part of the origin of the Down Low Phenomenon of the 1990s where so many Black men living heterosexual lives with family were secretly indulging their homosexual proclivities that they were forced to learn in prison. And in fact that is how some the researchers saw this: as an experiment in homosexuality as a *learned* behavior. In other cases the researchers *chemically* induce homosexual tendencies through such chemicals as cyproterone acetate and medroxyprogesterone acetate. But the U of P Research Program demonstrated something else: that through the "coercive persuasion" techniques suggested by Dr. Edgar Schein, homosexuality can be a learned culture. And Black men and boys were the human guinea pigs for this experiment. The Black Community suffers from the increasing infusion prison culture and the blending of prison culture and community culture due to the constant human traffic between the two; what Wacquant calls "Deadly symbiosis: when ghetto and prison meet and mesh."[322] The increasing homosexualization of the community and continued sky-rocketing of AIDS are two examples of such infusion.

VI.   *The Black Muslim Problem*

There were two primary ways a targeted man or boy could avoid being a victim of the homosexuality gang rape. The first was to enter into a coerced "voluntary" homosexual relationship for protection. The second way was to join the Nation of Islam. It was the Muslims who took the stand against the rape and homosexual culture of prison and it is stated that

---

[320] M. Dyan McGuire, "The Impact of Prison Rape on Public Health," **Cal. J. Health Promotion** 3 (2005): 72-83 (76).
[321] Edward Sagarin, "Prison Homosexuality and Its Effect on Post-Prison Sexual Behavior," **Psychiatry** 39 (1976): 245-257.
[322] Wacquant, "Deadly symbiosis."

youths who were targeted found instant sanctuary by joining the Black Muslims. It was the Black Muslims on D Block of Holmesburg that fought the U of P Research Program and helped to ultimately get the program shut down by 1974. Simon Khaadim Ahad, former member of the Nation of Islam in Holmesburg, recalled to Hornblum that "Muslims had taken a position opposed to the tests" and were not cooperative when U of P test recruiters came over to D Block "to try and solicit guinea pigs..."; D Block is where most of the Muslims were housed. "We knew white men were devils, and the tests were dangerous," recalled Ahad.[323]

Dr. Burt Cahn for example ran clinical experiments at Holmesburg between 1959 and 1965, after which he decided to leave. The Cahns (Burt and his brother Milton) tested tranquilizers on the Black inmates: Librium, Valium, Haldol, etc., the very psychopharmacological tools that will be used to tranquilize and zombify Black men in prisons around the country and inner-cities around the country. Why did Dr Burt Cahn shut down his program and leave Holmesburg? Because he feared the Black Muslims. As Hornblum explains:

[Dr. Burt Cahn said:] "I became concerned about the growth of the Muslim movement." The Nation of Islam, or Black Muslims...grew dramatically in the 1960s as America's prisons became a arena for recruitment and training in black nationalist and racial separatist ideology. Under the passionate and often confrontational leadership of Elijah Muhammad and Malcolm X, Muslims learned an antiwhite philosophy and a paramilitary code of behavior that many white prison employees found threatening. "Islam in the prison," a force with which he no longer wished to contend, combined with a "very taxing and time consuming" work schedule...and Dr. Cahn decided to leave Holmesburg Prison.[324]

Thus, it was the Muslims who resisted the violent and homosexual "prison masculinity" created by the prison authorities themselves; It was the Muslims who offered an alternative performance of Black Masculinity characterized by military discipline, hygiene, fearlessness, intellectuality, self-esteem and group solidarity or (brotherhood). Islam was the force against prison violence and homosexuality and a Muslim

---

323 Hornblum, *Acres of Skin*, 26.
324 Hornblum, *Acres of Skin*, 45.

code developed that said: "When a brother tries to deny a brother the right to be a man, he no longer deserves to live." Such a code struck fear in the prison experimenters and caused some to close up shop and get out of dodge for fear of their life. Ultimately this Muslim active resistance to the U of P Research Project and the homosexual culture that it was producing helped to get the project shut down in 1974.

Part II

Nixon's War

Chapter Seven:

President Nixon's War On Black America

President Nixon and John Ehrlichman

I.　*The War on Drugs as War on Black People*

It was Richard Nixon's political advisory Harry S. Dent who masterminded the so-called "Southern Strategy" that pried southern whites away from the Democratic Party and into Nixon's Republican camp by playing on white fears of Black Power and anger at the Civil Rights movement. The Nixon White House had clearly defined ideas of *the enemy,* and Dent's office provided the White House with a distinct language to identify them, including: *theyoungthepoortheblack.* This phrase bandied about in Dent's office and in the White House generally was the proper White House pronunciation of "the young, the poor, the black" rolling off of the tongue as if one word.[325] "The young" here are the young people protesting the Vietnam War, both the short haired white college students and

[325] Dan Baum, *Smoke and Mirrors: The War on Drugs and the Politics of Failure*, excerpt in *The Washington Post* @ https://www.washingtonpost.com/wp-srv/style/longterm/books/chap1/smoke.htm

the long-haired white hippies. The antiwar New Left exemplified a youthful defiance that Nixon "had no use for." The inner city was the home of the poor and the black that here identified as *the enemy*.

In June of 1971 President Nixon launched his War on Drugs. That this War on Drugs was explicitly a disguised War on Black People has now been confirmed by President Nixon's chief domestic policy advisor John Ehrlichman. Ehrlichman spent 18 months in prison for his central role in the Watergate scandal. In 1994 journalist Dan Braum interviewed Ehrlichman, excerpts of which appeared in last April's cover story of **Harper's**. Speaking with the bluntness of a man who, after public disgrace and federal prison, had little left to protect, Ehrlichman told Braum:

> [L]ook, we understood we couldn't make it illegal to be young or poor or black in the United States, but we could criminalize their common pleasure. We understood that drugs were not the health problem we were making them out to be, but it was such a perfect issue for the Nixon White House that we couldn't resist it.
>
> You want to know what this was really all about? The Nixon campaign in 1968, and the Nixon White House after that, had *two enemies*: the antiwar left *and black people*. You understand what I'm saying? We knew we couldn't make it illegal to be either against the war or black, but by getting the public to associate the hippies with marijuana *and blacks with heroin*, and then criminalizing both heavily, we could disrupt those communities. We could arrest their leaders, raid their homes, break up their meetings, and vilify them night after night on the evening news. Did we know we were lying about the drugs? Of course we did.[326]

This is astonishing. Associating Black people with heroin in order to wage a war against them is to associate Black people with the very drug that the U.S. government via the CIA-Mafia alliance deliberately flooded our communities with. As Hilary Hanson comments, this confession by Nixon's chief domestic advisor

---

[326] Dan Braum, "Legalize it all: How to win the war in drugs," **Harper's** April 2016.

pulls back the curtain on the true motivation of the United States war on drugs...the intense racial targeting that's become synonymous with the drug war wasn't an unintended side-effect-it was the whole point.[327]

The whole point, indeed. The "War on Drugs" was specifically the government's answer to Nixon's very real Negro Problem.

II.   *Nixon's Negro Problem*

"[Nixon] emphasized that you have to face the fact that the *whole* problem is really the blacks." H.R. Halderman, Diary, April 1969.

"It's all about law and order and the damn Negro-Puerto Rican groups out there." Richard Nixon, after viewing one of his 1968 campaign ads.

President Richard Nixon very much had a Negro Problem. Or, said better, America's Negro Problem was President Nixon's personal crusade. He shared American White Supremacy's attitude and view of Black people, as the released Nixon Tapes reveal unmistakably.[328]

The tapes reveal Nixon to be a deeply paranoid, deeply bigoted misanthrope. Nixon had the greatest fun spewing offensive racial epithets about blacks. While working on his first presidential address to Congress, Nixon told Henry Kissinger, then his national-security advisor, to leave Africa policy to Secretary of State William Rogers, saying, "Henry, let's leave the niggers to Bill, and we'll take care of the rest of the world."[329]

Investigative journalist Seymour Hersh exposed Nixon's and his National Security Advisor Henry Kissinger's deep racism is considerable detail in his book, ***The Price of Power:***

[327] Hilary Hanson, "Nixon Aide Reportedly Admitted Drug War Was Meant To Target Black People," *Huffington Post* March 22, 2016.

[328] Elspeth Reeve, "Some Newly Uncovered Nixon Comments on the Subject of Jews and Black People," *The Atlantic* August 21, 2013; Adam Nagourney, "In Tapes, Nixon Rails About Jews and Blacks," *The New York Times* December 10 ,2010.

[329] Earl Ofari Hutchinson, "The Nixon That Watergate Exposed," *HuffPost* August 8, 2014, updated October 8, 2014.

Kissinger in the Nixon White House (Simon and Schuster, 2013):

> There seems to have been an unrelenting stream of anti-black remarks from the President during his first year in office. In his telephone conversations with Kissinger, he repeatedly referred to blacks as "niggers," "jigs," and "jiga-boos." Some of the slurs were obviously results of Nixon drinking bouts, but [National Security Council] aides who monitored Kissinger-Nixon telephone calls came to believe that Richard Nixon, drunk or sober, was a racist. Far more disillusioning was their boss's [i.e. Kissinger's] attitude; Kissinger also repeatedly made clear his contempt for black people. Yet there was a constant stream of Kissinger asides to his staff about Nixon's racism. One theme was that Nixon had always been a racist but did not know the correct derogatory words until he moved from California to New York in the 1960s. After Nixon had referred to blacks as "jungle bunnies" during one of his telephone calls with Kissinger in 1969, Morris recalls, Kissinger whimsically explained that Nixon had seen *Hair* while in New York "and gotten educated." (One scene in the play consists of recitations, put to music, of various derogatory and slang phrases for blacks, including "jungle bunny.")

> Kissinger repeatedly made clear his lack of respect for the intelligence of blacks.

Kissinger's demonstrated anti-Blackness throws his draconian *National Security Memorandum 200,* which called for the *culling* of 2 billion people - into greater relief, and the *Memorandum* throws Nixon's views and agenda in greater relief. The *Memorandum* was actually prepared under Nixon and submitted to *him* in 1974. Thus, NSM 200 is a *Nixon* document.

Kissinger was not the only one on Nixon's staff that shared Nixon's sentiment. Earl Ofari Hutchinson reports: "In one tape, Nixon sat mute when White House advisor John Ehrlichman ranted that blacks are sexually degenerate, have no family values, and live in filthy neighborhoods."[330] Ehrlichman would later reveal that Nixon's anti-Blackness was not superficial: he actually was a convinced White Supremacist. As

---

[330] Earl Ofari Hutchinson, "Nixon's Ghetto Obsession," **HuffPost** March 18, 201, updated May 25, 2011.

the *Kingman Daily Miner* reported and *The New York Times* confirmed in 1981:

> Former President Nixon thought 'blacks were inferior to whites'...says Nixon's top domestic aide...[John] Ehrlichman says, "the racial issue was both a problem and an opportunity for President Richard Nixon...Twice, in explaining all this me, Nixon said he believed America's blacks could only marginally benefit from federal programs because blacks were genetically inferior to whites. All the federal money and programs we could devise could not change that fact, he believed. Blacks could never achieve parity – in intelligence, economic success or social qualities – but, he said, we should still do what we could for them, within reasonable limits, because it was "right".[331]

White House anti-Blackness had real-life consequences, as Hutchinson points out.

> Nixon's taped comments were much more than one man's loose-lipped racial abominations uttered in unguarded moments. Those remarks and the narrow racial mindset behind them fueled the Republican Party's nascent willingness to bash civil rights and social programs and *laid the groundwork for the repressive national-security state* (emphasis added-WM).[332]

And repressive this racism-driven national-security state indeed was/is toward Black people, in ways that most are unaware of. The urban rebellions or "insurrections" of the

---

[331] Louise Cook, "Ehrlichman says Nixon thought blacks were 'inferior,'" *The Kingman Daily Miner* December 11, 1981; Phil Gailey, "Report on Burger is Disputed," *The New York Times* December 11, 1981.

[332] Earl Ofari Hutchinson, "The Nixon That Watergate Exposed," *HuffPost* August 8, 2014, updated October 8, 2014.

1960s gave Nixon his mission, and he seems to have pursued it with intensity and commitment.

III.   *Nixon on the Riots*

"Richard Nixon...made law and order – and the revulsion of white suburbia against the violent images of rioters reacting to King's death – a central theme of his campaign," says Clay Risen.[333] "Law and order for Nixon boiled down to the 'damn Negroes'," affirmed Tali Mendelberg.[334]

> Whereas the liberal state portrayed the ghetto as something to be integrated into the rest of the society, the riots gave impetus to a new domestic militarism that saw the ghetto as an alien entity within the American borders, a cancer that had to be isolated from the rest of the body politic. In the wake of the riots suburban gun purchases skyrocketed, and Nixon, through the Law Enforcement Assistance Administration, funneled money to police departments to buy exotic anti-riot weaponry: body armor, tear gas, even surplus tanks. By the early 1970s *an anti-riot urban infrastructure was in place*, one that bureaucratically and even physically severed the ghetto from the rest of the city, and the city in turn from the suburbs.[335]

The young, Black, male revolutionaries or insurrectionists of America's inner-cities preoccupied Nixon and his administration, partly because he was personally offended by them. "Rioting and disorder offended many Americans and 'none so more than Richard Nixon for whom riots have always been offensive, emotionally disturbing, infuriating to his neat way of thinking'."[336] During his presidential campaign in October 1967 Nixon weighed in with a statement published in *The Readers Digest* entitled "What Happened to America?"

---

[333] Clay Risen, "The Legacy of 1968 Riots," *The Guardian* April 4, 2008.

[334] Tali Mendelberg, *The Race Card: Campaign Strategy, Implicit Messages, and the Norm of Equality* (Princeton and Oxford: Princeton University Press, 2001) 97.

[335] Clay Risen, "The Legacy of 1968 Riots," *The Guardian* April 4, 2008. See further Clay Risen, *A Nation in Flames: America in the Wake of the King Assassination* (Wiley, 2009).

[336] Katherine Scott, "Nixon and Dissent," in *A Companion to Richard M. Nixon*, ed. Melvin Small (Malden, MA: Wiley-Blackwell, 2011) 311-327.

What has happened to America?

Just three years ago this nation seemed to be completing its greatest decade of racial progress and entering one of the most hopeful periods in American History. Twenty million Negroes were at last being admitted to full membership in the society, and this social miracle was being performed with a minimum friction and without loss of our freedom or tranquility.

With this star of racial peace and progress before us, how did it happen that last summer (July 1967, i.e. Detroit Rebellion etc.) saw the United States blazing in an inferno of urban anarchy?

In more than 20 cities police and mayors were unable to cope with armed insurrection. Central cities were abandoned to snipers, looters and arsonists. Only the state militia or federal soldiers could regain the city and restore peace...

Why is it that in a few short years a nation which enjoys the freedom and material abundance of America has become among the most lawless and violent in the history of the free peoples?

There has been a tendency in this country to charge off the violence and the rioting of the past summer solely to the deep racial division between Negro and white. Certainly racial animosities--and agonies--were the most visible causes. But riots were also the most visible causes. But riots were also the most virulent symptoms to date of another, and in some ways graver, national disorder--the decline in respect for public authority and the rule of law in America. Far from being a great society, our's is becoming a lawless society...

Midsummer Madness. The nationwide deterioration of respect for authority, the law and civil order reached its peak this past summer when mobs in 100 cities burned and looted and killed in a senseless attack upon their society, its agents and its law...

The problems of our great cities were decades in building; they will be decades in their solution. While attacking the problems with urgency we must await the results with patience. *But we cannot have patience with urban violence. Immediate and decisive force must be the first response.* For there can be no progress unless there is an end to violence and unless there is respect for the rule of law. To ensure the success of long-range programs, we must first deal with the immediate crisis--the riots...

There can be no right to revolt in this society; no right to demonstrate outside the law, and, in Lincoln's words, "no grievance that is a fit object of redress by mob law."

Not only are violent rebellions to be dealt with by force, so too peaceful civil disobedience like civil rights or anti-war demonstrations (see Kent State and Jackson State). In a radio address Nixon said:

We have been amply warned that we face *the prospect of war* in the making in our own society. We have seen the gathering hate, we have heard the threats to burn and bomb and destroy. In Watts and Harlem and Detroit and Newark, we have had a foretaste of what *the organizers of insurrection* are planning...we must take the warnings to heart and prepare to meet force with force if necessary.[337]

And take them to heart Nixon did. He declared war on Black America before he declared "war of drugs". That war was simply one angle of his multi-level assault on Black America.

IV.   *Operation Garden Plot and Huston Plan*

The Nixon administration greatly expanded upon a program initiated by Lyndon Johnson in 1968 to use the military to quell riots and civil disobedience. The initiative, codenamed "Operation Garden Plot," is still in existence.[338]

Not only did the Nixon Administration expand on Operation Garden Plot, it was also the first to test it in a live situation. The opportunity presented itself to roll out the secret contingency plan February through May 1973 in the village of Wounded Knee on the Pine Ridge Reservation in South Dakota after a trading post and church were seized by "250 militant

---

[337] Quoted from Julian E. Elizer, "Is America Repeating the Mistakes of 1968?" *The Atlantic* Jul 8, 2016.
[338] Mark Nestmann, *The Lifeboat Strategy* (2011).

Indians". Operation Garden Plot was initiated, and the so-called militants surrendered "without heavy loss of life."[339]

A peek into the expansion of the Garden Plot powers under President Nixon, and his bellicose obsession with Black people, is provided by The Huston Plan, the White House's domestic security plan formalized in 1970. Seymour Hersh was the first to write on it after it came to light during the 1973 Watergate hearings:

> The Central Intelligence Agency, directly violating its charter, conducted a massive, illegal domestic intelligence operation during the Nixon Administration against the antiwar movement and other dissident groups in the United States, according to well-placed Governmental sources.
>
> An extensive investigation by The New York Times has established that intelligence files on at least 10,000 American citizens were maintained by a special unit of the C.I.A. that was reporting directly to Richard Helms, then the Director of Central Intelligence and now the Ambassador to Iran...
>
> The disclosure of alleged illegal, C.I.A. activities is the first, possible connection to rumers (sic) that have been circulating in Washington for some time. A number of mysterious burglaries and incidents have come to light since the breakin at Democratic party headquarters in the Watergate complex on June 17, 1972...
>
> It...could not be determined whether Mr. Helms had had specific authority from the President or any of his top officials to initiate the alleged domestic surveillance. Or whether Mr. Helms had informed the President of the fruits, if any, of the alleged operations...
>
> The official also said that the requirement to maintain files on American citizens emanated, in part, from the so-called Huston Plan. That plan, named after its author, Tom Charles Huston, a Presidential aide, was a White House project in 1970 calling for the use of such, illegal activities as burglaries and wiretapping to combat antiwar activities, and student turmoil that *the White House believed was being "fomented" – as the Huston plan stated – by black extremists.*

---

[339] The Washington Star, "Army Tested Secret Civil Disturbance Plan at Wounded Knee, Memos Show," *The New York Times* December 2, 1975.

Former President Richard M. Nixon and his top aides have repeatedly said that the proposal, which had been adamantly opposed by J. Edgar Hoover, then the director of the Federal Bureau of Investigation, was never implemented.[340]

This White House plan authorized illegal selective break-ins against domestic radicals and organizations, as well as telephone and mail surveillance, "to combat civil disturbances fomented by what was euphemistically referred to as 'black extremists'."[341] And "from the seeds of The Huston Plan came the Plumbers and, ultimately, the Watergate Scandal."[342]

Nixon brought together in a June 1970 meeting at his White House Richard Helms, CIA Director; J. Edgar Hoover, FBI Director; Lt. General Donald Bennet, Defense Intelligence Agency; Admiral Noel Gayler, National Security Agency; Robert Finch, Secretary of the Department of Health, Education and Welfare; H.R. Haldeman, Assistant to the President; John Ehrlichman, Domestic Affairs Advisor to the President; and Tom Huston, White House Staff Assistant. This circle would be called the Interagency Committee on Intelligence (ICI). They were tasked with operationalizing The Huston Plan.

It is demonstrably untrue that The Huston Plan, which is classified TOP SECRET till this very day, was never implemented, as was the common belief before the release of the Nixon Tapes. Douglas Brinkley reports for CNN:

> Recent releases of declassified Nixon White House tapes...suggest the National Security Agency at least partially implemented provisions of the Huston Plan...On May 16, 1973 White House special counsel J. Fred Buzhardt reported to

---

[340] Seymour M. Hersh, "Huge C.I.A. Operation Reported in U.S. Against Antiwar Forces, Other Dissidents in Nixon Years," *The New York Times* December 22, 1974. On the Huston Plan see further: "National Security, Civil Liberties, and the Collection of Intelligence: A Report on the Huston Plan," Supplementary Detailed Staff Reports on Intelligence Activities and the Rights of Americans. Book III: Final Report of the Subcommittee to Study Governmental Operations With Respect to Intelligence Activities United States Senate, April 23 (under authority of the order of April 14) 1976.

[341] Jussi Hanhimäki, *The Flawed Architect: Henry Kissinger and American Foreign Policy* (Oxford: Oxford University Press, 2004).

[342] Charles Peirce, "It's Official: Nixon Is the Worst," *Esquire* June 10, 2014.

Nixon that top NSA officials, including Deputy Director Louis Tordella, had told him the Huston Plan had been put into effect, according to a tape released in August 2013 by the National Archives...When the existence of the Huston Plan first became public during Watergate, we were led to believe that it was never implemented. Nixon ordered the plan and then recalled it, so the story goes. However, the reason the Huston Plan remains classified today is likely because at least portions of it were indeed implemented after all. The basis for its continued classification is to protect secrets that were operational.[343]

The possibility that a White House plan to employ illegal activities against "revolutionary (youth) protest movements" - a plan designed with Black people in mind - is the same Plan that brought Richard Nixon and his administration down, is simply delicious.

"The question will arise, undoubtedly," Judge John Sirica said during the trial of the burglars, "what was the motive for doing what you people say you did." Principal U.S. Attorney Earl Silbert also questioned the conventional wisdom behind Watergate in his diary, which he thought was important enough to future research to deposit at the National Archives.

Our chance to learn about the Huston Plan and whether it was the authority upon which the Watergate burglary took place slipped away when former White House counsel John W. Dean III turned over the White House copy to the U.S. District Court for the District of Columbia on May 14, 1973.

Dean took the plan with him when he was fired on April 30. As a result of his giving the document to the courts, it became out of the reach of congressional subpoena and out of the reach of the Freedom of Information Act, even though it was a document created by the executive branch and should have been reviewable under the FOIA. The document and associated records have been in the custody of the court ever since...

When word reached the intelligence community that the Huston Plan was no longer in the custody of the White House, panic swept across the FBI, CIA, and NSA on May 17. The FBI feared it could end up in the hands of congressional investigators then looking into Watergate, with the result being

---

[343] Douglas Brinkley, "Great mystery of the 1970s: Nixon, Watergate and the Huston Plan," *CNN* June 17, 2015.

that "inference is likely to be drawn by Congressional committees that this committee (the ICI) was a prelude to the Watergate affair and the Ellsberg psychiatrist burglary."

In the end, the intelligence community won. The Ervin Committee became, in effect, an unclassified inquiry into Watergate. Sens. Sam Ervin and Howard Baker were never given more than generic summaries of the Huston Plan. Baker and his counsel Fred Thompson were always skeptical, but their minority reports never went anywhere.

Later inquiries, such as the Church Committee, were the beginning of the classified investigation into Watergate and abuses of government power, but even the Church Committee published no more than excerpts of the Huston Plan in its multivolume public report.

When the Watergate investigation sharply focused on Richard Nixon, the problem was never an insufficient number of crimes or wrongdoing to send him to trial, whether in the U.S. Senate or a later criminal or civil courtroom. *The elephant in the room was the quantity of classified material that would be made public either in his prosecution or his defense.* That would have been unacceptable to the intelligence community and to the future ability of the government to function.

Cutting Nixon out

There was indeed a "cancer on the presidency," as Dean said to Nixon on March 21, and the apparent answer of the national security establishment was to cut it out -- to cut Nixon out. *The President had to resign, and he had to be pardoned to ensure that inquiries into broader U.S. government wrongdoing could not continue indefinitely.*

More than 40 years after Nixon's resignation, we still have him to kick around, to borrow his phrase. It will remain this way for as long as the Huston Plan remains classified. Virtually all of the Watergate grand jury records remain closed except for Nixon's testimony. A huge mystery of the '70s that still needs to be answered is whether the Watergate burglars, plumbers, and Elkbery psychiatrist office break-in artists derived their authority from the Huston Plan and its enhanced domestic surveillance provisions.[344]

---

[344] Douglas Brinkley, "Great mystery of the 1970s: Nixon, Watergate and the Huston Plan," *CNN* June 17, 2015.

## V.	Ronald Reagan's War Plans: Cable Splicer

Before Richard Nixon was either a U.S. president (1969-1974) or vice president (1953-1961) in Washington D.C., he was a Senator (1950-1953) and a member of the U.S. House of Representatives for the state of California where he was born. President Nixon's first Secretary of Health, Education and Welfare (H.E.W.), Richard Finch who was tasked with implementing the racist plan of Dr. Arnold Hutschnecker (Nixon's physician and advisor – see below) to put Black boys in concentration camps, was also from California. He served as Lieutenant Governor of California in (1967-1969). The Governor was Ronald Reagan (1967-1975). And according to *Napa Sentinel* investigative reporters Harry V. Martin and David Caul, "a mind-boggling tale of horror has been a part of California penal history for a long time," especially in the 1960s and 1970's.

> Mind control experiments have been part of California for decades and permeate mental institutions and prisons. But, it is not just in the penal society that mind control measures were used. Minority children were subjected to experimentation at abandoned Nike Missile Sites, veterans who fought for American freedom were also subjected to the programs...California has been in the forefront of mind control experimentation.[345]

Each region of the country (and Nixon divided the country into 10 Standard Federal Regions) would follow a sub-plan of Operation Garden Plot, the federal counterinsurgency plan to suppress urban uprisings. It was California governor Reagan who developed the first known (with any detail) sub-plan. This west coast sub-plan, called Operation Cable Splicer, covers four/five states (from what would become Regions IX and X): California, (Nevada)[346], Oregon, Washington, and Arizona. It was (is?) under the command of the Sixth Army.

> It is a plan that outlines extraordinary military procedures to stamp out unrest in this country. Developed in a series of California meetings from 1968 to 1972, Cable Splicer *is a war*

---

[345] Harry V. Martin and David Caul, "Mind Control. Part 1 of 13: Min Control in California," *Napa Sentinel* August-November 1991, p.1.
[346] Some reports include Nevada, others do not.

plan that has adapted for domestic use procedures used by the U.S. Army in Vietnam. The story began a decade ago.[347] In 1965 Watts exploded in riots and, across the Pacific, Marines landed in South Vietnam (emphasis added – WM).[348]

Cable Splicer, like the larger Operation Garden Plot, was organized to respond to "the revolution they (the Pentagon and the Justice Department) thought would blossom from race riots and antiwar protests of the late Sixties and early Seventies."[349] In May 1970 California Chief Deputy Attorney General Charles O'Brien told a gathering of Cable Splicer operatives: "We are in a revolution. Here in this room today we have at least the nucleus of people who should be able to, in some measure, contribute to the *counter-revolution* (emphasis added – WM)."[350]

Governor Reagan tapped retired National Guard General, Louis O. Giuffrida, to design Operation Cable Splicer as a martial law plans "to legitimize the arrest and detention of anti-Vietnam war activists and other political dissidents."[351]

During the late sixties and early seventies, Giuffrida had served as Governor Reagan's terrorism advisor and at Reagan's request founded the California Specialized Training Institute (GSTI), a school for police and military commandos. To quote from an early CSTI instruction manual: "Legitimate violence is integral to our form of government, for it is from this source that we can continue to *purge our weakness.*" Giuffrida and (Edwin) Meese (then Governor Reagan's chief assistant) helped develop a plan to purge

General Louis Giuffrida

---

[347] This was written in 1975.
[348] Ron Ridenhour with Arthur Lubow, "Bringing the War Home," **New Times** 5 (1975): 18, 20-24; Ron Ridenhour, "Garden Plot & SWAT: U.S. Police as New Action Army," **CounterSpy** 2:4 (Winter 1976): 16-25, 43-58.
[349] Ridenhour with Lubow, "Bringing the War Home," 18.
[350] Ridenhour with Lubow, "Bringing the War Home," 20.
[351] Diana Reynolds, "FEMA and the NSC: The Rose of the National Security State," **CovertAction** 33 (Winter 1990): 54-58 (54-55).

California of its militant *and* peaceful protestors. Operation Cable Splicer, a variation of the army Garden Plot, a "domestic counterinsurgency" scheme, spied on suspected radicals and marshaled maximum force to squash riots and legitimate demonstrations alike (emphasis added – WM).352

These plans were refined with the assistance of British counterinsurgency expert Sir Robert Thompson, who had used massive detention and deportation to deal with the 1950s Communist insurgency in what is now Malaysia. Thompson's plans for massive detention, adapted first by Giuffrida in California's Operation Cable Splicer, were further refined by Giuffrida and FEMA with the assistance of Oliver North.353

Advisers formed shadow government, probers say

But it was not just any "militants" that Giuffrida and later Attorney General Edwin Meese wanted to purge California of.354 In 1987 reporter Alfonso Chardy of the *Miami Herald*

---

352 Jonathan Vankin and John Whalen, *The 70 Greatest Conspiracies of All Time: History's Biggest Mysteries, Coverups & Cabals* (New Jersey: Carol Publishing Group, 1998 [1995]) 28-29.
353 Peter Dale Scott, *The American Deep State: Big Money, Big Oil, and The Struggle for U.S. Democracy* (Lanham: Rowman & Littlefield, 2017) 149.
354 On Meese's "enthusiastic cooperation" with Cable Splicer as a gubernatorial aide to Ronald Reagan see Sharon Churcher and Mary

broke the story about "Reagan Aides and the 'Secret Government'," in which he revealed:

> Some of President Reagan's top advisers have operated a virtual parallel government outside the traditional Cabinet departments and agencies almost from the day Reagan took office, congressional investigators and administration officials have concluded...

> Lt. Col. Oliver North, for example, helped draw up a controversial plan to suspend the Constitution in the event of a national crisis, such as nuclear war, violent and widespread internal dissent or national opposition to a U.S. military invasion abroad...

> The martial law portions of the plan were outlined in a June 30, 1982, memo by Giuffrida's deputy for national preparedness programs, John Brinkerhoff. A copy of the memo was obtained by The Herald.

> The scenario outlined in the Brinkerhoff memo resembled somewhat a paper Giuffrida had written in 1970 at the Army War College in Carlisle, Pa., in which he advocated martial law *in case of a national uprising by black militants*. The paper also advocated the roundup and transfer to "assembly centers or relocation camps" of *at least 21 million "American Negroes."*[355]

The paper written by Giuffrida mentioned here is his 1970 master's thesis from the U.S. Army War College entitled, "National Survival-Racial Imperative."[356] Written on the heels of the Urban Rebellions of the Sixties, the Giuffrida thesis tries "to figure out...when the system breaks down...what the Army's response should be."[357] His answer: mass detention of all Black people, militant and pacifist.

Murphy, "Meese Said to Have Cooperated With Secret Pentagon Plan," **New York Magazine** April 9, 1984, p. 13.
[355] Alfonso Chardy, "Reagan Aides and the 'Secret Government'," **Miami Herald** July 5, 1987.
[356] Louis O. Giuffrida, "National Survival-Racial Imperative," (Carlisle Barracks, Pennsylvania: U.S. Army War College, 1970) Master's thesis.
[357] Said the U.S. Army War College spokeswoman to Matthew Cunningham-Cook, who had to secure a copy of the thesis with some difficulty after an FOIA request. See Matthew Cunningham-Cook, "Contingency Plans," **Jacobin Magazine** (Online) September 11, 2014.

Specifically, Giuffrida's was a plan for the government's response to "the 'Black Peril'." He wrote:

> Faced by mounting death and destruction, as well as increasing demands that he do so, the President reluctantly declares a state of national emergency and puts the entire country on a war basis. The previously murmured suggestion that *all Negroes be locked up* now swells to a roar. It is like 1941 again, except that now it is the "Black Peril" rather than the "Yellow Peril."

> In the extremely unlikely event that the government were to order the evacuation and detention of *all blacks* from actual or potential trouble spots, how and by whom would the order be enforced? What are the yardsticks for collecting, evacuating, and interning either militant or pacifistic minority groups; or dissident, potentially disloyal elements; or law-abiding citizens whose only offense is accident of color? Where would the internees be kept? . . . What would be done with the blacks in the Armed Forces and in civil service and in Congress? The task would be far too large for the Justice Department; it would have to be greatly augmented by military forces, primarily from the United States Army.

> The government has historically had the right to protect itself. A government faced with prolonged, simultaneous, apparently coordinated riots disrupting the entire nation to the point where the government feared its very existence was in jeopardy would take many actions which in calmer times would never be considered. "The authority to decide whether the exigency has arisen, belongs exclusively to the President and . . . his decision is conclusive upon all other persons." (*Martin v. Mott*, US Supreme Court 1827).358

Giuffrida's ideas were in harmony with those of President Nixon's, who also considered a plan to intern Black people – young Black males in particular – in detention camps (see below). Giuffrida's plan also excited the leadership in California. According to Diana Reynolds, Research Associate and Director of the Edward R. Murrow Center at Tufts University,

> Giuffrida's creation of contingency emergency plans to round up 'militant negroes' while he was at the Naval War College *caught the attention of then-Governor of California Reagan*

---

358 Matthew Cunningham-Cook, "Contingency Plans," **Jacobin Magazine** (Online) September 11, 2014.

*and his executive secretary Edwin Meese III...*In 1971, Governor Reagan, with a $425,000 grant from the Federal Law Enforcement Assistance Administration (LEAA), established a counterterrorism training center--the California Specialized Training Institute (CSTI)--and made Giuffrida its commandant..[359]

The California Specialized Training Institute was established in May, 1971 as a government agency to train California authorities in emergency management tactics. In a GSTI textbook for the class "Civilian Violence and Terrorism: Officer Survival and Internal Security," Giuffrida wrote: "A white man cannot ever be black, red, or brown and so long as the white man remains superior in numbers *he will be the repressor* and the constant *target of the mad dog.*"[360] The tag "mad dog," which President Reagan would later call Libya's Colonel Muammar Qaddafi, was earlier used by Governor Reagan's "emergency czar" General Giuffrida for Black people: both uses were pretenses for murder. In the CSTI "Civil Emergency Management" course manual, a "virtual handbook for the counterrevolution," the author acknowledges that the "revolutionary activity" is based on sincere, well-justified feelings of frustration and the causes of that frustration are legitimate, which is "exactly why the threat is dangerous,"[361] and must be put down like a mad dog.

VI.   *Practicing War with Black People*

Cable Splicer is a series of *war games.* As Donald Goldberg and Indy Badhwar report:

> At first, the Garden Plot exercises focused primarily on racial conflict. But beginning in 1970, the scenarios took a different twist. The joint teams, made up of cops, soldiers, and spies, began practicing battle with large groups of protestors. *California, under the leadership of Ronald Reagan, was among the most enthusiastic participants in Garden Plot war games...*

---

[359] Reynolds, "FEMA and the NSC," Reynolds, "FEMA and the NSC," 54.

[360] Quoted in Matthew Cunningham-Cook, "Contingency Plans, " **Jacobin Magazine** (Online) September 11, 2014.

[361] Ridenhour with Lubow, "Bringing the War Home."

Garden Plot evolved into a series of annual training exercises based on contingency plans to undercut riots and demonstrations, ultimately developed for every major city in the United States. Participants in the exercises included key officials from all law enforcement agencies in the nation, as well as the National Guard, the military, and representatives of the intelligence community. According to the plan, teams would react to a variety of scenarios based on information gathered through political espionage and informists. The object was to quell urban unrest. [362]

In February 1969 Governor Reagan spoke to a gathering of 500 Cable Splicer personnel:

> Before an audience of 500 – including generals from the Pentagon, the Sixth Army and the National Guard, dozens of lesser officers, police chiefs and sheriffs from as far east as Washington D.C., California state legislators, a dozen Military Intelligence officers and executives from telephone, utility and defense-contract companies – Governor Ronald Reagan took the microphone. It was a week after he had promised to keep California's universities open at the point of a bayonet, if necessary. "You know," he began, "there are people in the state who, if they could see this gathering right now and my presence here, would decide that their worst fears and convictions have been realized – I was planning a military takeover.[363]

He would later engineer a quasi-military takeover of the federal government as president. A month after this speech, a series of Cable Splicer war games were conducted and the "enemy" in these war games was Black people (the "minority group") who are rioting because of a police shooting. Investigative journalist Ron Ridenhour broke the story on Cable Splicer in a 1976 *New Times* article based on internal documents which describe in some detail these war games. He describes:

> The games were organized around 23 existing political jurisdictions, usually at the city, county or regional level, across California. On the scheduled morning, the controllers, players,

---

[362] Donald Goldberg and Indy Badhwar, "Blueprint for Tyranny," *Penthouse Magazine* August 1985, p. 72; James W. Button, *Black Violence: Political Impact of the 1960s Riots* (Princeton: Princeton University Press, 1978) 133; Frank Morales, "U.S. Military Civil Disturbance Planning: The War At Home," *CovertAction Quarterly* 69 (Spring/Summer 2000).
[363] Ridenhour with Lubow, "Bringing the War Home."

monitors and observers gathered in the emergency operations center," usually the radio room of the county sheriff or of the largest participating police department. In some cases, a National Guard armory was used. Among the participants were senior National Guard officers and their Army advisers, senior police and sheriff's officers and telephone and utility company executives. The soldiers always wore civilian clothing and took all precautions to disguise the military's cooperation with the police.

By the time the participants gathered in the emergency operations center, anywhere from six weeks to six months of preparation had already been invested in the game. Initial orders had been transmitted from the Army command to the state National Guard headquarters, where, with the help of Army advisers, the scenarios were drafted. On every level, in every way, military men worked closely with police officers. In California the Guard prepared two special intelligence documents, titled "Special Intelligence Summary" and "Organizations and Personalities." Although their content is unknown, apparently they supply intelligence data on California citizens and political organizations. Asked if that were true, Lt. Col. Frank Salcedo, public information officer for the California Guard and a Cable Splicer planner since 1969, answered rhetorically: "Well, how else could you do it?" Copies of both documents were sent to Cable Splicer planners to help them create realistic skirmishes. On their end, local policemen prepared their own special intelligence summaries featuring the "best described dissident activity" for their community, targeting either racial, student or labor unrest. Finally, over 1,200 preplanned intelligence reports on supposedly imaginary events, people and organizations, carefully pasted to IBM cards, were provided to help generate *the make-believe war*.

With everything ready, it's time to begin. The clock reads 0800 hours. The players listen to a special intelligence summary, learning the background of the civil disturbance that has led up to the current "emergency." At that point, the "controllers" -- usually the senior National Guard officers and their Army advisers -- begin play, feeding the IBM-card preplanned intelligence reports of dissident activity to the players. Seated at rows of desks dotted with telephones, facing a "situation map" of their community, the players respond to the unfolding scenario. They are the thin blue line standing between order and anarchy.

150

The situation escalates. In Phase I of the scenario possessed by *New Times*, *an arrest and shooting provoke crowd unrest and threats against public officials.* Fourteen hours later (not real time: the riot unfolds like a time-phased movie of a chicken hatching) a "major incident" occurs -- a police car is ambushed and an officer is wounded, *a minority group* member is killed and two others are injured. This is followed by *"minority group charges* [that] police planned [the] shooting incident" and "threats of retaliation." A day passes. Intelligence reports indicate "probable widespread activity momentarily." Apparently the reports are accurate, for Phase I ends with the *arrival of a "chartered flight" carrying "70 persons" -- apparently radicals -- who are picked up at the airport by friends in 20 separate automobiles.*[364]

Phase II begins two hours later with the ambush of several police cars, the attempted assassination of the mayor, the bombing of local armories, the destruction of vehicles and ammunition stocks and the gathering of thousands of people in the streets. County and state police and police from other cities are called in. Previous intelligence reports have proved prophetic, but within the next few hours "two distinct and conflicting intelligence reports develop." The players decide that the first, which indicates "widespread support for general insurrection, is unreliable and invalid." They rely on the second one, which identifies "limited but violent activity planned and executed by a relatively few individuals with virtually no popular support. There are soon reports of "scattered incidents of guerrilla activity."

As Phase III opens, intelligence reports pouring into the Emergency Operations Center disclose more fire-bombings, attempted assassinations of public officials, hoarding of water in certain areas and sniping at fire trucks. The streets remain filled with thousands of people, and the National Guard is called to active duty. Intelligence notes that the "crowds [are] not violent yet and should be dispersed before becoming sympathetic to guerrillas." But the police and National Guard aren't quick enough. Reports soon come in of window-mashing and looting. The crowds are now violent, and as Phase III ends the Guard is unable to deal with the riots.

What happens next is unclear. The scenario possessed by *New Times* says only, "It is now 96 hours later," followed by these

---

[364] Like the Airport Detail for the Honorable Brother Minister Farrakhan.

cryptic entries: "Situation well under control. No major incidents last 24 hours. Intelligence: remaining loose militants cannot get support for further violence."

How has order been restored? We can only guess. It is known that during this period the U.S Army is called in to bail out the National Guard. At their disposal, according to the game plan, there are heavy artillery, armor, *chemical and psychological warfare teams* and tactical air support. "Complete coverage day and night" is offered by observation helicopters coordinated with ground patrols. To impress the populace, armored vehicles and "saturation of areas with police and military patrols" are two recommended tactics, Cable Splicer players are instructed to "evacuate civilians to preclude their interference with operation and/or to ensure their safety." They are also coached in techniques of emergency relief supply, temporary shelters "for civilians whose homes have been destroyed," collection of privately-owned weapons and other techniques useful for the rule of war-torn provinces.

Do the police detain radical leaders, leaving only some "remaining loose militants"? How do they extract the militants from the thousands of less committed supporters? At last the Military Intelligence domestic surveillance program begins to make some sense. In the winter of 1967-8, as Garden Plot and subplans such as Cable Splicer were developed, Military Intelligence sent domestic operatives countrywide to organize political intelligence units, compiling data eventually stored in *the Pentagon domestic war room computer.* Was that information the basis for the "hypothetical" war games? In the exercise directive's "security guidance" paragraph is the following order: "Names of real militant or dissident organizations will not be used. For development of problem play, fictitious names will be used." Are the directors of this secret military project worried about slander lawsuits? Or are they simply notifying local forces not to draw on the police or military intelligence lists of "real militant or dissident organizations?" (emphasis added – WM)[365]

These war games are no doubt part of the operationalization of Giuffrida's vision on how to deal with America's Negro Problem or the "Black Peril." But this planned and practiced war against Black people also had another aspect to it that was also piloted

---

[365] Ridenhour with Lubow, "Bringing the War Home."

in California under Ronald Reagan. This one was under the authority of the CIA and the Synagogue of Satan.

VII. *The Final Solution for Black People – With A Twist*

Henry Kissinger, Nixon's National Security Advisor, was a German Jew from Bavaria. So too was Nixon's former physician and advisor Dr. Arnold Hutschnecker, a Jew from Berlin. He was also under President Nixon a consultant to the National Commission on the Cause and Prevention of Violence, formed by President Johnson. This commission sent their final report, **Violent Crimes**, to Nixon in December 1969 and its conclusions, much to Nixon's liking, was that violent crimes are "chiefly a problem of the cities of the nation, and there

Dr. Arnold Hutschnecker

violent crimes are committed mainly by the young, poor, male inhabitants of the ghetto slum."[366] Like the Kerner Report before it, **Violent Crimes** urged that "only progress toward urban reconstruction can reduce the strength of the crime-causing forces in the inner city and thus reverse the direction of present crime trends." *That*, President Nixon was *not* trying to hear. Already by that time though Nixon was realizing the limitations of relying exclusively on beefed up law-enforcement. It was not sufficient to only lock up the Black male body. He had to also *modify* behavior and alter or "fix" the Black male mind. Enter his former physician who practiced *psychosomatic* medicine: Hutschnecker.

In a December 1, 1969 Oval Office meeting President Nixon asked Hutschnecker to review the commission's report and make recommendations. His review was as an unpaid consultant to the National Institute of Mental Health

---

[366] National Commission on the Causes and Prevention of Violence, **Violent Crime: The Challenge to Our Cities** (New York: George Braziller, 1969) 82.

(NIMH).[367] He prepared a confidential White House report with proposals that he submitted directly to the President. Three months later, on March 23, 1970 Nixon sent his counselor Daniel P. Moynihan to see Hutschnucker and they planned a meeting about his proposal with Dr. Stanley Yolles, director of NIMH, who in the meantime did "some staff work" on their behalf. Before that meeting could take place, however, a Black employee of HEW got a hold of that confidential White House report and, alarmed at what he read, leaked the report to the press. What alarmed this Black male employee of HEW? This first to break the story was the **Washington Post** on April 5, 1970, reporting:

> President Nixon has asked the Department of Health, Education and Welfare to study the proposals of a New York psychiatrist that psychological tests be administered to all the six-year-olds in the United States to determine their future potential for criminal behavior...Teenage boys later found to be persistently in incorrigible behavior would be remanded to camps.[368]

Hutschnecker proposed to Nixon that, in order to prevent crime in the U.S., children should be tested and screened for incipient anti-social behavior and a violent propensity or disposition. They should be genetically screened as well for a chromosomal anomaly in males, an XYY karyotype which,[369] at that time, was deliberately, falsely presented as a

---

[367] Jack Nelson, "Crime Tests for Kids," **San Francisco Chronical** May 7, 1970.

[368] Robert C. Maynard, "Crime Tests at Age 6 Urged," **Washington Post** April 5, 1970. See also R. Maynard, "Doctor Would Test Children to Curb Crime," **Los Aneles Times** April 5, 1970, p. 9; Erica Goode, "Arnold Hutschnecker, 102, Therapist to Nixon," **The New York Times** January 3, 2001.

[369] Peter Conrad and Joseph W. Schneider, **Deviance and Medicalization: From Badness to Sickness** (Philadelphia: Temple University Press, 1992) 228:"Likewise, the XYY chromosome theory has given rise to newly proposed programs of early warning and corrective therapy. For example, in 1970 Dr. Arnold Hutschnecker, one of President Nixon's personal medical advisors, proposed a massive program of chromosomal screening and psychological testing for every 6-year-old in the country. The policy was aimed at detecting evidence of criminal potential. He suggested that "hard-core 6-year-

genetic marker for male violence and sexual pathology, and young Black males were deceptively being tagged and stigmatized thusly.[370] The Black HEW employee received Hutschnecker's proposal with personal alarm for good reason. While the doctor would try to cover himself once the controversy erupted by claiming, "I wasn't just talking about black children and not just ghetto children, but all children – the total population should be tested,"[371] the fact is that he agreed and claimed in his "crime-prevention" proposals that "the breeding ground of violence (and crime) (is) in the predominantly black ghetto slums"[372] and that "violent crime in the cities stems disproportionately from the ghetto slum, where most Negroes live."[373]

Black inner-city young males thus *were* the primary population considered for these proposed crime and violence remedies. And the remedy, Hutschnecker argued, was neither urban reconstruction nor more robust law-enforcement. Rather, it is *mind-fixing* these young Black males:

> No doubt there is a desperate need for urban reconstruction, but I would like to suggest another, direct, immediate and what I believe effective way of attacking the problem at its very origin, by focusing on the "criminal mind" of the child. The aim is to *prevent* a child with a delinquent character structure from being allowed to grow into a full-fledged teen-age delinquent or adult criminal...A drive to violence and crime can be discovered as early as the age of six.[374]

This six-year old criminal-in-waiting, with the right intervention and "treatment," can be made to overcome his natural propensity. With the collaborative effort of NIMH along with "local chapters of mental health all over the country, and the psychiatric clinics in urban America, a wide scale program

---

olds" be sent to "therapeutic" camps where they could learn to be "good social animals."

[370] Wesley Muhammad, **Understanding The Assault**, 169-179.

[371] Jack Nelson, "Crime Tests for Kids," **San Francisco Chronical** May 7, 1970.

[372] Arnold Hutschnecker, **The Drive for Power** (New York: M. Evans, 1974) 158.

[373] Dr. Arnold Hutschnecker, "A Plea for Experiment," **The New York Times** October 2, 1970.

[374] Hutschnecker, **The Drive for Power**, 159.

could be set in motion as soon as approved and funded."[375] And what happens to the already (Black) "full-fledged teen age delinquent"? He is sent to a *concentration camp*, euphemistically called "rehabilitation camp," "preventive detention camp," "treatment camps," etc.

> For the severely disturbed, the young hard-core criminal, there may be a need to establish camps with group activities under the supervision of psychologists, who have empathy (important) but also firmness and who can earn the respect of difficult adolescents.[376]

While this German Jew tried to publicly present these "camps" for young Black "criminals" as benign summer camps full of fun, the true Nazi context was *not* missed on those familiar with the proposal.

> The most grotesque of proposals reached President Nixon, December 1969, by memorandum from Dr. Arnold Hutschnecker, a psychiatrist and consultant to the National Commission on the Causes and Prevention of Violence. He suggested that all 6- to 8-year-old U.S. children take psychological tests to determine whether they had a predilection for criminal behavior, and to weed out the potentially dangerous. This program would have been implemented by the construction of "rehabilitation camps," day-care centers and afterschool centers, where the children would be treated...Perhaps even more alarming, is the fact that the President sent this ludicrous thing to HEW for advice on setting up pilot projects.[377]

Indeed, the White House had every intention of implementing this Nazi-esque program, at least portions of it.

---

[375] Hutschnecker, *The Drive for Power*, 163.

[376] Robert C. Maynard, "Crime Tests at Age 6 Urged," *Washington Post* April 5, 1970; Arnold Hutschnecker, "Nixon-Era Plan for Children Didn't Include Concentration Camps," *The New York Times* October 15, 1988.

[377] Statement of Theodore J. Johnson of the Veteran's Administration at "Federal Involvement in the Use of Behavior Modification Drugs on Grammar School Children of the Right to Privacy Inquiry," Hearing Before a Subcommittee on Government Operations, House of Representatives, Ninety-First Congress, Second Session. September 29, 1970 (Washington, 1970) 44.

On December 30, Ehrlichman sent a memo to Robert Finch, Secretary of the Department of Health, Education and Welfare (HEW) stating: "The President asks your opinion as to the advisability of setting up pilot projects embodying some of these approaches."[378] On September 29, 1970 Congressman Cornelius Gallaghar (D-New Jersey) convened a hearing of his House Privacy Subcommittee condemning the proposal to psychologically and genetically test boys, and suggesting that "from this test result [the boys will be] possibly torn from his mother's arms by Federal agents taking him to an American Dachau."[379] Dachau: the German concentration camp for Jews. Go figure: the first White House plan to solve the Negro Problem by putting Black people in concentration camps was authored by a German Jew.

While Nixon clearly intended to implement Hutschnecker's proposal – and indeed *did implement it* a little later – the violent controversy in the press forced a public about face and distancing.

> The public reaction to this authoritarian scheme (Dr. Hutschnecker was born in Berlin) was so violent that the administration soon disowned it, although, at the instance of the President and his then top aide, John Ehrlichman, the proposal was given serious consideration at the highest level of the government.[380]

The "Blacks-in-Concentration-Camps" solution to the Negro Problem is far from dead with this public disowning of the Hutschnecker proposal. A reporter will later call him in 1974 to inform him that "you have been vindicated," because the Department of Justice moved on his Nazi-esque plans after all,[381] and they are today government policy (at least the concentration camps). The fact that Hutschnecker's proposed camps were apparently to be on the west coast is an important detail to be elaborated upon later.[382]

---

378 Jack Nelson, "Crime Tests for Kids," **San Francisco Chronical** May 7, 1970.
379 **Government Publishing Office – Extensions and Remarks, April 8, 1970**, pp. 10886-10887.
380 Clayton Fritchey, "A Political Prescription," **Los Angeles Times** July 28, 1973.
381 Hutschnecker, **The Drive for Power**, 189.
382 Norman K. Denzin, **Children and their Caretacker** (New Brunswick: Transaction Books, 1973) 72 quotes Hutschnecker

Chapter Eight:

Scientifically Taming The Black Bull

I.   *The Rise of Psychochemical Warfare and Weapons*

The Edgewood Arsenal facility on the Chesapeake Bay in Maryland is where the U.S. Army Chemical Corps conducted its chemical and biological warfare research from 1948 to 1975. The Edgewood ethos was: "better fighting through chemistry." In 1949 Luther Wilson Green, the Technical Director of the Chemical and Radiological Center at Edgewood, wrote a classified report entitled "Psychochemical Warfare: A New Concept of War." Green wrote:

> I am convinced that it is possible, by means of the techniques of psychochemical warfare, to conquer an enemy without the wholesale killing of his people or the mass destruction of his property...
>
> The symptoms which are considered to be of value in strategic and tactical operations include the following: fits or seizures, dizziness, fear, panic, hysteria, hallucinations, migraine, delirium, extreme depression, notions of hopelessness, lack of initiative to do even simple things, suicidal mania.[383]

The military is now pivoting to warfare that spares lives and architectural structures, but conquers an enemy population by incapacitating the mind. The Department of Defense argued that "certain types of 'psychochemicals' would make it possible to paralyze temporarily entire population centers without damage to homes and other structures."[384] "The psycho agents incapacitated primarily by interfering with cognitive mental abilities and produced delirium or hallucinations."[385] According to top military scientists psychochemicals were "the next step in

---

[383] Luther Wilson Green, "Psychochemical Warfare: A New Concept of War" (Maryland: Edgewood Arsenal, 1949).
[384] E. James Lieberman, "Psychochemicals as Weapons," **Bulletin of the Atomic Scientists** 18 (1962): 11-14.
[385] Reid Kirby, "Paradise Lost: The Psycho Agents," **The CBW Convention Bulletin** 71 (2006): 1-5 (1).

the evolution of warfare."[386] The aim of this new form of warfare without death was:

> the use of incapacitating but nonlethal agents from which a drugged and stupefied or sickened and prostrated enemy would quickly recover after being disarmed...According to one Army spokesman, the ideal mixture "would bring happily intoxicated enemy troops into our lines with their hands up, humming the Star-Spangled Banner."

> troops exposed to one of these agents were not even conscious of their abnormal condition, which was so changed that they were unable to follow simple commands and perform normal tasks with acceptable accuracy.

British pharmacologists Dr. William Maxwell Hollyhock reported in 1963 that psychochemical weapons were considered then (and now) "another technique in the war for men's minds."[387] The military objective of a psychochemical weapon is "so altering the subject's state of mind that he is incapable of continuing to function effectively." Then Dr. Hollyhock makes an observation of critical importance here, to which we shall return later: "Probably *the archetype of psychochemical compounds is hashish.*"[388] By hashish, of course, is meant cannabis.

II.   *The CIA, the Synagogue of Satan, and the Control of Human Behavior*

In 1977 **The New York Times** published the first public exposé of one of the U.S. Government's darkest and dirtiest secrets: the CIA's MKULTRA program.[389] The **Times** story began:

---

[386] Ben A. Franklin, "Drug War Study Pressed By Army," **NYT** November 22, 1964.

[387] Dr. W.M. Hollyhock, "Weapons Against the Mind," **New Scientist** April 22, 1963, pp. 224-226.

[388] Hollyhock, "Weapons Against the Mind," 224.

[389] Which we covered in some detail in Wesley Muhammad, **Understanding The Assault on the Black Man, Black Manhood and Black Masculinity** (Atlanta: A-Team Publishing, 2017) 213-218.

WASHINGTON, Aug. 1 – Several prominent medical research institutions and Government hospitals in the United States and Canada were involved in a secret, 25-year, $25-million effort by the Central Intelligence Agency to learn how to control the human mind. The existence of the agency's investigation into behavior and thought control was previously known. But through access to 2,000 C.I.A. documents and wide-ranging interviews, a group of New York Times reporters has developed new information about the cost of the program, the range of its penetration into prestigious research centers, the identities of some institutions, the secret funding conduits of the agency and the concern about the program expressed by some scientists (emphasis added – WM).[390]

The CIA sought "an offensive use for behavior control," not defensive. "They wanted to reduce a man to a bewildered, self-doubting mass in order to "subvert his principles." [391]

[The CIA] sought to crack the mental defenses of enemy agents- to be able to program them and its own operatives to carry out any mission even against their will and "against such fundamental laws of nature as self-preservation.[392]

The overall objective of this program was not necessarily death, though it is true that "they (the CIA) wanted to be able to get away with murder without leaving a trace."[393] But the main point was to "develop 'effective and practical techniques' to 'render an individual *subservient to an imposed will or control.*'"[394] By the 1960s the CIA was exploring "Ways for predictably influencing human behavior through the use of drugs."[395] In 1966, the Agency established a "behavioral pharmacology program" in order to develop the "capability to

---

[390] Nicholas Horrock, "Private Institutions Used in C.I.A. Effort to Control Behavior," **The New York Times** August 2, 1977.
[391] Mind-Control Studies Had Origins in Trial of Mindszentry," **The New York Times** August 2, 1977.
[392] Nicholas Horrock, "Private Institutions Used in C.I.A. Effort to Control Behavior," **The New York Times** August 2, 1977.
[393] "Mind-Control Studies."
[394] "Mind-Control Studies."
[395] CIA memorandum, Influencing Human Behavior, undated. (CIA), quoted in Hornblum, **Acres of Skin**, 139.

manipulate human behavior in a *predictable manner* through the use of drugs".[396]

> The C.I.A. was fascinated by LSD *and other psychochemicals* that they thought might be useful in getting people to talk or *in temporarily putting them out of action*. They were aware that it was considered unethical to experiment on people with drugs without their knowledge, but they decided *that "unwitting" testing was essential* if accurate information on LSD and other substances was to be obtained.[397]

This was a *secret* program because the CIA was fully aware of the fact that *its methods and agendas crossed the line*. Thus, there is always a "cover story" to hide the true operation.

> One thread running throughout the documents was the need for extreme secrecy about the project, minimum documentation of planning and approval of test programs, and a realization that any disclosure could severely embarrass the CIA. Its inspector general said in his report that testing MKULTRA substances or devices on "unwitting subjects," while important, was not as important as the "risk of serious damage to the agency in the event of compromise of *the true nature of this activity* (emphasis added – WM)."[398]

The CIA assembled "an extensive network of non-governmental scientists and facilities" to conduct much of this unethical and even *illegal* research and weaponization of chemical and biological agents. This network involved 80 institutions, including 44 colleges and universities.[399] "The mind control experiments were conducted by a network of doctors that included leaders of psychiatry and the major medical schools."[400] The CIA funded these "CIA Doctors" by clandestinely channeling money through private medical

---

[396] CIA memorandum, Influencing Human Behavior, undated. (CIA), quoted in Hornblum, *Acres of Skin*, 139.
[397] "Mind-Control Studies."
[398] John Jacobs, "CIA Papers Detail Secret Experiments on Behavior Control," *The Washington Post* July 21, 1977.
[399] Jo Thomas, "Extent of University Work for C.I.A. Is Hard to Pin Down," *The New York Times* October 9, 1977.
[400] Colin A. Cross, M.D., *The C.I.A. Doctors: Human Rights Violations By American Psychiatry* (Richardson, TX: Manitou, Inc., 2006) 33.

foundations and military offices, such as the Office of Naval Research.[401]

> There was an "urgent need," the C.I.A. and other agencies argued, to develop "effective and practical techniques" to "render an individual subservient to an imposed will or control." The C.I.A. men, who led the way, enlisting the support of the Army, the Navy, the Air Force, *the Departments of Agriculture, Health, Education, and Welfare* and several other agencies, acknowledged among themselves that much of what they were setting out to do was "unethical," bordered on the illegal and would be repugnant to the American people. So they made certain that these activities were tightly held, known only to the director, Allen W. Dulles, and a handful of operatives and high-ranking aides.[402]

The use of the Department of Health, Education and Welfare (HEW) by the CIA is important to our discussion, as is the use by the CIA of the Department of Agriculture. We will return to these institutions below.

CIA chief Allen Dulles hatched MKULTRA with Richard Helms, who would later become CIA Director himself. Helms was Director until President Nixon forced him out in 1973. Why? Because Helms refused to help cover up the Watergate burglary even though, in Nixon's words, "We protected Helms from one hell of a lot of things."[403] Their working relationship was thus close up until Helms refused to play ball. During the better days, the CIA's MKULTRA (name changed to MKSEARCH in 1964) techniques were at the Nixon administration's disposal and the Nixon administration was preoccupied with behavioral and mind control of Black males – the "enemy" – in particular. One of President Nixon's "pet agencies" was the Law Enforcement Assistant Administration (LEAA).[404] The LEAA was a U.S. federal agency within the U.S. Department of Justice that administered federal funding to

---

[401] Nicholas Horrock, "Private Institutions Used in C.I.A. Effort to Control Behavior," **The New York Times** August 2, 1977.
[402] "Mind-Control Studies Had Origins in Trial of Mindszentry," **The New York Times** August 2, 1977.
[403] Stanley Kutler, **Abuse of Power** (Simon and Schuster, 1999) 68.
[404] Harry V. Martin and David Caul, "Mind Control. Part 4: LEAA and Funding for Experimentation," **Napa Sentinel** August-November 1991.

state and local law enforcement agencies. LEAA funded state planning agencies, local crime initiatives and research programs. Some of those "research programs" was CIA MK-ULTRA research. "LEAA and the [National] Institute [of Mental Health] were named in secret CIA documents as those who provided research cover for the MK-ULTRA program," according to Harry Martin and David Caul's investigation.[405] The LEAA therefore subsidized 537 behavioral modification research projects by 1974.[406]

THE CIA'S "CHIEF DOCTOR AT LEXINGTON"

"Whenever the CIA came across a new drug...that needed testing," Martin Lee and Bruce Shlain inform us, "they frequently sent it over to their chief doctor at Lexington, where an ample supply of captive guinea pigs was readily available."[407] The chief doctor of whom Lee and Shlain speak is Dr. Harris Isabell, Director of Research (1945-1963) for the NIMH Addiction Research Center of the U.S. Public Health Service Hospital in Lexington, Kentucky, a Federal drug prison. For a decade he was a CIA-funded doctor and tried out the CIA's unproven drugs on inmates, "nearly all black drug addicts."[408] Lee and Shlain inform us that "Isabell and the CIA were interested in drugging people to gather more data *on the disruptive potential* of mind-altering substances.[409] Nor did the CIA overlook the potential of *un-incarcerated* Black guinea pigs. "For continued experimentation, [Dr. Sidney] Gottlieb (director of MK-ULTRA) now (in 1953) decided to begin widespread testing on the *urban poor*: street people, prostitutes, and other undesirables."[410] The CIA

> chose "the borderline underworld" – prostitutes, drug addicts, and other small-timers who would be powerless to seek any sort of revenge if they ever found out what the CIA had done to them.[411]

---

[405] Ibid.
[406] Chavkin, *Mind Stealers*, 80.
[407] Lee and Shlain, *Acids Dreams*, 24.
[408] Marks, *Search for the "Manchurian Candidate"*, 66-69 (68); Lee and Shlain, *Acids Dreams*, 24-25.
[409] Lee and Shlain, *Acids Dreams*, 76.
[410] Cockburn and St. Clair, *White Out*, 206.
[411] Marks, *Search for the "Manchurian Candidate"*, 96.

The CIA violated the Nuremberg Code for medical ethics by sponsoring experiments on unwitting subjects...Like the Nazi doctors at Dachau, the CIA victimized certain groups of people who were unable to resist: prisoners, mental patients, foreigners, the terminally ill, sexual deviants, ethnic minorities.[412]

As it turned out, most of the listed categories (prostitutes, drug addicts, prisoners, ethnic minorities) are simply code for "Black subjects."

III.   Chemical Mind Fixers

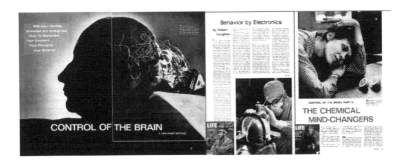

In March of 1963 a most important two-part article was published in **Life Magazine** announcing the science of manipulating human emotions, thoughts and behavior through electrical and chemical means. Brain power is an electrochemical force. Each nerve cell or neuron is actually like a tiny dynamo or electrical generator that is powered by chemistry. By manipulating the chemistry one can control the production of thought and thus of emotions and behavior. Robert Coughlan reported:

> Dr. Robert S. Morison, medical director of the Rockefeller Foundation, comments, "Knowledge of human behavior is becoming organized and accumulative...It is becoming scientific...It is not too early to prepare ourselves for the day when there will be a behavioral science which will make possible the control of human behavior with *a high degree of precision*. Dr. Carl R. Rogers, professor of psychology at the

---

[412] Lee and Shlain, **Acids Dreams**, 24.

University of Wisconsin, warns, "We have in the making...a science of enormous potential importance, an instrumentality whose social power will make atomic energy seem feeble by comparison."[413]

1963 was ten years after the beginning of MK -ULTRA, the CIA's chemical mind control project, but thirteen years before it first came to public attention during the Church Committee of the US Congress in 1975. Here, during a time when Black men and women were non-violently and violently exploding in cities across the country, *Life Magazine* - a long time CIA media asset - announces that control of human behavior with a *high degree of precision* is immanent and its *social power* will make that of the atomic bomb seem feeble. Highlighted in the first part of this series was Dr. Vernon Mark – one of the Project Ferdinand scientists - pictured on the first page, and Dr. José Delgado, who today is still considered "among the world's most acclaimed – and controversial – neuroscientists,"[414] and called "Legendary and Slightly Scary Pioneer of Mind Control."[415] We read in Part I of the *Life* article:

> Dr. José M.R. Delgado, professor of physiology and psychiatry at Yale, and his colleagues Dr. Warren E. Roberts and Dr. Neal E. Miller, have been among those most responsible for perfecting ESB [electrical stimulation of the brain] and showing what can be done with it. The Office of Naval Research has been among the main financial sponsors. In a paper titled "Control of Behavior by Electronic Stimulation of the Brain" in *Naval Research Reviews*, Dr. Delgado described some of ESB's effects in animals: "Under the influence of electrical stimulation of the brain the cats and monkeys performed like electrical toys. Depending on which "button" was pressed by the investigators, one of a great variety of motor responses was evoked...

---

[413] Robert Coughlan, "Behavior By Electronics," *Life* March 8, 1963, pp. 92-106.

[414] According to John Horgan, "The Forgotten Brain Chip: The work of Jose Delgado, a pioneering star in brain-stimulation research four decades ago, goes largely unacknowledged today. What happened?" *Scientific American* (October 2005): 66-73.

[415] John Horgan, "Tribute to Jose Delgado, Legendary and Slightly Scary Pioneer of Mind Control," *Scientific American* September 25, 2017.

However, Dr. Delgado and his research team probed on beyond the [motor] cortex to hitherto inaccessible regions deep in the brains interior. And here they encountered absolutely astonishing phenomena.

They had, in fact, arrived at the seat of emotions. They had found the central machinery of those violent and tender impulses, cravings and fears which, for better or for worse, account for such a large share of life's content...ESB *applied to the amygdala*, a part of the limbic system, evoked rage. A normally peaceable cat became a bundle of fury-claws out, back hairs bristling, pupils dilated, eager to attack any object or living creature put into the same pen with it. When the current was turned off, the rage too was turned off and the cat instantly reverted to its peaceable ways...

And yet, quite surprisingly, experiments show that when an electrode is implanted in the amygdala just a small fraction of an inch from the spot that brings rage, the result is exactly the opposite. There is a "significant increase in what we might call contactual activities: the stimulate animal sniffed and licked the other cats and rubbed and muzzled against them...

Other investigations have revealed that the amygdala has an important role in sexuality; if the amygdala is destroyed by disease or removed or blocked off by surgery, the consequence is extreme nymphomania in the female or stayrism (and homosexuality – WM) in the male...

Similarly, Dr. Delgado and investigators in other laboratories have found places in the brain that help regulate feelings of fear and anxiety, *attitudes of dominance and submissiveness*, and emotionally reaction to pain. They have also discovered that normal reactions can be reversed. ESB at the right places can cause a cat to purr contentedly when hurt, bristle angrily when being petted, *or shrink back in panic at the sight of a mouse* (emphasis added - WM).[416]

The effect of amygdala manipulation to sexuality is important here. Beginning in early 1950s the neuroscientist Arthur S. Kling also set out to discover the behavioral functions of the mysterious amygdala. His name actually became

---

[416] Robert Coughlan, "Behavior By Electronics," *Life* March 8, 1963, pp. 92-106 (99).

synonymous with the amygdala.[417] Kling's researches showed that damaging the amygdala can affect social rank, causing animals to fall from the top to the bottom of the dominance hierarchy. Dogs that previously won competition for bones showed a decrease in aggressiveness and began to lose.[418] Amygdala-lesioned rhesus monkeys failed to compete for food resources because of a pervasive fear produced by the lesions, which made them lower ranking on all indices of social dominance.[419] Kling focused his researches on a bizarre constellation of behaviors that followed damage to the temporal lobe (deep in which resides the amygdala), called the Kluver-Bucy syndrome, and described:

> the classic syndrome includes tameness toward normally threatening stimuli, hyperorality-placing food and nonfood objects in the mouth-and hyper- and inappropriate sexuality (e.g. mounting another species). Kling discovered that the basic elements of the syndrome could be produced by the bilateral ablation of the amygdala alone...[420]

Other researchers also found that with lesions on the amygdala "the preexisting components of sexual programs may be disturbed".[421] A 1966 report by Kling describes an amygdalotomy of rats, cats, and monkeys and the effects were a "marked taming effect in these animals," "relative docility," and the animals "showed reduction in both fear and defensive behavior in the presence of threatening stimuli. *The males, especially, exhibited increased and inappropriate sexual behavior toward both sexes and other species.*"[422] This is of

---

[417] See H. Dieter Steklis, "Arthur S. Kling: Pioneer of the Primate Social Brain," *American Journal of Primatology* 44 (1998): 227-230.
[418] B.N. Bunnell, "Amygdaloid lesions and social dominance in the hooded rat," *Psychon. Sci.* 6 (1966): 93-94.
[419] M.D. Bauman et al., "The Expression of Social Dominance Following Neonatal Lesions of the Amygdala or Hippocampus in Rhesus Monkeys (*Macaca mulatta*)," *Behavioral Neuroscience* 120 (2006): 749-760.
[420] Steklis, "Arthur S. Kling," 228.
[421] A. Kolarsky et al. "Male Sexual Deviation: Association With Early Temporal Lobe Damage," *Arch Gen Psychiat* 17 (1967): 735-743.
[422] Arthur Kling, "Ontogenetic and Phylogenetic Studies on the Amygdaloid Nuclei," *Psychosom Med* 28 (1966): 155-161.

extreme importance because it was specifically the Black male's *amygdala* that was the target of Project Ferdinand.

Effects of an incapacitating gas being tested by U.S. Army Chemical Corps send a cat recoiling with fright when two mice are let loose in its cage.

An amazing photo from Part II of the **Life** article showing results of some of the psychochemical manipulation: a cat recoiling in fright at the sight of two mice let loose in its cage. A cat terrified at the sight of mice? If you didn't see it with your own eyes you couldn't imagine that it could ever be possible. That type of stuff only happens in children's cartoons – and Satan's labs. This is a consequence of an experimental gas tested by the US Army Chemical Corps

In Part II of the **Life** article, "The Chemical Mind-Changers," we read further:

To manipulate the chemistry of behavior, one needs to know which reactions occur in what sequence in which parts of the brain to bring about a particular effect. One must then find ways to deliver the right doses of chemicals to the right locations through the 'blood-brain barrier' that surrounds the brain's cells and selectively admits or blocks substances passing by in the blood stream. These "psychochemicals," as they are called- or "chemical mind-changers," as author Aldous Huxley has more conveniently termed them-must not upset the body's other chemical processes and create unpleasant side effects...

Nature produces a number of these drugs, and apparently many of them have been known and used for thousands of years. The most familiar comes from the female hemp plant, Cannabis sativa. Americans call it marijuana, Moroccans call it kief...[423]

Again, cannabis is mentioned in this 1963 article on chemical mind-changers used by scientists to control thoughts and manipulate social behavior. This is because cannabis was one of the first substances investigated by the CIA and US Army as a psychochemical weapon and enhanced marijuana was and is one of the several psychochemical weapons used to subdue Black masculine hostility.[424] We will develop this in more detail below.

IV.   Dr. Delgado: Master of Mind Control

Delgado looms larger than anyone in this earlier

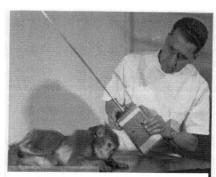

A young Delgado and his "remote controlled" monkey

governmental effort to scientifically control the Black male mind, for it was he who "pioneered that most unnerving of technologies, the brain chip-an electronic device that can manipulate the mind by receiving signals from and transmitting them to neurons."[425] He investigated both electrical and *chemical* manipulations of the brain and "explored

[423] Robert Coughlan, "The Chemical Mind-Changers," *Life* March 15, 1963, pp. 81-106.

[424] Wesley Muhammad, ***Understanding The Assault on the Black Man, Black Manhood and Black Masculinity*** (Atlanta: A-Team Publishing, 2017) 239-255 and below.

[425] John Horgan, "The Forgotten Brain Chip: The work of Jose Delgado, a pioneering star in brain-stimulation research four decades ago, goes largely unacknowledged today. What happened?" ***Scientific American*** (October 2005): 66-73.

the neural roots of aggress ion, pain, passivity, and social behavior."[426] By far Delgado's most famous act of mind and behavior control, his "signature experiment,"[427] was his sensational bull experiment. The experiment was conducted on September 1963 at a fighting bull-breeding ranch in Cordoba, Spain. Delgado inserted his brain chip or stimoceiver into the brains of several fighting bulls and stood in a bullring with one bull at a time. Delgado had only a handheld transmitter and when the bull "Lucero" charged the scientist he pressed the appropriate button, forcing the bull to skid to a halt only a few feet away from him.[428] Delgado had the black bull "maintaining in a state of 'disappeared aggressiveness."[429] John Osmundsen of *The New York Times* thought this "was probably the most spectacular demonstration ever performed of the deliberate modification of animal behavior through external control of the brain."[430] According to Delgado he was "trying to find out what makes brave bulls brave."

---

[426] José M.R. Delgado, "Neurological Mechanisms in Epilepsy and Behavior," Final Report to the Office of Naval Research on Contract SAR/Nonr 609 908) – NR 101 – 320, March 1965; idem, "Pharmacology of Spontaneous and Conditioned Behavior in the Monkey," in *Pharmacology of Conditioning, Learning and Retention*, ed. M. Ya. Mikhel'son, V.G. Longo, and Z. Votava (Oxford: Pergamon Press, 1965) 133-156; idem, "Aggressiveness, Hierarchy, and Rhythms in Monkeys," The Twelfth International Conference on the Unity of the Sciences, Chicago, Illinois November 24-27, 1983. See further Barry Blackwell et al., "Jose Delgado: A Case Study. Science, Hubris, Nemesis and Redemption," in Barry Blackwell, *Bits and Pieces of a Psychiatrist's Life* (XLIBRIS, 2012) 228-256.

[427] Jack El-Hai, "The Man Who Fought a Bull With Mind Control," *Discover* March 21, 2016.

[428] Horgan, "Forgotten Brain Chip," 70.

[429] Timothy C. Marzullo, "The Missing Manuscript of Dr. Jose Delgado's Radio Controlled Bulls," *The Journal of Undergraduate Neuroscience Education (JUNE)* 15 (Spring 2017): R29-R35.

[430] John Osmundsen, "'Matador' with a Radio Stops Wired Bull," *The New York Times* May 17, 1965, pp. 1, 20.

José Delgado performing his famous Bull experiment with "Lucero" in Spain

But Delgado's "signature experiment" was not about bovines. It was about the black bulls of the American inner-cities. Delgado always applied an "anthropomorphic interpretation" to his experiments.[431] Delgado confesses that his primary interest in these experiments is their *social* applicability.

> I do believe that an understanding of *the biological basis of social and antisocial behavior* and of mental activities which for the first time in history can now be explored in a conscious brain, may be of decisive importance in the search for intelligent solutions to some of our present anxieties, frustrations *and conflicts* (emphasis added).[432]

Delgado's research had an interest in dominance hierarchy – the relationships between dominant and subordinate males in a society[433] – as well as the US race riots of the 1960s, specifically the "cerebral basis of [the] anti-social behavior" and aggressiveness of the black "rioters" were a focus

[431] Horgan, "Forgotten Brain Chip," 69; José M. R. Delgado, "Animal Models for Brain Research," in *Animal Models in Human Psychobiology*, ed. George Serban and Arthur Kling (New York and London: Plenum Press, 1976) 203-218; Maggie Scarf, "Brain Researcher José Delgado Asks – 'What Kind of Humans Would We Like to Construct?" *The New York Times* November 15, 1970.
[432] John Osmundsen, "'Matador' with a Radio," 1.
[433] David Linden, *Brain Control: Developments in Therapy and Implications for Society* (Hampshire, UK: Palgrave Macmillan, 2014) 47-48.

of his.[434] He was considered "a specialist in technological control of human aggression," and he and his colleagues did research on "behavioral control technologies and psychopharmacology in the context, stated in their research applications, *of 'stress' and 'alienation' in U.S. cities.*"[435] Delgado's bull experiment demonstrated "the power of science stopping animal aggression in its tracks,"[436] but it's the "animal aggression" of the inner-city that is the target: Black masculine aggression. Delgado wrote:

> The radio stimulated bulls underscore the classic symbolism of the bullfight, that is – the triumph of intelligence over brute force, the supremacy of skill and grace over aggression and ferocity. The radio directed bulls also teach us that ancestral instincts of attack and destruction can be pacified by technology and human intelligence, giving a hope of peace that perhaps could benefit future humanity.[437]

---

[434] Chavkin, **Mind Stealers**, 176: "Delgado calls for 'experimental investigation of the cerebral structures responsible for aggressive behavior as an essential counterpart of social studies.' He contends that this should be recognized by sociologists as well as biologists. He deplores the fact that social upheavals are usually associated with 'economic, ideological, social and political factors . . . while the essential link in the central nervous system is often forgotten.' Like his colleagues at Harvard, Dr. Frank Ervin and Dr. Vernon H. Mark, who tied the civil disorders of the late sixties to individuals who suffered from brain damage, Delgado declares that this realization should play a role when investigating the causes of a riot. It would be an error 'to ignore the fact . . . that determined neuronal groups' in the brain of a rioter 'are reacting to sensory inputs and are subsequently producing the behavioral expression of violence.'"

[435] Dana Haraway, "Morphing in the Order: Flexible Strategies, Feminist Science Studies, and Primate Revisions," in **Primate Encounters: Models of Science, Gender and Society**, ed. Shirley C. Strum and Linda Marie Fedigan (Chicago: University of Chicago, 2000) 404.

[436] Amanda C. Pustilnick, "Violence on the Brain: A Critique of Neuroscience in Criminal Law," **Wake Forest Law-Review** 44 (2009): 183-238 (201).

[437] Timothy C. Marzullo, "The Missing Manuscript of Dr. Jose Delgado's Radio Controlled Bulls," **The Journal of Undergraduate Neuroscience Education (JUNE)** 15 (Spring 2017): R29-R35 (R34).

The government's "law-and-order" agencies certainly saw Delgado's work for what it was.

> Delgado's work seemed to hold tremendous and direct promise for law enforcement. Recruited by government agencies, Delgado worked for many years (although fruitlessly) on brain stimulation techniques to control human violence.[438]

When Delgado made the aggressive Black Bull passive and docile, that was just what the Nixon and later Administrations wanted for the Black Bulls of the inner-cites. As Chavkin observes, "Delgado has demonstrated movies of a violent, madly charging bull with electrodes implanted; the activation of an electric current stops the bull in his wild charge *and turns him into a docile Ferdinand.*"[439] Indeed, as John Horgan observes: "articles hailed Delgado's transformation of an aggressive bull into a real-life version of Ferdinand the bull, the gentle hero of a popular children's story."[440] ***Ferdinand The Bull*** is a children's story written in 1936 by Munro Leafe. Ferdinand is the gentile and kind natured bull who is yet the largest and strongest bull among his peers and is capable of ferocity when stung by a bee. Ferdinand is completely uninterested though in fighting and would rather sit under a tree all day and smell flowers rather than fight, even when forced into the bullfighting ring and suffers multiple provocations by the matador. The bull experiment of Delgado symbolized the objective of the Nixon Administration: he "tamed the bull," as the government sought to tame and transform the aggressive, *revolutionary* Black Bulls of America's cities into docile Ferdinands that refuse to fight.

Delgado personifies *both* the evil of the CIA and the evil of the Synagogue of Satan against the Black Man and Woman of America. "The Office of Naval Research has been among the main financial sponsors" of Delgado's research, revealed ***Life Magazine. The New York Times*** later revealed that

---

[438] [438] Amanda C. Pustilnick, "Violence on the Brain: A Critique of Neuroscience in Criminal Law," **Wake Forest Law-Review** 44 (2009): 183-238 (202).
[439] Jonas B. Robitscher, "Psychosurgery and Other Means of Altering Behavior," **Bulletin of the American Academy of Psychiatry and Law** 11 (1974): 7-33 (29).
[440] Horgan, "Forgotten Brain Chip," 70.

The C.I.A was also able to conduct research through military contracts. For 11 years, the agency tested mind-altering drugs...on prisoners at the United States Public Health Service hospital in Lexington, KY. *The money was channeled through the Office of Naval Research...*[441]

According to Dr. Colin Ross, who examined 15,000 pages of CIA documents obtained through the Freedom of Information Act, "Through MKULTRA Subproject 54, the CIA gave $62, 400.00 to the Office of Naval Research in 1955."[442] Among Delgado's other "Pentagon sponsors"[443] was the Air Force 657 1st Aeromedical Research Laboratory as well as the Public Health Service. It is also the case that his research was not only funded by the Nixon Administration, specifically through Rockland State Hospital/Rockland Psychiatric Center, operated by the New York State Office of Mental Health (a beneficiary of NIMH/LEAA collaboration and funding), but so too did the Nixon State Department intervene to assist him and his colleagues in securing protected gibbons from Thailand to be used in their "inner-city" simulation research, according to records revealed by the International Primate Protection League.[444] After Delgado returned to Spain the Spanish monthly magazine **Tiempo** interviewed him in 2000 and reported that he had ties with the Spanish secret police.[445]

Dr. José Manuel Rodriquez Delgado was born in 1915 in Ronda, Spain, in the province of Málaga. His paternal family name is Rodriquez and his maternal family name is Delgado. Delgado is a Sephardic (Spanish Jewish) name meaning "Great Door," from the Hebrew *del*= door and *gado*= "great." According to the **Jewish Encyclopedia** "After the year 1492 Jews were no longer allowed to live in Málaga, though Maronos

[441] Nicholas Horrock, "Private Institutions Used in C.I.A. Effort to Control Behavior," **The New York Times** August 2, 1977.
[442] Cross, M.D., **C.I.A. Doctors**, 104.
[443] Horgan, "Forgotten Brain Chip," 70.
[444] "The Hall's Island Gibbon Project," **the international primate protection league Newsletter** Vol. 3, No. 1 March 1976, p. 1.
[445] Magnus Bartas, Fredrik Ekman and Jose Delgado, "Psychocivilization and its discontents: An interview with José Delgado," **Cabinet** 2 (Spring 2001); Horgan, "Forgotten Brain Chip," 70.

were still found there in the eighteenth century."[446] But Jews will rebound in the city. The World Jewish Congress reports that "The two major centers of Jewish life in Spain are Madrid (4,500) and Barcelona (3,500), followed by Malaga, where a smaller number of Jews live." Confirmation that Delgado is a "quasi-secret" Jew comes from the fact that in the letters that he wrote he is known to include an insignia of Hebrew letters in what looks like a Torah scroll.[447]

---

[446] *Jewish Encyclopedia* s.v. Malaga by Richard Gottheil and Kayserling.
[447] Magnus Bartas, Fredrik Ekman and Jose Delgado, "Psychocivilization and its discontents: An interview with José Delgado," *Cabinet* 2 (Spring 2001).

Chapter Nine

Nixon's War on Black Masculinity

I.   *Organizing Against the Black Mind*

The development and acceptance of the idea of pinpointing those who may be potentially assaultive or crime-prone because of genetic, hormonal, or brain abnormality received major impetus during the Nixon administration... "Shape up or be zapped (with drugs - WM)" was to be the motto of the new generation. This was also the Nixon attitude when dealing with the civil protest disorders that continued to break out immediately before and after the assassination of Martin Luther King, Jr.[448]

During the Nixon administration, psychiatric and police organizations merged their efforts on many fronts. Richard Nixon and members of his staff met with agents of the Justice Department's Law Enforcement Assistance Administration, and Dr. Bertram Brown, director of the National Institute of Mental Health. LEAA was also involved in plans for the creation of a national police force, and urban warfare preparation that went by the names Operation Cable Splicer and Operation Garden Plot. Incredibly, the LEAA began the financing of 350 National Institute of Mental Health psychiatric projects, with LEAA directly monitoring the NIMH doctors.[449]

A distinguishing characteristic of the Nixon era is its organized, deliberate and well-funded assault of the Black male's *mind* and the attempts to biochemically *neuter* the Black male's masculinity. It was determined that this psycho-assault and biochemical neutering was the proper course of action to quell the "Black rage" that erupted in America's cities, a prelude to revolution.

The Law Enforcement Assistance Administration (LEAA) and other government agencies are pouring hundreds of millions of dollars into programs designed to reshape the delinquent by a

---

[448] Samuel Chavkin, ***The Mind Stealers: Psychosurgery and Mind Control*** (Boston: Houghton, Mifflin Company, 1978) 90-91.
[449] Jim Keith, ***Mass Control: Engineering Human Consciousness*** (Adventures Unlimited Press, 2003) 128.

177

host of behavior modification techniques...This (the National Institute of Mental Health) is one of a group of scientific institutes under the umbrella name of the National Institute of Health — all of which employ thousands of researchers, technicians, and scientists whose task is that of tracking down some of the country's worst scourges: heart disease, cancer, and mental illness, among others. During the Nixon administration, these institutes were forced to retrench and even abandon some of their programs because of the executive decision to reorder the nation's priorities, one of which was to create a society in keeping with Nixon's notion of law and order. Thus a good deal of the emphasis was shifted from tracking down disease to tracking down law violators. The NIMH was called on to do its part. In the process it became a bedfellow of the Department of Justice. At a meeting held in Colorado Springs in 1970, Dr. Bertram Brown, director of the NIMH, joined with Nixon, Attorney General John Mitchell, John Ehrlichman, H. R. Haldeman, and other key members of the White House staff to work out plans for close collaborative efforts between the NIMH and the newly organized Law Enforcement Assistance Administration...Scientists began to be answerable for their research directly to the LEAA and not to the NIMH. It is not surprising that the nature and form of some of the research projects seemed to bolster the prevailing philosophy that much of crime may have pathological origins. The LEAA began funding studies designed to associate fingerprints as well as chromosomal distinctions with violent behavior.[450]

Together the NIMH and the LEAA searched for effective ways to *biomedically control* the "juvenile delinquents" of the inner-city.

---

[450] Chavkin, **Mind Stealers**, 9, 185-187.

The above image appeared in the February 1973 edition of ***Ebony Magazine*** as an illustration to a "critical article" by B.J. Mason entitled: "New Threat To Blacks: Brain Surgery to Control Behavior." The focus of the article was on the theorizing of three Boston mind-doctors: Dr. William H. Sweet, Professor and Chief of Neurosurgery, Harvard; Vernon Mark, Chief of Neurosurgery at Boston City Hospital; Frank Ervin, psychiatrist, Harvard. In September 1967, responding to the Detroit Rebellion that July, these three submitted an article to the ***Journal of the American Medical Association*** ("Role of Brain Disease in Riots and Urban Violence") suggesting that the real cause of the urban rebellions was not economic inequality but a *brain disease* suffered by the Black male rioters.[451] Those who engage in peaceful social protest also suffer brain dysfunction, Sweet testified before the New York state legislature in 1968.[452] Their views were laid out more fully

---

[451] Frank Ervin, Vernon Mark and William Sweet, "Role of Brain Disease in Riots and Urban Violence," ***Journal of the American Medical Association*** 201 (September 11, 1967): 895.

[452] David Bird, "More Stress Urged on Cause of Civil Disorders," ***The New York Times*** August 14, 1968, p. 19; Vernon Mark and Frank

in their 1970 book, *Violence and the Brain* (Vernon Mark and Frank Ervin). Black rioters and social protesters suffer from a malfunctioning amygdala that causes poor impulse control and violent behavior. The solution: suppress the Black rioters and social protestors as well as their leaders through psychosurgery.[453] As John Horgan remarks: "In their book, *Violence and the Brain*, Ervin and Mark suggest that brain stimulation or psychosurgery might quell the violent tendencies of blacks rioting in inner cities."[454]

Dr. Ramamuthi Balasubramaniam, neurosurgeon from Government General Hospital in Chennai, India, often called "the Father of Neurosurgery of India," described psychosurgery as "sedative neurosurgery" because the patient is "made quite and manageable" by the operation. The focus of the Boston mind-doctors' psychosurgical efforts was the amygdala.[455] As B.J. Mason notes: "Since they believe it moderates emotions and drives, brain specialists agree that removing the amygdala curbs aggressive behavior and makes the patient docile"; "it can turn a person into a zombie."[456] Peter Breggin points out that "Amygdalotomy is *the* pacification operation *par excellence* (emphasis added - WM)"[457] and Black male pacification and docility, as Professor Gerald Horn of the University of California at Santa Barbara notes, "is precisely what certain U.S. elites desired for often-rebellious blacks," such as the Nixon Administration; "blacks who rebelled against their plight could be 'cured' by carving their brains or drugging them."[458]

This was the solution of the Nixon Administration: psychosurgery as a "therapeutic weapon" and as a "technology

Ervin, "Is There a Need to Evaluate the Individuals Producing Human Violence?" *Psychiatric Opinion* 32 (1968): 5.

[453] Vernon Mark and Frank Erwin, *Violence and the Brain* (New York: Harper & Row, 1970).

[454] John Horgan, "The Forgotten Brain Chip: The work of Jose Delgado, a pioneering star in brain-stimulation research four decades ago, goes largely unacknowledged today. What happened?" *Scientific American* (October 2005): 71 [art.=66-73].

[455] Chavkin, *Mind Stealers*, 33: "But it is the amygdala...that has taken the limelight over the past decade. It is the amygdala that is most strongly identified with rage, violence and aggression."

[456] Mason, "Brain Surgery," 63, 66.

[457] Breggin, "Psychosurgery for the control of violence," 359.

[458] Gerald Horn, "Race Backwards: Genes, Violence, Race, and Genocide," *CovertAction* 43 (1992-1993): 29-35 (30-31).

of violence control." "In the case of psychosurgery, the USA came close to an Orwellian scenario when Richard Nixon's administration planned to use brain operations to deal with 'difficult' prisoners."[459] Not just prisoners, but difficult Black youth as young as six-years old who showed revolutionary potential.[460] Nixon's agencies funded these efforts generously. As Conrad and Schneider note:

> The research reported in **Violence and the Brain** was supported by grants from the Department of Health, Education and Welfare (HEW)...the U.S. Public Health Services, and the Dreyfus Foundation, in short, the mental health establishment (...). Since 1970 the Neuro-Research Foundation, which is devoted to the "diagnosis and treatment of persons with poor control of violent impulses" (Mark, Ervin and Sweet are its trustees), has received a half million dollars to do the kind of research proposed in Mark and Ervin's book (...).[461]

Mason reports:

> Indeed, the Senate Appropriations Committee recently instructed the National Institute of Mental Health (NIMH) to award a $500,000 grant to Dr. William Sweet...to determine if there is any connection between violent behavior and brain disease. More specifically, he was asked to develop a way to identify *and control persons* who commit "senseless" violence as well as those "who are constantly at odds with the law for minor crimes, assaults, and constantly in and out of jail. This perked the interest of the Justice Department's Law and Enforcement Assistance Administration (LEAA), which invested $108,930 in further brain research by two of Dr. Sweet's colleagues, Dr. Frank Ervin...and Dr. Vernon Mark...It didn't matter that the Kerner Commission had already concluded that white racism was at the root of civil violence. The Justice Department ordered the grantees to "determine the incidence of brain disorders in a state penitentiary for men; to establish their presence" in a civilian population; and to "improve, develop and test the usefulness of electrodes and brain surgery "for the detection of such disorders in routine examination." Judging from the language of this directive, the

---

459 Charles Watson, Matthew Kirkaldie and George Paxinos, **The Brain: An Introduction to Functional Neuroanatomy** (Amsterdam: Elsevier, 2010) 136.
460 Mason, "Brain Surgery."
461 Conrad and Schneider, **Deviance and Medicalization**, 225-226

Justice department is interested in devising an early-warning system for riot control.[462]

The media and public outrage at the disclosures, with the 1973 *Ebony* exposé serving as a "critical article" in this regard, forced the government in 1974 to withdraw this funding and publicly distance itself from psychosurgery and behavior modification research.[463] However, such research, experimentation and brain mutilation continued through loopholes in the new policy.

Despite the LEAA's definitive statement that it would no longer support psychosurgical experimentation, word comes from the south indicating a strong possibility that psychosurgery is still being applied in certain state prisons.

Dr. L. A. Swan, a Fisk University sociologist specializing in criminal justice, believes it is conceivable that at least fifty psychosurgical operations were performed in 1975 at the Atmore State Prison in Birmingham, Alabama. Dr. Swan ran across this information while conducting an extensive interview project with relatives of black prisoners to find out what happens to the black family when the husband or father is sent to prison. The project is sponsored by the National Institute of Mental Health...It is Dr. Swan's belief that those prisoners who were operated upon were politically active....Atmore State Prison, in all likelihood, as all state prisons, receives part of its share of financial support from the block money grants that the LEAA distributes.[464]

If there were any doubt regarding the government's intention to continue such research, the NIMH disabused us of it in 1975 with the publication of its report, "Behavior Modification: Perspective on a Current Issue."

But others, such as Dr. Bertram S. Brown, director of the National Institute of Mental Health (NIMH), a unit of the Department of Health, Education, and Welfare, welcomes the government's participation in behavior research. Designed to counter the sort of anxiety and controversy voiced by Senator

---

[462] Mason, "Brain Surgery," 63.
[463] Lesley Oelsner, "U.S. Bars Crime Fund Use On Behavior Modification," *The New York Times* February 15, 1974.
[464] Chavkin, *Mind Stealers*, 81-82.

Ervin and others, the NIMH published a brochure on policy in 1975 in which Dr. Brown states:

"The Federal Government continues to support and encourage research and demonstrations that test new behavior modification techniques, that seek to refine existing ones and apply them to new clinical populations and new settings, and that promote the dissemination of techniques that have been positively evaluated . . . *Research is also needed in ways to deliver behavior modification techniques to larger numbers of persons in less restrictive settings than the institutions where much of the research, until now, has been done.*"[465]

How the Boston doctors succeeded in securing this funding has been described as a mystery.[466] But a partial answer may be that their success was due to the fact that they were doing CIA MKULTRA research. Frank Ervin, for example, did his residency at Tulane University in New Orleans under Dr. Robert Heath, Chairman of the Department of Psychiatry and Neurology and a documented "CIA Doctor" who was funded by the Agency to do MKULTRA research.[467] ***DigBoston*** reported this year:

Mark and Ervin are now dead, but given the nature of their research and its funding through the National Institute of Mental Health – now known to have served as a conduit for the

---

[465] Chavkin, ***Mind Stealers***, 67; National Institute of Mental Health, "Behavior Modification: Perspective on a Current Issue," (U.S. Department of Health, Education, and Welfare, 1975).

[466] Jonas B. Robitscher, "Psychosurgery and Other Means of Altering Behavior," ***Bulletin of the American Academy of Psychiatry and Law*** 11 (1974): 7-33 (18): "In 1970, *through various mysterious maneuvers that no one seems to be able to explain*, they persuaded Congress to direct the National Institute of Mental Health (NIMH) to award them a $500,000 grant to carry on their work...While Sweet's work was regarded with apprehension by the medical community, the law enforcement community has shown more enthusiasm: at about the same time the foundation obtained a grant of $108,000 from the Law Enforcement Assistance Administration of the Justice Department to test procedures for screening habitually violent male penitentiary inmates for brain damage."

[467] Nicholas Horrock, "Private Institutions Used in C.I.A. Effort to Control Behavior," ***The New York Times*** August 2, 1977; Colin A. Cross, M.D., ***The C.I.A. Doctors: Human Rights Violations By American Psychiatry*** (Richardson, TX: Manitou, Inc., 2006) 91.

Central Intelligence Agency at the time – it's likely their work was part of the CIA's behavior control efforts...We may never know the full extent of Mark and Ervin's dealings with intelligence agencies, but more pieces of the story continue to emerge [Dr. George Bach-y-Rita, a former colleague of Mark and Ervin] maintains they were "good professors working in the context of their time" yet also acknowledged that they probably received clandestine funding. "They might have been working for the CIA, but the CIA wasn't considered bad," Bach-y-Rita says. At the time, he added, "people hadn't learned to mistrust the Dulles brothers yet. They didn't how horrible the Dulles brothers were."[468]

Strengthening the case of their intelligence associations is the fact that these Boston mind-doctors and their research were in a way the "son" of the work of a notorious CIA doctor, Dr. José Delgado. They not only collaborated and co-authored with Delgado (who was lead author),[469] but Delgado appears to have kind of "mentored" the Boston 3.

Brain electrode research was also conducted independently at Harvard by Dr. Delgado's coauthors, Drs. Vernon Mark, Frank Ervin ad William Sweet...Dr. Delgado supplied brain electrodes to the Harvard team *through the Office of Naval Research contract* (=CIA conduit). Frank Ervin...was trained at Tulane by brain electrodes specialist Dr. Robert Heath (= "CIA Doctor"). He was recruited by Dr. Louis Jolyon West (= "CIA Doctor") to join the UCLA Violence Center...It is evident that the brain electrode doctors knew each other well.[470]

---

[468] Jonathan Riley, "Critical History: Lobotomass," ***DigBoston*** June 1, 2017.
[469] Jose Delgado, Vernon Mark, William Sweet, Frank Ervin, G. Weiss, G. Bach-y-Rita, R. Hagiwara, "Intercerebral radio stimulation and recording in completely free patients," ***Journal of Nervous and Mental Disease*** 147 (1968): 329-340. On this collaboration see John Horgan, "The Forgotten Brain Chip: The work of Jose Delgado, a pioneering star in brain-stimulation research four decades ago, goes largely unacknowledged today. What happened?" ***Scientific American*** (October 2005): 66-73 (71); Miquel A. Faria, "Violence, mental illness, and the brain – A brief history of psychosurgery: Part 3 – From deep brain stimulation to amygdalotomy for violent behavior, seizures, and pathological aggression in humans," ***Surgical Neurology International*** 4 (2013): 1-22; Breggin, "Psychosurgery for Political Purposes," 847-848.
[470] Cross, M.D., ***C.I.A. Doctors***, 91, 98.

III.   *Feminizing the Black Bulls*

In 1972, as a result of the Detroit Rebellion of 1967, the State of Michigan planned an experimental program aimed at the control of violence. This program was to be run out of the Lafayette Clinic, the research and teaching facility of Wayne State University. Beginning in 1954, according to investigative journalist Hank P. Albarelli Jr., several psychiatric facilities in the Detroit area, including the state-funded Lafayette Clinic, were being covertly used and funded by the CIA under the cover of the Human Ecology Fund of the MKULTRA program.

> human experiments on unwitting patients were conducted at the Lafayette Clinic, as well as at Michigan's Ionia State Hospital for the criminally Insane. Ionia State Hospital was particularly abusive and cruel to African American inmates, who were considered mere human fodder for any behavior-modification quackery that the CIA and the U.S. Army thought might yield domination over the minds of others...[T]he vast majority of CIA files on the Lafayette Clinic project have been destroyed, but a few surviving Agency documents reveal that covert work at the clinic included electronical brain stimulation, induced psychosis through psychotropic drugs, and other behavior modification techniques...
>
> Interviews with former CIA Chemical Branch and Technical Services Section staff, as well legal depositions and files from the Agency's Artichoke Project, reveal that a number of MK/ULTRA luminaries made MK/ULTRA-related visits to the clinic. These "visitors" included Dr. Jolyson (sic) West, and Dr. Amedeo Marrazzi (the Army Chemical Corps chief of clinical research). "Visitors" also included CIA officials such as chemist Robert Vern Lashbrook, psychologist John Gittinger (...), and chemist Henry Bortner. At the time, all three scientists were working under the direction of the CIA's Dr. Sidney Gottleib.[471]

Regarding Ionia State Hospital, Ross informs us:

> Ionia State Hospital was the site of MKULTRA Subproject 39, in which investigators cleared at TOP SECRET received $30,000.00 in 1955 for drug testing on prisoners and sexual

---

[471] H.P. Albarelli Jr., *A Secret Order: Investigating the High Strangeness and Synchronicity in the JFK Assassination* (Walterville, OR: Trine Day, LLC, 2013).

psychopaths including interrogations with hypnosis, LSD, and marijuana.[472]

In 1972 chief neurologist Dr. Ernst Rodin and psychiatrist Dr. Jacques Gottleib, both from Lafayette Clinic, proposed a controlled study comparing the effects of amaygdalotomy (surgery on the amygdala) and "chemical castration" on 24 Black inmates from Ionia State Hospital, many of whose Black inmates at that time were arrested during the 1967-1968 Rebellions.[473] The controlled study was thus called "Proposal for the Study of the Treatment of Uncontrolled Aggression at

Dr. Ernst Rodin

Lafayette Clinic." Rodin was a collaborator of the Boston trio (Mark, Ervin and Sweet); he visited their project site and assessed their psychosurgery patients.[474] Rodin was not satisfied with the Harvard trio's results.[475] He thus proposed his own experiment.

The project would be a comparison of two different methods of controlling aggression: The first is psychosurgery, specifically amygdalotomy, "destruction of tiny portions of the amygdala":[476] "implantation of depth electrodes into various brain structures of the limbic system; monitoring brain-wave activity; stimulating the different sections of the limbic system; and finally psychosurgery (of the amygdala) if the electric discharges indicated that defective brain cells were implicated in aggression."[477] Twelves inmates from Ionia State Hospital

---

[472] Cross, M.D., *C.I.A. Doctors*, 98.

[473] Metzl, *Protest Psychosis*, 11-15; Christopher Lane, Ph.D., "How Schizophrenia Became a Black Disease: An Interview with Jonathan Metzl," *Psychology Today* May 5, 2010.

[474] Breggin, "Psychosurgery for Political Purposes," 847.

[475] See e.g. Ernst A. Rodin, "Psychomotor Epilepsy and Aggressive Behavior," *Archives of General Psychiatry* 28 (1973): 210-213.

[476] Jane E. Brody, "Psychosurgery Will Face Key Test in Court Today," *The New York Times* March 12, 1973.

[477] Chavkin, *Mind Stealers*, 111-112.

would be transferred to Lafayette Clinic to undergo the psychosurgery.

Twelve other inmates would be experimented on with the second method: "chemical castration" by an experimental German drug that acts as an anti-androgen and inhibits the production of testosterone and other androgens. The experimental drug was cyproterone acetate (CPA).[478] CPA is a strong *feminizing* drug, said to be the most potent of the steroid anti-androgen drugs, out of hundreds.[479] It both decreases masculine secondary sexual characteristics in males and increase feminine secondary sexual characteristics in men, such as gynecomastia or "man-boobs." It does this by chemically demonstrating two properties:

1.) Anti-androgenic: CPA decreases testosterone in a male by binding to the androgen receptor and thereby disallowing the circulating testosterone or any other androgen to bind and thus "do its job." This demasculinizes men.

2.) Progestogenic/anti-gonadotropic: CPA exerts negative feedback on the hypothalamaic-pituitary axis by inhibiting secretion of Luteinizing hormone, leading to the diminished production of testosterone. CPA is chemically similar to the female hormone progesterone and it activates the progesterone receptor. CPA thus has some progesterone-like effects. For example, it induces extensive lobuloalveolar development of mammary glands. This helps the full

---

[478] Paul Lowinger, "Psychosurgery: The Detroit Case," *The New Republic* April 13, 1974, p. 18; "Kaimowitz v. Department of Mental Health For The State of Michigan. No. 73-19434-Aw (Mich. Cir. Ct., Wayne County, July 10, 1973)," *Mental Disability Law Reporter* 147 (September-October 1976): 147-154 (147).

[479] On cyproterone acetate see *PRODUCT MONOGRAPH: CYPROTERONE. Cyproterone Acetate Tablets BP 50 mg. Antiandrogen* (Vaughan, Ontario: AA PHARMA INC., 2010); Daniel Turner, Raphaella Basdekis-Jozsa and Peer Briken, "Prescription of Testosterone-Lowering Medications for Sex Offender Treatment in German Forensic-Psychiatric Institutions," *J. Sex Med* 10 (2013): 570-578; H. Steinbeck, F. Neumann and W. Elger, "Effect of an Anti-Androgen on the Differential of the Internal Genital Organs in Dogs," *J. Reprod. Fert.* 23 (1970): 223-227;

development of breasts in transgender women when CPA is used in combination with estrogen.

In male-to-female transsexual women, elimination of body hair growth, induction of breast formation, and a more feminine fat distribution are essential. A near-complete reduction of the biological effects of androgen secretion is required in order to achieve this. For the above reasons, in Europe and Canada CPA is *the preferred oral anti-androgen for transgender women*!

> In the hormonal treatment of transgender woman, an anti-androgen agent is used in combination with estrogen to block the effects of testosterone, enabling feminization to occur. Cyproterone acetate (CPA) is a commonly used anti-androgen agent in feminizing therapy in Europe and Canada.[480]

> "CPA is...widely used as a component of hormone replacement therapy (HRT) for transgender women."[481]

And *this* is the drug that Rodin and the Lafayette Clinic in Detroit planned to treat Black inmates with in order to quell and control aggression. But it wasn't just *Rodin's* plan. It was the State of Michigan's plan and the Nixon Administration's. It was Dr. Gordon Yudashkin, Director of the State Department of Mental Health, who recruited the subjects for the study. The Human and Animal Experiment Committee and the Human Rights Review Committee approved the procedures. The Michigan State Senate approved a budget of $164,000 for the project in 1972. This was two years after Nixon forced the shotgun marriage between LEAA and NIMH, and Dr. Bertram Brown sent a memo to his staff and the state mental health agencies to cooperate with LEAA-NIMH,[482] and the federal government (Nixon's LEAA and NIMH) matched state funds for the *same* program in California that same year (1972). There too black and brown prisoners *and middle schoolers* would be subjected to psychosurgery and chemical castration with the

---

[480] Raymond Fung, "Is a lower dose of cyproterone acetate as effective at testosterone suppression in transgender women as higher doses?" *International Journal of Transgenderism* 18 (2017).
[481] J.J. Janeson et al. *Endocrinology Adult and Pediatric: Reproductive Endocrinology* (Elsevier Health Sciences, 2013).
[482] Chavkin, *Mind Stealers*, 185-187.

feminizing drug cyproterone acetate (see Part II: Reagan's War). This is the smoking gun proving that the U.S. Government actively sought to chemically *demasculinize* and *feminize* Black men in route to "chemically subduing the threat" presented by "angry black masculinity." This seems to have begun in earnest under Nixon.

In a 1972 speech Rodin spoke about the implications of the riots that had rocked his city and he proposed that the solution *was both* psychosurgery *and* chemical castration of the urban males, which he compared - like Delgado before him - to aggressive bulls who should be turned into docile oxen through castration – Ferdinand. He said:

> Tolerance and encouragement of free thought is *probably* excellent for the high IQ bracket, but not advisable for the lower one, and one is reminded of the Roman saying: "Quod licet Jovi non licet bovi" (What is allowed for Jupiter is not allowed for the ox). The problem is that the ox may not recognize himself as an ox and demand Jupiter's prerogatives. [483]

In other words, the urban bulls agitate for better living conditions and for rights because they don't recognize their place in the hierarchal order. But much violence could be avoided, Rodin claimed, by castrating the "dumb young males":

> Farmers have known for ages immemorial that you can't do a blasted thing with a bull except fight or kill and eat him; the castrated ox [however] will pull his plow...It is also well known that human eunuchs, although at times quite scheming entrepreneurs, are not given to physical violence. Our scientific age tends to disregard this wisdom of the past...[484]

"The castrated ox will pull his plow": a call for incapacitated Black males to *serve* the beneficiaries of this society. They want a return to slavery. Rodin argued that *both* procedures were necessary in order to turn the targeted Black male into the "hopefully more placid dullard." However, in 1972

---

[483] Ernst Rodin, "A Neurological Appraisal of Some Episodic Behavioral Disturbances with Special Emphasis on Aggressive Outbursts," quoted in Peter R. Breggin, M.D., "Psychosurgery for Political Purposes," **Duquesne Law Review** 13 (1975): 853 [art.=841-862].
[484] See Breggin, "Psychosurgery for Political Purposes," 853.

before the project could officially take off a Michigan Legal Services lawyer Gabe Kaimowitz intervened in court on behalf of two dozen state psychiatric inmates scheduled for enrolment in the project. A media controversy ensued, and the state was compelled to pull funding for the project. A three-judge panel was convened and determined that psychosurgery was destructive and should not be performed on an involuntary basis. The project was killed.[485] Not really though. This Government was and is determined to subdue and feminize the Black Bull, and turn him into Ferdinand.

Like Delgado and Louis Jolyon West, Rodin was a "CIA Doctor." Kevin Ryan of *The Abakus Blog* reported: "In a message to me, Rodin ... did acknowledge having been a CIA asset and he believed that the CIA still wanted something from him."[486] And he collaborated with the *other* CIA Doctors: "Dr. Rodin met with Drs. Vernon Mark and Jose Delgado as part of his development of the Michigan brain electrodes project."[487]

According to his autobiography, *War and Mayhem: Reflections of a Viennese Physician* (1999), before Rodin was a CIA asset he was Nazi soldier. He was a member of the Hitler Youth and a soldier in the Nazi Wehrmacht. But if being CIA and a Nazi is not enough: Ernst Rodin is actually *of Jewish heritage*. Phillip L. Paul writes in Rodin's 2017 obituary:

> As a matter of accident not previously uttered in his household, he [Rodin] learned that his maternal grandfather was from a Hungarian Jewish family, even though he converted to Catholicism to marry who would become Ernst's mother. This made Ernst a Mischling, and thus racially mixed, i.e., non-Aryan, and ineligible to serve on the front. Although drafted into the army of the Third Reich and forced to serve ultimately against Russian soldiers, he mused that he may have been the one person to survive based on Jewish genealogy because all his friends sent to the front "died like flies.[488]"

---

[485] Breggin, "Psychosurgery for Political Purposes," 852; Breggin and Breggin, *War Against Children of Color*, 116.
[486] Kevin Ryan, "Ernst Rodin," *The Abakus Blog*, April 14.
[487] Cross, M.D., *C.I.A. Doctors*, 100.
[488] Phillip L. Pearl, "Ernst Rodin, MD (1925–2017): An Icon in Clinical Neurophysiology,A Searcher of Truth in the Midst of Horror," *Journal of Clinical Neurophysiology* 34 (2017): 296-297 (297).

Rodin's collaborator in this Detroit "Feminizing the Black Bull" project, Dr. Jacques Gottleib, seems to be Jewish as well. "Gottleib" is an Askenazi or German Jewish name. The leader of the California "Feminizing the Black Bull" being prepared at the same time, Dr. Louis Jolyon West, was both a CIA Doctor and a Jew. In these men – Delgado, Rodin, West – we have the intersecting of the CIA and the Synagogue of Satan, all serving the War interests of President Nixon: war with the Black Man, with his mind and his masculinity.

IV.   *The Psychopharmaceutical Assault on Black Boys: California*

If General Louis Giuffrida was Governor Reagan's *counterinsurgency* advisor, William Herrmann was his *counterintelligence* advisor, reports say. Herrmann was a CIA agent as well as an FBI asset. He would later, during the Iran-Contra period, be an Oliver North (thus Secret Government) operative as well.[489] Said to have worked in a Psychological Operation (psy-ops) in both Vietnam and Cambodia, in

---

[489] Joel Baineman, ***The Crimes of a President: New Revelations on Conspiracy & Cover-up in the Bush and Reagan Administrations*** (New York: SPI Books, 1992) 240: "Back in the early 1960s Herrmann...from time to time did contract work for the CIA...Herrmann worked with the FBI to infiltrate the "Action Directe" terrorist organization in Belgium." In 1985 Herrmann was in London on behalf of the US intelligence and law enforcement communities participating in an operation to break up a European counterfeiting ring printing US currency, an operation that also involved the sale of US and Israeli missiles through an Iranian arms dealer. "In early March 1985," Herrmann said, "I got orders from Oliver North to issue pro-forma invoices for 10,000 TOW missiles from Cyrus Hashemi via Bank Melli." But North turned on him and left him out to dry, ordering the legal attaché at the American Embassy in London to *not* make the necessary arrangements and provide cover for him. Herrmann was thus arrested in London hotel with a briefcase full of counterfeit US currency. "Report: Iranian Arms dealer suggested diversion to Contras,"***UPI.com*** December 27, 1986 described Herrmann as "An imprisoned man claiming to be a former C.I.A. agent..." and reported that "C.I.A. spokeswoman Kathy Pherson said...she...could not confirm whether Herrmann ever worked for the C.I.A....Herrmann said he served in both Iran and Iraq over the last 10 years for the C.I.A.." The ***Los Angeles Times*** December 29, 1986 ("The World") would only describe Herrmann as a "reputed former C.I.A. agent".

California, according to journalist Brad Schreiber, Herrmann oversaw behavior modification experiments at Atascadero State Hospital (repository for the criminal insane) and at Vacaville Medical Facility.[490] California Medical Facility at Vacaville in the 1970s is where "The CIA had funding to set up drug experiments and other coercion against black prisoners specifically. There was psychosurgery done there."[491]

> Vacaville already had CIA funding for psychological research...It was called Subproject 3 of a program known as MKSEARCH (which replaced MKULTRA Subproject 140).[492]

Governor Reagan's counterintelligence advisor Herrmann along with his Secretary of Health Dr. Earl Brian are associated with an idea in 1971 for a horrible assault on Black and Brown male youth.[493] They planned to pilot Sweet, Ervin, and Mark's psychosurgery "Boston Project" there in California.[494] A Center For The Study and Prevention of

---

[490] Brad Schreiber, ***Revolution's End: The Patty Hearst Kidnapping, Mind Control, and the Secret History of Donald Defreeze and the SLA*** (Skyhorse Publishing, 2016); Gregg Reese, "Down the rabbit hole of the radical Left," ***Our Weekly*** (Los Angeles) March 16, 2017.
[491] Brad Schreiber quoted in Bob Calhoun, "Yesterday's Crimes: LAPD Snitches, CIA Mind Control and the Birth of the SLA," ***San Francisco Weekly*** September 20, 2016.
[492] Brad Schreiber, ***Revolution's End***, page 3 of Chapter 3.
[493] Though others have attributed the origin of the idea to Dr. Louis Jolyon West, chairman of psychiatry and director of the Neuropsychiatric Institute at the University of California, Los Angeles and James M. Stubblebine, California state director of health. See Willard Gaylin and Ruth Macklin, "Pitfalls in the Pursuit of Knowledge," in ***Violence and the Politics of Research***, ed. Willard Gaylin, Ruth Macklin and Tabitha M. Powledge (New York: Springer, 1981) 3-21.
[494] "Testimony of Fred J. Hiestand, Public Advocate, INC. Before the Senate Health & Welfare Committee on Behalf of the NAACP, Western Region, the Black Panther Party, the National Organization for Women, the Mexican-American Political Association and the California Prisoners' Union, May 9, 1973." As Samuel Chavkin points out as well: "The link between the Mark-Ervin book (***Violence and the Brain***) and the proposal for the center as outlined by Dr. West, was obvious": ***Mind Stealers***, 106. On April 5, 1973 the Committee Opposing Psychiatric Abuse of Prisoners submitted a "Memorandum

Violence was to be established, a screening and treatment center to catch the "violence prone" before the commit violence. In 1971 the California Department of Corrections sought

---

on the Center for the Study of Violent Behavior" which made it into the Subcommittee on Constitution Rights Report and observed: "The proposal listed on page 27 of the current draft (of the West Center proposal) is the Ervin-Mark-Sweet research project. Dr. Ervin is presently on the faculty of U.C.L.A. An earlier draft (NO. 1, of the proposal indicates that he will take part In the research. Why is he not listed in the recent proposals when it is his ideas and his experience which forms the background of this program? ...And why did Dr. Ervin come to U.C.L.A. just as funding appeared to be imminent for continuation of his research in Boston? The proposal to equate violence with brain dysfunction, which is so prominently featured in several of the projects under submission in Draft No. 4, was considered recently by Congress when Ervin, Mark, and Sweet applied directly to Congress for an additional $1 million to continue their scientific exploits. Congress finally turned them down after investigation disclosed the shoddy operation they were running and the scientific invalidity of the approach they were taking. It was shortly after the denial of this money to Ervin-Mark-Sweet that the announcement was made by Dr. Earl Brian, Secretary of HEW, that $1 million would be given to fund the U.C.L.A. Center. Coincidence?" See "Memorandum on the Center for the Study of Violent Behavior. Prepared by the Committee Opposing Psychiatric Abuse of Prisoners-April 5, 1973, in *Individual Rights and the Federal Role in Behavior Modification*. A Study Prepared by the Staff of the Subcommittee on Constitutional Rights of the committee on the Judiciary, United States Senate, Ninety-Third Congress. Second Session, November 1974 (Washington: U.S. Government Printing Office, 1974) 352.

No coincidence at all. On May 23, 1972 Dr. William Sweet testified before Congress on behalf of a continuation of federal support for the psychosurgery work of his "Project Ferdinand" colleagues Dr. Vernon Mark and Dr. Frank Ervin. Sweet revealed that a much broader program of violence control was in the making including mass screening programs and large treatment centers for "violent individuals." Sweet disclosed that the pilot program will be in California. He therefore requested funds for the chief architect of the California program, saying: "The testimony is being presented on behalf of the Neuropsychiatric Institute of the University of California at Los Angeles – under the direction of Louis Jolyon West [and] of the Brain Research Institute of the same University under the direction of Professor John French..." See Hearings on H.R. 15417 Before the Senate Committee on Appropriation, 92nd Congress, 2nd Session, Part 5, at 4946 (Testimony of Dr. W. Sweet).

$300,000 from LEAA and $189,000 from the state for their proposal for an experimental program on prisoners involving psychosurgery and "chemical castration."[495] The State would propose the same program for Black and Brown middle school students, and this California center "was to serve as a model for future facilities to be set up throughout the United States."[496]

> The CIA, in the late 1960s and early 1970s, funded experiments at Vacaville during a time when Governor Reagan and his cabinet were cracking down on student protests, prisoners, and the mentally ill...Dr. Earl Brian, Reagan's Secretary of Health, felt that behavior modification, a.k.a. mind control, was important in the prevention of crime. The law-and-order doctrine of Reagan and Brian was concentrated on the volatility of the Black Panthers and leftist political activism in general, especially at UC Berkley and throughout the Bay area. Later in the 1970s, Dr. Brian and Reagan's counterintelligence advisor, William Herrmann, worked together on the Center for the Study and Reduction of Violence, a project that intended to explore social control of those prone toward violence, even children...Eventually, both Brian and Herrmann worked with Reagan when he became president.[497]

Martin and Caul says in addition,

> Dr. Earl Brian...was adamant about his support for mind control centers in California...The Violence Control Center was actually the brain child of William Herrmann as part of *a pacification plan for California*. A counterinsurgency expert for Systems Development Corporation and an advisor to Governor Reagan, Herrmann worked with the Stand Research Institute, the RAND Corporation, and the Hoover Center on Violence. Herrmann was a CIA agent who is now serving an eight year prison sentence for his role in a CIA counterfeiting operation. He was also directly linked with the Iran-Contra affair according to government records and Herrmann's own testimony...The London Sunday Telegraph confirmed Herrmann's CIA connections, tracing them from 1976 to 1986.

---

[495] Jonas B. Robitscher, "Psychosurgery and Other Means of Altering Behavior," *Bulletin of the American Academy of Psychiatry and Law* 11 (1974): 7-33 (19).
[496] Harry V. Martin and David Caul, "Mind Control. Part 5: Reagan Era – Violence Center," *Napa Sentinel* August – November, 1991.
[497] Brad Schreiber, *Revolution's End*, page 5 of Chapter 3.

He also worked for the FBI. This information was revealed in his London trial (emphasis added).[498]

While the original idea is attributed to Brian, Herrmann, and even California state Director of Health James Stubblebine, Brian himself clarifies in a November 8, 1973 press release, affirming: "Last January Governor Reagan proposed the formation of a Center for Study and Reduction of Violence, under the joint sponsorship of the Health and Welfare Agency and the University of California at Los Angeles."[499] This is of course a reference to Governor Reagan's State of the State address in January, 1973 during which he announced and hailed the Center, and on January 11 his Secretary of Health and Welfare, Dr. Brian, announced that in the fiscal year 1973-1974 more than $1 million would be invested in the Center, one-third coming from the state and two-thirds ($750,000) from the federal LEAA.[500] One thing we can thus confirm: the Center was a State and thus a State-controlled endeavor. "The center was described as part of a Reagan package for reform of California's mental institutions, correctional system, and health delivery system."[501]

---

[498] Harry V. Martin and David Caul, "Mind Control. Part 6: More on the Violence Center," *Napa Sentinel* August – November, 1991.

[499] "PRESS RELEASE FROM CALIFORNIA STATE HEALTH AND WELFARE AGENCY, NOVEMDER 8, 1973," in *Individual Rights and the Federal Role in Behavior Modification*, 358.

[500] Chavkin, *Mind Stealers*, 95; Gaylin and Macklin, "Pitfalls in the Pursuit of Knowledge."

[501] Gaylin and Macklin, "Pitfalls in the Pursuit of Knowledge." West says: "Discussions by the Secretary of Human Resources, the Director of the Department of Mental Hygiene, and the Medical Director of the Neuropsychiatric Institute at UCLA, have led to this proposal." Dr. Louis Jolyon West, "Project Description, September 1, 1972-Center for Prevention of Violence, Neuropsychiatric Institute, UCLA," in *Individual Rights and the Federal Role in Behavior Modification*. A Study Prepared by the Staff of the Subcommittee on Constitutional Rights of the committee on the Judiciary, United States Senate, Ninety-Third Congress. Second Session, November 1974 (Washington: U.S. Government Printing Office, 1974) 325. He says also: "The plan for establishing the Center for the Study and Reduction of Violence has been initiated by the State of California Health and Welfare Agency." 333.

Dr. Louis Jolyon West

The project director and "chief architect" for the Center was Dr. Louis Jolyon West who in 1969 was brought from his post as chairman of the Department of Psychiatry at the University of Oklahoma to dual posts at UCLA as director of its Neuropsychiatric Institute and chairman of its Department of Psychiatry. In his original proposal for the Center for the Study and Prevention of Violence West was clear – like Hutschnecker before him was – about the source of violence and crime: "The major known correlates of violence are sex (male), age (youthful), ethnicity (black), and urbanicity."[502] Thus, young, Black males of the inner city are the targets of this center and its mind-control, behavior modification experiments and procedures[503] that will be conducted there. But not just prisoners[504]; middle school students as well. West wrote:

> The task force on violence in the schools will continue to survey the community for approaches to the reduction of school violence that have had some success in practical application. These approaches will be combined into a more total approach that will be tested during the school year 1973-1974 in two junior high schools which have agreed to participate in the program. One of these junior high schools is located in a

---

[502] West, "Project Description," 341.

[503] In a CONFIDENTIAL letter written to Stubblebine dated January 22, 1973 West confirms that research at the Center will include programs on "modification of chronic antisocial or impulsive aggression" and for "the alteration of undesirable behavior": "Nike Nonsense: Army Offers Nike Bases to UCLA Violence Center," *Berkeley Barr* March 8-14, 1974, p. 8.

[504] West, "Project Description," 337: "A partial list of facilities which will be used to develop treatment models and implement pilot and demonstration programs are: Ataseadero State Hospital; Camarillo State Hospital; UCLA Neuropsychiatric Institute; California Medical Facility, Vacaville."

predominantly Black ethnic area; the other in a predominantly Chicano area. The plan of the task force is to survey the schools on the initial level of violence, and then to introduce new anti-violence programs.[505]

The stated purpose of the Center was to study the "pharmacology of violence-producing and violence-inhibiting drugs," i.e. which experimental drugs make the boys more or less violent; and to study "hormonal aspects of passivity and aggressiveness in boys," i.e. how to manipulate the hormones of boys to make them either passive or aggressive. West proposed a "biosocial approach" to the problem of violence in the cities committed by young, Black males.[506] The "bio-" aspect of this approach will focus on genetic factors such as the misrepresented "XYY defect,"[507] and on biochemical factors, specifically *testosterone*:

> Many investigators have hypothesized that hormones are an important determinant of aggressive behavior. *Excessive secretion of testosterone in males is thought to be related to uncontrolled aggression*, and in females there is a definite relationship between incidence of violent behavior and hormonal changes associated with the menstrual cycle. Much remains to be learned about such factors and about *effective remedial measures*...New drugs now being tested in Europe and (very recently) in America hold promise for diminishing violent outbursts without dulling other brain processes. These drugs should be tested in the laboratory and then in prisons, mental hospitals, *and special community facilities*. Preliminary studies reported thus far have been largely clinical, without

---

[505] West, "Project Description," 346.

[506] West, "Project Description," 326.

[507] West, "Project Description," 327: "Recent evidence from studies of violent prisoners suggests that a disorder in sex chromosomes (the XYY defect) may be associated with the presence of violent behavior. This line of inquiry should be pursued. At the same time, a long-range study should be instituted to identify children who have this type of genetic abnormality, and to compare their development with that of children who have normal chromosomes. Detailed studies should yield valuable clues to factors that inhibit or encourage development of violent behavior patterns in children of different genetic constitutions. Such research has great implications, especially with the growing development of means of practical intervention to overcome hereditary defects."

rigorous scientific controls. Proper experiments must be done as soon as possible (emphasis added – WM).[508]

Dr. West says further:

> The Center will investigate genetic, biochemical, neurological, and neurophysiological elements of violent behavior. The effects of hormones on aggressive behavior will be studied in biological laboratories. New drugs now being developed hold some promise for the lessening of violent outbursts without a negative effect on other brain mechanisms and processes. These drugs will be tested in laboratory situations within the Center programs, and in related Health and Welfare Agency programs. Other applications of pharmacology will be developed in the course of the Center's activities. Studies of abnormal electrical activities within the brain, involving various forms of brain diseases and brain lesions, will be carried out in the neurological and physiological laboratories to clarify their relationship to various types of violent behavior. The subjects of such studies will *include hyperkinetic* (hyperactive or, simply, "busy" -WM) *children* and individuals who have committed aggressive or violent sew crimes.[509]

The focus on these Black boys testosterone is part of the *pathologizing* of Black masculinity that followed the urban riots of the 1960s. West thus says:

> Violent behavior appears, additionally, to be related to participation in subcultures with particular attitudes towards the value of human life, *and with attitudes equating violent physical expression with "manliness."* "Subcultures" may be viewed as regionally based, that is, composed of neighborhood associations. One strategy to be utilized will be selective sampling of metropolitan neighborhoods in California, to discover and compare norms of violence among various ethnic groups (Caucasian, Black, Chicano, and Oriental).[510]

And if attitudes of "manliness" are a problem, *medicating the manliness* is a solution. West says:

> Task IV-C: Biological Aspects of Violence: This task includes four sub-components, all involving biological aspects of the

---

[508] West, "Project Description," 327.
[509] West, "Project Description," 336.
[510] West, "Project Description," 341.

development and the behavioral expression of violence in human beings...The senior investigator for this task force on the biological aspects of violence is Richard Green, M.D. He will carry out a special analysis of a group of boys presently under study who are characterized by low levels of aggression. He will compare these boys with groups of boys who display average levels of aggression and with another group of boys who have excessive levels of aggression involving episodes of violent behavior. There will be studies of hormonal levels in these males and also studies of their interactions with their families. This study has important implications for the theory of constitutional predisposition to violence, and it may also have important therapeutic implications in the design of parent education programs. A third task for Dr. Green's task force will be the investigation of the feasibility of using the drug *Cyproterone Acetate* in the treatment of violent sex offenders such as rapists and child molesters. Several investigators in other countries have reported that this drug produces a temporary, safe, and reversible suppression of androgen secretion in males. For this reason Cyproterone Acetate has been accepted for use in the United States for the treatment of certain types of cancer in males. It has been observed that suppression of androgen secretion often reduces or eliminates the urge toward violent activity in male sex offenders.[511]

Like the federal and state-funded experiment in Detroit that chose the feminizing drug Cyproterone acetate as the drug to quell Black masculine aggression as well as psychosurgery, so too has this federally and state-funded experiment in Los Angeles chosen the same drug and same psychosurgery for the same purpose. In both cases, the "project director" was a representative of both the CIA and the Synagogue of Satan.

West also proposed to implant brain electrodes into some prisoners at Vacaville State Prison, the site of CIA mind control experiments under MK-SEARCH (which MK-ULTRA became in June 1964). After discharge from the prison the men would be monitored remotely through the brain implant which is connected to radio receivers at a central location. If any of the men or boys entered a restricted area, or if they exhibited *any sexual arousal at all*, a signal would be sent to the brain implant

---

[511] West, "Project Description," 344.

completely *immobilizing him/them*, allowing law enforcement to be dispatched to their location to arrest them.[512]

And as West could boast: "Richard Nixon and Ronald Reagan were each going to put up half the money for us...,"[513] because both Nixon and Reagan were equally invested in the goal: taming the Black Bull. But like in Detroit, the public outcry shut the Center down before it got off the drawing board, but it *did not* stop the specific "research" and targeted experimentation that it was to house. These just went covert. As West would later boast:

> So our project to start a center at UCLA was blocked. This was the most frustrating experience of my career. *But it didn't stop us from going on to study violence*, and we've made a lot of progress in the care and understanding of victims, especially in the fields of child abuse and rape.[514]

Who then *is* Louis Jolyon West? Walter Bowart observes:

> Perhaps the greatest champion of a Zombie America is one of the most respected figures in American Psychiatry today, Dr. Louis Jolyon "Jolly" West. Beginning with Brainwashing work for the Air Force, MKULTRA work with the CIA, West has positioned himself smack in the midst of the Invisible War.[515]

---

[512] Colin A. Ross, M.D., ***Bluebird: Deliberate Creation of Multiple Personality by Psychiatry*** (Richardson, TX: Manitou Communications, 2000) 118-119.

[513] Dr. West quoted in The Hastings Center, "Researching Violence: Science, Politics, & Public Controversy," ***The Hastings Center Report*** 9 (1979) 1-19 (19).

[514] Marshall Berges, "Louis J. and Kathryn West: Probers of the Mind, Dedicated Activists: He is Director of the Neuropsychiatric Institute at UCLA," ***Los Angeles Times*** October 27, 1985.

[515] Bowart says: "The only safe way to wage war, the warriors realized, was to wage it silently. Toward the end of World War Two various forms of IW research began, and eventually modern warriors came up with a number of insidious ways to subdue enemy populations without their ever knowing that a war had even begun. Today secret "invisible weapons" pose a more ominous threat to life than even thermonuclear holocaust. These weapons have not only been developed without the knowledge of their intended victims, they cannot even be detected at the very moment they are murdering or robotizing civilian populations." Walter H. Bowart and Richard Sutton, ***The Invisible Third World*** (1990), 2.

West's career appears to be a carefully constituted espionage 'cover,' always in the forefront on [Invisible War] technology.[516]

Even more than José Delgado, "Jolly" West epitomizes the "CIA Doctor." Between 1952 and 1956 West was the Air Force chief of psychiatry at Lackland Air Force Base in San Antonio, Texas. He had a TOP SECRET clearance with Air Force Intelligence, as he interviewed returning American pilots downed and captured in Korea by Communist Chinese. In this way he studied and became expert in the Chinese methods of brainwashing.[517] He moved to the University of Oklahoma, where he was head of the Department of Psychiatry, Neurology and Behavioral Sciences between 1956 and 1969. He received TOP SECRET clearance for the CIA as a contractor on MK-ULTRA Subproject 43 and was funded $20,800 in 1956 by the CIA. His subproject that the CIA funding was entitled, "Psychophysiological Studies of Hypnosis and Suggestibility."[518] West was outed as a "CIA Doctor" in the 1977 *New York Times* exposé on the CIA's mind control program that revealed:

The agency's entry into the field of behavior control was widespread and on varying levels. For instance, Dr. Louis Jolyon West, chief of psychiatry at the University of California, Los Angeles, was asked to make a study of LSD by Dr. [Sidney] Gottlieb [the MK-ULTRA, Technical Services Division chief]. He, too, was paid by the [CIA conduit] Geschikter Foundation.[519]

---

[516] Walter H. Bowart and Richard Sutton, *The Invisible Third World* (1990), 19.
[517] I.E. Farber, Harry F. Harlow and Louis Jolyon West, "Brainwashing, Conditioning, and DDD (Debility, Dependency, and Dread)," *Sociometry* 20 (1957): 271-285.
[518] Ross, *The C.I.A. Doctors*, 106-117.
[519] Nicholas Horrock, "Private Institutions Used in C.I.A. Effort to Control Behavior," *The New York Times* August 2, 1977.

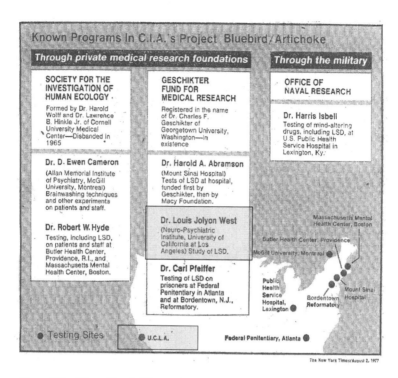

From *The New York Times* August 2, 1977 exposé of the CIA mind control operation.

But that's not all. "Like many other leading psychiatrists of his generation, West came from a family of Russian Jewish immigrants"[520] According to the *Los Angeles Times* Jolly West was

> The eldest of three children and the only son of Russian Jews who fled pogroms in their native Kiev and settled in Madison, Wis., Jolly grew up in poverty-but with a sense of power and destiny instilled by his mother...[H]e enlisted in the Army with a determination "to show Hitler there were Jews who knew how to fight, and to kill." With a grim chuckle, as if speaking of a dimly remembered acquaintance, West added: "I was a bloodthirsty young fellow."[521]

---

[520] Joel Paris, *Fall of an Icon: Psychoanalysis and Academic Psychiatry* (Toronto: University of Toronto Press, 2005) 131.
[521] Berges, "Louis J. and Kathryn West." Also Myrna Oliver, "Louis J. West; Psychiatrist, Rights Activists," *Los Angeles Times* January

West had working relationships with the Boston 3, but also with fellow Jewish CIA Doctors Delgado at Yale and Rodin in Detroit. These three – Delgado, Rodin, and West – personify the nexus between the CIA and the Synagogue of Satan, and these in the service of President Nixon's and Governor Reagan's war against the Black male.

VI.   *Methadone: Nixon's Magic Bullet*

While the Nixon Administration showed great interest in cyproterone acetate as a chemical solution to the problem of *black masculine hostility* in the inner cities, they found their magic bullet – or so they thought - elsewhere: methadone, the synthetic opioid used as a "treatment" for heroin addiction.

Prior to World War II heroin addiction in America was mainly a southern, white disease. As we reported in Volume I,[522] the War disrupted international shipping and drug smuggling operations and therefore nearly extinguished this drug problem in America. The number of addicts dropped down to a tenth: from 200,000 in 1924 to 20,000 in 1945. But after the War the U.S. military/intelligence apparatus in collaboration with Jewish and Italian Mafia elements deliberately revived the opium trade and the number of American heroin addicts resurged: 60,000 by 1952 and 150,000 by 1965. But there was a big difference with this new epidemic: while the pre-WWII addicts were mainly southern and white, the post-WWII addicts were largely northern, metropolitan and Black. By 1955 it could be said: "Addiction to opiates...is now more common in Negroes than whites."[523]

The heroin pattern of addiction has increased markedly since World War II and is currently associated with minority group status (predominantly from metropolitan centers)...A

07, 1999; Herbert Weiner, "Louis Jolyon West, MD (1924-1999)," ***Arch Gen Psychiatry*** 56 (1999): 669-670; "Louis West has died – a cult expert and member of AFF's *Cultic Studies Journal* editorial advisory," ***Reuters*** January 7, 1999.
[522] Wesley Muhammad, ***Understanding The Assault on the Black Man, Black Manhood, and Black Masculinity*** (Atlanta: A-Team Publishing, 2016) 236-237.
[523] Harris Isbell, "Medical Aspects of Opiate Addiction," ***Bull. N.Y. Acad. Med.*** 31 (1955): 886-901 (887).

comparison of the 1962 geographic distribution...reveals a marked change in the hospital population [admitted for drug use – WM]. In 1937, the highest rates of admission were from the southern states. Thus, what has occurred since 1937 has been a substantial increase in the number of patients from northern metropolitan centers... The change in place of residence of the addict patients between 1937 and 1962 has been accompanied by shifts in age and race. The median age of the 2713 male patients in 1962 was 30.2 years, the mean was 33.5 years...Patients less than 30 years of age constituted 49.3 percent of the total male population. In 1937 the median age of males was 38.3, the mean 39.1. Only 19.7 percent of the male patients were under 30 years of age. Thus, the median age has decreased by eight years. During this period the median age of males in the United States has remained fairly constant: in 1930 26.7 years, in 1940 29.1, in 1950 29.9 and, in 1960 28.7. The racial and ethnic composition of the hospital population has altered markedly during this twenty-five year period. In 1937 [however], 88.4 percent of the male patients were white, 8.9 percent Negro, 1.2 percent Mexican and, together, Chinese, Japanese, and Indian were 1.5 percent. In 1962, 51.0 percent of the male patients were white, 30.4 percent Negro, 12.2 percent Puerto Rican, 4.9 percent Mexican, and others 1.5 percent. There has, then, been a notable increase in the number of addicts from the minority groups in American society... What has occurred since the 1920's is the increased use of heroin among addicts and the concentration of this type of addiction among Negroes, Puerto Rican, and Mexican youth in metropolitan slum areas... As Clausen has observed, addiction in the United States has now become "clearly entwined with minority group status.[524]

What is important here is that there were two heroin "Negro epidemics": one started around 1944-45 and peaked around 1949, and then dropped off drastically.[525] The second

---

[524] John C. Ball, "Two Patterns of Narcotic Drug Addiction in the United States," *The Journal of Criminal Law, Criminology, and Police Science* 56 (1965): 203-211 (203).

[525] Jerome Jaffe et al., "The Natural History of a Heroin Epidemic," *AJPH* 62 (1972): 995-1001: "Chicago's Negro community experienced a serious epidemic of heroin addiction shortly after World War II... description of Chicago narcotic addicts during the early 1930s indicated that only about 17% were Negro... Immediately following World War II, older patients describe the onset of a poly-drug epidemic among teenage Negroes in association with a hip youth culture which included jazz musicians and well-known entertainers.

epidemic coincided with the Civil Rights agitations in the south and, more specifically, the urban rioting in the North.[526] This epidemic began around 1966 and peaked around 1969-1971.[527] This implies that this CIA-protected, Mafia-distributed heroin was poured into the Black communities in the 1960s as a result of – and with the intent of quelling - these national agitations and uprisings.

THE JEWISH MAFIA

Because of the key role played in the narcotics trade into Black ghettos by the Mafia's Five Families, New York became the home of the largest population of heroin addicts. Second to New York was Chicago, which served as a distribution point for other midwestern and southwestern cities. The Jewish element in this anti-Black drug conspiracy should not go unnoticed.

Night spots on Chicago's Negro South Side were swinging places for conventioneers and local well-to-do whites. Marijuana and heroin were part of this hip scene, and the lyrics of popular songs contained thinly disguised references to drugs... Our data delineate a major heroin epidemic among Chicago Negro youth which reached its peak in 1949..."

[526] Robert L. Dupont, "Profile of a heroin-addiction epidemic," *The New England Journal of Medicine* 285 (1971): 320-324: "Washington, D.C., is experiencing an alarming epidemic of heroin addiction. According to current estimates there are now about 17,000 heroin addicts in the city. Two thirds of the addicts are under 26 years of age, 91 per cent are black, 74 per cent are male, and 52 per cent began heroin use within the last four years. In one large part of the central city it has been estimated that 20 per cent of the boys from 15 to 19 and 38 per cent of the young men from 20 to 24 years of age are heroin addicts."

[527] Michael Agar and Heather Schacht Reisnger, "A Tale of Two Policies: The French Connection, Methadone, and Heroin Epidemics," *Culture, Medicine and Psychiatry* 26 (2002): 371-396 (371, 372): "Every data source we have looked at agrees that a heroin epidemic occurred in the U.S. in the 1960s (...). Heaviest impact was in urban areas at the low end of the socioeconomic scale, especially among African-Americans and Hispanics...Most everyone agrees that the 1960s heroin epidemic ended in the late 1960s or early 1970s. Epidemiologists wrote that incidence of heroin peaked, for the most part, in 1969-1971."

In the 1920s and 1930s, heroin's principle distributers were mobsters Meyer Lansky, Dutch Schultz, and Legs Diamond. (Because all three were Jewish, heroin was often called "smack," from the Yiddish word *schmecher*, meaning "addict".) In the mid-1930s the Italian Mafia took over, specifically, (Arnold Rothstein protégé) Charles "Lucky" Luciano who established the "French Connection (insert added-WM)."[528]

Beginning in the 1920s, Jewish and Italian traffickers, bankrolled by the (Jewish) underworld financier Arnold Rothstein, made heroin purchases in China and Europe and smuggled them back to New York.[529]

Into the min-1960s, New York's five Italian crime families and some Jewish underworld figures kept a grip on drug dealing – specifically heroin – in the city's black neighborhood, Harlem.[530]

Figure 1—Incidence of First Heroin Use in a Negro Patient Sample—A 3-Year Moving Average

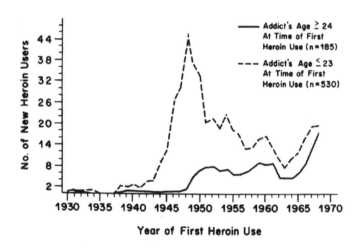

Year of First Heroin Use

[528] Paul A. Offit, *Pandora's Lab: Seven Stories of Science Gone Wrong* (Washington, D.C.: National Geographic, 2017) 26.
[529] Eric C. Schneider, *Smack: Heroin and the American City* (Philadelphia: University of Pennsylvania, 2008) 9.
[530] Jeff Burbank, *"Did Frank Matthews Get Away With It?* The New York Drug Kingpin Has Been At Large Since 1973," *The Mob Museum* @ Https://Themobmuseum.Org/Blog/Did-Frank-Matthews-Get-Away-With-It/

CAUSES ENDOCRINE DISRUPTION

It is not hard to understand why heroin would be used to chemically neutralize the aggression of Black people agitating and rioting in America's cities. Harris Isbell, who headed the Office of Naval Intelligence and CIA MK-ULTRA studies at the National Institute of Mental Health's Addiction Research Center (ARC) in Lexington, Kentucky (=the Narcotics Farm) from 1951 to 1962,[531] reported already in 1955 that opiates reduced aggression and antisocial impulses and caused "testicular depression."[532] The latter description includes depression of testosterone levels. Opioids exert inhibitory effects on the hypothalamus in the brain, the area responsible for production of gonadotropin-releasing-hormone (GnRH), whose release is necessary for the synthesis of testosterone. Opioids thus suppress testosterone in men and estradiol in women indirectly, but also directly through causing a reduction in testosterone synthesis in men. [533] Heroin was dropped in the 1960s Black neighborhoods no doubt with the hope that, due to the effects of testosterone reduction on the inner-city Black males, the cities would quiet down. But it didn't. 1967 and 1968 saw the devastating Detroit Rebellion and the 100 riots that resulted following the assassination of Dr. Martin Luther King Jr. in 1968. A better alternative was needed.

That better, more effective alternative was, according to the Nixon Administration, methadone. Methadone is a synthetic opioid created in a lab in 1939 for Adolf Hitler by the German chemical company I.G. Farben. The U.S. military/intelligence apparatus seized it after the war and sent it to their man in Kentucky, Harris Isbell, who conducted research on the drug using Black inmates.[534]

---

[531] Associated Press, "Addicts Paid Off With Narcotics in CIA-Funded Tests," *The Washington Star* November 8, 1975.

[532] Isbell, "Medical Aspects of Opiate Addiction," 890, 891.

[533] Todd T. Brown, Amy B. Wisniewski and Adrian S. Dobs, "Gonadal and Adrenal Abnormalities in Drug Users: Cause or Consequences of Drug Use Behavior and Poor Health Outcomes," *American Journal of Infectious Diseases* 2 (2006): 130-135 (130, 131).

[534] For example Harris Isbell and Victor H. Vogel, "The Addiction Liability of Methadone (Amidone, Dolophine, 10820) and its Use in the Treatment of the Morphine Abstinence Syndrome," *The American Journal of Psychiatry* 105 (1949): 909-914; Harris Isbell, "The Addiction Liability of Synthetic Substitutes for Codeine."

The differences between heroin and methadone made the latter preferable as a *masculinity neutralizer.* It is more potent than heroin and even potentially more addictive.

> Methadone, an addictive drug made in the laboratory, is similar in chemical structure to heroin...Methadone, then, is a heroin substitute. The important difference between it and heroin is its durability. Unlike heroin, which is fragile and dissipates itself quickly in the body, methadone has a lasting quality. Because of its durability, it can be taken orally, rather than intravenously, and it retains its potency even after it has gone through the digestive process and enters the bloodstream...But methadone is a dangerous drug. If taken orally by a nonaddict, it can cause euphoria and even death.[535]

Methadone's effect on the endocrine system is therefore more severe.

> The function of the secondary sex organs was found to be *markedly impaired* in 29 participants in a methadone maintenance program. The ejaculate volume and seminal vesicular and prostatic secretions were reduced by over 50 per cent in methadone clients, as compared to 16 heroin addicts and 43 narcotic-free controls. *Serum testosterone levels were also approximately 43 per cent lower in methadone clients than in controls or heroin users.* Although the sperm count of methadone clients was more than twice the control levels, reflecting a lack of sperm dilution by secondary-sex-organ secretions, the sperm motility of these subjects was markedly lower than normal. On all measures of secondary-sex-organ and testicular function, heroin addicts appeared to fall between the methadone and control subjects, but, with the exception of

---

Request to the Office of Naval Research for Renewal of Contract NR 101-149. January 27, 1958; Martin A. Lee and Bruce Shlain, **Acid Dreams. The Complete Social History of LSD: The CIA, the Sixties, and Beyond** (New York: Grove Weidenfeld, 1992) 24-25.
[535] Richard Severo, "Addiction: Chemistry Is the New Hope, but Degree of its Effectiveness is Still Disputed," **The New York Times** March 19, 1971. See also Joseph D. Sapira, John C. Ball and Emily S. Cottrell, "Addiction to Methadone among Patients at Lexington and Forth Worth," **Public Health Reports (1896-1970)** 83 (1968): 691-694.

sperm motility, the deviation from control values did not reach statistical significance.[536]

"In experimental models, methadone administration was found to significantly reduce testosterone concentrations *by over two-thirds of the baseline* values after 60 minutes".[537] Methadone treatment causes testosterone levels in men to plummet such that they can resemble a woman's level.[538] What is more, methadone has a *melanin affinity*, meaning it is a chemical that attracts to and binds tightly with *melanated* tissues, making methadone useful as an *ethnic weapon* against Black people who are the world's most melanated people.[539] All these factors make comprehensible President Nixon's selection of methadone as the *magic bullet* shot at the *black masculine hostility* of the inner city.

ROOTS OF THE METHADONE PLAN

The roots of the Methadone Plan (if you will) go back before the Nixon Administration. The U.S. Government's Lexington Narcotics Farm (the ARC) "represented big-government social engineering..."[540] There the "CIA Doctor" Harris Isbell investigated over 800 possible behavioral control chemicals for the CIA and the Office of Naval Research. With Isbell there worked two important individuals: Marie Nyswander and Jerome Jaffe. Nyswander did her medical

---

[536] T.J. Cicero et al., "Function of the male sex organs in heroin and methadone users," **N Engl J Med** 292 (1975): 882-887.

[537] Todd T. Brown, Amy B. Wisniewski and Adrian S. Dobs, "Gonadal and Adrenal Abnormalities in Drug Users: Cause or Consequences of Drug Use Behavior and Poor Health Outcomes," **American Journal of Infectious Diseases** 2 (2006): 130-135 (130, 131).

[538] Monica Bawar et al., "Methadone induces testosterone suppression in patients with opioid addiction," **Scientific Reports** 4:6189 (2014): 1-7; Adam Carter, "Methadone suppresses testosterone in men, McMaster research suggests," **CBC News** August 26, 2014.

[539] Suzanne J. Green and John F. Wilson, "The Effect of Hair Color on the Incorporation of Methadone into Hair in the Rat," **Journal of Analytical Toxicology** 20 (1996): 121-123.

[540] Claire Clark, " "Chemistry is the New Hope": Therapeutic Communities and Methadone Maintenance, 1965-1971," **Social History of Alcohol and Drugs** 26 (2012): 192-216 (194).

residency in Lexington beginning in 1944. Isbell was publishing results of his studies on methadone by 1947.

In 1963 Nyswander was recruited to the Rockefeller Institute for Medical Research by research associate Vincent P. Dole, who was during WWII a lieutenant commander at the Naval Medical Research Unit at Rockefeller. In 1964 Dole and Nyswander began a social engineering experiment among Black heroin addicts in New York: the investigators switched the addicts' addiction from that of heroin to that of the harsher opiate methadone. This "methadone maintenance" experiment involved setting up a clinic in New York that doled out daily and freely to heroin addicts high doses of the addictive drug methadone, *and getting them addicted to it* (the "maintenance" part).[541] "The objective of their (Dole and Nyswander) rehabilitation program was not to render the addict drug-free but to make him socially useful," explains Edward Jay Epstein.[542] Dole and Nyswander saw methadone as "an easily dispensable chemical solution to urban problems"[543]; as the "magic-bullet solution" to the problem of crime and violence in the inner city; a "Cinderella drug" that, once swallowed, transforms a criminal addict into a "decent, law-abiding citizen," i.e. one who does not engage in civil disobedience or urban rebellion. The "CIA Doctor" Isbell visited Nyswander and Dole at Rockefeller.

Jerome Jaffe, "the bespectacled Jewish psychiatrist," is from a Lithuanian Jewish family.[544] Jaffe arrived in Lexington in 1959. He would have lunch with the "CIA Doctor" Harris Isbell. Jaffe left Lexington and settled in New York, where he

---

[541] Claire Clark, "'Chemistry is the New Hope': Therapeutic Communities and Methadone Maintenance, 1965-1971," **Social History of Alcohol and Drugs** 26 (2012): 192-216 (194).
[542] Edward Jay Epstein, **Agency of Fear: Opiates and Political Power in America** Revised Edition (London and New York: Verso, 1990 [1977]) 129; idem., "Methadone: the forlorn hope," **The Public Interest** Summer (1974): 3-24.
[543] Epstein, "Methadone," 6.
[544] David T. Courtwright, **No Right Turn: Conservative Politics in A Liberal America** (Cambridge and London: Harvard University Press, 2010) 83. Michael Massing, **The Fix** (Berkeley: University of California Press, 2000) 87: "Jaffe was born in 1933 into a lower-middle-class household in the Germantown section of Philadelphia. His father, a Jewish immigrant from Lithuania, ran a grocery store on the ground floor of the family house."

started handing out this potent and addictive drug methadone to (Black) New Yorkers (addicts). He worked in Dole's lab for a time and then took that "methadone maintenance" program and piloted it among Black heroin users in Chicago in 1967. Jaffe saw Chicago as *his* "laboratory. He established his methadone clinics in high-crime, gang-infested Black areas such as East 79th Street and Stoney Island Avenue.[545] The top administrators of Jaffe's methadone operation were primarily white, the "clients" primarily Black.[546] Chicago courts even gave arrestees the option of methadone treatment as an alternative to prison.

Dole was able to convincingly demonstrate the utility of his and Nyswander's "methadone maintenance" program as an efficient means to quiet "Negro unrest". After a violent riot occurred in October 1970 at Tombs prison in Lower Manhattan (the Manhattan House of Detention for Men) Dole was called by the Department of Corrections to administer methadone treatment on the inmates and as a result "the prison calmed down." Dole then boasted that methadone treatment "can make the difference between a quite prison and a riot."[547] By 1972 he had used their methadone maintenance (addiction) treatment on 22,000 heroin addicts in detention jails in New York and "Violence and suicides, which occurred frequently before the treatment was started, have been completely absent in the detoxification areas."[548]

> the effect of the simple medical program has been dramatic. The ninth floor in The Tombs, which was the focal point of the riots six months before the program, is now (one year after the riots) the quietest area of the prison...[549]

In 1969 psychiatrist Robert Dupont, who worked at the Department of Corrections in Washington D.C., got the blessings of D.C. Mayor Walter Washington to pilot in that city

---

[545] Massing, *The Fix*, 92,

[546] Massing, *The Fix*, 95.

[547] Christopher S. Wren, "Holding an Uneasy Line In The Long War on Heroin; Methadone Emerged in City Now Debating Its Use," *The New York Times* October 3, 1998.

[548] Vincent P. Dole, "Detoxification of Sick Addicts in Prison," *JAMA* 222 (1972): 366-369.

[549] Dole, "Detoxification of Sick Addicts in Prison," 368-369.

.

the methadone program of Jerome Jaffe used in Chicago (whom he visited recently) and Dole and Nyswander in New York (whom he researched). In September 1969 the first methadone dispensary was established in Washington D.C. Over the next three years 15,000 primarily Black men (and women) in the D.C. area were put on methadone *chemical parole.*

NIXON'S WAR *THROUGH* DRUGS

This all inspired the "law-and-order" Nixon Administration who was looking for a solution to the problem of riots and crime in the inner cities, a chemical solution. Nixon's chief domestic policy advisor John Ehrlichman – who admitted that the War on Drugs was a ruse allowing the Nixon Administration to wage war on Black people – needed to deliver to his boss a proposal to fix these urban problems. So he turned to the "Mr. Fix It" on his staff, White House deputy domestic policy advisor Egil "Bud" Krogh Jr. Krogh himself turned to one of his own staff assistants.

White House domestic council staff assistant Jeffery Donfeld "was raised in an affluent Jewish household in Los Angeles," his father "one of the few Jewish Republicans around."[550] As a member of Krogh's staff he was responsible for crafting the administration's non-law-enforcement anti-drug abuse programs. Having discovered during his research Dole and Nyswander's New York, Jaffe's Chicago, and Dupont's D.C. methadone programs, Donfeld made the recommendation to Krogh to implement it nationally as the solution to urban Black "crime." Eventually this was accepted and methadone became the core of the Nixon Administration's "War on Drugs," i.e. the government's war on Black People through drugs. Not only did Donfeld expand Dupont's D.C. program through the establishment of the Narcotics Treatment Administration; but also Jaffe was named in June 1971 as head of the newly created Special Action Office for Drug Prevention with the task of orchestrating the national methadone program. He is the nation's first Drug Czar. Through Jaffe, the Nixon Administration opened legal opiate clinics throughout Black America and freely doled out a highly addictive opiate – legally (and illegally).

---

[550] Michael Massing, *The Fix* (Berkeley: University of California Press, 2000) 97.

The importance of this Methadone Plan for the Nixon Administration is evident in the federal dollars invested in it. In fiscal year 1969, the year of Nixon's ascension to the presidency, only $80 million was spent on drug issues. By fiscal year 1973, that number skyrocketed to $730 million. And the core initiative of this War on Drugs was the national dispensing of methadone to Black men (and women) across America: 450 clinics were established by 1972 with 7.5 million doses of methadone doled out to over 85,000 persons. And this is only the *licit* distribution. As we shall, there was an even greater *illicit* distribution of methadone into Black America through these clinics, and if the government is not actually at the root of this, it certainly applauded the development.

The U.S. Government had officially gone from narcotic suppression to narcotic distribution – a radicle change in government policy. Because methadone was seen as the chemical solution to the urban problem the Nixon Administration went into the business of *openly and freely distributing a highly addictive narcotic in the inner city.* There were set up "filling-stations" where addicts could get methadone as easy as motorists get gasoline, except the motorists had to pay. The Nixon Administration became the major supplier of narcotics into the inner city, "pouring out a synthetic drug in the ghettos".[551]

By 1970, the Nixon Administration was promoting methadone to reduce crime...The Nixon Administration's support of methadone as a crime-reducer led to suspicions among some black New Yorkers that the medication was a plot to render them docile.[552]

This is certainly beyond suspicion. Methadone was to be the tool of "pharmaceutical containment" of the inner city.

Thus no attempt was made to justify methadone as a "'normalizing" or a preventive medicine; instead, it was defined principally as *a powerful means of exerting a form of social control over street addicts.* Not only did it attract addicts into participating in government-sponsored programs and transfer

---

[551] Epstein, **Agency of Fear**, 247.
[552] Christopher S. Wren, "Holding an Uneasy Line In The Long War on Heroin; Methadone Emerged in City Now Debating Its Use," **The New York Times** October 3, 1998.

the object of their dependency from an opiate, procured illegally to an opiate obtained from licit sources; but it placed them on a highly effective kind of *chemical parole*. Their urine could be tested daily for illicit narcotics, and if they broke their parole-or the rules of the program-*they could be denied the methadone they had become dependent on...* In January 1969, when Richard Nixon assumed office, there were only 16 drug treatment programs receiving financial support from the federal government, and the main forms of treatment were detoxification and drug-free therapy. Almost all the agencies involved in the administration of these treatment programs, including the National Institute of Mental Health, the Office of Economic Opportunity, and the Department of Housing and Urban Development, were actively opposed to methadone maintenance. By 1973, however, the federal government was funding some 394 (*sic*) treatment programs offering methadone maintenance. In the intervening four years, there had obviously been a major shift in policy towards methadone... *The focus of policy thus changed accordingly from relieving the individual from the suffering and degradation of drug dependency to relieving the rest of society from the putative criminal behavior of addicts...*Since methadone maintenance, whatever its side effects, promised to transfer street addicts from a dependency on heroin, which they had to obtain at great cost from illegal suppliers, to a dependency on methadone, which could be dispensed legally under tight controls, it held great appeal to the young men in the Nixon Administration concerned with the problem of urban crime... To be sure, methadone users can be placed under a tighter form of chemical parole through more sophisticated urinalysis techniques and more rigorous requisites for remaining in the program; however, such forms of behavior control raise the most difficult sort of ethical and legal questions: *Can the state be justified in deliberately raising the tolerance of an addict for drugs by giving him higher dosages of an opiate than he would normally take, and then denying him the opiate when he fails to conform to the rules?*[553]

President Nixon is reported to have declared that the inner city addicts' move from heroin to the *more* potent, *more* addictive, and *more* endocrine disrupting methadone was "a wonderful move."[554] In order to facilitate this "wonderful" move

---

[553] Edward Jay Epstein, "Methadone: the forlorn hope," **The Public Interest** Summer (1974): 3-24.
[554] Courtright, **No Right Turn**, 83.

and force the drug addict to substitute methadone for heroin, heroin had to be made unavailable. The Nixon Administration accomplished this by cutting the supply off at the root: the French Connection. Nixon got Turkey to ban poppy growing and France to increase law enforcement and disrupt the heroin labs in Marseille. This concerted assault on the supply successfully produced a heroin drought in America between 1973 and 1975. "Most everyone agrees that the 1960s heroin epidemic ended in the late 1960s and early 1970s."[555] During this drought the heroin was replaced in the ghettos of America by Nixon's methadone.

> even though the heroin "epidemic" by all measures abated and the number of addicts turning up for treatment (and for free methadone) drastically declined after 1973, the methadone program continued to expand and *the amount of illicit methadone available to addicts increased in direct proportion to the number treatment programs.* The federal government, therefore, again assumed its unwitting (*sic*) role as a major supplier of illicit drugs.[556]

This role assumed by the government was not unwitting, we argue. The above- mentioned connection between the spread of treatment programs and the increase of *illicit* methadone in the community is important. Federal clinics and private treatment centers became hubs for the illicit distribution of methadone or diversion, the deliberate leaking of methadone pills from clinics/centers to the streets, creating a black market and a rapidly expanding population of new addicts. This "diverting" occurred in two primary ways:

1. Many of those enrolled in a methadone maintenance program were given "take home privileges," allowing them to take enough supplies back to the community and retail it. Users in one Brooklyn Bedford Stuyvesant section told researchers that, due to illicit methadone

---

[555] Michael Agar and Heather Schacht Reisnger, "A Tale of Two Policies: The French Connection, Methadone, and Heroin Epidemics," *Culture, Medicine and Psychiatry* 26 (2002): 371-396 (372).
[556] Epstein, *Agency of Fear*, 250.

supplies, "the drug was always available in the neighborhoods."[557]

2. The bigger culprit: clinic/center administrators and staff deliberately leaked the drug out the back door into the community, in startling amounts. For example:

- The operator of one of the largest private methadone programs in New York, Dr. Robert T. Dale and his wife, became fugitives from justice after 55,000 40 milligram methadone wafers turned up missing (one or two wafers could maintain an addict for a day).[558]
- Psychiatrist Dr. Elio Maggio, who ran a private program in the Bronx, passed methadone to customers through a slit in the office door.[559]
- There existed in Detroit, which was in 1972 thought to have the highest addiction per capita in the nation, a methadone black market which officials from the Food and Drug Administration attributed largely to diversion from methadone programs.[560]

This "leakage" of methadone from clinics and treatment centers into the street created not only a black market but also an epidemic of "nonaddict" addicts: "a new type of 'addict' – with no track marks, no established history, no morphine in the body."[561] These are thus methadone addicts who were not previously heroin addicts. In Detroit, more than two thirds of the methadone addicted population "did not have a clear history heroin addiction."[562] Many of these new addicts are young people, teenagers. Interesting in this connection is the fact Nyswander at Rockefeller Institute as well as physicians from

[557] James M. Markham, "New Problem in Drugs: Addiction to Methadone," *The New York Times* August 14, 1972.
[558] Markham, "New Problem in Drugs."
[559] Markham, "New Problem in Drugs."
[560] Markham, "New Problem in Drugs."
[561] Markham, "New Problem in Drugs."
[562] Markham, "New Problem in Drugs."

Johns Hopkins Medical School both experimented with giving the potent and dangerous drug to young teenagers.[563]

This methadone black marker is important to keep in mind. When we hear that by 1972 there were more than 85,000 "addicts" on methadone, these are numbers on for the *licit* market. When we account for the *illicit* market, the numbers drastically increase.

Government complicity in this leaking of a highly addictive narcotic into the community is suggested by Jeffery Donfeld's own words, according to Harvard trained investigative journalist Edward Jay Epstein:

> Donfeld granted that there was no way to prevent such leakage into the illegal market, but argued that even if this happened, it would work, at least in the short run, *to the advantage of the administration*...even suggested that the leakage of methadone from treatment programs to the black market would undercut the price of heroin, thereby diminishing the addicts level of criminal activity. He reasoned in the staff report: "...if heroin addicts were to obtain supplies of methadone (illegally) society is not hurt in a direct way because methadone will help to sustain an addict [who] will have less compulsion to commit crimes.[564]

Professor David Musto of the University of Pennsylvania, an expert on American drug policy, was told so much directly:

> That crime-reduction held first place among Nixon's priorities – not the care of addicts – is illustrated by Administration's surprising willingness to adopt methadone, a synthetic opiate, as its preferred treatment for heroin users. At the time, a high-ranking official in the Bureau of Narcotics and Dangerous Drugs told me that *the bureau would hand out heroin if it thought that would cut crime.* This attitude was surprising because the substitution of one addiction by another contradicted the previously adamant stand by Nixon's adherent's against drug use.[565]

Dr. Robert Dupont was interviewed recently by PBS Frontline and was asked about the controversy surrounding his

---

[563] Richard Severo, "Addiction: Chemistry Is the New Hope, but Degree of its Effectiveness is Still Disputed," *The New York Times* March 19, 1971.

[564] [564] Epstein, *Agency of Fear*, 129.

[565] David F. Musto, "Just Saying 'No' Is Not Enough," *The New York Times* October 18, 1998.

program in D.C. and the national program in general. He responded in part:

> Methadone was just horrible from a political point of view, just a total disaster...The fact that we were associated--that methadone and its expansion was associated with Nixon--that was a tremendous problem. And then there was the racial aspect of it, which was very difficult for me to deal with. Ninety percent of the patients were black. The city was seventy-one percent black, and I was obviously white. There was a charge that this was racist, that this was a form of enslaving the black, young men in the nation's cities. That was, I think, the most vicious of the anti-methadone kind of arguments. . .

> **[Frontline] What did methadone symbolize that was so terrible?**

> Enslavement. It was enslaving the black underclass. It was robbing, it was the narcotic, the opiate of the masses, being given out by the government for political purposes, to make docile the revolutionaries who were otherwise going to free themselves and change the society. That's the way people thought, what some people thought. And it was done for political purposes. I was the agent of Richard Nixon and it was anti-black, anti-poor. . .

But there is some direct evidence that *some* form of enslavement was indeed intended. Donfeld wrote in a report after returning from Jaffe's Chicago operation: "Methadone is a *benign addiction,* for it allows the addict to function normally, be employed, *pay taxes,* and stay out of jail."[566] This was the era before the boom of private prisons, so jailing someone was costly to the state and federal government; keeping undesirables *outside* but on a *chemical leash* ("[Methadone Maintenance] was a *successful* experiment in controlled availability of narcotics, a "harm reduction" measure that...held [addicts] hostage to clinic routines and brought them under clinic control."[567]) was a preferable state of affairs from the vantage point of the government. The drug prevents these Black men in particular from being rebellious or threatening in any way (makes them docile), while it allows them to *work* to...*pay the government* (taxes). The Methadone Plan was a win-win for

---

[566] Massing, **The Fix**, 103.
[567] Agar and Reisinger, "Tale of Two Policies," 387.

the Nixon Administration. Therefore, as far back as 1971 the Nation of Islam, through its publication **Muhammad Speaks**, properly warned the people against "Nixon's methadone package."

> the use of methadone perpetuates permanent addiction and guarantees that the addict is an eternal slave. Among other things, methadone attacks and dissembles the libido: it creates a metabolic lethargy, souring the individuals will and resolve – along with his sexual appetite – and his passion to strike out for self against the forces of oppression within society...it constantly assaults the centers of courage and aggressiveness...thereby potentially entombing the individual's manhood and psychologically vaulting the individual back into the womb...[568]

And I would be remiss if I did not point that the chief architects of this hideous Methadone plan were of Jewish background: Jeffery Donfeld and Jerome Jaffe.

And Richard Nixon, the apostle of law and order, was going to make treatment his principal weapon. As his general, he was enlisting a young Jewish Democratic psychiatrist with no experience in national politics. And so, at the age of thirty-seven, Jerome Jaffe was going to get a chance to apply to the nation as a whole the lessons he had learned during his long apprenticeship in Lexington, New York, and Chicago. [569]

---

[568] Leon Forrest, "Use of methadone pills perpetuates dependency," **Muhammad Speaks** March 19, 1971; idem, "Fight Nixon's methadone package," **Muhammad Speaks** December 3, 1971.
[569] Michael Massing, **The Fix** (Berkeley: University of California Press, 2000) 87.

Part III

Scientific Genocide

"The White man is a scientist. The Negro is a science project." -Dr. Wesley Muhammad

Chapter Ten

The Warning

In January 1975 the Most Honorable Elijah Muhammad revealed in **Muhammad Speaks** a plot against Black people by our 400-year enemies in America:

> At this very hour, eternal war against the Black man is planned as the Psalmist (Bible) prophesizes that they plan to destroy the poor secretly. All kinds of evil are planned against the once loyal slave of America today: in the drugs, in food and the water that the slave eats and drinks, to destroy his increase of his nation, making his women unproductive and turning her into the most disgraceful woman of the nations...[570]

Our former slave masters have secretly planned an eternal war against the Black man and woman in America, a plan that involves doing "all kinds of evil" to us through the food that we eat, the water that we drink and the drugs that we use. Speaking at the Chicago Coliseum on Saviour's Day 1966 the Honorable Elijah Muhammad gave us a little insight into *how* our enemies will execute this secret war against us:

---

[570] The Honorable Elijah Muhammad, "The Fall and Break Up of the Old World," **Muhammad Speaks** January 1975

This race of devils who has planned your destruction, who are leading you to total destruction, who want you to die and be destroyed with them, who are absolutely killing you daily and beating you for even asking them for justice...But their time is now up and they are doing everything to try to stay by planning the total termination of the Black man and they are practicing it on you today, the so-called American Negros. I even heard talk of their planning mass murder of the so-called Negros here in America. And planned to sterilize them to prevent them from continuing to produce a people like themselves. This is a plan that was made by Pharaoh (of Egypt)...they planned the total destruction of (the Children of Israel) by killing off the males. This *scientific* nation (inaudible) who have so much more *knowledge of chemistry* today (inaudible) and plan the total destruction of you and me (emphasis added – WM).

The secret war of destruction against Black America will thus be a *scientific* war that will utilize America's advanced knowledge of *chemistry* and the war aims to sterilize the Black woman and the Black man and *kill* the Black male (men and masculinity) *scientifically*, it appears from the words of the Messenger of God. He says further:

America is destroying herself in her effort to destroy her Black slave. The water and air of America are being polluted by chemico-bacteriologists. America's scientists of war conduct dreadful experiments on how best to kill human beings by the millions and wipe out the life of whole continents.[571]

Even the air that we breath is scientifically poisoned against us, says Mr. Muhammad: "In this poison world, there are scientists who are experimenting with poison and are experimenting on how to kill or maim people so that they will die later from eating the wrong foods and *from breathing this poison atmosphere.*" [572] Thus, our food, water, air and drugs were to be chemically manipulated in such a way as to render the Black Nation infertile or *non*reproductive. Muhammad Speaks:

---

[571] Muhammad, *Fall of America*, 222.
[572] Muhammad, *How to Eat To Live* II:147.

Food

This race of people experiments on everything other than good. This includes what they grow and prepare for us to eat. There is very little pure food on the market today. And, there will not be any pure food on the market tomorrow, if they prepare it for you, because they are experimenting on your life to see what can take you away and what they can keep you here with for a certain length of time.[573]

It is hard to get pure, good, healthy food for those who desire it. The enemy, the devil has poisoned everything. He has poisoned the Bible and the food that we eat. But, do the best that you can until he has been removed.[574]

This state of affairs is no accident, Muhammad reveals to us. It was done deliberately, scientifically.

It is very hard for a person who wants to eat the proper food to find anything like good food in this poison world, so that his life may be prolonged, because such people as the scientists have poisoned the food.[575]

The poisoning of food and drinks *is done deliberately* and there is no help coming from the government to stop such demoniac, evil freedom to maim and destroy life. Our only hope for survival is in Allah, Who has power over the evil plans of the devil (emphasis added).[576]

Water

The very water we drink is polluted from filth. We make the water filthy with our own refuse and then turn around calling ourselves cleaning the water to make it fit to drink. THIS IS NOT because the government is too poor to try and see that its citizens have pure water to drink. It is not because the government is too poor that we have to eat the poor and poison foods. *They deliberately cause this drink and food to be impure* (emphasis original and added).[577]

---

[573] Muhammad, *How to Eat To Live* I:114.
[574] Muhammad, *How to Eat To Live* II:70.
[575] Muhammad, *How to Eat To Live* II:147.
[576] Muhammad, *How to Eat To Live* II:190.
[577] Muhammad, *How to Eat To Live* II:21.

Take, for instance, the use of fluoride, chloride, and sodium, which if not used correctly can destroy our entire life. Maybe it is best to find something else that will clear our water without killing both us and the poison in our food and water. The scientists should not advocate the use of such poisonous chemicals as fluoride, chloride, and sodium, which may have a bad effect on our brains and our human reproductive organs.[578] The scientist that uses such poison on human beings wants to either minimize the birth rates or cause the extinction of a people.[579]

Drugs

The use of drugs as chemical weapons in a *Testosterone Conspiracy* against the Black Man was revealed by God through the Most Honorable Elijah Muhammad before I was even born.

The poison it (tobacco) contains is called nicotine. The full extent of the poisonous nicotine has not yet been known to scientists...The poison which tobacco contains is what *pacifies the smoker*, who thinks he is feeling fine...Tobacco and alcoholic beverages also affect *the organs of reproduction of young men*. You should never use tobacco, whisky, beer or wine. They ruin the reproductive organs and *waste away the man power*. Tobacco and alcoholic beverages also have this destructive effect upon the reproductive organs of woman (emphasis added).[580]

Alcohol and tobacco, with their poisonous effect upon the male, cut his life down, as far as his reproductive organs are concerned. He is unable to produce his own kind...In a few days (years), they lose sexual desires. Tobacco and whiskey will most certainly destroy it.[581]

The "man power" that is wasted away due to the effects of nicotine (tobacco) and ethanol (alcohol) is no doubt the

---

[578] Facts. See e.g. Douglass Main, "Water Fluoridation Linked to Higher ADHD Rates," **Newsweek** March 10, 2015; Shuang Liang et al., "Sodium fluoride exposure exerts toxic effects on porcine oocyte maturation," **Sci Rep 7,** 17082 (2017): 1-14; Curtis Chubb, "Reproductive toxicity of fluoride," **Journal of Andrology** 6 (1985).
[579] Muhammad, **How to Eat To Live** I:107.
[580] Muhammad, **How to Eat To Live** I:112-113.
[581] Muhammad, **How to Eat To Live** I:82.

hormone testosterone, and in this Volume we document the truth of this claim. The diminishing of testosterone indeed pacifies a man and diminishes his sex drive. This is what weaponized drugs do to the Black man, according to the Most Honorable Elijah Muhammad. It was The Most Honorable Elijah Muhammad who warned us of the scientific assault planned for us by our enemies. *Our* job in this book is merely to document the execution of this scientific assault; in other words, provide the verification for the revelation.

Chapter Eleven

The Scientific Assault: Weaponizing The Air We Breathe

America is destroying herself in her effort to destroy her Black slave. The water and air of America are being polluted by chemico-bacteriologists. America's scientists of war conduct dreadful experiments on how best to kill human beings by the millions and wipe out the life of whole continents – The Most Honorable Elijah Muhammad, **The Fall of America**

I.   *Segregation and Scientific Racism Today*

Segregation is one of our nation's most enduring and intractable problems. More than 60 years since the Supreme Court's landmark *Brown v. Board of Education* decision denounced racial segregation in primary and secondary public schools, and 50 years since the enactment of the federal Fair Housing Act, our neighborhoods and schools have yet to reflect the rich diversity of our nation as a whole. In far too many cases, racial segregation is as severe or worse today than a generation ago. Racially segregated neighborhoods and schools are visible in every part of the United States. *Segregation seems embedded in our nation's fabric...*[582]

Segregation is embedded in the fabric of America, not only for the purposes of the *social isolation* of White people from Black people but for the purposes *of scientific isolation* as well. In 1994 sociologist Dr. Robert D. Bullard rightly invoked the image and memories of South Africa to contextualize the situation in the U.S.

Residential apartheid is the dominant housing pattern for most African Americans-the most racially segregated group in the United States-and other people of color. Nowhere is this separate-society contrast more apparent than in the nation's

---

[582] Stephen Menendian and Samir Gambhir, "Racial Segregation in the San Francisco Bay Area, Part 1," Haas Institute for a Fair and Inclusive Society (October 29, 2018), https://haasinstitute.berkeley.edu/racial-segregation-san-francisco-bay-area.

large metropolitan areas. Residential apartheid did not result from some impersonal super-structural process. White racism created American apartheid...The nation's ghettos, barrios, and reservations, *are kept isolated and contained from the larger white society* through well-defined institutional practices, private actions, and government policies (emphasis added – WM).[583]

As Dr. Kenneth B. Clark saw also, the hood is a *colony* with subject peoples contained by *invisible walls*

The dark ghetto's invisible walls have been erected by white society who have power both to confine those who have *no* power and to perpetuate their powerlessness. The dark ghettos are social, political, educational, and-above all-economic colonies. Their inhabitants are subject people, victims of the greed, cruelty, insensitivity, guilt and fear of their masters.[584]

While Black people in America, as a largely colonized group, live a life of imposed *segregation*, White people – the domestic colonizer - exist in *self-separated communities*. In 1995 Research Atlanta conducted a survey and found that 90% of Whites surveyed in metro-Atlanta expressed a willingness to move into an area with one Black household. As the number of Black households increased to eight, the percentage of willing Whites dropped to 26%.[585] The reality of life in America for Black and for White is not different today. The Brookings Institution has reported that, while the level of segregation characteristic of the "chocolate city, vanilla suburb" map has modestly declined, still "Most white residents of large metropolitan areas live in neighborhoods that remain overwhelmingly white".[586] A segregation index (from 0 = complete integration to 100 = complete segregation) shows that

---

[583] Dr. Robert D. Bullard, "The Legacy of American Apartheid and Environmental Racism," *Journal of Civil Rights and Economic Development* 9 (1994): 445-474 (445).
[584] Kenneth B. Clark, *Dark Ghetto: Dilemmas of Social Power* (New York: Harper & Row, 1965) 11.
[585] Chris Geller, Keith Ihlanfeldt, and David Sjoquist, *Atlanta in Black and White: Racial Attitudes and Perspectives* (Atlanta: Research Atlanta, Inc., 1995) 13.
[586]William H. Frey, "Black-white segregation edges downward since 2000, census shows," The Avenue, Brookings. Institution, December 17, 2018

the twelve largest metro areas still score numbers from 65 to 79. In 2013-2017, according to the Brookings Institution, the average White resident of the nation's 100 largest metropolitan areas lived in a neighborhood that was 72 percent White.

Metro areas with highest black-white segregation
2000 and 2013-2017*

2000		2013-2017	
	Segregation Index**		Segregation Index**
1 Detroit	85.7	1 Milwaukee	79.8
2 Milwaukee	83.3	2 New York	76.1
3 Chicago	81.2	3 Chicago	75.3
4 New York	79.7	4 Detroit	73.7
5 Cleveland	78.2	5 Cleveland	72.9
6 Buffalo	78.0	6 Buffalo	72.2
7 St. Louis	74.0	7 St. Louis	71.7
8 Cincinnati	73.6	8 Cincinnati	67.3
9 Indianapolis	71.7	9 Philadelphia	67.0
10 Philadelphia	71.0	10 Los Angeles	66.8
11 Kansas City	70.8	11 Pittsburgh	66.1
12 Los Angeles	70.0	12 Hartford	65.7

* Among 51 metro areas with populations exceeding one million and with black populations exceeding 3 percent of metro population (metro area names are abbreviated).
** Segregation Index is a dissimilarity index, which represents the percent of blacks that would need to relocate to be fully integrated with whites across metropolitan neighborhoods.
A value of 100 indicates complete segregation; a value of 0 equals complete integration (See values for all metro areas and further details in Table A).

THE BAY AREA AS ILLUSTRATIVE

Illustrative of the intransigence of segregation in America and its ability to *hide in plain sight* is Northern California's Bay Area. The Bay Area is remarkably diverse racially, geographically, and economically. This region of more than seven million people consists of roughly 39% White, 26 % Asian, 24 % Hispanic, 6 % Black, and 5% "other" (Native American, Pacific Islanders, mixed-race, etc.). However, this remarkable diversity masks a severe segregation:

> Only a handful of cities in the region are both diverse *and* highly integrated...The San Francisco Bay Area, like most of the United States, is deeply segregated...we find racial segregation in every county and MSA [*metropolitan* statistical area] in the region. Despite the racial diversity that exists through most of the Bay

231

Area, segregated neighborhoods exist in every part of the region, from north to south, and east to west...far too few census tracts in the region resemble the populations in the Bay Area as a whole, let alone of the counties or MSAs in which they reside...Thus, although these cities are diverse in aggregate, they tend to contain some of the most racially segregated non-white neighborhoods in the Bay Area." [587]

To the extent that integration *does* exist in the Bay, it is *people of color* that are more or less integrated with *each other*.[588] Whites on the other hand are the most *(self-) separated* and *segregating* (colonizing) racial group. Whites make up over 50% of the population in 1206 of the 1582 census tracts that characterize the region. In 543 of the census tracts Whites constitute from 66% to over 75% of the population. On the other hand, African Americans are the most racially concentrated and segregated group in the Bay Area: 75% of the Bay's Black residents reside in just 26% of the region's census tracts, such as Hunter's Point in San Francisco and the flatlands of East Oakland and West Oakland. Oakland itself is exceptionally diverse (28% Hispanic, 27% White, 23% Black, 15% Asian) while containing *"some of the most segregated neighborhoods in the Bay Area."*[589] These patterns of segregation are the consequence of exclusionary policies and private housing discrimination. This forced segregation allows for the easy targeting of the group.

---

[587] Stephen Menendian and Samir Gambhir, "Racial Segregation in the San Francisco Bay Area, Part 1," Haas Institute for a Fair and Inclusive Society (October 29, 2018), https://haasinstitute.berkeley.edu/racial-segregation-san-francisco-bay-area.

[588] Menendian and Gambhir, "Racial Segregation in the San Francisco Bay Area, Part 1."

[589] Menendian and Gambhir, "Racial Segregation in the San Francisco Bay Area, Part 1."

II.   *Life and Death in White and Black*

A recent report from City Lab is revealing: "Life Expectancy Is Associated With Segregation in U.S. Cities."[590] It was found that in cities with the clearest lines of segregation, life expectancy shows the greatest gap between the segregated communities, a difference that can equal 20 to 30 years. For example, in Chicago which ranked just below Milwaukee and New York in the 2013-2017 Segregation Index with a score of 75.3

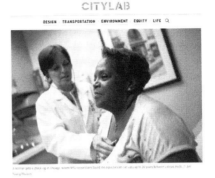

CITYLAB

Life Expectancy Is Associated With Segregation in U.S. Cities

SARAH HOLDER / DAVID MONTGOMERY   JUN 6, 2019

"Your neighborhood shouldn't influence your odds of seeing your grandchildren grow up," says a researcher for NYU's new analysis of City Health Dashboard data.

(between 0 = complete integration and 100 = complete sgregation), there is a *30 year life expectancy gap between Whites on the North side and African Americans on the South and West sides!* This means that northside Whites live on average 30 years longer than south- and westside African Americans. In segregated San Francisco there is a 25 year gap between segregated Black and self-seperated White populations. This is in contrast to San Jose, California - said to be the most-integrated metropolitan region in the Bay Area - where we don't see the same stark color divisions in terms of life expectany gap, because even in the worst-off neighborhoods of San Jose the average lifespan is near 80 years old. This is because *the magnitude of racial/ethnic segregation leads to the life expectancy gap.*[591]

There is a *cloud of living* that hovers over White communities and over "integreated" communities like San Jose, from which even poor people there benefit: "a Harvard analysis found that residents of rich neighborhoods <u>live on average 15 years longer</u> than residents of poor neighborhoods, and that

---

[590] Sarah Holder and David Montgomery, "Life Expectancy Is Associated With Segregation in U.S. Cities," **CitiLab** June 6, 2016.
[591] Holder and Montgomery, "Life Expectancy Is Associated With Segregation in U.S. Cities."

even lower-income residents of wealthy neighborhoods live longer than others in poorer ones."[592] That is because with this *spatial determinism* that characterizes American society the *determining* factor is race first, socioeconomic status second. "While there are some very poor white neighborhoods in Appalachia and some older rust belt cities, 75% of poor whites in the United States live in predominantly middle-income neighborhoods."[593]

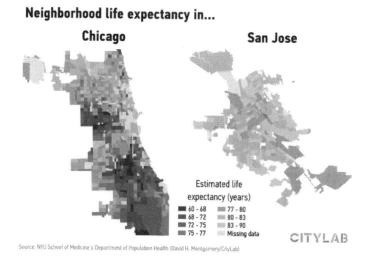

Neighborhood life expectancy in...

Source: NYU School of Medicine's Department of Population Health (David H. Montgomery/CityLab)

In America, Whites have (scientifically) insured that *clouds of living* hover over their seperated communites (even if they permit others within it) and *clouds of death* hover over segregated Black communities (with the poorest of whites who live there as acceptable casualties of war).

Segregation is so "embedded in the nation's fabric" because it serves Whites not only a *social* purpose but also a *scientific purpose*. Segregation creates localized geographic areas that can be targeted. Segregation provides *concentrated Blackness*. When I use the language *cloud of death*, I am being quite literal. The concentration of Black and Brown people into

---

[592] Holder and Montgomery, "Life Expectancy Is Associated With Segregation in U.S. Cities."

[593] Myron Orfield, "Segregation and Environmental Justice," 7 **Minnesota Journal of Law, Science & Technology** 7 (2005): 147-160 (148).

segregated areas and the self-separation of White people from those areas allow for *the easy and efficient targeting of Black People with chemical poisoning of the air, food, and water while hermitically sealing affluent White (and "integrated") communities off from the poisons and the consequences of the poisoning.* Thus, the life expectancy gaps between Black and White people.

Max life expectancy gap between neighborhoods

Among 50 largest U.S. cities.

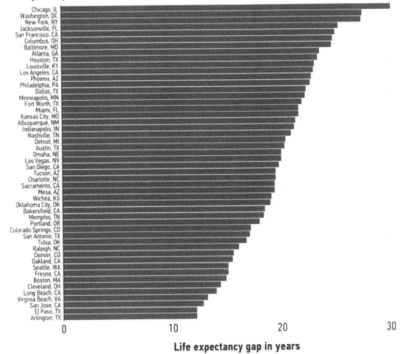

Source: NYU School of Medicine's Department of Population Health (David H. Montgomery / CityLab)

III. *Clouds of Death*

If one seeks evidence that Black zip codes have been scientifically targeted, we need go no further than the example of the *air* breathed in by the residents of segregated Black neighborhoods. And if the *air* is weaponized, how about the food? As ***Scientific American*** reported in 2012:

> Tiny particles of air pollution contain more hazardous ingredients in non-white and low-income communities than in affluent white ones, a new study shows. The greater the concentration of Hispanics, Asians, African Americans or poor residents in an area, the more likely that potentially dangerous compounds such as vanadium, nitrates and zinc are in the mix of fine particles they breath.[594]

Dr. Robert Bullard documented in his important work ***Dumping in Dixie*** that communities of color *are deliberately and consistently sought out for toxic dumping*, thus hazardous waste sites and other polluting facilities are likely to be deliberately placed near poor, Black and Brown areas, resulting in heavily polluted local environments.[595] In 2012 Yale University researchers found that in segregated cities with

---

[594]Cheryl Katz, "People in Poor Neighborhoods Breathe More Hazardous Particles," ***Scientific American*** November 1, 2012.
[595] Robert D. Bullard, ***Dumping in Dixie: Race, class, and environmental quality*** (Boulder, CO: Westview, 1990).

concentrations of poor Black and Brown residents like Los Angeles, St. Louis, etc., the air is most polluted with fine *particulate matter* (PM), which is microscopic particles suspended in the air from diesel fuel emissions, smog, soot, oil, ash, construction dust, etc. and when inhaled can penetrate deep into the lungs and are linked to asthma, cardiovascular disease and cancer. The most pervasive air pollutant is called $PM_{2.5}$. The researchers found that, of the 14 components[596] of $PM_{2.5}$, "non-Hispanic blacks had higher exposures than whites for 13 of the 14 components" and "Non-Hispanic whites had the lowest estimated exposure for 11 of the 14 components."[597] How convenient.

The researchers found that the profile of those with the highest exposure of $PM_{2.5}$ was "non-Hispanic black, the least educated, the unemployed, and those in poverty." In an assessment of whether geographic areas are in compliance with the National Ambient Air Quality Standards (NAAQS) which regulates air pollutant emissions, Miranda et al. found in 2011 that "non-Hispanic blacks are consistently overrepresented in communities with the poorest air quality (re: $PM_{2.5}$ and ozone exposure)."[598] The Environmental Protection Agency (EPA) itself in 2018 also confirmed that "results at national, state, and county scales all indicate that non-Whites tend to be burdened [by fine particulate matter] disproportionately to Whites," and that *race* is a stronger variable in this situation than poverty: *segregated* Black people[599] suffer long-term exposure to 1.5

---

[596] The researchers investigated the levels of sulfate ($SO_4{}^{2-}$), nitrate (NO_3), ammonium ($NH_4{}^+$), organic carbon matter (OCM), elemental carbon (EC), sodium ion (NA^+), aluminum (AI), calcium (Ca), chlorine (Cl), nickel (Ni), silicon (Si), titanium (Ti), vanadium (V), and zinc (Zn).

[597] Michelle L. Bell and Keita Ebisu, "Environmental Inequality in Exposures to Airborne Particulate Matter Components in the United States," **Environmental Health Perspectives** 120 (2012): 1699-1704.

[598] Marie Lynn Miranda et al., "Making the Environmental Grade: The Relative Burden of Air Pollution Exposure in the United States," **Int. J. Environ. Res. Public Health** 8 (2011): 1755-1771.

[599] Cheryl Katz, "People in Poor Neighborhoods Breathe More Hazardous Particles," **Scientific American** November 1, 2012: "The risks (of exposure) increase with degree of segregation in all racial and ethnic groups"; "Cities that are more segregated, you see higher pollution burdens for residents of color."

times more particulate matter than Whites.[600] Very importantly it was found that, while people of color *suffer* air pollution, it is largely *affluent White people who cause* that air pollution in segregated Black and Brown areas! Christopher W. Tessum et al. found that

> in the United States, $PM_{2.5}$ exposure is disproportionately caused by consumption of goods and services mainly by the non-Hispanic white majority, but disproportionately inhaled by black and Hispanic minorities.[601]

So it is affluent White society that created the clouds of death that hover over Black America, from which they themselves are largely separated and thus protected. As Bullard explains:

> Environmental racism is real. It is just as real as the racism found in housing, education, employment, and the political arena...Environmental racism combines with public policies and industry practices to provide *benefits* for whites while shifting *costs* to people of color...In the United States, race has been found to be independent of class in the exposure to lead, harmful pesticides, location of municipal landfills and incinerators, abandoned toxic waste dumps, and environmental protection and cleanup of Superfund sites.[602]

Again, the Bay Area is illustrative. People of color (Black, Hispanic, Asian) comprise 93% of East Oakland and 85% of West Oakland. Whites are 6.7% and 15.4% respectively. It is the highest poverty neighborhoods of Alameda County (Oakland is the county seat) that are the *darkest* (ethnically) and suffer the poorest health outcomes. This is because "Low-income neighborhoods and communities of color are often unjustly burdened by a disproportionate number of hazardous facilities

---

[600] Vann R. Newkirk II, "Trump's EPA Concludes Environmental Racism is Real," *The Atlantic* February 28, 2018.
[601] Christopher W. Tessum et al., "Inequality in consumption of goods and services adds to racial-ethnic disparities in air pollution exposure," *PNAS* 116 (2019): 6001-6006.
[602] Bullard, "The Legacy of American Apartheid," 452.

that pollute the air, ground water and soil with toxic contaminants."[603]

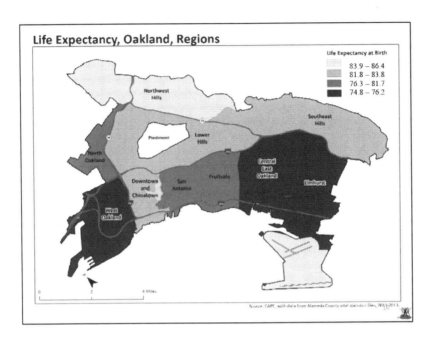

In Alameda County the density of industrial chemical and fuel release sites in high poverty neighborhoods is 4 times higher than in affluent neighborhoods. Thus, low-income Black and Brown communities of East and West Oakland disproportionately suffer from chronic disease complications and deaths. "East and West Oakland have some of the highest Emergency Department (ED) and hospitalization rates than both Oakland overall and Alameda County overall for causes that are linked to air pollution, including childhood asthma, overall asthma, and congestive heart failure."[604] Black people in East and West Oakland thus have the highest all-cause death rates in Oakland and in Alameda County overall. A White child born in the affluent Oakland Hills is expected to live 12.4 years

---

[603] *East and West Oakland Health Data Existing Cumulative Health Impacts*, Report from the Alameda County Public Health Department, September 3, 2015.
[604] *East and West Oakland Health Data Existing Cumulative Health Impacts*, Report from the Alameda County Public Health Department, September 3, 2015.

longer than a Black child born in West Oakland and 14 years longer that a Black child born in East Oakland.

> In Alameda County, the opportunity to live a long, healthy, and productive life is not evenly distributed throughout the County...with East and West Oakland populations living shorter lives on average. People living in the Northwest Hills can expect to live one decade or more longer than people living in West Oakland, Elmhurst, or Central East Oakland.

Atlanta, the "Black Mecca," is likewise illustrative of this *chemical war waged by zip code.* Central Atlanta has become increasingly Black and poor, encircled by middle-income, largely White suburbs. Even in the suburbs, though, African Americans are segregated from and by Whites.[605] The Black neighborhoods scattered across the urban landscape of metro Atlanta are deliberately made "toxic".

> According to the EPA's toxic release inventory data, African Americans and other people of color are disproportionately represented in the Atlanta region's "dirtiest" zip codes. While people of color comprise 29.8% of the population in the five largest counties contiguous to Atlanta (Fulton, DeKalb, Cobb, Gwinnett, and Clayton counties), they represent the majority of residents in five of the ten "dirtiest" zip codes in these large counties. Atlanta metro residents living in predominantly white areas are exposed to an average of 38.2 pounds of toxic releases per person annually, compared to an average of 208.6 pounds of toxic releases per person in majority minority locales. The "dirtiest" area (*i.e.* zip code 30354) in the five-county area is located in Fulton County and receives over 1.55 million pounds of toxic releases annually. Over 69% of the population of this area is composed of people of color. Another area which is predominantly black (98.2%), zip code 30336, is subjected to 879.9 pounds of toxic releases *per person* annually (emphasis added)."[606]

---

[605] Robert D. Bullard, Glenn S. Johnson and Angel O. Torres, "The Costs and Consequences of Suburban Sprawl: The Case of Metro Atlanta," **Georgia State University Law Review** 17 (Summer, 2001): 935-998 (946)

[606] Bullard, Johnson and Torres, "The Costs and Consequences of Suburban Sprawl," 958.

This is chemical warfare by zip code: "Overall, the zip codes with the highest percent minority population also had the highest total outputs of pollution per resident."[607] Thus, while Fulton County, which is 60.5% Black and Brown, receives 4.7 million pounds of total toxic releases annually (7.23 pounds per person), Gwinnett County, which is 89.1% White, receives only 290,930 pounds of total toxic releases annually (0.82 pounds per person).

Understanding The Scientific Assault Against Black America!

IV.   *Gender Neutering By Air*

And what are some of the health consequences of this excessive exposure (scientific assault) of segregated Black people to air pollution caused by self-separated White people? Among those listed above (asthma, cardiovascular disease, and cancer), we can add infertility, gender neutering, and less Black males being born into the world viz-a-viz Black females (an altered sex ratio at birth).

$PM_{2.5}$ is an endocrine disrupter. The Endocrine Society announced that particulate air pollution was linked with reduced sperm production in mice and this may be relevant to rising infertility rates among humans.[608] Exposure to $PM_{2.5}$ – which Black people in segregated America suffer disproportionately from – can cause testicular tubes to deteriorate and epigenetically alter genes related to testicular cell function, thus leading to poor sperm quality. A robust association has thus been reported between exposure to $PM_{2.5}$ and the decrease in normal sperm morphology.[609]

Parental (maternal and paternal) exposure to air pollution derived from diesel exhaust, often a component of particulate matter, is associated with altered sexual differentiation of the fetus. It was shown that diesel exhaust inhalation by pregnant lab rats can disrupt the development of

---

[607] Bullard, Johnson and Torres, "The Costs and Consequences of Suburban Sprawl," 960.

[608] Endocrine Society, "Particulate air pollution linked with reduced sperm production in mice," *Current Press Releases* March 24, 2019.

[609] Xiang Qian Lao et al., "Exposure to ambient fine particulate matter and semen quality in Taiwan," **Occup Environ Med** 75 (2018): 148-154.

the immune system and the reproductive organs of the fetus as well as *masculinize the female fetus* by the excessive elevation of maternal testosterone and decrease of maternal estradiol and progesterone.[610]

This air pollution can interfere with sex distribution (number of males-to-females) by altering testicular function in pollution-exposed males leading to an excess of X sperm production and to a reduction in the proportion of Y/X bearing sperm, thus lowering the Y:X sperm chromosome ratio. This then results in *fewer Black male births.*[611] All of this, the air quality that characterizes segregated Black areas can cause and no doubt *does* cause.

Another example of a hazardous air pollutant that disproportionately affects Black zip codes and can often be traced to U.S. military activity is polychlorinated biphenyls or PCBs. Banned in 1979, PCBs were used in insulating fluids to prevent fire in transformers and other electrical equipment. Along with being linked with cancer, asthma, and immune suppression, PCBs are endocrine disrupters. They have been known to interfere with the action of the thyroid gland and hormone and cause thyroid disease and disfunction.[612] In males PCBs are estrogenic and anti-androgenic (testosterone is the main "androgen" or *masculinizing* hormone) and in females they are anti-estrogenic.[613] "Exposure to PCBs has long been associated with reproductive disfunction in humans, including

---

[610] Nobue Watanabe and Masayuki Kurita, "The Masculinization of the Fetus During Pregnancy Due to Inhalation of Diesel Exhaust," *Environmental Health Perspectives* 109 (2001): 111-119.

[611] MichaÑ Radwan et al., "Air Pollution and Human Sperm Sex Ratio," *American Journal of Men's Health* 12 (2018): 907-912.

[612] Kelly J. Gauger et al., " Polychlorinated Biphenyls (PCBs) Exert Thyroid Hormone-like Effects in the Fetal Rat Brain but Do Not Bind to Thyroid Hormone Receptors," *Environmental Health Perspectives* 112 (2004): 516ff; Valerie J. Brown, "Blocking Brain Development: How PCBs Disrupt Thyroid Hormone," *Environmental Health Perspective* 113 (2005): A472–A473; R. Thomas Zoeller, "Polychlorinated Biphenyls as Disruptors of Thyroid Hormone Action," in *PCBs* ed. Robertson and Hansen 2001, The University Press of Kentucky, 2001) 265-271.

[613] Risheng Ma and David A. Sassoon, "PCBs Exert an Estrogenic Effect through Repression of the *Wnt7a* Signaling Pathway in the Female Reproductive Tract," *Environmental Health Perspectives* 114 (2006): 898-904.

decreased sperm motility, decrease in fecundity, earlier menarche, altered sex ratio, and altered gonadal hormones in newborns."[614] Sexual differentiation of the female neuroendocrine systems can be masculinized/defeminized and reproductive maturation disrupted (by masculinizing the hypothalamic neurons of the female brain that control reproduction). In men PCB exposure is correlated with reduced testosterone[615] and it influences childhood play behavior: prenatal PCB levels were related with less masculinized play in boys later and more masculinized play in girls, indicating prenatal and perinatal disruption of neurological sexual differentiation.[616] Finally, maternal exposure to PCBs may decrease the sex ratio of offspring (less boys, more girls).[617]

Urban Black America is hit the hardest with PCB exposure. "Despite a ban on U.S. production since 1979, urban centers such as Chicago still provide a site for slow release of PCBs into the environment today."[618] Indeed, "airborne PCBs in Chicago are widely present and elevated in residential communities,"[619] i.e. *Black residential communities*. In East Chicago, Indiana, which is 20 minutes from Downtown Chicago and 92% Black and Hispanic with 36% poor, the U.S. Army Chemical Corps dredged a highly contaminated canal along the shore of Lake Michigan consciously doubling the amount of

---

[614] Margaret R. Bell, "Endocrine-disrupting actions of PCBs on brain development and social and reproductive behaviors," **Curr Opin Pharmacol.** 19 (2014): 134-144.

[615] Sara M. Dickerson et al., "Endocrine Disruption of Brain Sexual Differentiation by Developmental PCB Exposure," **Endocrinology** 15 (2011): 581-594.

[616] Hestien J.I. Vreugdenhil et al., "Effects of Prenatal Exposure to PCBs and Dioxins on Play Behavior in Dutch Children at School Age," **Environmental Health Perspective** 110 (2002): A593-A598.

[617] Marc G. Weisskopf et al., "Decreased sex ratio following maternal exposure to polychlorinated biphenyls from contaminated Great Lakes sport-caught fish: a retrospective cohort study," **Environmental Health: A Global Access Science Source** 2 (2003): 1-14.

[618] Joseph E. McGraw Sr. and Donald P. Waller, "The Role of African American Ethnicity and Metabolism in Sentinel Polychlorinated Biphenyl Congener Serum Levels," **Environ Toxicol Pharmacol** 27 (2009): 1-24.

[619] Dingfei Hu et al., "Atmospheric PCB congers across Chicago," **Atmos Environ** 44 (2010): 1550-1557.

PCB pollution in the air to which these poor Black residents are subjected.[620] In the Bay Area as well, "San Francisco Bay is facing a legacy of polychlorinated biphenyls (PCBs) spread widely across the land surface of the watershed, mixed deep into the sediment of the Bay, and contaminating the Bay food web to a degree that poses health risks to humans and wildlife."[621] Thus, when a cohort study of 399 women who were pregnant between 1963-1967 was conducted, it was found that Black women from the San Francisco Bay Area had the highest level of PCBs detected in their blood.[622] Studies also found that pregnant Black women in Chicago also had a higher level of certain PCBs in their blood, indicating a greater level of airborne PCB exposure.[623]

V.   *The Military Poisons the Air*

It can be proved that much of the toxic pollutants composing the *clouds of death* hovering over segregated Black neighborhoods was deliberately introduced there as chemical and biological agents of and by the U.S. Government. In 1952 the CIA entered into a partnership with the Army to produce *offensive* chemical and biological weapons. The joint CIA-Army program was codenamed MK-NAOMI and was a part of MK-ULTRA. In 1955 and 1956 MK-NAOMI targeted two black housing communities with offensive biological weapons. In Carter Village in Miami, Florida and in Carter Village in Chatham County, Georgia – both black housing complexes – swarms of *Aedes aegypti* mosquitos bred by the Army Chemical Corps at Fort Detrick, Maryland laboratories and carrying both yellow fever and dengue fever were unleashed into the air on the

---

[620] Brian Bienkowski, "Dredging Could Unleash PCBs in Indiana Community," **Scientific American** December 5, 2012.
[621] J.A. Davis et al., "Polychlorinated biphenyls (PCBs) in San Francisco Bay," **Environment Research** 105 (2007): 67-86.
[622] Rebecca A. James et al., "Determinants of Serum Polychlorinated Biphenyls and Organochlorine Pesticides Measured in Women from the Child Health and Development Study Cohort, 1963–1967," **Environmental Health Research** 110 (2002): 617-624.
[623] J.E. McGraw and D.P. Waller, "Fish ingestion and congener specific polychlorinated biphenyl and p,p'-dichlorodiphenyldichloroethylene serum concentrations in a great lakes cohort of pregnant African American women," **Environ Int.** 35 (2009): 557-565.

black residents.[624] The purpose of this experiment was to test the effectiveness of the mosquitos as disease vectors to be used as first-strike biological weapons against "the Soviets." 1,080 Miami residents alone came down with whooping cough, some died. This spike in local disease and death convinced the MK-NAOMI operatives that the infected mosquitos indeed made effective bioweapons.

For sixteen years (1950-1966) U.S. Army scientists, as part of their germ warfare experiments, deliberately released the bacteria *Serratia marcescens* into the air of eight cities and military installations and then monitored the bacteria's spread. The bacterium was grown in Oakland, California at the U.S. Naval Biological Laboratory and tested in the Bay. In San Francisco, the Army scientists wanted to know if the Bay Area winds would carry the germs into the city. After the bacteria's release military personnel took air samples for testing. Within a week, San Francisco residents developed rare infections and at least one died. In another experiment conducted in the Bay code-named Operation Seaspray, the bacterium was put is a paste and then dropped into the water. The idea was to see if the breaking waves would toss the germs into the air where the winds would carry them into San Francisco or Oakland. The germs were carried into Berkeley and Oakland.[625]

In St. Louis, which has a 71.1 Segregation Index, the Army conducted secret biological weapons testing in impoverished Black neighborhoods in the mid-1950s and 1960s by using motorized blowers atop a low-income housing high-rise, at schools, and from the back of station wagons to send potentially dangerous chemical compounds – zinc cadmium sulfide - into the air in predominantly Black areas of St. Louis.[626] Residents also remember the Army using planes to drop a powdery substance down on the landscape *and on the inhabitants*. Thousands of people were unwillingly exposed so that the Army could "test" the health effects of one of their potential chemical-biological warfare agents. The Army used the claim of a "Russian-threat" as a smoke screen and lied even

---

[624] Washington, **Medical Apartheid**, 359-365.
[625] "Army Tested Biological War in S.F." **Newsday** December 22, 1976.
[626] "Secret Cold War tests in St. Louis cause worry," **CBS News** October 3, 2012.

to local officials regarding the true nature of their activities in these segregated Black neighborhoods.

The point of all of this? If the U.S. Government would *deliberately poison the air* of segregated Black communities, it would not hesitate to deliberately poison the food that *they* provide to segregated Black neighborhoods. As we saw, the U.S. government has been in the business of poisoning food to cause infertility and sending poisoned food secretly to communities for a long time.

Chapter Twelve

Waging War By Zip Code: Weaponizing The Food We Eat

This is the secret knowledge of the death they caused us to suffer through foods. - The Honorable Elijah Muhammad, **How To Eat To Live**

I.   *Scientific Genocide Through Food*

In 2013, the Honorable Minister Louis Farrakhan delivered an historic series of revelatory broadcasts entitled "The Time and What Must Be Done." In Part No. 36, "Farming is the Engine of Our National Life," he gives profound insight into the *operationalization* of this plot which his Teacher, the Most Honorable Elijah Muhammad, had warned us all of in 1975. The Honorable Minister Farrakhan said:

We are completely dependent on somebody else to feed us; and the Honorable Elijah Muhammad said, "No people can be free with their mouth in the kitchen of another, particularly, in the kitchen of our former slave masters and their children"... And you know, they don't know what to do with us. We've become a problem, nearly fifty million of us. They won't be able provide jobs for us. So many White scientists are thinking, what can we do with the Negroes?

Well, during my 2012 Saviours' Day message, we spoke on a plan by the government of the United States led by Dr. Henry Kissinger to engage in worldwide depopulation of the darker peoples of the world. Mr. Kissinger as Secretary of State under President Nixon signed National Security Study Memorandum 200 titled, "Implications of Worldwide Population Growth for U.S. Security Overseas Interests." It was adopted as official policy in 1975 by President Gerald Ford. Those who analyzed the report said, "Dr. Kissinger proposed that depopulation should be the highest priority of U.S. foreign policy toward the Third World." Think about that.

Although this plan of action was to be activated in developing countries, it was designed as a two-edged sword that could be swung with equal determination in both developed and developing countries alike because in developing countries, like America, a growing number of Third World people live.

This document was signed by Henry Kissinger and directed to the Secretaries of Defense, Agriculture, Central Intelligence and the Deputy Secretary of State, and the Administrator of the Agency for International Development with a copy to the Joint Chiefs of Staff. This was taken like a theatre of war and all factions of government were introduced to this to develop plans and activate plans internationally to cull between two to three billion people from the face of the earth.

Well, Kissinger prepared yet another depopulation manifesto for President Jimmy Carter called, "Global 2000," which detailed **using food as a weapon** to depopulate the Third World. So then Zbigniew Brzezinski, I think he was Carter's National Security Advisor said, "It's easier to kill a million people today than to control a million people." So the killing of millions is going on. Let's see what is happening to us.

These groups: The Department of Defense, Agriculture, CIA, Agency for International Development and the Joint Chiefs of Staff, I'm sorry to tell you, they're planning death on a worldwide scale. They have used a series of methods to affect global depopulation, depleted uranium bombs, genetically engineered and modified foods, chemical additives in foods, poison in vaccines, famine, AIDS, Chemtrails, illegal wars. This plan for culling the population is not only in the Third World, but it comes right back home to the United States of America...

The importance of this data is: When we juxtapose the decrease in farming with this Memorandum 200 by Kissinger and the culling of the population of the planet with a policy of population control or depopulation in the United States, then we can see now **how food is used as a weapon** in that process. Then the control of the means of production of food and the methodology in producing the food, all of this is a part of the policy now of the Department of Agriculture, the FDA, the CIA, they are all linked together.

This Part III documents how the U.S. Government and allied interests actually *executed this plot* that the Most Honorable Elijah Muhammad warned us of in 1975 and the Honorable Minister Farrakhan shined great light upon for us in 2013. Specifically, it can be demonstrated that the food made available in Black neighborhoods – fast food, supermarket food, even fished food - has been deliberately, chemically poisoned. Poisoned by whom? By U.S. Government agencies (examples include the Department of Agriculture, the U.S. Army and the C.I.A.) and allied interests such as the Monsanto Chemical Company, just to name a single example. Black America is indeed being deliberately sterilized through our food, our water, our drugs, even our air. The result today is the many aspects of Black America's current *Health Crisis*: a cancer crisis, autism spectrum disorder, ADHD, an obesity epidemic, a disproportionately high rate of infertility as well as male feminization and female masculinization in Black America, among other conditions. This can all, in large measure, be traced back to the food made available to Black communities and to which we avail ourselves. To put it bluntly, our food has been *weaponized* against us.

II.   *Food as Chemical Warfare*

This race of people experiments on everything other than good. This includes what they grow and prepare for us to eat. There is very little pure food on the market today. And, there will not be any pure food on the market tomorrow, if they prepare it for you, because they are experimenting on your life to see what can take you away and what they can keep you here with for a certain length of time. - The Most Honorable Elijah Muhammad, **How To Eat To Live**

In pursuit of their MK-ULTRA psychochemicals the CIA assembled "an extensive network of non-governmental scientists and facilities" to conduct much of this unethical and even *illegal* research and weaponization of chemical and biological agents. This network involved 80 institutions, including 44 colleges and universities.[627] "The mind control experiments were conducted by a network of doctors that included leaders of psychiatry and the major medical schools."[628] The CIA funded these "CIA Doctors" by clandestinely channeling money through private medical foundations and military offices, such as the Office of Naval Research.[629]

> There was an "urgent need," the C.I.A. and other agencies argued, to develop "effective and practical techniques" to "render an individual subservient to an imposed will or control." The C.I.A. men, who led the way, enlisting the support of the Army, the Navy, the Air Force, *the Departments of Agriculture, Health, Education, and Welfare* and several other agencies, acknowledged among themselves that much of what they were setting out to do was "unethical," bordered on the illegal and would be repugnant to the American people. So they made certain that these activities were tightly held, known only to the director, Allen W. Dulles, and a handful of operatives and high-ranking aides.[630]

The use of the Department of Health, Education and Welfare (HEW) by the CIA is important to our discussion, as is the use by the CIA of the Department of Agriculture. Not to be left out, the Food and Drug Administration (FDA), claiming to be "The Nation's Foremost Consumer Protection Agency," in fact assisted the CIA's secret mind and behavior control program; indeed, the FDA is described as the CIA's "junior partner."[631] The CIA's "junior partner" the FDA allowed the CIA

---

[627] Jo Thomas, "Extent of University Work for C.I.A. Is Hard to Pin Down," *The New York Times* October 9, 1977.

[628] Colin A. Cross, M.D., ***The C.I.A. Doctors: Human Rights Violations By American Psychiatry*** (Richardson, TX: Manitou, Inc., 2006) 33.

[629] Nicholas Horrock, "Private Institutions Used in C.I.A. Effort to Control Behavior," *The New York Times* August 2, 1977.

[630] "Mind-Control Studies Had Origins in Trial of Mindszentry," *The New York Times* August 2, 1977.

[631] John Marks, ***The Search for the "Manchurian Candidate": The CIA and Mind Control*** (New York: W.W. Norton & Company, 1979) 73; Martin A. Lee and Bruce Shlain, ***Acid Dreams. The Complete Social History of LSD: The CIA, the Sixties, and Beyond*** (New York: Grove Weidenfeld, 1985) 26.

to test its chemical and biological agents in its laboratories and testing facilities.[632] The Department of Agriculture aided the CIA mind-control program by importing "various botanicals" that could be tested as behavior modification agents.

Why solicit the aid of the Department of Agriculture and the FDA? The CIA sought **"a way to manufacture food that looked and tasted normal but, when eaten, would create 'confusion-anxiety-fear'."**[633] We are talking about *weaponized food* here. We know that the CIA is squarely in the business of weaponizing food and releasing it upon an unsuspecting population. In August 1951 the inhabitants of the quiet village of Pont-Saint-Esprit in southern France suddenly fell ill, struck down with mass insanity and frightful hallucinations of terrifying beasts and fire. Five people died, dozens were interned in asylums, and hundreds were afflicted. For 50 years it was assumed that the outbreak was inadvertently caused by a local baker who unknowingly served the villagers bread contaminated with ergot, the hallucinogenic mould that infects rye grain. In fact, the local bread was *deliberately contaminated with LSD by the CIA and the US Army as part of a human chemical warfare experiment.*[634]

The U.S. Government has openly considered such chemical manipulation of food to increase infertility in populations of color, domestic and foreign, as a solution to the alleged "population crisis." A 1969 *The New York Times* article says enough:

> A possibility that the government might have to put sterility drugs in reservoirs and in food shipped to foreign countries to limit human multiplication was envisioned today by a leading crusader on the population problem. [635]

---

632 John Jacobs, "CIA Papers Detail Secret Experiments on Behavior Control," *The Washington Post* July 21, 1977.
633 "Mind-Control Studies Had Origins in Trial of Mindszentry," *The New York Times* August 2, 1977.
634 H.P. Albarelli Jr., *A Terrible Mistake: The Murder of Frank Olson and the CIA's Secret Cold War Experiments* (Walterville, OR: Trine Day LLC, 2009).
635 Gladwin Hill, "A Sterility Drug in Food is Hinted," *The New York Times* November 25, 1969.

On November 24, 1969 the 13th National Conference of the U.S. UNESCO (United Nations Educational, Scientific, and Cultural Organization) Commission was held in New York City. UNESCO is a 100-member commission consisting of representatives of Government, outside organizations, and the public, but appointed by the U.S.

A STERILITY DRUG IN FOOD IS HINTED

Biologist Stresses Need to Curb Population Growth

By GLADWIN HILL
Special to The New York Times

SAN FRANCISCO, Nov. 24 —A possibility that the Government might have to put sterility drugs in reservoirs and in food shipped to foreign countries to limit human multiplication was envisioned today by a leading crusader on the population problem.

Secretary of State. This 13th National Conference was keynoted by President Richard Nixon's chief science advisor Dr. Lee DuBridge, who introduced the discussion of the global and domestic "population crisis" and called for zero population growth rate. President Nixon had already pointed to the "underprivileged (read: "the poor" and "the Blacks") in America as birth control targets.[636] Dr. DuBridge admonished that population control should be the prime task of every government. Dr. Paul Ehrlich of Stanford University declared,

> Our first move must be to convince all those we can that the planet Earth must be viewed as a spaceship *of limited carrying capacity*. I think that 150 million people (50 million fewer than there are now) would be an optimum number to live comfortably in the United States.

So a reduction of the 1969 American population by 50 million is here envisioned. The methods entertained during the discussion included compulsory family regulation, changing tax laws to discourage reproduction, and even *"the addition of a temporary sterilant to staple food, or to the water supply"*.[637] Staple foods. This could be done by "doctoring foods sent to underdeveloped countries," but other nations "already are suspicious of our motives," said Dr. Ehrlich. But the American Negro is not sufficiently suspicious of his 400-year open enemy so that method will work domestically. In any case, according to Dr. Ehrlich these draconian methods are a better "alternative to

---

[636] Hill, "A Sterility Drug in Food is Hinted."
[637] Hill, "A Sterility Drug in Food is Hinted."

Armageddon." "Every human institution – school, university, church, family, government and international agencies such as Unesco – should set [retarding population growth] as its prime task."

In 1977 Dr. Paul Ehrlich co-authored with his wife Ann and John Holdren the book, *Ecoscience: Population, Resources, Environment* in which they at least entertained or even endorsed the use of such horrifying measures to reduce population as compulsory abortions as well as the sterilizing of segments of the population by introducing drugs into the water supply and their staple foods. Who is John Holdren? He later became President Barack Obama's Science Czar, appointed Director of the White House Office of Science and Technology and Co-Chair of the President's Council of Advisors on Science and Technology.

We thus see that the Government has never been shy about "doctoring" food with chemicals that could induce infertility, just as the Most Honorable Elijah Muhammad warned our enemies would do.

III. *Weaponized Food, Vaccines and the AIDS Epidemic: The U.S. and South African Collaboration*

In the early 1980s, fears of a "black tidal wave" drove white scientists to try to develop a variety of means that could ensure the survival of white South Africa...[R]eportedly part of Project Coast was genetic engineering research, which was being conducted to produce a "black bomb," bacteria or other biological agents that would kill or weaken blacks not whites. The black bomb could be used to wipe out or incapacitate an entire area where an insurrection was taking place.[638]

If we *really* want to know what the U.S. Government is capable of vis-à-vis Black people, study the evils of apartheid South Africa, because the mind (and actions) of the apartheid regime mirror the mind (and actions) of its biggest allies, supporters and tutors: America and Israel. The US, Israel and South Africa worked closely together because they all shared the same problem: their most immediate enemy to be disposed of

[638] Dr. Stephen Burgess and Dr. Helen Purkitt, *The Rollback of South Africa's Chemical and Biological Warfare Program* (Maxwell Air Force Base, Alabama: Air University, 2001) 21.

was not another nation-state threatening them from outside. Rather, in all three cases the real enemy threat came from *pockets of ethnic populations within their own borders*. The U.S. propped up the horrifically racist apartheid regime of South Africa (and Israel) for decades and the US repressed the anti-apartheid movement in South Africa. In fact, it was the CIA who tipped off the apartheid government of the whereabouts of Nelson Mandela, leading to his capture in 1962. The US had pegged Mandela as "the world's most dangerous communist outside the Soviet Union."[639]

Everything was fine in South Africa – from the Afrikaner rulers' point of view – until the Soweto Uprisings in 1976, which initiated unrest throughout the country. The eruptions in the Black townships of South Africa put the regime in the mind of "total war" and "total onslaught" against the Black South Africans. In 1981 the regime initiated its chemical and biological weapons (CBW) program called Project Coast, headed by Dr. Wouter Basson, later known as "Dr. Death." Why the nickname? Because: "There are many people who think Basson was a war hero—because he killed the blacks big time,"[640] in the words of Daan Goosen, Basson's subordinate in Project Coast.

The South African CBW program was the protégé of the United States CBW establishment. During the 1940s and 1950s South African military officers were trained in CBW by the United States and the United Kingdom.[641] As William Finnegan in **The New Yorker** observes: "According to Basson, Project Coast was modelled on the American chemical-weapons program, which he first managed to penetrate in the early nineteen-eighties."[642] Basson received his training in CBW at Fort Detrick in Maryland and Porton Down in the U.K. From

---

[639] Ben Norton, "How the CIA helped apartheid South Africa imprison Nelson Mandela for 27 years – and is now facing lawsuits," **Salon** May 17, 2016.

[640] Boateng Osei, "Did This Man 'Kill Blacks Big Time'? (Special Report: south Africa)," **New African** November 2001.

[641] Stephen Burgess and Helen Purkitt, "The Secret Program: South Africa's Chemical and Biological Weapons," in **War Next Time: Countering Rogue States and Terrorists Armed with Chemical and Biological Weapons** (USAF Counterproliferation Center, 2004) 27-66 (28); Jerome Amir Singh, "Project Coast: eugenics in apartheid South Africa," **Endeavour** 32 (2008): 5-9 (5).

[642] William Finnegan, "The Poison Keeper," **The New Yorker** January 15, 2001: 58-74 (63).

the U.S. he got knowledge, equipment, and viruses to weaponize. Basson himself would later confess: "I must confirm that the structure of the [CBW program] project was based on the U.S. system. That's where we learnt the most."[643] Thus,

> The South African bioterrorist campaign depended upon very close relationships with U.S. scientists...From 1981 to 1993, the United States supported Wouter Bassoon's (sic) weaponization programs by financing close collaborations with U.S. scientists and by sponsoring Basson's sojourns to the United States for conferences education.[644]

The close working relationship between the U.S. and the South African CBW programs is demonstrated here: In 1984, the Center for Disease Control and Prevention (CDC) in Atlanta, Georgia provided Project Coast's original viral samples of the deadly hemorrhagic fevers Ebola, Marbug, and Rift Valley, which the regime weaponized. The CDC sent eight separate shipments to Pretoria and "suddenly, South Africa possessed viruses that could be used with devastating effect in surrounding countries."[645] South Africa would return the favor. Soviet scientists developed and shared with Basson their nasty flesh-eating bacteria *necrotizing fasciitis* and its antidote. In 1994, Basson gave both to the U.S.[646] The programs – the US and South Africa – were close because they shared the same *mindset*.

The main aim of Project Coast was the development of a *kaffir-killer* or ethnic weapon designed to target Black people specifically. *Kaffir* is the N-word of choice for South African racists. An ethnic weapon is a genetically engineered virus that is coded to, upon entering an organism, scan cells looking for a specific genetic marker or specific combination of genetic markers. When a cell with such genetic markers is found, the virus would insert itself into the host DNA and start the process of infection. In this way the virus attacks only people who have these genetic markers.   The South African Defense Force

---

[643] Washington, ***Medical Apartheid***, 372.

[644] Washington, ***Medical Apartheid***, 372.

[645] Burgess and Purkitt, ***Rollback***, 29-30; Tom Mangold and Jeff Goldberg, ***Plague Wars: The Terrifying Reality of Biological Warfare*** (New York: St. Martin's Press, 1999) 244.

[646] Stephen Burgess and Helen Purkitt, "The Secret Program: South Africa's Chemical and Biological Weapons," 34.

(SADF) Surgeon General Dr. Neil Knobel, who oversaw Project Coast, described the development of a bacterial ethnic weapon or "pigmentation weapon" that would specifically target pigmented or Black people as "the most important project for the country."[647] This bacterial *kaffir-killer*, called a "black bomb," was delivered to South Africa *by an American scientist that did CBW work for the U.S. government*, Dr. Larry Creed Ford.[648]

---

[647] Jerome Amir Singh, "Project Coast: eugenics in apartheid South Africa," ***Endeavour*** 32 (2008): 5-9 (6).
[648] Edward Humes, "The Medicine Man," ***Los Angeles Magazine*** July 2001, 94-99, 166-168; Marlene Burger and Peta Thornycroft, "Larry and the teabags of death," ***IOL*** March 11, 2000; Arthur Allen, "Mad Scientist," ***Salon*** June 26, 2000.

One of the *Kaffir-killing* viruses that Basson used to "kill the Blacks big time" was a version of HIV, the AIDS virus. In a safe in the director's office there was a refrigerator that kept Basson's personal bottle of freeze-dried blood in which was the weaponized HIV.[649] Basson deployed this weaponized HIV against Black South Africans through three primary ways:

1. Infect a person with the virus, and then send that person on a mission to sexually expose as many Africans as he or she can. As Stefan Elbe documents:

HIV/AIDS can be used as a weapon of war independent of the practice of rape. One highly disconcerting example involved the apartheid regime in South Africa. In 1998, following the transition to democracy, the country's Truth and Reconciliation Commission heard testimony that the regime may have planned to use HIV against its political enemies. ...Bacteriologist Mike Odendaal has stated that the head of the Roodeplaat Research Laboratories near Pretoria, which functioned as a front company for the apartheid military, had given him a bottle with HIV-infected blood taken from a man who had died of AIDS in a military hospital. Odendaal testified that he had received orders to freeze-dry the blood for Wouter Basson, a chemical-warfare specialist who allegedly wanted to use it "against a political opponent." ... Willie Nortje and Andries van Heerden, security officers under the apartheid regime, requested amnesty from the Truth and Reconciliation Commission for their part in a different plan. They tried to use four HIV-positive freedom fighters from the African National Congress and the Pan Africanist Congress, who had switched sides to work for the state security forces, to spread HIV/AIDS among sex workers in two Hillbrow hotels in the 1990s. Nortje and Van Heerden apparently hoped that the sex

[649] "'Basson had HIV blood freeze-dried'," *IOL* May 24, 2000; Tim Butcher, "South African 'Dr Death' learned from Saddam," *The Telegraph* July 24, 2001; Tom Mangold and Jeff Goldberg, *Plague Wars: The Terrifying Reality of Biological Warfare* (New York: St. Martin's Press, 1999) 253, 265.

workers would then spread the virus to their other clients.[650]

2. Under the cover of vaccinations.

One arm of the SADF which served Project Coast was the South African Institute of Maritime Research (SAIMR). SAIMR was not only linked to the country's CBW program, but also "operated with support from the CIA and British intelligence."[651] SAIMR was headed by Keith Maxwell. Maxwell had no medical qualifications but ran clinics in poor, mostly Black areas around Johannesburg while claiming to be a doctor. That gave him the opportunity for sinister experimentation."[652] He claimed that "AIDS would ultimately be good for humanity and would decimate the black population in South Africa," and to insure that that happens, Maxwell and SAIMR "used phony vaccinations in the early 1990s to spread H.I.V...in an attempt to wipe out the black population," according to former SAIMR intelligence officer Alexander Jones who worked for Maxwell.[653] This was an orchestrated campaign to spread HIV/AIDS among Black people in Africa (including Mozambique as well).[654] "We were at war. Black people in South Africa were the enemy," Jones says. According to *The Independent* "The group's leader (Maxwell) is said to have posed as a philanthropic doctor to give impoverished black South African's 'false injections',"[655] injections containing Basson's weaponized HIV. Jones says:

---

[650] Stefan Elbe, "HIV/AIDS and the Changing Landscape of War in Africa," *International Security* 27 (2002): 159-177 (170-171).
[651] "'CIA-backed' mercenaries spread HIV in S. Africa, ex-member claims," *RT News* January 28, 2019.
[652] Emma Graham-Harrison, "Ex-mercenary claims South African group tried to spread Aids," *The Guardian* January 27, 2019; idem, "Coups and murder: the sinister world of apartheid's secret mercenaries," *The Guardian* January 20, 2019.
[653] Matt Apuzzo, "Quest to Solve Assassination Mystery Revives an AIDS Conspiracy Theory," *The New York Times* January
[654] Baffour Ankomah, "Former intelligence officer confesses: 'We Deliberately Spread AIDS in South Africa," *New African* March 2019: 17-20;
[655] Adam Lusher, "South African paramilitary unit plotted to infect black populations with Aids, former member claims," *Independent* January 27, 2019.

258

Black people have got no rights, they need medical treatment. There's a white 'philanthropist' coming in and saying, "You know, I'll open up these clinics and I'll treat you." And meantime [he is] actually a wolf in sheep's clothing.

While Maxwell presented a public face of a benevolent philanthropist who was trying to discover a cure for AIDS, he was in actuality offering free "healthcare" in order to secretly infect Black people with HIV/AIDS through phony vaccinations. SAIMR was supported by the CIA, who also uses "phony vaccinations" in covert operations.[656]

3. Contaminating food sources.

Isak Niehaus and Gunvor Jonsson record:

Allegedly, Dr. Basson distributed HIV by various means. He put it in the food, water reservoirs, and clothes of black people; in the injections given to hospital patients; in TB and smallpox vaccines; and even in the free, government-distributed condoms. However, most informants saw black soldiers as the prime agents for transmitting HIV. Dr. Basson allegedly placed the virus in the rivers from which soldiers of the ANC 's [African National Council] military wing, *Umkhonto We Sizwe* (MK), drank, and he laced the malaria tablets given to black South African Defense Force soldiers with HIV. Dr. Basson purposefully created a slow virus so that the soldiers could spread it to as many women as possible.[657]

According to these reports. Basson secretly added the virus in *free, government-distributed condoms* and even *in the medicine* (malaria tablets) *made available to Black South Africans!* It was the U.S. – governmental CBW researcher Dr. Larry Ford in particular – who taught Project Coast operatives these techniques. How was HIV put in the food? Niehaus and Jonsson report as well:

---

[656] "How the CIA's Fake Vaccination Campaign Endangers Us All," *Scientific American* April 16, 2013.
[657] Isak Niehaus with Gunvor Jonsson, "Dr. Wouter Basson, Americans, and Wild Beasts: Men's Conspiracy Theories of HIV/AIDS in the South African Lowveld," *Medical Anthropology* 24 (2005):179–208 (197-198)

ANC activists claimed that members of white right-wing movements distributed poisoned bread at the schools of Bushbuckridge and dumped poisoned milk in the forest. It was thought that the whites wished to ensure that few votes were cast for the ANC. At a series of meetings some ANC organizers warned civil servants and ordinary villagers that whites would employ any devious method to defeat the ANC. They alleged that the undergrade potatoes white farmers distributed free of charge in the villages were stained with invisible election ink. When people's hands were scanned under ultraviolet rays at the polling stations it would appear as though they had already voted. The organizers also cautioned people against accepting T-shirts from seemingly generous whites as these were likely to have been doctored with dangerous chemicals. These allegations were widely accepted as truthful.

The advent of HIV/AIDS saw renewed scares. Some men claimed that in 1996 and 1997 white farmers dumped tons of undergrade oranges and sweet potatoes, which were doctored with blood containing HIV, at a shopping center and at schools. In the village of Brooklyn parents beat children who ate the oranges and warned them that they could contract AIDS. Parents were extremely suspicious of the motives of these farmers. They were hard pressed to believe that racist whites would all of a sudden give away tons of their produce. One informant, Ben Nyambi, raised the following questions: "It happened here. A white farmer brought us sweet potatoes for free. I saw the truck and the white man. How could this happen? The farmer does not pay his workers well and never transports them to work. But he spent lots of money on petrol and on his truck to bring us sweet potatoes. How can he rob his workers but give us sweet potatoes for free? I think he wants to kill us."[658]

Many of Project Coast's chemical and biological weapons were covertly deployed through the food and beverages made available to Black South Africans. For example, at African National Congress meetings the food and beverages would be poisoned in order to disrupt the proceedings. Botulinum toxin, the most acutely lethal toxin known, laced chocolates and

---

[658]Niehaus with Jonsson, "Men's Conspiracy Theories of HIV/AIDS in the South African Lowveld," (195-196).

milk[659]; cigarettes and lipstick were injected with anthrax[660]; food was injected with Hepatitis A; tinned cans of corned beef fed to villagers was injected with thallium, a poison which can cause mental retardation; sugar cubes were laced with salmonella[661]; alcohol was mixed with the weedkiller paraquat as well as with thallium. [662] In fact, it is reported that Basson had thallium-infused beer passed out for free to Black Africans at bus stops.[663]

Thus, food, water, and alcohol were thoroughly – and grossly – weaponized against Black Africans of southern Africa by the chemical and biological weapons program of the apartheid regime. The U.S. supported the regime *and* the CBW program, tutoring the operatives in techniques and providing some chemical and biological weapons. The tactics used by the South African bioterrorists against Black people in Africa were also used by U.S. bioterrorists against Black people in America. *That's* the point.

IV.   *Poisoned Catfish: Tuskegee Experiment Part II*

While airborne PCBs pollute the air of segregated Black communities, the main route of PCB exposure and poisoning is through the food, especially the fish. According to Max Weintraub and Linda S. Birnbaum, "For the 10% of the US population that remains most exposed to PCBs, fish consumption is the primary source. National Health and Nutrition Examination Survey (NHANES) data indicates that the highest remaining PCB levels exist in a non-Hispanic black population."[664] But it is demonstrable that there is deliberate

---

659 Raymond Whitaker, "SA planned chemical war on blacks," *Independent* June 13, 1998; Chandré Gould and Peter I. Folb, "The South African Chemical and Biological Warfare Program: An Overview," *The Nonproliferation Review* (Fall-Winter 2000): 10-23 (18).

660 Boateng Osei, "Did This Man 'Kill Blacks Big Time'? (Special Report: south Africa)," *New African* November 2001.

661 William Finnegan, "The Poison Keeper," *The New Yorker* January 15, 2001: 58-74 (62).

662 Mangold and Goldberg, *Plague Wars*, 246, 257-259.

663 "The deeds of Dr. Death," *The Guardian* October 4, 1999.

664 Max Weintraub and Linda S. Birnbaum, "Catfish consumption as a contributor to elevated PCB levels in a non-Hispanic black

U.S. military involvement in the poisoning of fish and other food sources upon which Black people rely.

The small town of Anniston, Alabama has the unfortunate distinction of being known as "Toxic Town U.S.A." Roughly half white and half Black, the races are segregated around a chemical plant of the Monsanto Chemical Company that produced PCBs. African Americans are concentrated downhill on the north and east of the plant, while Whites are concentrated uphill on the south and west sides. In 2002 an Alabama jury found Monsanto guilty on six counts including "outrage," which the law describes as conduct "beyond all possible bounds of decency...atrocious and utterly intolerable in civilized society." This is because Monsanto was found to have "knowingly poisoned Anniston residents and then had hidden the dangers from public knowledge."[665] In documents

---

subpopulation," *U.S. Environmental Protection Agency Papers* 23 (2008): 412-417.

[665] Ellen Griffith Spears, *Baptized in PCBs: Race, Pollution, and Justice in an All-American Town* (Chapel Hill: The University of North Carolina Press, 2014; Laura Dillon Burgess, Glenn S. Johnson and Steven C. Washington, "An African American Community and The PCB Contamination in Anniston, Alabama: An Environmental Justice Case Study," *Race, Gender & Class* 21 (2014): 334-361.

Monsanto executives admitted to deliberately dumping large quantities of PCBs on a daily basis into Snow Creek, which flows downhill into the Black areas, polluting the soil, water, and food chain of the Black residents of West Anniston, including the fish upon which the local residents depended.[666] Whites were uphill, and thus able to avoid the contaminated water. Black residents of Anniston had an average toxic body burden of PCBs that is four times higher than the national average and three times greater than the Whites of Anniston- some of the Black residents had a body burden *27 times higher than the national average*.[667] One Monsanto official candidly referred to the PCB work in Anniston as "quite a little human experiment," and the racial differences in reaction to exposure were noted.[668] Monsanto also dumped tons of liquid mercury into its waste system, exposing the residents.

MONSANTO AND THE MILITARY

Monsanto was held liable for the PCB poisoning and agreed to a $700 million settlement.[669] However, that "little human experiment" using Black residents of Anniston was unquestionably a joint Monsanto-*Military* operation. Anniston was not only a highly *militarized* town, it was a *chemical weapons and warfare hub*. And as Ellen Griffith Spears notes, "In Anniston, as in the nation, chemical contamination has been inextricably linked with the machinery of war."[670] By 1951 Camp McClellan, adjacent to the city of Anniston, was the home of the U.S. Army Chemical Corps Training School and from 1960 the Chemical Corps Command was in Anniston. The Army's cache of nerve gas and mustard gas was stored at the Anniston Army

---

[666] "In Dirt, Water and Hogs, Town Got Its Fill of PCBs," *The Washington Post* January 1, 2002.
[667] Spears, *Baptized in PCBs*, 11; Brett Israel, "Pollution, Poverty and People of Color: Dirty Soil and Diabetes," *Scientific American* June 13, 2012; Kevin Sack, "PCB Pollution Suits Have Day in Court in Alabama," *The New York Times* January 27, 2002.
[668] Spears, *Baptized in PCBs*, 10.
[669] Michael Grunwald, "Monsanto Held Liable For PCB Dumping," *The Washington Post* February 23, 2002; "$700 Million Settlement in Alabama PCB Lawsuit," *The New York Times* August 21, 2003.
[670] Spears, *Baptized in PCBs*, 7.

Depot since 1963. In fact, more than 7% of the U.S. chemical weapons stockpile was housed in the Anniston Army Depot.

The lab at Camp/Fort McClellan was one of two sites in the U.S. - the other was Edgewood Arsenal in Maryland – authorized to make chemicals for use in *live agent testing*. Open air testing of chemical and biological agents was thus routine in Anniston. In 1952 the U.S. Army released a live biological agent, *Serratia marcescens*, into the air of Anniston (as well as major cities like San Francisco). This led to twice the normal pneumonia occurrence in Calhoun County for that year.[671]

The Monsanto-Military alliance is deep and intimate. Monsanto had extensive involvement in WWII and Cold War military projects. Monsanto did secret work in Anniston for the Chemical Warfare Service in the 1950s, work which included the production of offensive and defensive chemicals for the armed forces, specifically the "precursors for chemical warfare agents." We know also from internal documents that Monsanto carried out "investigation and research" for the Army Chemical Corps.[672] So who is responsible for this "little human experiment" that turned Black Anniston into "Toxic Town U.S.A."? The U.S. Government (the Army) and allied interests (Monsanto). The food upon which the people depended – fish from the creek, hogs, and any food grown from the soil – was deliberately contaminated with PCBs, mercury, and several other toxins. And the people suffered dearly. Anniston, Alabama = Tuskegee, Alabama.

---

[671] "Army Tested Biological War in S.F.," *Newsday* December 22, 1976.
[672] Spears, *Baptized in PCBs*, 7, 80, 81.

New Scientist 26 May 1983   527

Triana: a town poisoned by DDT

Kathleen Johnston, Washington DC

THE TWELVE hundred poor, mostly black citizens of Triana, a small town in northern Alabama, have won an unprecedented $19 million settlement from a chemical company that contaminated them and their town with DDT. But government scientists seem set to pass up the chance to study this unique population for the long-term effects of the pesticide.

The Olin Corporation, one of the world's largest manufacturers of chemicals, made DDT for many years at a plant on the army's Redstone arsenal near Triana, until the factory closed in 1971. Now it has agreed to compensate the townspeople, clean up the DDT in the soil and waters within 10 years, and spend $5 million to monitor the health of local citizens.

The DDT ran from a waste ditch near the plant into the Indian Creek as it flowed past the arsenal and through the town, contaminating water, sediments, wildfowl, fish and, finally, the people that ate the fish. DDT levels in five species of fish in the creek averaged 204 parts per million and peaked at 450 ppm, according to a government survey carried out in the late 1970s.

Poisoning deep in Alabama

Wildfowl in a nearby swamp were found with up to 2252 ppm of DDT in their flesh. The Tennessee Valley Authority claimed that at least 4000 tonnes of DDT had found its way into sediments in a local branch of the Tennessee river.

For several years, the population of

Triana had eaten fish and drunk water contaminated by DDT from the Olin plant. In 1979, eight years after the plant closed, epidemiologists from the Centers for Disease Control in Atlanta, Georgia, first took blood samples from residents of the town. In one case, the results showed a level of DDT twice as high as any previously reported in the medical literature. Other samples were comparable to those previously seen only in the most heavily-exposed workers at pesticide plants. Thirty-three people were found with DDT levels in their blood above 500 parts per billion. Six had levels above 1000 ppb.

A spokesman for the army said it had insisted on the plant being closed and, after an initial clean-up, had assumed that the residues would degrade. But in 1977 army scientists found this had not happened. The Environmental Protection Agency (EPA) ordered the army to conduct a study of the effect of the DDT on the local population. But it refused, according to Howard Zeller, the EPA's second-in-command in the region. The two agencies settled on a study of the pollution and how to contain it—but not on the health effects.

THIS WEEK

Triana is a small, rural settlement in northern Alabama with a population that is 75% Black. The poor Black residents are largely subsistence anglers who depend on fish caught in the Indian Creek and Tennessee River. While the U.S. Army through Monsanto Chemical Company was poisoning the air, water, food and people of Anniston, Alabama with PCBs, the U.S. Army through Olin Chemical Corp was poisoning the air, water, food and people of Triana with DDT, which was introduced during World War II as an insecticide. The DDT that poisoned the town of Triana was manufactured six miles away on the grounds of the Army's Redstone Arsenal, adjacent to Huntsville, from 1947 to 1971. Olin Corp (who was leased the Redstone property in 1954) released DDT-contaminated water into brick-lined trenches that ultimately released into Huntsville Spring Branch and Indian Creek, both of which emptied into the Tennessee River. The polluted water contaminated the fish (catfish, perch, carp, goldfish, and gar) which the Black residents of Triana consumed. The residents got highly contaminated. 99% of the U.S. population has DDT in their blood, and the average DDT level in people 12 – 74 years old at that time was 15 nanograms per milliliter (ng/ml). A 1979 CDC analysis of Triana blood samples found that the average sample had a DDT level of 159.4 ng/ml: "They found that DDT was higher in Blacks than in Whites and higher in males than in females."[673] Of course.

The mayor of Triana from 1964 to 1984, Clyde Foster, who was also a NASA administrator (director of the Equal Opportunity Office at the NASA-George C. Marshall Space Flight Center in Huntsville from 1956 to 1957) and mathematician technician   for the Army Ballistic Missile Agency at Redstone Arsenal itself, said that state and federal agencies knew of excessive levels in the fish consumed by Triana residents for years but refrained from making the information public *because they wanted to use them as guinea pigs.*[674] According to a 1979 **The New York Times** report in that year the CDC swooped in to conduct "the most extensive inquiry to date into the effects of longterm consumption of food contaminated with high levels of DDT."[675] The study was, according to the **Times**,

> intended to determine what health problems, if any, could be correlated with high levels of consumption of DDT...in a previous study, a small number of volunteers were given an oral intake of 35 milligrams of DDT a day, about twice that of the highly exposed DDT industrial workers, for 21 months without measurable effects on health. [676]

This explains the indifference toward the wellbeing of the Triana residents. As Dorceta E. Taylor observes:

> Though evidence of DDT contamination was identified as early as 1948 and research indicating that the chemical might be harmful to humans began surfacing in the 1950s, Blacks who lived close to the Olin plant and who drank the contaminated water and ate large quantities of toxic fish were not tested or alerted to the problem till three decades after the problem was identified.[677]

---

[673] Dorceta E. Taylor, **Toxic Communities: Environmental Racism, Industrial Pollution, and Residential Mobility** (New York and London: New York University Press, 2014) 11.
[674] Taylor, **Toxic Communities**, 10.
[675] Wayne King, "Tests in an Alabama Town Seek to Trace DDT's Effects on Humans," **The New York Times** May 12, 1979.
[676] King, "Tests in an Alabama Town."
[677] Dorceta E. Taylor, **Toxic Communities: Environmental Racism, Industrial Pollution, and Residential Mobility** (New York and London: New York University Press, 2014) 10.

The Tuskegee Experiment all over again. Further evidence of deliberateness in this case is this small detail.

> The (1980 CDC) study revealed that Triana residents had high levels of polychlorinated biphenyls (PCBs) in their blood stream. The discovery of PCBs in residents' bloodstream triggered a search for the source of the cancer-causing agent, *but no major source of PCBs were found.*"[678]

The reason no major source was "found" is likely because the major source was the U.S. Army, who at the same time was poisoning Black residents of Anniston with PCBs.

During World War II DDT was a chemical weapon (U.S. Army Chemical Warfare Service field officers sprayed the insecticide) aimed at the elimination of bugs (lice and mosquitos) carrying malaria and typhus in the European and Pacific Theaters. "The atomic bomb and DDT were the two technological icons of the second World War."[679] The War Production Board secured mass production of the insecticide, and DuPont and Monsanto were two of the biggest producers of DDT for the military during the war. After the war DDT was repurposed: "Quickly approved by the U.S. Department of Agriculture (USDA), stockpiles of DDT held by DuPont for military use...entered the domestic front largely *untested.*"[680] The Department of Agriculture again.

The *testing* seems to have occurred *covertly*, and with *Black test subjects.* DDT was released for public sale in 1945. In 1946 the U.S. Public Health Service (re: Tuskegee Experiment!) initiated a domestic use campaign that clearly targeted Black areas because by 1967, as shown in numerous studies, Black males nationally were reported as having two to four times the amount of DDT in their blood and tissue than Whites.[681] Triana,

---

[678] Taylor, ***Toxic Communities***, 12; Mike Hollis, "The Persistence of a Poison," ***The Washington Post*** June 15, 1980.

[679] James Erwin Schmitt, "From the Frontlines to *Silent Spring*: DDT and America's War on Insects, 1941-1962," ***CONCEPT*** 39 (2016): 1-29.

[680] John Wills, ***US Environmental History*** (Edinburgh: Edinburgh University Press, 2012) 89.

[681] Suzanne M. Snedeker, "Pesticides and Breast Cancer Risk: A Review of DDT, DDE, and Dieldrin," ***Environmental Health Perspectives*** 109 (2001): 35-47 (42): "Survey studies conducted in

Alabama *was no isolated phenomenon.* DDT poisoning "clustered" in Black areas around the country. In a national survey for the years 1973-1974 from 75 collecting sites in 48 states, Blacks had twice the level of serum DDT than whites. DDT was thus a chemical warfare weapon first targeting bugs and then, after the war, redeployed against Blacks.

FOOD FROM GENDER-BENDING WATERS

And what are the consequences of sufficient DDT poisoning? For starters, arthritis, breast cancer, and diabetes. But also, hear the *Los Angeles Times*:

> In the gender-bending waters of Lake Apopka, alligators aren't quite male. They aren't quite female either. They may be both. Or neither.

> This sexual confusion in the wild, discovered in this steamy Florida swamp last year, is so disturbing to scientists that they keep performing test after test on the scaly reptiles, trying to prove themselves wrong. But the more they look, the more evidence they find. In fact, hardly any young alligators with

---

the 1970s and 1980s consistently demonstrated that adipose tissue levels were higher in American blacks than in whites (...)". See further: Stephen A. Martin, Jr. et al., "DDT Metabolite and Androgens in African-American Farmers," *Epidemiology* 13 (2002): 454-458; F.W. Kutz, A.R. Yobs, and S.C. Strassman, "Racial Stratification of Organochlorine Insecticide Residues in Human Adipose Tissue," *Journal of Occupational Medicine* 19 (1977): 619-622; B.T. Woodard, B.B. Ferguson and D.J. Wilson, "DDT Levels in Milk of Rural Indigent Blacks," *Am J Dis Child* 130 (1976): 400-3; J.E. Keil, C.B. Loadholt and S.H. Sandifer, "Sera DDT Elevation in Black Components of Two Southeastern Communities: Genetics or Environment?" in *Pesticides and the environment: A continuing controversy*. Vol. 2. ed. W. B. Diechmann, 203–213. New York: Intercontinental Medical Book Corp, 1973) 203-213; John Finkles et al., "Polychlorinated Biphenyl Residues in Human Plasma Expose a Major Urban Pollution Problem," *AJPH* 62 (1972): 645-651; Walter F. Edmundson et al., "P,p'-DDT and p,p'-DDE in Blood Samples of Occupationally Exposed Workers: Community Studies on Pesticides, Dade County, Fla.," *Public Health Reports (1896-1970)* 84 (1969): 53-58; John E. Davies et al., "A Epidemiologic Application of the Study of DDE Levels in Whole Blood," *AJPH* 59 (1969): 435-441.

normal sexuality can be found in this vast lake on the suburban outskirts of Orlando.

Elsewhere around the world, the same astonishing phenomenon is turning up in a menagerie of fish, birds and other wild animals. Testosterone levels have plummeted in some males, while females are supercharged with estrogen. Both sexes sometimes are born with a penis and ovaries, and some males wind up so gender warped they try to produce eggs.

"Everything is really fouled up. It is indeed real, and it is scary," said Tim Gross, a University of Florida wildlife endocrinologist on the team that discovered the feminized alligators. "We didn't want to believe it, in all honesty."

This is no fluke of Mother Nature, no quirk of evolution. *This is probably a legacy of pollution.*

Wildlife scientists have uncovered persuasive evidence that artificial pesticides and industrial chemicals are infiltrating wombs and eggs, where they send false signals imitating or blocking hormones, which control sexuality. Although the parents are unharmed, their embryo's sexual development is disrupted, and some male offspring are left chemically castrated and females sterile.

The potential consequences, if unabated, are almost unthinkable.
If males aren't male and females aren't female, they cannot reproduce, and some outwardly healthy populations could be a generation away from extinction.[682]

The alligator population of Lake Apopka, Florida crashed in 1990 because *the alligators were changing sex.* 80% of the male gators showed some form of sex-reversal. Blood tests revealed that the male alligators had high levels of estrogen and lowered levels of testosterone. The cause? In 1980 Tower Chemical let a waste pond overflow and spill into the lake, pouring *large amounts of DDT into the lake.* The alligators were exposed to DDE, a metabolite of DDT which is anti-androgenic. 90% of the alligators disappeared. The gator penis was 75%

---

[682] Marla Cone, "Sexual Confusion in the Wild: From gators to gulls, scientists say, pollution may be playing havoc with animals' hormones. Some males try to lay eggs; some females nest together. Certain species risk extinction," *Los Angeles Times* October 2, 1994.

shorter than normal and the testosterone levels were so low that the gators hormonally resembled females. Nancy McVicar of the *Sun-Sentinel* referred to these gators as "nature in drag."[683] Commercial DDT is a composite of two chemicals: *o,p'-DDT* which is estrogenic and *p,p-DDT* which anti-androgenic.

> So, in effect, DDT has a double action on the sex hormones. One of its component ingredients can act like an estrogen; the other is an anti-androgen and blocks the action of the male hormone.[684]

It is believed that DDT exposure lowers sperm counts in men and contributes to prostate and testicular cancer as well. DDT contamination off the cost of Los Angeles and in Lake Michigan crashed the sea gull and herring gull populations because the males were being born dead or *hermaphrodite* (having both testes and ovaries). DDT is blamed for the missing or neutralized males. Female gulls thus started pairing and nesting with each other in what we would call "lesbian" relationships.[685] Sound familiar? And it is *Black people* who are most exposed to DDT (as well as BPA, PCBs, $PM_{2.5}$, and more).

Even more disturbing is the fact that DDT has epigenetic affects, which deliver their consequences to *future generations*.

> In 2013, (Michael K. Skinner, a professor at Washington State University and the founding director of the Center for Reproductive Biology in the School of Biological Sciences) and

---

[683] Nancy McVicar, "Nature In Drag: Male Gators Becoming Female," *Sun-Sentinel* September 3, 1994.

[684] Deborah Cadbury, *Altering Eden: The Feminization of Nature* (New York: St. Martin's Press, 1997) 83.

[685] D. Michael Fry, "Injury to Seabirds Caused by Estrogenic Effects of DDT Contamination in the Southern Califor0na Bright," Report, September 30, 1994; Gary W. Shugart, Mary A. Fitch and Glen A. Fox, "Female Pairing: A Reproductive Strategy for Herring Gulls?" *Condor* 90 (1988): 933-935; David B. Peakall and Glen A. Fox, "Toxicological Investigation of Pollutant Related Efffects in Great Lakes Gulls," *Environmental Health Perspective* 71 (1987): 187-193; Michael R. Conover, "Female-Female Pairings in Caspian Terns," *Condor* 85 (1983): 346-349; D.M. Fry and C.K. Toone, "DDT-induced feminization of gull embryos," *Science* 213 (1981): 922-924; Glen A. Fox, Carl R. Cooper and John P. Ryder, "Predicting the Sex of Herring Gulls By Using External Measurements," *Journal of Field Ornithology* 52 (1981): 1-9.

his team published research showing that direct exposure to DDT left mice with a slightly elevated rate of certain diseases. But by the time those mice had grandchildren, more than 50 percent of the male mice developed obesity. In fact, Skinner's research found that DDT left 90 percent of the progeny of the mice originally exposed more likely to develop obesity, experience lower sperm counts, or contract other even more serious health conditions. This pattern continued through four generations, to the great-grandchildren of the mice originally exposed to DDT.[686]

Thus, the Most Honorable Elijah Muhammad was right on when he warned us as far back as 1967:

Poisonous food and drink we are now eating and drinking...D.D.T., which is sprayed on food while it is growing up from the earth, is also a poison that should not be put into the human body, regardless of the desire to kill the insects, that love to dine on the same food on which we dine.[687]

But DDT-poisoning is not restricted to Alabama catfish. Chicago salmon – and salmon in general - is even *more* contaminated. It was reported in 1969 that the Coho salmon of Lake Michigan was contaminated with DDT *and* PCBs![688] We

---

[686] Janell Ross, "Epigenetics: The Controversial Science Behind Racial and Ethnic Health Disparities," *The Atlantic* March 20, 2014.

[687] Elijah Muhammad, *How To Eat to Live* Vol. I (Chicago: Muhammad's Temple of Islam No. 2, 1967) 107-108.

[688] Ronald Kotulak, "DDT Killing Lake Michigan Coho, Scientist Says," *Chicago Tribune* November 14, 1968; Gilman D. Veith, "Baseline Concentrations of Polychlorinated Biphenyls and DDT in Lake Michigan Fish, 1971," *Pesticides Monitoring Journal* 9 (1975): 21-29; Stevenson Swanson, "DDT, PCBs Still Lurk in Lake Michigan Waters," *Chicago Tribune* November 23, 1992.

know that state governments were not averse to deliberately dumping such toxic chemicals near Lake Michigan.[689] Marla Cone reported in 2009: "The most contaminated wildlife on Earth-killer whales in the Pacific Northwest-are picking up nearly all of their chemicals from Chinook salmon in polluted ocean waters off the West Coast, according to new scientific study."[690]

While PCBs are the main contaminant of the Pacific salmon that the killer whales dine on, DDT is the main contaminant of the salmon we land creatures consume. In 2009 Arnold Schecter of the University of Texas and colleagues studied the food contamination from five supermarkets in Dallas, Texas testing for 50 chemicals in 310 food samples representing 31 different food types.[691] They found that the highest level of chemical contamination of the food was from DDT and that salmon was the most contaminated food sample. Emily Elert, writing in *Scientific American*, notes as well:

Farmed fish are even more contaminated. A 2004 study found that farmed salmon contained 10 times higher levels of [persistent organic pollutant] than wild salmon. The source of the pollutants, said Dr. David Carpenter, director of the Institute for Environmental Health at the University of Albany, New York...is the contaminated mixture of fish fats and proteins in fishmeal.[692]

---

[689] William Jones, "Fight Pesticide Use Near Lake Michigan," *Chicago Tribune* November 11, 1967.
[690] Marla Cone, "Poisoned Killer Whales? Blame Salmon," *Scientific American* January 20, 2009.
[691] Arnold Schecter et al., "Perfluorinated Compounds, Polychlorinated Biphenyls, and Organochlorine Pesticide Contamination in Composite Food Samples from Dallas, Texas, USA," *Environmental Health Perspective* 118 (2010): 796-802.
[692] Emily Elert, "U.S. Food Still Tainted with Old Chemicals," *Scientific American* April 22, 2010.

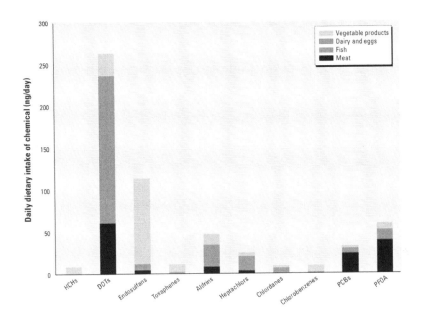

VI.   *Toxic Blood Through Poisoned Food*

Scientific   American reported a startling finding in its December 2, 2009 edition, stating: "U.S. minority children are born carrying *hundreds* of chemicals in their bodies, according to a report released today by an environmental group."[693] The group is the watchdog Environmental Workers Group (ewg). In 2009 ewg partnered with Rachel's Network to commission five laboratories in the U.S., Canada and Europe to analyze umbilical cord blood from 10 anonymous African American, Asian and Hispanic infants born between December 2007 and June

[693] Sara Goodman, "Tests Find More Than 200 Chemicals in Newborn Umbilical Cord Blood," ***Scientific American*** December 2, 2009.

2008 in Michigan, Florida, Massachusetts, California and Wisconsin. The tests found up to 232 toxic chemicals in *each of* the 10 cord blood samples. Their cord blood resembled a toxic mixing bowl and showed these non-white newborns to be "contaminated with an average of more than 100 chemicals known or suspected to cause cancer, birth defects or other health problems."[694] These stews of potential neurotoxins such as mercury, endocrine disrupters such as BPA, and carcinogens such as dioxin may have a synergistic effect, resulting in more significant adverse effects than single chemical exposures.

In 2013 the ewg in collaboration with Keep A Breast Foundation published a list of 12 of the "dirtiest" of the hundreds of chemicals that turned up in the cord blood of babies of color. ewg called them the "Dirty Dozen" Endocrine Disrupters, the twelve worst hormone-altering chemicals that pollute the environment today:

1. Bisphenol A (BPA)
2. Dioxin
3. Atrazine
4. Phthalates
5. Perchlorate
6. Fire Retardants
7. Lead
8. Arsenic
9. Mercury
10. Perfluorinated Chemicals
11. Organophosphate Pesticides
12. Glycol Esters

Table 1. Examples of pesticides found in the U.S. inner-city environment.

Chemical group	Examples	Toxic effects
Organochlorines (halogenated hydrocarbons)	DDT, lindane, dieldrin, chlordane	Carcinogenic, hormonal agonists, neurotoxic
Organophosphates	Parathion, chlorpyrifos	Neurotoxic, dermatotoxic
Carbamates	Malathion, aldicarb	Neurotoxic, dermatotoxic
Pyrethroids	Cyfluthrin, permethrin, fenvalerate	Possibly immunotoxic and neurotoxic, hormonal agonists, antagonist
Herbicides		
Dipyridyl	Paraquat, diquat	Pulmonary fibrosis
Other	Atrazine, alachlor	Carcinogenic

[694] Environmental Working Group, "Pollution in Minority Newborns," *ewg.org* November 23, 2009; "Toxic Chemicals Found in Minority Cord Blood," *ewg.org* December 2, 2009.

While natural and industrial products have poisoned almost the whole of the environment, ewg reports that "It is clear that minority populations in the U.S. have higher exposures to many chemical pollutants"[695] because "Racial and ethnic minority communities in the U.S. are often *bombarded* with environmental pollutants (emphasis added)."[696] As we showed above, this "bombardment" is deliberate. Philip J. Landrigan and colleagues in their 1999 study "Pesticides and Inner-City Children," likewise documented that poor children of color of the inner city, i.e. Black and Brown children, "are a group within the American population that is at disproportionately high risk of exposure to numerous environmental toxins," including some of the "Dirtiest" chemicals such as atrazine and organochlorines.[697]

The developing human brain is exceptionally sensitive to injury caused by toxic chemicals. In 2014 scholars from the prestigious universities of Harvard and Mount Sinai School of Medicine announced that a "silent pandemic" of toxins has been damaging the brains of unborn children leading to widespread behavioral and cognitive problems.[698] Twelve chemicals were identified, the *in utero* and developmental

exposure of which can help cause lowered IQ, ADHD, autism spectrum disorder, dyslexia, and increased aggressive and anti-social behavior in young children – *our children*. Exposure to these neurotoxins was associated with changes in neuron

[695] Environmental Working Group, "Pollution in Minority Newborns," *ewg.org* November 23, 2009.

[696] Environmental working Group, "Toxic Chemicals Found in Minority Cord Blood," *ewg.org* December 2, 2009.

[697] Philip J. Landrigan et al., "Pesticides and Inner-City Children: Exposures, Risks, and Prevention," *Environmental Health Perspective* 107 (1999) Supplement 3: 431-437.

[698] Philippe Grandjean and Philip J Landrigan, "Neurobehavioural effects of developmental toxicity," *Lancet Neurol* 13 (2014): 330–38.

development in the fetus and among infants. Other researchers even used MRI testing to show that these chemicals appear to change children's brain structure, causing thinning of the cortex.[699] A growing body of research is finding links between higher levels of these chemicals in the blood and urine of expectant mothers and brain disorders in their children.[700]

VII.   *The Plot to Target Black Women Through The Food They Buy*

At the top of the ewg's Dirty Dozen list is bisphenol A or BPA, which is a synthetic estrogenic/antiandrogen endocrine disrupter widely used in the production of plastics and the lining of canned goods. BPA is bad, bad news. BPA exposure has been linked to diabetes and cancer, particularly prostate cancer. It also is a gender-bending chemical. In a study of the effect of BPA on aromatase expression in rat testicular Leydig cells JY Kim et al. found that BPA induced and increased aromatization – thereby increasing estrogen levels - and reduced testosterone synthesis.[701] A 2015 study of painted turtles with BPA applied on their eggs found that BPA reversed sex (male turtles developed female sex organs) and reprogramed male turtle brains to show female-typical behavior.[702] Turtles are considered "indicator species" because they can be used as a barometer for the health of the entire ecosystem. In humans, adult exposure can lower natural hormone levels – testosterone in males and estrogen in females (it can be anti-estrogenic in females). Child and *in utero* exposure effects brain development, sexual differentiation, open-field and play

[699] James Hamblin, "The Toxins That Threaten Our Brains," *The Atlantic* March 18, 2014.
[700] Alice Park, "Children Exposed to More Braain-Harming Chemicals Than Ever Before," *Time* February
[701] JY Kim et al. "Bisphenol A-induced aromatase activation is mediated by cyclooxygenase-2-regulation in rat testicular Leydig cells," *Toxicol Lett* 193 (2010): 200-208.
[702] Lindsey K. Manshack "Effects of developmental exposure to Bisphenol A and ethinyl estradiol on spatial navigational learning and memory in painted turtles (*Chrysemys picta*)," *Hormones and Behavior* 85 (2016): 48-55; Caitlin M. Jandegian, "Developmental exposure to bisphenol A (BPA) alters sexual differentiation in painted turtles (Chrysemys picta," *General and Comparative Endocrinology* 216 (2015): 77-85.

behavior as well. In fact, early BPA exposure can interfere with the brain sex differentiation process and eliminate or reverse sexual dimorphisms in brain structure and behavior, making boys act like girls and girls act like boys. As Kundakovic et al. note:

> This study provides evidence that low-dose maternal BPA exposure induces long-lasting disruption to epigenetic pathways in the brain of offspring...One of the most striking neurobiological effects of BPA is the loss of sexual dimorphism in brain structure and behavior illustrated by animal studies (...), findings concordant with human epidemiological studies (...).[703]

Every year over two million tons of BPA are used in the manufacture of epoxy resins (which line food cans) and polycarbonate plastics. As a result, BPA is ubiquitous in the environment and exposure is universal. The CDC suggests that BPA is in the body of 93% of Americans over 6 years old.[704] However, *poor Black people carry the greatest body burden.* "Urinary metabolites of BPA are detected in 90% of the U.S. population with higher exposures observed in non-Hispanic Blacks, children, females, and those of lower socioeconomic status..."[705] And the major source of the Black BPA body burden is *our food sources.* As ***The San Diego Union-Tribune*** reported:

> Canned foods in grocery stores continue to contain the toxin BPA., according to a report by the Center for Environmental Health...Low-income people are more likely to face exposure to the chemical, since many live in areas with limited access to fresh produce and other food..."African Americans and low income families have, on average, higher amounts of BPA in

---

[703] Marija Kundakovic et al. "Sex-Specific epigenetic disruption and behavioral changes following low-dose in utero bisphenol A exposure," ***PNAS*** 110 (2013): 9956-9961 (9960); P. Negri-Cesi, "Bisphenol A Interation With Brain Development and Functions," ***Dose-Response*** 2015: 1-12.

[704] https://www.niehs.nih.gov/health/topics/agents/sya-bpa/index.cfm

[705] Ami R. Zota et al., "Recent Fast Food Consumption and Bisphenol A and Phthalates Exposures among the U.S. Population in NHANES, 2003-2010," ***Environmental Health Perspective*** 124 (2016): 1521-1528 (1521).

their bodies than people of other races and people of higher incomes," the report stated.[706]

In the first study to investigate maternal-fetal BPA concentrations by racial and ethnic group, Black pregnant women from a South Carolina cohort were found to have the highest maternal serum BPA concentrations, *10-fold higher than Caucasian mothers* (30.13 vs. 3.14 ng ml^{-1}).[707] In a study of inner-city Black and Dominican mothers and their children from New York "widespread BPA exposure" was detected among this group: BPA detected in 94% of samples.[708] N. Ranjit and colleagues thus explains:

> a growing body of evidence suggests that African Americans may be more likely to be at higher risk of exposure to EDCs. As noted, BPA has been shown to account for most estrogenic activity that leaches from landfills into the surrounding ecosystem i.e. *communities in which African Americans are more likely than Whites to reside.* Furthermore, *communities with higher proportions of African Americans have a disproportionate number of fast food restaurants* compared to communities with lower proportions of African Americans, and fewer sources of fresh food. Studies of the spatial distribution of fast food restaurants and supermarkets found that all African American areas, regardless of income, were less likely to have access to healthy food options than predominantly White higher income communities. Specifically, stores in predominantly black areas have been found to carry less fresh produce and higher proportions of canned foods than stores in predominantly white areas. African American households are overrepresented among the food insecure; in 2005, 23. 6% of

---

[706] Deborah Sullivan Brennan, "Canned food still contains toxin BPA," **The San Diego Union-Tribune** March 17, 2017. See also Jessica W. Nelson et al. "Social disparitities in exposures to bisphenol A and polyflurooalkyl chemicals: a cross-sectional study within NHANES 2003-2006," **Environmental Health** 11 (2012): 1-15: "People with lower incomes have higher body burdens of BPA."

[707] E.R. Unal et al. "Racial disparity in maternal and fetal-cord bisphenol A concentrations," **Journal of Perinatology** 32 (2012): 844-850.

[708] Lori A. Hoepner et al. "Urinary Concentrations of Bisphenol A in an Urban Minority Birth Cohort in New York City, Prenatal Through Age 7 Years," **Environ Res.** 122 (2013): 38-44; Frederica Perera et al., "Prenatal Bisphenol A Exposure and Child Behavior in an Inner-City Cohort," **Environmental Health Perspectives** 8 (120): 1190-1194.

African American households were food insecure, compared with only 8. 6% of White households. Given these high rates of food insecurity, *African American households are more likely to rely on cheap, energy dense fast food and on food banks, which typically distribute canned foods* as noted, a known and significant source of BPA exposure. *Food pantry use is more than twice as high among blacks than among non-Hispanic whites (7.8% vs. 2.7%)* (emphasis added - WM).[709]

Not only is the environment where poor Black people are forced to live made toxic by the intentional "dumping" of these chemicals nearby, but the food that is made available in Black areas which are deemed "food deserts" - fast food and canned foods – are contaminated with chemicals such as BPA.

When E.R. Unal et al. report that "findings show significantly higher serum BPA concentrations in pregnant African American women compared with Caucasians,"[710] there is evidence that this disparity is not accidental but the result of the deliberate targeting of pregnant Black women with BPA products. In May 2009 lobbyists for industry giants who use BPA in their products, such as Coca Cola and Del Monte, convened for five hours at the exclusive Cosmo Club in Washington D.C. to secretly collude and plot a major public relations campaign aimed at defeating legislative initiatives to remove BPA from items designed for small children. The **Washington Post** obtained the internal notes from the meeting and published them along with the **Journal Sentinel**.[711]

---

[709] N. Ranjit, K. Siefert and V. Padmanabhan, "Bisphenal-A and disparities in birth outcomes: a review and directions for future research," **Journal of Perinatology** 30 (2010): 2-9.
[710] Enal et al., "Racial disparity," 849.
[711] Lyndsey Layton, "Strategy Is Being Devised to Protect Use of Bisphenol A and Block U.S. Ban," **Washington Post** May 31, 2009, A02; Susanne Rust and Meg Kissinger, "BPA industry seeks to polish image," **Journal Sentinel** May 29, 2009.

The purpose of the meeting, as ewg reported, was to "plot to scare mothers *and minorities* into consuming more BPA."[712] In order to defeat efforts to ban BPA, the industry would target "young mothers" with a message to resist BPA-free products and remain loyal to BPA-use products. According to the notes, the lobbyists' "'holy grail' spokesperson would be a 'pregnant young mother' who would be willing to speak around the country about the benefits of BPA."[713] But it wouldn't be *any* pregnant young mother showcasing the "good" of BPA; according to the notes the focus of this campaign "to dissuade people from choosing BPA-free packaging" is specifically "minorities" or "Hispanic and African Americans."[714] The industry lobbyists were prepared to invest $500,000 to come up with a message trying to sell BPA to Black people and frightening pregnant Black and Brown mothers into staying away from BPA-free food packaging for their children. As the *Journal Sentinel* reports:

---

[712] Environmental Working Group, "Coca-Cola and Del Monte Caught in Plot to Deceive Moms and Minorities Over Dangers of BPA," *ewg.org* June 4, 2009.
[713] Layton, "Strategy Is Being Devised."
[714] Meg Kissinger "What goes on behind closed doors," *Journal Sentinel* June 1, 2009.

Other strategies discussed at the meeting included focusing on how BPA bans would disproportionately put minorities at risk, particularly Hispanics and African Americans who are more inclined to be poor and dependent on canned foods. Committee members said they would try to get stories in the media that spread the message that canned goods made without BPA would be more likely to become contaminated [with bacteria].[715]

It should be very clear now why Black pregnant women have serum BPA concentrations *10-fold higher than Caucasian women*. It is not an accident. Pregnant Black and Brown women are specifically targeted with BPA products so they could feed BPA-poisoned food to their fetus.

VIII. *WIC and the Mystery of the Missing Zinc*

Zinc (Zn) is an essential nutrient necessary in small amounts for health. As one of the most abundant biological trace metals, zinc is easy to get in developed countries in foods like beef, poultry, and beans. Zinc deficiency in humans can cause an assortment of pathological conditions such as growth retardation, cell-mediated immune disfunction, among others.[716] Zinc deficiency is rare in the U.S. because, due to the easy access to zinc-containing foods, most diets provide more than the recommended dietary intake. So an important 2010 study seems then to reveal to us more than the circumstances of an exceptional case of zinc deficiency in an American population,[717] but also *hints of a scientific conspiracy.*

Scientists from Emory University, Grady Hospital and the Center for Disease Control and Prevention (CDC) studied a group of low-income Black and Hispanic pre-school children (1-5 years of age) in urban Atlanta, Georgia who were on government insurance and were enrolled in the Women, Infants, and Children (WIC) nutrition program 2006-2007. WIC is a federal assistance

---

[715] Susanne Rust and Meg Kissinger, "BPA industry seeks to polish image," *Journal Sentinel* May 29, 2009.

[716] Ananda S. Prasad, "Discovery of Human Zinc Deficiency: Its Impact on Human Health and Disease," *Adv. Nutr.* 4 (2013): 176-190.

[717] Conrad R.Cole et al., "Zinc and Iron deficiency and their interrelations in low-income African American and Hispanic children in Atlanta," *Am J Clin Nutr* 91 (2010): 1027-1034.

program that provides (among other things) free food packages to low-income pregnant and breastfeeding women, infants, and children under age 5 in order to supplement diets and provide nutrition. It is administrated by the U.S. Department of Agriculture (!). Annual Race/Ethnicity Data indicates that, in general, around 60% of WIC recipients are White and 20% are Black.[718] WIC participation is historically associated with good zinc levels. A 2003 study of a national sample of 7474 mostly non-urban (67%) Whites (61%) found "Less than 1% of (preschool) children had usual zinc intakes below the adequate intake or estimated average requirement" and that "WIC participation was positively associated with zinc intake".[719] In other words, the food provided through the WIC program provided at least some of the zinc needed to achieve healthy levels. Fifteen years later a 2018 national random sample of 3,235 children found that WIC participants who received the food packages tested better for zinc intake than low-income *as well as high-income* non-WIC participants.[720] This suggests that the WIC package was a source of zinc for these participants. Jun et al. found that only 2% of this national sample of young infant (0- to 5.9-months-old) WIC recipients and 1.5% of toddlers (12- to 23.9-months-old) had zinc intakes below the estimated average requirement.

Even Black children have historically benefited from WIC in this regard. The Third National Health and Nutrition Examination Survey, 1988-1994 surveyed the zinc status of a nationwide sample of 29,103 (10,533 White, 8392 Black, 8421 Mexican American) aged two years and older and found that, while Whites do have a better zinc status than African Americans and Mexican Americans in part due to the larger percentage of Whites (mainly female) who can afford to use zinc supplements, "Mean *dietary* zinc intakes were not statistically

---

[718] Thorn, B., Kline, N., Tadler, C., Budge, E., Wilcox-Cook, E., Michaels, J., Mendelson, M., Patlan, K. L., & Tran, V., *WIC Participant and Program Characteristics 2016* (Alexandria, VA: U.S. Department of Agriculture, Food and Nutrition Service, 2018) 24-27.
[719] Joanne E Arsenault and Kenneth H Brown, "Zinc intake of US preschool children exceeds new dietary reference intakes," *Am J Clin Nutr* 78 (2003): 1011-7.
[720] Shinyoung Jun et al. "Usual Nutrient Intakes from the Diets of US Children by WIC Participation and Income: Findings from the Feeding Infants and Toddlers Study (FITS) 2016," *The Journal of Nutrition* 148 (2018): 1567S–1574S.

different among non-Hispanic whites, non-Hispanic blacks, and Mexican Americans of the same age and sex group for age/sex groups aged < 51y."[721] The national zinc status of African Americans (mean 9.5) did not depart significantly from that of the national mean (10.0). So a zinc deficiency is uncharacteristic in America, for both Whites and African Americans. Thus, what was discovered in Atlanta in 2006-2007 is indeed an anomaly that demands explanation.

Conrad R. Cole et al.'s 2010 report is an analysis of the zinc status of 280 Black and Hispanic children of urban Atlanta.[722] This is a study of a defined, single metropolitan area group of Black and Hispanic preschoolers dependent (to one degree or another) upon WIC food supplies. The authors found evidence of a zinc deficiency in *from 19.4% to upwards of 44% of the Black children*: "Mean serum zinc concentrations were significantly lower among African American preschool children than among Hispanic preschool children, and they were significantly lower among those covered by government-sponsored insurance programs than among those with private health insurance".[723] The risk of zinc deficiency among these Black children was 4-fould that of the Hispanic children. This zinc-deficiency was so prevalent among Black children on WIC that "African American" ethnicity as well as "government-sponsored insurance status" were deemed risk factors for zinc-deficiency.[724]

This unexpectedly high prevalence of zinc deficiency among Black preschool WIC recipients in Atlanta is remarkably contrary not only to the reported good zinc status of White WIC recipients nationwide but is contrary also to the zinc status of nationwide samples of African Americans as well. Our 2006-2007 Atlanta population of Black preschoolers with a high prevalence of zinc deficiency thus *stands out radically as a national outlier.*

---

[721] Ronette R. Briefel et al., "Zinc Intake of the U.S. Population: Findings from the Third National Health and Nutrition Examination Survey, 1988-1994," *Journal of Nutrition* 130 (2000): 1367S-1373S.

[722] Conrad R. Cole et al., "Zinc and Iron deficiency and their interrelations in low-income African American and Hispanic children in Atlanta," *Am J Clin Nutr* 91 (2010): 1027-1034.

[723] Cole et al., "Zinc and Iron deficiency," 1029.

[724] Cole et al., "Zinc and Iron deficiency," 1027, 1030.

The consequences of zinc deficiency are significant. Zinc deficiency can cause growth retardation, mental lethargy and endocrine disruption, specifically male hypogonadism (=low testosterone), testicular atrophy (shrinkage of testicles), and male and female infertility.

> Zinc plays an essential role in the synthesis and secretion of luteinizing hormone (LH) and follicle-stimulating hormone (FSH), gonadal differentiation, action of the Müllerian inhibiting factor, testicular growth and development of seminiferous tubules, spermatogenesis, testicular steroidogenesis, androgen metabolism and interaction with steroid receptors (...). In zinc deficiency, testicular cells are able to take up cholesterol and neutral lipids which are precursors of sex steroids but are incapable of converting them into sex steroids, leading to the arrest of spermatogenesis and the impairment of fertilization...[725]

Not only does zinc deficiency cause male reproductive disruption, it causes male feminization. Zinc inhibits the process called *aromatization* i.e., the conversion of the male hormone testosterone into the feminizing hormone estrogen by the enzyme aromatase. Zinc deficiency therefore results in *excessive* aromatization, which leads to an excessive amount of testosterone converting into estrogen, thus an increased estrogen/testosterone ratio. Zinc deficiency also decreases the available number of *androgen receptors* necessary to potentiate the testosterone and increases the number of *estrogen receptors* that potentiate the extra estrogen: "Such (zinc) deficiency plays a pathogenic role in feminization and reproductive dysfunction," reports Om and Chung.[726]

So a condition – zinc deficiency - that causes male feminization as well as reproductive disfunction leading to infertility in males and females is a rare occurrence in America among African Americans and Whites, yet it "unexpectedly"

---

[725] Ae-son Om and Kyung-Won Chung, "Dietary Zinc Deficiency Alters 5a-Reduction and Aromatization of Testosterone and Androgen and Estrogen Receptors in Rat Liver," *Journal of Nutrition* 126 (1996): 842-848 (842). See also Ananda S. Prasad, "Discovery of Human Zinc Deficiency: Its Impact on Human Health and Disease," *Adv. Nutr.* 4 (2013): 176-190; Ananda S. Prasad et al., "Zinc status and serum testosterone levels of healthy adults," *Nutrition* 12 (1996): 344-348.
[726] Om and Chung, "Dietary Zinc Deficiency Alters 5a-Reduction," 847.

occurs in a population of Black preschoolers in the CDC's Atlanta, as "discovered" by a CDC funded study?! What is the cause of this "unexpected" find? Our authors don't give us an answer, but they do offer us a hint:

> Food intake was not a problem in either group (Black or Hispanic), as documented in the food diaries, especially those of the African American children who consumed very high mean daily energy. However, *the bioavailability of zinc in the foods consumed* and the interactions between zinc and other components of the diet might be responsible for the zinc status among these children.

In other words, it is not the case that the Black children are not consuming the right foods in order to have a better zinc status. Rather, it is possible that the zinc in these foods is not rendered bioavailable when consumed by these Black children. Or: the food does not contain the zinc that it is *expected* to contain. Both can be accomplished scientifically.

Zinc deficiencies have been experimentally induced by diet in animals by scientists since 1967 and by 1983 it was "considered desirable to develop a *human model* which would allow a study of the effects of a mild zinc deficient state in man."[727] In other words, after mastering the induction of a zinc deficiency in animals through manipulation of food sources, scientists were ready to try their skills with human guinea pigs. The first human models were groups of volunteers enrolled in scientific experiments.[728] But *in vitro* (in the lab) results need *in vivo* (in real life) confirmation. Did the *in vivo* phase of the project to develop and study a human model of zinc deficiency involve those 146 Black children of metro Atlanta who participated in the 2006-2007 zinc study supported by the CDC and the National Institutes of Health? Were they unwitting human guinea pigs?

---

[727] R.B. Williams and C.F. Mills, "The experimental production of zinc deficiency in the rat," **Br. J. Nutr.** (1970): 989-1003; Ananda S. Prasad, "Experimental Zinc Deficiency in Humans: An Overview of Original Studies," **Nutritional bioavailability of zinc**, ed. George E. Inglett (Washington, DC: American Chemical Society, 1983) 1-14; Parviz I. Rabbani et al., "Dietary model for production of experimental zinc deficiency in man," **Am J Clin Nutr** 45 (1987): 1514-1525.

[728] Prasad, "Experimental Zinc Deficiency in Humans."

The American Journal of Clinical Nutrition

Dietary model for production of experimental zinc deficiency in man[1-3]

Parviz I Rabbani, PhD; Ananda S Prasad, MD, PhD; Rita Tsai, RD; Barbara F Harland, PhD, RD; and MR Spivey Fox, PhD

ABSTRACT   A semipurified diet based on soy protein was developed to induce mild zinc deficiency in five male volunteers. Each of seven daily menus provided (mean ± SD) 2248 ± 128 kcal, 56.6 ± 5.7 g protein, 261 ± 30 g carbohydrate, 110 ± 21 g fat, 8.5 ± 1.4 g fiber, and 4.8 ± 1.3 mg zinc. The analytical value for phytate:zinc molar ratio was 21 ± 9. One subject, who received five of the menus for 28 wk, lost ~200 mg body zinc and 7% weight; zinc concentration declined 25% in plasma, 30% in lymphocytes, and 55% in neutrophils. This dietary model allowed simple formulation of new menus for subjects in diverse states of health. It caused no ill effects after prolonged consumption, and all deficiency symptoms were reversed by zinc supplementation of 30 mg/d for 20 wk. With simple manipulation, this dietary model may be used safely for gradual induction of zinc and/or other micronutrient deficiencies in humans.   *Am J Clin Nutr* 1987;45:1514–25.

KEY WORDS   Dietary model, zinc deficiency in humans, textured soy protein

Introduction

In 1974, the National Academy of Sciences (1) first published a recommended dietary allowance (RDA) for zinc. The recommendation was based on radioisotope and zinc-balance data. Radioisotope data (2) showed that zinc turnover was ~6 mg/d for adults. Daily obligatory zinc losses with no dietary zinc intake totaled 2 mg/d (3, 4). Assuming that 40% of the dietary zinc is biologically available (5), the recommended zinc intake for adults would fall between 5 and 15 mg/d.

Such a study would have to be monitored closely to reduce errors involved in estimation of zinc balance.

We developed a 2-d cycle diet for two groups of two volunteers each and fed it for ~1 yr (19). One of the most difficult problems we encountered was dissatisfaction with prolonged consumption of such a monotonous diet. To reduce the monotony of the diet and to increase its palatability, the original diet was extensively modified and new recipes were added according to the principles of the American Diabetic Association's (ADA) ex-

---

There are a variety of techniques capable of experimentally inducing a zinc deficiency in a human model through dietary means. Foods can be scientifically modified to deplete zinc in a human consumer and to cause a zinc deficiency without the consumer having a clue. This can be achieved via two primary methods of food manipulation: 1. Stripping a food item of its natural zinc content or 2. Introducing into the food a chemical inhibitor that reduces the zinc's bioavailability once the food is consumed. In the case of Black WIC recipients in Atlanta, both of these methods could be performed by the food manufacturer before the food is packaged and shipped to the zip codes where the destination stores are located.

In terms of the first method, food can be stripped or "purified" of its zinc by being "washed" with the disodium salt of the chemical ethylenediaminetetraacetic acid (EDTA). Because EDTA binds to zinc, its disodium salt (Na_2EDTA) acts as a chelator or *extractant* that "pulls out" all or most of the zinc in the food, which is then washed off of the food with deionized water. Once dried, the food can be packaged and shipped, and the store personnel and the consumer of the food is none the wiser. EDTA-washed foods have been extensively used by scientists to induce zinc-deficiency. Thus, theoretically if the "purified-then-packaged" food is sent to stores in selected areas (zip codes) and purchased with a WIC voucher, only *those* WIC costumers in *that* area would show any signs of a zinc deficiency. This hypothetical is very consistent with what we actually find in our Atlanta cohort of 2006-2007.

The second method of modifying food to covertly induce a zinc deficiency is by inserting an *additive* into the food that, once consumed, inhibits the bioavailability of the zinc. Incidentally, it is public knowledge that WIC products – on a state-by-state basis - *contain such chemical inhibitors* which fall under the title "Functional Ingredients." A "Functional Food" is a food that is modified by a functional ingredient, which is a substance added to a food through the manufacturing process and that is purported to improve bodily function or is intended to produce a desired physiological effect.[729] WIC offers such "Functional Foods" that have been modified by chemical additives, such as baby formula, infant cereal, eggs, juice, and bread.[730] One of the recognized "functional ingredients" used to modify food is soy protein isolate. Soy products have been a staple of the WIC package since 2009. But as a recognized *functional ingredient*, soy protein isolate can be added to any WIC-offered food by the manufacture. Even though WIC is a fully federally-funded program, the decision to offer modified or "enhanced" foods is not a national decision but is made on a state-by-state basis, and *not* by the state WIC office but by the manufacturers! Because soy protein isolate is a highly refined product processed to remove "off flavors," beany tastes and flatulence producers and increase digestibility, it is much easier to conceal its presence in a food item.

---

[729] Kristi M. Crowe and Coni Francis, "Position of the Academy of Nutrition and Dietetics: Functional Foods," ***Journal of the Academy of Nutrition and Dietetics*** 113 (2013): 1096-1103; Institute of Food Technologies, "Functional Foods: Opportunities and Challenges," March 2005. http://www.ift.org/ Knowledge-Center/Read-IFT-Publications/ Science-Reports/Expert-Reports/w/media/ Knowledge%20Center/Science%20Reports/ Expert%20Reports/Functional%20Foods/ Functionalfoods_expertreport_full.pdf. Accessed June 23, 2019
[730] Zoë Neuberger, "WIC Package Should Be Based on Science: Foods with New Functional Ingredients Should Be Provided Only If They Deliver Health or Nutritional Benefits," ***Center on Budget and Policy Priorities*** June 4, 2010.

SOY THE ENEMY

Why is adding soy protein isolate to a food as a functional ingredient a problem and of potential relevance to our discussion of Black WIC recipients in Atlanta with an "unexpected" zinc deficiency? Because, in the case of the *in vitro* phase of the human experiment, in "the nature and composition of a diet that could be used to produce a deficiency of zinc...in man," "[t]he principle ingredient used to formulate the [menu] was texturized soy protein."[731] This is because soy contains a substance called phytate which is released in the body (after consumption) as phytic acid. Phytic acid has been referred to as an "anti-nutrient" substance because it promotes mineral deficiency. When soy is added to a food and that food is consumed, the phytic acid impairs the absorption by the body of iron, zinc, and calcium by binding to these minerals in the intestine, making them less available to the body, i.e. not "bioavailable." Soy-enhanced foods thus can cause zinc deficiency.

Soy is also a feminizer on its own. The soybean contains isoflavones like genistein that are estrogenic-they bind to and activate the estrogen receptors. Soy protein also depletes testosterone in men.[732] In addition, "Soy phytoestrogens have contraceptive effects," impairing male and female fertility.[733] Nevertheless, soy is recognized by the FDA – the CIA's own "junior partner" - as a "functional food" that can be added to foods, and today it is reported that 60% of foods found in the supermarket and natural food stores contain soy as an ingredient, often a "hidden" ingredient in products where soy would not ordinarily be expected, such as fast-food hamburgers.[734] According to Slate.com "A quick scan of a McDonald's ingredients list revealed soy in more than 200 items—and not just in expected things like French fries and chicken nuggets, but also breakfast sausages, grilled onions,

---

[731] Prasad, "Experimental Zinc Deficiency in Humans"; Rabbani et al., "Dietary model for production of experimental zinc deficiency in man."

[732] See Dr. Kaayla T. Daniel, *the whole soy story: the dark side of America's favorite health food* (Washington, DC: New Trends Publishing, Inc., 2005).

[733] Daniel, *the whole soy story*, Chapter 28.

[734] Daniel, *the whole soy story*, 88.

chicken patties, BBQ ranch sauce, sesame buns, liquid margarine, cinnamon melts, hash browns, griddle cakes, chocolate chips, and bagels."[735]

Prior to this current *dominance* of labeled and unlabeled (hidden) soy-infused foods, it is not inconceivable that such a practice was piloted by programs that offered food to poor Black people in urban areas-the WIC program for example - in order to test the ability to dietarily induce a zinc deficiency in an *in vivo* human model. This would most certainly give context to the "discovery" of a rare prevalence of zinc deficiency among Black WIC recipients of urban Atlanta, 2006-2007 by the CDC.

At around this same time another isolated, captive population was punitively force-fed a soy-based diet. In 2010 prisoners from Danville Correctional Center sued the Illinois Department of Corrections (IDOC) in federal court alleging that the prisoners were being "tortured" by excessive soy in the diets. Well into the 1990s prisoners were fed a beef-based meat diet and even operated prison farms and abattoirs, producing much of their own food. But in 2003 when Rob Blagoyevich became governor of Illinois, he fired the Black woman in charge of food service and instituted a 60-70% soy-based diet: soy protein "meat," soy cheese in the macaroni, soy sausage, sour flour used for baked goods, etc.[736]

The soy was provided to the IDOC by Archer Daniel Midlands, who reportedly was a big contributor to the Blagoyevich campaign. The prisoners were being fed as many as seven soy-enhanced "meat" entrées a week, amounting to as much as 100 grams of soy protein a day while the USDA (!) was recommending no more than 25 grams of consumption per day as safe. Some of the soy was Monsanto's genetically modified soy. At the same time, the IDOC staff were provided soy-free food. The suit alleged that feeding a soy-laden diet constitutes cruel and unusual punishment in violation of the eighth amendment of the Constitution. Men were suffering from heart

---

[735] Rachel E. Gross, "Why Soy Is Everywhere?" **Slate.com** May 21, 2015.

[736] Andrea Billups, "Soy diet prompts prisoners' lawsuit," *The Washington Times* Tuesday February 28, 2012; Sally Fallon Morell, "State of Illinois Still Poisoning Male Prisoners with Soy Diet," @ http://nourishingtraditions.com/state-illinois-still-poisoning-male-prisoners-soy-diet/ ; "Illinois Prisoners Sue over Soy-Based Food," *Prison Legal News* April, 2010.

issues, thyroid damage, severe digestive problems, vomiting, constipation, debilitating diarrhea, and hormonal changes that caused men to grow breasts and become infertile. "The main problem was the high estrogen levels in the soy," said Larry "Rocky" Harris, a "prisoner lawyer" and one of the plaintiffs in the suit.[737] Yet, this same soy is classed as a *functional ingredient* and indiscriminately added to food. This soy can cause zinc deficiency.

Zinc deficiency can cause infertility in males and females and feminization of males. This is a rare condition in America, yet it made an "unexpected" appearance among Black children in Atlanta dependent upon government-issued food sources. Using secretly manipulated food to covertly induce a condition of infertility and male feminization would not have been a new idea in 2006-2007, as we saw. The spatial isolation of Black communities through segregation makes it easy to target this specific group.

IX. *Fast Food and Food Oppression*

We know we are in a bona fide "Food Crisis" when it could be said that in Black neighborhoods "it is easier to get fried chicken than a fresh apple."[738] Fast food has become "entrenched" in urban neighborhoods and diets. "NHANES data indicate that non-Hispanic blacks are more likely than other racial/ethnic groups to eat fast food."[739] As Dr. Chin Jou documents in her **Super Sizing Urban America. How Inner Cities Got Fast Food With Government Help**, "many urban, low-income African-American neighborhoods are both saturated with fast food and disproportionately affected by the obesity epidemic."[740] According to Dr. Andrea Freedman, fast food is *"oppression through poor nutrition"*:

---

[737] "Larry 'Rocky' Harris Innocence Project," @ https://freelarryrockyharrisx2.com/
[738] Naa Oyo A. Kwate, "Fried chicken and fresh apples: Racial segregation as a fundamental cause of fast food density in black neighborhoods," **Health & Place** 14 (2008): 32-44 (34).
[739] Wendee Nicole, "Phthalates in Fast Food," **Environmental Health Perspective** 124 (2016): 191.
[740] Chin Jou, **Super Sizing Urban America. How Inner Cities Got Fast Food With Government Help** (Chicago and London: The University of Chicago, 2017) 17.

Fast food has become a major source of nutrition in low-income, urban neighborhoods across the United States. Although some social and cultural factors account for fast food's overwhelming popularity, *targeted marketing, infiltration into schools, government subsidies, and federal food policy each play a significant role in denying inner-city people of color access to healthy food.* The overabundance of fast food and lack of access to healthier foods, in turn, have increased African American and Latino communities' vulnerability to food-related death and disease.' Structural perpetuation of this race- and class-based health crisis constitutes "food oppression."[741]

NHANES data indicate that non-Hispanic blacks are more likely than other racial/ethnic groups to eat fast food. This raises questions about disproportionate exposures to phthalates found in fast food. © Finbarr O'Reilly/Reuters

This "structural perpetuation" is obvious:

West Oakland, California, a neighborhood of 30,000 people populated primarily by African Americans and Latinos, has *one supermarket and thirty- six liquor and convenience stores.* The supermarket is not accessible on foot to most of the area's residents. The convenience stores charge twice as much as grocery stores for identical items. Fast food restaurants selling cheap and hot food appear on almost every corner. West Oakland is not unique. The prevalence of fast food in low-income urban neighborhoods across the United States,

---

[741] Andrea Freeman, "Fast Food: Oppression through Poor Nutrition," *California Law review* 95 (2007): 2221-2260 (2221-2222).

combined with the lack of access to fresh, healthy food, contributes to an overwhelmingly disproportionate incidence of food-related death and disease among African Americans and Latinos as compared to whites (emphasis added – WM).742

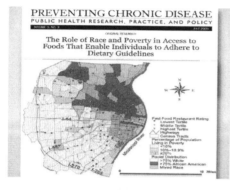

A 2006 audit by Elizabeth A. Baker et al. of food quality options in the St. Louis (!) area found that the highest quality supermarkets that provide the best options for meeting dietary guidelines (fresh fruits and vegetables, lean, low-fat and fat-free meats and dairy options) clustered in white higher-income communities and *none in Black census tracts*, while the poorest quality fast food restaurants and poor quality super markets – to the extent that super markets exists at all - that offer low quality food (high fat), disallowing consumers to meet recommended dietary intake clustered in predominantly Black census tracks.743

In a 2004 study researchers mapped fast food restaurants in New Orleans and discovered that shopping districts in communities that were 80% Black were exposed on average to six fast food outlets more than majority white areas of the same size.

> Fast-food restaurants are geographically associated with predominately black and low-income neighborhoods after controlling for commercial activity, presence of highways, and median home values. The percentage of black residents is a more powerful predictor of [fast food restaurant density] than median household income. Predominantly black neighborhoods (i.e., 80% black) have one additional fast-food restaurant per square mile compared with predominantly white neighborhoods (i.e., 80% white). These findings suggest that black and low-income populations have more convenient access to fast food. More convenient access likely leads to the increased

---

742 Freeman, "Fast Food: Oppression through Poor Nutrition."
743 Elizabeth A. Baker et al., "The Role of Race and Poverty in Access to Foods That Enable Individuals to Adhere to Dietary Guidelines," **Prev Chronic Dis** [serial online] 2006 Jul, 1-11.

consumption of fast food in these populations, and may help to explain the increased prevalence of obesity among black and low-income populations.[744]

THE ORIGIN OF BLACK AMERICA'S FAST FOOD DEPENDENCY

While it true that Black and Hispanic communities disproportionately patronize fast food restaurants, this is a *new phenomenon*.

> But despite its current popularity, there was a time not too long ago when fast food was *entirely absent from the diets of inner-city African-Americans*. McDonald's and most of the major fast food chains only opened in urban areas starting in the late 1960s and early 1970s. Brady Keys, a former pro-football player and African-American fast food franchising pioneer, recalls that before the emergence of fast food, African Americans consumed more meals at home; there was simply "no opportunity to eat anywhere else [relatively cheaply]."[745]

And believe it or not, Black People had *a better diet than Whites in many cases*. In a 1939 U.S. Department of Agriculture dietary survey it was revealed that during the summer months African Americans' diets contained more vitamins, minerals, and proteins than whites' diets in cases where households spent the same money on food. In 1965, African Americans were still consuming dietitians recommended quantities of fat, fiber, fruits, and vegetables at twice the rate of whites. However, by 1996 a near-reversal had occurred. "Dietary surveys indicated that 28 percent of African Americans, and only 16 percent of whites, now consumed unhealthy diets."[746] This diet revolution was caused largely by the new availability of fast food.

> During the heyday of fast food in the United States-roughly the 1970s to 1990s-Americans' appetite for Big Macs and Whoppers seemed to cut across socioeconomic divides more than they do now...*Today's* typical fast food habitué is more likely to be

---

[744] Jason P. Block et al., "Fast Food, Race/Ethnicity, and Income," *Am J Prev Med* 27 (2004): 211-217 (214-215).
[745] Jou, *Super Sizing Urban America*, 47.
[746] Jou, *Super Sizing Urban America*, 49.

relatively young, low-income, and African-American (emphasis added).[747]

It was the relentless targeting of the Black poor, with the aid of the U.S. Government, that transformed the urban food landscape: "federal programs were...part of a remaking of inner cities as fast food havens"[748]

> Fast food companies' aggressive pursuit of African Americans since the early 1970s has been reflected in the inordinate share of their promotional budgets dedicated to reeling in minority consumers. One report in 1990 found that the three major fast food chains-McDonald's, Burger King, and Wendy's-earmarked up to one-fifth of their advertising budgets on African-American consumers even though African-Americans made up only about 12 percent of the total U.S. population at the time.[749]

The fast food industry is particularly "unrelenting in its appeal to young urban African Americans".[750] According to one 2012 report Black children (ages two through eleven) and teenagers viewed almost 60% more television advertisements for fast food than white children and teens. *The Washington Post* took notice of this "food oppression" in 2014 reporting "The disturbing ways that fast food chains disproportionately target black kids," noting the research that "fast food chains (such as **Popeye's** and **Papa John's**) in predominantly black neighborhoods were more than 60 percent more likely to advertise to children than in predominantly white neighborhoods."[751]

The concentration of African-Americans into segregated neighborhoods made us "compact sales targets," in marketing jargon, and made the direct, geographic targeting of us easy and efficient: *waging war by zip codes.* As Naa Oyo A. Kwate points out:

---

[747] Jou, *Super Sizing Urban America*, 152-153.
[748] Jou, *Super Sizing Urban America*, 16.
[749] Jou, *Super Sizing Urban America*, 117.
[750] Jou, *Super Sizing Urban America*, 16.
[751] Roberto A. Ferdman, "The disturbing ways that fast food chains disproportionately target black kids," *The Washington Post* November 12, 2014.

A primary reason why Black neighborhoods have a high prevalence of fast food restaurants is because African Americans are actively sought by fast food companies, and segregation creates a ready, spatially concentrated target area. From a purely rational business perspective, the high prevalence of fast food restaurants in Black neighborhoods is itself suggestive of purposeful targeting. When opening a business, owners must consider location characteristics, including neighboring shops and local business climate, the crime rate, quality of public services, condition of homes, buildings, and lots, relationship to competition, and the spatial relationship to the target market (...). In many Black neighborhoods, such a location analysis would reveal: a retail climate that generates few customers; a relatively high crime rate; public services that have faced years of cutbacks and neglect; visibly deteriorated buildings; and several competing fast food restaurants. *In other words, there would be few incentives to open a store in a neighborhood with these characteristics, unless a primary goal was to target the individuals who reside there.*[752]

And it seems to be urban young Black men who are the real target audience.

Living near fast food restaurants may indeed constitute a "risky" physical environment, at least if one is low-income and male. A 2011 analysis of a longitudinal nationwide survey of 5,155 U.S. adults between the ages eighteen and thirty found that low-income men who lived within 3 kilometers (1.9 miles) of fast food chain restaurants consumed fast food more frequently than those who did not. These low-income men, researchers reasoned, were less likely to own cars, which made them more dependent on their immediate environs for meals and other services. This geographic constraint, coupled with limited cash for food, made it more likely that these low-income men would be ordering double cheeseburgers...off McDonald's Dollar Menu. [753]

The Dollar Menu was targeted toward poor Black people, a strategy to ensnare African Americans into a fast-food diet. As McDonald's vice president for United States business research Steve Levigne quasi-confessed: "The Dollar Menu appeals to lower-income, ethnic consumers...It's people who don't always

---

[752] Kwate, "Fried chicken and fresh apples," 35.
[753] Jou, **Super Sizing Urban America**, 16.

have $6 in their pockets."[754] This disproportionate patronizing of fast food by Black and Hispanic communities is thus not an organic or natural phenomenon but the desired end of a government and industry process. And this process has contributed to the "obesity crisis" of Black America. According to the U.S. Department of Health and Human Services, in 2015 African Americans were 1.4 times as likely as Whites to be obese. 69.6% of Black men and 82% of Black Women are either obese (body mass index > 30.0) or overweight (body mass index > 25.0). "African American Women have the highest rates of being overweight or obese compared to other groups in in the U.S.," HHS.gov reports.[755]

X. How McDonalds is making Us Sterile

CNN reported recently under the title, "Junk food loving young men have lower sperm counts than healthier eaters, researchers say"[756]:

Junk food loving young men have lower sperm counts than healthier eaters, researchers say

By Susan Scutti, CNN

Updated 6 hrs ago | Posted on Jun 26, 2019 | 0

Burgers, fries, pizza and high energy drinks impact testicular function in young men, new research suggests. Specifically, the sperm counts for men who typically eat "Western" meals of high fat foods were 25.6 million lower, on average, than the counts of men noshing on fish, chicken, fruits, vegetables and other more "prudent" foods, a new Harvard study found. Full Credit: Thomas Northcut/Photodisc/Getty Images

Getty Images

Burgers, fries, pizza and high energy drinks impact testicular function in young men, new research suggests. Specifically, the sperm counts for men who typically eat "Western" meals of high fat foods were 25.6 million lower, on average, than the counts of men noshing on fish, chicken, fruits, vegetables and other more "prudent" foods, a new Harvard study found."

The Harvard researchers believe that a high processed food diet characteristic of American fast food may be responsible for the

---

[754] Jou, **Super Sizing Urban America**, 154.
[755]   @
https://minorityhealth.hhs.gov/omh/browse.aspx?lvl=4&lvlid=25
[756] Susan Scutti, "Junk food loving young men have lower sperm counts than healthier eaters, researchers say," **CBS46** June 26, 2019.

known trend that has been recorded over the recent past of progressively decreasing sperm counts and increasing male infertility. According to the World Health Organization (WHO) a normal sperm count is 39 million or more per ejaculation. Consumers of a Western diet (processed red meats, chips, fried foods, potatoes, snacks, pre-packaged foods, high-fat dairy, high-sugar drinks, sweets) have on average a slashed sperm count (25.6 million lower), while those with healthier diets (such as the "Mediterranean diet": fruit, vegetables, fish, beans, extra-virgin olive oil, healthy grain, small amount of meat and dairy) showed an elevated sperm count (42.8 million more). Pizza, chips, and red meat increases oxidative stress on cells, while healthier foods are more anti-oxidant and associated with higher fertility.[757]

Researchers believe that processed foods irreversibly damage the sperm-producing Sertoli cells in males. In addition, a Taiwanese study in 2018 described an association between the high-fat diet characteristic of fast foods and diminished testosterone levels in men (hypogonadism), affirming results which suggests that "individuals who prefer Western-style food..., *eat out, and eat fewer homemade foods*, noodles, and dark green vegetables are more likely to have an unhealthy body composition (e.g. increased visceral fat and deceased skeletal muscle mass) and low serum total [testosterone] levels, and are likely to develop hypogonadism."[758] Slashed sperm count and diminished testosterone levels contribute to male infertility. On the other hand, in a study of 5598 nulliparous (never given birth) women Jessica A. Grieger and colleagues presented an association between consumption of fast foods and female infertility.[759] Greater consumption of foods with a high glycemic index and a higher intake of energy from trans fats as well as sodium and sugar are associated with increased risk of ovulatory infertility.

---

[757] Estefania Toledo et al., "Dietary patterns and difficulty conceiving: a nested case–control study," **Fertility and Sterility** 96 (2011):1149-1153.

[758] Tzu-Yu Hu et al., "Testosterone-Associated Dietary Pattern Predicts Low Testosterone Levels and Hypogonadism," **Nutrients** 10 (2018): 1-16.

[759] Jessica A. Grieger et al., "Pre-pregnancy fast food and fruit intake is associated with time to pregnancy," **Human Reproduction** 33 (2018): 1063-1070.

Thus, fast food consumption is believed to lead to infertility in men and women. And because *"non-Hispanic blacks are more likely than other racial/ethnic groups to eat fast food,"*[760] and because fast food is "entrenched" in Black neighborhoods today *not* because Black people have a cultural predilection to it but because Black communities are victims of *food oppression*, the reproductive capability of Black America is most effected.

As the United States hit a 40-year low in its fertility rate in 2018, "the decline in fertility has been *far* greater among minorities than among non-Hispanic whites," according to the Institute for Family Studies, who admits that

> in racial or ethnic terms, America's 'Baby Bust' is kinda, sorta, a little bit racist: it's hammered Native Americans and Hispanics particularly hard, and hit even African Americans harder than whites generally, and certainly harder than non-Hispanic whites.[761]

Black people are famously a very fecund people and White people have stopped reproducing themselves such that the "browning of America" is now an inevitability: Whites will become the minority in America in this century, it is predicted. Thus, one may be surprised to know that fertility rates have *decreased* for Black women over the past several years at a much greater rate than that of White women at the same time.[762] Fertility rates for Black women have dropped from 2.5 births per woman in 1990 to 2.0 births in 2010, while White women had 1.9 births per woman in 1990 and 1.8 in 2010.

Even more to the point, however: in multiple recent semen analysis studies of Black and White men, Black men are found to have lower average sperm counts (92.43 million vs. 175.23 million), lower average sperm motility (39.87% vs. 49.22%), and a lower amount of normal sperm (4.89% vs. 7.28%) than White and Hispanic men and are more likely today

---

[760] *Environmental Health Perspective* 124 (2016): 191.

[761] Lyman Stone, "Baby Bust: Fertility is Declining the Most Among Minority Women," *Institute for Family Studies* May 16, 2018.

[762] Melissa F. Wellons et al., "Racial Differences in Self-Reported Infertility and Risk Factors for Infertility in a Cohort of Black and White Women: The CARDIA Women's Study," *Fertil Steril* 90 (2008): 1640-1648.

to suffer from azoospermia (no sperm in the ejaculate).[763] In another, multi-city study

> total sperm count and total motile sperm count were almost 50% lower for Black men compared to men in the other two groups (P<0.0001)...The percentage of men with semen volume, sperm concentration and total sperm count below current WHO reference values (...) was greater for Black men compared to White and Hispanic/Latino men.[764]

Thus, in a study of infertility among U.S. active service men between 2013 and 2017, crude overall incident infertility rates were highest among Black men vs. Whites and Hispanics.[765] This is quite astounding. The whole Western world is currently experiencing a "male fertility crisis," and the U.S. is smack dab in the middle of it. Sperm concentrations fell by 52% between 1973 and 2011 among Western men, from 99 million per milliliter to 47.1 million.[766] And in the midst of all of this male infertility, *this relatively small subpopulation of Black men has developed the highest infertility rates of all other U.S. groups!* The number of live births per woman must be roughly 2.1 in order to keep a country's population stable through birth alone. The U.S. fertility rate has drastically dropped to 1.8. Black America's fertility rate, having dropped from 2.5. to 2.0, has thus dropped below the number (2.1.) of births per woman necessary for our national stability.

XI.   *How Papa John's Is Making Us Feminine*

Black America's "obesity epidemic" and fertility crisis are not the only consequences of a heavy fast food diet. So too is *gender disruption*, including the feminizing of Black boys and the masculinizing of Black girls. Yes, through Whoppers and Big Macs. CNN said it succinctly: "A new study finds that those

---

763 American Society for Reproductive Medicine, "Ethnicity Affects sperm Quality in Infertility Patients," Press Release, October 9, 2018.
764 J. Bruce Redmon et al., "Semen Parameters in Fertile US Men: The Study for Future Families," ***Andrology*** 1 (2013): 1-21.
765 Valerie F. Williams, Irene Atta, and Shauna Stahlman, "Brief Report: Male Infertility, Active Component, U.S. Armed Forces, 2013-2017," ***Health.mil*** March 1, 2019.
766 Bryan Walsh, "Male Infertility in the U.S. Has Experts Baffled," ***Newsweek*** September 12, 2017

fast food drive-thru hamburgers and take-out pizzas could increase your exposure to hormone-disrupting chemicals called phthalates."[767] According to a recent report, people who eat fast food have higher levels of these chemicals called *phthalates* in their urine. Phthalates are chemicals commonly used to soften plastic. Phthalates exposure has been associated with breast cancer, diabetes and insulin resistance, obesity, and metabolic disorders in adults, as well as adverse child neurodevelopment (e.g. ADHD, ASD, lower cognitive and motor development).

Like BPA, PCBs, and DDT, phthalates are endocrine disrupters. Phthalates are anti-androgen chemicals that inhibit the synthesis of testosterone by Leydig cells, thereby reducing fetal testosterone,[768] and that interfere with androgen signaling during the critical periods of sexual differentiation prenatally

and perinatally. Prenatal, neonatal and peripubertal exposure can disrupt testis structure and function, reduce testosterone production, delay pubertal onset, and reduce androgen-dependent male organ weights (i.e. cause "shrinkage"),[769] thus producing a "phthalate syndrome": reduced anogenital distance, impaired testicular descent and reduced genital size. Phthalates target a key pregnancy hormone made by the placenta, human chorionic gonadotropin (hCG). hCG is essential to the normal differentiation of fetal testes. Phthalates exposure raises hCG in women carrying a female fetus and

---

[767] Carina Storrs, "Fast food serves up phthalates, too, study suggests," *CNN* April 18, 2016.

[768] S.H. Swan et al., "Prenatal phthalate exposure and reduced masculine play in boys," ***Int J Androl.*** 33 (2010): 259-269.

[769] Andrew K. Hotchkiss et al., "Of Mice and Men (and Mosquitofish): Antiandrogens and Androgens in the Environment," ***BioScience*** 58 (2008): 1037-1050, 1046-1047; S.H. Swan et al., "First trimester phthalate exposure and anogenital distance in newborn," ***Human Reproduction*** 30 (2015): 963-972; Lung-Cheng Lin et al. "Associations between maternal phthalate exposure and cord sex hormones in human infants," ***Chemosphere*** 83 (2011): 1192-1199.

lowers hCG in women carrying a male. This lowered hCG in the male placenta disrupts male sexual differentiation and masculinization of the genitals. In males this also results in a shortened (feminized) anogenital distance which is associated with decreased sperm count and infertility. Because exposure can reduce fetal and maternal testosterone secretion, brain sexual differentiation (of which testosterone is a critical mediator) may be altered. This demasculinizing of the neurology of the male fetus leads to a feminization of his *behavior* as early as adolescence, or "make little boys behave a bit more like little girls."[770]

Phthalates are thus *very scary contaminants*. But it is *Black People* who are disproportionately exposed to these nasty chemicals – and largely through fast food. An important study was published in 2016.[771] With a study population of nearly 9000 people and using data from the National Health and Nutrition Examination Survey (NHANES) collected by the CDC between 2003 and 2010, researchers looked at the relationship between how much fast food people consume and the level of certain phthalates (DEHP and DiNP) in their urine. One-third of the

Environmental contaminants phthalates linked to obesity in African-American children

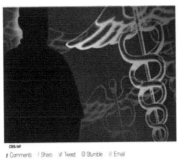

CBS/AP
↲ Comments ↑ Share ⅋ Tweet ⊙ Stumble @ Email

A new study shows that African-American children who have high levels of an environmental contaminant called phthalates are more likely to be obese.

participants in the study – and 43.8 % of the Black respondents - said they had eaten fast food in the last 24 hours and those who consumed a modest or a high amount of fast food had 15.5 - 23.8% (DEHP) and 24.8 - 39% (DiNP) higher levels than those

---

770 Ford Fox, M.D., "Phthalates Threat: Les Boy, More Girl," *U.S. News & World Report* November 7, 2009; S.H. Swan et al., "Prenatal phthalate exposure and reduced masculine play in boys," *Int J Androl.* 33 (2010): 259-269;

771 Ami R. Zota et al., "Recent Fast Food Consumption and Bisphenol A and Phthalates Exposures among the U.S. Population in NHANES, 2003-2010," *Environmental Health Perspective* 124 (2016): 1521-1528.

who did not consume. Young Black men were both the greater consumers of fast food and the group with the highest levels of phthalates in their body.

> Participants who ate fast food were more likely to be < 40 years old, male, and non-Hispanic black and to have higher [total energy intake] and total fat intake. Fast food consumers had higher levels of ΣDEHPm, DiNPm, and BPA than did nonconsumers.[772]

> Exposure to ΣDEHPm was positively associated with fast food intake in all three racial/ ethnic groups; however, the association did not reach statistical significance among Hispanics. Moreover, the highest tertile estimate for fast food intake was greater in magnitude for non-Hispanic blacks compared to non-Hispanic whites or Hispanics.[773]

Wendee Nicole reports:

> The authors also found that the associations between phthalates and fast food *were not uniform across the population.* They speculate that *the pronounced association they saw between fast food consumption and DEHP in black consumers* could reflect higher overall consumption of fast food and/or different food choices among this population. *Prior research suggests that predominately black neighborhoods in urban areas have a greater density of fast food restaurants than white neighborhoods.* "The fact that non-Hispanic blacks showed a steeper dose–response curve to fast food and DEHP is an important contribution to the environmental justice field since it suggests a potential *connection between neighborhood environments, food choices, and phthalates exposure,*" says lead author Ami Zota, an assistant professor of environmental and occupational health at George Washington University. Environmental justice research has found that minority populations often have greater environmental exposures to potentially harmful agents than other groups (emphasis added – WM).[774]

But this "pronounced" association between the Black fast food consumer and a high phthalates body burden needs

---

[772] Zota et al., "Recent Fast Food Consumption," 1523.
[773] Zota et al., "Recent Fast Food Consumption," 1524.
[774] Wendee Nicole, "Phthalates in Fast Food," **Environmental Health Perspective** 124 (2016): 191.

further consideration. The theory is advanced that the food was contaminated on secondarily, when the phthalates from the vinyl gloves (that all food handlers wear) or from the packaging leaches onto and contaminates the food. However, there is evidence that *the food itself was contaminated independent of the plastic gloves and wrappings.* Using data from the 2003-2004 NHANES a 2010 study by University of Michigan researchers to determine which food types are most contaminated with phthalates demonstrated that poultry – chicken – is specially associated with high levels of DEHP and high molecular weight phthalates and that consumers of a lot of chicken – a hood staple - tend to have a heavy phthalate body burden.[775] They also note:

> Additionally, the finding that egg consumption is significantly associated with levels of MEHP suggests that *chickens themselves may be contaminated with phthalates and that food is not being contaminated just through packaging and processing* (emphasis added – WM)." [776]

XII.   *Is Our Food Making Us Gay? D.C. As Compelling Evidence*

We have demonstrated that more than *any* other American demographic Black babies are born with a "complex cocktails of chemicals" in their blood. The chemicals are the very ones femininizing males and masculinizing females of lower species, and we know that these chemicals also disrupt the endocrine system of humans as well. "A huge body of data," reports P. Negri-Cesi, "demonstrate that developmental exposure to low BPA interferes with the brain sex differentiation process with enduring effects on brain structure and function."[777] Prenatal BPA exposure can even "reverse sex

---

[775] Justin A. Colacino, T. Robert Harris and Arnold Schecter, "Dietary Intake Is Associated with Phthalate Body Burden in a Nationally Representative Sample," ***Environmental Health Perspectives*** 118 (2010): 998-1003.
[776] Colacino, Harris and Schecter, "Dietary Intake," 1002.
[777] P. Negri-Cesi, "Bisphenol A Interaction With Brain Development and Functions," ***Dose-Response: An International Journal*** (2015): 1-12 (4).

differences in brain morphology, function and behavior,"[778] thereby reprogramming a male brain to show female typical behavior.[779] Prenatal exposure to PCBs, as we saw above, defeminizes and masculinizes the female neuroendocrine system.[780] DDT, phthalates, atrazine, etc. – *all* of these "gender bending" chemicals mix in *Black blood* to an extent that they do not in other groups in America, and our *food* is the main source of these chemicals. With so much "gender bending chemistry" running through our veins, how in the world *could* Black America escape having a "Gender Bender Crisis"?

And "Gender Bender Crisis" we *do* have. When Historian Allan Bérubé every year (up to 2001) asked his students what they think of when envisioning a gay man, the response was always the same: "white and well-to-do."[781] For a long time gay *was* an "Affluent White Thing" in America.

But when the 2012 Gallup Poll revealed its results, we learned that now "Nonwhites are more likely than white segments of the U.S. population to identify as LGBT." Specifically, "Poor blacks and Asians are more likely to be gay than whites."[782]   African Americans made up the largest individual percentile of LGBT at 4.4%; Asian 4.3% Hispanic 4.0%; White 3.2%. Between 2013 and 2017, Hispanics took and consistently held first place in terms of largest percentile.[783] Nevertheless, the Black adult LGBT population grew to 5.0 in

---

[778] Frederick S. vom Saal, "Bisphenol A Eliminates Brain and Behavior Sex Dimorphisms in Mice: How Low Can you Go?" **Endocrinology** 147 (2006): 3679-3680.

[779] Marija Kundakovic et al., "Sex-specific epigenetic disruption and behavioral changes following low-dose in utero bisphenol A exposure," **PNAS** 110 (2013): 9956-9961.

[780] Sarah M. Dickerson et al., "Endocrine Disruption of Brain Sexual Differentiation by Developmental PCB Exposure," **Endocrinology** 152 (2011): 581-594.

[781] Allan Bérubé, "How Gay Stays White and What Kind of White it Stays," in **The Making and Unmaking of Whiteness**, ed. (Durham: Duke University Press, 2001) 234-265.

[782] Tom Leonard, " 'White people are less likely to be gay': Poll reveals African-American community has highest percentage of 'LGBT' adults in U.S.," **Daily Mail** October 19, 2012; Gary J. Gates and Frank Newport, "Special Report: 3.4% of U.S. Adults Identify as LGBT," **Gallup** October 18, 2012, 1-10.

[783] Frank Newport, "In U.S., Estimates of LGBT Population Rises to 4.5%," **Gallup** May 22, 2018.

2017, while the White adult LGBT population was only 4.0 in that year. Whites now consistently register *the lowest percentile group*. Such a wide pendulum swing – from "rich White thing" to "poor Black thing" - *cannot* be considered a natural phenomenon or organic process. And when we now consider all of the gender bending chemicals that poison the blood of Black (and Brown) people due to the deliberate targeting of Black America by the U.S. government and allied interests, this state of affairs makes much sense.

An illustrative case is Washington D.C. One of the most segregated metropolitan areas in the country, the District of Columbia has a Segregation Index for 2013-2017 of 61.3, considered "severe black-white segregation." According to the 2017 census, 47.1% of D.C. is Black, overwhelmingly concentrated in the census tracks on the east side of D.C., and 45.1% is White, overwhelmingly concentrated in the west side census tracks. Segregation "almost divides the city right down the middle,"[784] as we see from the map below. There is a high level of poverty in Black D.C. Census findings indicate that 27.9% of African Americans are in poverty, which is four times higher than the White poverty rate of 7.9%. The median income for White households was in 2017 $125,747, compared to the median household income of Black D.C., $37,891.[785]

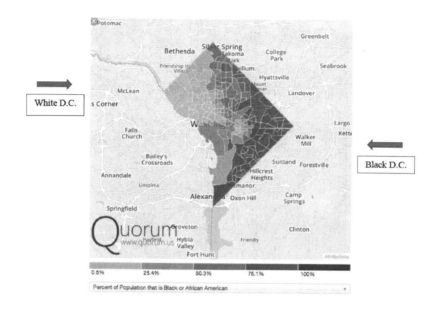

Percent of Population that is Black or African American

Black D.C. is also a very "food insecure" place. Food insecurity is defined by the USDA as the limited or uncertain availability of nutritionally adequate and safe food or the limited or uncertain ability to acquire such food for a household. People living in food insecure areas are often forced to turn to quick marts, gas stations, convenience stores and fast-food restaurants for their primary nutrition. In D.C. 1 in 7 households experience some form of food insecurity. These food insecure areas are usually what's called "food deserts," geographic areas where people have limited access to healthy food. In

---

[784] Aaron Blake, "The remarkable racial segregation of Washington, D.C., in 1 map," *The Washington Post* June 19, 2015.
[785] Courtland Milloy, "Even in a prosperous city like D hungry, report finds," *The Washington Post* Sep Randy Smith, "Food access in D.C. is deeply connected to poverty and transportation," *D.C. Policy Center* March 13, 2017.

Washington D.C. 14.5% of the residents are food insecure and 11 percent of the District's total area – 6.5 square miles – is food desert. D.C.'s food deserts are almost all concentrated in the southeast side of the District, the Black side, particularly the poorest and Blackest Wards 7 and 8 where more than three-fourths of D.C.'s food deserts are located. In contrast, the very White Ward 3 has no food desert. There are 49 full-service grocery stores in D.C., and only three are located in Wards 7 and 8. By comparison, in the Whiter and more affluent Ward 6, at least 10 full service grocery stores service an estimated 80,000 residents.[786] D.C. has one of the highest fast-food restaurant densities, and Black D.C. is the densest. Thus, there is a lot of fast-food consumption by poor, Black residents and this means a lot of phthalates exposer. The high poverty and food insecurity in Black D.C. mean a lot of canned foods are procured which thus means a lot of BPA exposer.

Washington D.C. Wards. Wards 7 and 8 are the poorest and the Blackest, while Wards 6 and 3 are affluent and White.

Food deserts in D.C.

Areas of limited food access in the District (in red) based on grocery or supermarket location, household income, and transportation access.

---

[786] Courtland Milloy, "Even in a prosperous city like D.C., many still go hungry, report finds," *The Washington Post* September 19, 2007; Randy Smith, "Food access in D.C. is deeply connected to poverty and transportation," *D.C. Policy Center* March 13, 2017.

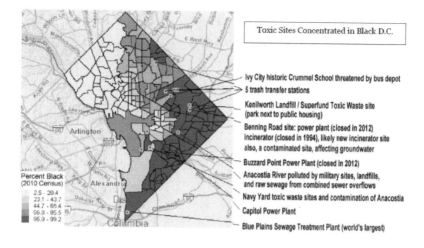

Toxic Sites Concentrated in Black D.C.

Ivy City historic Crummel School threatened by bus depot

5 trash transfer stations

Kenilworth Landfill / Superfund Toxic Waste site
(park next to public housing)

Benning Road site: power plant (closed in 2012)
incinerator (closed in 1994), likely new incinerator site
also, a contaminated site, affecting groundwater

Buzzard Point Power Plant (closed in 2012)

Anacostia River polluted by military sites, landfills,
and raw sewage from combined sewer overflows

Navy Yard toxic waste sites and contamination of Anacostia

Capitol Power Plant

Blue Plains Sewage Treatment Plant (world's largest)

Percent Black
(2010 Census)
2.5 - 20.4
23.1 - 43.7
44.7 - 65.4
66.8 - 85.5
86.9 - 99.2

Black D.C. is the victim of profound environmental injustice.[787] The map below definitively documents the reality of "environmental racism." Toxic sites are concentrated in the *Black side* of Washington D.C.: waste transfer stations, landfill/Superfund site, power plant, trash incinerator, all situated in Black D.C., polluting the air, land, and people with a host of noxious chemicals, many of which are endocrine disrupting.

Flowing through Black D.C. is the Anacostia River, which essentially separates the Federal Buildings and upscale housing from the poor, Black communities to the south. These communities have historically depended on the Anacostia River as a food source. As ***National Geographic*** reports:

> Fish from the river have fed some of the city's African Americans for many generations from bonded Africans sold on the shores of the Chesapeake Bay to refugees of the Civil War South, to some of today's unemployed and poor residents east of the river. They are joined by recent immigrants, mostly Spanish-speakers who have continued their custom of fishing for dinner from the rivers of Central America.[788]

---

[787] David Alpert, "Environmental justice for Ivy City," ***The Washington Post*** December 14, 2012; Naomi Todd, "Of Rubbish and Injustice: Environmental Racism in DC," ***The Beacon*** February 8, 2019; Editorial Board, "A Tale of Two Rivers: Environmental Injustice in D.C.," ***The Georgetown Voice*** April 22, 2016.
[788] Krista Schlyer, "Fishing the Forgotten River in the Nation's Capital," ***National Geographic*** July 24, 2012.

The Potomac River is not surrounded by poor, Black neighborhoods,[789] and unlike Rock Creek, which is in the suburbs, the Anacostia River is highly toxic. In fact, it is notorious as one of the nation's dirtiest. Industry but mainly the federal government (military) "was largely responsible for despoiling" this historical food source of Black people in D.C.[790] Runoff from the adjacent Washington Navy Yard pollutes the river. Landfills were deliberately situated near it and factories discharged waste into the Anacostia. As Mike Bolinder, the Anacostia Riverkeeper acknowledged: "We've been dumping toxic waste in there for 100 years."[791] The map below shows these military, government and industrial toxic sites along the Anacostia River.

---

[789] Editorial Board, "A Tale of Two Rivers: Environmental Injustice in D.C.," *The Georgetown Voice* April 22, 2016: "The neighborhood surrounding the Anacostia is largely poor and black. The neighborhood surrounding the Potomac is not."

[790] Schlyer, "Fishing the Forgotten River"; Editorial Board, "A Tale of Two Rivers: Environmental Injustice in D.C.," *The Georgetown Voice* April 22, 2016.

[791] Schlyer, "Fishing the Forgotten River."

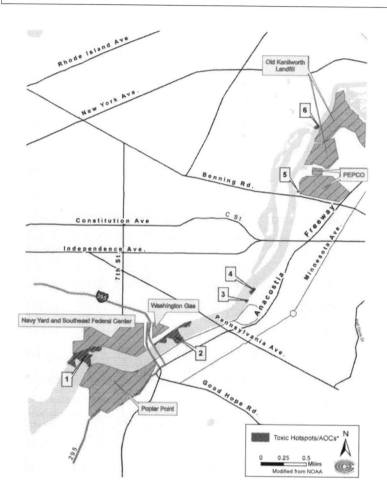

It is the marginalized, Black communities along the borders of the Anacostia that are most impacted by this *targeted toxicity*. The river "has all the markings of a Superfund site,"[792] and the fish are thoroughly contaminated (upwards of 68% of the bullhead catfish have liver tumors), yet as many as 17,000 Black and Brown residents (65% of the anglers are Black) are believed to be consuming the contaminated fish of the Anacostia

---

[792] Schlyer, "Fishing the Forgotten River."

River.[793] In contrast, as ***National Geographic*** points out, "In the more affluent neighborhoods of the (northwestern) Washington, D.C., metro area, the idea that anyone would eat a fish caught in the Anacostia seems unthinkable."[794] But most of D.C.'s neighborhoods with the highest poverty rates and greatest food insecurity are located east of the Anacostia River. Black D.C. has among the highest rates of food insecurity among children in the country. In 2013, there were 31,000 children who did not know where their next meal was coming from.[795] The poor communities of the Anacostia watershed have only three alternatives to

Black children fishing at the Anacostia River. Most of the local consumers of this fish are poor, Black residents dependent on the fish for subsistence

relying on this poisoned river fish: fast food, foo d bank, or hunger. But even the food banks may lead these food insecure residents to the same poisoned food because "Even fishermen who don't eat the fish themselves, who understand there are health risks, will share the fish with others in need."[796] So benevolent.

The health toll of this dependency on Anacostia fish by poor Black and Brown residents is great. As Dr. Harriette Phelps reports,

---

[793] Catherine Krikstan, "New Study shows Anacostia fishermen are sharing, consuming contaminated fish," ***Chesapeake Bay Program*** November 8, 2012.

[794] Schlyer, "Fishing the Forgotten River."

[795] Kelly Vandersluis Morgan, Ph.D., "Food Insecurity and its Effects in Washington, D.C.," ***Roots For Life*** November 12, 2018.

[796] Schlyer, "Fishing the Forgotten River."

There is a high incidence of cancer and other diseases in this minority community, where there is also subsistence fishing in the Anacostia in spite of a fishing advisory. Anacostia estuary catfish have tumors related to high polycyclic hydrocarbon (PAH) levels in sediment (...), and dangerous tissue levels of polychlorinated biphenyls (PCBs) and chlordane which can be associated with cancer.[797]

What exactly has the military and industry poisoned the water and the food with? The river and its fish host a cocktail of toxic and gender bending chemicals to *an astounding degree.* The number of these chemicals in the toxic stew is scary, and some of these are *the same chemicals that the military and allied interests* (Monsanto, for example) were poisoning Black communities within the South. Jeff Day notes:

> Polychlorinated biphenyls, or PCBs, are the main contaminant in locally caught fish...But the legacy pesticides DDT and chlordane...were detected in carp or eel at levels that exceed safe-consumption limits recommended by the Environmental Protection Agency.[798]

In the Anacostia River PCBs are above FDA action (!) levels. Sediment from the Anacostia River is contaminated with PCBs but also DDT, polycyclic aromatic hydrocarbons (PAHs), chlordane, *phthalates,* lead and mercury.[799] A 2007 government report (U.S. Geological Survey Open-File Report 2006-1392) analyzed the ground-water quality in the Anacostia River watershed within Washington D.C. and also found the water contaminated with, among other pollutants, PCBs, *phthalates, atrazine* and even *cyanide.*[800] Cyanide? Really?! PCBs, DDT, phthalates, and atrazine are notorious gender bending

[797] Dr. Harriette L. Phelps, "Identification of PCB, PAH and Chlordane Source Areas in the Anacostia River Watershed." (DC Water Resources Research Center Report, 2005) 1-9 (1).

[798] Jeff Day, "PCB Levels in Some DC-Caught Fish Decline, But Rockfish Are Off Limits," **Bay Journal** February 19, 2016.

[799] David J. Velinsky et al., "Historical contamination of the Anacostia River, Washington, D.C.," **Environ Monit Assess** 183 (2011): 307-328.

[800] Cheryl A. Klohe and Linda M. Debrewer, **Summary of Ground-Water-Quality Data in the Anacostia River Watershed, Washington, D.C., September-December 2005** (Reston, Virginia: U.S. Geological Survey, 2007).

chemicals in their own right (as we saw).[801] Polycyclic aromatic hydrocarbons (PAHs) are toxic particulate air pollutants that have mutagenic (causing DNA mutations) and/or carcinogenic (cancer causing) properties as well as gender bending properties. "The testis is an important target for PAHs" and "disruption of testosterone production by these chemicals can result in serious defects in male reproduction," reports Seunghoon Oh.[802]

The Georgetown Voice writes: "The neighborhood surrounding the Anacostia is largely poor and black. The neighborhood surrounding the Potomac is not."[803] It is this *poor, Black community* that is exposed to water and food sources so contaminated with this *toxic stew* of gender bending and cancer-causing chemicals. The consequences of this chemical targeting of Black D.C. are:

- Black and Brown residents breathe air that has been poisoned with particulate matter which negatively effects testosterone production and sperm quality in boys and men and masculinizes the neurology of female fetuses;
- Black D.C., having one of the highest fast food densities in the country, has a high exposure to and dependency on fast food that is laced with phthalates;
- The high level of food insecurity in Black D.C. means a high level of dependency on canned foods and thus an excessive exposure to BPA.

---

[801] On atrazine see Tyrone B. Hayes, "There Is No Denying This: Defusing the Confusion about Atrazine," *BioScience* 54 (2004): 1138-1149; Tyrone B. Hayes et al, "Atrazine induces complete feminization and chemical castration in male African clawed frogs (*Xenopus laevis*)," *PNAS* 107 (2010): 4612-4617; Tyrone B. Hayes et al, "Demasculinization and feminization of male gonads by atrazine: Consistent effects across vertebrate classes," *Journal of Steroid Biochemistry and Molecular Biology* 127 (2011): 64-73; Wesley Muhammad, *Understanding The Assault on the Black Man, Black Manhood and Black Masculinity* (Atlanta: A-Team Publishing, 2016) 376-379.
[802] Seunghoon Oh, "Disturbance in Testosterone Production in Leydig Cells by Polycyclic Aromatic Hydrocarbons," *Dev. Reprod.* 18 (2014): 187-195.
[803] Editorial Board, "A Tale of Two Rivers: Environmental Injustice in D.C.," *The Georgetown Voice* April 22, 2016.

- The high concentration of food deserts east of the Anacostia River means poor Black residents must consume the river's poisoned fish, fish from water contaminated with a "Who's Who" of chemical gender benders: PCBs, DDT, atrazine, PAHs, chlordane.
- Pregnant Black and Brown mothers may eat contaminated fish exposing their unborn child to a cocktail of DDT, PCB, PAH and atrazine.

What would we expect from a community so heavily *bombarded* by such a cocktail of gender-bending chemistry? Maybe we would expect this:

LGBT People Rankings: United States		AREA RANKINGS	
RANK	STATE	% OF LGBT INDIVIDUALS WITH CHILDREN	LGBT PERCENTAGE ↓
1	District Of Columbia	9%	9.8%
2	Oregon	23%	5.6%
3	Nevada	22%	5.5%
4	Massachusetts	21%	5.4%
5	California	24%	5.3%
6	Washington	28%	5.2%
7	Vermont	23%	5.2%
8	New York	22%	5.1%
9	Maine	21%	4.9%
10	New Hampshire	31%	4.7%
11	Hawaii	30%	4.6%
12	Florida	24%	4.6%
13	Colorado	25%	4.6%
14	Rhode Island	19%	4.5%
15	New Mexico	29%	4.5%
16	Indiana	34%	4.5%
17	Georgia	27%	4.5%
18	Delaware	35%	4.5%
19	Arizona	25%	4.5%
20	Ohio	30%	4.3%

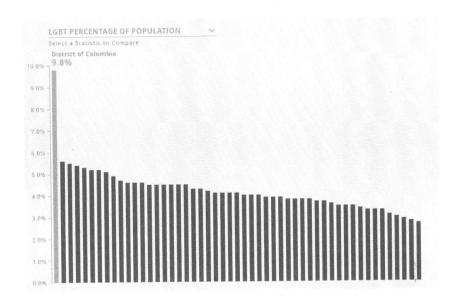

In 2013 ***The New York Times*** crowned Washington D.C. "The Gayest Place in America."[804] In a Gallup ranking of the states with the greatest percentage of adult LGBT self-identifiers it was concluded that "Residents in the District of Columbia were most likely to identify as LGBT." The District topped the rankings with 10% of adults identifying as LGBT at the time, which was 3 times the national percentage of 3.5% and double the percent of the second-placed state of Hawaii with 5.1%.[805] How did it happen that D.C. would be so head and shoulders and even waist above every other state in the country in terms of percent of gay and transgender persons, *a disproportionate percentage of whom are Black and Brown?*

Not only does D.C. stand out in terms of numbers, but it also defies national trends. In 2017, for example, 4.5% of the U.S. population (11 million people) identified as LGBT; 58% female and 42% male, because "Women continue to be more likely to identify as LGBT than men," which has remained consistent since recording started in 2012.[806] As 61% of the U.S. population, Whites constituted 58% of the LGBT population.

---

[804] Jeremy W. Peters, "The Gayest Place in America?" ***The New York Times***

[805] Gary J. Gates, "LGBT Percentage Highest in D.C., Lowest in North Dakota," ***Gallup*** February 15, 2013.

[806] Frank Newport, "In U.S., Estimates of LGBT Population Rises to 4.5%," ***Gallup*** May 22, 2018.

African Americans were 12% of the U.S. and 12% of the LGBT population, which is at least proportionate.

In D.C. 57% of self-identified LGBT were White in 2017 and 26% were Black, with 65% male and 35% female, which contradicts the national trend: males were more gay in D.C. than females. The *transgender* numbers are much more revealing. In 2014 Whites constituted 66% of the U.S. adult population and 55% of the adult transgendered population; this is proportionate. African Americans, on the other, constituted 12% of the U.S. adult population and 16% of the adult transgender population; this is disproportionate. In D.C. 2.8% of all adults were transgender. Whites constituted 39% of D.C. adults and 22% of adult transgenders. At the same time, 46% of D.C. adults were Black and *62% of adult transgenders were Black.* Thus, of the 14,550 transgenders in D.C. in 2014, 3,150 were White and 9,000 were Black![807] While nationally it is the *American Female* who is representative of the LGBT, in Washington D.C. *it is the Black Male (transgendered)!*

Such a high proportion of Black transgenders can easily be – and no doubt is - a direct result of the neurological gender-bending and gender-*reversing* characteristics of *each* of the chemicals that make up the toxic stew that Black D.C. is so heavily assaulted by through the air, the food and the water. In fact, just as we *must* expect the high level of cancer that we see among this population given the prevalent exposure to carcinogens, we also *must* expect a high level of transgenderism and homosexuality in this population given the same prevalence of exposure to these gender-bending toxins. And our expectations were in no ways disappointed.

XIII.   *Food and Black America's Health Crisis*

Black people in America are the subpopulation that suffers the greatest exposure to and body burden of a deadly cocktail of nasty industrial chemicals: $PM_{2.5}$, Atrazine, PCBs, BPA, DDT, phthalates, and more. We have demonstrated that

---

[807] Andrew R. Flores, Taylor N.T. Brown and Jody L. Herman, **Race and Ethnicity of Adults who Identify as Transgender in the United States** (Los Angeles: The Williams Institute, 2016); The Williams Institute, "LGBT Data & Demographics. Area Selection: United States," 2017; The Williams Institute, "LGBT Data & Demographics. Area Selection: District of Columbia," 2017.

the over-exposure *is not* accidental or circumstantial, but consciously and deliberately created by the U.S. Government (military) and allied (industrial) interests, who have more or less successfully separated and quarantined White Americans from these poisons. The body burden of these chemicals that Black people disproportionately carry in our blood is likely at the root of many of the symptoms of our "Black Health Crisis." For example, Black America's autism epidemic.

Autism was once a White disorder, but several studies have demonstrated that Black boys are disproportionately suffering from the neurological disorders that characterize the Autism Spectrum.[808] While it has been persuasively demonstrated that the ethylmercury preservative used in the MMR vaccine, thimerosal, is the cause for much of the autism epidemic that Black America suffers from, studies also make clear that *another cause* of certain phenotypes on the Autism Spectrum is the chemicals that segregated Black communities have been deliberately *bombarded* with. Links have been established between autism and the prenatal exposure to environmental pollutants.[809] These chemicals cause neurological damage prenatally that manifests later as childhood disruptive behavior, such as ADHD. A direct association has been established between maternal exposure to

---

[808] Wesley Muhammad, **Understanding the Assault on The Black Man, Black Manhood and Black Masculinity** (Atlanta: A-Team Publishing, 2016) 309-313.

[809] Philippe Grandjean and Philip J. Landrigan, "Neurobehavioural effects of developmental toxicity," **Lancet Neurol** 13 (2014): 330-338; Kathryn Doyle, "Study links pesticide exposure in pregnancy to autism," **Reuters** June 23, 2014; Nicholas Kristof, "Do Toxins Cause Autism?" **The New York Times** February 24, 2010.

BPA and childhood ASD,[810] as has an association between phthalates exposure and ASD been established.[811]

The other example is Black America's Cancer Crisis.

Most health specialists agree that the loss of the health of Black people is directly related to the foods we consume. - The Honorable Brother Minister Farrakhan

Of all the crises that Black America is experiencing, none is comparable to our ***Food Crisis***. -Dr. Wesley Muhammad

---

[810] T. Peter Stein et al., "Bisphenol A Exposure in Children with Autism Spectrum Disorders," ***Autism Res.*** 8 (2015): 272-283; Zaleh Md. Nor et al., "Does Bisphenol A contribute to autism spectrum disorder?" ***Current Topics in Toxicology*** 10 (2014): 63-73; D. Sarroulhe and C. Dejean, "Autism spectrum disorders and bisphenol A: Is serotonin the lacking link in the chain?" ***Encephale*** 43 (2017): 402-404; Mia de Graaf, "The plastic plaque: Hormone-disrupting chemicals in everyday things like water bottles DO cause cancer, diabetes, ADHD and autism – and cost US $340 Billion a year," ***Daily Mail*** October 18, 2016.

[811] Fatih Kardas et al., "Increased Serum Phthalates (MEHP, DEHP) and Bisphenol A Concentrations in Children With Autism Spectrum Disorder," ***Journal of Child Neurology*** October 8, 2015; Chiara Testa et al., "Di-[2-ethylhexyl] phthalate and autism spectrum disorders," ***ASN NEURO*** 4 (2012): 223-229; Marla Cone, "Scientists Find 'Baffling' Link between Autism and Vinyl Flooring," ***Scientific American*** March 31, 2009.

Chapter Thirteen

Black America's Prostate Cancer Epidemic and The Testosterone Conspiracy

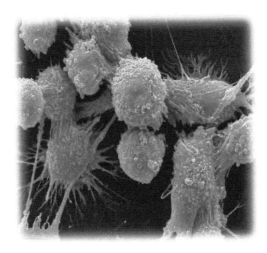

"For decades African-American men have had the highest prostate cancer incidence rate *of any racial/ethnic group in the world*...Researchers have yet to find a definitive reason..." Hugh McIntosh, "Why Do African-American Men Suffer More Prostate Cancer?" ***Journal of the National Cancer Institute*** 89 (1997): 188.

"There is unequivocal evidence that African-American men are disproportionately affected by carcinoma of the prostate. They develop it at an earlier age (manifesting a higher PSA level than their white counterparts at a given age), present with the disease at a more advanced stage, are more likely to be diagnosed with the disease, may be less likely to respond to treatment for cure and are more likely to die of the disease. At issue is *why*." Ian M. Thompson et al., "Association of African-American Ethnic Background With Survival in Men With Metastatic Prostate Cancer," ***Journal of the National Cancer Institute*** 93 (2002): 222.

I.   *Black America's Cancer Crisis*

According to the Cancer Facts & Figures for African Americans 2016-2018 Report:

Blacks have the highest death rate and shortest survival of any racial/ethnic group in the US for *most cancers*...Although the overall racial disparity in cancer death rates is decreasing in 2012, the death rate for all cancers combined was 24% higher in black men and 14% higher in black women than in white men and women, respectively.[812]

According to this report, about 1 in 2 Black men and 1 in 3 Black women will be diagnosed with cancer in their lifetime. The lifetime probability of dying from cancer is about 1 in 4 for Black men and 1 in 5 for Black women. Why are Black people so cancerous? While breast cancer is the most commonly diagnosed cancer in Black women and prostate cancer is the most common in Black men, we also have high rates of colorectal and lung cancer. Since 2005, colorectal cancer death rates have been 50% higher in Black men than in white men[813] and lung cancer is 36% more common in Black than in white men. Black women have now closed the gap with white women in terms of breast cancer incidence rate and still are more likely to die from it and develop the disease much younger.

Black America, it can be said, is right now experiencing a Cancer Crisis. Black America's Cancer Crisis is not a natural phenomenon. Black women, for example, suffer so much breast and ovarian cancer as well as fibroids *not* because they are naturally cancerous but because, as the **Daily Mail** headline announced: "Nearly 80% of hair products aimed at black women contain chemicals linked to cancer, infertility and obesity, study finds."[814] These estrogenic and toxic chemicals that increase breast cancer risk - such as parabens and phthalates - are found in only 7.7% of products used by white women and they mainly go *unlabled* on the products that target Black women *and children* such as hair relaxers, root

---

[812] American Cancer Society, Cancer Facts & Figures for African Americans 2016-2018 (Atlanta: American Cancer Society, 2016) 1.

[813] See also Ian M. Paquette et al., "African Americans should be screened at an earlier age for colorectal cancer," Gastrointest Endoes 82 (2015): 878-883.

[814] Alexandra Thompson, "Nearly 80% of hair products aimed at black women contain chemicals linked to cancer, infertility and obesity, study finds," Daily Mail (Online) April 26, 2018. See also: Inga Vesper, "Hair Products Popular with Black women May Contain Harmful Chemicals," Scientific American May 11, 2018.

stimulators, lotions, and even douching products.[815] Black America is suffering a Cancer Crisis because we are under an intense *scientific assault* by estrogenic and other toxic chemicals.

An aspect of this Cancer Crisis and a spawn of America's scientific war on her former slaves is Black America's *prostate cancer epidemic*. The evidence strongly indicates, I believe, that this cancer epidemic in particular is the textbook illustration of what I have called the "Testosterone Conspiracy and the Estrogen Assault" against Black America. The Assault is, I believe, a fruit or a result of this secret scientific (chemical) war against the so-called Negro in America that the Honorable Elijah Muhammad revealed to us from Allah. The aim of the Estrogen Assault, coming out of the American white man's "Crisis of White Masculinity," is the scientific creation of "the Negro as the Lady of the Races" that sociologist Robert Ezra Park envisioned at the turn of the last century. A byproduct of this assault, I believe, is Black America's Cancer Crisis and the poster child of this assault is Black America's prostate cancer epidemic.

II.   *The Black Male's Distinct Prostate Cancer*

Prostate cancer (hereafter PCa) presents the highest disparity in mortality between Black and white people of any cancer in the US. Black men in America have a 60% greater risk of diagnosis of PCa than white men, a 67% higher incidence rate

---

[815] Jessica S. Helm et al., "Measurement of endocrine disrupting and asthma-associated chemicals in hair products used by Black women," Environmental Research, available online April 2018, doi: 10.1016/j.envres.2018.03.030; Tamarra James-Todd, Ruby Senie, and Mary Beth Terry, "Racial/Ethnic Differences in Hormonally-Active Hair Product Use: A Plausible Risk Factor for Health Disparities," Journal of Immigrant and Minority Health 14 (2012): 506-11; Ami R. Zota and Bhavna Shamasunder, "The environmental injustice of beauty: framing chemical exposures from beauty products as a health disparities concern," American Journal of Obstetrics & Gynecology (2017): 1-5; Francesca Branch et al. "Vaginal douching and racial/ethnic disparities in phthalates exposures among reproductive aged women: National Health and Nutrition Examination Survey 2001-2004," Environmental Health (2015): 1-8; Laura Stiel et al., "A review of hair product use on breast cancer risk in African American women," Cancer Medicine 5 (2016): 597-604.

of PCa than white men, and a PCa mortality rate that is 2.4 x's higher than that of white men. We suffer from the disease at a much younger age than white men and with a more aggressive disease.[816] Certain models project that from 30% to 43% of Black men develop preclinical prostate cancer by age 85, a risk that is (respectively) 28% to 56% higher than that of the general US population. Add to all of this the fact that Black men in America have the highest incidence of PCa of all racial or ethnic groups *in the world*, one might be tempted to see PCa as an *ethnic disease.*[817] Indeed, "Black Race" has in fact been identified as an independent prognostic factor for the disease.[818] Gaines et al. found in a multivariable analysis that "black race was significantly predictive of PC overall...and high-grade PC" and that "black race is integrally linked with more aggressive PC grade at diagnosis".[819]

Prostate Cancer is a heterogenous disease. In 2015 Cambridge scientists discovered five distinct "types" of PCa, each with a characteristic genetic fingerprint.[820] They suggest that "pussy cat" cancers that grow slowly and cause few problems might be a different disease than the "lion" PCa which

---

[816] See Alex Tsodikov et al., "Is Prostate Cancer Different in Black Men? Answers From 3 Natural History Models," Cancer June 15, 2017: 2312-2319; Otis W. Brawlan, "Trends in Prostate Cancer in the United States," Journal of the National Cancer Institute Monographs 45 (2012): 152-156; Ian M. Thompson et al., "Association of African-American Ethnic Background With Survival in Men With Metastatic Prostate Cancer," Journal of the National Cancer Institute 93 (2002):219-225; Isaac J. Powell and Frank L. Meyskens, Jr. "African American Men and Hereditary/Familial Prostate Cancer: Intermediate-Risk Populations For Chemoprevention Trials," Urology 57 (Supplement 4A) (2001): 178-181.
[817] See also Therese Lloyd et al., "Lifetime risk of being diagnosed with, or dying from, prostate cancer by major ethnic group in England 2008-2010," BMC Medicine 13 (2015): 1-10.
[818] J.W Moul et al., "Black race is an adverse prognostic factor for prostate cancer recurrence following radical prostatectomy in an equal access health care setting," J Urol. 155 (1996): 1667-1673.
[819] Alexis R. Gaines et al. "The association between race and prostate cancer risk on initial biopsy in an equal access, multiethnic cohort," Cancer Causes Control 25 (2014): 1029-35.
[820] H. Ross-Adams et al., "Integration of copy number and transcriptomics provides risk stratification in prostate cancer: A discovery and validation cohort study," EBioMedicine 2 (2015): 1133-1144.

is fast spreading and aggressive. The *nature* of PCa differs between Black and white men as well, suggesting possibly different biological etiologies.[821] As Dr. Edward Schaeffer, Chairman of Urology at Northwestern University confirms: "*Biologically, their cancers are different* (emphasis original)."[822] James Farrell summarizes:

> The racial disparity exists from presentation and diagnosis through treatment, survival, and quality of life...AA [=African American] men have a significantly higher PSA [=prostate-specific antigen] at diagnosis, higher grade disease on biopsy, greater tumor volume for each stage, and a shorter PSA doubling time before radical prostatectomy. Biological differences between prostate cancers from CA [=Caucasian] and AA men have been noted in the tumor microenvironment with regard to stress and inflammatory responses. Although controversy remains over the role of biological differences, observed differences in incidence and disease aggressiveness at presentation suggest a potential role for *different pathways of prostate carcinogenesis between AA and CA men* (emphasis added).[823]

This means that Black and white men may get the disease *differently* or may even get *different diseases* (different genotype as well as phenotype). Why do Black men in America have a higher susceptibility to prostate cancer and a greater tendency to develop aggressive disease than any other group in the world? "The observation that prostate cancer diagnosis is more common and more lethal among black men than among white men has never been fully explained," acknowledges Alex Tsodikov and colleagues.[824] However, there is evidence pointing to a startling explanation: The Black male's naturally high

---

[821] Lizzie Parry, "Black men are 'TWICE as likely to develop prostate cancer as white men', study warns," Daily Mail July 30, 2015.

[822] Quoted in Janet Farrar Worthington, "How Prostate Cancer is Different in Men of African Descent," Prostate Cancer Foundation (Online) October 6, 2016. See also Divya Shenoy et al. "Do African-American men need separate prostate cancer screening guidelines? BMC Urology 16 (2016): 1-6.

[823] James Farrell et al. "Genetic and molecular differences in prostate carcinogenesis between African American and Caucasian American men," International Journal of Molecular Sciences 14 (2013): 15510-15531.

[824] Tsodikov et al., "Is Prostate Cancer Different in Black Men?" 2315.

testosterone levels have been deliberately weaponized against him through an *estrogen assault* on his person.

III. *The Black Man's Testosterone is Protective Against Cancer*

During the 1980's Dr. R.K. Ross of the University of Southern California School of Medicine published an important series of studies. In 1979 Ross et al. published an epidemiological study of testicular and prostatic cancers in the Los Angeles area.[825] They noted that, while the Black/white prostate cancer ratio was already high in 1970s (likely due to certain governmental practices of the 1950s and 1960s – see below), this is contrasted markedly with the low black:white testicular cancer ratio. "Perhaps the most striking finding in examining the 2 diseases simultaneously is *the virtual absence of testicular cancer among blacks* in Los Angeles County, while prostatic cancer among blacks is twice as frequent as among the other racial-ethnic groups," they report.[826] During the 1970s increasing rates for cancer of the testis in white males were recorded, while no such increase with Black males and only a modest but steady increase in prostate cancer in Black men. It was Mexican Americans who saw the greatest increase in PCa incidence in the area, catching up and surpassing that of whites, who showed a decline. Ross et al. wanted to know the reason for these trends. "African blacks, like American blacks, have extremely low rates [of testicular cancer], making cancer of the testis, together with Ewing's sarcoma, *unique among non-melanin-related sites*," they affirm.[827] Why do white men get testicular cancer and Black men (generally) don't? And why do Black men get so much PCa, regardless of social class? In both cases, Ross et al. suggest a "hormonal influence theory," according to which black men are characterized by "increased 'maleness'" due to their naturally higher androgen/estrogen levels, leading to more prostate cancer and less testicular cancer.

In 1986 Ross et al. confirmed their theory, at least the presupposition of the theory: the elevated "maleness" of Black

---

[825] R.K. Ross et al., "Descriptive Epidemiology of Testicular and Prostatic Cancer in Los Angeles," Br. J. Cancer 39 (1979): 284-292.
[826] Ross et al., "Descriptive Epidemiology," 285.
[827] Ross et al., "Descriptive Epidemiology," 290.

men. Studying the circulating steroid hormone levels in white and Black college students in Los Angeles, they discovered that the Black males had mean T levels 19% higher and free T levels 21% higher than white males. When adjusted for covariance, Black males still had 15% and 13% higher T, respectively.[828] Black males thus *are* characterized by "increased 'maleness'." And this biochemical "maleness" starts in the womb of his mother, and this "increased maleness" affords the black male certain protections against cancer, both PCa (as we shall see) and testicular cancer, as Ross et al. suggested in a 1988 follow-up report.

> Another important descriptive feature of the disease, the rarity of testis cancer in black males...During the past several decades, while the incidence of testis cancer has been increasing in white males, the rates in black males have remained stable and are considerably lower. In searching for an explanation for this *'protection'* afforded black males, we studied the hormone levels in maternal blood of black and white women during early pregnancy...(emphasis added)

> Black women had testosterone levels that were 48% higher than those of white women during the early weeks of gestation (...). Black women had total E2 levels that were 37% higher, free E2 levels that were 30% higher and SHBG-bc levels that were 22% higher than those of white women, but none of these results was statistically significant... Testosterone is necessary for the virilization of the male urogenital tract (...). High maternal testosterone levels such as those observed in black women in this study may ensure this orderly process by crossing the placenta into the foetal circulation... the excess of testosterone in the early gestational blood of black women provides a possible explanation for the subsequent lower incidence of testis cancer in black male offspring as it may counteract the effects of elevated oestrogen.[829]

In 2005 Potischman et al. made the same observation regarding this "protection" that Black mothers bequeath to their male children:

---

828 R. Ross et al, "Serum testosterone levels in healthy young black and white men," J Natl Cancer Inst 76 (1986): 45-8.

829 B.E. Henderson et al., "The early in utero oestrogen and testosterone environment of blacks and whites: Potential effects on male offspring," Br. J. Cancer 57 (1988): 216-218 (216).

African-American males are at substantially reduced risk of testicular cancer compared with Caucasian males. Henderson and coworkers hypothesized that the in utero hormonal environment might influence the development of germ cell tumors of the testes. Later they evaluated blood from first trimester pregnant African-American and Caucasian women, matched on a variety of factors, and found testosterone to be 48% higher in the African-American women. Troisi and coworkers reported testosterone to be 84% higher and androstenedione to be 52% higher in maternal serum of African-American compared with Caucasian women. Our results are consistent with previous findings. In the overall group, we found 69% and 31% higher testosterone and androstenedione levels, respectively, in the African-American compared with the Caucasian women. Furthermore, we observed higher concentrations of prolactin and nonsignificantly elevated estrogens among the African-American women, generating the hypothesis that these hormones could be involved in decreasing the risk of testicular cancer.[830]

This is very important: The high T uterine environment of Black mothers in which Black male fetuses gestate is believed to provide protection against the testicular cancer that white males fall victim to at much greater numbers. Elevated T also, we now know, is protective against the *onset* of PCa *unless it is made toxic by estrogenization*. It is an *estrogenized* environment that can predispose a male fetus to adult onset testicular and prostate cancer (see below). And while Black women indeed have a more estrogenized uterine environment than white women, the male fetus is protected from this estrogen by α-fetoprotein which binds to and thus inactivates this natural estrogen. However, by *excessively* estrogenizing the uterine environment in which Black males gestate – by means of exogenous estrogen mimicers – the α-fetoprotein protection can be overwhelmed and the Black male fetus can be imprinted by the excess estrogen, thereby predisposing him to PCa risk. We can document that this is exactly what was done. Further, we argue that the PCa epidemic among Black men is a direct result of a chemical assault against the heightened

---

[830] Nancy Potischman et al., "Pregnancy Hormone Concentrations Across Ethnic Groups: Implications for Later Cancer Risk," Cancer Epidemiology, Biomarkers & Prevention 14 (2005): 1514-1520 (1518).

androgenicity or "manness" of Black men, weaponizing both our elevated testosterone and our more effective androgen receptors against us:

> The AR signaling pathway has been implicated as one of critical biological mechanisms associated with PCa disparities. For instance, it has been reported that AA men have higher mean serum testosterone levels compared to CA men. Furthermore, the expression of AR protein is 22% higher in benign and 81% higher in malignant prostate tissues of AA patients compared to their CA counterparts undergoing radical prostatectomy. Genetic mutations contributing to higher serum dihydrotestosterone to testosterone ratios have been forwarded as another mechanism underlying PCa disparities. Thymine-Adenine (TA) dinucleotide repeat and A49T variants of the SRD5A2 gene, which encodes a type II 5α-reductase, are prevalent in AA men. In addition, these two polymorphisms were shown to correlate with the elevated 5-α-reductase activity and higher conversion rate of testosterone to dihydrotestosterone (DHT), respectively, in AA patients. The architecture of the AR gene has also provided hints into the mechanism of the PCa health disparities. Exon 1 of the AR gene, encoding the N-terminal transactivation domain, was found to have two polymorphic trinucleotide repeats (CAG and GGC, the codons for glutamine and glycine, resp.). The CAG repeat length is inversely correlated with AR transcriptional activity, and previous reports have revealed that AA men tend to have significantly shorter CAG repeats than CA men. The shorter CAG and GGC repeats have been associated with a higher risk for developing PCa. Taken together, these findings suggest that *differences in androgenic activities between AA and CA populations may play an important role in PCa health disparities* (emphasis added).[831]

Differences in androgenic activities = heightened "manness" in Black men vs. white men.

IV.   *Testosterone, Superior "Manness" and Prostate Cancer*

Despite much research over the decades, it could still be said in 2015 that "the biological mechanism related to the

---

[831] Bi-Dar Wang et al., "Androgen Receptor-Target Genes in African American Prostate Cancer Disparities," Prostate Cancer Volume 2013: 1-13 (1-2).

development and progression of PCa remains largely unknown."[832] Prostate cancer is generally assumed to be an androgen[833] dependent tumor, but the androgen hypothesis of PCa as first articulated by Huggins and Hodges in 1941 has never been demonstrated and is, in fact, self-contradictory.[834]

> The concept that human prostate cancer represents a prototype of age-related, androgen-dependent tumor is widely accepted. *Paradoxically, however, both total and bioavailable serum testosterone significantly decline with age,* eventually leading to an inverse relationship between circulating testosterone and the risk of developing prostate cancer. Many epidemiologic studies have investigated the association between circulating androgens and prostate cancer, but the resulting data have been inconsistent and largely inconclusive...Hence, several authors have raised the question why has it been so difficult to prove that circulating androgens are associated with the risk of

---

[832] Xiaohui Xu et al., "Current opinion on the role of testosterone in the development of prostate cancer: a dynamic model," BMC Cancer 15 (2015): 1-8 (1).

[833] Androgens are the male hormones like testosterone and androstenedione. Estrogens like estrone and estradiol are the female hormones.

[834] Xiaohui Xu et al., "Current opinion on the role of testosterone in the development of prostate cancer: a dynamic model," BMC Cancer 15 (2015): 1-8 (1): "the prevailing opinion that high levels of testosterone increase the risk of prostate cancer. To date, this claim remains unproven...The landmark study by Huggins and Hodges in 1941 suggested a direct correlation between circulating levels of testosterone and PCa progression [6]. It was the first study to show that both progression and regression of PCa are testosterone-dependent. These findings led to the prevailing hypothesis that elevated androgen levels increase the risk of PCa. However, Huggins and Hodge's study only provided evidence on the role of testosterone in the progression of PCa. Therefore, this widely accepted opinion fails to distinguish the role of testosterone in PCa development. Despite more than 70 years passing since the study was conducted, little progress has been made in understanding the role of testosterone in the development of PCa"; Hui Hu et al., "Racial Differences in Age-Related Variations of Testosterone Levels Among US Males: Potential Implications for Prostate Cancer and Personalized Medication," J. Racial and Ethnic Health Disparities 2 (2015): 69-76 (72): "The prevailing wisdom that high-testosterone levels are a risk factor for PCa is not supported by extensive evidence. In fact, recent studies refute this notion."

developing prostate cancer? The most obvious answer to this question is that circulating androgens are simply *not* associated with prostate cancer risk (emphasis added).[835]

To say that circulating androgens are *not* associated with PCa risk is an overstatement, but the current "androgen hypothesis" definitely does need refinement and revision.[836] Androgens are traditionally considered to be the main hormones regulating normal and malignant cell growth in the prostate, and it is assumed that "huge amounts of androgen are required to induce prostate cancer," specifically the testosterone metabolite dihydrotestosterone (DHT).[837] This may be true, but it is likely only *half* of the story. New evidence points to androgens (including normal testosterone levels) being *protective* against the *onset* of PCa and only playing a supportive role promoting PCa progression *after* the disease has occurred.[838]

There is currently a medical and scientific controversy over the role of androgens in the development and progression of PCa. While older medical orthodoxy posited a relationship between high T levels and the onset or worsening of PCa, a number of recent studies either showed no relation with T levels at all or a relation between PCa and *low T levels*.[839] However,

---

[835] Giueseppe Carruba, "Estrogen and Prostate Cancer: An Eclipsed Truth in an Androgen-Dominated Scenario," Journal of Cellular Biochemistry 102 (2007): 899-911 (901-902).

[836] Hendrik Isbarn et al., "Testosterone and Prostate Cancer: Revisiting Old Paradigms," European Urology 56 (2009): 48-56; Abraham Morgentaler, "Testosterone and Prostate Cancer: An Historical Perspective on a Modern Myth," European Urology 50 (2006): 935-939.

[837] Hugh McIntosh, "Why Do African-American Men Suffer More Prostate Cancer?" Journal of the National Cancer Institute 89 (1997): 188.

[838] Xiaohui Xu et al., "Current opinion on the role of testosterone in the development of prostate cancer: a dynamic model," BMC Cancer 15 (2015): 1-8; Michele Algarte-Genin, Olivier Cussenot, Pierre Costa, "Prevention of Prostate Cancer by Androgens: Experimental Paradox or Clinical Reality," European Urology 46 (2004): 285-295; Gail S. Prins, Jason L. Nelles and Wen-Yang Hu, "Estrogen action and prostate cancer," Expert Rev Endocrinol Metab 6 (2011): 437-451.

[839] Peter Boyle et al., "Endogenous and exogenous testosterone and the risk of prostate cancer and increased prostate specific antigen (PSA): a meta-analysis," BJU International 118 (2016): 431-741; A.W.

the contradictory conclusions drawn from the numerous studies are due largely to conflicting and inadequate study designs, definitions and methodologies. Most studies, for example, failed to adhere to professional society guidelines on such matters as T measurement. As Klap, Schmid and Loughlin point out:

> Contradictory findings have been reported, largely due to the disparate methodologies used in many studies. Most studies did not adhere to professional society guidelines on total testosterone (TT) measurements...TT variations (throughout the day or across several days) can be large enough to render a single measurement inadequate to accurately characterize levels in an individual...It is treacherous to posit a relationship between TT and PCa using a single measurement. Few trials in this review (of studies) used repeat determination of TT but guidelines recommend doing so, especially for low TT...Thus, TT identified as low in some studies may have been normal on another day or at another hour during the day. Therefore, many apparent contradictions in the literature may represent methodological heterogeneity rather than biological differences.[840]

Nevertheless, new research has significantly advanced the discussion and supported the basic premise of the "androgen hypothesis," i.e. greater exposure to testosterone during the course of one's life is associated with increased risk of (aggressive) PCa. In 2017 University of Oxford researchers reported the breakthrough findings of a 58-year, multigenerational population study using blood samples of 19,000 men between 1959 and 2004. They found a 20% decreased risk of developing PCa in men with low concentrations of testosterone: "men with naturally low levels

---

Roddam, Allen, N.E., Appleby, P. and Key, T.J. for the Endogenous Hormones and Prostate Cancer Collaborative Group, "Endogenous sex hormones and prostate cancer: a collaborative analysis of 18 prospective studies," J Natl Cancer Inst 100 (2008): 170-183; EL Rhoden, CL Riedner and A Morgentaler, "The ratio of serum testosterone-to-prostate specific antigen predicts prostate cancer in hypogonadal men," J Urol 179 (2008): 1741-1745.

[840] Julia Klap, Marianne Schmid and Kevin R. Loughlin, "The Relationship between Total Testosterone Levels and Prostate Cancer: A Review of the Continuing Controversy," The Journal of Urology 193 (2015): 403-413 (403, 411).

of the male sex hormone are less likely to develop prostate cancer than those with higher blood levels of the hormone," Prostate Cancer UK reports.[841] Thus "scientists finally confirmed that testosterone does play a role," **Consumer Health Digest** announced.[842] This is consistent with Porcaro et al.'s 2016 study of a contemporary cohort of patients demonstrating that preoperative levels of total testosterone were directly and independently associated with high grade PCa. They determined that a single unit increase in TT plasma levels increases the odds of having high grade PCa by 4%.[843]

Professor Louis Calistro Alvarado of the University of New Mexico has made the most sense out of the seemingly conflicting reports on the relation of high T levels and PCa. Because cancer risk is mediated by *life-time exposure* to steroid hormones and because PCa risk increases with age while testosterone levels naturally and robustly diminish with age – serum T levels drop by about 35% between the ages of 21 and 85 – studies that concentrate on T levels near the later ages that PCa is diagnosed is of limited value in assessing the role of high T in PCa incidence. Rather, testosterone's influence on PCa risk is better observable in the steroid hormone physiology of *young men*.

> African-American men have repeatedly shown higher testosterone levels than other Western ethnic groups (...), though this relationship becomes inconsistent at later ages (...). And accordingly, African-American men exhibit the highest incidence of prostate cancer, an incident rate which is nearly twice that of their Caucasian counterparts in some areas of the United States (...). This disparity is noticeable as early as age 45, suggesting that prostate cancer risk is determined at a relatively

---

[841] "Testosterone and prostate cancer risk: the plot thickens as study reveals intriguing clues," Prostate Cancer UK (Online) November 6, 2017; Elanor Watts, "Low circulating free testosterone is associated with reduced incidence of prostate cancer: A pooled analysis of individual participant data from 20 prospective studies," NCRI Cancer Conference abstracts 2017.

[842] Dr. Ahmed Zayed, "Low Testosterone Levels Can Cut Down Prostate Cancer Risk," Consumer Health Digest (Online). Accessed May 5, 2018.

[843] Antonio B. Porcaro et al., "Preoperative Plasma Levels of Total Testosterone Associated with High Grade Pathology-Detected Prostate Cancer: Preliminary Results of a Prospective Study in a Contemporary Cohort of Patients," Current Urology 10 (2016): 72-80.

young age (...). Moreover, autopsy examinations have revealed fairly high rates of latent prostate carcinoma among younger men (...), which is also suggestive that etiological factors during early adulthood affect prostate cancer development in later life.

If cumulative exposure to testosterone across the life- span determines prostate cancer risk, then the steroid physiologies of late-middle aged and elderly men, *the typical age range sampled in prospective case–control studies*, would offer limited information on lifetime androgen exposure. As such, it is predicted that population differences in the testosterone levels of young men will be positively associated with population disparities in prostate cancer among older men.[844]

Later life is thus not the most appropriate period for comparative analysis of men's testosterone levels. Testosterone levels of young men more appropriately capture relative differences of circulating hormone exposure. This is why the 2008 meta-analysis by Roddam et al. of 18 prospective studies of men with PCa compared with age-matched controls is of little consequence.[845] The meta-analysis found no significant difference in T levels between the patients and the controls and thus they found no relationship between T levels and PCa. However, the studies analyzed there measured the hormone levels of *late-middle aged and elderly men*, age-groups in which intra- and inter-population variation in T levels is *least detectable due to the natural decline of T in older age.* Alvarado's meta-analysis however showed that "Population differences in total testosterone levels *of young men* were associated with population disparities in prostate cancer incidence, $r(9) = 0.833$, $p = 0.001$, as were population differences in free testosterone, $r(9) = 0.661$, p. $= 0.027$."[846] He explains further:

---

[844] Louis Calistro Alvarado, "Population Differences in the Testosterone Levels of Young Men are Associated with Prostate Cancer Disparities in Older Men," American Journal of Human Biology 22 (2010): 449-455.

[845] A.W. Roddam, Allen, N.E., Appleby, P. and Key, T.J. for the Endogenous Hormones and Prostate Cancer Collaborative Group, "Endogenous sex hormones and prostate cancer: a collaborative analysis of 18 prospective studies," Journal of the National Cancer Institute 100 (2008): 170-183.

[846] Louis Calistro Alvarado, "Total testosterone in young men is more closely associated than free testosterone with prostate cancer disparities," Therapeutic Advances in Urology 3 (2011): 99-106.

the findings of this meta-analysis are consistent with the androgen-dependent nature of prostate disease, and furthermore demonstrate a dose-dependent relationship in which proportional differences in testosterone are associated with proportional disparities in prostate cancer incidence. This suggests an alternative explanation for the null relationship found by the Endogenous Hormones and Prostate Cancer Collaborative Group: Androgen production among older men is often diminished to the extent that meaningful differences between prostate cancer cases and controls are no longer apparent. Comparisons of early age testosterone production more appropriately capture relative differences in cumulative androgen exposure, and the positive association found here is consistent with the observed influence of testosterone on prostate cell proliferation.[847]

And it is *young Black men* that have the highest levels of testosterone in this country, as we saw above. Now, left alone high T levels are *protective* against PCa as testosterone has anti-inflammatory influence. However, the Black male's own testosterone can be *weaponized against him* by being *toxified* through exposure to excess estrogen. We will describe that process below.

Those studies that report an association between low T and high grade PCa are not all meaningless. There *is* such an association but it occurs *after the fact,* i.e. after the onset of disease and as a consequence of it. Testosterone levels in PCa patients seem to be lowered secondary to chronic disease or as a consequence of advanced disease. A number of studies have suggested that T levels are actually altered by the very presence of PCa. It has been theorized that PCa secretes a biochemical agent that suppresses testosterone indirectly by negative feedback on the hypothalamic-pituitary axis. This is supported by the observed fact that after radical prostatectomy (removal of the cancerous prostate gland and the surrounding tissue) hormone levels and gonadotropin levels (luteinizing hormone and follicle stimulating hormone) increase. The diseased tissue itself thus seems to inhibit the production of testosterone by suppressing the release of the gonadotropins.[848] The *resulting*

---

[847] Alvarado, "Population Differences," 454.
[848] Mauro Gacci et al., "Changes in sex hormone levels after radical prostatectomy: Results of a longitudinal cohort study," Oncology

low T is thus associated with high-grade cancer, more aggressive disease, advanced pathological stage at radical prostatectomy, and shorter survival.

And this affects Black men more than it does white men. In a 2017 study of the effect that race and demographic characteristics have on the association between testosterone level and PCa de Albuquerque et al. found that it is specifically among Black men as compared to white men that hypogonadism (=low T) is associated with high-grade PCa.

> In our data, Black men had a higher incidence of hypogonadism compared to Caucasians (p-value = 0.0103). Variations of TT levels had a higher impact on predicting high-grade disease (GS ≥ 7) among Black men compared to White men (p=0.02)...In our results, low TT was an independent predictor for high-grade PCa among patients undergoing (radical prostatectomy). This effect was significantly more pronounced among Black men, who also had higher incidence of hypogonadism. These results may reveal an underlying mechanism for high-grade PCa found in Black race, and may also partly explain inconsistencies between previous investigations regarding association between TT and PCa grade...[W]e hypothesize that low serum testosterone may be an underlying mechanism involved in higher-grade PCa found in both obese and Black men in previous reports.[849]

Letters 60 (2013): 529-533; George Yu et al. "Circulating levels of gonadotropins before and after prostate ablation in cancer patients," Horm Mol Biol Clin Invest 11 (2012): 355-362; T Imamoto et al., "Does presence of prostate cancer affect serum testosterone levels in clinically localized prostate cancer patients?" Prostate Cancer and Prostate Disease 12 (2009): 78-82; ibid., "The role of testosterone in the pathogenesis of prostate cancer," International Journal of Urology 15 (2008): 472-480; S Madersbacher et al. "Impact of radical prostatectomy and TURP on the hypothalamic-pituitary-gonadal hormone axis," Urology 60 (2002): 869-74.

[849] George AM Lins de Albuquerque et al., "Low serum testosterone is a predictor of high-grade disease in patients with prostate cancer," Rev Assoc Med Bras 63 (2017): 704-710.

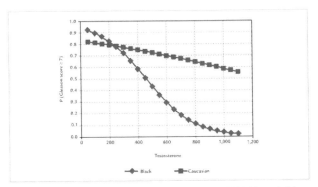

FIGURE 1 Interaction between TT levels and race in predicting the risk of high-grade PCa. Among Black individuals, hypogonadism had a stronger effect in predicting high-grade disease (p=0.038), although there was a similar trend among Caucasians (p=0.06). Both groups differed significantly on this behavior (p=0.02).

According to this graph, as the T levels among men drop, the PCa grade rises. This effect is much more pronounced among Black men than among white men.

Andrea Salonia and colleagues found a U-shaped rather than a linear association between testosterone and high-grade PCa: high risk prostate cancer was in fact significantly more frequent *both* for those with the highest *and* the lowest levels of circulating testosterone.[850] We believe we can explain that: it is the naturally higher levels of T of Black men that, *when made toxic*, predisposes us to PCa. On the other hand, as a *consequence* of the cancer there is a dramatic diminishing of T, which in turn makes the disease more severe. The U-shaped association thus connects the *high T* of the pre-cancer (Black) male to the *low T* of the post-cancer (Black) male. Both are associated with a higher grade of PCa. In contrast, white males have less natural T which is why PCa incidence is so much lower among them and their disease phenotype is much less severe than that of Black males.

Edward Giovannucci and coworkers argued that "androgenicity influences the development of prostate cancer"[851] and that "Both androgen levels and the AR, which mediates the effect of testosterone and dihydrotestosterone in

---

[850] Andrea Salonia et al. "Serum Sex Steroids Depict a Nonlinear U-Shaped Association with High-Risk Prostate Cancer at Radical Prostatectomy," Clinical Cancer Research 18 (2012): 3648-3657.

[851] Edward Giovannucci, "Is the Androgen Receptor CAG Repeat Length Significant for Prostate Cancer?" Cancer Epidemiology, Biomarkers & Prevention 11 (2002): 985-986 (985).

androgen-responsive tissues, determine androgenicity."[852] "Androgenicity" is the state or quality of being androgenic, which pertains to the development of male characteristics. Androgenicity is thus the quintessence of "maleness" or "manness." The Black male's heightened androgenicity as expressed both by his high T levels and in his AR profile also makes him vulnerable to PCa, but to a peculiar disease phenotype that is distinguished from the disease phenotype of most whites. For example, the shorter (and thus more effective) AR repeats of Black males are significantly correlated with younger age at diagnosis and with more aggressive disease.[853]

> a consistent finding (of studies) was that *AR* CAG repeats appeared most relevant for prostate cancers diagnosed at younger ages...the prostate cancer cases that tend to occur at younger ages tend to be most strongly related to *AR* CAG repeat number (...) The relation between fewer *AR* CAG repeats and higher risk of aggressive prostate cancer in younger men suggests that a heightened state of androgenicity directly influences a pool of relatively aggressive, early onset "androgen-driven" prostate cancers. Possibly, prostate cancers that tend to occur at older ages may be less driven by androgenicity and more related to pathologic processes such as oxidative insults, although andro- gens may play a permissive role. Although speculative, this "two pool" model is consistent with several observations. First, African-Americans, presumably exposed to higher androgenicity through shorter *AR* CAG repeats and higher testosterone at younger ages, are particularly susceptible to early onset, highly aggressive prostate cancer, but the rate differences with Caucasians diminish with increasing age.[854]

Giovannucci et al. in a large prospective nested case-control study found that

---

[852] Elizabeth A, Platz et al., "Racial Variation in Prostate Cancer Incidence and in Hormonal System Markers Among Male Health Professionals," Journal of the National Cancer Institute 92 (2000): 2009-2017 (2014).

[853] Dianne O. Hardy et al. "Androgen Receptor CAG Repeat Lengths in Prostate Cancer: Correlation with Age of Onset," Journal of Clinical Endocrinology and Metabolism 81 (1996): 4400-4405; Kevin A. Nelson and John S. Witte, "Androgen Receptor CAG Repeats and Prostate Cancer," American Journal of Epidemiology 155 (2002): 883-890.

[854] Giovannucci, "Is the Androgen Receptor," 985-986.

An association existed between fewer androgen receptor gene CAG repeats and higher risk of total prostate cancer...[S]horter CAG repeat lengths of the AR was closely related to an aggressive phenotype of prostate cancer, as defined by high histological grade, extension through the prostate gland, presence of distant metastasis at diagnosis, and mortality from the disease...African-American men have about a 2-fold higher rate of metastatic prostate disease and mortality, and have larger tumor volumes, even when they have equal access to health care as whites. Although the similar access to care does not assure equivalent utilization, it would appear that black men are prone to a more aggressive tumor biology. Because black men tend to have considerably shorter AR CAG repeats than white men, we speculate that CAG repeat length may be a factor contributing to an increased risk of metastatic and fatal prostate cancer in blacks. However, our population was predominantly caucasian (> 95%), so this hypothesis needs to be studied directly in an African-American population.[855]

The Black male's AR was shown to be expressed 22% higher than a white male's in benign prostate and 81% higher in malignant prostate. "[PCa] may occur at a younger age and progress more rapidly in black than in white men due to racial differences in androgenic stimulation of the prostate," found Gaston et al.[856]

So it is the Black man's own distinct "androgenicity" or superior "manness" that is turned against him in prostate cancer. How so? By means of an estrogen assault.

---

[855] Edward Giovannucci et al. "The CAG repeat within the androgen receptor gene and its relationship to prostate cancer," Proc. Natl. Acad. Sci. 94 (1997): 3320-3323.
[856] KE Gaston et al., "Racial differences in androgen receptor protein expression in men with clinically localized prostate cancer," Journal of Urology 170 (2003): 990-993.

V.   *Estrogen: The True Villain*

High testosterone is necessary but it is not sufficient to cause the Black man's peculiar form of PCa. "[W]e now know that androgens *alone* are insufficient to induce tumourigenesis (emphasis added)," affirms Ellem and Risbridger.[857] It is now believed that high testosterone *coupled by an excess of estrogen* actually collaborate to *induce* prostate tumors.

> A growing body of evidence suggests that estrogen signaling may play a significant role in both normal and abnormal growth of the prostate gland; likewise, estrogens and their receptors have been implicated in PCa development and progression...Overall, preclinical data support the concept that 17b-estradiol (E2) *may potentiate the carcinogenic effects of androgens* through the specific ERα [estrogen receptor alpha], which is localized predominantly in the stromal compartment (emphasis added).[858]

---

[857] Stuart J. Ellem and Gail P. Risbridger, "Aromatase and regulating the estrogen: androgen ration in the prostate gland," Journal of Steroid Biochemistry and Molecular Biology 118 (2010): 246-251 (247).
[858] Andrea Salonia et al., "Circulating estradiol, but not testosterone, is a significant predictor of high-grade prostate cancer in patients undergoing radical prostatectomy," Cancer November 15, 2011: 5029-5038 (5029-5030).

A world-wide study found an association between PCa incidence and mortality and the use of female oral contraceptives.[859] The birth control pill contains high doses of the synthetic estrogen ethinyloestradiol which is excreted in women's urin without degradation. This then contaminates the environment and ends up in the drinking water supply and passed up the food chain. David Margel and Neil F. Fleshner of the University of Toronto speculate that every day use of water contaminated with birth control pill metabolites exposes the world to PCa risk.

Together testosterone (T) and estrogen (E) in concert can stimulate proliferation of prostate cancer cells or, in the formulaic phrasing of Maarten C. Bosland: "T plus E2...induces cancer".[860] Evidence suggests that estrogen – and an estrogenized uterine milieu during gestation – plays a causative role in human prostate cancer. In fact, "The human prostate progenitor cells appear to be estrogen targets, whereas E2 [estradiol], *when combined with testosterone*, acts as a carcinogen in human prostate epithelium (emphasis added)."[861] E2, acting as a "chemical carcinogen" and through the estrogen receptors (ERα and ERβ), is believed to exert synergistic activity and toxifying effects on androgens and facilitate tumor growth.[862]

Doubtlessly, since the pioneering work of Charles Huggins, prostate cancer has become a paradigm of androgen-dependent tumor, with androgens being universally considered critical regulators of normal prostatic function and inducers of malignant prostate growth. This general concept has endured

---

[859] David Margel and Neil E. Fleshner, "Oral contraceptive use is associated with prostate cancer: an ecological study," BMJ Open 1 (2011): 1-5.
[860] Maarten C. Bosland, "A Perspective on the Role of Estrogen in Hormone-Induced Prostate Carcinogenesis," Cancer Lett. 334 (2013): 28-33 (30).
[861] Zakaria Y. Abd Elmageed et al., "High Circulating estrogens and selective expression of ERβ in prostate tumors of Americans: implications for racial disparity of prostate cancer," Carcinogenesis 34 (2013): 2017-2023 (2017).
[862] Eileen M. McNerney and Sergio A. Onate, "New Insights in the Role of Androgen-to-Estrogen Ratios, Specific Growth Factors and Bone Cell Microenvironment to Potentiate Prostate Cancer Bone Metastasis," Nuclear Receptor Research 2 (2015): 1-12 (3).

against a bulk of experimental evidence suggesting that estrogen and other growth factors may play a role in the development and/or progression of human prostate cancer. Presently, the view of androgens as all-seasoned and sole determinants of prostate tumor development and progression appears to be a never-ending persuasion that has, faultily, led to neglect different areas of research with promising perspectives for both treatment and prevention of this disease.[863]

Early work on the hormonal basis of prostate cancer focused on the role of androgens, but more recently estrogens have been implicated as potential agents in the development and progression of prostate cancer...an ample body of evidence suggests that estrogens may play a critical role in predisposing, or even causing, prostate cancer.[864]

In recent years there is a growing body of evidence that oestrogens play crucial role in prostate tumourgenesis. Here we presented data showing that oestrogen, acting via its receptors, regulates various cellular processes including: proliferation, differentiation, apoptosis, EMT, invasiveness and chronic inflammation in prostate cancer cells. It seems that ERα possesses oncogenic role in prostate cancer, whereas ERβ suppressive role has been disputable so far...Taken together, oestrogen plays an important role in prostate carcinogenesis through direct or indirect participation in molecular mechanism which are crucial for tumourgenesis...[865]

Studies with mice have shown that elevated testosterone in the absence of estrogen leads to the development of hypertrophy and hyperplasia, *but not malignancy.* On the other hand, raised estrogen and *lowered* testosterone can lead to the development of inflammation of the prostate upon aging and the emergence of pre-malignant lesions: "the mechanism of hormonal induction of PCa requires both androgens and

---

[863] Carruba, "Estrogen and Prostate Cancer," 902, 907.
[864] Jason L. Nelles, Wen-Yang Hu and Gail S. Prins, "Estrogen action and prostate cancer," Expert Rev Endocrinol Metab 6 (2011): 437-451 (438).
[865] Karolina Kowalska and Agnieszka Wanda Piastowska-Ciesielska, "Oestrogens and oestrogen receptors in prostate cancer," SpringerPlus 5 (2016): 1-9 (7).

estrogens."[866] Thus, while the Black man's high testosterone has been villainized as the cause of his disease, it is actually estrogen that is the true villain along with a steep and unnatural *decline* of T. "Estrogen alone *or in synergy with androgen* is responsible for the pathogenesis of prostate cancer (emphasis added),"[867] argues Ho et al. And it is specifically the Estrogen Receptor alpha (ERα) that may potentiate the carcinogenic effects of androgens according to McNerny and Onate.[868]

The natural androgen:estrogen balance is critical to maintaining a healthy prostate. At age 50 a man's prostate can start to swell due to the natural age-related increase of the estrogen:testosterone ratio.

Although androgens and estrogens both play significant roles in the prostate, it is their combined action – and specifically their balance – that is critically important in maintaining prostate health and tissue homeostasis in adulthood. In men, serum testosterone levels drop by about 35% between the ages of 21 and 85 while estradiol levels remain constant or increase. This changing androgen:estrogen (T:E) ratio has been implicated in the development of benign and malignant prostate disease.[869]

Estrogen levels do not have the same PCa-inducing effect on white men,[870] no doubt due to their naturally low T

---

[866] Stuart J. Ellem et al., "Increased Endogenous Estrogen Synthesis Leads to the Sequential Induction of Prostatic Inflammation (Prostatitis) and Prostatic Pre-Malignancy," The American Journal of Pathology 175 (2009): 1187-1199; Stuart J. Ellem and Gail P. Risbridger, "Aromatase and regulating the estrogen: androgen ration in the prostate gland," Journal of Steroid Biochemistry and Molecular Biology 118 (2010): 246-251 (247).

[867] Shuk Mei Ho et al., "Estrogen and Prostate Cancer: Etiology, Mediators, Prevention, and Management," Endocrinol Metab Clin North Am 40 (2011): 591-614 (591).

[868] McNerny and Onate, "New Insights," 4.

[869] Stuart J. Ellem and Gail P. Risbridger, "Aromatase and regulating the estrogen: androgen ration in the prostate gland," Journal of Steroid Biochemistry and Molecular Biology 118 (2010): 246-251 (246).

[870] Andrew W. Roddam et al., "Endogenous Sex Hormones and Prostate Cancer: A collaborative Analysis of 18 Prospective Studies," Journal of the National Cancer Institute 100 (2008): 170-183: "The findings from this collaborative study indicate that endogenous estrogen concentrations are not related to prostate cancer risk (178)";

levels and naturally long AR CAG repeats; thus, their naturally low androgenicity or "manness." It is the steep decline in testosterone characteristic of Black men and not white men that is suspected of inducing compensatory mechanisms that result in tumorigenesis. As Algate-Genin and colleagues write:

> It appears that a *withdrawal* in androgens induced the adaptation and/or selection of cells responsive to very low levels of hormones. Mutations or increased expression of androgen receptors, upregulation of androgen coactivators or enrichment in the population of neuroendocrine cells have been analyzed in tumor cells deprived in androgens...A hypothesis is that low levels of testosterone induce changes in molecular balance of epithelial prostate cells... It is possible that accumulation of changes during years in the cells may induce deregulations that lead to tumorigenesis.[871]

A new theory or "dynamic model" on the origin of prostate cancer has thus been recently (2015) put forward by scientists out of the Texas A&M Health Science Center. Xiaohui Xu and colleagues propose that it is not *elevated* testosterone that is the problem but the *decline of the naturally elevated* T:

> The risk of PCa increases *when testosterone levels fall below a threshold*...As testosterone level falls below the threshold, prostatic cells reach the limit of their compensatory capabilities, thus impairing adaption to lower levels of testosterone and finally triggering the prostatic carcinogenesis process...As the model suggests, the prostatic carcinogenesis may be a process by which the normal prostate cells first adjust themselves to progressive declining testosterone levels at the cellular and receptor levels. As testosterone levels *fall below the threshold* when normal prostate cells are not able to make additional adjustments without mutations, some of the normal prostate cells may evolve into cancer cells. If additional

Song Yao et al., "Serum estrogen levels and prostate cancer risk in the prostate cancer prevention trial: a nested case-control study," Cancer Causes Control 22 (2011): 1121-1131. The studied populaton in both studies were predominantly Caucasian.
[871] Michele Algarte-Genin, Olivier Cussenot, Pierre Costa, "Prevention of Prostate Cancer by Androgens: Experimental Paradox or Clinical Reality," European Urology 46 (2004): 285-295 (290, 291).

testosterone is added before reaching the threshold level, it may change the course of the disease.[872]

They suggest that this is particularly relevant to Black men:

> With the dynamic model, the increased risk of PCa for blacks could be due to more significant *reductions* in testosterone levels, relative to that of whites. Evidence from previous studies indicates that testosterone levels in black males declines quicker with age when compared to white men. During young adulthood, testosterone levels are higher in blacks than in whites; *but the difference diminishes with age* and completely disappears after the age of 60 years of age (emphasis added).[873]

Ellem and Risbridger also note:

> Epidemiological evidence provides further support for the relationship between a shift in the T:E ratio and the development of PCa. This ratio is significantly lower in African-American men (who have the highest incidence of PCa in the USA), due to higher levels of serum estrogens, compared to Caucasian-American men. Conversely, the T:E ratio is higher in Japanese men (who are known to have a low risk of PCa), due to lower levels of serum estrogens, compared to Caucasian-Dutch men.[874]

Studies confirm that in Black PCa patients excess estrogen is found, compared to non-patients.

> Significant elevation of circulating E2 levels was detected in [African Americans] (P = 0.0011), but not in [Caucasian Americans] (P = 0.1814), with PCa *compared with their corresponding age- and race-matched normal subjects.* Interracial analysis demonstrates a significant increase ($P < 0.0046$) in circulating E2 levels in AA (30.97 } 14.99 pg/ml) compared with CA men (19.01 } 9.51 pg/ml) with PCa...Consistent with other studies, our ethnicity-based study revealed selective

---

[872] Xiaohui Xu et al., "Current opinion on the role of testosterone in the development of prostate cancer: a dynamic model," BMC Cancer 15 (2015): 1-8 (2, 5).

[873] Xu et al., "Current opinion," 3.

[874] Stuart J. Ellem and Gail P. Risbridger, "Aromatase and regulating the estrogen: androgen ration in the prostate gland," Journal of Steroid Biochemistry and Molecular Biology 118 (2010): 246-251 (247).

elevation of serum E2 levels in AA compared with CA men and corresponding race-, and age-matched normal subjects. Estradiol increases cell proliferation in LNCaP cell line and induces carcinoma *in situ* and adenocarcinoma in the prostates of transgenic mice. Likewise, E2 metabolism has been shown to play a key role in prostate carcinogenesis. In contrast, low circulating E2 has been detected in Japanese men, known to have a low risk of PCa...The aforementioned findings argue that high circulating estrogens may pose risk for PCa in aging populations, *especially at young age among AA men*...Taken together, our study implicates a pivotal role of estrogen-ERβ axis in PCa risk, progression and poor prognosis, especially among AA men.[875]

The mechanism of the change in this T:E ratio is believed to be aromatization.

Combined evidence supports the concept that aromatase expression and activity in the prostate may be up-regulated in the tumor site, eventually resulting in an altered testosterone-to-estrogen ratio. Moreover, epidemiologic evidence suggests African-American men, who have the highest incidence of PCa in the United States, suffer from a *shift* of the circulating testosterone-to-estrogen ratio because of higher levels of serum estrogens compared with white American men.[876]

In the normal prostate the aromatase enzyme is expressed by the stromal (connecting) tissue but not in the epithelial (surface) tissue. In the malignant prostate however, aromatase is expressed in both.[877] The decreased androgen-to-estrogen ratio that results from aromatase *over-expression* is believed by many now to be a risk factor for PCa.[878] "Raised E2 levels stimulate the developing epithelial cells of the prostate to

---

[875] Zakaria Y. Abd Elmageed et al., "High circulating estrogens and selective expression of ERβ in prostate tumors of Americans: implications for racial disparity of prostate cancer," Cancinogenesis 34 (2013): 2017-2023 (2018).

[876] Salonia et al., "Circulating Esteradiol," 5036.

[877] Habibur P. Rahman, Johannes Hofland, Paul A. Foster, "In Touch with your Feminine Side: How Oestrogen Metabolism Impacts Prostate Cancer," Endocrine-Related Cancer 23 (2016): r249-R266.

[878] Staurt J. Ellem and Gail P. Risbridger, "Aromatase and regulating the estrogen:androgen ratio in the prostate gland," Journal of Steroid Biochemistry and Molecular Biology 118 (2010): 246-251.

proliferate and also cause morphological changes."[879] But it is estrogen *plus the testosterone* (and its necessary withdrawal) that induces PCa, as the mouse models suggest:

> Aromatase knockout mice (i.e. lab mice that lack the aromatase enzyme) and mice overexpressing aromatase suffer from androgen metabolism abnormalities that limit their potentially interesting use for carcinogenesis studies. Aromatase knockout mice lack estrogen production but have elevated circulating T levels and their prostate is enlarged but does not develop cancer. In aromatase overexpressing mice estrogen production is elevated, while T levels are considerably reduced and no neoplastic or preneoplastic prostate lesions develop. These observations are consistent with the idea that *both hormones are necessary for prostate carcinogenesis*.[880]

Because Black men have naturally high T levels, by increasing the amount of aromatase enzyme in the body (through food, alcohol and drugs, for example) more estrogen (E2) can be synthesized and react toxically with the rest of the testosterone. We believe that we can show that neither the Black male's diminishing T levels nor his elevated E:T ratio is natural or accidental but are in fact deliberately provoked scientifically.

We intend to show in this report that the causes of the prostate cancer epidemic among American Black men can be convincingly illuminated. This epidemic is the poster boy, if you will, for what we have termed "The Testosterone Conspiracy and the Estrogen Assault" against Black America. The PCa epidemic, we strongly believe we can document, is the result of this society deliberately targeting the Black male's natural endowment of higher levels of androgenicity or physiological "manness." The American Black male's testosterone levels are assaulted through deliberately manipulated environmental exposure to estrogenic chemicals that both unnaturally diminish his T levels below a dangerous threshold and *toxifies* his T, making it interact with the estrogen in a cancerous way.

VI.   *BPA and Black America's Prostate Cancer Epidemic*

---

[879] Rahman, Hofland and Foster, "In touch with your feminine side," R251.
[880] Bosland, "A Perspective," 4.

TECH & SCIENCE

BPA LEVELS HIGHER IN MEN WITH PROSTATE CANCER: STUDY

BY ZOE SCHLANGER ON 3/3/14 AT 6:44 PM

Men with prostate cancer have BPA in their urine at levels 2- to 4-fold
higher than those who are cancer-free, a study claims

STEVE MCKINLEY/REUTERS

These endocrine disrupting chemicals or "gender benders" are relevant to our discussion of Black America's Cancer Crisis. As Gail S. Prins observes:

> There is increasing evidence both from epidemiology studies and animal models that specific endocrine-disrupting compounds may influence the development or progression of prostate cancer. In large part, these effects appear to be linked to interference with estrogen signaling, either through interacting with ERs or by influencing steroid metabolism and altering estrogen levels within the body. In humans, epidemiologic evidence links specific pesticides, PCBs and inorganic arsenic exposures to elevated prostate cancer risk. Studies in animal models also show augmentation of prostate carcinogenesis with several other environmental estrogenic compounds including cadmium, UV filters *and BPA*. Importantly, there appears to be heightened sensitivity of the prostate to these endocrine disruptors during the critical developmental windows including in utero and neonatal time points as well as during puberty. Thus, infants and children may be considered a highly susceptible population for ED exposures and increased risk of prostate cancers with aging.[881]

Dr. Shuk-mei Ho, Chair of the Department of Environmental Health at the University of Cincinnati, led a study in 2014 that found that men with prostate cancer have BPA in their urine at levels 2-to-4-fold higher than cancer-free

---

[881] Gail S. Prins, "Endocrine disruptors and prostate cancer risk," Endocrine-Related Cancer 15 (2008): 649-656 (649).

men.[882] This was the first evidence of a direct link between BPA exposure and PCa. While PCa is usually associated with old age, BPA is a contributing factor to the development of the disease in men *under the age of 40*. Ho et al. found that " patients with PCa are more likely than those without PCa to have higher levels of BPA in their urine" and that "Higher urinary BPA may be associated with early onset prostate cancer."[883] This is important because: "African-American men have earlier onset of prostate cancer, higher prostatic-specific antigen (PSA) levels, more advanced stage at diagnosis, and higher mortality than white men."[884] Ho et al.'s work thus preliminarily identifies

---

[882] Shuk-mei Ho et al., "Prostate "Exposure to Bisphenol A Correlates with Early-Onset Prostate Cancer and Promotes Centrosome Amplification and Anchorage-Independent Growth In Vitro," PLOS 9 (2014): 1-11; Zoë Schlanger, "BPA Levels Higher in Men with Prostate Cancer: Study," Newsweek March 3, 2014.

[883] See further Shuk-Mei Ho et al., "Prostate Cancer Risk and DNA Methylation Signatures in Aging Rats following Developmental BPA Exposure: A Dose-Response Analysis," Environmental Health Perspective 11 July 2017: 1-12; "Bisphenol A and its analogues disrupt centrosome cycle and microtuble dynamics in prostate cancer," Endocrine-related Cancer 24 (2017): 83-96; "DNA methylome changes by estradiol benzoate and bisphenol A links early-life environmental exposures to prostate cancer risk," Epigenetics 11 (2016): 674-689; "Environmental Epigenetics and its Implications on Disease Risk and Health Outcomes," ILAR Journal 53 (2012): 289-305; "Estrogen and Prostate Cancer: Etiology, Mediators, Prevention, and Management," Endocrinol Metab Clin North Am 40 (2011): 591-614; "Perinatal Exposure to Oestradiol and Bisphenol A Alters the Prostate Epigenome and Increases Susceptibility to Carcinogenesis," Basic Clin Pharmacol Toxicol 102 (2008): 1-8; "Developmental Exposure to Estradiol and Bisphenol A Increases Susceptibility to Prostate Carcinogenesis and Epigenetically Regulates Phosphodiesterase Type 4 Variant 4," Cancer Res 66 (2006): 5624-5632; Shuk-Mei Ho and Mengchu Wu, "PMP24, a gene identified by MSRF, undergoes DNA hypermethylation-associated gene silencing during cancer progression in an LNCaP model," Oncogene 23 (2004): 250-259; Shuk-mei Ho and Mary Ellen Taplin, "The Endocrinology of Prostate Cancer," The Journal of Endocrinology & Metabolism 86 (2001): 3467-3477; Shuk-mei Ho and Pheruza Tarapore, "Bisphenol A exposure and prostate cancer outcomes, 'Beyond the Abstract'," UroToday.com.

[884] Ian M. Thompson et al., "Association of African-American Ethnic Background With Survival in Men With Metastatic Prostate Cancer," Journal of the National Cancer Institute 93 (2002):219.

347

urinary BPA level as an independent prognostic biomarker of PCa.

In animal studies BPA was found to be able to switch on or off genes that promote or block tumor growth. In *in vitro* studies with human prostate cells, treatment with BPA was found to cause in those cells the development of abnormal centrosomes, the organelle responsible for cell division. Abnormal centrosomes are a hallmark of malignant transformation. Ho and colleagues found that early BPA exposure sensitized the prostate to later estrogenic exposure and primed it to over-respond to later-life estrogenic triggers. This early exposure predisposes the prostate to later disease. This is the researchers "Two-Hit" model of carcinogenesis. The first hit is exposure to xenoestrogens like BPA during the fetal period thereby sensitizing the prostate to later exposure. The second hit could be exposure to excess estrogen via the natural age-related rise of the estrogen:testosterone ratio of older men or adult exposure to any one of the environmental xeno-estrogens or endocrine disrupting chemicals that we discussed above, including BPA.

Ho et al. also found that elevated estrogen and BPA may even *reprogram* the *Black man's genetics*. **ScienceNews** announced on July 4, 2009: "Estrogen may reprogram prostate cancer gene in black men." Laura Sanders reports:

A new study shows how chemical tags on DNA may lead to higher rates of prostate cancer in black men. And estrogen may play a role, researchers reported June 12 at a meeting of the Endocrine Society in Washington, D.C.

"It may be that estrogen can reprogram the genome," says study coauthor Wan-yee Tang of the University of Cincinnati in Ohio.

In black men, Tang and her colleagues found fewer of the chemical tags, called methyl groups, near the portion of DNA that encodes a gene active in the prostate than the team found in white men. The lack of these epigenetic tags may alter the gene's activity and upset the balance of other proteins in the cell, making the cell more vulnerable to becoming cancerous, the researchers propose.

Earlier studies have shown that black men face a higher risk of prostate cancer than white men. Black men also have higher average levels of estrogen than white men. And experiments on rats have shown that high doses of estrogen take away methyl groups near the prostate gene PDE4D4, leading to abnormally high levels of the PDE4D4 protein.[885]

PDE4D4 is a gene active in the prostate. As men age, this gene is naturally eventually "silenced" by the accumulation of chemical "tags" called epimarks (methyl groups) which turn this gene "off." This is important because an active PDE4D4 gene stimulates processes involved in cell proliferation and differentiation. The natural silencing of this gene through the accumulation of these chemical tags (a process called DNA hypermethylation) is therefore necessary to enhance apoptosis (cell death) and prevent excess cell proliferation and neoplastic transformation (the transformation of normal human tissue into malignant tumor). But exposure to BPA and other xenoestrogens during the prenatal and perinatal period of development strips these silencing chemical tags away (resulting in DNA hypomethylation or demethylation) resulting in the gene staying "on" throughout the life of the male. When this gene fails to shut down as it is supposed to with age, it is over expressed and this over expression promotes abnormal cell proliferation and prostate disease.

---

[885] Laura Sanders, "Estrogen may reprogram prostate cancer gene in Black men," ScienceNews Vol. 176 #1, July 4, 2009, p.13.

But Ho and colleagues found a critical difference in Black and white PCa patients: white patients showed demethylation (absence of these chemical tags) only in their cancerous cells while Black men show demethylation in both cancerous and normal cells. "The *PDE4D4* promoter in white men had DNA demethylation in prostate cancer cells but not in normal prostate cells. In black men, even normal prostate cells had substantial demethylation in the *PDE4D4* promoter, perhaps setting the stage for earlier neoplastic transformation," explains co-investigator Dr. Winnie Wan-yee Tang.[886] "These methyl groups may be stripped away by higher levels of estrogen in black men," we are assured.[887]

It is no doubt the Estrogen Assault against Black America – the estrogenizing and thus weaponizing of our environment, food and water – that is at the root of our Cancer Crisis. This BPA which is a prognostic biomarker of PCa is the same BPA which contaminates Black blood at far higher levels than it does white blood; the same BPA that companies target pregnant Black women for use; the same BPA that is reprogramming Black genes by stripping away protective chemical tags, thus causing higher rates of PCa among Black men. How are Black people exposed to BPA? "*The major route of exposure to BPA is diet,*" Shuk-mei Ho and Pheruza Tarapore inform us.[888] Black people's dietary options and habits makes us most vulnerable to BPA exposure. As **San Diego Union Tribune** reported: "Canned food still contains toxin BPA" and because Black people used canned foods at such a high rate, "African Americans and low-income families have, on average, higher amounts of BPA in their bodies than people of other races and people with higher incomes."[889]

Jean-Marc A. Lobaccaro and Amalia Trousson announced: "The Holy Grail has been found: environmental estrogen exposure will modify the fate of prostate stem cells, making them more sensitive to estrogen during adulthood and

---

[886] John Schieszer, "Estrogen May Explain Higher PCa Risk in Blacks," Renal & Urology News September 18, 2009.
[887] Laura Sanders, "Estrogen may reprogram prostate cancer gene in Black men," ScienceNews Vol. 176 #1, July 4, 2009, p.13.
[888] Shuk-mei Ho and Pheruza Tarapore, "Bisphenol A exposure and prostate cancer outcomes, 'Beyond the Abstract'," UroToday.com
[889] Deborah Sullivan Brennan, "Canned food still contains toxin BPA," The San Diego Union-Tribune March 17, 2017.

more prone to develop PCa."[890] They affirm further that BPA is "the paradigm of these environmental estrogen-like molecules."

VII.   *Breast Cancer Among Black Women and Black Men*

BPA and other xeno-estrogens are the culprits in Black women's breast cancer as well:

> exposure to estrogens throughout a woman's life, including the period of intrauterine development, is a risk factor for the development of breast cancer. The increased incidence of breast cancer noted during the last 50 yr may have been caused, in part, by exposure of women to estrogen-mimicking chemicals that have been released into the environment from industrial and commercial sources. Epidemiological studies suggest that exposure to xenoestrogens such as DES during fetal development, to DDT around puberty, and to a mixture of xenoestrogens around menopause increases this risk. Animal studies show that exposure *in utero* to to he xenoestrogen BPA increases this risk. Moreover, these animal studies suggest that estrogens act as morphogens and that excessive perinatal exposure results in structural and functional alterations that are further exacerbated by exposure to ovarian steroids at puberty and beyond. These altered structures include preneoplastic lesions, such as intraductal hyperplasias, and carcinomas *in situ.*[891]

Giuseppe Carruba thus rightly noted: "cancer of the human prostate and cancer of the breast can be viewed as brother and sister tumors, where dietary factors and hormones, notably estrogens, are crucial and interactive players in many biological and pathological process."[892] And Black men suffer from both the "brother" *and* "sister" cancers. In 2007 ABC News reported: "Black men are more likely than white men to die of breast cancer, concludes a study that urges more research into

---

[890] Jean-Marc A. Lobaccaro and Amalia Trousson, "Environmental Estrogen Exposure During Fetal Life: A Time Bomb for Prostate Cancer," Endocrinology 155 (2014): 656-658 (656).

[891] Evanthia Diamanti-Kandarakis et al., "Endocrine-Disrupting Chemicals: An Endocrine Society Scientific Statement," Endocr Rev. 30 (2009): 293-342. (IV.E.2.)

[892] Giueseppe Carruba, "Estrogen and Prostate Cancer: An Eclipsed Truth in an Androgen-Dominated Scenario," Journal of Cellular Biochemistry 102 (2007): 899-911 (900).

racial disparities in male breast cancer."[893] *Breastcancer.org* also announced that "African American Men Hit Harder by Breast Cancer," noting: "And like African American women, African American men are hit harder by breast cancer than their white counterparts. After diagnosis, African American men are three times more likely to die from breast cancer than white men. This difference is probably due to the same factors suggested by research involving African American women."[894] The study, by Dawn L. Hershman and colleagues, noted that "The male-to-female breast cancer incidence ratio is higher among black patients than among white patients, and black men have higher age-adjusted incidence rates (1.65/100,000) than do white men (1.31/100,000)."[895]

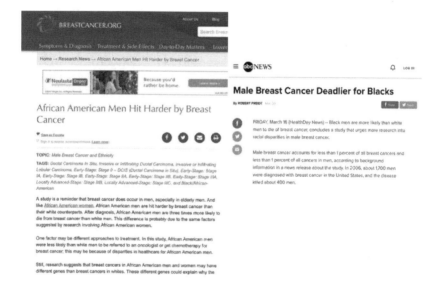

And what is the cause of this breast cancer among Black men (and women)? *ScienceDaily* reports: "Men with naturally high levels of the female hormone estrogen may have a greater risk of developing breast cancer, according to research

[893] Robert Preidt, "Male Breast Cancer Deadlier for Blacks," ABC News March 23, 2007.
[894] "African American Men Hit Harder by Breast Cancer," Breastcancer.org April 6, 2007.
[895] Dawn L. Hershman et al., "Racial Disparities in Treatment and Survival of Male Breast Cancer," Journal of Clinical Oncology 25 (2007): 1089-1098.

by an international collaboration...Men with highest levels of estrogen were two and a half times more likely to develop breast cancer than men with the lowest levels of the hormone."[896] The breast cancer phenomenon among Black men and Black women is thus another consequence of the Estrogen Assault against Black America and, as a "female cancer," is part of the chemical feminizing of Black men.

VIII.   *The Prostrate Cancer Treatment that Castrates, Feminizes and then Kills Black Men*

Abraham Morgentaler has pointed out that "the primary thrust of the last 7 decades of research into treatment of advanced prostate cancer has been to find ways to *more completely deprive PCa of androgen.*"[897] The main means of doing that is Androgen Deprivation Therapy (ADT). Through actual surgical castration (bilateral orchiectomy) or through the use of testosterone depleting drugs called luteinizing hormone-releasing hormone (LHRH) agonists or gonadotropin releasing-hormone (GnRH) agonists, a man's testosterone is brought down to castrate levels (< 50 ng/mL). The goal of this hormone therapy is twofold: 1.) to reduce androgen levels in order to stop them from stimulating prostate cancer cells to grow and 2.) to shrink the prostate to make it easier to cover the entire area with radiation seed treatment (brachytherapy).

In August 2016 **The Washington Post** had a startling headline: "Hormone therapy for prostate cancer may pose a risk for black men" (August 5, 20016) and stated: "Black men treated with hormone therapy for prostate cancer may have a higher risk of death than white men undergoing the same therapy, according to a new study. But the deaths aren't actually caused by prostate cancer."[898]

The treatment in question is of course ADT. The study conducted by researchers at Brigham and Women's Hospital in Boston, Massachusetts assessed the impact of race on the risk

---

[896] "Men with high estrogen levels could be at greater risk of breast cancer," ScienceDaily May 11, 2015.
[897] Abraham Morgentaler, "New Concepts Regarding Testosterone and Prostate Cancer: A Breadth of Fresh Air," Oncology 28 (May 16, 2014): 3.
[898] Lateshia Beachum, "Hormone therapy for prostate cancer may pose a risk for black men," The Washington Post August 5, 2016.

of mortality among men on ADT.[899] The researchers found that Black men had a 77% higher risk of death from all causes compared with men of other races when treated with a short-term course of ADT. "When African-American men," says Konstantin Kovtum, MD a lead researcher of the study,

> were exposed to an average of only four months of hormone therapy, primarily used to make the prostate small enough for brachytherapy, they suffered from higher mortality rates due to causes other than prostate cancer than non-African American men. This leads us to believe that there may be something intrinsic to the biology of African-American men that predisposes them to this increased risk of death and that this deserves further study.[900]

Indeed there is something intrinsic to the biology of the Black Man. Most of these ADT-related deaths of Black men seem to involve cardiovascular health issues. "African American men have an onset of cardiovascular problems that are linked to ADT use," reported Dr. Kovlum.[901] This makes sense. The aim of ADT or *androgen deprivation* therapy is to *deprive* the male patient of his testosterone by reducing his testosterone to castration levels. But, as Jerald Bain reported, "The current evidence...strongly suggests that testosterone may be cardioprotective,"[902] meaning that a lot of T is *good for the heart* because it protects the heart. T levels are now found to correlate positively with cardio-protective high-density lipoprotein (HDL) cholesterol and negatively with atherogenic low-density lipoprotein (LDL) cholesterol and triglycerides.[903] Intracoronary artery infusion of testosterone causes significant

---

[899] Konstantin A. Kovtum et al., "Race and mortality risk after radiation therapy in men treated with or without androgen-suppression therapy for favorable-risk prostate cancer," Cancer 122 (2016): 3608-3014 (Epub: August 4, 2016).
[900] Quoted by Nick Mulcahy, "ADT for Prostate Cancer May Increase Death Risk in Black Men," Medscape August 17, 2016.
[901] Lateshia Beachum, "Hormone therapy for prostate cancer may pose a risk for black men," The Washington Post August 5, 2016.
[902] Jerald Bain, "The many faces of testosterone," Clinical Interventions in Aging 2 (2004): 567-576.
[903] Paul D. Morris and Kevin S. Channer, "Testosterone and cardiovascular disease in men," Asian Journal of Andrology 14 (2012): 428-435.

artery dilation rather than constriction as previous believed.[904] Men with coronary artery disease tend to have *lower testosterone*. As Morris and Channer document,

> current evidence suggests that normal and physiological levels of testosterone are not deleterious to the male heart and are, in fact, beneficial. It is hypotestosteronaemia (= low T) which is associated with adverse coronary risk profiles and with coronary morbidity and mortality in men...Contrary to the notion that higher testosterone levels account for the higher burden of coronary disease in men than women, there is an increasing body of literature indicating that men with coronary artery disease (CAD) have significantly lower testosterone levels than men without CAD...[I]t has now been demonstrated in several large longitudinal cohort studies of men with and without coronary disease that low baseline testosterone is a significant risk marker of increased all-cause and cardiovascular mortality.[905]

So low T increases the risk of cardiovascular morbidity and thus men rendered hypogonadal (= low T) as a result of ADT through hormone therapy are associated with greater CAD risk. Along with plummeting testosterone levels the LHRH/GnRH agonists also significantly increase fat mass and fasting insulin levels and decrease insulin sensitivity, all of which contribute to cardiovascular disease and diabetes. In a large, population-based study of older men with local or regional PCa on ADT treatment Keating and coworkers found that

> Androgen deprivation therapy with GnRH agonists was associated with increased risk of incident diabetes, coronary heart disease, acute myocardial infraction, and sudden cardiac death, Moreover, short-term GnRH agonist treatment was significantly associated with greater risk of disease and the elevated risks persisted in men on longer-term therapy.[906]

---

904 CM Webb et al., "Effects of testosterone on coronary vasomotor regulation in men with coronary heart disease," Circulation 100 (1999): 1690-1696.
905 Morris and Channer, "Testosterone and cardiovascular disease in men," 428, 429, 433.
906 Nancy L. Keating, A. James O'Malley, and Matthew R. Smith, "Diabetes and Cardiovascular Disease During Androgen Deprivation

Saigal et al. found a 20% higher risk of serious cardiovascular morbidity in men newly diagnosed with PCa and receiving ADT than similar men who did not receive ADT.[907] We can thus understand why Black men are at such higher risk of death due to ADT treatment than any other group. Because Black men have the highest levels of testosterone we are affected more and more severely by the medically induced hypogonadism that is the outcome of ADT. Plummeting *our* T levels puts us at much greater risk of cardiotoxicity, and cardiotoxicity is thought to be a main cause of non-PCa death in those Black men with PCa on ADT. Not only is the *disease* an assault on our testosterone, but the *treatment for the disease* is an assault on our testosterone!

But ADT is not only killing Black men, it is profoundly *feminizing* Black men on the way to the grave. ADT is accompanied by an array of gruesome side effects and toxicities. The castrate level of testosterone produced is associated with a constellation of symptoms that together are now recognized as "androgen deprivation syndrome" and includes[908]:

- Loss of testicular volume and penile length (shrinkage)
- Loss of lean muscle mass
- Development of a characteristically post-menopausal female pattern of fat distribution
- Gynecomastia (development of breasts)
- Loss of body hair
- Hot flashes "similar to those experienced by women at the time of menopause."

Therapy for Prostate Cancer," Journal of Clinical Oncology 24 (2006): 4448-4456 (4452).

[907] Christopher S .Saigal et al., "Androgen Deprivation Therapy Increases Cardiovascular Morbidity in Men With Prostate Cancer," Cancer 110 (2007): 1493-1500.

[908] Paul L. Nguyen et al., "Adverse Effects of Androgen Deprivation Therapy and Strategies to Mitigate Them," European Urology 67 (2015): 825-836; Petros Sountoulides and Thomas Rountos, "Adverse Effects of Androgen Deprivation Therapy for Prostate Cancer: Prevention and Management," ISRN Urology Volume 2013, Article ID 240108, pages 1-8; Rowan G Casey, Niall M Corcoran and S Larry Goldenberg, "Quality of life issues in men undergoing androgen deprivation therapy: a review," Asian Journal of Andrology 14 (2012): 226-231; "Managing Hot flushes in men after prostate cancer-A systematic review," Maturitas 65 (2010): 15-22.

- Decrease in bone mineral density with potential increased risk of fractures
- Emotional lability such as increased tearfulness
- Decreased cognitive sharpness

ADT's effect by continuously assaulting testosterone production and androgen action is to produce a "border body" that is neither masculine nor fully feminine, leaving "a man without masculinity," according to one patient. Dr. Richard Wassersug, currently adjunct professor in the Department of Urologic Sciences at the University of British Columbia and the Australian Research Centre in Sex, Health and Society at La Trobe University in Melbourne, Australia, is currently one of the leading voices highlighting what he calls "the emasculating reality of ADT" for men on the treatment, noting:

> ADT typically leads to a loss of body hair, genital shrinkage, the development of fat in a postmenopausal female pattern of distribution, loss of muscle mass, hot flashes, and, depending on the drugs used, various amounts of gynecomastia. Thus, ADT both emasculates and feminizes.[909]

Many men who suffer from "androgen deprivation syndrome" have a very tortured sense of self as men.

> Many males castrated to treat prostate cancer have expressed during interviews their inability to find an effective narrative or template to interpret their experience (...). They struggle to describe who they are and what they have become, both to others and to themselves. As one patient stated, 'Whenever I saw my body, I wondered, "Who am I? A woman? A man?" It's a very confusing situation' (...). Others echo this statement. One patient said, for example, that he is 'a man who's not a man' (...). Another claimed, 'I'm no longer a viable man – I'm a eunuch, I'm a gelding', and one more asserted, 'You're not male, you're not female, you're just a *neuter gender*' (emphasis added).[910]

---

[909] Richard J. Wassersug, "Mastering Emasculation," Journal of Clinical Oncology 27 (2009): 634-636 (634).

[910] Richard J. Wassersug, Emma McKenna and Tucker Lieberman, "Eunuch as a gender identity after castration," Journal of Gender Studies 21 (2012): 253-270 (256). See also Karen D. Fergus, Ross E. Gray and Margaret I. Fitch, "Sexual dysfunction and the preservation of manhood: experiences of men with prostate cancer," Journal of Health Psychology 7 (202): 303-316.

Because Black men suffer the greatest androgen depletion impact, we can imagine the "neuter gender" effects experienced by some Black men on ADT. And the case can be made that Black men have been *targeted* for this treatment. Today ADT is standard of care for men with advanced PCa. Its use was initially restricted as a palliative treatment for symptomatic, metastatic as well as inoperable locally advanced disease. Because ADT through LHRH agonists is one of the costliest of all PCa treatments (Medicare reimbursements totaled > $1 billion in 2001), it's initial use was among the more high-income white males. Black men more often opted for the least costly method of ADT: surgical castration or orchiectomy. However, the 1990s (1991-1999) were a watershed period. There was a sharp and striking (and inexplicable) increase in ADT use, *especially among low-risk patients* (local, non-metastatic PCa) and *low-income patients.*[911] In 1991 11.5% of patients with non-metastatic PCa received LHRH agonists but by 1999 this increased to 41.1%.[912] Black men were still during this period less likely to receive this treatment than white men, but the numbers (both white and Black) who used ADT either as the primary treatment or in conjunction with other treatments (and for low as well as high grade cancer) grew dramatically.[913]

---

[911] Matthew R. Cooperberg et al., "National Practice Patterns and Time Trends in Androgen Ablation for Localized Prostate Cancer," Journal of the National Cancer Institute 95 (2003): 981-989.

[912] Vahakn B. Shahinian et al., "Increasing Use of Gonadotropin-Releasing Hormone Agonists for the Treatment of Localized Prostate Carcinoma," Cancer 103 (2005): 1615-1624.

[913] April P. Carson et al., "Trends and Racial Differenes in the Use of Androgen Deprivation Therapy for Metastatic Prostate Cancer," Journal of Pain Symptom Management 39 (2010): 1-17; Nancy L. Keating et al., "Use of androgen deprivation therapy for metastatic prostate cancer in older men," Urological Oncology 101 (2008): 1077-1083; Laurens Holms Jr., "Impact of androgen deprivation therapy on racial/ethnic disparities in survival of older men treated for locoregional prostate cancer," Cancer Control. 16 (2009): 176-185; Steven B. Zeliadt et al., "Racial Disparity in Primary and Adjuvant Treatment for Nonmetastatic Prostate Cancer: SEER-Medicare Trends 1991 to 1999," Urology 64 (2004): 1171-1176.

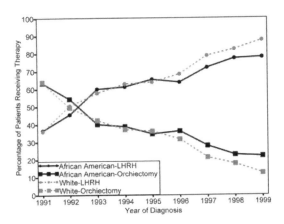

Fig. 3.
Proportion of men treated with an orchiectomy or an LHRH agonist by race, among those receiving ADT, SEER-Medicare 1991–1999.

But the efficacy of this treatment is controversial and has not been demonstrated clinically. Not only does ADT fail to increase survival of PCa, almost all patients on the treatment eventually develop a more aggressive ADT-*resistant cancer*. Why then has its use skyrocketed? A national survey in 1998 showed that 53% of urologists who did not believe in the efficacy of ADT in locally advanced cancer *still prescribed it!*[914] Dr. Wassersug argues that physicians prescribe ADT in a cavalier fashion and without adequately informing patients of the side effects.[915] One reason to over-prescribe this treatment might be the financial incentive.

> financial incentive may be a motivating force for some physicians to prescribe GnRH agonist therapy. During the study period, Medicare drug reimbursement was set at 95% of the average wholesale price (approximately $600 per dose of leuprolide). However, a report in 2001 by the U.S. General Accounting Office showed that, on average, physician providers purchased the drugs at 82% of the average wholesale price, allowing a substantial profit for every dose administered.[916]

---

[914] Shahinian et al., "Increasing Use," 1622.
[915] André Picard, "Why Castration Makes You No Less of a Man," The Globe and Mail (Halifax, Canada), September 18, 2007, http://www.theglobeandmail.
[916] Shahinian et al., "Increasing Use," 1622.

We suspect that money was not the only consideration in making this costly testosterone depleting treatment so available to men who can't afford it (low-income) and who don't need it (low-risk). While there was a steady increase of use of LHRH agonists through the 1990s, there was a dramatic decline in its use by Black men in 1996. In 1997 the National Cancer Institute published in its journal a commentary *advocating the preventive use of ADT by high-risk but healthy men, starting with Black men!*

> Androgens are required for the normal development and function of the prostate gland. Prostate cancer and benign prostatic hyperplasia are common in men and develop in an environment of continuous androgen exposure. The utility of androgen deprivation as a treatment for advanced prostate cancer was first demonstrated in 1941, and many new classes of drugs that interfere with androgen production and function have been introduced in recent years. These agents are effective in treating prostate cancer and benign prostatic hyperplasia and may have an important role in *chemoprevention*...Chemoprevention refers to *prevention* of cancer or reduction of risk *in susceptible individuals* by administration of natural or synthetic drugs with little or no toxicity that suppress, delay, or reverse carcinogenesis...[A] strategy directed toward interrupting or decreasing exposure to androgens can significantly decrease prostate cancer incidence...Prostate cancer chemoprevention trials directed at African-American men or men with a strong familial predisposition for prostate cancer could potentially include highly motivated target populations. African-American men have the highest rates of prostate cancer in the world (emphasis added).[917]

Whatever strategy was devised, the rate of ADT use by Black men shot up after 1997. In fact, between 2000 and 2007 the likelihood of use flipped: white men were 48% *less likely* than Black men to receive ADT vs. radical prostatectomy, and white men were 71% *less likely* to receive ADT than radical prostatectomy compared to Black men for low-risk disease:

---

[917] Joseph W. Aquilina, James J. Lipsky, David G. Bostwick, "Androgen Deprivation as a Strategy for Prostate Cancer Chemoprevention," Journal of the National Cancer Institute 89 (1997): 689-696.

"Our data show that nonwhite men are less likely to undergo surgery for prostate cancer when analysis is controlled for multiple factors. African American men, in particular, are more likely to receive ADT for low-risk disease compared with their white counterparts...whites were much less likely to receive ADT for low-risk disease (...) than were African Americans." [918]

---

[918] Kelvin A. Moses et al., "Impact of Ethnicity on Primary Treatment Choice and Mortality in Men With Prostate Cancer: Data From CaPSURE," Journal of Clinical Oncology 28 (2010): 1069-1074.

Chapter Fourteen

The Toxic Assault Against
The Black Woman and Child

I.   *The Estrogen Assault*

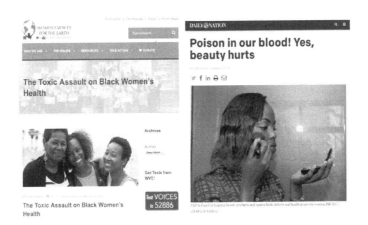

Fast food consumption is not the only source of Black America's disproportionately high phthalates body burden. A 2013 study showed a race-specific association of phthalate exposure and childhood obesity in Black Children in a nationally representative sample. In a data set of 2,884 children aged 6-19, obese and overweight Black children were found to have high levels of phthalates detected in their urine and have higher body concentration of these chemicals than whites.[919]

> A new study...showed that African American children had higher levels of the chemicals (i.e. phthalates) compared to white and Hispanic children...There was no association found between urinary levels of phthalates in white and Hispanic children and increased body mass index (BMI). However, a

---

[919] Leonardo Trasande et al., "Race/Ethnicity-Specific Associations of Urinary Phthalates with Childhood Body Mass in a Nationally Representative Sample," *Environmental Health Perspectives* 121 (2013): 501-506.

strong relationship between weight, body mass...and phthalate levels was found for African-American kids.[920]

However, the phthalates in these obese children did not derive from fast food.

Black children have much higher levels of the chemicals (i.e. phthalates) in their bodies than children of other races...The phthalates associated with black children's obesity were the kind commonly added to *personal care products* to make fragrances last longer. Other phthalates are used to make vinyl and can be found in food packaging, medical devices and flooring... For the personal care product-type

Daily **Mail**
.com

Home | U.K. | News | Sports | U.S. Showbiz | Australia | Femail | Health | Science | Money

Shampoo for Hair Los
Recommended By Top Dermat
USA. Learn More Now.
VISIT SITE

Nearly 80 percent of hair products aimed at black women contain cancer-causing chemicals (stock)

Nearly 80% of hair products aimed at black women contain chemicals linked to cancer, infertility and obesity, study finds

• Up to 78% of relaxers contain hormone-disrupting chemicals called parabens
• Parabens have been linked to cancer, weight gain and reduced muscle mass
• Up to 78% also contain phthalates, which extend the products' shelf lives
• Phthalates are associated with breast and ovarian cancer, and early menopause
• Black women are thought to use such products to meet social beauty norms

By ALEXANDRA THOMPSON HEALTH REPORTER FOR MAILONLINE
PUBLISHED: 10:45 EDT, 26 April 2018 | UPDATED: 12:08 EDT, 26 April 2018

phthalates, black children had levels 81 percent higher than white children, 45 percent higher than Mexican American children and 4 percent higher than other Hispanic children...[921]

Endocrine disrupting, cancer causing chemicals are found in most scented personal grooming products that target Black women and girls, such as perfume, nail polish, skin lighteners, feminine hygiene and hair products.[922] More

[920] Michelle Castillo, "Environmental contaminants phthalates linked to obesity in African-American children," **CBS News** February 6, 2013.
[921] Brian Bienkowski, "Chemicals Linked to Obesity in Black Children," **Scientific American** February 4, 2013.
[922] Jessica S. Helm et al., "Measurement of endocrine disrupting and asthma-associated chemicals in hair products used by Black women," **Environmental Research**, available online April 2018, doi: 10.1016/j.envres.2018.03.030; Tamarra James-Todd, Ruby Senie, and Mary Beth Terry, "Racial/Ethnic Differences in Hormonally-Active Hair Product Use: A Plausible Risk Factor for Health Disparities," **Journal of Immigrant and Minority Health** 14

personal care products marketed toward Black women than used by White women contain placenta, which is high in estrogens.[923]

> hair products commonly used by African Americans often vary from those used by Whites. For example, White women rarely use hair relaxers, but one study found that 94% of African American women surveyed under age 45 and 89% aged 45 and above used them. According to one review, some studies have found that African Americans use more personal care products that contain hormones and placenta than Whites, and may be exposed to them as infants, toddlers, and in utero through their pregnant mothers. Further, the authors hypothesize that penetration and absorption of hair products are increased with the use of heat, which is regularly used in their application... A study...discovered premature sexual characteristics developed in African American girls as young as 14 months of age following topical application of hair products containing hormonally active ingredients.[924]

It is reported that while up to 78% of Black hair care products contain phthalates and other EDC's linked with breast and ovarian cancer which is high among Black women, only 7% of those used by white women contain them.[925] And as Olga

---

(2012): 506-11; Ami R. Zota and Bhavna Shamasunder, "The environmental injustice of beauty: framing chemical exposures from beauty products as a health disparities concern," **American Journal of Obstetrics & Gynecology** (2017): 1-5; Francesca Branch et al. "Vaginal douching and racial/ethnic disparities in phthalates exposures among reproductive aged women: National Health and Nutrition Examination Survey 2001-2004," **Environmental Health** (2015): 1-8; Laura Stiel et al., "A review of hair product use on breast cancer risk in African American women," **Cancer Medicine** 5 (2016): 597-604.

[923] Laura Stiel et al., "A review of hair product use on breast cancer risk in African American women," **Cancer Medicine** 5 (2016): 597-604.

[924] Stiel et al., "A review of hair product use," 599.

[925] Alexandra Thompson, "Nearly 80% of hair products aimed at black women contain chemicals linked to cancer, infertility and obesity, study finds," **Daily Mail** (Online) April 26, 2018. See also: Inga Vesper, "Hair Products Popular with Black women May Contain Harmful Chemicals," **Scientific American** May 11, 2018; T. James-Todd, R. Senie and M.B. Terry, "Racial/ethnic differences in hormonally-active hair product use: a plausible risk factor for health disparities," **J Immigr Minor Health** 14 (2012): 506-511.

Khazan points out, "Phthalates seem to have the greatest effect *in the womb*, so they are most concerning for women of reproductive age."[926] And reproductive age and pregnant Black women are targeted. In several studies it was shown that young reproductive age and pregnant Black women have higher levels of phthalates such as DEHP in their blood than White women.[927] Phthalates have been linked to reproductive problems in women, as well the premature appearance of secondary sexual characteristics among Black infants and toddlers, early puberty, and obesity.[928] Thus, 62% of Black girls reach menarche by age 12 compared to 35% of White girls.[929]

> Virtually all U.S. women are exposed to multiple phthalates. Among reproductive-aged women in the U.S. general population, non-Hispanic black and Mexican American women have higher metabolite concentrations of the low-molecular weight phthalates (e.g. DEP, DnBP) than non-Hispanic white women. Similar exposure disparities between non-white and white subpopulations have also been observed in pregnant women and girls aged 6–8 years.[930]

> Nationally representative data of US reproductive aged women suggest that women of color have higher levels of certain endocrine disrupting chemicals, such as phthalates and parabens, in their bodies compared with white women and that

---

[926] Olga Khazan, "The Toxins in Feminine-Hygiene Products," **The Atlantic** July 20, 2015.

[927] T.M. James Todd et al. "Racial and Ethnic Variations in Phthalate Metabolite Concentration across Pregnancy," J Expo Sci Environ Epidemiol. 27 (2017): 1-17; Ami R. Zota and Bhavna Shamasunder, "The environmental injustice of beauty: framing chemical exposures from beauty products as a health disparities concern," **American Journal of Obstetrics & Gynecology** (2017): 1-5; Roni W. Kobrosly et al. "Socioeconomic factors and phthalate metabolite concentrations among United States women of reproductive age," Environmental Research 115 (2012): 11-17.

[928] Maryann Donovan et al., "Personal care products that contain estrogens or xenoestrogens may increase breast cancer risk," **Medical Hypothesis** 68 (2007): 756-766.

[929] Tamarra M. James-Todd1, Yu-Han Chiu, and Ami R. Zota, "Racial/ethnic disparities in environmental endocrine disrupting chemicals and women's reproductive health outcomes: epidemiological examples across the life course," **Curr Epidemiol Rep**. 3 (2016): 161–180 (161).

[930] James-Todd, Chiu, and Zota, "Racial/ethnic disparities," 161.

these racial/ethnic differences are not explained by socioeconomic status.[931]

African American women are more likely than white women to use vaginal douches and other fragranced feminine cleansing products such as sprays and wipes. In a nationally representative sample of reproductive aged women, those who reported frequent douching had 150% higher exposures to diethyl phthalate, which is a chemical commonly found in fragrances, than douch nonusers...vaginal douching may contribute to racial/ethnic disparities in phthalates exposure. Prenatal exposure to diethyl phthalate can alter maternal sex steroid hormone concentrations during pregnancy...Advertisers used targeted marketing towards African American women with messages that encouraged self-consciousness of potential vaginal odors.[932]

The most alarming aspect of this toxic problem is that "Five of the compounds studied had the *highest concentrations in products aimed at children*" and "The majority of such compounds *were not mentioned on the products' ingredient labels.*"[933]

Some of the substances were not mentioned on the product packaging at all whereas others were referred to by vague terms such as "fragrances." In the U.S. companies are required to list intentionally added chemicals on product packaging. [934]

Erin Switalski thus summarizes "The Toxic Assault on Black Women's Health":

[931] Ami R. Zota and Bhavna Shamasunder, "The environmental injustice of beauty: framing chemical exposures from beauty products as a health disparities concern," **American Journal of Obstetrics & Gynecology** (2017): 1-5, 1.
[932] Zota and Shamasunder, "The environmental injustice of beauty," 3.
[933] Inga Vesper, "Hair Products Popular with Black women May Contain Harmful Chemicals," **Scientific American** May 11, 2018.
[934] Inga Vesper, "Hair Products Popular with Black women May Contain Harmful Chemicals," **Scientific American** May 11, 2018. Also Jessica S. Helm et al., "Measurement of endocrine disrupting and asthma-associated chemicals in hair products used by Black women," *Environmental Research*, available online April 2018, doi: 10.1016/j.envres.2018.03.030.

Black women bear a greater burden of chronic diseases that have been linked with exposure to toxic chemicals in the United States. For example, 90% of the individuals diagnosed with the autoimmune disease, lupus, are women. Lupus affects African-American women at three times the rate of white women. African American women are also more likely to have premature births and infants with low birth rates, which are also linked to environmental contamination. According to the CDC, African American women are 34% more likely to die of breast cancer than white women... The toxic assault on Black women doesn't end there. It gets intimate, as many products marketed to Black women, like skin lighteners, hair relaxers and dyes, contain some of the most toxic chemicals on the market...Getting even more intimate, a recent study looking at phthalates (a hormone-disrupting chemical) and douching found that black women have 48% higher levels of phthalates than white women in their bodies. In a particularly egregious example of this attack on Black women's health, Johnson & Johnson intentionally marketed talc baby powder to Black women, despite knowing since 1979 that talc could potentially cause cancer. It's not a coincidence that a Black woman spends nearly twice as much on skin care products than a white woman, or that she douches at higher rates than her white counterpart. That is the result of a lifetime of subtle (or sometimes blatant) messages that have told her she is not beautiful enough, or clean enough, or worthy enough, or white enough – and the answer to her "problems" lies in a product.[935]

These toxic personal care products marketed to Black women are thus another major source of the high phthalate body burden that they and Black children suffer from.

II. *The Aspirin Conspiracy*

In 2014 this government made a head-scratching move: it recommended pregnant, primarily Black women take aspirin daily after 12 weeks of pregnancy. This is remarkable because pregnant women were for the longest and with good reason warned to stay away from pain killers such as aspirin and ibuprofen except for occasional, doctor-prescribed cases

---

[935] Erin Switalski, "The Toxic Assault on Black Women's Health," **Women's Voices For The Earth** August 3, 2016 @ https://www.womensvoices.org/2016/08/03/toxic-assault-on-black-womens-health/

because aspirin is well-known to cause both maternal and fetal hemorrhaging: intracranial hemorrhaging or bleeding inside the skull and gastrointestinal hemorrhaging or bleeding in the gut.[936] But that was all dismissed in 2014. The pretext was that an aspirin a day will keep preeclampsia away, which is a condition in pregnant women characterized by high blood pressure and protein in the urine.

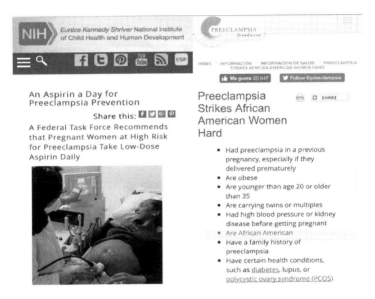

Black women are indeed most at risk for preeclampsia: Black women develop the condition at a 70% higher rate than white women, but no one knows the cause of this.[937] In other words, the Black Woman's is the only case where her very ethnicity "African American" is a listed high risk factor for preeclampsia. There *was* a study in 1994 that suggested that low-dose aspirin might be helpful in treating severe preeclampsia once that

---

[936] Sheena Derry and Yoon Kong Loke, "Risk of gastrointestinal haemorrhage with long term use of aspirin: meta-analysis," **BMJ** 321 (2000): 1183-1187; Carol M. Rumack et al., "Neonatal Intracranial Hemorrhage and Maternal Use of Aspirin," **Obstetrics & Gynecology** 58 (1981): 52S-56S;

[937] Annettee Nakimuli et al., "Pregnancy, parturition and preeclampsia in women of African ancestry," **American Journal of Obstetrics and Gynecology** 210 (2014): 510-520; Dr. Linda Burke-Galloway, "Preeclampsia Strikes African Women Hard," **Preeclampsia Foundation** February 6, 2013;

condition actually developed. But the government is *here* encouraging otherwise healthy "high risk" women - Black Women - to take aspirin daily on the false pretense that it will "prevent" the onset of preeclampsia.

So what? What are we suggesting is the real reason Black Women are encouraged to take aspirin while pregnant?

Ten years before this recommendation was made, behavioral neuroscientists from the University of Maryland made a startling announcement:

> A new study finds that male rat fetuses exposed to aspirin have a less masculinized brain and a reduced sex drive as adults. The results reveal a surprise twist in how testosterone makes males out of fetal rats.[938]

Exposing a male fetus to enough aspirin can reduce his masculinization because Aspirin acts as a class of chemicals called *Endocrine Disrupters.*

> Mild analgesics like aspirin have recently been incriminated by several epidemiological and toxicological studies to act as endocrine disrupters. Aspirin treated rat had decreased level of testosterone production.[939]

Aspirin acts as a Gender Bender to a male fetus by decreasing testosterone: it de-masculinizes the male fetus and that de-masculinization won't be apparent until adulthood.[940]

---

[938] Mary Beckman, "Aspirin Kills More Than Pain for Male Rats," **Science** May 24, 2004.

[939] Fahar Ibtisham et al., "Effect of Aspirin on Reproductive Profile of Male Rat An-Overview," **International Journal of Research and Development in Pharmacy and Life Sciences** 5 (2016): 5-12.

[940] Mehmet Gokhan Culha and Ege Can Serefoglu, "Prolonged exposure to acetaminophen during pregnancy reduces testosterone production by the human fetal testis," **Ann Transl Med** 2017. doi: 10.21037/atm.2017.01.57; Millissia Ben Maamar et al., "Ibuprofen results in alterations of human fetal testis development," **Nature: Scientific Reports** 10 March 2017: 1-15; David M. Kristensen et al., "Analgesic use – prevalence, biomonitoring and endocrine and reproductive effects," **Nature Reviews: Endocrinology** May 6, 2016: 1-13; O. Albert et al., "Paracetamol, aspirin and indomethacin display endocrine disrupting properties in the adult human testis *in vitro*," **Human Reproduction** 28 (2013): 1890-1898; Claudia A.

And *that*, I submit, is the reason Black Women are asked to disregard the known risk to their own health that daily aspirin intake while pregnant presents. The target is the boy child growing in her womb. "Kill the Male" does not only mean physically murder Black boys and men. "Kill the male" also means eradicate the masculinity of the black male.

Snijder et al., "Intrauterine exposure to mild analgesics during pregnancy and the occurrence of cryptorchidism and hypospadias in the offspring: the Generation R Study," **Human Reproduction** 27 (2012): 1191-1201; David M. Kristensen et al., "Intrauterine exposure to mild analgesics is a risk factor for development of male reproductive disorders in human and rat," **Human Reproduction** 26 (2011): 235-244; Stuart K. Amateau and Margaret M. McCarthy, "Induction of PGE_2 by estradiol mediates developmental masculinization of sex behavior," **Nature Neuroscience** 7 (2004): 643-650; Domenico Conte et al., "Aspirin inhibits androgen response to chorionic gonadotropin in humans," **Am J Physiol.** 277 (1999):E1032-7;

Part IV

.*The Pot Plot*

Chapter Fifteen

Newports: An Early Ethnic Weapon

In order to fully appreciate this weaponizing of weed we must see the Pot Plot in the context of the broader chemico-biological assault on the Black man and woman. It is *not* an accident that Black men chase their weed down with menthol cigarettes and alcohol. Before marijuana was ethnically weaponized against the Black Man and Woman, tobacco actually was one of the first chemical weapons targeting the post-1960s urban Black Males. A landmark legal decision of 1998 forced Big Tobacco companies to release previously secret internal documents going back decades, documents many of which detail the ways that Big Tobacco companies – often with Jewish executives at the helm - targeted the Black community in the 1960s-1970s with a relentless advertising assault and literally conspired to coerce the adoption by Black males in particular of a specific type of cigarette, menthol cigarettes, which are *more* addictive than regular (non-mentholated)

cigarettes.[941] As Philip S. Gardiner, research scientist at the Tobacco Related Disease Research Program at the University of California, describes this process of "the African Americanization" of menthol cigarettes:

> Today, over 70% of African American smokers prefer menthol cigarettes, compared with 30% of White smokers. This unique social phenomenon was principally occasioned by the tobacco industry's *masterful manipulation* of the burgeoning Black, urban, segregated, consumer market in the 1960s. Through the use of television and other advertising media, coupled with culturally tailored images and messages, the tobacco industry "African Americanized" menthol cigarettes. The tobacco industry successfully positioned mentholated products, especially Kool, as young, hip, new, and healthy. During the time that menthols were gaining a large market share in the African American community, the tobacco industry donated funds to African American organizations hoping to blunt the attack on their products (emphasis added – WM).[942]

In the 1960s these companies employed a mobile van program in which representatives were sent on "Ethnic field" trips to Black neighborhoods where they would stay for hours and give away menthol cigarettes.[943] Tobacco companies enticed Black Media, civil rights organizations and Black

---

[941] Phillip S. Gardiner, "The African Americanization of menthol cigarette use in the United States," **Nicotine & Tobacco Research** 6 (2004): S55-S65; idem, "African American Teen Cigarette Smoking: A Review," In D. Burns (Ed.), **Changing adolescent smoking prevalence: Where is it and why** (Smoking and Tabaco Control Monograph 14, 2001) 213-226; Jim Edwards, "Why big Tobacco Targeted Blacks With Ads for Menthol Cigarettes," **CBS News** January 5, 2011; Tom McNichol, "Mint That Kills: The Curious Life of Menthol Cigarettes," **The Atlantic** March 25, 2011; David J. Moore, Jerome D. Williams and William J. Qualls, "Target Marketing of Tobacco and Alcohol-Related Products to Ethnic Minority Groups in the United States," **Ethnicity & Disease** 6 (1996): 83-98; V.B. Yrger, J. Przewoznik and R.E. Malone, "Racialized geography, corporate activity, and health disparities: tobacco industry targeting of inner cities," **J Health Care Poor Underserved** 18 (2007): 10-38.
[942] Gardiner, "The African Americanization of menthol cigarette use," S58.
[943] Taryn Finley, "How Tobacco Companies Led A Devastating 50-Year Infiltration Into Black Communities," **HuffPost** April 11, 2016.

politicians into a Quid Pro Quo: for their monetary support there will be no participation in tobacco control efforts or criticism of tobacco's damaging health effects on the community and these financial beneficiaries would support tobacco industry positions.[944]

Our music, including Hip Hop, was used by Big Tobacco to market menthol cigarettes to Black people, in violation of the Master Settlement Agreement of 1998 for forbids marketing to minors. This "music campaign" aim was to get Black people "emotionally hooked." These campaigns often involved cigarette brands sponsoring concerts, MC competitions, and using DJ's to distribute free keychains, lighters, flying disks, CD-ROMS featuring rap music and interactive games, clothes and, of course, cigarettes.[945] In 2004 tobacco giant Brown & Williamson was sued by the states of Illinois, New York and Maryland for violating the terms of the Settlement by "improperly using hip-hop music, cigarette-package art, promotions such as lighters, flashlights and CD-ROMs, and a 'House of Menthol' Web site in a slick campaign to lure children to smoke."[946] The company agreed to pay a nearly $1.5 million settlement and cease their marketing tactics to minors.

Menthol is a chemical compound that is the chief ingredient in peppermint oil and is used as an additive to flavor cigarettes. It cools and numbs the throat, reducing the harshness of cigarette smoke and making it easier to inhale. Menthols were originally, from the 1930s to the 1960s, an affluent white woman's cigarette.

---

[944] Phyra M. McCandless et al., "Quid Pro Quo: Tobacco Companies and the Black Press," *American Journal of Public Health* 102 (2012): 739-750; V.B. Yerger and R.E. Malone, "African American leadership groups: smoking with the enemy," *Tobacco Control* 11 (2002): 336-345; Myron Levin, "The Troubling History of Big Tobacco's Cozy Ties With Black Leaders," *Mother Jones* November 17, 2015

[945] Navid Hafez and Pamela M. ling, "Finding the Kool Mixx: how Brown & Williamson used music marketing to sell cigarettes," *Tobacco Control* 15 (2006): 359-366.

[946] Al Swanson, "Analysis: Tobacco giant cuts back hip hop," *UPI* October 7, 2004

How did Black men start chasing their weed down with Newports[947]?

There are approximately 42 million Black people in this country. 30% of Black adults reported tobacco use in 2015: 21 % of Black men smoke cigarettes and 13.3% of Black women. 80% of Black smokers smoke menthol cigarettes, vs. only 30% of white smokers. Black smokers are 4X's more likely to smoke menthol brand cigarettes than their white counterpart is.[948] This is because the tobacco industry deliberately, successfully and at great financial expense to themselves created a demand among inner-city Black males for menthol cigarettes that did not previously exist and an attachment to those cigarettes which to this day still resonates, with severe consequences.[949]

> In essence, the tobacco industry successfully created an attachment to menthols that still resonates in the Black community today. Initially targeted to a high-end clientele when they were first broadly advertised in the 1930s, and though consumed primarily by women, menthol brands became the cigarette of choice for African American smokers by the 1970s (...)."[950]

Why target Black men and women with menthol cigarettes?

Because according to internal documents companies like Lorillard who makes Newports funded studies and thus knew back in the 1970s what Penn State University scientists are only reporting now in 2015:

> Higher concentrations of melanin -- the color pigment in skin and hair -- may be placing darker pigmented smokers at increased susceptibility to nicotine dependence and tobacco-

---

[947] Grace Kong et al., "Menthol Cigarette and Marijuana Use Among Adolescents," **Nicotine & Tobacco Research** 15 (2013): 2094-2099.

[948] Campaign For Tobacco-Free Kids, "Impact of Menthol Cigarettes on Youth Smoking Initiation and Health Disparities," (2017) @ https://www.tobaccofreekids.org/assets/factsheets/0390.pdf.

[949] Stephanie Saul, "A Flavoring Seen as a Means of Marketing to Blacks," **The New York Times** May 13, 2008; Phillip S. Gardiner, "The African Americanization of menthol cigarette use in the United States," **Nicotine & Tobacco Research** 6 (2004): S55-S65.

[950] Gardiner, "The African Americanization of menthol cigarette use," S58.

related carcinogens than lighter skinned smokers, according to scientists.[951]

It was known since the 1970s, when Big Tobacco was targeting the Black Community, that nicotine has a biochemical affinity for melanated tissues: nicotine binds tightly to melanin pigments and then lingers and accumulates in other melanin-containing tissues like the heart, lungs, liver and brain.[952] When you add menthol, the menthol increases the body's absorption of nicotine. The higher the levels of melanin in the skin, the greater the accumulation of nicotine and its cancer-causing compounds in the body. And when the tobacco companies switched the target community of menthols from affluent white women to poor, urban Black males they increased the nicotine content, according to their own documents, and they lied about it.[953] Thus, with all of our melanin, the 30% of Black adults who are smokers have been potentially made into walking reservoirs or nicotine storage containers.

And what are the consequences of our being targeted with this chemico-biological ethnic weapon, the menthol cigarette?

According to the CDC smoking-related illness kills more Black people than AIDS, car crashes, murder, and drug and alcohol abuse combined. There are reported 45,000 preventable Black deaths a year caused by tobacco. Smoking rates between Black and white adults are comparable, yet Black

---

[951] Jenny Leonard, "Skin Color Clue to Smoking Addiction," *Futurity* May 11, 2009 @ https://www.futurity.org/skin-color-clue-to-smoking-addiction/

[952] Valerie B. Yerger and Ruth E. Malone, "Melanin and nicotine: A review of the literature," **Nicotine & Tobacco Research** 8 (2006): 487-498; Gary King et al., "Link between facultative melanin and tobacco use among African Americans," **Pharmacology, Biochemistry and Behavior** 92 (2009) 589-596.

[953] Gardiner, "The African Americanization of menthol cigarette use," S59 and ff: "Many people assumed that menthols had less tar; however, nothing could be further from the truth. Not only were Kools' tar and nicotine content comparable with the leading nonmenthol brands, but by the mid-1960s, Brown & Williamson's menthol offering contained more tar and nicotine than either of its main menthol rivals, Salem or Newport (...)"; Philip J. Hilts and Glenn Collins, "Records Show Philip Morris Studied Influence of Nicotine," **The New York Times** June 8 ,1995.

men suffer the greatest burden of tobacco-related deaths of any racial or ethnic group in the United States. Black people smoke fewer cigarettes than whites and take fewer puffs, yet – because of our melanin *that was targeted* - Black smokers maintain higher blood levels of nicotine and its metabolite. It is predicted that 1.5 million African Americans alive today under the age of 18 years old will become regular tobacco users, and 500,000 of them will die prematurely from tobacco-related illness.

And if that was not bad enough: Your enemy Brother never wants to simply kill you and me. He always wants to feminize us on the way to our grave. The nicotine in tobacco reduces a male's testosterone levels by producing carbon monoxide in the blood which travels to the testes and damages the Leydig cells which produce the testosterone in the testicles.[954] And when you add menthol to that cigarette, you not only increase the nicotine absorbed and thus available in the body to interfere with testosterone production, but the menthol itself also decreases testosterone levels in men.[955] Nicotine deforms sperm as well and contributes to infertility in men. Smoking has also been shown to cause changes to the brain's serotonergic system including a decrease in serotonin receptors in the brain. And while a short-term increase in serotonin stimulation after nicotine intake has been documented, over a prolonged period of smoking serotonin production inhibited.[956]

---

[954] Mohamed Shaarawy and Kamal Zaki Mahmoud, "Endocrine profile and semen characteristics in male smokers," *Fertility and Sterility* 38 (1982): 255-257; M.H. Briggs, "Cigarette smoking and infertility in men," *Med J Aust* 12 (1973): 616-617;

[955] D. Kapoor and T.H. Jones, "Smoking and hormones in health and endocrine disorders," *European Journal of Endocrinology* 152 (2005): 491-499; Mehmet Akdogan et al., "Effects of Peppermint Teas on Plasma Testosterone, Follicle-Stimulating Hormone, and Luteinizing Hormone Levels and Testicular Tissue in Rats," *Urology* 64 (2004): 394-398.

[956] Jun'ichi Sembaand Maki Wakuta, "Chronic effect of nicotine on serotonin transporter mRNA in the raphe nucleus of rats: Reversal by co-administration of bupropion," *Psychiatry and Clinical Neurosciences* 62 (2008): 435–441; Kevin M. Malone, "Cigarette Smoking, Suicidal Behavior, and Serotonin Function in Major Psychiatric Disorders," *Am J Psychiatry* 160 (2003):773–779; Ghada I Mohamed and Yasser R Lasheen, "Correlation between smoking, serum serotonin level, and peripheral fatigue of back extensors: cross-sectional study," *Bulletin of Faculty of Physical*

MASCULINIZING BLACK WOMEN

13.3% of adult Black women reportedly smoke cigarettes and, of course, Black Girls Toke too in greater numbers today. So when we add together the cigarettes Black Women smoke and the marijuana they toke, this all contributes to, with other factors of course, the fact that 56.6% of Black Women are obese. Cigarette smoking can cause weight gain and obesity. What's the connection and what the relevance is that to our discussion today?

Just like the marijuana, the cigarettes have the opposite effect on women than it does on men because "men are not like women and women are not like men." While nicotine enhanced by menthol lowers testosterone and raises estrogen in him, by different processes it is anti-estrogenic in her: it lowers the feminizing estrogen levels in the female and it raises her testosterone levels, like marijuana.[957]

The ratio of T/E in the male and E/T in the female determines gender body patterns: men are naturally tubular and women are naturally curvy. That's done by these ratios. The

---

Therapy 22 (2017):83–88; M.E. Benwell, D.J. Balfour and J.M. Anderson, "Smoking-associated changes in the serotonergic systems of discrete regions of human brain," *Psychopharmacology (Berl)* 102 (1990): 68-72; A.M. Attia et al, "Cigarette Smoking and Male Reproduction," *Archives of Andrology* 21 (1989): 45-49. On the assault on the Black male's serotonin see Wesley Muhammad, *Understanding The Assault on The Black Man, Black Manhood and Black Masculinity* (Atlanta: A-Team Publishing, 2016) 181-200.

[957] Jesse Oliver Tweed et al., "The endocrine effects of nicotine and cigarette smoke," *Trends Endocrinol Metab* 23 (2012): 334-342; Judith S. Brand et al., "Cigarette Smoking and Endogenous Sex Hormones in Postmenopausal Women," *J Clin Endocrinol Metab* 96 (2011): 3184-3192; Ami P. Raval, "Nicotine Addiction Causes Unique Detrimental Effects on Women's Brains," *Journal of Addictive Diseases* 30 (2011): 149-158; D. Kapoor and T.H. Jones, "Smoking and hormones in health and endocrine disorders," *European Journal of Endocrinology* 152 (2005): 491-499; M.F. Sowers et al., "Testosterone Concentrations in Women Aged 25-50 Yeas: Associations with Lifestyle, Body Composition, and Ovarian Status," *American Journal of Epidemiology* 153 (2001): 256-264; A.M. Attia et al, "Cigarette Smoking and Male Reproduction," *Archives of Andrology* 21 (1989): 45-49.

estrogen in a female with normal testosterone levels produces her characteristic low waist/high hip ratio.

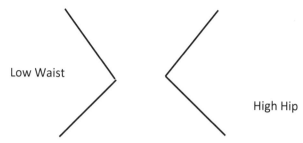

Low Waist

High Hip

Excess testosterone in a female causes the accumulation of fat cells around the waist area producing abdominal weight gain and it inhibits the accumulation of fat cells in the hip region. This produces in a female a high waist/ low hip ratio.

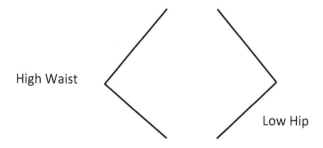

High Waist

Low Hip

This hormonal inversion or changes caused by smoking thus results in changes in fat distribution that can make a female form more tubular like a male rather than curvy like a female or, with other cofactors, can help make her obese.[958] The nicotine can deepen her voice, increase her facial and body hair growth and inhibit the estrogen signaling in her brain. Steve Harvey said, "Think Like A Man, Act Like A Lady." But these drugs or psychochemical ethnic weapons have got women thinking like a man, acting like a man and even looking like a man, while they got too many Black men thinking like a woman, behaving like a woman and - with your pants sagging exposing your butt – looking like a woman.

---

[958] Mari Pökki, "Smoking Affects Women's Sex Hormone-Regulated Body Form," *American Journal of Public Health* 99 (2009): 1350.

Of course, everybody isn't affected by marijuana and tobacco the same way or to the same degree, at the same time: diet matters, genetics matter, and life-style matters. But every time we puff puff pass, we open ourselves up to these effects. I'm talking about the Feminization of the Black Man and The masculinization of the Black Woman. Between the blunts that we smoke and the Newports that we chase it with, not to mention the alcohol, the Black community has become the poster child for gender-bending gone wild.

There is no such thing today as "Recreational drug use" among us. Black America's whole drug culture, from cigarettes to marijuana, to alcohol; from heroin to crack to molly; all have been deliberately imposed on Black America by our Enemy for a specific purpose. Our recreational drugs are his psychochemical technologies of control that have been weaponized against the Black Man, Black Manhood and Black Masculinity.

Chapter Sixteen

Cannabis and the Ancient Cult Of the White Feminine

She, the genus *Cannabis*, has been seen and felt as a being or a deity in multiple cultures. I say *she* because both historically and right now in Western culture, that is the gender that so many of us experience when we engage with cannabis.

> Kathleen Harrison (2017), "Who Is She? The Personification of Cannabis in Cultural and Individual Experience." In: ***Cannabis and Spirituality: An Explorer's Guide to an Ancient Plant Spirit Ally***, Stephen Gray (ed.) Park Street Press, Rochester

In 2008, an international research team analyzed a cache of cannabis discovered at a remote gravesite in northwest China. The well-preserved flower tops had been buried alongside a light-haired, blue-eyed Caucasian man, most likely a shaman of the Gushi culture, about twenty-seven centuries ago. Biochemical analysis demonstrated that the herb contained tetrahydrocannabinol (THC), the main psychoactive ingredient of marijuana. "To our knowledge, these investigations provide the oldest documentation of cannabis as a pharmacologically active agent," concluded Dr. Ethan Russo, lead author of the scientific study.

> Martin A. Lee (2012), ***Smoke Signals: A Social History of Marijuana-Medical, Recreational and Scientific***. Scribner, New York

I.   *The Herbal Divine Feminine*

According to many of her devotees ancient and modern the cannabis plant is not just a herb but is also the embodiment of a deity, specifically of *the* female deity. The Divine Feminine not only incarnates in this ancient botanical medicine but, we are assured, cannabis is the *antidote* to the rule of man (male), "Mother Goddess's way to help overthrow patriarchy." As marijuana enthusiast and author Chris Bennet notes,

> From the collected evidence it is clear that cannabis has been associated with worship of the Goddess since antiquity. Now, as we stand on the verge of a new millennia, in what seem to be the death throes of the patriarchy, it is as if the Goddess is once again reaching out her hand and offering her sacred Tree of Life to us in our time of collective need.[959]

Ethan Indigo Smith laid it out in more detail in his "Waking Times" article, "Cannabis Represents the Divine Feminine in the Patriarchal Oligarchy" (2015):

> Marijuana is the embodiment of the Divine Feminine...The feminine influence on our cultures, and correspondingly, the manifestation of feminine nature of our collective consciousness, has diminished throughout an era of increasingly patriotic global elitism. As our reverence for the nature of 'the feminine' and natural has diminished, so too has the influence of women and 'feminine' values (such as nurturing and sustainability) on the priorities of our cultures. Around the world, entire civilizations have lost their energetic balance, becoming overtly 'masculine', and the symptoms of this energetic imbalance are have manifested in the foundations of our societies.

> Without the natural feminine balance, our most influential institutions are competitive and not co-operative, controlling not empowering, scientific not spiritual. Our society has been built only on the 'masculine' principles of consumption, militarism, collectivism and the irrational belief in perpetual growth on a finite planet...

---

[959] Chris Bennet, "Marijuana and the Goddess," **Cannabis Culture** (Online) September, 1 ,1998.

It's time we reconnect to the Divine Feminine and embrace the innately supportive relationship we have with our Earth Mother and her perfect creations. To do that, we must be free to (re)discover the nature of our nature itself, without prohibition or limitation. So beneficial, so nurturing of our needs, and so healthful for humans and birds alike, marijuana *is* a gift from nature ~ the Divine Feminine embodied in our gardens.[960]

II.   *Not Originally "African"*

Cannabis has been growing under the hot sun of Mother Africa for many centuries, but it is not native to Africa. It was brought to the continent via trade (ancient Egypt) and migration (eastern and southern Africa).[961]

As far as can be ascertained, cannabis has been growing in southern Africa for the past four or five centuries. While it was originally an imported plant, most likely carried southward by early migrants, it has long since become naturalized, and grows with much vigor in the warmer regions.[962]

When the natives first began using cannabis as a drug is not known. The plant is not indigenous to Africa. The only way the African natives could have learned about it would have been through their contact with outsiders, and the most likely point of contact was the Arabs. The earliest evidence for cannabis in Africa outside of Egypt comes from fourteenth-century Ethiopia, where two ceramic smoking-pipe bowls containing traces of cannabis were recently discovered during an archaeological excavation. From Ethiopia, cannabis seeds were

---

[960] Ethan Indigo Smith, "Cannabis Represents the Divine Feminine in the Patriarchal Oligarchy, " ***Waking Times*** (Online), May 25, 2015.
[961] On Cannabis in Africa see further: Chris Bennett, ***Cannabis and the Soma Solution*** (Walterville, OR: TrineDay LLC, 2010), "*Shemshemet*: A Ladder to the Heavens – Egypt," 225-250; John Edwards Phillips, "African Smoking and Pipes," ***The Journal of African History*** 24 (1983): 303-319; Brian M. du Toit, "Man and Cannabis in Africa: A Study of Diffusion," ***African Economic History*** 1 (1976): 17-35; N.J. van der Merwe, "Cannabis Smoking in 13-14th Century Ethiopia," in ***Cannabis and Culture***, ed. V. Rubin (The Hague: Mouton, 1975) 77-80; Theodore James, "Dagga: A Review of Fact and Fancy." ***S.A. Medical Journal*** May 16, 1970.
[962] Brian M. du Toit, "Dagga: The History and Ethnographic Setting of *Cannabis sativa* in Southern Africa," in ***Cannabis and Culture***, ed. V. Rubin (The Hague: Mouton, 1975) 81-116.

carried to the south by Bantu-speaking natives who originally lived in North Africa, and from them the use of cannabis as an intoxicant spread to other native Africans such as the Bushmen and the Hottentots.[963]

Pollen samples indicate the presence of cannabis in sub-Saharan Africa for at least two millennia. Introduced by overland traders from the Arab Middle East and later by Portuguese seamen traveling from India, the herb quickly spread throughout the continent.[964]

Cannabis entered Eastern Africa via Egypt and Ethiopia, most likely carried by Arab merchants...Its diffusion throughout the African continent included the central role played by Zanzibar and Arab settlements on the east African coast; indeed, for most of its African history cannabis was closely associated with migrant Muslim populations. From there, it gradually spread to Bantu speakers in the interior, and was in use in the Zambezi River valley by the time the Portuguese arrived in 1531. It likely spread to the west by Swahili-speaking traders. Known as dagga, psychoactive cannabis has been consumed in southern Africa for at least five centuries.[965]

Evidence of cannabis pollen has reportedly been found at Egyptian sites from the Predynastic/Early Dynastic period (ca. 3000 BCE) and the medicinal use of the herb is documented in Egyptian medical texts dating to 1700 BCE. Nevertheless, the ancient cannabis *cult* was apparently an Indo-European cult.[966]

---

[963] L. Ernest Abel, "The African Dagga Cultures," in idem, *Marijuana: The First Twelve Thousand Years* (New York: Springer Science & Business Media, 1980) 136-147.
[964] Martin A. Lee, *Smoke Signals: A Social History of Marijuana-Medical, Recreational and Scientific* (New York: Scribner, 2012) 14.
[965] Barney Warf, "High Points: An Historical Geography of Cannabis," *Geographical Review* 104 (2014): 414-438.
[966] Burned cannabis seeds were found in kurgan mounds of Pazryk tribes in Siberia dating back 3000 BCE and tombs of Caucasoid nobles buried in Xinjiang and Siberia dated 2500 BCE included large quantities of mummified cannabis.

III.   *The European Cult*

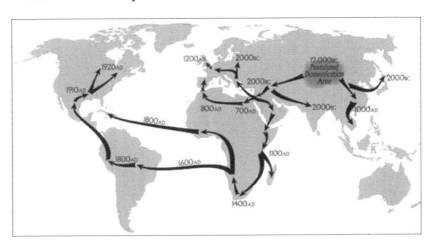

Proposed historical diffusion of Cannabis Sativa

While it grows in almost any environment, the cannabis plant is native to the cold steppes of Central Asia, the presumed ancestral homeland being the Kush in the Himalayan foothills. It is among the Proto-Indo-Europeans where we currently find the oldest documented use of cannabis for ritual purposes,[967] and Europe reportedly has the earliest archaeological evidence of the psychoactive use of cannabis *ca.*3500 BCE.[968]

---

[967] Chris Bennet, **Cannabis and the Soma Solution** (Walterville, OR: TrineDay LLC, 2010) 48: "The ancestors of the Indo-Europeans, are known as the Proto-Indo-Europeans and were located in the Eastern Ukraine and Southern Russia, and, in relation, it is important to note that it is there we can find the oldest evidence of the use of cannabis for ritual purpose."

[968] Bennet, **Cannabis and the Soma Solution**, 48, 52: "Europe has the oldest archaeological evidence of the use of cannabis for psychoactive purposes"; "Archaeological evidence from 3,500 BC gives clear proof that European man was using cannabis as an incense and inebriant very early on."

Detail from a felt rug found in a cave in the Altai Mountains, southern Siberia *ca.* 5th-3rd century BCE. From a Pazyrk tomb of the Scythian Iron Age. The Pazyrks appear to be closely related to the Scythians. This rug depicts on its frame a likely Pazrk/Scythian horseman approaching their Great Goddess Tabiti. In the cave also was found a fur bag containing cannabis seeds.

Cannabis use was widespread among Aryan nomadic herds of the Central Asian steppes. The Scythians, a Caucasian nomadic warrior group from the Russian steppes who ruled Eurasia for 1000 years, is credited with spreading the cannabis cult throughout the ancient world.[969] It was a death cult with rituals involving cannabis and opium.[970] The ancient Indo-European cannabis cult was also a Goddess cult.

---

[969] Bennet, ***Cannabis and the Soma Solution***, 58, 152: "cannabis is thought to have been spread around much of the ancient world by the later descendants of the Sredeni Stog, the Scythians, whose mobility was due to their early use of the horse," "The Nomadic Scythians travelled extensively, bringing their cultural influence and their holy plant cannabis everywhere they went"; Warf, "High Points," 421: "The primary vehicle for its early diffusion seems to have been the Scythians..."

[970] Karen Graham, "Ancient Scythians spread use of cannabis in death rituals," ***Digital Journal*** May 25, 2015; Andrew Curry, "Gold Artifacts Tell Tale of Drug-Fueled Rituals and 'Bastard Wars',"

With the strong elements of Goddess worship in the Scythian culture, it is not surprising to find a matriarchal hierarchy as well, and we know from surviving artefacts that Scythian women took powerful leadership roles in the tribe. As well, 'Both men and women probably smoked [hemp], since we found two sets of apparatus for smoking with the burial of a man and a woman'.[971]

The Scythian goddess was Tabiti. "The Nomadic Scythians travelled extensively, bringing their cultural influence and their holy plant cannabis everywhere they went."[972] "It is generally accepted that it was the horseback-riding Scythians who spread the combination of cannabis and goddess worship throughout much of the ancient world," reports Bennet.[973] Tabiti's Germanic cognate is the goddess Freya whose spirit was said to be incarnated within the

The Goddess Freya

cannabis plant. According to ethnobotanist Christian Ratsch "in ancient Germanic culture cannabis was used in honor of the Goddess Freya as both a ritual inebriant and an aphrodisiac and...the harvesting of the plant was connected with an erotic festival...*It was believed Freya lived as a fertile force in the plant's feminine flowers and by ingesting them one became influenced by this divine force.*"[974] By ingesting the female cannabis plant one is ingesting the feminine force. This is important.

National Geographic May 22, 2015; Lambros Comitas, "The Social Nexus of *Ganja* in Jamaica," in *Cannabis and Culture*, ed. V. Rubin (The Hague: Mouton, 1975) 119-132; Bennet, *Cannabis and the Soma Solution*, 125-153 "The Scythian 'Haoma-Gathers."

[971] Bennet, *Cannabis and the Soma Solution*, 148.

[972] Bennet, *Cannabis and the Soma Solution*, 152.

[973] Chris Bennet, "Marijuana and the Goddess," *Cannabis Culture* (Online) September, 1 ,1998.

[974] Bennet, *Cannabis and the Soma Solution*, 60. Lee, *Smoke Signals*, 21: "It was customary to honor Freya, the German fertility goddess, with hemp as a pagan sacrament."

The ancient Chinese agreed. The earliest reference to the medical use of cannabis is possibly ca. 2800 BCE in the Chinese medical compendium the *Pen Ts'ao* of the legendary Chinese emperor Shin Knung, called the "Father of Chinese Medicine."[975] Cannabis preparations were used as an anesthetic. In Chinese cosmology the universe and everything in it is composed of two principles: the masculine *Yang* (strong, active, positive) and the feminine *Yin* (weak, passive, negative). A healthy human body has a balance of these two principles

Portrait of the Red Emperor
Shen Nung
(2838 - 2698 B.C.)

which is appropriate to that body. The Chinese knew that there was a male cannabis plant (*ma*) which contained Yang, the masculine principle, and a female cannabis plant (*chu-ma*) that contained Yin, the feminine principle. The female plant *Chu-ma* was used to add Yin to an imbalanced body. In other words: the world's earliest documented user of medicinal cannabis knew that the psychoactive cannabis (*chu-ma*) specifically increases the Yin or *female energy* in the body of he or she who partakes of *her*.[976]

Those who honor cannabis today as the embodiment of the Divine Feminine or female energy invest hope in *her* to overthrow or upset the patriarchal order of male rule. The Indo-European Goddess who was incarnated within the plant was associated with the moon-sickle with which she castrated the male God. The moon-sickle or *scythe* was named after the Scythians who used the long-handled tool with its curved blade in the harvesting of cannabis.[977] In the hands of Scythian Goddess however this scythe was a weapon that castrated the

---

[975] While the *Pen Ts'ao* was attributed to the time of the Shen-Nung, the oldest copy of the text dates to about 100 AD.
[976] See Bennet, **Cannabis and the Soma Solution**, 158-159.
[977] Bennet, **Cannabis and the Soma Solution**, 137.

God. Barbara Walker claims in her ***The Woman's Book of Myths and Secrets***

> This image of the cannibal mother was typical everywhere of the Goddess as Time, who consumes what she brings forth; or as Earth, who does the same. When Rhea was given a consort in Hellenic myth, he was called Kronus or Chronos, "Father Time," who devoured his own children, in imitation of Rhea's earlier activity. He also castrated and killed his own father, the Heaven-god Uranus; and he in turn was threatened by his own son, Zeus. These myths reflect the primitive succession of sacred kings castrated and killed by their supplanters. It was originally Rhea Kronia, Mother Time, who wielded the castrating moon-sickle or scythe, a Scythian weapon, the instrument with which the Heavenly Father was "reaped." Rhea herself was the Grim Reaper.[978]

The Goddess behind the plant castrates the God. As we will show, this "divine feminine" is still castrating God, the Black God. Her moon-sickle is the cannabis plant itself; not the natural herb but the weaponized drug. The marijuana of today castrates the Black male twice: the White Goddess's moon-sickle castrates him at his testicles and at his brain.

---

[978] Barbara G. Walker, ***The Woman's Encyclopedia of Myths and Secrets*** (New York: Harper & Row, San Francisco, 1983) 855-56 s.v. Rhea.

Chapter Seventeen

Militarized Marijuana
How "Loud" Was First Created

Well before the hippies ever took marijuana as the official drug of peace and love, the U.S. Army took it as the official drug of crippling one's enemies...[979]

nearly every drug that appeared on the black market during the sixties — marijuana, cocaine, heroin, PCP, amyl mitrate, mushrooms, DMT, barbiturate, laughing gas, speed and many others — had previously been scrutinized, tested and in some case refined by CIA and army scientists... (emphasis added).[980]

I.   *The Beginning of The Pot Plot*

It is not a coincidence that Lee and Shlain above list marijuana first among the drugs that were processed through CIA labs before they appeared on the streets. Indeed, in their search for a behavior modification agent the Office of Strategic Services (OSS) and the Federal Bureau of Narcotics (FBN) very early tested cannabis and then they *produced a new, more potent form* of cannabis unknown anywhere in the world to be used as a covert chemical agent.

On December 5, 1938 twenty-three scientists and government officials gathered at a Marihuana Conference held in Room 3003 of the United States Bureau of Internal Revenue Building in Washington, D.C. The conference was presided over by Harry J. Anslinger, Commissioner of the newly-formed Federal Bureau of Narcotics (FBN), and H.J. Wollner, a Consulting Chemist from the Treasury Department. The purpose of the conference was a planning meeting to implement the prohibitive Marihuana Tax Act of 1937. There was also an information session to learn about the cannabis plant. One of the scientists who presented at the conference was Dr. Walter Siegfried Loewe, a pharmacologist from Cornell University

---

[979] Robert Brockway, "The U.S. Army's Weed Weapon: A Paranoid But True Conspiracy," ***Cracked.com*** June 3, 2010.
[980] Lee and Shlain, ***Acids Dreams***, xxiv-xxv.

Medical College. Loewe had been testing cannabis on monkeys. During his talk Loewe highlighted the fact that the active principles of cannabis were still chemically unknown.[981]

To hunt down cannabis's active principles Wollner and Loewe recruited the generation's leading organic chemist in the United States: Roger Adams.[982] Adams served thirty years as head of the Department of Chemistry at the University of Illinois, Urbana- Champagne (1926-1954). During World War I

Roger Adams,
Grandfather of
Militarized Marijuana

Adams got an assignment at the National Defense Research Council (NDRC) and served as a Major in the Chemical Warfare Services in Washington, D.C. where he developed gases for use on the battlefield. When World War II began, Adams returned to the NDRC's Division B to develop bombs, fuels, tactical gases, and chemical weapons. Adams took charge of the wartime U.S. chemistry programs. After being recruited by Wollner and Loewe, "In 1939 this problem of marijuana became the central focus of Adam's research."[983] The three collaborated to isolate THC

($\triangle$9-Tetrahydrocannabinol), the active principle of cannabis. From 1940 through 1949, Adams and his associates carried out over 27 studies on cannabis.[984] They inferred the structures of

---

[981] Marihuana Conference, December 5, 1938 <http://www.druglibrary.org/schaffer/hemp/taxact/1938_mhc.htm>

[982] D. Stanley Tarbell and Ann Tracey Tarbell, *Roger Adams: 1889-1971. A Biographical Memoir* (Washington D.C.: National Academy of Sciences, 1982) 3.

[983] Ronald E. Doel, "Roger Adams: Linking University Science with Policy on the World Stage," in *No Boundaries: University of Illinois Vignettes*, ed. Lillian Hoddeson (Urbana-Champagne: University of Illinois, 2004) 124-144 (129).

[984] See e.g. Roger Adams, Madison Hunt and J.H. Clark, "Structure of Cannabinol, a Product Isolated form the Marihuana Extract of Minnesota Wild Hemp. I," *Journal of the American Chemical Society* 62 (1940): 196-200; Roger Adams, D.C. Pease, J.H. Clark and B.R. Baker, "Structure of Cannabinol. I. Preparation of an Isomer, 3-Hydroxy-1-*n*-amyl-6,6,9-trimethyl-6-dibenzopyran," *Journal of*

the American Chemical Society 62 (1940): 2197-2200; Roger Adams, C.K. Cain and B.R. Baker, "Structure of Cannabinol. II. Synthesis of Two New Isomers, 3-Hydroxy-4-*n*-amyl-and 3-Hydroxy-2-*n*-amyl 6,6,9--trimethyl-6-dibenzopyran," *Journal of the American Chemical Society* 62 (1940): 2201-2204; Roger Adams, B.R. Baker, and R.B. Wearn, "Structure of Cannabinol. III. Synthesis of Cannabinol, 1-Hydroxy-3-*n*-amyl-6,6,9-trimethyl-6-dibenzopyran," *Journal of the American Chemical Society* 62 (1940): 2204-; Roger Adams, D.C. Pease, C.K. Cain, and J.H. Clark, "Structure of Cannabidiol. VI. Isomerization of Cannabidiol to Tetrahydrocannabinol, Physiologically Active Product. Conversion of Cannabidiol to Cannabinol," *Journal of the American Chemical Society* 62 (1940): 2402-2405; Roger Adams and B.R. Baker, "Structure of Cannabinol. VII: A Method of Synthesis of a Tetrahydrocannabinol which Possesses Marihuana Activity," *Journal of the American Chemical Society* 62 (1940): 2405-; Roger Adams, "Marihuana," *Science* 92 (1940): 115-119; Roger Adams, "Tetrahydrocannabinol Homologs with Marihuana Activity. IX," *Journal of the American Chemical Society* 63 (1941): 1971-1973; Roger Adams, C.M. Smith and S. Loewe, "Tetrahydrocannabinol Homologs and Analogs with Marihuana Activity. X," *Journal of the American Chemical Society* 63 (1941): 1973-1977; Roger Adams, C.K. Cain and S. Loewe, "Tetrahydrocannabinol Analogs with Marihuana Activity. XI," *Journal of the American Chemical Society* 63 (1941): 1977-1978; Roger Adams, C.K. Cain, W.D. McPhee and R.B. Wearn, "Structure of Cannabidiol. XII. Isomerization to Tetrahydrocannabinols," *Journal of the American Chemical Society* 63 (1941): 2209-2213; Roger Adams, S. Loewe, C.M. Smith and W.D. McPhee, "Tetrahydrocannabinol Homologs and Analogs with Marihuana Activity. XIII," *Journal of the American Chemical Society* 64 (1942): 694-697; H.J. Wollner, John R. Matchett, Joseph Levine and S. Loewe, "Isolation of a Physiologically Active Tetrahydrocannabinol from Cannabis Sativa Resin," *Journal of the American Chemical Society* 64 (1942): 26-29; Roger Adams, "Marihuana: Harvey Lecture, February 19, 1942," *Bulletin of the New York Academy of Medicine* 18 (1942): 705-730; S. Loewe, "Studies on the Pharmacology and Acute Toxicity of Compounds with Marihuana Activity," *The Journal of Pharmacology and Experimental Therapeutics* 88 (1946): 154-161; Edwin G. Williams et al., "Studies on Marihuana and Pyrahexyl Compound," *Public Health Reports (1896-1970)* 61 (1946): 1059-1083; Roger Adams, Morton Harfenist and S. Loewe, "New Analogs of Tetrahydrocannabinol. XIX," *Journal of the American Chemical Society* 71 (1949): 1624-1628; S. Loewe, "The Active Principles of Cannabis and the Pharmacology of the Cannabiiols," originally published in German, "Cannabiswirkstoffe

THC, cannabidiol (CBD) and cannabinol (CBN) and basically got them right, except for the final placement of one double linkage.

In 1942 during the second World War General George Veazey Strong, chief of Military Intelligence Service (MIS), which was the intelligence branch of the National Defense Research Council (Strong was one of eight managing members of the NDRC), established a committee of prestigious American scientists to undertake a top-secret research program. The program was to investigate the viability of efficiently using drugs during the interrogation of German U-boat POW's in order to extract information about German submarine movement. The NDRC, through its Division 19 (a highly secret unit of the NDRS that devised covert weapons and sabotage devices), worked closely in this endeavor with the Office of Strategic Services (OSS), the precursor of the CIA. Division 19 was run by Dr. H. Marshall Chadwell, former deputy manager of the New York office of the Atomic Energy Commission and then CIA deputy director of the Office of Scientific Intelligence. The OSS was run by William "Wild Bull" Donovan. The committee of scientists that was established included, among others: Dr. John Whitehorn of Johns Hopkins University; Winfred Overholser Sr., superintendent of St. Elizabeth's Hospital in Washington D.C.; Harry J. Anslinger, head of the Federal Bureau of Narcotics; Roger Adams, National Defense Research Council; Watson W. Eldridge, also of St. Elizabeth's Hospital; Lawrence Kubie, a prominent psychiatrist and psychoanalyst with the New York Neurological Institute at Columbia University; and Edward Stricker of the University of Pennsylvania, among others.[985]

"Wild Bull" Donovan ordered Stanley Lovell, OSS Director of Research and Development, to find a "potion" to be used on high-value POWs, enemy agents, and traitorous Americans. Lovell was the OSS's real life "Inspector Gadget."

From a cramped basement room in the headquarters building, Lovell headed the Office of Scientific Research and

---

und Pharmacologie der Cannabinole," **Arch Exper Path u Phurmakol** 211 (1950): 175-193. Translation by Dr. Carl C. Pfeiffer, New Jersey Bureau of Research in Neurology and Psychiatry, Princeton, New Jersey.
[985] Albarelli Jr., **A Terrible Mistake,**214-215.

Development, with free rein to develop any spy gadget he could dream up. For that mission, Lovell had a mind even more creative than Donovan's. Thousands of pistols with silencers, lightweight submachine guns, miniature cameras, agent radios, exotic knives, and special explosives were manufactured and shipped out to operatives. Invisible ink was developed to write secret messages on paper or even an agent's shirt. Explosives shaped like lumps of coal (nicknamed "Black Joe") and pocket-sized incendiaries with time-delayed fuses to start fires were sent to Europe. Bombs fashioned with explosive powder made to look like flour (called "Aunt Jemima"), which could be kneaded and backed into bread, were produced and sent to Asia...Some of his gadgets were comical. Lovell had gland experts produce female sex hormones an agent could inject into vegetables Hitler ate to make the hair from his mustache fall out and his voice turn soprano...But Lovell had other gadgets that were deadly serious, such as tasteless poisons that could be slipped into food and drink.[986]

Lovell conducted secret research on chemical and biological agents, which was the charge of the committee established by the NDRC. The committee surveyed and rejected numerous drugs, including alcohol, barbiturates, caffeine, peyote and scopolamine.[987] Ultimately "the drug that showed promise when injected into food or cigarettes was tetrahydrocannabinol acetate, an extract of Indian hemp,"[988] i.e. a cannabis preparation. A de-classified O.S.S. document dated 2 June 1945 entitled "Report on T.D." reveals:

Exhaustive review of all relevant pharmacological literature narrowed the field to a half-dozen drugs. Preliminary experiments found attention on some variety of *cannabis as the drug of choice*. Three varieties of cannabis were studied: Cannabinol from Indian Charis, tetrahydrocannabinol acetate derived from the above, and synthetic cannabinol. Of these, the acetate derivative was found to be preferable. Various routes of administration were explored; oral administration, burning in smokeless charcoal, spraying, and inhalation in cigarettes. Of these, inhalation in cigarettes is the only route which can be recommended at the present time. Standard

986 Douglas Waller, *Wild Bill Donovan. The Spymaster Who Created the OSS and Modern American Espionage* (New York: Free Press, 2011) 101-102,
987 Lee and Shlain, *Acids Dreams*, 4.
988 Waller, *Wild Bill Donovan*, 103.

cigarettes (see attached package) may be loaded with .02 grams of Loewe's acetate. The drug is introduced into the cigarette with a 1/4cc tuberculin syringe and a specially prepared #22, 1/12" hypodermic needle. The level of the latter's point is sanded away to form a blunt, rounded tip which slides easily through the center of the tobacco. Effort is made to achieve an even distribution of the drug through all but ½" at each extremily (sic). The acetate is injected at maximum viscosity compatibel (sic) with delivery from the needle. A dilution with more than 1% with 95% alcohol is required to achieve this viscosity. Cigarettes prepared as above outlined are perfectly normal in appearance and in taste...The drug may be administered, via cigarettes, without the subject's knowledge.

Note here that the chief method of delivering this weaponized THC is through a "proto-Blunt," if you will. That is to say, mixing the THC analogue with tobacco in a cigarette. This "proto-Blunt" used by the government to deliver its weaponized weed will take on greater significance when we discuss the Weaponization of Hip Hop later.

Division 19 chief Chadwell instructed Lovell to work closely with Roger Adams in pursuit of this cannabis "potion" desired by the NDRC. Alberelli Jr reports:

According to Narcotics Bureau files, in 1941, Adams and Dr. Walter Siegfried Loewe of the University of Utah produced "by chemical modification, two highly active tetrahydrocannabinols," as well as "a synthesized tetrahydrocannabinol."...[S]cientists at Camp Detrick and Edgewood Arsenal had begun spending the $1.5 million allocated for extensive classified research with Dr. Loewe's THC, or synthetic marihuana. The central purpose of the research, according to army records, was to explore the potential of marihuana to create "hypnotic like states," among other things...After weeks of trial and error, it was the Adams-Loewe synthetic compound derived from marihuana that the OSS decided was its most promising drug." [989]

This collaboration between Roger Adams and Siegfried Loewe - one gentile and one German Jew[990] - is a template

---

[989] Albarelli Jr., *A Terrible Mistake*,214-215, 216.
[990] Walter Siegfried Loewe was a Jew born in Fuerth, Bauern, Germany. See Noah J. Efron, *Judaism and Science: A Historical Introduction* (Westport, Connecticut: Greenwood Press, 2007) 162;

characterizing the history of The Pot Plot. Lee and Shlain go on to report:

> OSS scientists created a highly potent extract of cannabis, and through a process known as esterification a clear and viscous liquid was obtained. The final product had no color, odor, or taste. It would be nearly impossible to detect when administered surreptitiously, which is exactly what the spies intended to do. "There is no reason to believe that any other nation or group is familiar with the preparation of this particular drug," stated a once classified OSS document.[991]

Various ways of administering this cannabis potion were tried on witting and unwitting subjects.

> Further experiments with the marijuana extract concerned the feasibility of administering it to an unknown subject not only in ordinary cigarettes but also in candy, in a vapor composed of carbon dioxide gas and, apparently, in specially impregnated facial tissues to be thrust upon unsuspecting enemy agents.[992]

The committee chose the sadomasochist Lt. Col. George White of the OSS as the man to test the "potion" on unsuspecting hoods, spies, and assassins.

> In August 1943 a quantity of the extract was carried by Colonel White on a train from Washington, where it had been produced under elaborate secrecy, to New York City, and guarded during the journey by a contingent of armed counterintelligence officers. [993]

> In a quest for truth serums, White and other OSS agents slipped concentrated tetrahydrocannabinol acetate (THCA) into the food and cigarettes of suspected communists, conscientious objectors, and mobsters in the 1940s.[994]

Jews and Sciences in German Contexts, ed. Ulrich Charpa and Ute Deichmann (Tübingen: Mohr Siebeck, 2007) 285.
[991] Lee and Shlain, *Acids Dreams*, 4.
[992] John M. Crewdson, "Files Show Tests For Truth Drug Began in O.S.S.," *The New York Times* September 5, 1977.
[993] John M. Crewdson, "Files Show Tests For Truth Drug Began in O.S.S.," *The New York Times* September 5, 1977.
[994] Troy Hooper, "Operation Midnight Climax: How the CIA Dosed S.F. Citizens with LSD," *SFWeekly* March 14, 2012.

Colonel George H. White

Visualize this Top Secret weed being transported under armed guard to D.C. to be used as a chemical weapon clandestinely slipped into the cigarettes and the *food* of unsuspecting citizens, particularly "undesirables." While ultimately this cannabis potion failed as a "truth serum," other assets as potential chemical weapon were discovered.

> Moderate amounts produce elation, loquacity, euphoria, and *irresponsible behaviour*(sic). Large amounts produce stupor and lethargy...Tetrahydrocannabinol acetate is not a perfect "truth drug" in the sense that it's administeation(sic) is followed immediately and automatically by the revelation of all the secrets which the subject wishes to keep to himself...However, the drug does produce a psychological state of relaxation, talkativeness and *irresponsibility* which might be extremely useful to a skilled interrogator (emphasis added – WM).[995]

> It accentuates the senses and makes manifest any strong characteristics of the individual. Sexual inhibitions are lowered, and the sense of humor is accentuated to the point where any

---

[995] "Report on T.S." 2 June 1945. De-classified O.S.S. document.

statement or situation can become extremely funny to the subject...[996]

Weaponized Weed is a reality.

In 1939 Mayor Fiorello LaGuardia of New York appointed a committee to study mental and physical effects of marijuana and the social consequences of its use, noting in the 1944 report that "The majority of marihuana smokers (in New York) are Negroes and Latin-Americans."[997] During this study a population of 77 prisoners (35 White, 26 Black, 11 Puerto Rican, 65 males and 7 females) from Riker's Island, Hart Island, and the House of Detention for Women were exposed to both a concentrate of natural THC supplied by Dr. H.J. Wollner of the Treasury Department who co-chaired the 1938 Marihuana Conference with Harry Anslinger, as well as some of Roger Adams' synthetic THC analogues. The different effects on the test subjects were noted. Siegfried Loewe reported the findings in the Pharmacology section of the LaGuardia Report. A few years later (1946) Adams' synthetic, militarized weed would be tested on an exclusively White male population (with one Puerto Rican) at Harris Isbell's Lexington ARC, and noted that

comprehension and analytical thinking were made more difficult and an adverse effect was noted in accuracy on those tests which require concentration and manual dexterity. Personality changes in the direction of lessened inhibitions were also observed. Individuals became more spontaneous and more responsive to external stimuli under the influence of pyrahexyl compound...In conclusion, it appears that the changes produced by these drugs are related to lessening of inhibition and removal of restraint."[998]

---

[996] OSS Memorandum for the File, Subject: Truth Drug (T.D.), April 5, 1946.
[997] Mayor's Committee on Marihuana, by the New York Academy of Medicine, "The LaGuardia Committee Report New York, USA: The Marihuana Problem in the City of New York," City of New York, 1944.
[998] Edwin G. Williams et al., "Studies on Marihuana and Pyrahexyl Compound," *Public Health Reports (1896-1970)* 61 (1946): 1059-1083.

II.   The Military Origins of "Super" Pot

In 1949 Roger Adams synthesized a "super pot," called DMHP (Dimethylheptylpyran), also referred to as "Adams' 9-carbon compound," a synthetic analogue similar in structure to THC, differing from the latter only by the arrangement of a couple of electrons. DMHP produces similar activity to THC, such as <u>sedative</u> effects, but it is considerably more potent – about 60 times the biological activity of natural THC.

Adams' **9-carbon** compound

This "super pot" caught the interest of the chemical warfare scientists at Edgewood Arsenal, who concluded that "The combination of strong incapacitating effects and a favorable safety margin" made DMHP and its derivatives "promising non-lethal incapacitating agents." From 1955 to 1959 Edgewood's U.S. Army Chemical Center contracted Dr. Edward Domino and other scientists from the University of Michigan to conduct animal studies with Adams' DMHP and other synthetic cannabis compounds, which the Army labeled EA 1476.[999] One of the main discoveries of the super pot is that

---

[999] Edward F. Domino, "Why I Came...and Why Did I Stay?" in *Sixty -One Years of University of Michigan Pharmacology*, ed. Edward F. Domino (Ann Arnor, Michigan: NPP Books, 2004) 165-170; Edward F. Domino, Interviewed by Christian j. Gillin, San Juan, Puerto Rico, December 11, 1985; Edward F. Domino, Philip Rennick and Joseph H. Pearl, "Dose-effect relations of marijuana smoking on various physiological parameters in experienced male users Observations on limits of self-titration of intake," *Clinical*

it causes docility and passivity in the face of assault or injury: "you can step on their (dogs) feet without any response." Once the effects kicked in, "we were unable to arouse the animals from their depressed state by any form of painful stimuli."[1000] That's the "Negro" on that "Loud." From 1957 to 1960 the CIA tested this "super pot" on 142 prisoners at Michigan's Iona State Hospital.[1001]

Pharmacology and Therapeutics 15 (1973): 514-520; Harold F. Hardman, Edward F. Domino and Maurice H. Seevers, "General Pharmacological Actions of Some Synthetic Tetrahydrocannabinol Derivatives," *Pharmacological Review* 23 (1971): 295-315; Edward F. Domino, "Neuropsychpharmacologic Studies of Marijuana: some Synthetic and Natural THC Derivatives in Animals and Man," *Annals of the New York Academy of Sciences* 191 (December 1971): 166-191; Edward F. Domino et al., "Effects of Marihuana Smoking on Sensory Thresholds in Man," in *Psychotomimetic Drugs. Proceedings of a Workshop Organized by the Pharmacology Section, Psychopharmacology Research Branch, National Institute of Mental Health Held at the University of California, Irvine, on January 25-29, 1969*, ed. Daniel H. Efron (New York: Raven Press, 1970) 299-321., 325-343; Ernst A. Rodin and Edward F. Domino, "The Marihuana-Induced 'Social High'," *JAMA* 213 (1970): 1300-1302;; Harold F. Hardman and Maurice H. Seevers, "A Pharmacological Comparison of EA 1476 (Tetrahydrocannabinol) Isomers," Progress Report December 1, 1956.
[1000] Harold F. Hardman and Maurice H. Seevers, *THE CHEMISTRY AND PHARMACOLOGY OF CERTAIN COMPOUNDS AFFECTING THE CENTRAL NERVOUS SYSTEM OF ANIMALS AND MAN. A PHARMACOLOGICAL COMPARISON OF EA 1476 (TETRAHYDROCANNABINOL) ISOMERS. PROGRESS REPORT* December 1, 1956. P. 5; Edward F. Domino, "Neuropsychpharmacologic Studies of Marijuana: some Synthetic and Natural THC Derivatives in Animals and Man," *Annals of the New York Academy of Sciences* 191 (December 1971): 166-191 (167, 173)
[1001] Nicholas M. Horrock and Joseph B. Treaster, "Records Show C.I.A. Tested LSD on Sex Psychopaths," *The New York Times* August 5, 1977.

III.   The Army's Conquer-By-Cannabis Plan

During the 1960s, the U.S. Army tested a potent form of synthetic marijuana on soldiers to develop a secret weapon. Martin A. Lee. 2008

We weren't looking for medical benefits (of cannabis). We were trying to subdue people. Lt. Col. James Ketchum, U.S. Army Chemical Corps, Edgewood, Arsenal.

The cannabis compounds that Domino and colleagues at the University of Michigan were testing showed promise but were not ideal chemical warfare agents. They were "crude" preparations that contained chemical baggage (cannabis components other than THC) and they thus weighed too much. The Army scientists

were intrigued by the possibility of amplifying the active ingredient of marijuana, tweaking the mother molecule, as it were, to enhance its psychogenic effects. So the Chemical Corps set its sights on developing a synthetic variant of THC that could clobber people without killing them.[1002]

Col. James Ketchum, chief of the Army's "Conquer-By-Cannabis Plan"

This was the Army's "Conquer-by-Cannabis Plan" and Col. James Ketchum, who led the classified research program at Edgewood Arsenal starting in 1961,[1003] was "the man who tried to harness THC as a weapon of war," as Martin Lee described him.[1004] Ketchum declared: "We weren't looking for medical benefits (of cannabis). We were trying to subdue people."[1005]

[1002] Martin A. Lee, "The Counterculture Colonel," ***Bohemian.com*** July 2, 2008.

[1003] Fred Gardner, "Army's conquer by cannabis plan," ***SFGate*** April 8, 2007.

[1004] Lee, ***Smoke Signals***, 87.

[1005] James S. Ketchum, ***Chemical Warfare: Secrets Almost Forgotten*** (Santa Rosa, California: ChemBooks, Inc., 2006) 35-36;

The ideal chemical weapon would make the "population manageable."[1006] "Ketchum was into weapons of mass elation, not weapons of mass destruction."[1007] According to Ketchum, "the goal [of nonlethal incapacitating substances] has been to weaken an enemy without the use of lethal force"; "using psychochemicals to produce temporary ineffectiveness."[1008]

> The drugs of greatest military interest are those that tend to affect predominantly "higher integrative" or "cognitive" functions, which process sensory data or conscious decision-making, including attention, orientation, perception, memory, and motivation. Working together, these capabilities regulate conceptual thinking, planning, and judgment.[1009]

As we shall demonstrate, "Loud" is their man.

Ketchum started with Adams' super potent DMHP and made it *more potent*. Actually, Edgewood Arsenal contracted this job to the Cambridge, Massachusetts firm Arthur D. Little, Inc. and their scientist Dr. Harry Pars, who frequently traveled to Edgewood to present progress reports on the synthesis of the cannabis weapon. Two critical developments in the weaponization of marijuana occurred here. First, Pars and the Edgewood scientists were able to separate the synthetic THC (DMHP), which was a mixture of isomers (=compounds with the same molecular formula but different bonding arrangement of atoms), into its eight component stereoisomers (compounds with the same formula and bonding arrangement but different spatial arrangement of atoms), and then produced the acetate esters or forms of each of the eight (The acetate ester is the neutral molecule formed by the negative ion and positive ion). This collection of acetate esters is known collectively as EA 2233,

---

Martin A. Lee, "The Counterculture Colonel," **Bohemian.com** July 2, 2008; Lee, **Smoke Signals**, 82-83.

[1006] "The Army's Conquest-by-Cannabinoid Fantasy," **O'Shaughnessy's** Winter/Spring 2008.

[1007] Martin A. Lee, "The Counterculture Colonel," **Bohemian.com** July 2, 2008.

[1008] James S. Ketchum and Harry Salem, "Incapacitating Agents," in **Medical Aspects of Chemical Warfare**, ed. Shirley P. Tuorinsky (Virginia and Washington, D.C.: Office of the Surgeon General and Walter Reed Army Medical, 2008) 411-439 (412, 413).

[1009] Ketchum and Salem, "Incapacitating Agents," 415.

and at least two of these esters were super-duper potent or "loud."[1010]

     Incapacitating an enemy population with this "loud" marijuana, EA 2233, would effectively *de-militarize that population* through its ability to take the fight out of the soldier. EA 2233 "left soldiers virtually immobilized, either lacking the motivation or simply unable to defend themselves in the event of an attack."[1011] Ketchum acknowledged that EA 2233 "might be an ideal way to produce temporary inability to fight (or do much else) without toxicological danger to life";[1012] "Essentially [the enemy] would be immobilized for any military purpose until the effects wore off."

IV.   *Making Weed The New Heroin*

     The second critical development in the weaponization of weed achieved under Ketchum was manipulating the THC molecule to make marijuana addictive, similar in ways to heroin or morphine. Alkaloids are a class of nitrogenous ("nitrogen containing"), organic compounds of plant origin that have pronounced psychological action in humans. THC is unique among psychotropic materials from plants in that it is *non-alkaloid*, i.e. it has *no nitrogen* atom. Harry Pars and the Army scientists "fixed" that problem, but not without important help.

At the outset of this project, Pars had sought the advice of Dr. Alexander Shulgin, then a brilliant young chemist employed by Dow Chemical. Shulgin was a veritable fount of information regarding how to reshape psychoactive molecules to create novel mind-altering drugs...Shulgin gave Pars the idea to tinker with nitrogen analogs of tetrahydrocannabinol (THC).[1013]

[1010] Herbert S. Aaron and C. Parker Ferguson, "Synthesis of the Eight Stereoisomers of a Tetrahydrocannabinol Congener," **The Journal of Organic Chemistry** 33 (1968): 684-689.
[1011] Bertram Joyner, "Marijuana Testing in the Military was an Attempt to Save Lives," @ https://www.marijuanapackaging.com/blog/marijuana-testing-in-the-military/.
[1012] "The Army's Conquest-by-Cannabinoid Fantasy," **O'Shaughnessy's** Winter/Spring 2008.
[1013] Martin A. Lee, "The Counterculture Colonel," **Bohemian.com** July 2, 2008.

It was Shulgin's idea to insert a nitrogen atom into THC. Shulgin said:

> it occurred to me that Mother Nature, which thoroughly loves alkaloids, kind of blew it in letting the Cannabis plant make a psychoactive compound devoid of nitrogen...What would THC look like pharmacologically if it were a phenethylamine? I said to myself, "Let's make it!" So I hied myself off to the library to begin unraveling some possible paths to the synthesis.[1014]

A young Dr. Alexander Shulgin in his lab at Dow Chemical

Shulgin looms exceptionally large in our story, in regards both to the Pot Plot as well as the Weaponization of Hip Hop. We will return to him again later. The fact that this man – Alexander Shulgin – gave the U.S. Army chemical warfare scientists the technical guidance in the production of EA 2233; that the government was *dependent on him* for this breakthrough in the weaponization of marijuana is no small matter. Shulgin gives two accounts of this indebtedness: one in the Forward to Ketchum's memoirs, *Chemical Warfare: Secrets Almost Forgotten* and one in his own book, *PiHKAL: A Chemical Love Story.*

[First] My first two interactions with the world of US Government chemical warfare were in the 1950s or maybe the 1960s when I was still a senior research chemist at the Dow Chemical Company in the San Francisco Bay Area...
    The first meeting was with two or three chemists in dark suits and ties who were introduced to me and a half dozen other research chemists as being government researchers in the area of potentially interesting synthetic organic chemicals. We were not told from which laboratory they came and the only

---

[1014] Alexander and Ann Shulgin, *PiHKAL: A Chemical Love Story*, 41-44

clues to their areas of interest were two synthetic reaction sequences which had been drawn on the conference room blackboard. The man with the chalk told us that these two pictures had been worked out successfully, and their question was: could any of us propose a last step which might link them together. The bottom compounds in the two schemes were followed by arrows which pointed to an empty area at the bottom of the blackboard. I asked them why not draw in the structure of the desired product and they said that they were not at liberty to do so.

"Oh, nonsense," I said and got up and went to the blackboard and drew the structure of the target. I drew the isomeric homologue of tetrahydrocannabinol with the terpene double bond down in the terpene 3,4-position and a 1,2-dimethylheptyl chain at the aromatic 3- position. "This is the obvious product you want," I added as I returned to my seat, "So why don't we discuss how this coupling could be achieved."

There was an unmistakable discomfort shared by the gentlemen from Washington. After a bit of discussion I volunteered the statement, "Of course, with three chiral centers, there will be eight distinct optical isomers possible, all of different pharmacology, and some may not resemble marijuana at all in action." The meeting broke up shortly thereafter. A lot of things just couldn't be talked about.[1015]

And, as a throw-away, I mentioned that if they really wanted to remedy Nature's sloppiness, they should consider synthesizing this unnameable target compound with a nitrogen atom in it, so as to emulate an alkaloid. That, I added in conclusion, might be a really super-potent phenethylamine![1016]

[Second] "I have a radio communication from RCA International for you," he said, handing it to me. I found a flashlight and read it. Some 500 words from a Dr. Frederick Pearsman at A.R.L. Company [=Harry Pars at Arthur D. Little Inc. – WM], in Cambridge, Mass. saying - nay, demanding - that I call him from Trinidad collect when I arrived (we were due there the next day). I had no sooner gotten back to sleep, than there was another knock on the door. Mr. Munoz, again. He said that he had just received another radio communication for me, this time via ITT or something, but not to bother reading it as it was, word for word, identical to the first one. "Okay, okay," I muttered, "I've got it: I'm supposed to make a call from Trinidad."

[1015] In Forward to Ketchum, *Chemical Warfare*, 1-2.
[1016] Shulgin, *PiHKAL*, 42.

Morning came, and with it came Trinidad, along with heat and humidity. I spent almost an hour in a telephone booth, talking to Fred Pearsman at A.R.L. [=Harry Pars at Arthur D. Little Inc. – WM]

Dr. Pearsman [Dr. Pars] said something like this, "We have been asked to submit a contract proposal, by a group which we can't really identify, to synthesize a nitrogen-containing phenethylamine analog of THC. You will be arriving in London at such and such a time on such and such a day (he was correct to the minute) and we want you to please send us a complete synthetic procedure at that time by airmail special delivery the very minute you arrive. It will get to us here just in time for our submission."

"But," I protested, "I'm aboard a luxury liner, and the most up-to-date reference book in its library is an 1894 edition of Roget's Thesaurus!"

"Then write it out from memory," said he, and that was that. I cannot begin to describe what forty minutes in a Trinidad telephone booth at 90% humidity and 92 degrees temperature can do to one's rational defenses.

So, for the rest of the way across the Atlantic Ocean, I reviewed, with what modest photographic recall I could muster, the appropriate texts of Beilstein and Chemical Abstracts, and put together a chemical flow- sheet and proposal for the phenethylamine analogues of THC. It was mailed from London and got to A.R.L. Company [=Arthur D. Little Inc. – WM] apparently in time for the contract proposal to be awarded to them. It must have been somewhat successful in showing CNS activity, since Dr. Pearsman [Dr. Pars] left A.R.L. [=Arthur D. Little Inc.] and became the founder of a consulting group in Boston that promoted nitrogen-containing THC analogs to industry, apparently with some success.

I got my name on a patent that was subsequently issued to the Simpson Winter Corporation, and for which I received a token dollar; that is the way things are done when one works for industry. I never found out what the connection was between Blackwood Arsenal [Edgewood Arsenal], A.R.L. [=Arthur D. Little Inc.] and Simpson Winter [Sterling-Winthrop Research Institute]. I also never met the man I privately dubbed "Frantic Freddy," although I did run into people at several scientific meetings in following years who knew him. His company has

411

continued to grow, and today it is pursuing a large number of research projects in the area of pharmaceuticals. Their work occasionally touches the THC molecule with imaginative variations, but as to the putting of a nitrogen atom in there, not much more has been done. I did put out a few more materials with that THC-nitrogen combination from my own lab sometime later, which earned me a trip to Sweden. But I found nothing of psychedelic interest.[1017]

While at Dow Shulgin prepared for the government a synthetic THC that was *512 times more potent than natural THC*: a nitrogen-containing phenethylamine. *This* is **LOUD** weed. Again, the fact that Alexander Shulgin, "The Godfather of MDMA," gave the U.S. Army/CIA the secrets to weaponize cannabis is big.[1018] This will become clear as we continue.

The alkaloid THC or nitrogenous THC was achieved in 1966.[1019] Harry Pars acknowledged his debt to Shulgin in the published report:

[1017] Shulgin, *PiHKAL*, 43-44.
[1018] Alexander T. Shulgin, "Recent Developments in Cannabis Chemistry," *Journal of Psychedelic Drugs* 2 (1968): 15-29; idem., "Psychotomimetic Agents," *Psychopharmacological Agents.* **Volume IV: Use, Misuse and Abuse**, ed. Maxwell Gordon (Academic Press, 1976) 59-146
[1019] H.G. Pars et al. "Physiologically Active Nitrogen Analogs of Tetrahydrocannabinols. Testrahydrobenzopyrano[3,4-*d*]pyridines," *Journal of the American Chemical Society* 88 (1966): 3664-3665. See further: William Dewey et al (Harry Pars etc.), "Pharmacology of some Marijuana Constituents and Two Heterocyclic Analogues," *Nature* 226 (1970): 1265-1267; Harry G. Pars and Raj K. Razdan, "Tetrahydrocannabinols and Synthetic Analogs," *Annals of the New York Academy of Sciences* 191 (1971): 15-22; H.G. Pars et al., "Water-Soluble Derivatives of Δ¹-Tetrahydrocannabinol," *Science* 177 (1972): 442-444; Harry G. Pars and Raj K. Razdan, "Heterocyclic Analogs of the Cannabinoids," in *The Therapeutic Potential of Marihuana*, ed. S. Cohen et al (Plenum Publishing Corporation 1976) 419-437; David B. Uliss et al, "Hashish: Synthesis of dl-Δ¹,⁶-Cis-Tetrahydrocannabinol (THC)," *Tetrahedron Letters* No. 49 (1975): 4369-4372; Raj K. Razdan, "The Total Synthesis of Cannabinoids," in *The Total Synthesis of Natural Products.* Volume 4. Ed. John ApSimon (New York: John Wiley & Sons, 1980) 185-262; V.K. Mahesh et al, "Analogs of cannabinoids: synthesis of some 7*H*-indolo-, 5*H*-imidazolo, 7*H*-benzimidazolo[1,2-*c*] [1,3]benzoxazines – novel ring systems," *Can. J. Chem.* 63 (1985): 632-635; Bill R. Martin et al, "Pharmacological Characterization of

We wish to report the successful synthesis of nitrogen analogs (testrahydrobenzopyrano[3,4-*d*]pyridines) of Adam's conjugated double-bond isomers of natural tetrahydrocannabinol...We are indebted to Dr. A.T. Shulgin of the Dow Chemical Co. for drawing our attention to the synthesis of these nitrogen analogs and to Dr. F. W. Hoffmann of the research Laboratories, U.S. Army Edgewood Arsenal, for his encouragement of this work...Carried out for the U.S. Army Edgewood Arsenal in collaboration with the Sterling-Winthrop Research Institute, Rensselaer, N.Y., under Contract No. DA18-108-AMC-103(A).[1020]

Fig. 10

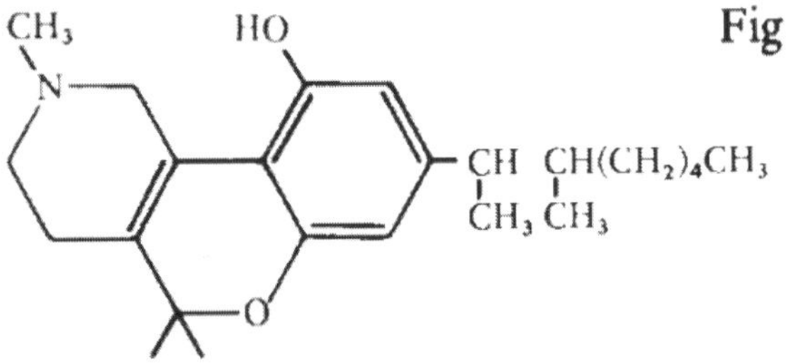

Pars' nitrogen analog

The new nitrogen THC analogs have "points of similarity" with morphine: "With nitrogen in the C-ring of THC, other points of striking structural similarity become evident between the nitrogen analog I and LSD, and between the nitrogen analog II and morphine."[1021] Like heroin, the nitrogen THC analogues

---

Novel Water-Soluble Cannabinoids," *The Journal of Pharmacology and Experimental Therapeutics* 318 (2006): 1230-2006.

[1020] Pars et al. "Physiologically Active Nitrogen Analogs of Tetrahydrocannabinols."

[1021] Harry G. Pars and Raj K. Razdan, "Heterocyclic Analogs of the Cannabinoids," in *The Therapeutic Potential of Marihuana*, ed. S. Cohen et al (Plenum Publishing Corporation 1976) 419-437 (420); Harry G. Pars and Raj K. Razdan, "Heterocyclic Analogs of the Cannabinoids," in *The Therapeutic Potential of Marihuana*, ed. S. Cohen et al (Plenum Publishing Corporation 1976) 419-437 (433).

have an addiction risk that natural cannabis does not. The government succeeded in making weed the New Heroin.

THC Analogue

Morphine

This new military "super pot" EA 2233 (or the acetate of its separated isomers) was tested on GIs at Edgewood. When the THC analogues triggered a dangerous drop in blood pressure, tests on these American GIs were suspended and instead in 1964 *transferred to Holmesburg Prison in Philadelphia and tested on the Black inmates under the charge of Dr. Albert Kligman* under Edgewood Arsenal contract DAAA15-70-C-0324![1022] EA 2233 proved effective as Col. Ketchum's "knock-'em-out-but-don't-kill-'em" agent.

V.   *Israel's "Godfather of THC"*

It was Roger Adams and colleagues who discovered in the 1940s the cannabinoids THC, CBD, and CBN and elucidated their basic structure. Adams was able to correctly infer chemical structure, though no pure form of THC had been isolated. That was accomplished in 1964. With the benefit of modern technology at the time – Nuclear Magnetic Resonance (NMR) spectroscopy - Dr. Rafael Mechoulam at Weizmann Institute of Science, Hebrew University, in Israel was able to clearly detect the chemical structure of THC, CBD, and CBN, confirming the instincts of Adams who did not have the benefit of NMR. Mechoulam went on to isolate, elucidate the structure and fully synthesize THC.[1023] He prepared a crystalline

---

[1022] Lee, **Smoke Signals**, 85. Ketchum, **Chemical Warfare**, 41; Frederick R. Sidell et al, "Dimethylheptyl-Delta 6a-10a-Tetrahydrocannabinol: Effects After Parenteral Administration to Man," Edgewood Arsenal Technical Report, December 1972.
[1023] Y. Gaoni and R. Mechoulam, "Isolation, Structure, and Partial Synthesis of an Active Constituent of Hashish," **J. Am. Chem. Soc.**

derivative from which pure THC could be obtained. For this reason, Mechoulam is popularly known as the "Godfather of THC," the "Father of Cannabis' and "the man Who Discovered Why Weed Makes You High."[1024] Mechoulam's work made Israel the birthplace of the modern medical marijuana industry.

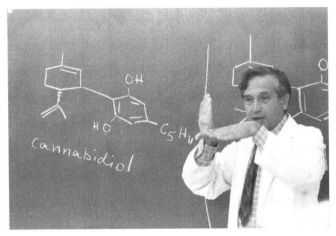

MECHOULAM DURING A LECTURE, WITH THE STRUCTURE OF TETRAHYDROCANNABINOL BEHIND HIM, CIRCA 1964. COURTESY OF ZACH KLEIN, FROM HIS DOCUMENTARY 'THE SCIENTIST'

Mechoulam's cannabis work was a U.S.-Israel collaborative effort. The National Institute of Mental Health (NIMH) and the National Institute on Drug Abuse (NIDA) had been financing his work for sixteen years.[1025] The NIMH is one of the agencies that the CIA used to channel funds to institutions and individuals doing covert drug experimentation.[1026] Mechoulam returned to Israel in the early 1960s after a post-doctoral stay at

86 (1964): 1646-1647; Raphael Mechoulam, "Marihuana Chemistry," **Science** 168 (June 1970): 1159-1165; Raphael Mechoulam and Lumír Hanuš, "A historical overview of chemical research on cannabinoids," **Chemistry and Physics of Lipids** 108 (2000): 1-13; Raphael Mechoulam, "Marihuana Chemistry," **Science** 168 (June 1970): 1159-1165 (1162).

[1024] Juan Camilo Maldonado Tovar, "Meet the 'Father of Cannabis,' the Man Who Discovered Why Weed Makes You High," **Vice** February 19, 2016.

[1025] "Conversation with Raphael Mechoulam," **Addiction** 102 (2007): 887-893 (890).

[1026] Lee and Shlain, **Acid Dreams**, 24.

the infamous Rockefeller Institute in New York.[1027] After Mechoulam's isolation of pure THC Dan Efron, head of the pharmacology section of NIMH, flew to Israel in 1965 to claim his property on behalf of the U.S. government. As Mechoulam recounts.

> Elfron...took with him the entire "world supply" of THC which we had. This sample was used for many of the original cannabinoid investigations in the United States, although our contribution was seldom recognized. NIH has supported my research with grants ever since for over four decades.[1028]

VI.   *Government Tests New THC on Black Bodies*

One of those many "original cannabinoid investigations in the United States" was testing the effects of pure THC on Black bodies. Not long after Elfron and the NIMH claimed Mechoulam's newly isolated THC in 1964 and brought it back to

the U.S., it was sent to the CIA's "chief doctor at Lexington," Harris Isbell at the NIMH Addiction Research Center. Remember, the human guinea pigs on whom Harris tested every new drug the CIA sent him for over a decade were "nearly all black drug addicts."[1029] By testing both Adams' DMHP and Mechoulam's isolated Δ⁹-THC at the ARC on "former opiate addicts who were serving sentences for violations of the United States Narcotic Laws," Isbell was the first to demonstrate THC activity in man.[1030]

Dr. Harris Isbell, the CIA's "chief doctor at Lexington"

[1027] "Conversation with Raphael Mechoulam," **Addiction** 102 (2007): 887-893 (887).

[1028] "Conversation with Raphael Mechoulam," **Addiction** 102 (2007): 887-893 (890).

[1029] Marks, **Search for the "Manchurian Candidate"**, 66-69 (68); Lee and Shlain, **Acids Dreams**, 24-25.

[1030] Harris Isbell et al., "Effects of (-)Δ⁹-trans-tetrahydrocannabinol in man," **Psychopharmacologia** (Berlin) 11 (1967): 184-188; Harris Isbell and D.R. Jasinski, "A Comparison of LSD-25 with (-)Δ⁹-Trans-Tetrahydrocannabinol (THC) and Attempted Cross Tolerance

Δ9-THC was isolated from hashish by countercurrent distribution...Its structure and purity was proved by chemical measurements and by infrared and nuclear resonance spectroscopy. Δ9-THC (and other materials) was then studied in man at the Addiction Research Center. Subjects were healthy former opiate addicts wo were serving sentences for violations of the United States Narcotic Laws...When the drug was to be smoked it was deposited in the middle third of a tobacco cigarette and the cigarette died overnight.[1031]

Isbell found that THC is more potent when smoked than when taken orally. Isabell reports:

A number of tetrahydrocannabinols and related compounds have been studied in man for activity at the Addiction Research Center...Two compounds that are active in man are homologs originally derived by Adams and his coworkers from d,l-synthetic tetrahydrocannabinol (THC). These two homologs are the n-hexyl derivative known as synhexyl or pyrahexyl, and the dimethylheptyl derivative (DMHP), also known as CA-101 or SKF-5350...

Utilizing total dosages of 1 .0-5.0 mg administered orally (approximately 10-70 pg/kg), Isbell found that DMHP elicited marijuana-like identifications and symptoms in experienced marijuana users in the lower dose ranges. Larger doses of DMPH produced psychotic reactions. Outstanding characteristics of the effects of DMHP in man, in addition to its potency, are relatively long duration of action, *marked sedative effects*, and postural hypotension associated with tachycardia... On the basis of studies in man at the Addiction Research Center with Δ9-THC, pyrahexyl, and DMHP, the following observations can be made in this regard. Δ9-THC is a hallucinogen whose hallucinogenic activity is related to dose, and in sufficient amounts Δ9-THC will produce a toxic psychosis. Based on quantitative assessment in man under experimental circumstances, Δ9-THC, pyrahexyl, and DMHP produce a common set of subjective effects and physiologic

between LSD and THC," ***Psychopharmacologia*** (Berl.) 14 (1969): 115-123;
[1031] Harris Isbell et al., "Effects of (-)Δ9-trans-tetrahydrocannabinol in man."

changes, and may differ only in such characteristics as potency, onset, and duration of action.[1032]

When Isbell measured the subjective effects of these compounds he found that the test subjects who smoked the government's "proto-Blunts" were put in a subjective state expressed like this:

"I couldn't get mad at anyone right now"/ "I feel detached from the problems of everyday life."[1033]

This reminds us of the words of the great Jazz icon Louis Armstrong: "[Marijuana] makes you feel good, man. [It] makes you forget all the bad things that happens to a Negro." To an even greater degree, this weaponized weed can *de-militarize the Negro*. Isbell says further: "Sedative effects are prominent after the initial euphoriant phase. Psychologically, the most striking phenomenon appears to be impairment of ability to think in a connected fashion to a goal..."[1034]

[1032] Donald R. Jasinki, Charles A. Haertzen and Harris Isbell, "Review of the Effects in Man of Marijuana and the Tetrahydrocannabinols on Subjective State and Physiologic Functioning," ***Annals of the New York Academy of Sciences*** 191 (1971): 196-205.

[1033] Jasinki, Charles A. Haertzen and Harris Isbell, "Review of the Effects in Man," 197.

[1034] Harris Isbell, "Clinical Pharmacology of Marihuana," ***Pharmacological Reviews*** 23 (1971): 337-338.

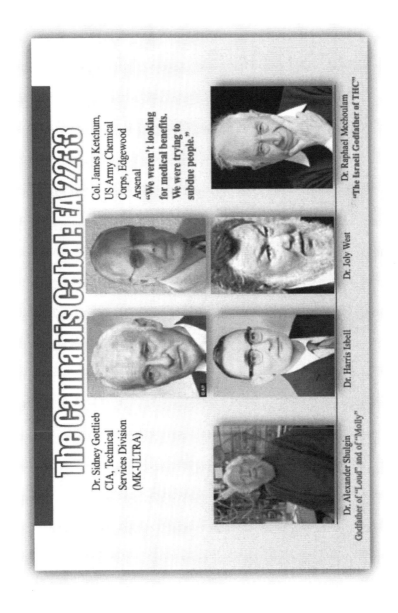

The Cannabis Cabal: EA 2233

Dr. Sidney Gottlieb
CIA, Technical
Services Division
(MK-ULTRA)

Col. James Ketchum,
US Army Chemical
Corps, Edgewood
Arsenal

"We weren't looking
for medical benefits.
We were trying to
subdue people."

Dr. Alexander Shulgin
Godfather of "Loud" and of "Molly"

Dr. Harris Isbell

Dr. Joly West

Dr. Raphael Mechoulam
"The Israeli Godfather of THC"

Chapter Eighteen

The Neuroendocrinology of Weaponized Weed

I.   *Cannabis vs. Loud*

Cannabis in its natural state is one of the many gifts God gave to man for our benefit. It is indeed a *holy herb* with great medicinal value when used properly. But the cannabis that God planted thousands of years ago, probably in Central Asia, is not the marijuana that we smoke today in south Chicago or Los Angeles. God is not responsible for "loud." In fact, as we have shown, the first "loud" form of marijuana was produced by the U.S. military and intelligence services as a prospective chemical weapon. God's cannabis and our "Loud" have very different chemical profiles.

The cannabis plant contains over 100 cannabinoids, chemical compounds unique to cannabis. The two principle cannabinoids, the psychoactive delta-9-tetrahydrocannabinol (Δ9-THC, shortened to THC) and the non-psychoactive cannabidiol (CBD), are structurally distinct and engender markedly different, even antagonistic molecular, pharmacological and neurological effects. In isolation THC can elicit psychosis, anxiolysis, intoxication, and cognitive impairment, while CBD reportedly has anti-anxiety actions, anti-psychotic effects, serves as an anti-oxidant, and has anti-inflammatory effects.[1035] CBD modulates the pharmacokinetics of THC[1036]; in other words, CBD *tames* THC by mitigating its negative effects while potentiating THC's positive effects. This

---

[1035] Zerrin Atakan, "Cannabis, a complex plant: different compounds and different effects on individuals," ***Ther Adv Psychopharmacol*** 2 (2012): 241-254; Paolo Fusar-Poli et al., "Distinct Effects of Δ9-Tetrahydrocannabinol and Cannabidiol on Neural Activation During Emotional Processing," ***Arch Gen Psychiatry*** 66 (2009): 95-105; Ethan Russo ad Geoffrey W. Guy, "A tale of two cannabinoids: The therapeutic rationale for combining tetrahydrocannabinol and cannabidiol," ***Medical Hypothesis*** 66 (2006): 234-246.

[1036] John M. McPartland, "Cannabis and Cannabis Extracts: Greater Than the Sum of Their Parts?" ***Journal of Cannabis Therapeutics*** 1 (2001): 103-132 (106).

is why the ratio of CBD to THC in a cannabis preparation determines the effects of that preparation. In natural cannabis the CBD:THC ratio is such that the synergistic effect makes the plant medicinal. However, today the THC:CBD ratio is *8 times greater* than before.[1037] This is one reason weed is "loud."

Confiscated marijuana samples in 1975 had THC content averaging between 0.5% to 1%.[1038] Since then the THC content of street marijuana has grown hugely.[1039] Dr. Sidney Cohen, professor of psychiatry at UCLA Medical School and a drug consultant for the U.S. State Department, noted in 1986: "A lot of stuff on the streets is now more than 10 times stronger than what people had been used to; its almost a completely different drug."[1040] And that was in 1986! He continues: "Ten years ago people would have laughed at the idea that marijuana could cause such an adverse reaction or that users would have a difficult time giving up smoking. But now," he said, "several patients a month check into the detoxification clinic because they cannot quit smoking the potent pot." And as **CNN** reported: "The stronger marijuana is of particular concern because the high concentrations of THC have the opposite effect of low concentrations;"[1041] "The higher the THC content, the stronger the effects on the brain."[1042]

[1037] Bertha K. Madras, "Tinkering with THC-to-CBD ratios in Marijuana," **Neuropsychopharmacology** 1 (2018).

[1038] Miles Corwin, "Stronger Marijuana Spurs New Concern," **Los Angeles Times** March 25, 1986; **Marijuana Research Findings: 1980**, ed. Robert C. Petersen, Ph.D. (Rockville, Maryland: Department of Health and Human Services, 1980) 2.

[1039] Mahmoud A. ElSohy et al., "Potency Trends of Δ^9-THC and Other Cannabinoids in Confiscated Marijuana from 1980-1997," **J Forensic Sci** 45 (2000): 24-30; Desmond Slade et al., "Is Cannabis becoming more potent?" in **Marijuana and Madness**, Second Edition, ed. David Castle, Robin M. Murray and Deepak Cyril D'Souza (Cambridge: Cambridge University press, 2012) 35-54 .

[1040] Miles Corwin, "Stronger Marijuana Spurs New Concern," **Los Angeles Times** March 25, 1986.

[1041] James Meserve and Mike M. Ahlers, "Marijuana potency surpasses 10 percent, U.S. says," **CNN.com** May 14, 2009.

[1042] Alice G. Walton, "New Study Shows How Marijuana's Potency Has Changed Over Time," **Forbes** March 23, 2015.

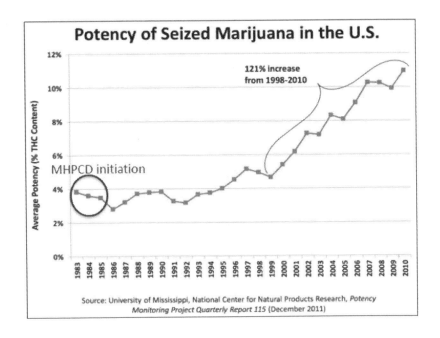

Potency of Seized Marijuana in the U.S.

121% increase
from 1998-2010

MHPCD initiation

Source: University of Mississippi, National Center for Natural Products Research, *Potency Monitoring Project Quarterly Report 115* (December 2011)

While the THC content in recreational marijuana is steadily and hugely rising, CBD content has shrunk: "it's being bred out," says Alice G. Walton.[1043] In a 2011 study of marijuana seized in California from 1996 to 2008, they tracked the CBD:THC ratio. Over this period THC % increased dramatically: 4.56 % in 1996 to 11.75 % in 2008. On the other hand, CBD % *dropped*: 0.24 % in 1996 to 0.08% in 2008. The two cannabinoids are trending in *opposite* directions. The median ratio or "Gap" between the percentages grew from 26.21 in 1996 to 187.99 in 2008![1044]

[1043] Alice G. Walton, "New Study Shows How Marijuana's Potency Has Changed Over Time," ***Forbes*** March 23, 2015.

[1044] Burgdorf, James Richard et al. "Heterogeneity in the Composition of Marijuana Seized in California," ***Drug Alcohol Depend.*** 117 (2011): 59-61; Mahmoud A. ElSohly et al., "Changes in Cannabis Potency over the last Two Decades (1995-2014) – Analysis of Current Data in the United States," ***Biol Psychiatry*** 79 (2016): 1-16.

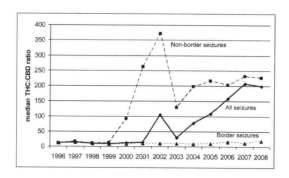

Figure 2. Increasing THC:CBD ratio in California seizures is driven by non-border seizures
Border seizures include those that took place at a Mexican border crossing or town: San Ysidro, Otay Mesa, Tecate, Calexico, and Andrade.

This amounts to the potential negative effects of THC not only being intensified by the increased potency but also being *unchecked* due to the diminishing presence of CBD.

Neuro relates to the nerves or the nervous system and the Central Nervous System is composed of the brain and spinal cord. *Endocrinology* relates to the endocrine system, the collection of glands that secretes hormones. Weaponized marijuana has adverse effects on both neural and endocrinal processes.

II.   *Castrating the Divine (Higher) Mind*

On June 16, 2019 ***The New York Times*** published a piece entitled "Marijuana Damages Young Brains," which read in part:

> It's tempting to think marijuana is a harmless substance that poses no threat to teens and young adults. The medical facts, however, reveal a different reality.
>
> Numerous studies show that marijuana can have a deleterious impact on cognitive development in adolescents, impairing executive function, processing speed, memory, attention span and concentration. The damage is measurable with an I.Q. test. Researchers who tracked subjects from childhood through age 38 found a consequential I.Q. decline over the 25-year period among adolescents who consistently used marijuana every week. In addition, studies have shown that substantial adolescent exposure to marijuana may be a predictor of opioid use disorders.

The reason the adolescent brain is so vulnerable to the effect of drugs is that the brain — especially the prefrontal cortex, which controls decision making, judgment and impulsivity — is still developing in adolescents and young adults until age 25...

In addition, researchers now have a good understanding of how marijuana in particular affects the brain. The chemical in marijuana responsible for producing mood elevation and relaxation, THC, interferes with the exchange of information between neurons. Regular exposure to THC in adolescents can permanently change neuropathways that are related to cognition, including learning, attention and emotional responses. In some adolescents, it can also lead to long-term dependence...

The risk that marijuana use poses to adolescents today is far greater than it was 20 or 30 years ago, because the marijuana grown now is much more potent. In the early 1990s, the average THC content of confiscated marijuana was roughly 3.7 percent. By contrast, a recent analysis of marijuana for sale in Colorado's authorized dispensaries showed an average THC content of 18.7 percent.[1045]

There are a number of points here worth highlighting. First, the noted path from marijuana use to opioid abuse is perfectly understandable in the context of weaponized weed which, through the insertion of a nitrogen atom into the THC molecule, gave it a certain affinity to opiates such as morphine. Young developing minds today are exposed to marijuana with a THC content of nearly *twenty percent*, and this is not street marijuana but authorized dispensary weed. The neurological impact on all users can be significant, especially on *higher cognitive* processes. The prefrontal cortex (PFC) carries out executive cognitive functions such as reasoning, complex thought, planning, judgement, and decision making and is also responsible for impulse control and emotional response. The impact of weaponized weed on cognitive function is "subtle but definitive."[1046] As Nadia Solowij explains:

[1045] Kenneth L. Davis and Mary Jeanne Kreek, "Marijuana Damages Young Brains," *The New York Times* June 16, 2019.
[1046] Johannes G. Ramaekers, et al. "High-Potency Marijuana Impairs Executive Function and Inhibitory Motor Control," *Neuropsychopharmacology* 31 (2006): 2296-2303 (2296); Ester

There is now good evidence that heavy and long-term use of marijuana can result in subtle impairments of memory, attention and executive function and that the functioning of prefrontal cortical, hippocampal and cerebellar regions can become compromised. Human research has used increasingly sophisticated and sensitive techniques to examine the cognitive consequences of marijuana use and their neural concomitants, improving upon the methodology that produced equivocal results in past studies...The scientific evidence from past research has been inconclusive. However, recent research with improved methodology continues to demonstrate definite but subtle impairments...

It is apparent from many years of research that long-term use of marijuana does not result in gross cognitive deficits. However, recent reviewers agree that there is now sufficient evidence that it leads to a more subtle and selective impairment of higher cognitive functions (...) which arises from altered functioning of the frontal lobe, hippocampus and cerebellum (...). The findings from recent methodologically rigorous research provide evidence for impaired learning, organization and integration of complex information in tasks involving various mechanisms of attention, memory processes and executive function. It is not clear to what extent the alterations in brain function and cognitive impairments as detected in laboratory testing might impact upon daily life, although users themselves complain of problems with memory, concentration, loss of motivation, paranoia, depression, dependence and lethargy ... The nature of the cognitive deficits as assessed by psychological testing suggests that long-term users would perform reasonably well in routine tasks of everyday life, although they may be more distractible and short-term memory may be compromised. Difficulties are likely to be encountered in performing complex tasks that are novel or that cannot be solved by automatic application of previous knowledge, or with

Fride and M. Clara Sañudo-Peña, "Cannabinoids and endocannabinoids: behavioral and developmental aspects," in *Biology of Marijuana* ed. Emmnauel S. Onaivi (London and New York: Taylor & Francis, 2002) 192-222 (193); Rebecca D. Crean, et al. "An Evidence Based Review of Acute and Long-Term Effects of Cannabis Use on Executive Cognitive Functions," *Journal of Addict Med* 5 (2011): 1-8.

tasks that rely heavily on a memory component or require strategic planning and multi-tasking.[1047]

Modern state-of-the-art technology allows us to actually observe this cognitive impairment caused by THC. Brain activity can be compared to a philharmonic orchestra in which string, brass, woodwind and percussion sections are rhythmically synchronized by the conductor. Brain structures tune in to one another, and this tuning gives rise to brain waves which allow for the processing of information used to guide our behavior. Two different sets of researchers, one from the University of Bristol, England (2011) and the other from Rutgers University, New Jersey (2006), have demonstrated that THC's effect on the brain can lead to "disorchestrated" neural networks, the disruption of the symphony of the synchronous firing of brain cells: "the drug completely disrupted co-ordinated brain waves across the hippocampus and prefrontal cortex, as though two sections of the orchestra were playing out of synch."[1048] The resulting neurophysiological and behavioral impairments are said to be reminiscent of those seen in schizophrenia.

Another important area targeted by THC is the amygdala, our "threat-processing center." Australian researchers in 2008 reported that brain scans of heavy marijuana users showed their hippocampus and amygdala were smaller than that of nonusers, 15 percent and 7 percent less volume, respectively.[1049] As we saw, one of the amygdala's main duties is to pick up social signals of threat and prompt a response to it. It has been demonstrated that THC significantly reduced amygdala perception of and reactivity to threat

---

[1047] Nadia Solowij, "Marijuana and cognitive function," in *Biology of Marijuana* ed. Emmanuel S. Onaivi (London and New York: Taylor & Francis, 2002) 326-327, 341-342.

[1048] M. T. Kucewicz, M. D. Tricklebank, R. Bogacz, M. W. Jones, "Dysfunctional Prefrontal Cortical Network Activity and Interactions following Cannabinoid Receptor Activation," *Journal of Neuroscience* 31 (2011); "How cannabis causes 'cognitive chaos' in the brain," *Science Daily* October 28, 2011; David Biello, "Marijuana's High Times Not Memorable with Neurons Out of Sync," *Scientific American* November 20, 2006.

[1049] Will Dunham, "Heavy marijuana use shrinks brain parts: study," *Reuters* June 2, 2008.

signals.[1050] The amygdala has endocannabinoid receptors (CB$_1$ and CB$_2$) which THC targets and hijacks.[1051] THC activates the CB$_1$ receptors of the amygdala and *dulls it*, making the amygdala non-responsive to aversive stimuli. The THC-attenuated amygdala is unable to pick up on threatening environmental stimuli such as predators and it decreases defensive behavior responses: a rat exposed to a cat or a Negro exposed to his 400-year Enemy *will both* fail to respond defensively under the influence of this marijuana. Remember the dogs on the government's weed? "you can step on their (dogs) feet without any response"; "we were unable to arouse the animals from their depressed state by any form of painful stimuli."[1052] This is **Project Ferdinand**. Remember, the results of damaging the amygdala and/or by diminishing testosterone to a level too low to act on the amygdala are

4. No threat can even be perceived and therefore no appropriate physical and psychological response to the threat can be mounted.
5. The person with a damaged or inactivated amygdala can be made "docile, subdued, and easy to manage" by an enemy because such damage mutes the instinct to fight, like Ferdinand.
6. Depending on which part of the amygdala is damaged, even an apex predator can be made to fear its easy prey

---

[1050] S.F. Lisboa et al., "Cannabinoid modulation of predator fear: involvement of the dorsolateral periaqueductal gray," *International Journal of Neuropsychopharmacology* 17 (2017): 1193-1206; K. Luan Phan et al., "Cannabinoid Modulation of Amygdala Reactivity to Social Signals of Threat in Humans," *The Journal of Neuroscience* March 5, 2008.
[1051] Christopher Bergland, "Cannabis Targets Receptors in the Amygdala Linked to Anxiety," *Psychology Today* March 6, 2014.
[1052] Harold F. Hardman and Maurice H. Seevers, *THE CHEMISTRY AND PHARMACOLOGY OF CERTAIN COMPOUNDS AFFECTING THE CENTRAL NERVOUS SYSTEM OF ANIMALS AND MAN. A PHARMACOLOGICAL COMPARISON OF EA 1476 (TETRAHYDROCANNABINOL) ISOMERS. PROGRESS REPORT* December 1, 1956. P. 5; Edward F. Domino, "Neuropsychpharmacologic Studies of Marijuana: some Synthetic and Natural THC Derivatives in Animals and Man," *Annals of the New York Academy of Sciences* 191 (December 1971): 166-191 (167, 173)

– like a cat terrified by a mouse; or the prey can be made to fail to perceive and respond to the threat posed by his natural, long time enemy - like a mouse that continues to sniff around casually as a hissing snake approaches, or like a cat who continues to clean its fur unbothered by the barking dog approaching. This is how the Negro is in the presence of his 400-year tormentor.

This is what Weaponized Weed does.

III.   *Endocannabinoids vs. Marijuana*

Spread throughout the human body and brain is a widespread network of "cannabinoid" receptors (CB_1 and CB_2) that however are *not* intended for THC, CBD or any cannabis constituent. Rather these receptors are activated by a range of natural substances produced by our own body called *endocannabinoids*. *Endo-* means "from within"; *Exo-* means "from without." Just as *endorphins* are the body's own natural version of morphine, an *exorphin,* THC and CBD are *exocannabinoids.* The body's primary *endo*cannabinoids, anandamide (AEA) and 2-arachidonoylglycerol (2-AG), act as neurotransmitters sending messages between nerve cells. Unlike classical neurotransmitters, AEA and 2-AG are not synthesized and stored for future release. Instead, they are synthesized "on demand." THC is structurally very different from endocannabinoids but it mimics them and hijacks the cannabinoid receptor, displacing the natural endocannabinoids and disrupting the normal, finely balanced neurosignaling system. By binding to the CB_1 receptor THC interferes with downstream endogenous signaling pathways.[1053]

The body's endocannabinoid system (EDS) controls some of our most vital life functions. The endocannabinoid system and the endocrine system interact extensively. The ECS seems to function as a gatekeeper preventing maladaptive excess activation of the HPG and HPA axes.[1054] The ECS

[1053] A.A. Amoako et al, "Anandamide modulates human sperm motility: implications for men with asthenozoospermia and oligoasthenoteratozoospermia," **Human Reproduction** 28 (2013): 2058-2066 (2059, 2064);
[1054] Boris B. Gorzalka and Silvain S. Dang, "Minireview: Endocannabinoids and Gonadal Hormones: Bidirectional

maintains hormones at the correct physiological levels and prevents overactivation of the axes. Endocannabinoid signaling through the CB1 receptor plays a pivotal role in spermatogenesis and testosterone production.[1055] In the hypothalamus and the pituitary endocannabinoid signaling (when activated) suppresses the release of GnRH and LH, which in turn reduces gonadal hormone (testosterone in males and estrogen in females) release. In this way the ECS appears to help regulate serum levels of gonadal hormones by regulating levels of gonadotropins.

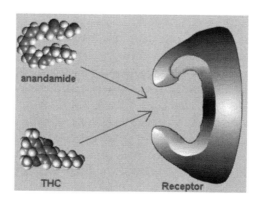

By hijacking and binding to the CB1 receptor THC interferes with downstream endogenous signaling pathways, disrupting the endocrine system and thereby disturbing reproduction and the development of natural biochemical masculinity in males and femininity in females.

It is to be expected that exogenous cannabinoids, such as those present in marijuana, compete with endocannabinoids for binding on the cannabinoid receptors. This can disturb the ECS, and the resultant imbalance can impact fertility. It is not

---

Interactions in Physiology and Behavior," ***Endocrinology*** 153 (2012): 1016-1024 (1020).
[1055] A.A. Amoako et al, "Anandamide modulates human sperm motility: implications for men with asthenozoospermia and oligoasthenoteratozoospermia," ***Human Reproduction*** 28 (2013): 2058-2066 (2059, 2064).

surprising then that studies consistently conclude that marijuana negatively affects male fertility.[1056]

THC could affect the normal balance of anandamide leading to impaired semen quality.[1057]

The *ENDO*cannabinoids AEA and 2-AG safeguard the reproductive and gender processes while the *EXO*cannabinoid THC disrupts them.

IV.   *Serotonin*

Serotonin is an important brain chemical which we discussed in detail in our previous writing. This is what we documented in **Understanding The Assault Volume I**:

> What the UCLA scientists discovered was that serotonin was the "Rosetta Stone" for decoding the mysteries of aggression, violence and also social hierarchy, among other things. They found that high levels of serotonin were distinctly related to male social dominance and low levels of serotonin was associated with low social status or subordination... Serotonin is our brain's key modulator of several physiological processes, including our primitive drives and emotions. It is the brain's chemical *breaks*, our impulse inhibitor (it puts a lid on our impulsive behavior). High serotonin is required to rein in our basic drives – appetite, sex, aggression, etc. – and keep them from racing out of control. When serotonin is low, "all the basic drives that it regulates can burst out of control," because low serotonin results in loss of impulse control.
>
> If serotonin is the brain's chemical breaks, noradrenalin is the chemical *accelerator*... Serotonin and noradrenalin are the two "brain buttons" that scientists discovered they can push and thereby determine a person's future, "two potent brain

---

[1056] Stefan S. du Plessis, Ashok Agarwal, Arun Syriac, "Marijuana, phytocannabinoids, the endocannabinoid system, and male fertility," **J Assist Reprod Gene** 32 (2015): 1575-1588 (1580).

[1057] Tina Djernis Gundersen et al., "Association Between Use of Marijuana and Male Reproductive Hormones and Semen Quality," **Am J Epidemiol** 182 (2015): 473-481. Also M. Rossato, C. Pagano and R. Vettor, "The Cannabinoid System and Male Reproductive Functions," **Journal of Neuroendocrinology** 20 (2008): 90-93 (91); Giovanna Cacciola et al., "Cannabinoids and Reproduction: A Lasting and Intriguing History," **Pharmaceuticals** 3 (2010): 3275-3323 (3285).

chemicals that researchers have successfully manipulated to make animals more violent or less violent," in the words of [*Chicago Tribune* writer Ronald] Kotulak. "[A]ggression can be controlled by manipulating brain levels of serotonin." By "twisting the architecture of the brain" scientists can "push noradrenalin production into overdrive and serotonin into low gear," thereby making an individual or group hyper-impulsive, hyper-aggressive and violent: "*the raging monster* was being forced into the open where scientists could begin to understand and tame it."

It is important to point out here that all violence is *not* the same. Not all aggression is associated with low serotonin; only impulsive, emotion-driven, reactionary aggression which is socially maladaptive and characteristic of low social status is. This is to be distinguished from proactive, premeditative, deliberate, predatory aggression characteristic of dominant males. Impulsive aggression is often severe, unrestrained, dysfunctional, and frequently results in the wounding or death of the aggressor. This is the aggression artificially produced by evil scientists who have mastered the manipulation of these chemical buttons of the brain.

In terms of dominance hierarchy, low serotonin among subordinate males favors dominant males, because in the interest of self-preservation low serotonin discourages the conspicuous challenging of dominant males who are, by virtue of their high-status, in a position to punish such insolence. So the aggression, the raging monster, *is unleashed instead against fellow subordinate males only*: "Even as low (serotonin) keeps him from challenging dominant males, he may behave recklessly toward those closer to him on the social ladder," explains Robert Wright.[1058]

The endocannabinoid system has been shown to provide regulatory control of functions of the serotonergic system. AEA and 2-AG signaling influences the release of serotonin and activation of the CB1 receptors have been shown to inhibit serotonin release in areas such the prefrontal cortex.[1059] When THC hijacks the cannabinoid receptors the result is an over-inhibition of serotonin release. It is reported that a low acute

---

[1058] Wesley Muhammad, *Understanding The Assault of the Black Man, Black Manhood and Black Masculinity*, **Volume I** (Atlanta: A-Team Publishing, 2017) 190.
[1059] Samir Haj-Dahmane and Roh-Yu Shen, "Modulation of the Serotonin System by Endocannabinoid Signaling," *Neuropharmacology* 61 (2011): 414-420.

dose of marijuana increases serotonin in the short term while high doses and chronic use "plummets" serotonin levels. THC and other agonists of the CB_1 receptor markedly attenuate serotonin neurotransmission,[1060] and accumulating evidence indicates that sustained THC exposure may precipitate the onset of some neuropsychiatric disorders that are associated with disfunction of serotonin 2A receptor signaling in the brain.[1061] This is how weaponized weed "plummets" serotonin levels. In addition, prenatal and perinatal exposure to THC can alter the normal development of serotonergic neurons and affect the organization of the serotonergic system, particularly in male offspring.[1062]

V.   *Diminishing Testosterone*

Testosterone is "The He Hormone"[1063] and "is at the root of what we call 'masculinty'".[1064] This Weaponized Weed diminishes male testosterone, thereby potentially feminizing males to one degree or another, including the shrinkage of genitals, the feminizing of body-type, and development of breasts (gynecomastia), and well as behavioral feminizations such as high emotionality. It is now known that THC cuts off testosterone production at the root by blocking the pulsatile release of GnRH in the brain.[1065] When I stated this from the rostrum of Mosque Maryam on January 29, 2017, it generated

---

[1060] Francis Rodriquez Bambico et al., "Cannabinoids Elicit Antidepressant-Like Behavior and Activate Serotonergic Neurons through the Medial Prefrontal Cortex," **The Journal of Neuroscience** 27 (2007): 11700-11711.

[1061] Jade M. Franklin, "Cannabinoid Regulation of Serotonin 2A (5-HT$_{2A}$) Receptor Signaling." Ph.D. dissertation, University of Kansas, 2013.

[1062] Francisco Molina-Holgado et al., "Effect of maternal Δ^9-tetrahydrocannabinol on developing serotonergic system," **European Journal of Pharmacology** 316 (1996): 39-42.

[1063] Andrew Sullivan, "The He Hormone," The New York Times Magazine April 2, 2000.

[1064] Joe Herbert, **Testosterone: Sex, Power,** and the Will to Win (Oxford: Oxford University Press, 2015) 33.

[1065] C. Michael Gammon et al., "Regulation of Gonadotropin-Releasing Hormone Secretion by Cannabinoids," **Endocrinology** 146 (2005): 4491-4499

a lot of controversy. Considering this, I will let the scientists speak for themselves in this matter.

- Jack Harclerode, "The Effect of Marijuana on Reproduction and Development," in ***Marijuana Research Findings: 1980***, ed. Robert C. Petersen (NIDA Research Monograph 31 June 1980; Rockville, Maryland: National Institute of Drug Abuse, 1981) 137-154ff (142):

The effects of marijuana are observed in all phases of reproductive physiology, including decreases in the weight and functions of organs associated with reproduction and decreases in hormones that control development of the fetus...In terms of endocrine effects, the human male appears to respond to marijuana in much the same way rats and mice do. Acute marijuana smoking decreased both LH and testosterone levels in the blood, an effect which lasted for up to three hours, whereas no change was detected in FSH levels...marijuana affects male reproductive function in all species studied. This is observed as a decrease in organ weight and organ function after both short- and long-term treatment. The mechanism by which this occurs seems to be due to the effect of the active ingredients in marijuana to depress release of LHRF with the subsequent depression of the gonadotropins. This lack of gonadotropin stimulation of Leydig cells is probably responsible for the observed decreased testosterone production. Many of the changes seen in decreased weight of the testes and associated reproductive organs are probably caused by the decreased testosterone production...

- Dr. Todd T. Brown and Dr. Adrian S. Dobs, "Endocrine Effects of Marijuana," ***Journal of Clinical Pharmacology*** 42 (2002): 90S-96S (91S-92S).

Marijuana and Δ^9-THC can have direct effects on the testes. Reductions in testicular size have been observed in rodents and dogs with administration of cannabis extract. Degeneration of the seminiferous tubules may provide an explanation for this observation and is dose dependent, with lower doses showing no appreciable effect. Abnormal sperm morphology has been characterized in rodents exposed to marijuana smoke or Δ^9-THC for a 5-day period.

434

In vitro studies have demonstrated that cannabinoids directly inhibit Leydig cell function... In humans, effects on sperm production and morphology have also been observed...a 58% decrease in sperm concentration was reported in chronic users after intensive marijuana smoking without a significant change in LH or testosterone.

- Laura Murphy, "Marijuana and endocrine function" in *Biology of Marijuana* ed. Emmnauel S. Onaivi (London and New York: Taylor & Francis, 2002) 351-361:

Marijuana and its cannabinoids have profound effects on hormone secretion in humans and experimental animals. The most studied aspect of the cannabinoid effects on endocrine function is how marijuana and cannabinoids affect the hormones of reproduction. Cannabinoids inhibit the hormones of the hypothalamic-pituitary-gonadal axis, i.e. gonadotropin-releasing hormone (GnRH), luteinizing hormone (LH)/follicle-stimulating hormone (FSH), and the sex steroids estrogen, progesterone and testosterone. Inhibition of this axis may be responsible for the ability of marijuana to cause anovulation, oligospermia, and changes in sexual behavior...

In human males, cannabis smoking has been shown to decrease serum LH, FSH, and testosterone levels when compared to pre-smoking baseline hormone levels ... or when compared to nonsmoking individuals...In the male rhesus monkey, an acute dose of THC produced a 65% reduction in plasma testosterone levels by 60 min of treatment that lasted for approximately 24 h ... Long-term cannabinoid exposure in male mice disrupts spermatogenesis and can induce aberrations in sperm morphology...Together, all of these studies suggest that THC inhibits LH and FSH secretion, consequently decreasing testosterone production, altering spermatogenesis, and influencing male sexual behavior.[1066]

[1066] Dr. Laura Murphy (Department of Physiology at Southern Illinois University), "Marijuana and endocrine function" in *Biology of Marijuana* ed. Emmnauel S. Onaivi (London and New York: Taylor & Francis, 2002) 351-361.

- Zaki S. Badawy et al., "Cannabinoids inhibit the respiration of human sperm," *Fertility and Sterility* 91 (2009): 2472-2476 (2474):

The cannabinoids (Δ^9-THC and Δ^8-THC) are known to reduce sperm count, disrupt spermatogenesis, induce aberrations in sperm morphology, decrease sperm fertilizing capacity, inhibit sperm protein and nucleic acid synthesis, and impair sperm glycolysis. Clinically, studies are still needed to confirm whether the use of marijuana adversely affects the fertilizing capacity of human sperm...Our results show that the cannabinoids are potent inhibitors of sperm mitochondrial O_2 consumption (sperm respiration...)...The results add further emphasis to the adverse effects of these toxins on human health, including fertility.[1067]

- Paola Grimaldi, Daniele Di Giacomo and Raffaele Geremia, "The endocannabinoid system and spermatogenesis," *frontiers in Endocrinology* 4 (2013): 1-6 (1, 3):

It is known that marijuana, the commonest recreational drug of abuse, has adverse effects on male reproductive physiology. Its use is associated with impotence, decreased testosterone plasma level, impairment of spermatogenesis, production of spermatozoa with abnormal morphology, reduction of sperm motility and viability and, more recently, with the occurrence of non-seminoma germ cell tumors...Several studies on human males smoking cannabis, reported a decrease in plasma levels of testosterone, FSH, and LH and this effect was also evident in animal studies after acute and chronic administration of THC. Decreased levels of testosterone correlate to an inhibitory effect of cannabinoids on male sexual behavior. Moreover *in vitro* studies on Leydig cells showed a decrease in testosterone secretion induced by THC.[1068]

[1067] Zaki S. Badawy et al., "Cannabinoids inhibit the respiration of human sperm," *Fertility and Sterility* 91 (2009): 2472-2476 (2474).
[1068] Paola Grimaldi, Daniele Di Giacomo and Raffaele Geremia, "The endocannabinoid system and spermatogenesis," *frontiers in Endocrinology* 4 (2013): 1-6 (1, 3).

- Stefan S. du Plessis, Ashok Agarwal, Arun Syriac, "Marijuana, phytocannabinoids, the endocannabinoid system, and male fertility," *J Assist Reprod Gene* 32 (2015): 1575-1588:

epidemiological and experimental studies have shown that episodic marijuana use has long been associated with decreased testosterone release, reduced sperm counts, motility, viability, morphology, and inhibition of the acrosome reaction in humans. All of these factors can have drastic implications in the long term with regards to impairing male reproduction as well as negatively impacting the offspring.

a number of animal studies have reported direct effects on various reproductive organs. Prolonged cannabis exposure reduced the ventral prostate, seminal vesicle, and epididymal weights in both rats and mice. These findings were accompanied by histological evidence showing disruption of the basement membrane, significant shrinkage of the seminiferous tubules marked by appearance of giant cells in their lumen, reduction in the number of spermatogonia, and furthermore spermatogenic cells showing degeneration, vacuolated/scanty cytoplasm, and small dense nuclei. It was also reported that testicular degeneration and necrosis was induced in dogs after only 30 days of cannabis administration. Results from various experiments of a very eloquent study not only showed a significant decrease in weight and increase in apoptosis of mice testes (in vivo) after cannabis treatment, but it also reports on significantly decreased testicular LH receptor (LHR) and FAAH expression, thus suggesting that cannabis has a direct action on testicular activity. Hypogonadism was also reported by Harclerode et al. A number of other animal studies correspondingly reported that THC reduces the activities of the enzymes, beta-glucuronidase, alpha-glucosidase, acid phosphatase, and fructose-6-phosphatase in a dose-related manner in the testis, prostate as well as in the epididymis. From these findings, it can be concluded that THC interfere with the normal physiology and functioning of the male reproductive organs.[1069]

- Tina Djernis Gundersen et al., "Association Between Use of Marijuana and Male Reproductive Hormones and Semen Quality: A Study Among 1,215 Healthy Young Men," *American Journal of Epidemiology* August 16, 2015: 1-9:

  Regular marijuana smoking more than once per week was associated with a 28% (...) lower sperm concentration and a 29% (...) lower total sperm count after adjustment for confounders...In this study on more than 1,200 healthy young men, of whom 45% had smoked marijuana during the past 3 months, we found associations between regular use of marijuana more than once per week during the past 3 months and reduced semen quality, whereas no adverse association was found for irregular use.[1070]

There are a number of studies which focused specifically on Black African populations. For example:

- EM Adu, OA Popoola and NA Adikema, "Serum Testosterone Level in Nigerian Marijuana and Cigarette Smokers," *African Journal of Cellular Pathology* 2 (2014): 35-39: In this study Nigerian scientists demonstrated that, between 30 marijuana smokers, 15 cigarette smokers and 25 controls, "There was a significant decrease (P<0.05) in testosterone level in marijuana smokers (5.33+/-3.5ng/ml) when compared with non-smokers (8.5+/-2.4ng/ml) but showed no significant difference statistically (P>0.05) when compared with cigarette smokers (5.4+/-5ng/ml)."

  Our results in this study show a statistically significant decrease in testosterone level in the mean of marijuana

---

[1069] Stefan S. du Plessis, Ashok Agarwal, Arun Syriac, "Marijuana, phytocannabinoids, the endocannabinoid system, and male fertility," *J Assist Reprod Gene* 32 (2015): 1575-1588 (1575).
[1070] Tina Djernis Gundersen et al., "Association Between Use of Marijuana and Male Reproductive Hormones and Semen Quality: A Study Among 1,215 Healthy Young Men," *American Journal of Epidemiology* August 16, 2015: 1-9.

smokers (5.35 ± 3.5ng/ml) when compared with non-smokers (8.5±2.4ng/ml). This is in accordance with the work of Kelodny et al., (1976) but in contrast with the work of Freidrich et al., (1990) who found no significant difference between the serum testosterone level of marijuana smokers and non-smokers. This decrease in testosterone can be attributed to inhibition of the Gonadotrophin Releasing Hormone (GnRH) pulse generator in the hypothalamus by Δ^9-THC (Murphy et al., 1994). Our study also showed no significant difference between the means of marijuana smokers (5.35± 3.5ng/ml) and cigarette smokers (5.4±1.5ng/ml) when compared (P>0.05)... Serum testosterone decrease following cigarette smoking is due to the presence of nicotine in cigarette smoke which produces free radical and causes oxidative stress thereby altering the biological system... Conclusively, it has be affirmed that both marijuana and cigarette smoking alter the reproductive endocrine organ of males which ultimately leads to low level of testosterone, an important androgen needed in spermatogenesis.

- R.E. Okosun, H.B. Osadolor, O. Uso and E.M. Adu, "Serum Testosterone Levels in Nigerian Male Marijuana and Cigarette Smokers," *JMBR: A Peer-reviewed Journal of Biomedical Sciences* 13 (2014): 93-98:

In this study, we report a significantly decreased (p ≤0.05) serum testosterone levels in marijuana smoking Nigerian males compared with non-smokers. This is in consonance with earlier reports elsewhere but at variance with others who observed that chronic use of marijuana have no significant effect on serum testosterone in the population studied. The decreased effect of marijuana on serum testosterone is attributed to inhibition of the gonadotrophin releasing hormone (GnRH) pulse generator in the hypothalamus by THC; an action mediated by central cannabinoid CB1 receptors located in the hypothalamus. CB1 Receptors have also been found in the testis and ovaries of experimental animals, suggesting a possible direct effect of cannabinoids on the gonads. Furthermore, THC inhibits binding of dihydrotestosterone (DHT) to the androgen receptors and noncannabinoid components of marijuana extract have been shown to bind estrogen receptors... The observed significantly higher BMI of marijuana users than those of cigarette smokers and non-smokers in our study is in agreement with the work [which] attributed this to the weight gain associated with marijuana smoking. Others have reported similar observation in patients on dronabinol; a drug that has THC as its basic component. This may be due to accumulation of breast tissue in men which results from increases in circulating estrogen/androgen ratio; a common feature with marijuana smokers. Marijuana has been associated with the development of gynecomastia in early case series, but a case control study shows no association. Nevertheless, given the effectsof marijuana on HPG axis in males, and the possibility that non-THC components of marijuana smoke have affinity for estrogen receptors, an association with gynecomastia appears plausible.

Our study also shows that cigarette smokers have significantly reduced testosterone levels compared with non- smokers. This corroborates the reports of earlier investigators.

- Rania Abd Elazeem et al. "Assessment of Serum Luteinizing hormone, Follicle-stimulating hormone and Testosterone Level among Sudanese Marijuana abuse People," *Scholars Bulletin* 1 (2015): 148-150. In this study Sudanese scientists tested 60 smokers and 60 controls 18-60 years old.

Alterations in endocrine function in conjunction with marijuana use have caused considerable concern. Researchers efforts in many investigation in the recent past have made it abundantly clear that exposure to marijuana had significant effects upon the reproductive system on both male and female, altered testicular function and depressed hormonal secretion, LH and FSH, secreted by pituitary in the male. The tetra hydro cannabinol induced blockage of gonadotropins release and results in lowered LH and FSH which are responsible for a reduced testosterone production by the leydig cells of the testes. Acute and chronic marijuana smoking resulted in decreased plasma testosterone and LH concentration and large doses produced oilgospermia with decreased FSH... Cannabis smoke is mutagenic, in vitro and in vivo thus also suggesting carcinogenicity. Chronic intensive use of marijuana may produce alteration in male reproductive physiology through central hypothalamus or pituitary action. Cannabinoid administration actually alters multiple hormonal systems, including the suppression of the gonadal steroids, growth hormone, prolactin, and thyroid hormone and the activation of the hypothalamic – pituitary – adrenal axis."

- B. Humphrey Osadolor and Orhue E. Samuel, "Evaluation of Some Reproductive Hormones and Liver Enzymes Amongst Male *Cannabis sativa* Smokers in Benin City, Nigeria," ***Journal of Harmonized Research*** 4 (2017): 36-39: Scientists from the University of Benin, Benin City, confirmed the effect of cannabis smoking on Black male testosterone levels using 200 smokers and 100 controls. They found that TET (testosterone), FSH, LH were "highly significantly decreased" in smokers compared to non-smokers: "This study indicates a gradual damage to the liver and an impaired fertility hormone of male marijuana smokers in Benin-city."

Table 1: Mean ± SEM of Fertility Hormones in Male Cannabis smokers and Non-smokers subject.

Parameter	Smokers	Non-smokers	P-value	Level of Significance
TET (ng/ml)	3.08±0.05	7.50±0.22	0.000	$P<0.001$
FSH (mIU/ml)	1.08±0.06	2.89±0.17	0.000	$P<0.001$
LH (mIU/ml)	2.85±0.07	4.41±0.20	0.000	$P<0.001$

This deleterious effect of marijuana smoking on testosterone levels in males has many consequences. In addition to low testosterone's well-known effect on sexuality, low T is also associated with mental disorders and cognitive impairment.[1071] Testosterone is "brain food" as several cerebral areas are strongly testosterone-dependent, such as the amygdala and the hypothalamus. "In hypogonadal (= low testosterone) men, there is a significant decrease in many cognitive functions, such as episodic memory, working memory, processing speed, visual spatial processing, and executive function, which are regulated by the androgen receptor-regulated regions of the brain...low testosterone

---

[1071] Giacomo Ciocca et al. "Is Testosterone a Food for the Brain," ***Sex Med Rev*** 4 (2016): 15-25.

levels...are responsible for a deterioration in cognitive functioning."[1072]

VI.   *Cortisol*

When humans are faced with psychological and physical stressors, the HPA axis is operationalized. A process is initiated in the hypothalamus that results in the ultimate release of cortisol into the bloodstream. Cortisol is the "stress hormone" or the "fight or flight" hormone. Although activation of the HPA axis is necessary to cope with acute, time-limited stressors, frequent or chronic HPA axis activation has been shown to have damaging effects. High cortisol levels are linked to stress and high anxiety. Once a stressor triggers the release of cortisol, the hormone is supposed to be spent by our body, either through our response to the threat or by using the hormone up through aerobic exercise, for example. If the cortisol doesn't get spent, it builds up in the body and poisons the body, causing a whole host of mental and physical disorders: lower immune function, reduced bone density, high blood pressure, depression, shortened life span, etc. But it also decreases *dominance* potential in a male.

Cortisol is the inhibitor of testosterone. The interplay of these two (T and C) is believed to regulate status related behavior. When testosterone efficiently influences behavior, it motivates status-related or dominance related behavior. Cortisol is said to inhibit the pathway from testosterone to behavior; it blocks testosterone's influence on dominance. High testosterone levels can facilitate dominance only when cortisol is low. When cortisol levels are high, cortisol blunts the impact of testosterone.[1073]

Marijuana has a significant impact on cortisol levels: smokers have been shown to have significantly higher levels

---

[1072] Ciocca et al. "Is Testosterone a Food for the Brain," 16.

[1073] Pranja H. Mehta and Robert A. Josephs, "Testosterone and cortisol jointly regulate dominance: Evidence for a dual-hormone hypothesis," **Hormones and Behavior** 58 (2010): 898-906; Pranja H. Mehta and Smrithi Prasad, "The dual-hormone hypothesis: a brief review and research agenda," **Current Opinion in Behavioral Sciences** 3 (2015): 163-168.

than non-smokers.[1074] In the lab setting administration of THC increases cortisol levels.[1075] "Contrary to the (suppressive) effect of THC on gonadotropins, prolactin, and thyrotropin, the apparent effect of THC on corticotropin, and hence, adrenal cortical activity, is activation."[1076]

In 2015 University of Michigan researchers, having tracked around 200 African Americans of the Flint, Michigan area from 9th grade to early adulthood, published a study announcing that "African American youth whose anxiety levels are elevated by the everyday struggles they encounter will overproduce the stress hormone cortisol into adulthood."[1077] Black *male* youth who transition to adulthood in inner cities filled with trauma and other stressors overproduce cortisol because the chronic stress triggers their HPA axis. As one of the authors of the study noted: "Living all their lives in a very stressful environment, which is associated with higher levels of anxiety, is not very good for the brains of these black youth, and such exposures will have long lasting effects, which is potentially preventable."[1078] Imagine these inner city Black youth coping with their stress and anxiety by smoking weed.

[1074] George R. King et al., "Altered Brain Activation During Visuomotor Integration in Chronic Active Cannabis Users: Relationship to Cortisol Levels," *The Journal of Neuroscience* 31 (2011): 17923–17931; European Society of Endocrinology, "Smoking marijuana may cause early puberty and stunts growth in boys," *Science Daily* May 18, 2015; Mohini Ranganathan et al., "The effects of cannabinoids on serum cortisol and prolactin in humans," *Psychopharmacology (Berl)* 203 (2009): 737-744.
[1075] Dr. Laura Murphy (Department of Physiology at Southern Illinois University), "Marijuana and endocrine function" in *Biology of Marijuana* ed. Emmnauel S. Onaivi (London and New York: Taylor & Francis, 2002) 351-361 (354-356).
[1076] Carol Grace Smith, "Effects of Marijuana on Neuroendocrine Function," in *Marijuana Research Findings: 1980*, ed. Robert C. Petersen (NIDA Research Monograph 31 June 1980; Rockville, Maryland: National Institute of Drug Abuse, 1981) 120-136 (122-123).
[1077] Shervin Assari et al., "Anxiety Symptoms During Adolescence Predicts Salivary Cortisol in Early Adulthood Among Blacks; Sex differences," *Int J Endocrinol Metab* 13 (2015): e18041.
[1078] "U-M finds anxiety impacts future cortisol production in gender specific ways," *M Prevention Research Center* November 4, 2015 @ https://news.umich.edu/u-m-finds-anxiety-impacts-future-cortisol-production-in-gender-specific-ways/

This would contribute to their already high cortisol levels. And high cortisol levels antagonize and even *neutralize* testosterone.

VII.   *Estrogenization*

We have shown that the global Black Man is the world's "Mr. T," as he possesses the highest levels of testosterone than any other population. However, the Black Man in America has been made into the world's "Mr. E," i.e. Mr. Estrogen, because our estrogen levels have been excessively elevated. Part of this estrogenization process involves smoking this Weaponized Weed.

Marijuana extracts were shown to possess effects like endocrine disrupting chemicals (EDCs), such as the inhibition of activity of the enzymes progesterone 17alpha-hydroxylase, testosterone 6beta- and 16alpha-hydroxylase as well as androstenedione formation. "These results indicate that there are some metabolic interactions between cannabinoid and steroid metabolism and that the constituents showing estrogen-like activity exists in marijuana."[1079] Among the chemicals in marijuana that produce EDC effects are the flavone apigenin found in the plant flowers and ß-sitosterol, a phytosterol found in the plant root in cannabis.[1080] Apigenin has low-to-moderate estrogenicity (it can bind to estrogen receptors) but high progestational (progesterone) activity.[1081]

β-Sitosterol has a chemical structure similar to that of cholesterol. It is classified as a phytoestrogen or plant-based estrogen because its chemical structure shares the same 4-ring structure as estradiol, the more potent of the estrogens. β-sitosterol can therefore bind to estrogen receptors. At certain

---

[1079] K. Watanabe et al., "Marijuana extracts possess the effects like the endocrine disrupting chemicals," **Toxicology** 206 (2005): 471-8.

[1080] John M. McPartland, "Cannabis and Cannabis Extracts: Greater Than the Sum of Their Parts?" **Journal of Cannabis Therapeutics** 1 (2001): 103-132 (106).

[1081] Rachel S. Rosenberg et al., "Steroid hormone activity of flavonoids and related compounds," **Breast Cancer Research and Treatment** 62 (2000): 35-49; George G.J.M. Kuiper et al., "Interaction of Estrogenic Chemicals and Phytoestrogens with Estrogen Receptor β," **Endocrinology** 139 (1998): 4252-4263; Marrk A. Sauer et al., "Marijuana: Interaction with the Estrogen Receptor," **The Journal of Pharmacology and Experimental Therapeutics** 224 (1983): 404-407;

levels β-sitosterol has thus been demonstrated to be an endocrine disrupter, though it disrupts endocrine system function primarily in a *non-estrogen-like* manner. β-sitosterol can interfere with the production of both *testosterone in males* and *estrogen in females* by disrupting cholesterol concentration, thus decreasing the synthesis of steroid hormones (hormones made from cholesterol) like testosterone and estrogen. In addition, β-sitosterol can block in men the metabolism of dihydrotestosterone (DHT), the most potent form of testosterone in the male. β-sitosterol has already been implicated in gender-neutering fish and is officially classified as an Endocrine Disrupting Chemical (EDC).[1082] Hemp oil, for example, has 100-148mg of β-sitosterol.

Also estrogenic is the marijuana smoke produced when we light up. As Lee, Oh and Chung report:

> Marijuana smokers are actually exposed to not only marijuana plant elements, such as cannabinoids, but also the numerous components generated by marijuana cigarettes while they are smoking...Marijuana produces...numerous other compounds due to the heat generated during smoking. These pyrogenic chemicals, some of which are estrogenic, disturb the steroid system and have harmful effects on human health...[O]ur research clearly confirmed that smoking marijuana has an [estrogen receptor]-mediated estrogenic effect on the

---

[1082] M.I. Qasimi, K. Nagaoka, G. Watanabe, "Feeding of phytosterols reduced testosterone production by modulating GnRH and GnIH expression in the brain and testes of male Japanese quail (*Coturnix coturnix japonica*)," **Poultry Science** 97 (2018):1066–1072; Singh, K., and R. Gupta, "Antifertility activity of β-sitosterol isolated from *Barleria Prionitis* (L.) roots in male albino rats," **Int. J. Pharm. Pharma. Sci.** 8 (2016):88–96; Rainie L. Sharpe, Melissa Drolet and Deborah L. MacLatchy, "Investigation of de novo cholesterol synthetic capacity in the gonads of goldfish (Carassius auratus) exposed to the phytosterol beta-sitosterol," **Reproductive Biology and Endocrinology** 4 (2006): 1-11; **Environmental Endocrine Disrupters: An Evolutionary Perspective**, ed. Louis J. Guillette and D. Andrew Crain (New York: Taylor & Francis, 2005) 245-246; D.L. MacLatchy and G.L. van der Kraak, "The phytoestrogen beta-sitosterol alters the reproductive endocrine status of goldfish," **Toxicol Appl Pharmacol** 134 (1995): 305-12; S. Hendrich, "Phytoestrogens and phytosterols," in **Endocrine-disrupting chemicals in food**, ed. Ian Shaw (Oxford: Woodhead Publishing Limited, 2009) 444ff.

endocrine system, and that this effect is mostly caused not by the cannabinoid compounds themselves but by the complex ingredients generated by smoking marijuana. Furthermore, the in vivo results demonstrated the estrogenic activity of MSC and strongly supports our findings...Therefore, these results suggest that marijuana abuse is considered an endocrine-disrupting factor, and that the phenolic compounds are the causative chemicals responsible for the estrogenic effect of MSC.[1083]

Excursus: Paraquat and Atrazine

In 1975 the U.S. State Department paid Mexico to spray a dangerous weed killer called paraquat on Mexican marijuana fields.[1084] Much of American weed comes from Mexico via California. Paraquat, produced by the chemical giant Syngenta based in Basel, Switzerland, can not only cause severe lung damage when inhaled and death when ingested; a growing body of research has also linked it to the onset of Parkinson's disease.[1085] The Reagan administration began spraying the poison domestically on pot fields in national parks,[1086] and as recently as 2003 street marijuana tested positive for paraquat contamination.[1087]

What does this have to do with Black people? Paraquat is a toxic chemical with a strong melanin affinity, meaning it

---

[1083] Soo Yeun Lee, Seung Min Oh and Kyu Hyuck Chung, "Estrogenic effects of marijuana smoke condensate and cannabinoid compounds," *Toxicology and Applied Pharmacology* 214 (2006): 270-278 (270).

[1084] "Panic over Paraquat," *Time Magazine* May 1, 1978; John Trux and Lee Torrey, "Poison Pot Probe," *New Scientist* April 27, 1978, pp. 242-243.

[1085] Danny Hakim, "This Pesticide Is Prohibited in Britain. Why Is It Still Being Exported," *The New York Times* December 20, 2016; Andrew C. Revkin, "Paraquat: A Potent Weed Killer is Killing People," *Science Digest* 91 (1983): 36-38, 42, 100-104.

[1086] Poisoning Pot – and People," *The New York Times* August 19, 1983; Dale Russakoff, "Use of Paraquat to Kill Marijuana Stirs Protests," *The Washington Post* August 25, 1983; "U.S. to Resume Using Paraquat on Marijuana," *The New York Times* July 14, 1988.

[1087] "Govt. Tests for Toxic Paraquat on US Marijuana Supply According to ProCon.org FOIA Request," *ProCon.org* January 15, 2009; Michael Isikoff, "DEA Finds Herbicides in Marijuana Samples," *The Washington Post* July 26, 1989.

binds on melanin. Melanin is a naturally occurring pigment that colors hair, skin, and eyes. There is also melanin in the brain. This neuromelanin is mainly produced in the part of the brain called the substantia nigra. Paraquat binds and accumulates on melanin and the toxicant is gradually released into the cytosol (the aqueous component of the cytoplasm of a cell), causing damage to the melanin-containing tissue.[1088] Paraquat is believed to damage the melanated brain tissue of the substantia nigra, contributing to the onset of Parkinson's.[1089] Black people are of course the most melanated people on the planet, and this toxic chemical remains in Black bodies throughout life causing many physical and mental disorders.[1090] Paraquat's strong melanin affinity therefore makes paraquat contaminated weed effectively an ethnic weapon, causing particular damage to Black (melanated) people.

Syngenta, the Swiss company that makes paraquat, also makes another wicked pesticide: atrazine. In wildlife atrazine causes the reduction of androgen (the male hormone) and elevation of estrogen (the female hormone) and thus demasculinizes males of various species, including humans.[1091] Dr. Tyrone Hayes, integrative biologist from the University of California, Berkeley, has demonstrated that in lower species atrazine completely reverses sex, physically feminizing male African clawed frogs, for example. Atrazine is not only used on America's largest crop, corn, but it is also the most detected pesticide contaminant of ground, surface, and drinking water therefore exposing humans to the chemical's feminizing effects.

[1088] B. Larsson, A. Oskarsson and H. Tjälve, "Binding of Paraquat and Diquat on Melanin," *Exp. Eye Res.* 25 (1977): 353-359.

[1089] Oskar Karlsson and Nils Gunnar Lindquist, "Melanin affinity and its possible role in neurodegeneration," *Journal of Neural Transmission* July 3, 2013.

[1090] Carol Barnes, *Melanin: The Chemical Key to Black Greatness* (Chicago: Lushena Books, Inc., 1988) 2.

[1091] Tyrone B. Hayes, "There Is No Denying This: Defusing the Confusion about Atrazine," *BioScience* 54 (2004): 1138-1149; Tyrone B. Hayes et al, "Atrazine induces complete feminization and chemical castration in male African clawed frogs (*Xenopus laevis*)," *PNAS* 107 (2010): 4612-4617; Tyrone B. Hayes et al, "Demasculinization and feminization of male gonads by atrazine: Consistent effects across vertebrate classes," *Journal of Steroid Biochemistry and Molecular Biology* 127 (2011): 64-73.

Chapter Nineteen

How Weaponized Weed
Feminizes the Black Male
And Masculinizes the Black Female

I.   *Biochemical Feminization*

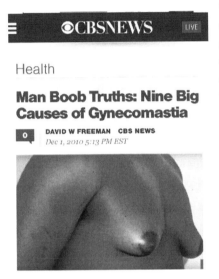

CBSNEWS LIVE

Health

Man Boob Truths: Nine Big Causes of Gynecomastia

DAVID W FREEMAN   CBS NEWS
Dec 1, 2010 5:13 PM EST

The endocrine effects of this weaponized weed on males – diminished testosterone, elevated cortisol, lowered serotonin, and elevated estrogen exposure – produces a biochemical profile that is more feminine and less masculine. Youth who begin smoking early are most susceptible to gender-disrupting effects. As Marry Brett notes correctly: "A boy of 16, smoking cannabis (marijuana) since the age of 11, suffered from retarded development of the secondary sexual characteristics and growth."[1092] Male secondary sexual characteristics (vs. female) include such things as:

More body hair
Heavier skull and bone structure
Increased muscle mass
Larger bodies, hands, feet and nose
Broader shoulders

Traditional masculinity is characterized by a more robust physique compared to the more delicate frame of the female.

[1092] Mary Brett, "Cannabis and the Reproductive System, Pregnancy and Development of Children (2015)" @ https://www.cannabisskunksense.co.uk/uploads/site-files/Cannabis_and_the_Reproductive_system_July_2015.pdf.

However, long-time weed smokers who started indulging early tend to have a markedly less robust and more delicate physical frame – think of the rappers Snoop Dogg, Wiz Khalifa, and Young Dolph.

THC has an anti-androgenic potency in that it can antagonize biochemical changes produced by testosterone on DNA, RNA and protein content. As S.P. Ghosh, T.K. Chatterjee and J.J. Chosh report:

> Marihuana and its psychoactive constituent delta-9-tetrahydrocannabinol (THC) have been implicated in the alteration of male reproductive functions. This drug reduces plasma testosterone concentrations in rats and men (...), inhibits testosterone secretion (...), alters glucose metabolism (...) and marker proteins of testicular tissue (...), suppresses spermatogenesis and produces change in sperm head proteins (...). In man, reduced sexual potency and gynaecomastia (...) have also been reported in heavy marihuana users. A reduction in certain androgen-dependent behavioural responses, copulatory behaviour in male rats and mice (...) and reduced weight of testes and accessory reproductive organs (...) has also been observed.[1093]

Long-time weed-smoking can feminize the body more overtly as well through the development of male breasts, a condition called gynecomastia, which is the accumulation of breast tissue in men due to increase of the estrogen:androgen ratio. A connection between chronic marijuana use and gynecomastia has been established due to the estrogenization of the body caused by the phenols in the weed smoke as well as the estrogenic chemicals in the plant itself.[1094] Dr. Adrian Lo, plastic

---

[1093] S.P. Ghosh, T.K. Chatterjee and J.J. Chosh, "Antiandrogenic effect of delta-9-tetrahydrocannabinol in adult castrated rats," *J. Reprod. Fert.* 62 (1981): 513-517.

[1094] J. Harmon, MA Aliapoulios, "Gynecomastia in marihuana users," *N Engl J Med.* 18 (1972) :936; idem, "Marijuana-induced gynecomastia: clinical and laboratory experience," *Surg Forum.* 25 (1974):423-5; Rebekah C. Allen et al., "Marinol-Induced

surgeon at Pennsylvania Hospital who specializes in breast reduction in men, noted

> "What we're left with are doctors, endocrinologists, and surgeons with clinical acumen saying we notice a trend," he says. Of the 100 or so patients who come to him for breast surgeries each year, more than one-third report regular marijuana use. "Some men are more susceptible to gynecomastia than others," he says.[1095]

II.   Non-Physical Feminization: Emotionalism

One of the chief characteristics of the feminized Black male is not necessarily homosexuality (though of course that applies); rather, it is hyperemotionality.

While the statement, "women are more emotional than men" stands true, this should not imply that men don't naturally have and display emotion.[1096] Rather, behavioral research has demonstrated that males have a higher capability of *regulating* their emotions, and this capability has a sex-related neuroanatomical basis.[1097] The male and female brains differ in architecture and activity, showing variation in structure, chemistry and function. The two brains are wired differently, particularly in areas that control emotion.[1098] Men and women

---

Gynecomastia: A Case Report," **The American Journal of Medicine** 120 (2007): e1.

[1095] Melissa Dribben, "Male Breast Growth and Pot," **Philly.Com** Sunday, November 24, 2013.

[1096] Ann M. Kring and Albert H. Gordon, "Sex Differences in Emotion: Expression, Experience, and Physiology," **Journal of Personality and Social Psychology** 74 (1998): 686-703.

[1097] Feng Kong, "Sex-Related Neuroanatomical Basis of Emotion Regulation Ability," **PLOS ONE** 9 (2014): 1-7.

[1098] Stuart J. Ritchie et al., "Sex Differences in Adult Human Brain: Evidence from 5216 UK Biobank Participants," **Cerebral Cortex** 28 (2018): 2959-275; Amber N.V. Ruigrok et al., "A meta-analysis of sex differences in human brain structure," **Neuroscience and Biobehavioral Reviews** 39 (2014): 34-50; Zeenat F. Zaidi, "Gender Differences in Human Brain: A Review," **The Open Anatomy Journal** 2 (2010): 37-55; Mark Prigg, "Men really DO have bigger brains: The amazing image that reveals just how male and female brains are wired differently," **Daily Mail** February 11, 2014; Larry Cahill, "His Brain, Her Brain," **Scientific American Mind** 292 (2005): 40-47.

have different emotional profiles.[1099] The field of affective neuroscience has helped us understand the neurobiology of emotion. It is believed now that men and women recruit different neural networks for emotional processing.[1100] The most compelling evidence for sex differences in emotion exists in the domain of negative emotions. Observational data of women's written and verbal behavior tends to find women express more negative emotion than men. Women respond more strongly to negative emotional stimuli than men.

Cerebral blood flow (CBF) refers to the supply of blood to the brain in a given period of time. Before puberty CBF decreased similarly in males and females. However, during puberty males and females diverge in this regard: CBF levels continue to decrease in males but reverse course in females and starts to increase. Thus, women have a notably higher CBF than men,[1101] particularly in the "emotional" areas of the brain such as the limbic cortex which manages mood and anxiety and the prefrontal cortex which helps control impulses and maintain focus. Elevated CBF in the orbitofrontal cortex (part of the prefrontal cortex) help make women empathetic while decreased blood flow makes men apathetic and indifferent. Men have more blood flow in visual and coordination centers of the brain.

Higher blood flow in emotional brain regions such as the left amygdala is associated with higher levels of anxiety and

---

[1099] TMC Lee et al., "Neural activities associated with emotion recognition observed in men and women," *Molecular Psychiatry* 10 (2005): 450-455; Larry Cahill et al., "Sex-Related Hemispheric Lateralization of Amygdala Function in Emotionally Influenced Memory: An fMRI Investigation," *Learning & Memory* 11 (2004): 261-266; Larry Cahill et al., "Sex-Related Difference in Amygdala Activity during Emotionally Influenced Memory Storage," *Neurobiology of Learning and Memory* 75 (2001): 1-9.

[1100] G. Einstein, J. Downar and S.H. Kennedy, "Gender/sex differences in emotions," *Medicographia* 35 (2013): 271-280; Stephan Hamann, "Sex Differences in the Responses of the Human Amygdala," *The Neuroscientist* 11 (2005): 288-293.

[1101] Shweta Iyer, "Cerebral Blood Flow Changes During Puberty Differentiate Emotions Among Men and Women," *Medical Daily* May 26, 2014; Guido Rodriguez et al., "Sex Differences in Regional Cerebral Blood Flow," *Journal of Cerebral Blood Flow and Metabolism* 8 (1988): 783-789.

mood symptoms, i.e. emotionality, in females.[1102] Women have approximately two times the risk of these as men.[1103] Women are up to three times more likely than men to develop major depressive disorder in response to a stressful event, and women show a greater number of severe depressive symptoms than men. Women attempt suicide three times more than men.

Weaponized Weed can cause in men a female emotional profile. While CBD has been shown to be anxiolytic (anxiety inhibiting), THC has been associated with an increase of anxiety.[1104] Marijuana smoking has been associated with a significant increase in CBF, and plasma levels of THC and CBF have been shown to correlate significantly.[1105] There is a particular increase of CBF in brains regions with extensive interconnections with the limbic system (the "emotional brain").[1106] As Professor Ester Fride, in the Department of Behavioral Sciences at the College of Judea and Samaria, Israel, and Dr. M. Clara Sanudo-Pena, from Brown University's Schrier Research Laboratory, Department of Psychology, reported in 2002:

> We have shown that following marijuana intoxication (both after smoking and after infusion of THC) there are significant increases in CBF over most of the brain. However, there are clear regional differences, and in particular in the frontal cortex, cingulate and cerebellum...Analyses indicated a significant

---

[1102] Antonia N. Kaczkurkin et al., "Elevated Amygdala Perfusion Mediates Developmental Sex Differences in Trait Anxiety," **Biol Psychiatry** 80 (2016): 775-785.

[1103] Jennifer S. Stevens and Stephan Hamann, "Sex differences in brain activation to emotional stimuli: A meta-analysis of neuroimaging studies," **Neuropsychologia** 50 (2012): 1578-1593.

[1104] Paolo Fusar-Poli et al., "Distinct Effects of $\triangle$9-Tetrahydrocannabinol and Cannabidiol on Neural Activation During Emotional Processing," **Arch Gen Psychiatry** 66 (2009): 95-105.

[1105] Ronald I. Herning et al., "Cerebrovascular perfusion in marijuana users during a month of monitored abstinence," **Neurology** 64 (2005): 488-493; Katharine Davis, "Marijuana makes blood rush to the head," **Daily News** 7 February 2005; Roy J. Mathew, "Regional Cerebral Blood Flow After Marijuana Smoking," **Journal of Cerebral Blood Flow and Metabolism** 12 (1992): 750-758;

[1106] Daniel S. O'Leary et al., "Effects of Smoking Marijuana on Brain Perfusion and Cognition," **Neuropsychopharmacology** 26 (2002): 802-816.

relationship to age of first use of marijuana for height, weight, global CBF and percentages of ray matter volume...the mean CBF for males who started smoking before age 17 was significantly higher than males who started after 17, and their mean CBF *was not different from females*...THC also has an inhibitory effect on serum testosterone levels, and it has been shown to reduce testicular weight...Of interest here also would be the possible effects of marijuana on sexual differentiation of the brain. It has been demonstrated that there are sexually dimorphic structural differences in the normal human brain. It is generally recognized that normal brain development follows a different course depending on sex. Sexual differences in brain organization are dependent on hormone levels occurring at critical periods. Prenatal exposure to marijuana administered to female rats has been shown to alter gonadal function. Studies show the testes actively produce hormones beginning in utero, and marijuana has been reported to decrease plasma levels of testosterone. Marijuana has been shown to have significant effects on weight (smaller), height (shorter) and head circumference (smaller) of newborns to mothers' who used it during pregnancy and while breast feeding. It is interesting to note that males may be more at risk of the effects of drugs because of the effects on hormones...It is the application of male hormones that masculinize the brain. It is in this context that we wish to note that males who start (smoking marijuana) early *have a more female like global CBF.* It is generally accepted that females have a higher resting CBF than males, and in the present study this expected main effect of sex was confirmed. However, *CBF of males who started using marijuana early was not different from females,* but was significantly higher than males who started smoking after age 17.[1107]

On the other hand, marijuana smoking has been shown to *decrease* regional CBF in brain regions involved in attentional modulation of sensory processing. What we perceive and our ability to behaviorally respond to what we perceive in an appropriate manner depends critically on our ability to direct our attention, i.e. the speed and accuracy of our focus, and the efficiency in reducing interference from non-relevant distractions in the environment. There are brain regions that appear to control attention modulation, and studies show that marijuana smoking dampens these processes by decreasing the

---

[1107] M. Clara Sañudo-Peña and Ester Fride, "Marijuana and movement disorders," in **Biology of Marijuana** ed. Emmnauel S. Onaivi (London and New York: Taylor & Francis, 2002) 288-290.

blood flow in these areas. [1108] For example, a 2016 large scale brain imaging study of 1000 marijuana users demonstrated deficient blood flow compared to controls in the hippocampus, the brain's key memory, *learning*, and *attention* center, and this distinguished the marijuana users.[1109] Thus, marijuana use can intensify the "emotional brain" and dampen the critical brain.

III.   Marijuana and the Masculinization of the Female

While in males THC is an antiandrogen that lowers male testosterone and marijuana smoke is estrogenic, Shuso Takeda et al. suggests that THC "may exhibit endocrine-disrupting effects as an antiestrogen"[1110] as well. In females THC is *antiestrogenic* and disrupts normal estrogen and progesterone production and it raises female testosterone.[1111] Estrogen and progesterone are responsible for production of the female reproductive tract and female secondary sex characteristics (e.g. breast enlargement, lower waist to hip ratio, fat distribution, wider hips, etc.). By decreasing a woman's feminine hormones and increasing her masculine hormones, smoking weed can lead to levels of masculinization of the female and female infertility. In addition, it has been demonstrated that THC has anti-estrogenic activity in that THC abrogates estrogen receptor A (ERα) signaling and interferes with ERα-mediated transcriptional activation by up-regulating the activity of estrogen receptor B (ERβ), which is a repressor of ERα's activity.

[1108] O'Leary et al., "Effects of Smoking Marijuana on Brain Perfusion and Cognition";

[1109] Daniel G. Amen et al., "Discriminative Properties of Hippocampal Hypoperfusion in Marijuana Users Compared to Healthy Controls: Implications for Marijuana Administration in Alzheimer's Dementia," *Journal of Alzheimer's Disease* 56(2016):1-13.

[1110] Shuso Takeda et al., "△9-Tetrahydrocannabinol Disrupts Estrogen-Signaling through Up-Regulation of Estrigen Receptor β (ERβ)," *Chemical Research Toxicology* 26 (2013): 1073-1079;

[1111] Lisa K. Brents, "Marijuana, the Endocannabinoid System and the Female Reproductive System," *Yale Journal of Biology and Medicine* 89 (2016): 175-191 (1975); Hailing Wang, Sudhansu K. Dey, and Mauro Maccarrone, "Jekyll and Hyde: Two Faces of Cannabinoid Signaling in Male and Female Fertility," Endocrine Reviews (2006): 427-448 (428).

- Shuso Takeda, "$\triangle^9$-Tetrahydrocannabinol Targeting Estrogen Receptor Signaling: The Possible Mechanism of Action Coupled with Endocrine Disruption," *Bio. Pharm. Bull.* 37 (2014): 1435-1438.

Among Δ^9-THC's biological activities, its recognized endocrine-disrupting effects, including anti-estrogenic activity, have been the subjects of previous investigations. It has been reported that chronic oral administration of marijuana resin is able to reduce fertility in female rats. An influence of Δ^9-THC on reproductive behavior has been suspected for at least 40 years: mechanistically in females, Δ^9-THC modulates the estrous cycle and inhibits ovulation, and in males, Δ^9-THC attenuates the mobility of mouse sperm. A Δ^9-THC inhibitory effect on ovulation is also suggested in the case of the human female... Although the benefits of Δ^9-THC are apparent as an adjuvant in the treatment of cancer-related side effects during cancer chemotherapy, the recent results reported here also suggest that the cannabinoid has endocrine-disrupting potential through the possible up-regulation of ERβ. Δ^9-THC may have inhibitory effects on breast cancer cell proliferation by means of up-regulation of ERβ (possibly through the formation of inhibitory ERα/ERβ dimers) if Δ^9-THC is selectively accumulated in cancer cells. On the other hand, at the same time, Δ^9-THC may disrupt the balanced relationship between ERα and ERβ *via* up-regulation of the β type ER in normal cells, since Δ^9-THC can be accumulated up to 20-fold in some tissues (*i.e.*, fat tissue) due to its highly lipophilic nature. In addition to the recreational use of marijuana, the clinical use of Δ^9-THC (dronabinol) may give rise to adverse effects on the endocrine system. We suggest that Δ^9-THC may be categorized as an EDC, but clearly, further studies coupled with *in vivo* experiments are needed to validate our hypothesis presented here. [1112]

[1112] Shuso Takeda, "$\triangle^9$-Tetrahydrocannabinol Targeting Estrogen Receptor Signaling: The Possible Mechanism of Action Coupled with Endocrine Disruption," *Bio. Pharm. Bull.* 37 (2014): 1435-1438.

- Lisa K. Brents, "Marijuana, the Endocannabinoid System and the Female Reproductive System," *Yale Journal of Biology and Medicine* 89 (2016): 175-191:

  findings from human and animal studies suggest that acute Δ^9-THC suppresses the release of gonadotropin-releasing hormone (GnRH) and thyrotropinreleasing hormone (TRH) from the hypothalamus, preventing these hormones from stimulating the release of prolactin and the gonadotropins, follicle stimulating hormone (FSH) and luteinizing hormone (LH), from the anterior pituitary. The gonadotropins maintain the menstrual cycle by promoting ovarian follicle maturation, stimulating production of the ovarian steroids estradiol and progesterone, and inducing ovulation, and alterations in circulating gonadotropin can disrupt these processes... daily administration of $\Delta 9$-THC (2.5 mg/kg iM) throughout the follicular phase disrupted follicle development, decreased estrogen and progesterone production, blocked LH surge and prevented ovulation, which was rescued by mid-cycle gonadotropin administration.[1113]

- Laura Murphy, "Marijuana and endocrine function" in *Biology of Marijuana* ed. Emmnauel S. Onaivi (London and New York: Taylor & Francis, 2002) 353:

  The gonadotropins LH and FSH in the female, when released from the anterior pituitary gland, act on the ovaries to stimulate the synthesis and release of the sex steroids estrogen and progesterone, and maintain folliculogenesis...The effects of THC exposure during the different phases of the menstrual cycle have been studied in both humans and monkeys. When a marijuana cigarette was smoked by women during the luteal phase, there was a 30% suppression of plasma LH levels within an hour of smoking when compared to placebo-smoking control subjects (...). However, there were no changes in plasma LH levels following marijuana smoking by women in their follicular phase of the cycle (...), or in post-menopausal women (...)...In the rhesus monkey, an acute injection of THC during the luteal phase of the menstrual cycle significantly reduced circulating progesterone levels (...). When THC was administered for 18 days during the follicular and

---

[1113] Brents, "Marijuana, the Endocannabinoid System and the Female Reproductive System," 180.

457

preovulatory phases of the monkey's menstrual cycle, the preovulatory estrogen and LH surges were blocked and ovulation did not occur during the treatment cycle or in the following post-treatment cycle (...). The long-term exposure of female monkeys to thrice weekly injections of THC resulted in a disruption of menstrual cycles that lasted for several months and was characterized by decreased LH and sex steroid hormone levels and anovulation (...).[1114]

- Jack Harclerode, "The Effect of Marijuana on Reproduction and Development," in *Marijuana Research Findings: 1980*, ed. Robert C. Petersen (NIDA Research Monograph 31 June 1980; Rockville, Maryland: National Institute of Drug Abuse, 1981) 137-154ff (144):

Cannabinoids also affect the ovary, for studies have shown an atrophy in ovarian function, including a decrease in ovarian weight and changes in rat vaginal smears which indicated a complete halt of the ovarian cycle...Other changes included inhibition of luetinization and corpus luteum degeneration along with a decrease in uterine RNA, protein and glycogen content...At least some of the changes that occur in the female reproductive tract caused by cannabinoids can partially be explained by their depressive action on LH secretion with the subsequent reduction of estrogen secretion by the ovary...These changes were probably caused by lowered estrogen production in the ovary caused by the cannabinoids' action to depress gonadotropin re- lease from the pituitary.[1115]

- Dr. Joan Bauman in *Health Consequences of Marihuana Use. Hearings Before the Subcommittee on Criminal Justice of the Committee on the Judiciary United States Senate. Ninety-Sixth Congress. Second Session*

[1114] Dr. Laura Murphy (Department of Physiology at Southern Illinois University), "Marijuana and endocrine function" in *Biology of Marijuana* ed. Emmnauel S. Onaivi (London and New York: Taylor & Francis, 2002) 353.

[1115] Jack Harclerode, "The Effect of Marijuana on Reproduction and Development," in *Marijuana Research Findings: 1980*, ed. Robert C. Petersen (NIDA Research Monograph 31 June 1980; Rockville, Maryland: National Institute of Drug Abuse, 1981) 137-154ff (144).

on Marihuana Usage. January 16 and 17, 1980 83-84:

> Mean serum testosterone levels were significantly higher in (female) marihuana users than in controls. Previous reports from our laboratory suggested that the chronic use of marihuana lowers plasma testosterone in young adult males. This apparent inconsistency is most likely attributable to differences in sites of androgen synthesis in men and women; almost all circulating testosterone derives from the gonads in men, whereas in women a large fraction of testosterone production is of adrenocortical origin...marihuana has been shown...to stimulate the pituitary-adrenal axis.[1116]

IV.   *Don't Smoke Weed While Pregnant (Assault in the Womb)*

Experiments with radioactively labelled THC (enabling its progress through the body to be traced) clearly indicate that the drug appears in the milk of nursing monkey mothers and in their offspring when the drug is administered to the mothers. There is also good evidence that THC and other cannabinoids pass through the placental barrier, reaching the fetus during uterine development where they tend to concentrate in the fetus's fatty tissue (including the brain).[1117]

Because THC crosses the placenta easily, when a pregnant mother uses marijuana, so does her child. And in states where marijuana use has been legalized, an increasing number of pregnant women and girls are turning to marijuana to alleviate nausea and other symptoms. Dispensaries are even marketing their product to pregnant women for morning sickness. The largest growing group is young, Black pregnant girls. According to **Reuters** "Adolescent girls are more than twice as likely to smoke marijuana if they're pregnant, a U.S.

[1116] Dr. Joan Bauman in **Health Consequences of Marihuana Use. Hearings Before the Subcommittee on Criminal Justice of the Committee on the Judiciary United States Senate. Ninety-Sixth Congress. Second Session on Marihuana Usage. January 16 and 17, 1980** 83-84.

[1117] **Marijuana and Health. Eighth Annual Report to the U.S. Congress From the Secretary of Health, Education, and Welfare 1980** (Rockville, Maryland: National Institute on Drug Abuse, 1981) 16-17.

study suggests...Among pregnant women, black women were more likely to report marijuana use than other racial and ethnic groups."[1118] While in earlier years there was some ambiguity and controversy over the effects of marijuana use on the fetus, today the picture is much clearer. *The New York Times* summarized in 2017:

> Often pregnant women presume that cannabis has no consequences for developing infants. But preliminary research suggests otherwise: Marijuana's main psychoactive ingredient — tetrahydrocannabinol, or THC — can cross the placenta to reach the fetus, experts say, potentially harming brain development, cognition and birth weight. THC can also be present in breast milk...
>
> In Pittsburgh, 6-year-olds born to mothers who had smoked one joint or more daily in the first trimester showed a decreased ability to understand concepts in listening and reading. At age 10, children exposed to THC in utero were more impulsive than other children and less able to focus their attention...
>
> "Prenatal exposure can affect the adolescent pretty significantly," said Dr. Lauren M. Jansson, the director of pediatrics at the Center for Addiction and Pregnancy at the Johns Hopkins University School of Medicine.
>
> Several studies have found changes in the brains of fetuses, 18 to 22 weeks old, linked to maternal marijuana use. In male fetuses who were exposed, for instance, researchers have noted abnormal function of the amygdala, the part of the brain that regulates emotion.
>
> "Even early in development, marijuana is changing critical circuits and neurotransmitting receptors," said Dr. Yasmin Hurd, a neuroscientist and the director of the addiction center at Icahn School of Medicine at Mount Sinai in Manhattan. "Those are important for regulation of emotions and reward, even motor function and cognition"...
>
> So far, prenatal cannabis exposure does not appear to be linked to obvious birth defects. "That's why some providers and lay people alike think there's no effect," said Dr. Erica Wymore, a

---

[1118] Lisa Rapaport, "Pregnant teens more likely to smoke pot than other girls," *Reuters* April 17, 2017; Nora D. Volkow, "Self-reported Medical and Nonmedical Cannabis Use Among Pregnant Women in the United States," *JAMA* 322(2019): 167-169.

neonatologist at Children's Hospital Colorado. But she warned, "Just because they don't have a major birth defect or overt withdrawal symptoms doesn't mean the baby's neurological development is not impacted."

Most research in this area was done when the drug was far less potent. Marijuana had 12 percent THC in 2014, while in 1995 it was just 4 percent, according to the National Institute on Drug Abuse.[1119]

Patrizia Campolongo et al. report as well.

In recent years, both clinical and preclinical studies have shown that exposure to cannabis preparations during pregnancy and lactation can induce behavioral teratogenic consequences...since the endocannabinoid system is present and already functional in early pregnancy (...), the active ingredients of cannabis and their metabolites could directly affect the brain by altering endocannabinoid signaling and related neurotransmitter and neuroendocrine systems.

A common problem in neurobehavioral teratology is that the identification of subtle neurodevelopmental phenotypes after exposure to drugs of abuse during pregnancy and lactation is often elusive (...). The effects of drugs that alter brain development without a physical phenotype or an easily identified neurodevelopmental behavioral phenotype such as seizures or retardation may go undetected and under- reported, despite significant impact on brain development and behavior...

Clinical studies have shown that cannabis use during pregnancy induces selective, deleterious effects on executive functions in the offspring both at childhood and adolescence (...). Executive functions comprise capacities such as cognitive flexibility, sustained and focused attention, and working memory. The deficits in executive functions induced by prenatal cannabis exposure seem to be long lasting, since 18–22-year-old young adults exposed to cannabis in utero also showed altered neuronal functioning during visuospatial working memory processing...the cognitive impairments observed in THC-exposed adult offspring were associated with long-lasting alterations in the cortical expression of genes related to glutamatergic neurotransmission, together with a decrease in the cortical extracellular levels of this neurotransmitter (...).

[1119] Catherine Saint Louis, "Pregnant Women Turn to Marijuana, Perhaps Harming Infants," *The New York Times* February 2, 2017.

Taken together, these preclinical studies show that maternal cannabis exposure alters cognitive performances in the adult offspring, and strongly suggest that changes in glutamatergic neurotransmission might be responsible for these effects...We demonstrated that perinatal exposure to THC (5 mg/kg, per os, from gestational day 15 to postnatal day 9) induced long-lasting changes in the emotional reactivity of the offspring (...).[1120]

A 2014 study demonstrated that fetal exposure to THC caused permanent neurobehavioral and cognitive impairments, including disruption of endocannabinoid signaling, the degradation of axon morphology (axons are the long threadlike part of a nerve cell along which impulses are conducted to other cells), and thus the "[permanent impairment of] the wiring diagram of neuronal networks during corticogenesis," as well as reduced levels of stathmin-2, a protein involved in learning and memory.[1121] In 2018 it was reported that DNA of sperm is altered by THC, possibly impacting the health of a future baby.[1122] Studies also show that the degrading effects of fetal exposure has epigenetic consequences as well, with the metabolic and behavioral effects of THC visiting sons three generations down.[1123]

Prenatal exposure to Weaponized Weed is also capable of feminizing the male offspring and masculinizing female offspring. As Ester Fride and M. Clara Sañudo-Peña document:

[1120] Patrizia Campolongo et al., "Developmental consequences of perinatal cannabis exposure: behavioral and neuroendocrine effects in adult rodents," *Psychopharmacology* 214 (2011): 5-15.

[1121] Giuseppe Tortoriello et al., "Miswiring the brain: "$\triangle^9$-Tetrahydrocannabinol disrupts cortical development by inducing an SCG10/stathmin-2 degradation pathway," *The EMBO Journal* January 27, 2014.

[1122] Susan Murphy et al., "Cannabinoid exposure and altered DNA methylation in rat and human sperm," *Epigenetics* 13 (2018): 1208–1221.

[1123] Henrietta Szutorisz and Yasmin L. Hurd, "Epigenetic Effects of Cannabis Exposure," *Biol Psychiatry* 79 (2016): 586-594; idem, "High times for cannabis: Epigenetic imprint and its legacy on brain and behavior," *Neuroscience and Biobehavioral Reviews* (2017): 1-7; John Gever, "Cannabis Effects Visit Sons Unto the 3rd Generation," *Medpage Today* November 14, 2013.

alterations in development of brain, behavior and health parameters have been reported as the result of exposure to cannabinoids during the fetal (prenatal) or early postnatal period in humans...close inspection of a number of studies on the adult offspring of Δ9-THC-treated mothers, reveals a pattern of alterations...These include: "Demasculinization" of prenatally stressed males ...or in males which were prenatally exposed to cannabinoids...[1124]

Some of the most extensive scientific work in this regard was done by Dr. Susan Dalterio of the University of Texas Health Science Center, San Antonio, who over several studies showed that "Maternal exposure to psychoactive or non-psychoactive cannabinoids produces long-term changes in body weight regulation, pituitary-gonadal feedback, testicular function, and also affects adult sexual behavior in male offspring" and that "maternal exposure to cannabinoids may interfere with the process of sexual differentiation in their male offspring as a result of decreased fetal androgen production."[1125]

In the human, the critical period of sexual differentiation occurs toward the end of the first trimester of pregnancy. In the mouse,

---

[1124] Ester Fride and M. Clara Sañudo-Peña, "Cannabinoids and endocannabinoids: behavioral and developmental aspects," in *Biology of Marijuana* ed. Emmnauel S. Onaivi (London and New York: Taylor & Francis, 2002) 208-209.

[1125] Susan L. Dalterio, Richard W. Steger and Andrzej Bartke, "Maternal or Prenatal Exposure to Cannabinoids Affects Central Neurotransmitter Levels and Reproductive Function in Male Offspring," in *Marihuana and Medicine*, ed. G.G. Nahas et al. (Totowa, NJ: Humana Press, 1999) 441-447; S.L. Dalterio and D.G. deRooij, "Maternal cannabinoid exposure Effects on spermatogenesis in male offspring," *International Journal of Andrology* 9 (1986): 250-258; S.L. Dalterio, SD Michael and PJ Thomford, "Perinatal cannabinoid exposure: demasculinization in male mice," *Neurobehav Toxicol Teratol* 8 (1986): 391-7; S. Dalterio et al., "Early Cannabinoid exposure influences neuroendocrine and reproductive functions in male mice: I. Prenatal exposure," *Pharmacol Biochem Behav* 20 (1984): 107-13; S. Dalterio et al., "Effects of Cannabinoids and Female Exposure on the Pituitary-Testicular Axis in Mice: Possible Involvement of Prostaglandins," *Biology or Reproduction* 24 (1981): 313-322; S. Dalterio and A. Bartke, "Fetal testosterone in mice: effect of gestational age and cannabinoid exposure," *J Endocrinol* 3 (1981): 509-514.

these critical periods occur just prior to birth and during the first few days of life. It has been demonstrated that alterations in testosterone levels during these critical periods, both in the human and in laboratory animals, result in profound and long-term changes in the maturing individual. Thus, exposure to high levels of testosterone can produce male-appearing external genitals in a female infant and result in delay or suppression of fertility later in life. In contrast, interference with testosterone action in a male fetus can result in a genetically male individual with a characteristic female appearance and inadequate development resulting in sterility... At birth, there was no evidence that the mice had been adversely affected by their mother's exposure to constituents of marihuana. Indeed, up to weaning at 21 days of age, these marihuana-exposed mice could not be distinguished from the untreated control males. However, just prior to puberty—about 30 to 37 days of age-those male mice whose mothers had received THC or CBN were lighter than the control mice in this study. It has been well documented that the growth spurt that occurs just before puberty in the maturing male is related to the rapid increase in testosterone at this time. Therefore, it is conceivable that cannabinoid exposure may result in lower levels of testosterone production during this period. In addition to the effects on body weight just prior to puberty, testicular weights were significantly reduced in the THC-exposed males, and the plasma levels of the pituitary reduced in the THC-exposed males, and the plasma levels of the pituitary hormone LH were considerably elevated. These effects persisted into adulthood. Since the function of the pituitary LH is to stimulate the testes and levels of LH normally increase in response to reduce testosterone levels, the presence of elevated LH and decreased testicular weights with low normal plasma testosterone levels may suggest that early exposure to THC may have interfered with the ability of the testis to respond to the stimulation by pituitary hormones...

We feel that the most likely explanation for these findings is that both the psychoactive and nonpsychoactive constituents of marihuana produced subtle alterations in the hormonal environment, particularly testosterone levels, during the critical period. At that time the brain is being primed to respond to testosterone in adulthood with the normal pattern of the male sexual behavior.

This hypothesis was supported by our recent findings that treatment of female mice during the midportion of pregnancy with THC or CBN significantly reduced the content of testosterone in their male fetuses... It is always difficult to extrapolate from results obtained in studies with laboratory animals to predict effects in man. However, the design of our studies was such that the results could probably be relevant to the heavy marihuana user... The possibility that marihuana use by pregnant women could affect the development of their sons should probably be seriously considered before a generation or two of children have been exposed to this substance."[1126]

V.   *Does Smoking Weed Make You Gay?*

In October of 1986 **Newsweek** published a most sensational report: "Reagan Aide: Pot Can Make You Gay."[1127] The aide in question was Dr. Carlton E. Turner, the White House Drug Czar and one of the world's leading experts on the botany and pharmacology of marijuana. According to the **Newsweek** article: "He believes that pot smoking may lead to homosexuality". The report continues:

> Turner offers scant scientific backing for his claims. But he says that when he visits drug-treatment centers for patients under 18, he finds that roughly 40 percent of them have also engaged in homosexual activity. "It seems to be something that follows along from their marijuana use," says Turner, who is convinced that the drugs come first, the homosexuality second. "My concern is, how is the biological system affected by heavy marijuana use? The public needs to be thinking about how drugs alter people's lifestyles."

Such a headline couldn't help but spark controversy and, according to another headline, a "great debate."[1128] Subsequently, Turner denied he made the headline's claim and clarifies his point: "I never said marijuana will make you

---

[1126] in *Health Consequences of Marihuana Use. Hearings Before the Subcommittee on Criminal Justice of the Committee on the Judiciary United States Senate. Ninety-Sixth Congress. Second Session on Marihuana Usage. January 16 and 17, 1980* 94-95
[1127] Terry E. Johnson, Margaret Garrard Warner and George Raine, "Reagan Aide: Pot Can Make You Gay," **Newsweek** October 1986, p. 95.
[1128] Elizabeth Kastor, "The Great Drug Debate," **The Washington Post** October 22, 1986.

homosexual. I don't know why someone made a quantum jump on that." Rather, he explains: "When you talk to young people who use drugs, you find *their inhibitions against everything are gone.* This is one of the things that goes along with it. That was the context under which it was discussed (emphasis added – WM)."[1129] The disappearance of inhibitions is no doubt related to THC's effect on serotonin and the serotonergic system. According to Margaret Garrard Warner who interviewed him for the story, she had pressed Turner on that question of homosexuality and marijuana abuse, asking: "Weren't these men gay first?" to which she says Turner replied: "Oh no, the drug came first." So, he *did* imply a causal connection. What did Turner know that might have led him to such a sensational conclusion? Could someone considered to be an "Einstein" be guilty of "deep ignorance, prejudice and stupidity"?[1130] Other administration officials co-singed Turner's observation. Donald Ian Macdonald, Administrator of the U.S. Alcohol, Drug Abuse and Mental Health Administration said in Turner's defense:

"One of the things I think Carlton is saying is that one of the things about marijuana and alcohol is that they do change sexual behavior *in kids* ... The question of homosexual behavior is interesting because indeed in treatment situations homosexual activity is a problem. Young people at that age, trying to establish sexual identities, they can become confused.

"As kids become involved in progressive drug use, thrill-seeking and experimentation is advanced. With homosexuality -- to say it's a casual thing would be very difficult to do."[1131]

As "drug czar," Carlton Turner was the director of the Drug Abuse Policy Office during President Ronald Reagan's administration (1981-1986) and he was Special Assistant to the President for Drug Abuse, responsible for directing drug-

[1129] Elizabeth Kastor, "The Great Drug Debate," *The Washington Post* October 22, 1986.
[1130] Jim Spencer, "The Drug Warrior: My Job Is To free America Of Addiction," *Chicago Tribune* October 26, 1986; Elizabeth Kastor, "The Great Drug Debate," *The Washington Post* October 22, 1986.
[1131] Elizabeth Kastor, "The Great Drug Debate," *The Washington Post* October 22, 1986.

control policies in America.[1132] But his job before the White House gig is even *more important.* He worked in the M-Project facility from 1971-1980. What is the M-Project?

> In 1968, four years after Oxford erupted into a bloody riot over the admission of Ole Miss' first African-American matriculant, James Meredith, and at the height of the turbulent, dope-loving 1960s, the National Institute on Mental Health awarded contracts to Mississippi and several other states to start growing cannabis.[1133]

It was Ole Miss itself – the University of Mississippi in Oxford where the "James Meredith Riot" occurred – who ended up with the exclusive contract to literally grow marijuana for the federal government. The Marijuana Research Project, M-Project for short, was established at Ole Miss in 1968 and was commissioned by the National Institute on Drug Abuse, a branch of the National Institutes of Health, not only to study the botanical, pharmacological and chemical properties of the cannabis plant but also to literally grow, process and *sell marijuana*! This government-produced pot is sold to approved researchers. Located on 12 acres in the rolling hills of northeast Mississippi and at the coy Waller Laboratory Complex, the M-Project lab is officially "the U.S. government's weed dealer," "America's legal weed supplier."[1134] The NIDA provides all legal and clinical-use marijuana and ingredients.

[1132] ***Encyclopedia of Drug Policy*** Volume 1, ed. Mark A.R. Kleiman and James E. Hawdon s.v. Turner, Carlton by Kathrine Ritter and Todd Moore.

[1133] R.L. Nave, "How A Mississippi Lab Taught Us Everything We Know About Marijuana, For Better or Worse," ***International Business Times*** April 22, 2015.

[1134] R.L. Nave, "How A Mississippi Lab Taught Us Everything We Know About Marijuana, For Better or Worse," ***International Business Times*** April 22, 2015.

The outdoor fields of marijuana plants at the government-backed Marijuana Research Project at the University of Mississippi. (Photo: University of Mississippi School of Pharmacy)

Turner eventually headed the M-Project and in 1980 became director of the Research Institute for Pharmaceutical Studies at the University of Mississippi. He was the head of the U.S. government's marijuana-growing project; literally, "the government's pot farmer." He was the chief researcher of the plant as well.[1135] Turner's lab eventually grew 228 strains of seeds from different geographical locations originating from 61 countries, from Columbia, Thailand, Jamaica, India, Pakistan,

---

[1135] Carlton E. Turner et al., "Cultivation, Extraction, and Analysis of *Cannabis sativa* L.," **Annals New York Academy of Sciences** 1991 (1971): 3-14; Carlton E. Turner et al., "Marijuana and Paraquat," **JAMA** 240 (1978): 1857; Carlton E. Turner et al., "Detection and analysis of paraquat in confiscated marijuana samples," **United Nations Office on Drugs and Crime** January 1, 1978: 47-56; Carlton E. Turner, "Chemistry and Metabolism," in **Marijuana Research Findings: 1980**, ed. Robert C. Petersen (Rockville, Maryland: National Institute on Drug Abuse, 1981) 81-97; C.E. Turner, H.N. Elsohly, and G.S. Lewis, "Constituents of *Cannabis sativa* L. XX: the cannabinoid content of Mexican variants grown in Mexico and in Mississippi, United States of America," **Bulletin on Narcotics** 34 (1982): 45-59; Jim Spencer, "First Pot, then The Hard Stuff," **Chicago Tribune** August 13, 1985; Jim Spencer, "The Drug Warrior: My Job Is To free America Of Addiction," **Chicago Tribune** October 26, 1986; Dr. Carlton E. Turner, "'Medical' Marijuana a Con," acdemoncracy.org. Nov 19, 2016.

the Middle East, Russia, Afghanistan, Brazil, Hungary, Turkey, etc.[1136] The lab genetically engineers seeds. As Mahmoud A. ElSohly, Turner's understudy and successor as head of the M-Project, responded to the question: "Does this mean that one could make genetically modified cannabis?"

> ElSohly: "Yes. Absolutely. That actually has been the trend over the years in the cultivation in the illicit market, and also in the legal market, where *we are* doing genetic selection, where we select the specific materials that have the genes that produce higher levels of THC or some of the other ingredients."[1137]

This wide range of natural and genetically modified seeds and the marijuana they produce are kept locked behind a steel vault. As the **Los Angeles Times** reported on this "one of the nation's most impressive stockpiles of marijuana":

> Inside, marijuana buds are packed into thousands of baggies filed in bankers boxes. Fifty-pound barrels are brimming with dried, ready-to-smoke weed. Freezers are stocked with buckets of potent cannabis extracts. Large metal canisters sit, crammed full of hundreds of perfectly rolled joints...What makes the cannabis here on the campus of the University of Mississippi unique is that it is grown, processed and sold by the federal government.[1138]

The DEA guards the stockpile and strictly controls the marijuana farm. So if any of this weed "slips" out of the lab and into the streets, it is because the federal government *wanted it to*. And this is exactly what has happened. Turner acknowledged that some of his lab marijuana slipped into the black market via "some of his lab assistants."[1139] According to "the most reliable anecdotal evidence," one of those "slips" involved the legendary

---

[1136] Carlton E. Turner et al., "Constituents of *Cannabis sativa* L., XIV: Intrinsic Problems in Classifying Cannabis Based on a Single Cannabinoid Analysis," **Journal of Natural Products** 42 (1979): 317-319.
[1137] Claudia Dreifus, "Growing Marijuana With Government Money. A conversation with Mahmoud A. ElSohly," **The New York Times** December 22, 2008.
[1138] Evan Halper, "Mississippi, home of federal government's official stash of marijuana," **Los Angeles Times** May 28, 2014.
[1139] Jim Spencer, "The Drug Warrior: My Job Is To free America Of Addiction," **Chicago Tribune** October 26, 1986.

yet mysterious G13 strain of marijuana, an Aafghani Indica. This is the famous strain featured in Kevin Spacey's classic movie "American Beauty," where Wes Bentley's character explains: "This shit is top of the line. It's called G-13. It's genetically engineered by the U.S. government. It's extremely potent, but a completely mellow high. No paranoia."[1140] Reportedly, this strain was "stolen" from the U of Mississippi M-Project lab under Turner's direction in 1970s. From that stolen sample, a clone was produced which made its way into the hands of the Australian Neville Schoenmaker and his Seed Bank. The story goes that Shoenmacker received the strain from a Sandy Weinstein. Weinstein had a friend in Turner's lab, a first-year botany student who was a lab assistant. This unidentified lab assistant "snuck" the potent Afghani strain – it allegedly originally had a THC content of 28% - out of the lab and into the hands of Weinstein. With the enormously tight controls of the DEA over this lab and farm, it is impossible to believe that such a parochial operation could have been pulled off without the awareness of the governmental overseers. It was as a consequence of this "operation" that one of the most potent and legendary marijuana strains hit the streets. This is not the only example. So when R.L. Nave writes, "Regardless of how it came to be, it's clear that most of what we know about marijuana can be linked to Mississippi and the M-Project,"[1141] this should include what we have learned from marijuana on the streets.

So Dr. Carlton Turner's sensational claims about marijuana cannot be dismissed as coming from "deep ignorance, prejudice and stupidity." When it is mentioned "the monumental role [the M-Project] has played in shaping America's drug policy and much of what we think we know about marijuana for the past five decades," much credit must go to Turner himself. For example, Turner's research concluded that the younger the people are when they first use THC, the greater the long-term effects on the body; and "Δ9-THC and other cannabinoids imbed themselves in the cellular wall of the fatty parts of the body, *primarily the brain and reproductive*

[1140] JessE, "Urban Legend: G13," **Treating Yourself Magazine** February 2009.
[1141] R.L. Nave, "How A Mississippi Lab Taught Us Everything We Know About Marijuana, For Better or Worse," **International Business Times** April 22, 2015.

organs..."[1142] Thus, his claims of a connection between **child** marijuana use and homosexuality *was not divorced from a scientific context*. He was in fact representing the science as it was already available in his day.

VI.   *The Kolodny Studies*

Robert C. Kolodny, endocrinologist and specialist in human sexuality, was in 1971 a researcher at the Reproductive Biology Research Foundation in St. Louis, Missouri. He was also a captain in the U.S. Army Medical Corps Reserves. Kolodny's research focused on the effects of drugs (illicit and prescription) on endocrinology and sexual function and orientation. In a 1971 study of 30 homosexual men ages 18-24 compared to 50 heterosexual men 17-24, Kolodny reported that the homosexual group had plasma T levels "significantly below" the control (heterosexual) group: 372 ng/ml vs. 689 ng/ml[1143]: "men who were judged to have been exclusively homosexual throughout their lives had an average of about 40 per cent as much testosterone in their blood (than the average heterosexual man)," he reported.[1144] Kolodny subsequently reported the implications of this observation and the experimental outcomes of it:

> Data gathered by many researchers clarifying embryologic sexual differentiation and sex differences in pituitary gonadotrophin release clearly show that the process of sexual differentiation is dimorphic. Unless sufficient amounts of androgens are present during critical stages of fetal (or neonatal) development, differentiation will always occur as a female, regardless of genetic programming. By use of this

---

[1142] ***Hearings Before the Subcommittee on Crime of the Committee on the Judiciary House of Representatives. Ninety-Eighth Congress, First Session on Eradication of Marijuana with Paraquat October 5 and November 17, 1983***, 8-9, Statement of Carlton E. Turner,

[1143] Robert C. Kolodny et al., "Plasma Testosterone and Semen Analysis in Male Homosexuals," ***The New England Journal of Medicine*** 285 (1971): 1170-1174.

[1144] Boyce Rensberger, "Homosexuality Linked to Hormone Level," ***The New York Times*** Nov. 18, 1971.

principle, *homosexual behavior in male and female animals has been experimentally induced and prevented.*[1145]

It is the fetus that is most vulnerable to hormonal disruption or manipulation and sexual disorientation. In the lab, scientists have successfully used this method to experimentally induce homosexual behavior, Kolodny was able to report in 1973.

Kolodny then turned to the effect of marijuana use on sexuality. In 1972 he suggested that marijuana influences sexual response by "acting on the higher centers of the brain to relax inhibitions and reduce the usual restraints on behavior."[1146] In 1974 he conducted another testosterone study: 20 heterosexual men 18-28 years of age who smoked an average of four days a week over six months or more showed a mean plasma testosterone level of 416 +/- 34 ng/100 ml vs. non-smoking controls who had a mean level of 742 +/- 29 ng/ml.[1147] *The New York Times* did a story on Kolodny's research under the title: "Male Sex Debility Traced to Marijuana":

A new study of men who smoked marijuana daily under controlled conditions has shown that the drug can interfere with production of reproductive hormones, in some cases suppressing the male sex hormone, testosterone, to levels that could result in impotence or infertility.

Although there have been earlier reports linking marijuana use to lowered testosterone levels, the new study clearly indicates that the drug is the actual cause of this hormonal effect and that the effect can be reversed within two weeks of stopping marijuana use...

The new study, described last weekend at the first meeting of the newly formed International Academy of Sex Research, showed that the testosterone effects of marijuana do not show up until five weeks after continued heavy use of the drug.

[1145] Robert C. Kolodny and William H. Masters, "Hormones and Homosexuality," *Ann Itern Med* 79 (1973): 897.
[1146] *Marihuana: a signal of misunderstanding. The Technical Papers of the First Report of the National Commission on Marihuana and Drug Abuse March 1972.* Appendix, 436.
[1147] Robert C. Kolodny et al., "Depression of Plasm Testosterone Levels after Chronic Intensive Marihuana Use," *The New England Journal of Medicine* 290 (1974): 872-874.

Thereafter, testosterone levels continued to fall as long as the men continued smoking marijuana.

The study was conducted jointly by researchers at the Reproductive Biology Research Foundation in St. Louis and the University of California at Los Angeles. Its findings were reported by Dr. Robert C. Kolodny of the St. Louis Foundation, directed by Dr. William H. Masters, the noted sex researcher.

Dr. Kolodny told the meeting, held at State University of New York at Stony Brook, that 20 men who had volunteered for the study were housed for its duration in the metabolic research ward of a hospital. They were not allowed to smoke cigarettes or drink coffee or alcohol or use drugs. They were given no marijuana for 11 days, after which their testosterone levels were measured.

Each man was then given five marijuana cigarettes a day, each containing a known quantity of the active ingredient. After four weeks, significant drops in the men's blood levels of a substance called luteinizing hormone, or LH, began to appear.

LH, a hormone produced by the pituitary gland, stimulates the testes to produce testosterone, which develops and maintains male sex characteristics.

After the fifth week of daily marijuana smoking, testosterone levels began dropping significantly, Dr. Kolodny reported, and after the eighth week production of another reproductive hormone, the follicle stimulating hormone, or FSH, also fell significantly. FSH stimulates sperm production.

Decreasing Levels

Within nine weeks, the men's average testosterone production had fallen off by one-third. Although the average stayed within the range of normal, the levels for some men fell to below normal and to within the range where impotence or infertility could occur, Dr. Kolodny reported.[1148]

In 1975 Kolodny presented his findings before Senate Subcommittee Hearings, with a focus on the embryological impact of marijuana use:

[1148] Jane E. Brody, "Male Sex Debility Traced to Marijuana," *The New York Times* September 16, 1975.

Testimony of Dr. Robert Kolodny, Reproductive Biology Research Foundation, St. Louis, MO:

We investigated blood levels of a variety of hormones that are important in reproduction. The principal male sex hormone, testosterone, was found to be approximately 44 percent lower in the group of men using marihuana chronically and frequently than in the group of men who had never used this drug. This finding was not uniform in all the men studied, however, and it appeared to be related to the amount of marihuana used...Since at least some of the active constituents of marihuana have been shown to cross the placenta, there may be a significant risk of depressed testosterone levels within the developing fetus when this drug is used by a pregnant woman. Since normal sexual differentiation of the male depends on adequate testosterone stimulation during critical stages of development, occurring approximately at the third and fourth months of pregnancy, it is possible that such development might be disrupted...Alcohol, when used with high frequency in terms that would generally be considered alcohol abuse, certainly can produce disruption of normal hormone balance and lowering of testosterone and can produce actual wasting of the testicular tissue as well as other feminizing changes in the male such as enlargement of the breasts...There is in existing literature a correlation between levels of testosterone and aggression, and I use that term in the scientific sense, not in a sense of socially deviant behavior. When testosterone levels get low, usually ambition and aggression get low. This has been documented in animals, in primates and in the human in a variety of different studies over the past 5 years. In theory, if the reports of alteration of behavior patterns in heavy cannabis users are accurate, the basis for this so-called amotivational syndrome may potentially be the decreased testosterone level.[1149]

In 1976 Kolodny testified before Congress:

Some apparent inconsistencies in research findings regarding reduced plasma levels of the male hormone, testosterone, may be explained by the differing length of time users had been

[1149] *Marihuana-Hashish Epidemic and its Impact on United States Security.* Hearings Before the Subcommittee to Investigate the Administration of the Internal Security Act and Other Internal Security Laws of the Committee on the Judiciary United States Senate, Ninety-third Congress, Second Session. May 9, 16, 17, 20, 21, qne Hune 13, 1974 (Washington: U.S. Government Printing Office, 1975)117-126.

smoking before such levels were assessed...With regard to hormonal aspects, two other adverse effects remain possibilities: 1) Interference with normal growth and sexual development *of adolescent heavy users* and, 2) Abnormal sexual differentiation of the male fetus developing in a mother who heavily uses marihuana during early pregnancy. No actual evidence for either of these speculative possibilities has yet appeared in the scientific literature...the data from research finding no marihuana-related hormone changes (...) are quite consistent with studies that do (...) if the different time periods of marihuana use are taken into account...Such alterations might be expected to be more important for prepubertal or pubertal males or males with already impaired sexual functioning. There might also be adverse effects on sexual differentiation of the fetus of mothers using cannabis.[1150]

The emphasis here is on adolescents and fetuses. These are most vulnerable to sexual disorientation by marijuana/THC exposure. In a 1974 report by the National Institute for Drug Abuse (director Dr. Robert L. DuPont), the NIDA highlighted marijuana's

effects on male sex hormone levels, interference with the body's immune response and effects on fundamental cell metabolism. The implications of these preliminary studies are, at this point, speculative. There is concern that alteration in hormone levels as a result of chronic use *may interfere with normal adolescent development* or with sexual differentiation of *male fetuses* if cannabis is used by pregnant women at critical periods of fetal development.[1151]

Since the early 1970s, these mattes have become much less speculative.

[1150] ***Marihuana and Health. Fifth Annual report to the U.S. Congress From the Secretary of Health, Education, and Welfare 1975*** (Maryland: National Institute on Drug Abuse, 1976) 5-6, 81-82.

[1151] Statement of Senator Javits Introducing S. 1450 Marihuana Control Act of 1975. In ***Marijuana Decriminalization. Hearing Before the Subcommittee to Investigate Juvenile Delinquency of the Committee on the Judiciary United States Senate. Ninety-Fourth Congress, First Session. May 14, 1975***, 201.

VII. THC and Female Sexual Behavior – in Males

Lordosis is the posture assumed by some female mammals, particularly rodents, during mating, in which the back is arched downward and the rear is raised to receive the male. This sexually receptive female reflex is regulated in the brain by the ovarian hormones estrogen and progesterone. The cooperation of these two hormones are in fact essential for the production of female sexual behavior.

Progesterone's synergizing with estrogen is critical to the process: "progesterone acts synergistically with estrogen to facilitate lordosis and is essential for the species-typical expression of proceptivity (soliciting the male) and sexual receptivity in estrogen-primed females"[1152]

This female sexual receptive behavior (lordosis) can be produced in males.

> there are suggestive evidences indicating that the differentiation of sexual behavior can be modified by the changes in the perinatal hormonal environments (...). The absence or suppression of testicular activity in during neonatal period has been found to induce feminization and demasculinization of sexual behavior in male rats. Such males show high levels of lordosis responses when they are treated with estrogen and progesterone (...).[1153]

[1152] Diane M. Witt, Larry J. young, and David Crews, "Progesterone and Sexual Behavior in Males," **Psychoneuroendocrinology** 19 (1994): 553-562 (554).

[1153] Korehito Yamanouchi and Yasumasa Arai, "Heterotypical Sexual Behavior in Male Rats: Individual Difference in Lordosis Response," **Endocrinol. Japan** 23 (1976): 179-182 (181).

This is important. The process of the feminization of a male rodent's sexual behavior is this: inhibit the testosterone production of a fetus or infant and then expose the fetus/infant to estrogen and progesterone. That male will grow up inclined to perform lordosis in the presence of other males.[1154]

We have documented in this volume that the Black man in America has been made into the world's "Mr. E": we have the highest levels of estrogen in our blood than any other male population on the planet. So, we reach teenage years already testosterone-diminished and "estrogen-primed." All that needs to happen now is that we are exposed to progesterone. That is where this weaponized weed comes in.

THC and progesterone are isomers.[1155] Isomers are compounds that have the same chemical formula but different structure (arrangement of the atoms). Both THC and progesterone have the chemical formula $C_{21}H_{30}O_2$. Exposure to THC thus can be tantamount to exposure to a progesterone shot. The danger with isomers is that the body may not be able to tell the difference between the two totally different chemicals. A molecule must have the right structure (shape) in order to function properly within a living cell. But in this case, THC can effectively stimulate the progesterone receptors.

[1154] Korehito Yamanouchi and Yasumasa Arai, "Heterotypical Sexual Behavior in Male Rats: Individual Difference in Lordosis Response," *Endocrinol. Japon.* 23 (1976): 179-182; idem, "Female Lordosis Pattern in the Male Rat Induced by Estrogen and Progesterone: Effect of Interruption of the Dorsal Inputs to the Preoptic Area and Hypothalamus," *Endocrinol. Japon.* 22 (1975): 243-246; J.M. Davison and S. Levine, "Progesterone and Heterotypical Sexual Behaviour in Male Rats," *J. Endocr.* 44 (1969): 129-130; Ingeborg L. Ward, JoAnn E. Franck, and William R. Crowley, "Central Progesterone Induces Female Sexual Behavior in Estrogen-Primed Intact Male Rats," *Journal of Comparative and Physiological Psychology* 91 (1977): 1417-1423; C. Schaeffer, A. Chabli and C. Aron, "Endogenous Progesterone and Lordosis Behavior in Male Rats Given Estrogen Alone," *J. Steroid Biochem.* 25 (1986): 99-102; DH Olster and JD Blaustein, "Progesterone facilitation of lordosis in male and female Sprague-Dawley rats following priming with estradiol pulses," *Horm Behav* 3 (1988): 294-304
[1155] Nivaldo J. Tro, *Chemistry in Focus: A Molecular View of Our World* Second Edition (Boston: Cengage Learning, 2019) 151.

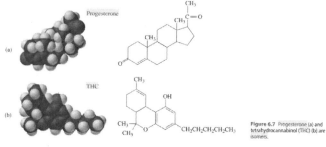

Figure 6.7 Progesterone (a) and tetrahydrocannabinol (THC) (b) are isomers.

Tetrahydrocannabinol has the ability to work on neurochemical substrates normally activated by progesterone and may also work via cell-signaling cascades that activate progesterone receptors. In essence, THC has the ability to mimic progesterone...[1156]

In rats as in people, sexual behavior requires certain hormones. If the ovaries are removed from a female rat, for example, she will no longer raise her rump when she is ready to mate. This behavior can be restored with injections of the sex hormones estrogen and progesterone-and also with shots of marijuana's active ingredient, 9-tetrahydrocannabinol (THC).[1157]

THC facilitates the display of lordosis: "Thus, it appears that THC is capable of enhancing sexual receptivity of female rats by a direct action on the central nervous system"[1158]; "these data indicate that THC can stimulate female sexual behavior and suggest that this effect reflects a direct, nonhormonal, effect of THC on brain mechanisms for behavior."[1159] This is true in

---

[1156] Arooka, **James Bong's Ultimate Spyguide To Marijuana** (Colorado: Free World Press, Ltd.) 46.

[1157] Caroline Seydel, "Sex, Drugs, and Brain Receptors," **Science** Jan 24, 2001.

[1158] John H. Gordon et al. "Δ^9-Tetrahydrocannabinol enhancement of Lordosis Behavior in estrogen treated female rats," **Pharmacology Biochemistry and Behavior** 8 (1978): 593-596.

[1159] William A. Turley Jr. and Owen R. Floody, "Δ-9-tetrahydrocannabinol stimulates receptive and proceptive sexual behaviors in female hamsters," **Pharmacology Biochemistry and Behavior** 14 (1981): 745-747; Carol Sue Carter, Sharon J. Michael and Alan H. Morris, "Hormonal induction of female sexual behavior in male and female hamsters," **Hormones and Behavior** 4 (1973): 129-141.

males as well as females, especially male rodents primed with synthetic estrogens.[1160] This, the confluence of diminished testosterone, estrogen exposure and exposure to THC (=progesterone) could indeed feminize the sexual behavior of males in lower species and even in humans if the exposure is prenatal or adolescent.

This is the scientific background of Dr. Carlton Turner's claim.

Excursus: White Scientists and Black Zombies

This photo was posted on social media with the caption suggesting that these brothers from Baltimore are suffering the effects of using K2, the synthetic marijuana that is reportedly 10 times stronger than regular marijuana. K2 is a popular "monster weed" and the language "zombies" was used in

---

[1160] Shailaja K. Mani, Andrea Mitchell and Bert W. O'Malley, "Progesterone receptor and dopamine receptors are required in Δ^9-Tetrahydrocannabinol modulation of sexual receptivity in female rats," **PNAS** 98 (2001): 1249-1254; Nelphi Stella, "How might cannabinoids influence sexual behavior?" **PNAS** 98 (2001): 793-795.

reference to these Brothers from Baltimore. What is the origin of K2? Uncle Sam, as the personification of the federal government, is the origin of K2. Specifically, Uncle Sam as represented by organic chemist Dr. John William Huffman, dubbed the "Godfather of synthetic marijuana" and "arguably the nation's most prolific inventor of outlawed synthetic marijuana."[1161] Spice, Skunk, K2 are all his creations.

K2 was designed and synthesized in Huffman's Clemson University laboratory in 1995. The technical, scientific name of K2 is JWH-018. "JWH" are his initials and "018" represents that this compound was the 18th that he synthesized in a series of over 470 analogs and metabolites of THC, all

Social Issues

How this chemist unwittingly helped spawn the synthetic drug industry

John Huffman at his home in Sylva, N.C. (John Fletcher, Jr./The Washington Post)

By Terrence McCoy

of them carrying Huffman's initials.[1162] "JWH" are described as the most notorious initials in the world of synthetic drugs, because John W. Huffman is credited with spawning the synthetic marijuana epidemic. He is blamed for "turning an entire generation onto 'monster weed'."[1163] According to own his colleague, Marilyn Huestis, senior investigator at the National Institute on Drug Abuse (NIDA), Huffman's work "is how it all started."[1164] She would know because the NIDA funded

---

[1161] Terrence McCoy, "How this chemist unwittingly helped spawn the synthetic drug industry," *The Washington Post* August 9, 2015.
[1162] Linda Wang, "John W. Huffman," *Chemical & Engineering News* 88 (2010).
[1163] David Zucchino, "Scientist's research produces a dangerous high," *Los Angeles Times* September 28, 2011.
[1164] McCoy, "How this chemist."

Huffman in his work. "Funded by the National Institute on Drug Abuse, he produced hundreds of synthetic cannabinoids".[1165] Between 1984 and 2011 JWH and his team created their 470 + synthetic cannabinoids under a $2 million federal grant.[1166]

Huffman's K2 or JWH-018 has a chemical formula $C_{24}H_{23}NO$ and is a chemical descendent of WIN 55,212-2, a cannabimimetic (THC-mimicking) compound produced by Sterling-Winthrop Research Institute.[1167] Sterling-Winthrop did work in the 1960s for the U.S. Army Edgewood Arsenal's "Conquer-By-Cannabis" project under contract No. DA 18-108-AMC – 103 (A).[1168] This was the project to weaponize marijuana by inserting a nitrogen atom into the THC molecule, making the synthetic marijuana "heroin-like" in its properties. This is why the new weed is addictive whereas the old weed is not. Dr. Alexander Shulgin, the "Godfather of MDMA," gave the Army the formula to add a nitrogen atom to the THC molecule.

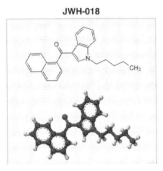

How did this government-funded creation (K2) hit the streets?

How that happened is a familiar tale of unintended consequences in a rapidly interconnected world. Like ecstasy or LSD, synthetic cannabinoids mark the latest example of a substance hatched in medical research that metamorphosed into a rampant street drug.[1169]

[1165] McCoy, "How this chemist."

[1166] Zucchino, "Scientist's research."

[1167] Jenny L. Wiley et al., "Hijacking of Basic Research: The Case of Synthetic Cannabinoids," *Methods Rep RTI Press* November 2011: 1-11 (3); John W. Huffman et al., "Design, Synthesis and Pharmacology of Cannabimimetic Indoles," *Bioorganic & Medicinal Chemistry Letters* 4 (1994): 563-566.

[1168] H.G. Pars et al. "Physiologically Active Nitrogen Analogs of Tetrahydrocannabinols. Testrahydrobenzopyrano[3,4-*d*]pyridines," *Journal of the American Chemical Society* 88 (1966): 3664-3665; James S. Ketchum, *Chemical Warfare: Secrets Almost Forgotten* (Santa Rosa, California: ChemBooks, Inc., 2006) 36.

[1169] McCoy, "How this chemist."

Unintended the consequences certainly were not. It has become common practice since the CIA's MK-ULTRA days to clandestinely seed synthetic drugs to the public market and then sit back and observe the effects as a way to get around the high requirements of clinical trials and regulatory oversight. K2 – or JWH-018 - now saturates the prisons[1170] as a mechanism to control the largely Black and brown prison population.

[1170] Tim Lammers, "Prisons around the country face a growing K2 problem," *FOX61* September 25, 2018.

Part V

The Weaponization of Hip Hop

Chapter Twenty

Black Music as a Province
Of Jewish Art

Nelson George remarks that the 'majority of [white] men and women [involved in record companies associated with early hip hop] were Jews who carried on a long tradition of black and white collaboration in grassroots music that stretches back, at least, to the '40s when Jewish record men like Leonard and Phil Chess in Chicago and Jerry Wexler in New York led the pioneers who put electrified blues and R&B on vinyl' ...[1171]

I.   *Fabricators and Merchandizers of Blackness*

For almost a century a typical role of Jewish entertainers in the United States was that of mediating between Black music and white audiences.[1172] Jews would play a key part in determining which particular images of Blackness would be disseminated and by whom,[1173] because many Jews saw themselves as the "true interpreters of black culture."[1174] The process of "repositioning African American music as a province of Jewish art" began with the likes of Irvin Berlin, George Gershwin, Jerome Kern, Harold Arlen, etc.[1175] From there Jews became important "creators" of what would be popularly taken as "black culture." Jews were "extensively immersed" in "the manufacture and merchandizing of Blackness" and the popular culture productions of Blackness.[1176] White Americans have an insatiable appetite for the sights and sounds of "pretend" blackness and by dominating the writing, publishing, performing, and promotion of American popular song, Jews made names for themselves by *constructing an urbane vision*

[1171] Jon Stratton, "The Beastie Boys: Jews in Whiteface," **Popular Music** 27 (2008): 413-432, quoted in 416-417.

[1172] Jon Stratton, "The Beastie Boys: Jews in Whiteface," **Popular Music** 27 (2008): 413-432 (414).

[1173] Jeffrey Melnick, "Tin Pan alley: The Black-Jewish Nation," in **American Popular Music**, ed. Rachel Rubin and Jeffrey Melnick (Amherst: University of Massachusetts Press, 2001) 29-45 (35).

[1174] Justin Joffe, "The Music Industry's Long History of Dividing Blacks and Jews," **Observe** February 9, 2017.

[1175] Melnick, **A Right to Sing the Blues**, 42.

[1176] Melnick, **A Right to Sing the Blues**, 97

of blackness, "a kind of musical translation of what *many white Americans imagined 'black' to represent.*"[1177]

> While African Americans and various representations of 'Blackness' (via stereotyped 'coon' song lyrics, syncopation, an overall 'raciness,' and so on) were important commodities, it was Jews who were coming to have most control over these performances, both in the crude sense of owning the means of production, and through the more complex process of gaining status as the best interpreters of African American culture. In early twentieth-century music culture, the success of Jews was inseparable from their management of African American styles, resources, and careers. [1178]

Jews traded in a Blackness which was actively worked to exclude Black people from positions of cultural power. An illustrative case is the American craze of blackface minstrelsy.

> One element in the Jewish relationship with Black culture has been blackface. As Michael Rogin writes: 'Jews - Al Jolson, Eddie Cantor, George Jessel, George Burns, Sophie Tucker - had pretty much taken over blackface by the turn of the century, Jewish songwriters - Irving Berlin, George Gershwin, and Jerome Kern to name only the most famous - created melting-pot American music in the Jazz Age from African American sources'...[1179]

> [Jews] made their first major incursion into the market as blackface performers...Jews were quite successful at selling themselves in blackface...American popular culture is drenched in the props, tropes, and imagery of minstrelsy; it comes as no surprise, then, to find that Jews made their first major appearance in the national marketplace of popular culture through their travesties of African Americans...Jews in the music business participated fully in the American project of making money out of making fun of African Americans...Jews making money out of African Americans and representations of

---

[1177] Jeffrey Melnick, "Tin Pan alley: The Black-Jewish Nation," in **American Popular Music**, ed. Rachel Rubin and Jeffrey Melnick (Amherst: University of Massachusetts Press, 2001) 29-45 (41).
[1178] Jeffrey Melnick, "Tin Pan alley: The Black-Jewish Nation," in **American Popular Music**, ed. Rachel Rubin and Jeffrey Melnick (Amherst: University of Massachusetts Press, 2001) 29-45 (31).
[1179] Jon Stratton, "The Beastie Boys: Jews in Whiteface," **Popular Music** 27 (2008): 413-432 (414).

Blackness...By the 1910s and 1920s stage blackface was widely understood to have become a special offering of the Jewish entertainment complex...the ubiquity of Jews in blackface disclosed in perhaps the most visible fashion that this group, rather new to the American racial scene, would be defining images.[1180]

II.   *Pansies and Bully Coons*

Blackface minstrelsy was translated into musical form as well as "offstage modes of behavior." An example of that musical form is the so-called coon songs, which represent "a kind of Jewish musical fulfillment of blackface," a Jewish translation of blackface from stage performance into song.[1181] Coon songs are a distillation of the sights and sounds of minstrelsy into a usable modern musical grammar. While coon songs were often blatantly racist,

Jim Crow

they offered an opening for African Americans to break into the music business and so Blacks are found alongside Jews as prolific composers. The coon song became a national craze.[1182] One of the earliest Blackface depictions produced by Jews of Tin Pan Alley was the "cultured, pansy-like negro," "slight and effeminate." This Negro pansy even appeared in drag and was represented as infantile, an effeminate man-child. "The production of effeminacy-which is, in this context, synonymous with homosexuality- as a major modality for these Jewish men in blackface was tied up with their display as children."[1183]

[1180] Jeffrey Melnick, *A Right to Sing the Blues: African Americans, Jews, and American Popular Song* Cambridge and London: Harvard University Press, 1999) 41, 108.

[1181] Melnick, *A Right to Sing the Blues*, 42.

[1182] J. Stanley Lemons, "Black Stereotypes as Reflected in Popular Culture, 1880-1920," *American Quarterly* 29 (Spring, 1977):102-116.

[1183] Melnick, *A Right to Sing the Blues*, 111.

Unlike the clumsy, dimwitted, non-threatening character of Jim Crow, the star of the coon songs was a threatening black dandy, a slick, urban, razor-toting bully, often called Zip Coon. The coon songs portrayed Blacks as posing a threat to the American social order and thus needed to be controlled. The coon songs were a sociopsychological mechanism justifying the segregation and subordination necessary to "control" the coons. Coon songs defining characteristic was its caricature of African Americans: we were portrayed as making money through gambling, theft, and hustling, rather than working to earn a living. Coons were promiscuous and libidinous (hypersexualized) and were inclined toward acts of provocative violence (hyperviolent). This hyperviolence is symbolized by a long razor in the possession of a "street-patrolling bully coon," the main character of these coon songs. James Dormon explains:

> In the songs...blacks began to appear as not only ignorant and indolent, but also devoid of honesty or personal honor, given to drunkenness and gambling, utterly without ambition,

sensuous, libidinous, even lascivious. "Coons" were, in addition to all of these things, razor-wielding savages, routinely attacking one another at the slightest provocation as a normal function of their uninhibited social lives. The razor - the flashing steel straight razor - became in the songs the dominant symbol of black violence, while the "coon" himself became that which was signified by this terrible weapon. The subliminal message was clear and clearly part of the connotative code: Blacks are potentially dangerous; they must be controlled and subordinated by whatever means necessary... Although black violence lay somewhere near the surface of virtually every episode or event described in coon songs, notably, the violence was uniformly perpetrated by blacks on blacks. Whites were never directly involved. To involve whites would eliminate the comic veneer altogether, and one simply did not write or perform comic songs about race riots. The black threat remained a subliminal threat, and "coons" remained hilariously funny...The "toughest" and "meanest" coon - the "bully coon" - was another stock figure prominent among the characters about whom coon songs were written. [1184]

But the coon songs and its antagonist the Bully Coon provided White America with more than comic relief: they also provided the necessary justification and psychological balm for the horrendous methods of socially controlling African Americans, such as lynchings.

> The coon song craze in its full frenzy was a manifestation of a peculiar form of the will to believe - to believe in the signified "coon" as represented in the songs - as a necessary sociopsychological mechanism for justifying segregation and subordination...Blacks were not only the simple-minded comic buffoons of the minstrel tradition; they were also potentially dangerous. They were dangerous not only in the way that animals are dangerous if allowed to roam unrestrained, but dangerous as well to white bourgeois culture itself. They constituted a threat to the American social order. For this reason, they had to be controlled and subordinated by whatever means, so the coon songs signaled. The songs also argued, implicitly at least, for coercion, for lynching if necessary, to maintain control and the domination of white over black. Such was their connoted message...The coon songs were

---

[1184] James H. Dormon, "Shaping the Popular Image of Post-Reconstruction American Blacks: The 'Coon Song' Phenomenon of the Gilded Age," *American Quarterly* 40 (1988): 450-471 (455, 460).

as popular as they were because they provided psychic balms by way of justifying the unjustifiable to white Americans who were as delighted with "coons" as they were determined to believe in them...In their very willingness to participate in the coon song phenomenon, black performers and song writers were able to profit commercially and to produce, among other things, an entirely new black musical theater based, at least in part, in authentically black musical materials.[1185]

The music industry has commodified "Black Authenticity," an ideal constructed by white corporate interests using controlling images and which reflects dominant socio-cultural ideologies. Controlling images are stereotypes constructed by the dominant society and portrayed in popular media which create and perpetuate popularized symbolic Black identities, designed to serve the interests of the dominant society (white males). The music industry today more or less restricts would-be hip hop stars - male or female - to two controlling images: the Black male as a dangerous, hyper-violent, libidinous, intellectually inferior thug and the Black female as a promiscuous, hypersexualized, non-virtuous Jezebel. White framing (the corporate label) and a White target audience (75% of consumers of hip hop or White) determine the portrayal of "Black Authenticity" in hip hop. It is Whites who largely purchase and consume this commodified Blackness, but it is primarily Black youth who try to *emulate* these controlling images of "Black Authenticity." Commercial rap music panders to White appetites for *pretend* "Blackness" and widely distributes a script that normalizes these controlling images produced by and for American White supremacy. The Jewish project of the production of Blacknesses that satisfied the appetites of racist White America gave birth to the Bully Coon and its descendent, the Gangsta Rapper; it also gave birth to the Negro Pansy and his descendent, the Drag Rapper (for example Young Thug) or Queer Rapper (for example Lil Nas X); and it gives birth to the Black Jezebel and her descendent today, the Bag-Getting-Slut Rapper (for example Megan Thee Stallion). These are arguably all Jewish fabricated expressions of Blackness.

[1185] James H. Dormon, "Shaping the Popular Image of Post-Reconstruction American Blacks: The 'Coon Song' Phenomenon of the Gilded Age," *American Quarterly* 40 (1988): 450-471 (467).

Chapter Twenty-one

Why Weaponize Hip Hop?
The Farrakhan Factor

I. *Historical Precedent: Black Rage and White Victims in Miami. 1980*

Unparalleled in modern American history for its random anti-white violence - **Miami Herald** May 15, 2016.

They say bounds were crossed in Miami in 1980 in an unprecedent and frightening way. The three-day riot that began on May 17, 1980 after Dade County police officers were acquitted by an all-white jury in the beating death of a Black motorist Arthur McDuffie, wasn't a standout riot in terms of the basic statistics: 18 dead, 400 injured, 1,100 arrested, $100 million in property damage. Rather, the so-called McDuffie Riot was unique in a very specific way: "it was the killing-the manner of the killing and who was killed-that most clearly separates Miami from the earlier riots."[1186]

> What was shocking about Miami was the intensity of the rage directed by blacks against white people: men, women and children dragged from their cars and beaten to death, stoned to death, stabbed with screwdrivers, run over with automobiles; hundreds more attacked in the street and seriously injured. In contrast, the disturbances of the 1960s could be regarded as "property riots," wherein blacks directed their anger largely against buildings. The deaths that did occur during those disorders were overwhelmingly those of blacks killed by white policeman and National Guardsmen. The few white deaths...occurred as a byproduct of the disorder. In Miami, attacking and killing white people was the main object of the riot... Indeed, to find a precedent for the random killing of whites, one would have to reach back before the twentieth century, to the Nat Turner-style slave rebellions before the Civil War, when blacks rose and killed the whites at hand.[1187]

[1186] Bruce Porter and Marvin Dunn, **The Miami Riot of 1980** (Lexington: D.C. Health and Company, 1984) xiii, 173.
[1187] Porter and Dunn, **The Miami Riot of 1980**, xiii, 173.

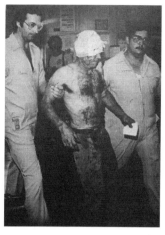

Two months after the uprising (July 1980) the Ford Foundation conducted a study, published exactly a year to the date of the riot (May 17, 1981), and determined that the Miami rebellion differed dramatically from the racial disturbances of the 1960s such as Watts (1965), Newark (1967) and Detroit (1967). Those were "merely a warning about the hostility that lay beneath the surface." Marvin Dunn, associate professor of psychology at Florida International University and Bruce Porter, director of the journalism program at Brooklyn College, concluded that "the antiwhite violence in the Miami riot was 'unprecedented in this century'": "not since the slave uprisings before the Civil War had blacks risen spontaneously with the sole purpose of beating or killing whites"; "In 1,893 individual racial disorders from 1964 to 1969...there was not one report of blacks rising up spontaneously to beat and kill whites as they did in Miami."[1188] In Miami a 55-year old White woman in her car had gasoline poured on her through the window and set on fire in her vehicle. Whites were dragged from their cars and viciously beaten to death; others were stoned to death in their cars. The rioters burned and looted specifically white owned businesses but they can't be described as "looters": "judging from the kinds of property that were burned, the rioters seemed often driven more by the desire to destroy than to steal."[1189]

The young Blacks of Miami who showed such fearlessness that the older Blacks thought they were literally crazy. While older Blacks were singing "We Shall Overcome" and the gospel song "Amen," the Black youth were declaring *no more singing and talking.*[1190] Some of these older Blacks were horrified at what they saw in the young rioters. 47-year old Willie Matthews, a Black business owner who witnessed the carnage himself from inside his store, said: "The young people I

[1188] Jo Thomas, "Study Finds Miami Riot was Unlike Those of 60's," *The New York Times* May 17, 1981.
[1189] Porter and Dunn, *The Miami Riot of 1980*, 131.
[1190] Porter and Dunn, *Miami Riot*, 61-62.

watched, they had no heart, no heart whatsoever...These kids, they just got no God in them. No God."[1191] Metro Sgt. Robert Hoelscher, who led SWAT teams into the 1980 riot, said "it was like chasing phantom guerrilla warriors"[1192] Not only were these Black youth shooting at cops on the streets with shot guns; *they fearlessly attacked the police headquarters with police in it.* They smashed the glass doors of the Metro Justice Building, the seat of the county's justice system, and set fire inside its marble lobby. One witness said: "When I saw men attack the police headquarters with the police *inside*, then I knew they were really crazy."[1193] Of course, "Fearlessness looks like insanity to a coward," as the Honorable Minister Farrakhan teaches us.

The Miami insurrection of 1980 illustrated the costs of the extinguishing of hope which gives way to hostility. Archie Hardwick, director of the James E. Scott Community Association, observed Miami's two major riots: 1968 and 1980.

> In the Miami riot of 1968 people did it because they [thought], 'Maybe now we'll get results. Something will happen.' But this (1980) riot was a lot different. It was brutal; it was done out of pure hostility, out of intense hatred. They weren't out there to get something. They wanted to hurt people.[1194]

This gravely concerned the interests behind the report. Their fear was that the so-called "Miami style" insurrection would become "the national norm,"[1195] and wanted to know if the 1980 Miami riot "introduced a new style to urban disorders of the future-whether crossed once, the bounds will be easier to cross again" or if this was an isolated aberration not likely to be repeated.[1196] How did the U.S. government respond to this jaw-dropping display of Black Rage against Whites? With crack cocaine. Crack debuted in Miami the very next year in 1981 – the year of the report - right in the area that was ground zero for the insurrection: Liberty City.[1197] Los Angeles and Miami were

---

[1191] Porter and Dunn, ***Miami Riot***, 58.

[1192] Celia W. Dugger, "The day Miami was rocked by riot after cops cleared in McDuffie beating," ***Miami Herald*** May 15, 2016.

[1193] Porter and Dunn, ***Miami Riot***, 62.

[1194] Porter and Dunn, ***Miami Riot***, 176.

[1195] Thomas, "Study Finds Miami Riot was Unlike Those of 60's."

[1196] Porter and Dunn, ***Miami Riot***, 178.

[1197] G. Witkin and G. Mukenge, "The Men Who Invented Crack," ***U.S. News & World Report*** August 19, 1991; James A. Inciardi, "Crack-

thus the "two cradles of 'crack' cocaine" in Black America.[1198] As Garry Webb documented for us, the CIA was at the root of the crack explosion in Cradle I (Los Angeles) that began in 1981. The same is true in Cradle II: Miami. It is usually said that Caribbean immigrants introduced crack to Miami, but these Jamaican posses had been organized by the CIA in the 1970s to destabilize the Michael Manley government of Jamaica and to move its (the CIA's) cocaine.[1199]

So, in 1981 the U.S. government unleased crack cocaine on Black LA and Black Miami. But something else happened that year. In 1981 the very first Saviours Day occurred in Chicago, signaling the Honorable Minister Farrakhan's success in rebuilding the Nation of Islam after its fall in 1975. The Nation is officially back. That too was 1981. Also important 1981-event: Edgar Bronfman Sr. became president of the World Jewish Congress. The significance of this co-incidence will become clear later.

II.   *The Government Prepares for War with the Black Muslims*

Immediately upon his ascent to the presidency in 1980 Reagan established his "Secret Team."[1200] They were largely his California team when he was governor. Earl Brian, William Herrmann, Edwin Meese, and Louis Giuffrida are just a few of Reagan's California team that also helped him execute his presidential agenda in Washington D.C. A consequence of this fact is that the "Black Peril" exercises and preparation that were conducted on a state level were now made a part of *national* planning. "The cadres developing Cable Splicer (headed by Louis Giuffrida) were with Reagan's

Cocaine in Miami," in *The Epidemiology of Cocaine Use and Abuse* ed. Susan Schober and Charles Schade (Washington D.C., 1991) 263-274.

[1198] Gary Webb, "Drug Expert: 'Crack' born in San Francisco Bay Area in '74," *San Jose Mercury News* August 19, 1996.

[1199] Casey Gane-McCalla, *Inside the CIA's Secret War in Jamaica* (Over The Edge Books, 2016); idem., "How The CIA Created The Jamaican Shower Posse," *NewsOne* June 3, 2010

[1200] Chardy, "Reagan Sides and the Secret Government."

elevation to the presidency transferred into FEMA,"[1201] Peter Dale Scott informs us. Diana Reynolds elaborates:

When Ronald Reagan came to power he gave FEMA vastly expanded executive emergency powers and appointed retired National Guard General Louis O. Giuffrida as his "emergency czar"... Shortly after he assumed the directorship of FEMA in 1981, Giuffrida had flooded high-level FEMA posts with friends from CSTI and the military police, had created a Civil Security Division of FEMA, and had established a Civil Defense Training Center in Emmitsburg, Maryland–based on the CSTI model. By 1984, the Center had trained one thousand civil defense personnel in survival techniques, counterterrorism and military police methods.[1202]

Between 1982 and 1984 FEMA Director Giuffrida and Lt. Col. Oliver North collaborated "in revising [U.S.] contingency plans for dealing with nuclear war, insurrection or massive military mobilization."[1203] Then, "In early 1984, FEMA, military, and other government officials met in portentous secrecy to plan a 'readiness exercise' code-named Rex-84."[1204] Rex-84 stands for "readiness exercise 1984," with "readiness" implying emergency preparedness. Rex-84 is a classified nation-wide drill that postulated a scenario of massive civil unrest and the need to detain and intern large numbers of citizens deemed to be a national security threat. The first exclusive story on Rex-84 was provided by James Harrer writing for the Liberty Lobby's *Spotlight*. Based on the confidential reporting of two Army officers, one stationed at Fort Benning, Georgia and the other at Fort Chaffe, Arkansas, the April 23, 1984 edition of *Spotlight* featured the headline: "Reagan Orders Concentration Camps," and read in part:

Mass detention facilities–otherwise known as concentration camps–are being set up at a number of major U.S. military installations on the secret orders of President Ronald Reagan.

[1201] Scott, *American Deep State*, 206 n. 4.
[1202] Reynolds, "FEMA and the NSC," 54-55.
[1203] Chardy, "Reagan Sides and the Secret Government."
[1204] Jonathan Vankin and John Whalen, *The 70 Greatest Conspiracies of All Time: History's Biggest Mysteries, Coverups & Cabals* (New Jersey: Carol Publishing Group, 1998 [1995]) 30.

The SPOTLIGHT has learned that on April 5 the White House issued a highly classified National Security Decision Directive (NSDD) which sets forth urgent instructions for the "activation" of 10 huge prison camps at key defense commands located across the nation... The SPOTLIGHT received information from two trustworthy confidential sources–patriotic career Army officers–stationed at Ft. Benning, Georgia, and Ft. Chaffee, Arkansas, revealing that preparations were being set in motion for an unprecedented roundup of aliens and "security suspects" coast to coast.

According to these sources, the primary goal of the vast police operation, codenamed "Rex 84," is to detain and deport illegal immigrants.

But these sources say "Rex 84" has another, even more closely guarded and carefully orchestrated objective: To apply so-called "C&C" ("capture and custody") measures against political opponents, resisters or even outspoken critics whom the administration considers "dangerous"...

"The first roundup–and the publicly announced one–will be of illegal aliens and refugees," a military source told The SPOTLIGHT. "But under the secret provisions of 'Rex 84' there will be also broad arrests of security suspects, who can be held in these centers, under this emergency order, whether they're U.S. citizens or not."

Americans whom the administration suspects of belonging to so-called "violence-prone" groups, or of "supporting" such groups–which may mean only that a citizen subscribes to the wrong newsletter–may find themselves hauled in with hordes of illegal immigrants if the bureaucrats find them "dangerous."[1205]

Freedom of Information Act disclosures reveal that Harrer's sources and reporting were "substantially accurate." On April 5, 1984 President Reagan issued a highly classified National Security Decision Directive (NSDD) "which sets forth *urgent instructions* for the 'activation' of 10 huge prison camps at key defense commands located across the nation." The "urgency," whatever the source, was real. Immediately this White House directive was operationalized. Between April 5-13, 1984 FEMA

[1205] James Harrer, "Reagan Orders Concentration Camps," ***Spotlight*** April 23, 1984.

in association with 34 other federal departments and agencies conducted a civil readiness exercise *in coordination with the Joint Chiefs*. This "readiness exercise" has two parts: Rex-84 Alpha and Rex-84 Bravo, "both of which are conducted in conjunction with a Joint Chiefs exercise known as Night Train 84..."[1206] Rex-84 Alpha focuses of nuclear fallout. On the other hand, "During [Rex-84 Bravo], the government practices plans for imposing martial law, deploying military forces in U.S. cities, and arresting civilians considered threats to national security."[1207] Reynolds informs us further:

> In the combined exercise (FEMA and Joint Chiefs), Rex-84 Bravo, FEMA and DOD led the other federal agencies and departments, including the Central Intelligence Agency, the Secret Service, the Treasury, the Federal Bureau of Investigation, and the Veterans Administration through a gaming exercise to test military assistance in civil defense. The exercise anticipated civil disturbances, major demonstrations and strikes that would affect continuity of government and/or resource mobilization. To fight subversive activities, there was authorization for the military to implement *government ordered movements of civilian populations* at state and regional levels, the arrest of certain unidentified segments of the population, and the imposition of martial rule.[1208]

What created the urgency in 1984 that FEMA and the Joint Chiefs engage in nation-wide *war* and mass detention drills? The **Miami Herald** alerts us to it:

> The martial law portions of the (secret contingency) plan were outlined in a June 30, 1982, memo by Guiffrida's deputy for national preparedness programs, John Brinkerhoff. A copy of the memo was obtained by The Herald. The scenario outlined in the Brinkerhoff memo resembled somewhat a paper Guiffrida had written in 1970 at the Army War College in Carlisle, Pa., in which he advocated martial law *in case of a national uprising by black militants*. The paper also advocated the roundup and transfer to "assembly centers or relocation

---

[1206] Douglas E. Campbell, **Continuity of Government: How the U.S. Government Functions After All Hell Breaks Loose** (Syneca Research Group, Inc., 2016) 69.
[1207] Douglas E. Campbell, **Continuity of Government**, 69.
[1208] Diana Reynolds, "FEMA and the NSC: The Rose of the National Security State," **CovertAction** 33 (Winter 1990): 54-58 (56).

camps" of *at least 21 million "American Negroes."* When he saw the FEMA plans, Attorney General [William French] Smith became alarmed.[1209]

If the Brinkerhoff memo outlines a scenario that "resembled somewhat" the "Black Peril" plan of 1970 Giuffrida, then in 1982 Reagan's Secret Team were planning the roundup and internment in detention camps of Black people in general or Black militants. Something was going on in 1984, however, that created an urgency from the White House's perspective to practice implementing the plan. We might have a subtle clue as to what that might have been. Some documents suggested that the urgent scenario was "uncontrolled population movement" sparked by a possible U.S. invasion of Nicaragua, setting off hordes of refugees swarming over the Mexican border and into the U.S. But this can't be the true concern. As Jonathan Vankin and John Whalen observe:

> the Mexican border's daunting terrain made an influx of gate crashers on the border of hundreds of thousands highly unlikely. In fact, more than one critic has suggested that Rex-84 was really a drill to practice rounding up crowds of *American citizens*...That Rex-84 dealt with more than merely apprehending illegal immigrants is certain.[1210]

As was disclosed to the ***Spotlight***, detaining our Brown Family under the pretense of "illegal immigrants" was always just a cover for the true objective, the rounding up of a particular group of American citizens, namely Black militants.

There is a very curious detail. During the Rex-84 Bravo drill FEMA, the 34 federal departments and agencies, and the Joint Chiefs anticipate intercepting a "mass exodus" of specifically *400,000* "aliens."[1211] How did the government come up with this figure, 400,000? Was it a purely arbitrary abstraction? Probably not. While I cannot say I that I have any information at all that will shine light on the motive behind this number 400,000 for the "mass exodus" that the White House

---

[1209] Alfonso Chardy, "Reagan Aides and the 'Secret Government'," *Miami Herald* July 5, 1987.
[1210] Vankin and Whalen, ***70 Greatest Conspiracies of All Time***, 30.
[1211] Vankin and Whalen, ***70 Greatest Conspiracies of All Time***, 30.

plans to intercept within a six hour period, I do draw our attention to a curious fact: In Ridley Scott's 2014 epic **Exodus: Gods and Kings** (20th Century Fox), recounting the Biblical story of Moses, Pharaoh, and the Exodus out of Egypt of the Children of Israel, the number of the *emigrating* or fleeing Hebrews is 400,000 and Pharaoh is found proclaiming in anger: "We are going to *recapture 400,000 slaves*" (see trailer). The Biblical Hebrew narrative *does not* give warrant for the number 400,000 so critics have declared that the movie "got it wrong."[1212] I can speculate on Ridley Scott's use of this number "400,000" no more than I can speculate on FEMA's. However, while I cannot prove it, I strongly believe that there is a connection between these two uses. I have a feeling (that I can't prove at this stage) that the architects of Rex-84 acknowledged Black Americans as the Biblical Children of Israel and Rex-84 is actually Pharaoh's (the White House's) plan to *intercept the Exodus*, not *into* this country by Nicaraguans but *out of this country* by the So-called Negro. As Ridley Scott's Pharaoh says: "We are going to *recapture* 400,000 slaves." The Most Honorable Elijah Muhammad in his lecture, "The Final War," said: "They (the Devils) don't want the so-called American Negro to go, but they don't want him to return to his own people. But they will be *forced* one of these days to give him up."

What happened in 1984 that created such "Rex-84" urgency?

Farrakhan happened in 1984. He burst onto the media scene as a surrogate of the presidential campaign of the Rev. Jesse Jackson during a speech at a rally for Rev. Jackson on February 25. On February 27, Farrakhan was dubbed "Black Hitler" by Nathan Pearlmutter of the Anti-Defamation League of B'nai B'rith and then by Nat Hentoff, Jewish columnist of the **Village Voice**. On March 11 in a radio broadcast from the Final Call Building in Chicago Minister Farrakhan's remarks on Adolf Hitler and **Washington Post** columnist Milton Colman

---

[1212] "I'm not sure where the EXODUS movie got 400,00 slaves, but it didn't come from a careful analysis of the Hebrew Bible." "Exodus: Movie and English Bible Get The Story Wrong," *reenactingtheway.com* November 23, 2014.

ignited further controversy.[1213] This is how Fred Barnes of the *New Republic* wrote.

> Eighteen months ago Farrakhan was the boss of a fringe Muslim sect with no more than 10,000 adherents nationwide. He was not an influential force among blacks nationally, and was scarcely known at all outside the black community. In 1984 he hooked up with Jesse Jackson's presidential campaign, threatened a *Washington Post* reporter who disclosed that Jackson had used the term "Hymie," trumpeted his own anti-Semitic views, and became infamous. Now he's a bigger draw than Jackson, who couldn't even defeat Jerry Falwell in a TV debate on South Africa. And money is pouring in. Farrakhan got five million dollars from Libyan dictator Muammar al-Qaddafi alone to finance a grandiose scheme to manufacture soap, napkins, and toothpaste in black neighborhoods.
>
> Those who have tried to isolate Farrakhan as a racist have only made matters worse. "There's a feeling in the black community, 'If whites are that upset, it must be good for black people,' " says George A. Dalley, the chief aide to New York representative Charles Rangel.
>
> The denunciations of Farrakhan It's mainstream black politicians, not Farrakhan, who have suffered as a consequence of the fuss.[1214]

After the February and March controversies, the National Security Decision Directive was issued by President Reagan on April 5 and the Rex-84 Bravo exercises began on April 5-13. Also that month, the U.S. Attorney's Office opened an investigation into Minister Farrakhan.[1215] After the Honorable Minister Farrakhan *burst* onto the scene in 1984 (though I'm sure the White House took notice in 1981 of his return) and after a year of Farrakhan sounding the Trumpet of Elijah across this country, Reagan, it appears, was ready to operationalize Garden Plot, Cable Splicer, and Rex-84. It appears that, by September

---

[1213] "Farrakhan and the Jewish Rift: How It All Started," *The Final Call* On-line Edition, 2001; Eleanor Randolph and Rick Atkinson, "Second Farrakhan Controversy Caused by Calling Hitler 'Great,'" *The Washington Post* April 12, 1984; "Farrakhan in Race, Politics and the News Media," *The New York Times* April 17, 1984.
[1214] Fred Barnes, "The Farrakhan Factor," *The New Republic* October 26, 1985.
[1215] "The U.S. attorney's office has opened an investigation into..." *UPI* April 11, 1984.

of 1985, the Rex-84 war drill had become a part of a *war plan*. President Ronald Reagan had met with his Joint Chiefs of Staff to plan the war that *he* had been literally and physically preparing for since his California governorship days. President Reagan was ready for his long-sought war against Black People, starting with the Black militants in particular – the Nation of Islam.

As the Crack Holocaust was burning in South Central Los Angeles for fears now, Farrakhan arrived there in September of 1985 and drew 18,000 Black people to the Forum sports arena. "The crowd was predominantly black, largely male and ranged from young to middle-age," declared the *Los Angeles Times*.[1216] The *New York Times* reported also:

> The cars parked at the Forum sports arena, Chevrolets and Toyotas, Mercedes-Benzes and BMW's, family sedans and clunkers, represented the whole spectrum of southern California incomes and lifestyles. They were driven by people who turned out Saturday night to hear a speech by Louis Farrakhan, the leader of a Black Muslim sect. Mr. Farrakhan drew nearly 15,000 (*sic*) people, evidence that in the last year he has gained recognition, if not followers, substantially beyond the Nation of Islam, a small extremist religious sect he heads.[1217]

Farrakhan went from LA to New York. On October 7, 1985 Farrakhan rode triumphantly into the city of the largest Jewish population in the U.S. at the time and brought 50,000 Black people out to the Madison Square Gardens and the Felt Forum. *The Washington Post* lamented that "Farrakhan Draws Huge Crowd" of "cheering blacks."[1218] Outside the Garden the Jewish Defense Organization protested holding placards calling for "death to Farrakhan."[1219]

How did President Reagan and the U.S. government respond to Farrakhan's wildly triumphant ride into New York?

[1216] Penelope McMillan and Cathleen Decker, "Israel a 'Wicked Hypocrisy'--Farrakhan: Forum Speech Before 14,000 Touches on Foreign Policy, Economics," *Los Angeles Times* September 15, 1985.

[1217] Judith Cummings, "Diverse Crowd Hears Farrakhan in Los Angeles," *The New York Times* September 16, 1985.

[1218] Margot Hornblower, "Farrakhan Draws Huge Crowd," *The Washington Post* October 8, 1985.

[1219] "Farrakhan Brings His Message of Bigotry and Anti-semitism to N.y.c.," *Jewish Telegraphic Agency* October 9, 1985.

That next month crack cocaine made its first official appearance in New York.

> The word 'crack' was first used to refer to a type of cocaine in a 1985 newspaper article. By the end of 1986 more than a thousand articles about crack had appeared in major newspapers and magazines and CBS News had aired a prime-time report on the crack epidemic viewed by fifteen people (...)[1220]

The newspaper article referred to was the November 17, 1985 edition of *The New York Times*, where the term "Crack" was used for the very first time in the press and introduced to the American lexicon, saying: "Three teen-agers have sought treatment already this year...for cocaine dependence resulting from the use of a new form of the drug called "crack," or rock-like pieces of prepared 'freebase' (concentrated cocaine)."[1221] "already this year" is certainly a euphemism which really should be read, "in the days between October 8 and November 16."

It wasn't until November 29, 1985 that *The New York Times* announced: "A new form of cocaine is for sale is for sale on the streets of New York, alarming officials and rehabilitation experts...the substance (is) known as crack..."[1222] While it is claimed that "Crack appeared on the streets of the Bronx last year," the article goes on to confess that it was "Earlier this month (i.e. November)" that "what is believed to be one of the country's first raids of a crack factory" occurred. What is indisputable is that the world was introduced to "crack" cocaine use in New York for the very first time one month after Farrakhan's magnetic visit to the city. The circumstances strongly suggest that this is when crack was first introduced to the Black population of New York. Thus, the riot of Miami in 1980 led to the appearance of the government's crack in 1981 and the Farrakhan Draw of 50,000 in New York in October 1985 led to the appearance of the government's crack there in November of 1985.

[1220] Jean Ruth Schroedel, *Is the Fetus a Person? A Comparison of Policies Across the Fifty States* (Ithaca: Cornell University Press, 2000) 101.

[1221] Donna Boundy, "Program For Cocaine-Abuse Under Way," *The New York Times* November 17, 1985.

[1222] Jane Gross, "A New, Purified Form of Cocaine Causes Alarm as Abuse Increases," *The New York Times* November 29, 1985.

III.   *Hip Hop and the Shadow of Farrakhan*

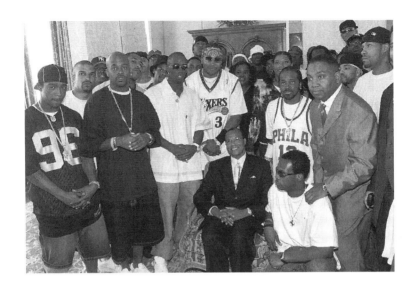

It is not inappropriate to take notice of the many Hip Hop superstars who have recently dinned with, shout outed or has been mentored to one degree or another by The Honorable Minister Farrakhan. One can mention for starters: Kanye West, Young Jeezy, Killer Mike, Jay Z, 2 Chainz, Young Thug, David Banner, Jay Electronica, Rick Ross, Ludacris, Ice Cube, Snoop Dog, Common, Birdman, The Game, Ja Rule, T.I., and more. One should not, however, as **Salon** did, describe this as a "recent trend in hip-hop."[1223] Rather, as Salim Muwakkil wrote in 2003: "Nation of Islam leader Farrakhan and hip hop go way back...Farrakhan's voice has been popping up on rap records since the genre's earliest years and rappers ranging the spectrum (from "conscious" to "gangsta") often speak his praises on record and off."[1224]

A pivotal moment in the relationship between Farrakhan and the Hip Hop community occurred in 1980. That year Minister Farrakhan was chosen to give the keynote address

---

[1223] Matthew Pulver, "Louis Farrakhan, rising: White Rap's superstars at his side, the Nation of Islam leaders steps forward in the new fight for civil rights," **Salon** April 28, 2015.
[1224] Salim Muwakkil, "Farrakhan and the Beefs of Rap," **In These Times** December 15, 2003.

at the 4th annual Jack The Rapper Family Affair convention, which brought Black music executives and artists together in Atlanta (and then in Orlando) for two decades. During the Minister's incredible message he referenced the Miami Riot as a sign of people rising up against the hand of tyranny. Further, Farrakhan "accurately predicted the co-opting of black radio, black labels and artists,"[1225] as it would happen only decades later. The Minister said:

> You know Brothers and Sisters, the wickedly wise who rule this world understand that thought is produced by what you see, hear, and taste and feel; that through your senses messages come in to create thought. And if they can control what you see, what you hear, what you taste, what you smell, they also can control how you feel, and how you think [and they] can predict your action and master you without you ever knowing that you are in 1980 a bigger slave than your parents were in 1680.
>
> White folks is into the business of mind control. Don't you know why Black people are not productive? It's because their minds are being controlled and you are the agent that they are using, you in Black Music![1226]

The co-opting of Black music as a tool of mind control and behavior modification is here laid out clearly by the Honorable Minister Farrakhan *in 1980*. It will occur exactly as revealed to the Minister.

IV.   *Public Enemy*

Public Enemy changed everything about Black America. They made [Louis] Farrakhan popular. They helped make the Million Man March. They put red, black, and green shit around niggas' necks instead of chains. They did everything. They were amazing.[1227] – Russell Simmons

---

[1225] Alex Ogg, **The Men Behind Dej Jam: The Radical Rise of Russell Simmons and Rick Rubin** (London: Omnibus Press, 2009).

[1226] "Minister Louis Farrakhan - Heed The Call Y'all (1980)" @ https://www.youtube.com/watch?v=cDDFxzo89lE&t=2857s.

[1227] https://allhiphop.com/news/russell-simmons-public-enemy-made-louis-farrakhan-popular-H8Qr3FTVKUSR9d6xpHMbqw/

The late 1980s and early 1990s are said to have marked the "Golden Age of Rap Nationalism." This was a nationalism anchored in the teachings and the vision of the Nation of Islam. As Charise Cheney observes regarding the rap politicos of this era, "Black nationalism shapes their political position and, with few exceptions, the teachings of Elijah Muhammad informs their nationalist perspective."[1228] Mattias Gardell elaborates:

> The Hip-Hop movement's role in popularizing the message of Black militant Islam cannot be overestimated. What reggae was to Rastafarianism in the 1970's, so Hip Hop is to the spread of Black Islam in the 1980s and 1990s. Teenagers dance into black consciousness and internalize the NOI creed through hip-hop albums...Expressing thanks and support for the Nation of Islam and Louis Farrakhan has become almost standard practice on the rap albums, and long quotations from NOI literature are often included in the lyrics.[1229]

> Most of the more influential message rap artists are either members or sympathisers of the Nation of Islam or other, related, black Islamic organisations, such as the Moors or the Nation of Gods and Earths. This include renown stars like Public Enemy, Brand Nubian, Poor Righteous Teachers, Lakim Shabazz, Paris, KAM, Ice Cube, Queen Latifah, Sister Souljah, Prince Akeem, KRS-One, Professor Griff, Big Daddy Kane, Mister Cee, Paris, Skinny Boys and Afrika Bambaataa, to name but a few. They all preach black Islam and address issues like police brutality, gang violence, and social injustice. Aiming at reversing self-destructive patterns among black youth, rappers call for community up-building and black liberation.

> Rap lyrics frequently include quotations from black Muslim teachings, or make implicit allusions, using metaphors unintelligible to those unfamiliar with black Islamic beliefs, like "dead niggaz" (non-Muslim blacks), "Yacub's crew (whites) or "cave bitch" (white female).[1230]

[1228] Charise Cheney, "Representin' God: Rap, Religion and the Politics of a Culture," *The North Star: A Journal of African American Religious History* 3 (1999): 1-12 (1).

[1229] Mattias Gardell, *In The Name of Elijah Muhammad Louis Farrakhan and The Nation of Islam* (Durham: Duke University Press, 1996) 295-296.

[1230] Mattias Gardell, "Hip-Hop, Black Islamic Nationalism and the Quest Of Afro-American Empowerment," Presented at the 1st World

No group during this period illustrates the nexus between early Rap Nationalism and Islam, specifically the Honorable Minister Louis Farrakhan, better than Public Enemy. The success of the musically and politically radical rap group Public Enemy was spectacular. Arguably, Public Enemy as we came to know them were a product of the work of Farrakhan across the nation. "[T]he Black Muslim ideology supplied a moral energy to the verbal denunciations" in PE's music. [1231] Chuck D famously belted out:

> The follower of Farrakhan.
> Don't tell me that you understand
> Until you hear the man. ("Don't Believe The Hype," **It Takes A Nation of Millions To Hold Us Back** 1988)

> Farrakhan's a prophet and I think you ought to listen to
> What he can say to you, what you ought to do. ("Bring The Noise" **It Takes A Nation of Millions To Hold Us Back** 1988)

> Ain't nothing changed, still down with Farrakhan
> Yeah, some seconds ticked, but still a time bomb (Chuck D on Terminator X, "Buck Whylin'," from **Terminator X & The Valley of the Jeep Beets** (1991)

As Russell Myrie put it, "The shadow of Farrakhan and the Nation of Islam had always loomed large in PE's background."[1232] But Myrie also makes the important, but often unrecognized point: "Even more than Chuck, Griff then was a 'follower of Farrakhan'."[1233] Indeed, the "Black Muslim moral energy" of PE was supplied by Professor Griff, PE's Minister of Information. As Chuck D recounts in a 2001 interview with **The Final Call Online**:

Conference on Music and Censorship, Copenhagen 20-22 November, 1998.

[1231] Lewis Cole, "Public Enemy: Def or Dumb?" **Rolling Stone** October 19, 1989.

[1232] Myrie, **Don't Rhyme For The Sake of Riddlin'**, 131.

[1233] Russell Myrie, **Don't Rhyme For The Sake of Riddlin': The Authorized Story of Public Enemy** (New York: Canongate, 2008) 131.

In 1980, I was introduced to Min. Farrakhan by Professor Griff, who had been two years past his DJ days with Hank Shocklee's Spectrum City. Griff used to bring records by occasionally and one record he brought was Min. Farrakhan's address to the Jack The Rapper convention in 1979 (=1980).

In that speech he (Min. Farrakhan) directly dealt with the co-opting of Black Radio, The DJs, Record Companies, and Artists for their use of the musical art form; and with the media for manipulating the Black community into a "take from, not give back" mentality.[1234]

We thus see the impact that Minister Farrakhan's 1980 Jack The Rapper address had on the course of Hip Hop's development. Public Enemy later used samples of that 1980 Jack The Rapper speech on "Terminator X To The Edge of Panic" (***It Takes A Nation of Millions To Hold Us Back***)."

The "Farrakhan Energy" that permeated PE's sound and whole vibe (with the S1Ws drilling on stage, FOI-style) all but guaranteed a collision with all of the Jews that surrounded the group. As PE publicist Bill Stephany put it: "There were so many people of Jewish background around them, more than black, by the way, that it would be pretty stupid to consider the group anti-Semitic...essentially Pubic Enemy's whole support system was people of Jewish background...There was the famous line: 'Public enemy were not anti-Semites, they were filo-Semites.'"[1235] The inevitable collision occurred in 1989 when Professor Griff gave the now infamous interview to David Mills of the ***Washington Times*** and allegedly declared that "Jews are responsible for the majority of the wickedness in the world." It can be said that "all hell broke out."

Shortly thereafter, the Jewish Defense Organization (JDO) — a militant group that claims a membership of 3,000 — announced a boycott of Public Enemy. Mordechai Levy, its main spokesman, said the JDO was going to "break PE in half." This threat was more bluster than anything else. Adler received two calls from wholesalers saying they were refusing to sell Public Enemy's records; the identifications left by both callers

---

[1234] Chuck D, "Eyes on Hip Hop," ***The Final Call On-Line Edition*** August 5, 2001
[1235] Myrie, ***Don't Rhyme For The Sake of Riddlin'***, 137.

proved fictitious. (Levy was later arrested after shooting at the leader of the rival Jewish Defense League.)[1236]

But the threats were not actually pure "bluster." Bill Adler, the Jewish publicist of the group, recounted:

> After that interview, I got a visit to the office by a sweaty guy called Mordechai Levy, who claimed to represent the Jewish Defense Organization. He said there was a truckload of armed Jews looking for Public Enemy! Thankfully, nothing came of it.[1237]

The JDO is the group that protested the Honorable Minister Farrakhan outside Madison Square Gardens with placards reading "death to Farrakhan." Rick Rubin, who initially signed the non-radicalized Chuck D and is Jewish, was actually a *fan* of this Jewish terrorist group led by Mordechai Levy. Rubin recounts how the JDO was outraged by his promotion of "violently anti-Jewish lyrics by Black ghetto groups" and they thus reportedly came looking to beat him up. Rubin couldn't make sense of their anger *at him*. He told an interviewer that:

> They (the JDO) should've talked to me and found out what I felt before coming to attack me, because I was a JDO [Jewish Defense Organization] supporter. When I was at NYU I saw [right wing rabbi] Meir Kahane speak and he blew me away – he was amazing ... After hearing him speak, I wanted to pack my bags and go to Israel ... I called the JDO several times, wanted to join, but they never returned my calls.[1238]

The Jew Rick Rubin, who supported the JDO, didn't like Black political/cultural consciousness at all, especially in Hip Hop. As **Spin** reported in 1990: "he doesn't deny...his dislike for Afrocentric-style hip hop."[1239] In fact, Rubin calls it "bullshit." Rubin even dismissed Public Enemy's political posture as simply a later "angle" or gimmick to be different. He said:

[1236] Lewis Cole, "Public Enemy: Def or Dumb?" **Rolling Stone** October 19, 1989.

[1237] Hardeep Phull, "Def Jam's wild early days: An oral history," **New York Post** October 11, 2014.

[1238] Farr, **Moguls and Madmen**, 123.

[1239] Frank Owen, "Geto Boys and Rick Ruben: Spin's 1990 Feature, 'Censorship Isn't Def American'" **Spin** November 1990.

508

"To be honest, I think the majority of that stuff is bullshit," says Rubin. "People wear Africa medallions because it's this week's fashion. If next week it was cool to wear a KKK hood, then they'd wear that."

"I don't think the reason people listen to hip hop is to be preached at. I don't think that artists are valid politicians. I'm uncomfortable with people thinking that Chuck D's politics are either brilliant or not 100 percent valid. He's a rapper, he's not running for President. *You listen to the first P.E. album and Chuck's talking about riding around in his '89 Oldsmobile and people treating him like Kareem Abdul-Jabbar.* The political side of Public Enemy only came into things as an angle, as something to write about that's different from 'I've got more gold.' They were college students who had an idea to make cool records. I don't think that anybody in Public Enemy *at the beginning* had any thoughts about being able to change the world."[1240]

According to Rubin, the Chuck D that *he* originally signed was less political and more urban typical, i.e. braggadocious. But between the first PE album (***Yo Bum Rush the Show*** 1987) and the second (***It Takes a Nation of Millions to Hold Us Back***), which was their markedly political and pro-Farrakhan offering, Rubin lost interest in Hip Hop. Rubin abandoned political PE and abandoned hip hop for rock n roll. Rubin would not have another interest in Black rap music until he heard the slasher and morbid Geto Boys, which was the first rap group he had signed since Public Enemy. [1241] So the Jewish Rick Rubin who admired the racist Meir Kahane also had a disdain for Black cultural and political consciousness, at least in hip hop.

But the fallout after Professor Griff's published remarks was significant. CBS Records CEO Walter Yetnikoff, the most powerful man in the music industry and a Brooklyn Jew who was said to wear his Jewishness "like a gaberdine,"[1242] describes his reaction after being informed of the Griff affair in his book, ***Howling at the Moon***:

[1240] Frank Owen, "Geto Boys and Rick Ruben: Spin's 1990 Feature, 'Censorship Isn't Def American'" ***Spin*** November 1990.
[1241] Frank Owen, "Geto Boys and Rick Ruben: Spin's 1990 Feature, 'Censorship Isn't Def American'" ***Spin*** November 1990.
[1242] Fred Goodman, "The Rolling Stone Interview: Walter Yetnikoff," ***Rolling Stone*** December 15, 1988.

My first instinct was to can Public Enemy and throw Griff in the East River. But that wouldn't work. Their *It Takes a Nation of Millions to Hold Us Back*, a brilliant work, sold millions, and their new one...was poised to sell even more. I had a responsibility to CBS shareholders. I was the responsible guy. But this was [Tommy Mottola]'s problem. "You handle it." I told him.'"

Myrie notes:

Yetnikoff was not wrong. The controversy helped PE sell even more albums, to those curious to find out what all the fuss was about...If PE's second album had been a modest seller like its predecessor *Yo! Bum Rush the Show*, they would have most likely found themselves removed from the Def Jam roster swiftly. We shouldn't be too surprised by the label's business-minded attitude.[1243]

But there was some shaking up. As Bill Adler recalls:

I don't think Chuck bought into any of the specifics of anti-Semitism. And how could he, by the way! He was signed to a record contract by a Jewish guy named Rick Rubin. All the photos that the group cherished and that promoted the group – the album covers and the press releases – were shot by a Jew named Glen Friedman. His publicist was a guy named Bill Adler, who happened to be Jewish. His manager day-to-day was a Jew named Lyor Cohen. So if there was any kind of a Jewish conspiracy, it wasn't anti-Public Enemy, it was pro-Public Enemy! They were not the victims, they were the beneficiaries of a philo-Semitic conspiracy...And for me after I spoke to Chuck I thought, well, this is basically a mess and I'm not gonna help them manage this crisis. And so I withdrew. I told Lyor: you handle it. Let someone else handle it, but it ain't me."[1244]

Lyor Cohen took it upon himself to "handle" the Professor Griff "anti-Semitism" problem. He said:

When Professor Griff from Public Enemy said what he said, and it caused this whirlwind, the whole industry asked me, 'What

---

[1243] Myrie, *Don't Rhyme For The Sake of Riddlin'*, 134.
[1244] "Interview: Def Jam Publicist Bill Adler on Run–D.M.C.'s Lost Year and the Professor Griff Controversy," @
https://daily.redbullmusicacademy.com/2014/03/bill-adler-interview.

the fuck are you doing?'" Every president of every record company called and said, 'Drop them.' But I believe part of being Jewish is education. *And I believe I was instrumental in changing Public Enemy's views.* I said, 'Your voice is being muted because you say Jews are this or that. You can't make blanket statements. If you want your message out there' – and it was profound, I think – 'stop generalizing.' And I was the only Jew in their lives. What if I resigned? They would only be more alienated. I hadn't quit being a Jew. I can't quit being a Jew. Instead, I tried to have an impact. I felt I was doing the right thing. Not just as a Jew, as a person. They had a big voice – 'a nation of millions,' to quote their album. I had the Holocaust Museum shut down, and we had a private tour. The first thing we see is a Jewish skull plus a black person's skull equals a baboon. The last thing is a monkey with enormous lips dressed with a Star of David holding a trumpet and a sign saying, 'It's these Jews that are bringing in this music called jazz.'[1245]

Cohen arranged a meeting between Chuck D and Rabbi Abraham Cooper of the Simon Wiesenthal Center, who educated the rapper about "Jewish sensitivities."[1246] Chuck will subsequently rap:

Crucifixion ain't no fiction
So-called chosen, frozen
Apology made to whoever pleases
Still they got me, just like Jesus." Chuck D, "Welcome to the Terror-dome," *Fear of a Back Planet* 1990.

Rabbi Cooper took these lyrics as a personal slight and said these are "the code words of Farrakhan": "The phrase 'so-called chosen,' Cooper said, is pulled right out of the lexicon of Farrakhan's ideology."[1247]

The shadow of Farrakhan did indeed cover the black self-awareness of Public Enemy and most if not *all* of the Rap Nationalism of the era, and this was unacceptable to the powers that be in hip hop.

[1245] Rich Cohen, "The Story of Lyor Cohen: Little Lan$ky and the Big Check," **Rolling Stone** June 21, 2001.
[1246] "Public Enemy Cause Stir Again Tying Jews to Jesus' Crucifixion," **Jewish Telegraph Society** December 28, 1989.
[1247] "Public Enemy Cause Stir Again Tying Jews to Jesus' Crucifixion," **Jewish Telegraph Society** December 28, 1989.

V.   *From Gods to N.I.G.G.A.Z.*

no medallions / dreadlocks / or Black fist it's just that
gangsta glare/ with gangsta rap that gangsta shit,/ brings a
gang of snaps – Dr. Dre, "Dre Day" 1992.

      Gangsta Rap originally offered a critique of the societal and governmental criminalization of Black youth. However, after the major labels hijacked hip hop, gangsta rap became devoid of its subversive edge and promoted the dehumanizing representations of Black men and women. An instructive example of this development is Los Angeles's N.W.A. Most people are not aware of the fact that Dr. Dre initially was inspired by the aggressive politics of Public Enemy.

> And Dre, meanwhile, would listen to Public Enemy on the way to the studio. "That was our go-to," says Dre. "I was the biggest Public Enemy fan — I think it's what inspired the aggression of N.W.A. We just took a different route lyrically."[1248]

      This is very important. Early N.W.A. did produce some revolutionary protest music, but it reflected protest from Ground Zero of the Crack Apocalypse with its attendant gang violence, high tech weaponry, death, and carnage. There's *was* a counterculture rebellion against Reaganomics and its consequences, particularly as they effected South Central Los Angeles. Ice Cube's comically cautionary "Dope Man" (1987) is a realistically ambivalent portrayal of the original trapper, alternatively glamorizing the money and girls that the dealer possesses and threatening the drug pusher for the death he pushes. N.W.A.'s debut album *Straight Outta Compton* (1988) was (appropriately) a mix of nihilistic gunplay, casual misogyny, ghetto reportage (e.g. *Gangsta Gangsta*) and furious protest (e.g. *Fuck Tha Police*).
      But N.W.A.'s Gangsta Rap would devolve from "Keep It Real" commentary on the bleakness of urban Black life in the Crack Zone to caricature and self-parody. As Dr. Dre would admit:

[1248] Brian Hiatt, "N.W.A: American Gangstas," ***Rolling Stone*** August 27, 2015.

I wanted to make people go 'I can't believe he's saying that shit.' I wanted to go all the way left. Everybody trying to do this Black Power and shit, so I was like, let's give 'em an alternative, 'nigger nigger nigger fuck this fuck that bitch bitch bitch suck my dick, all types of shit, you know what I'm saying?[1249]

Ren was candid as well: *"It's just an image. We got to do something that would distinguish ourselves. We was just trying to be different."*[1250] The persona of N.W.A as it will evolve was a carefully crafted image that didn't really reflect reality. As Mark Blackwell of **Spin** perceived already in 1991:

N.W.A. is a lot like the WWE. Its members are always in character, blurring the distinction between fantasy and reality. What's being sold is a carefully constructed world of carefully crafted personae.[1251]

Will.i.am is thus not incorrect to note: "When you listened to N.W.A. you forget that Cube went to college and that Dre was in an electro funk band called World Class Wreckin' Cru."[1252]

[1249] Brian Cross, ed. *It's not about a salary: Rap, race and resistance in Los Angeles*. (London: Verso, 1993) 197.

[1250] Terry McDermott, "The Secret History of Gangsta Rap," *Los Angeles Times Magazine* Sunday April 14, 2002.

[1251] Mark Blackwell, "Niggaz 4 Dinner," *SPIN* September 1991: 55-57, 101 (56).

[1252] Keith Murphy, "Eazy-E: The Ruthless Life of an American Gangsta," *Vibe* September 2015.

If it can be said – and I think it can – that the Bully Coon with his shinny steel razor of the early 19th century coon songs is the ancestor of the late 20th century Gangsta Rapper with his nickel platted 9 mm, then as with the former the latter must be understood as the product of Jewish fabrication. N.W.A. did not devolve from "reality rappers" to caricatures of Black self-destruction on their own.

Reflecting on hearing N.W.A.'s "Straight Outta Compton" and "Boyz N Tha Hood" for the first time Jerry Heller said: "It blew me away. I thought it was the most important music I had ever heard. *This was music that would change everything.*" So Heller put up $250,000 to Eazy E's $7000 toward the establishment of Ruthless Records. But Ruthless needed distribution. Enter fellow Jew Bryan Turner.

Jerry Heller   Bryan Turner

A Winnipeg, Manitoba native and son of a Canadian Jewish junk peddler, Turner is a Jewish rags-to-riches pop music success story who knew Jerry Heller from the industry. In 1985 Turner and Mark Cerami founded Priority Records and became rap impresarios.

> The real-life Winnipeg (Bryan Turner) expat helped foster the careers of most of the first generation of U.S. gangsta rappers. It was Turner who signed Ice Cube after he quit N.W.A. It was Turner who shuttled back and forth between Louisiana and Suge Knight's California prison cell to get Snoop Dogg out of his deal with Death Row Records. It was Turner who signed Ice T after Warner Music dropped the rapper over his song Cop Killer.[1253]

By 1998 Priority Records dominated the rap scene, such that *The New York Times* dubbed Turner "The Secret Power in Big Rap":

> When the pioneering gangsta rap group N.W.A was looking for its first record deal, it found a distributor in Priority Records, which released an album so obscene it prompted a letter of complaint from the F.B.I. When Ice-T left Warner Brothers Records after police groups and the company's shareholders objected to his song "Cop Killer," he found a new home at Priority. When Suge Knight, the imprisoned head of Death Row Records, who is known for his pugnacious business tactics, was looking for his first deal, Priority gave it to him.

> Through all the violence and controversy of hardcore rap music... the Los Angeles label Priority Records has been a major player. Yet Priority has somehow escaped censure... "And let me tell you something, man, that takes strategy," said Mr. Turner... In quietly distributing the rap albums that large corporations would not touch, Priority became the country's largest independent label in the mid-90's...Mr. Turner has remained in the shadows.[1254]

But it all started for Turner and Priority Records with N.W.A. Turner said Public Enemy and KRS-One "prepared me for

---

[1253] Bartley Kives, "Straight outta West K," *Winnipeg Free Press* September 8, 2015.
[1254] Neil Strauss, "The Secret Power in Big Rap; Bryan Turner Makes Rap Records but Escapes the Criticism," *The NYT* September 3, 1998.

N.W.A."[1255] Turner said he could not relate to the gangs, drugs, police brutality and racial profiling found in N.W.A.'s music. "I couldn't relate to it. Being from Winnipeg, how could I possibly? It was frightening to me. I knew it would scare the shit out of a lot of people"[1256] Scare the shit out of people and make him a lot of money in the process.

> The music was startling. Turner admits he didn't get it at first. He was sold when Jerry [Heller] brought him to an N.W.A. gig at Sherman Square Roller Rink in Reseda (Jerry taking him through the stage door so he wouldn't get a glimpse of the weapons folks tossed before going through the metal detectors). The label head (Turner) was dumbstruck seeing the crowd chant "Fuck tha Police"-the most controversial of the three recordings he had previewed...A week after the concert, Turner and Cerami agreed to finance and distribute **Straight Outta Compton** and **Eazy-Duz-It** through Priority via Eazy's Ruthless Records.[1257]

Turner had the appetites of *White people* in mind when promoting N.W.A., similar to the Jewish producers of the 19th century Coon Songs.

> "One day Jerry Heller brought the group in," Mr. Turner remembered. "They were 18 years old. And I was like, 'Let's do it. This is some scary stuff. *It will scare some white people here.*' From a business perspective, N.W.A completely fit in with what our success had been... Radio wasn't going to play any of those songs. It was strictly retail marketing, which was our strength... After working with N.W.A and Eazy-E's label, Ruthless, Mr. Turner became a gangsta rap mogul, making deals with Rap-a-Lot, the Houston label responsible for one of the genre's most extreme acts, the Geto Boys, and No Limit Records, which released six of the eight records Priority has in this week's Billboard top 100 pop album chart.[1258]

[1255] Robert Hilburn, "Making Music the Priority," **Los Angeles Times** January 6, 1999.

[1256] Bartley Kives, "Straight outta West K," **Winnipeg Free Press** September 8, 2015.

[1257] Gerrick D. Kennedy, **Parental Discretion Is Advised: The Rise of N.W.A and the Dawn of Gangsta Rap** (New York: Atria, 2018) 105-106.

[1258] Neil Strauss, "The Secret Power in Big Rap; Bryan Turner Makes Rap Records but Escapes the Criticism," **The NYT** September 3, 1998.

Turner told writer Jeff Chang: "That's how we sold two million. White kids in the valley picked it up and they decided they wanted to live vicariously through this music. Kids were just waiting for it"; [1259] "I heard 'Fuck Tha Police and I thought, 'I'm going to scare the shit out of a lot of white people with this stuff'"[1260]; "I know white kids in the suburbs, would love to hear the message being spit about the life of black urban youth in 517ere517ca (sic)."[1261] After Milt Ahlerich, assistant director of the FBI's Office of Public Affairs sent a threatening letter to Priority Turner thought: "It made them even more dangerous. So then kids were like, 'I gotta hear this record. The FBI doesn't want me to hear it!' We probably sold about a million records in conjunction with that letter."[1262] Turner and Priority Records gave Dr. Dre the $200,000 needed to produce his debut solo album, **The Chronic**.[1263] Thus when **Time Magazine** points out that "Priority has built a financial fortune and a reputation as the music industry's House of Raunchy Rap"[1264] this *must be* seen in the historical context of the Jewish fabrication and merchandizing of Blackness for White America's amusement. "The best visual," Turner would later recollect, "is my elderly Jewish parents, surrounded in their den by these gangsta-rap plaques. What are the odds?"[1265] The odds were quite great, in fact.

> The more rappers were packaged as violent black criminals, the bigger their white audiences became...Rap's appeal to whites rested in its evocation of an age-old image of blackness: a foreign, sexually charged, and criminal underworld against which the

[1259] Ernest Hardy and August Brown, "Los Angeles riots: Gangsta rap foretold them and grew after them," **LA Times** May 2, 2012.
[1260] Brian Hiatt, "N.W.A: American Gangstas," **Rolling Stone** August 27, 2015.
[1261] "Is Rap Music A Black Man's Hustle and A White Man's Paradise," **Is Hip Hop Dead** January 3, 2017.
[1262] Brian Hiatt, "N.W.A: American Gangstas," **Rolling Stone** August 27, 2015.
[1263] Jory Farr, **Moguls and Madmen** (New York: Simon & Schuster, 1994) 94.
[1264] Thomas McCarroll, "Taking The Bad Rap" **Time** July 24 2001.
[1265] Bartley Kives, "Straight outta West K," **Winnipeg Free Press** September 8, 2015.

norms of white society are defined, and, by extension, through which they may be defied.[1266]

These Jewish managers of the career and image of N.W.A. helped make sure they *lived up* to the fabricated persona. Heller records that "He (Easy-E) had more guns than Charlton Heston. Little derringers, homemade zip guns, plastic laser-scope Glock-style automatics undetectable by metal scanners."[1267] Where did he gets these high-tech weapons from? Dave Brooks, writing for **Amplify**, shares a number of "little known facts" about Heller, including the following remarkable scenario:

> It's probably no surprise that Eazy-E and the rest of the N.W.A./Ruthless crew loved their guns. Eazy had special compartments built into his cars where he could hide weapons. Heller said the group spent so much money on guns — both as stage props and real life Uzis and machine guns — that the band was able to take $80,000 in IRS deductions by labeling their arsenal as "stage ordinance."

Whose mind is behind this tax-guns arrangement? It is highly doubtful that these particular "Niggaz Wit Attitude" came up with this on their own. Brooks continues:

> Of course traveling with that type of weaponry is extremely dangerous, so *Heller devised a simple system to avoid friendly fire incidents.* When the band was on tour, ammunition and weapons traveled on separate busses. There were plenty of incidents when shooting almost broke out — Heller remembers one time when Cube and NWA's head of security were angry that someone inside a concert venue threw ice at Ice Cube during a soundcheck. Ice at Ice Cube, get it? KJ and Cube didn't think it was funny. The tour manager, a guy named Atron Gregory, cornered Heller and emphatically announced "KJ says he wants his bullets."

> "It was nearing the end of the tour. Everyone was sick of each other. I was tired of playing the authority figure," Heller wrote. "'Okay,' I said, laughing. 'Give him the fucking bullets.' I

[1266] David Samuels, "The Rap on Rap: The 'black music' that isn't either," **The New Republic** November 11, 1991.
[1267] Dave Brooks, "Let's Be Real About Jerry Heller," **Amplify** September 6, 2016.

walked away laughing. The bullets were indeed broken out, but never used. Cube and KJ never shot the ice tossers."[1268]

Jerry Heller clearly was the "boss man" when it came to N.W.A.'s arsenal, and he was *not* averse to greenlighting the use of these weapons against other Black people. In fact, Heller clearly found the prospect amusing.

A *N.I.G.G.A* AT THE WHITE HOUSE

Both Jerry Heller and Eazy E were rewarded by the Bush White House for their cultural productions that so entertained White America as the Coon Songs once did and which served the anti-Black policy interests of the Bush Administration. In March 1991 Eazy E and Jerry Heller were invited by Republican Senate leader Bob Dole to attend an exclusive Republican Senatorial Inner Circle "Salute to the Commander in Chief" luncheon in Washington D.C. where President Bush was to speak. The Inner Circle was the largest group-membership fund-raising arm of the National Republican Committee, "dedicated to advancing America's heritage of freedom and prosperity by capturing a Republican majority in the U.S. Senate." It's 1,400 members are mostly White, middle-aged Republicans. Both Eazy *and Heller* received invitations to the Inner Circle Dinner.[1269] As Chuck Philips reported:

> "The last time Wright (=Eazy E) heard from anyone from the federal government was in 1989, when an FBI official sent a letter to N.W.A.'s record company—Los Angeles-based Priority Records—claiming that a song on the group's "Straight Outta Compton" album encourages violence against law enforcement officers."
>
> ...
>
> "Wright, 23, a self-professed ex-gangster and former drug dealer, received his invitation to the closed-door fund-raiser after he contributed $2,490 to the Republican Party at the

---

[1268] Dave Brooks, "Let's Be Real About Jerry Heller," *Amplify* September 6, 2016.
[1269] Dave Brooks, "Let's Be Real About Jerry Heller," *Amplify* September 6, 2016.

urging of Sen. Phil Gramm (R-Texas), said Wright's spokesman, Norman Winter.

...

"Sources suggested that Wright's name may have been taken from fund-raising lists, pointing out the rapper donated $10,000 last year to a City of Hope charity banquet in Los Angeles. Winter said that Wright is a big "Bush fan" and departed on a flight Sunday to attend the luncheon.

The Inner Circle is a group of Republican campaign contributors–including brewing magnate Joseph Coors, actor Arnold Schwarzenegger, retailer Sam Walton and former Secretary of State George Shultz–that meets on a regular basis to discuss national and regional topics in a "comfortable mix of business and social settings," according to Dole's letter."[1270]

While at the luncheon Eazy E attended political strategy briefings. The invite meant that Eazy was "a member of the Republican Senatorial Inner Circle."[1271] He paid his $1000 annual dues, provided his Social Security Number and passed the Secret Service security clearance necessary for Inner Circle events with the president and vice president" !!! A former drug dealer and gun brandisher! Texas Senator Phil Gramm's letter of invitation to Eazy included: "I placed your name in nomination [for membership] because I believe your accomplishments and commitment prove you worthy of membership in this important organization." Also a warm letter from Sen. Robert Dole (R-Kansas): "Elizabeth and I are especially excited about the news of your nomination, because we will the chance to be with you."

The full-court press was on!

Wendy Burnley, Committee Director of Communications for the Inner Circle, explained the group's policy against divulging the selection process, but said: "This is clear and convincing evidence of the success of our new Rap-Outreach program.

[1270] Chuck Philips, "Rap's Bad Boy to Get Lunch With the Pres," **Los Angeles Times** March 18, 1991.
[1271] Martha Sherrill, "Guess Who's Coming To Lunch?" **The Washington Post** March 19, 1991.

Democrats, eat your heart out."[1272] Attempts to chalk Eazy's invitation up to a "computer foul up" therefore fails. And Eazy made it clear that he was not there because of his politics:

> SPIN: Was your contributions to the Republican Senatorial Inner Circle and luncheon with George Bush just a brilliant publicity stunt?
> Eazy: You know it! Everybody was dumb to that fact. Like Spike Lee, little bastard. He thought I was selling out or something. I paid $2,500 for a million dollars worth of publicity! I'm not a Republican or a Democrat. I don't give a fuck. I don't even vote.[1273]

A CBS Evening Report in 1991 by Washington Correspondent Bob Schieffer sums up the situation (from the White House's perspective) precisely and *revealingly*: "Finally, he's not a presidential advisor yet but *his rap has gained him entry into the Republican elite*." Wow.

THE NOI-ISRAELI SECURITY CONFLICT AND THE DEATH OF EAZY E

Around Eazy E's person the conflict between Jewish interests in Hip Hop and the influence of the Nation of Islam played out. During Ruthless Records hostilities with Death Row Records and Suge Knight, Heller brought into Ruthless Records both the Jewish Defense League and Israeli security personnel,[1274] specifically the "mysterious" Michael Klein. Heller says of Klein that he "had a background in the Israeli security forces". When Heller hired him as the new security director for Ruthless Records, Heller says:

> The effect was immediate and extreme. Somehow, the Suge Knight camp had Klein checked out and realized they were now

---

[1272] Martha Sherrill, "Guess Who's Coming To Lunch?" **The Washington Post** March 19, 1991; "N.W.A.'s Easy-E Lunched With President Bush," **Jet** April 15, 1991, p. 8.

[1273] Mark Blackwell, "Niggaz 4 Dinner," **SPIN** September 1991: 55-57, 101 (56).

[1274] "Jerry Heller, Jewish Gangsta-rap Impresario Behind N.W.A., Dies at 75," **Haaretz** Sep 04, 2016: "As a result of a spat following Dr. Dre's departure from Ruthless Records, Heller was said to have used the services of the extremist Jewish Defense League to protect him."

dealing with a Mossad-type mutherfucker who didn't fool around. Suge vanished. His crew vanished. An easy calm descended.[1275]

That makes sense. Before Klein moved to Los Angeles, says someone who knows him, the Israeli-born Klein "led a commando raid into southern Lebanon when they caught those guys that blew up the kibbutz kids on the school bus."[1276] Heller's cousin Gary Ballen, stage and production manager for N.W.A., likewise reported: "The first time I ever saw Mike Klein, it was a picture of him holding up two severed heads. He was one of those crazy Israeli army guys"[1277] As head of security "Klein tapped the Jewish Defense League to protect Ruthless in 1989."

On the other hand, Eazy E had begun aligning himself with the Nation of Islam, and at the time of his death, members of the Nation's security detail were guarding his hospital room. B.G. Knocc Out, a hip-hop artist and friend of Eazy, in a 2011 interview with HipHopDX recalled one important incident in particular.

> Before everything hit the fan with Eric and [manager] Jerry Heller, these brothers from the Nation of Islam from Chicago — some of [Minister Louis] Farrakhan's right hand men ... walked up in the [Ruthless Records] office ... [They] stormed in the office, into Jerry Heller's office, and told Eric to 'come here.' Eric got up and went into the conference room. They were in there for like two or three hours. And I swear, when they came out of there, Eric had a different look on his face. He seemed like he was shook up about something ... And like a week or so later, he started firing Jerry [and the rest of Heller's relatives at Ruthless]. He fired Jerry Heller. He fired Terry Heller. He fired Gary Ballen. And they were all family.

> The night before we go into the studio Eric had an episode with his bronchitis. He go to the hospital, [and] they kept him overnight. That next day he came directly from the hospital straight to the studio ... I went into the hallway [and] the man

---

[1275] Jerry Heller with Gil Reavill, **Ruthless: A Memoir** (New York: Simon Spotlight Entertainment, 2006) 193-194.

[1276] RJ Smith, "It Ain't Eazy," **Vibe** June-July 1998, pp. 118-124, 178 (124).

[1277] Bernadette Glacomazzo, "Eazy-E Allegedly Hired Ex-Israeli Soldier To 'Deal With' Suge Knight," **Hip Hop DX** May 17, 2018.

522

was in there by himself, sittin' on the floor wheezing, like, terribly. And I was like, 'You all right?' I sat down next to him, and he was tryin' to talk, and he had this big manila envelope in his hand, pulling out these faxes and all this stuff. He had records from where money was missing from the label — millions of dollars that he said Jerry was stealing from him. And Jerry was sending him idle threats, faxes and stuff like that.

On March 26, 1995 Eazy E was pronounced dead from complications of AIDS. He had been admitted on February 24 to Cedars-Sinai Medical Center in Los Angeles for a violent cough and was diagnosed with HIV/AIDS. The timing of his death raises a number of questions. N.W.A. were on the verge of a reunion shortly before Eazy's 1995 death. "If Eric hadn't passed away," says Dre, "we'd have definitely been working on another N.W.A record, and it would've been amazing. Eric and I talked about how stupid we were with dissing each other."[1278] In addition, and maybe *more consequentially*, "Five months before his 1995 death, Eazy-E was busy being Eric Wright. With the help of Tomica (his wife), he cleaned house at Ruthless, officially cutting ties with Heller and others on the payroll."[1279] Many close to Eazy smell foul play in his death. B.G. Knocc Out, for example, who is perhaps best known for appearing on Eazy-E's 1993 Dre diss, *Real Muthaphuckkin G's*, said in his 2011 song, "N My Prime" from his album, *Easy-E's I*: "the way my big homie went out, he didn't deserve it/they say he died of AIDS, but Eazy was cold murdered. I filtered out all the bullshit with my third iris/full blown AIDS but Tamica ain't got the virus?" In his HipHopDX interview he says further:

I believe in my heart somebody did something to Eric. Whether it was Jerry [Heller], whether it was [his widow] Tomica [Woods-Wright], I have yet to really know the truth about it. But, for a person to have full-blown AIDS [that quickly is suspicious]. My little brother, his father died from full-blown AIDS ... from sharing a needle ['cause] he was [an addict]. Now, I seen this man go through these stages, from HIV to full-blown AIDS. And, when you get a cold, any little thing like that, your whole immune system shut down. So you have to go into the hospital just to recover. Now, to be around Eric for the last three

[1278] Brian Hiatt, "N.W.A: American Gangstas," **Rolling Stone** August 27, 2015.
[1279] Keith Murphy, "Eazy-E: The Ruthless Life of an American Gangsta," **Vibe** September 2015.

years of his life and he never had an episode like this – never ever – something is strange, something is real odd. And then you gon' come out and tell me when the man go in there for bronchitis, you gon' come out and tell me this man had full-blown AIDS. And we done been to New York, we done been to Chicago in below zero weather [and] he never got sick. He never had an episode. Like, c'mon bruh. Who are you kidding?[1280]

Eazy E protégé Layzie Bone of **Bone Thugs-N-Harmony** also had reason to be suspicious. He told Angela Yee.

I have my own theory. He went in for the common cough, or pneumonia, which was January. Then in February, diagnosed as HIV-positive. Then March, full-blown AIDS [and] dead. I was kinda thinking, [what] kind of doctors did he go to? Even [Eazy-E's kids] that were born after he died, weren't positive. Even their mothers weren't positive. Nobody was positive. I believe [it's] just like the mystery of 'who killed Tupac' and 'who killed Biggie?'[1281]

Jerry Heller too put an interesting comment on the record:

"Do I think something fishy happened to Eazy? Absolutely," Heller told First Fam Radio. "I don't believe for a second that someone with as much money as we did—and could afford whatever like Magic Johnson could—who doesn't even test positive anymore. I don't believe that he could have possibly died that quickly from full-blown AIDS. I don't believe that. I think that something went on there. And like I say, I have my own ideas who I think was involved. But all I'm willing to say is this: I'm the only one who didn't profit from him passing away."[1282]

Did Heller *know* something? We don't know. He brought the Israeli killer Michael Klein and the Jewish Defense League (JDL) into the picture and put them around Eazy. We *now know* that the JDL was threatening the life of Eazy E – and Tupac – and trying to extort him/them. According to FBI documents the JDL ran an extortion racket against hip hop artists on the West

---

[1280] Alec Banks, "The Conspiracy Surrounding Eazy-E's Death," **High Snobiety** September 12, 2017.
[1281] Alec Banks, "The Conspiracy Surrounding Eazy-E's Death," **High Snobiety** September 12, 2017.
[1282] Banks, "The Conspiracy Surrounding Eazy-E's Death."

Coast, making death threats and then offering protection for a fee. A JDL operative would bombard the artist with phone calls threatening his life and that of his family until he paid the extortion money. The artist and his family would be taken to a safe house where the money is exchanged and several heavily armed JDL "bodyguards" would serve as the artist's protection. Prior to his execution in Las Vegas Tupac had been threatened by the JDL, as had Eazy-E before he died.[1283] As *High Snobiety* reports:

> In 2011, unsealed FBI documents linked both Eazy-E and Tupac Shakur to an alleged extortion attempt by the Jewish Defense League—who Jerry Heller had employed to combat threats from Suge Knight, as well as neo-Nazi skinhead groups who had threatened them. The report stated,
>
>> On September 11, 1996 [omitted] reported that JDL, and others yet unidentified have been extorting money from various rap music stars via death threats. The scheme involves [omitted] and other subjects making telephonic death threats to the rap star. Subjects then intercede by contacting the victim and offering protection for a 'fee.' Source reported that ERIC WRIGHT, also known as EAZY-E, who owned RUTHLESS RECORDS, Woodland Hills, California, was a victim of this extortion scheme prior to dying from AIDS. [Omitted] had also reportedly targeted TUPAC SHAKUR prior to his recent murder in Las Vegas, Nevada." [1284]

Recall that other Jewish groups like the JDO tried to muscle the influence of Farrakhan and the Nation of Islam out of Hip Hop. By 1995 Eazy had come to rely on the Nation of Islam. And Miami DJ Joe Stone who worked with Heller recounts Heller telling him that, while Easy was dying in the hospital "the Nation of Islam kept him (Heller) from being there"[1285] But the

---

[1283] "FBI Files on Tupac Shakur Murder Show He Received Death Threats From Jewish Gang," *Haaretz* April 14, 2011; "Who killed Tupac? The Jewish Defense League and an Unsolved Mystery," *Times of Israel* April 14, 2011.

[1284] Alec Banks, "The Conspiracy Surrounding Eazy-E's Death," *High Snobiety* September 12, 2017.

[1285] Jacob Katel, "Jerry Heller Remembered By Joe Stone: 'Jerry Made Sure Eazy E's Kids Were Taken Care Of," *Henry Stone Music* September 8, 2016 @ https://www.henrystonemusic.com/jerry-

Nation was not around Eazy's hospital bed simply to provide security. As Ben Westhoof details:

> But the Nation of Islam wasn't just interested in protecting Eazy and his belongings. They were interested in *curing* him...Dr. Abdul Alim Muhammad personally procured (the [AIDS] experimental drug from Kenya called) Kemron for Eazy, [according to] Shaheed Muhammad. "Dr. Alim shipped it from D.C. on a plane, having made sure it was fresh and potent, so it would go right into his system," Shaheed said, adding that he helped administer it to the rapper and it seemed, for a time, to make a difference...According to Shaheed, it had temporally perked Eazy up. "His vitals picked up again and he really got better," he said, though he added that before long his pain returned. "We were all so hopeful," Tracey Jernagin said. But though many close to Eazy were in favor of him continuing the alternative medicine, [Tomica] Woods was against it. She didn't know what they were giving him, she reasoned. Perhaps it could kill him. Shaheed Muhammad said she called it a "miracle potion" that wasn't going to work, and that she and Ron Sweeny promptly removed him [Shaheed] from the security detail. He was also told to cease administering the Kemron. [1286]

The Jewish Defense League was threatening to kill Eazy E. The Nation of Islam was trying to save Eazy E's life. In March, 1995 Eazy E died under mysterious circumstances.

VI.   *Hip Hop and The Million Man March (MMM)*

Most people are not aware of the fact that the decade of the 1960s was marked more by Black violent eruptions – so-called riots – than by non-violent protests. As we showed below, there were according to some counts over 1000 riots between 1960 and 1971. Then, nothing. This convulsive wave of Black rage and retaliatory violence that characterized a whole decade – what some sociologists described as "black masculine hostility" – was all but quelled and quieted. Between 1972 and 1992 – twenty years – there was only one notable "race riot": Miami in 1980. How did this "quieting" happen? We began the

---

heller-remembered-by-joe-stone-jerry-made-sure-eazy-es-kids-were-taken-care-of/
[1286] Ben Westhoff, *Original Gangstas: The Untold Story of Dr. Dre, Eazy-E, Ice Cube, Tupac Shakur, and the Birth of West Coast Rap* (New York: Hachette, 2016)

discussion of the process of the biomedical control of the inner city in our **Volume I**,[1287] and continued that discussion in this **Volume II**. The Nixon Administration inaugurated the scientific assault on this "Black masculine hostility" that would successfully quelle the Black Rage of the Inner City. So, the violent expression of Black frustration in Los Angeles in 1992 following the Rodney King incident and verdict was not supposed to happen from the perspective of those responsible for the biomedical control of the inner cities. And when it did happen, the biomedical controllers were taken aback and had to take this "situation" back to the White House "Situation Room."

In addition, an extraordinary but equally terrifying event (from the perspective of the "Situation Room") occurred *the day before* the LA Riots broke out. On April 28, 1992, outside the Nickerson Gardens housing project in Watts, hundreds of young Black men from warring factions of the Bloods and Crips gangs gathered and declared a truce to the bloody war that had killed hundreds. "After shooting at each other for years, Crips and Bloods partied all night together."[1288] One gang member who was present said to the press: "I do drive-by shootings, I kidnap babies. I kill people, so what? I'm an active gang member, I'm going to stop."[1289] The truce held for several years and gang crime fell as a result. Yet, the LAPD was no friend of the gang truce and, out of fear the gangs would unite against the police, actually worked to undermine the truce.

The ceasefire achieved on that day in April 1992 had been in the works for several years. Critical to that process was the work of the Honorable Minister Farrakhan. In 1988 he brought the nationwide 'Stop The Killing' tour to Los Angeles and in 1989 returned to that troubled city at the request of gang members to deliver a private message to 900 gang leaders, some

---

[1287] Wesley Muhammad, *Understanding The Assault of the Black Man, Black Manhood and Black Masculinity*, **Volume I** (Atlanta: A-Team Publishing, 2017) 153ff.
[1288] Frank Stoltze, "Forget the LA Riots – historic 1992 Watts gang truce was the big news," *89.3 KPCC* April 28, 2012 @ https://www.scpr.org/news/2012/04/28/32221/forget-la-riots-1992-gang-truce-was-big-news/
[1289] Frank Stoltze, "Forget the LA Riots – historic 1992 Watts gang truce was the big news," *89.3 KPCC* April 28, 2012 @ https://www.scpr.org/news/2012/04/28/32221/forget-la-riots-1992-gang-truce-was-big-news/

of whom said: "if the minister will talk to them, they would stop all killing activity for that day..."[1290] When the Minister spoke at the Los Angeles Sports Arena on February 2, 1990, Crips and Bloods were present and the *Los Angeles Times* even reported afterwards:

> To a standing ovation and an audience bristling with raised-fist salutes, Farrakhan entered the arena at 9:25 p.m...He smiled toward the balcony as a group of Crips gang members, more accustomed to retaliating with gunfire than cash, contributed $625 to exceed an earlier $500 donation by some Bloods rivals. The Bloods countered with another $500.[1291]

> [Former member of the Crips Andre Ransom said] "Black people around here, they see what's taking place. A lot of blacks are waking up. Before (Nation of Islam leader Louis) Farrakhan came to deliver that message, there were a lot of brothers blinded. But something is happening now. We're coming together...Even some Crips are willing to say: 'We aren't going to gang bang,"...Since Farrakhan's speech Friday Night, gang members "are willing to stop some of this killing," he said.[1292]

The "Farrakhan Factor" was thus no doubt involved in that extraordinary event of "Black (Male) Unity" on April 28, 1992, a day before the explosion of "Black (Male) Rage" engulfed the city on April 29th. When presidential candidate Bill Clinton stood on Rev. Jesse Jackson's Rainbow Push Coalition stage in the summer of 1992 and attacked the rapper Sister Souljah,[1293] Farrakhan strongly came to her defense in the national media and *called on Black male rappers to rise up in our sister's defense*:

> Now is the time for Black men to stand up for the Black woman, particularly those who are willing to take the point in the struggle for our liberation. All Black male rappers, particularly those who are the most conscious, should stand with and

---

[1290] Charisse Jones, "Farrakhan to Speak to 900 Gang Leaders to 'Stop the Killing'," *Los Angeles Times* October 6, 1989.
[1291] Andrea Ford and Charisse Jones, "Respect Life, Farrakhan Asks L.A. Crowd," *Los Angeles Times* February 3, 1990.
[1292] Darrell Dawsey, "One Neighborhood Where Farrakhan's Words Seem to Hit Home," *Los Angeles Times* February 4, 1990.
[1293] Gwen Ifill, "Clinton Stands by Remark on Rapper," *The New York Times* June 15, 1992.

behind Sister Souljah and let the enemies know that we will not stand for any harm coming to our sister...The Nation of Islam stands with and behind Sister Souljah.[1294]

This successful effort of the Honorable Minister Farrakhan to unite *Black Men* is an important precedent to the "miracle on the Mall," the unparalleled Million Man March (MMM) in 1995 called and led by The Honorable Minister Farrakhan. The MMM was the largest gathering of Black people in American history – close to two million primarily Black men. More importantly, it was a demonstration of Black manhood and masculinity that stunned and even terrified America. For the first time ever, masses of (primarily) Black men were televised across the country "as leaders and pillars of their communities, rather than as predators, deviants or criminals."[1295]

You must understand that this country has always been hell-bent against any collective display of Black manhood. American author Mark Twain did not misspeak when he wrote in a December 24, 1885 letter to Yale Dean Francis Wayland that "We have ground the manhood out of them (i.e. Black men), & the shame is ours, not theirs; & we should pay for it."[1296]

[1294] The Honorable Minister Louis Farrakhan, "Statement on Sister Souljah," **The Final Call** July 13, 1992, p. 3.
[1295] Kendrea Mekkah, "Hip-hop and the Million Man March," **Creative Loafing Charlotte** October 24, 2012.
[1296] Edwin McDowell, "From Twain, A letter on Debt to Blacks," **The New York Times** March 14, 1985.

Indeed, you should. But America never developed the capacity to countenance or even stomach any collective display of Black manhood and masculinity. Daniel P. Moynihan, the Assistant Secretary of Labor in President Lyndon B. Johnson's administration, likewise acknowledged in his 1965 Report "The Negro Family: The Case for National Action."

> (T)530ere centuries of sometimes unimaginable mistreatment have taken their toll on the Negro people...Of the greatest importance, the Negro male...became an object of intense hostility, an attitude unquestionably based in some measure on fear...Keeping the Negro "in his place" can be translated as keeping the Negro *male* in his place: the female was not a threat to anyone...The very essence of the male animal, from the bantam rooster to the four star general, is to strut. Indeed, in 19th century America, a particular type of exaggerated male boastfulness became almost a national style. Not for the Negro male. The 'sassy nigger' was lynched...(T)he Negro community has been forced into a matriarchal structure which...seriously retards the progress of the group as a whole, and imposes a crushing burden on the Negro male and, in consequence, on a great many Negro women as well.

American sociologist and radical feminist scholar Jessie Bernard also shared a candid moment in her book, ***Marriage and Family Among Negros*** (1966):

> Negro men have been more feared, sexually and occupationally, than Negro women...[The] institution of slavery in the United States...inflicted grievous wounds on the Negro man...*The Negro man had to be destroyed as a man [in order] to 'protect' the white world*...The Negro man...was put in a situation in which *conformity to masculine norms was all but impossible*...One does not have to resort to psychoanalytic figures of speech to see that the Negro men were castrated by the white world-sometimes literally as well as figuratively (emphasis added).

This is why the urban rebellions of the 1960s resulted not only in the criminalizing but also the pathologizing of Black masculinity[1297]: sociologists described the "black masculine hostility" that erupted in the inner cities as a symptom of a "brain disease," or "mild epilepsy" of young Black males caused

---

[1297] See below, Chapter 1.

in large part (they claimed) by their listening to the Islam of the Honorable Elijah Muhammad and the Nation of Islam.[1298] The U.S. government thus decided to "medicate" Black masculinity by chemically neutralizing it.[1299] And it worked, for a long time. But the 1992 LA Riot shattered their comfort, and then the 1995 MMM sent a terrifying message. In this Michael Eric Dyson wrote well:

what we witnessed (at the MMM) was the public choreography of black male identity, a ballet of black masculine self-revelation and reinvention that had been rehearsed in millions of miniature but meaningful gestures, both in individual psyches and on the historical stage of collective aspiration...The Million Man March afforded black men the occasion of a symbolic solidarity that had a practical and profound purpose: By combining our resources, we consolidated a vision of black masculinity that had been largely ignored by the media and other cultural myth makers.[1300]

The alarm that this display of Black manhood and masculinity caused is well illustrated by the Black feminist reaction to the MMM and the Honorable Minister Farrakhan. Feminist scholar bell hooks said the MMM was a "celebration of fascist patriarchy" and Professor Nikol G. Alexander-Floyd alleged a "patriarchal macho at the core of the March's message" and

---

[1298] See below pp....
[1299] See Wesley Muhammad, *Understanding The Assault of the Black Man, Black Manhood and Black Masculinity*, **Volume I** (Atlanta: A-Team Publishing, 2017) Part Four and below, Chapter 5.
[1300] Michael Eric Dyson, "Black Men Triumphed," *The Washington Post* October 13, 1996, p. C03.

claimed that a "problematic Black macho imperative" provided the impetus for the MMM. [1301] They were big mad.

Also characteristic of the MMM – and troubling to this government – was the awesome involvement of the Hip Hop community. Indeed, in that historic effort to bring nearly two million Black men to D.C. "Farrakhan had help – big help. The hip hop community played a large role in appealing to young black men."[1302] The biggest artists of the day appeared on the hip hop compilation album *One Million Strong* released the following month: Chuck D, Ice Cube, Pac, Mobb Deep, Biggie, Snoop, Dre, etc. Leading up to the MMM there was within Hip Hop a strong current of what Charise Cheney describes as *rap nationalism* which, like the political philosophy of Black Nationalism, embraced *a masculinist agenda* in that it emphasized a reclamation of Black manhood. Rap nationalism – from Public Enemy's 1988 *It Takes a Nation of Millions to Hold Us Back* to Ice Cube's 1993 *Lethal Injection* – evolved as a politics of masculine protest, an outlet for Black male frustrations over our compromised gender identity.

> From East Coast groups such as Public Enemy, Boogie Down Productions, and X-Clan to West Coast artists Ice Cube, Paris, and Kam, rap nationalists intentionally conjured a tradition of model, and militant, black manhood. With these politicized rap artists the performative race/gender politics of the black nationalist tradition (re)emerged with a vengeance. Raptivists (= rap activists) offered young black males the opportunity to reassert a masculine presence in the public domain...In fact, the embodied-social politics of rap music in the late 1980s and early 1990s was similar to the sexual politicking of such Black Power notables as Eldridge Cleaver, Stokely Carmichael, and H. Rap Brown – it was profound, as well as profane – and it stands as the postmodern revisioning of black nationalism as a politics of masculine protest.[1303]

[1301] Nikol G. Alexander-Floyd, " "We Shall Have Our Manhood:" Black Macho, Black Nationalism, and the Million Man March," *Meridians* 3 (2003): 171-203.

[1302] Kendrea Mekkah, "Hip-hop and the Million Man March," *Creative Loafing Charlotte* October 24, 2012.

[1303] Charise Cheney, "In Search of the 'Revolutionary Generation': (En)gendering the Golden Age of Rap Nationalism," *The Journal of African American History* 90 (2005): 278-298 (283, 285).

The late 1980s and early 1990s marked, according to Cheney, the "Golden Age of Rap Nationalism" and its Black masculinist agenda. It thus comes as no surprise that so many of these raptivists (rap activists) supported the MMM in 1995. On the other hand, if in both Black Nationalism and rap nationalism "masculinity is defined as not-femininity,"[1304] then the *weaponizing* of rap music against the masculinist agenda laid out at the MMM would involve promotion of the *feminizing* of Black males through Hip Hop. Thus, Kendrea Mekkah, writing on Hip Hop and the MMM, offers a very important analysis supporting "a direct connection between the Million Man March and *the decline in positive mainstream hip-hop acts*":

> In '95, gangsta rap was shooting up the pop charts, but you could still hear and see balanced depictions of black America in the wider cultural lens of hip-hop. On one hand, 2Pac was baring his soul in songs like "Me Against the World," while conscious rappers such as KRS-One were calling for justice for death-row inmate and former Black Panther Party member Mumia Abu-Jamal, whom many felt was railroaded because of his political activism. Down in Atlanta, Goodie Mob and Outkast were bringing a Southern sensibility to hip-hop that would take the music by storm within the next decade.
>
> For a whole generation, hip-hop had represented a complete social commentary, with history, struggle, life lessons, love songs and gangstas all woven into its spine. This was the atmosphere in popular culture when the National African American Leadership Summit announced it was holding a Million Man March in the nation's capital in October 1995...*The year 1996 marked a paradigm shift for rappers and a turning point in hip-hop's relationship with the music industry.* It was the end of rap's golden age and the beginning of the major-label rush to sign any violent hip-hop coming down the pike.[1305]

While the major labels after the MMM severely narrowed signed acts to promoters of violence, they also helped guarantee that such promotion could only result in *a specific type of violence*: "subordinate male" violence, i.e. impulsive, emotional, *feminized* violence, rather than "dominant male" violence. As we show in **Volume I**:

[1304] Cheney, "In Search of the 'Revolutionary Generation'," 288.
[1305] Mekkah, "Hip-hop and the Million Man March."

[The brain chemicals] Serotonin and noradrenalin are the two "brain buttons" that scientists discovered they can push and thereby determine a person's future, "two potent brain chemicals that researchers have successfully manipulated to make animals more violent or less violent," in the words of [*Chicago Tribune* writer Ronald] Kotulak. "[A]ggression can be controlled by manipulating brain levels of serotonin"...

It is important to point out here that all violence is *not* the same. Not all aggression is associated with low serotonin; only impulsive, emotion-driven, reactionary aggression which is socially maladaptive and characteristic of low social status is. This is to be distinguished from proactive, premeditative, deliberate, predatory aggression characteristic of dominant males. Impulsive aggression is often severe, unrestrained, dysfunctional, and frequently results in the wounding or death of the aggressor. This is the aggression artificially produced by evil scientists who have mastered the manipulation of these chemical buttons of the brain.

In terms of dominance hierarchy, low serotonin among subordinate males favors dominant males, because in the interest of self-preservation low serotonin discourages the conspicuous challenging of dominant males who are, by virtue of their high-status, in a position to punish such insolence. So the aggression, the raging monster, *is unleashed instead against fellow subordinate males only*: "Even as low (serotonin) keeps him from challenging dominant males, he may behave recklessly toward those closer to him on the social ladder," explains Robert Wright.[1306]

As we shall show below, government-affiliated scientists found a way to chemically induce a feminized violence profile in males causing non-dominant males to fight and kill each other only. This aggression and violence *are never* directed at society's dominant male, i.e. the White male. Hip Hop will be used to promote these chemicals, such as MDMA (Ecstasy/Molly), among Black males. We call this the "Molly-fication of Hip Hop."

[1306] Wesley Muhammad, *Understanding The Assault of the Black Man, Black Manhood and Black Masculinity*, **Volume I** (Atlanta: A-Team Publishing, 2017) 190.

Chapter Twenty-two

The Neuroscience of Music

The Science of Music...is at the root of the true religion of God.
- The Honorable Minister Farrakhan

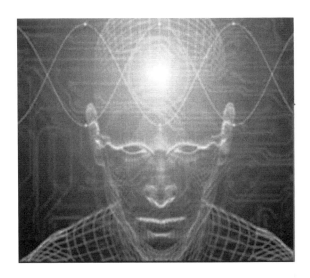

I.   *Mind Moving To The Beat*

In 2012 **Scientific American** published an article on the well-known power of rhythmic sound to tap into the brain circuits controlling emotion and movement and to actually control the brain circuitry of sensory perception; in other words, the power of music to control the human mind and behavior.[1307] Through this power of music both individual as well as group-think and behavior can be coordinated: "Rhythmic sound 'not only coordinates the behavior of people in a group, it also coordinates their thinking-the mental processes of individuals in the group become synchronized."[1308]

[1307] R. Douglas Fields, "The Power of Music: Mind Control by Rhythmic Sound," **Scientific American** October 19, 2012.
[1308] Diana Kwon, "Brain Rhythms Sync to Musical Beat," **Scientific American** November 10, 2015.

Brain cells are like little clocks with intrinsic frequencies: some fire slowly, others fire more rapidly. There is normally no neural chaos because groups of cells synchronize in order to get things done.

> The internal cadences of the brain and nervous system appear to play an important role in everything from walking to thinking...And abnormal rhythms...have been associated with problems including schizophrenia, epilepsy, autism and Parkinson's disease. The rhythms of the brain begin with the firing patterns of individual brain cells.[1309]

The rhythms of the brain can be manipulated by outside sources. Neural activity is electrochemical. And as Speech-Language pathologist Dr. Suzanne Evans Morris observed back in 1998: "Through EEG studies, it is known that carefully selected and programmed sounds are capable of changing the brain's electrical energy patterns."[1310] *Optogenetics* is the use of light to turn certain neurons of the brain on and off. *Sonogenetics* is the control of the brain through sound.[1311] Entrainment is the process of synchronization, where the vibrations of one object or source (e.g. music) will cause that of another object (the brain) to oscillate at the same rate. Musical frequencies can cause the human brain's neurons to fire in sync, i.e. "Rhythmic sound synchronizes brain waves."[1312] This brainwave entrainment is applied to alter a target's state of mind because the music-mind syncing can induce neurological states within the body and can *drive* brainwave activity to a desired state.[1313]

[1309] Jon Hamilton, "Your Brain's Got Rhythm, And Syncs When You Think," **NPR** June 17, 2014.

[1310] Suzanne Evans Morris, "Hemi-Sync and the Facilitation of Sensory Integration," **New Visions** (February 1998): 1-7.

[1311] Tim De Chant, "New Neuro-Manipulation Technique 'Sonogenetics' Controls Brains with Sound," @ https://www.pbs.org/wgbh/nova/article/new-neuro-manipulation-technique-sonogenetics-controls-brains-with-sound/

[1312] Diana Kwon, "Brain Rhythms Sync to Musical Beat," **Scientific American** November 10, 2015.

[1313] Udo Will and Eric Berg, "Brain wave synchronization and entrainment to periodic acoustic stimuli," **Neuroscience Letters** 424 (2007): 55-60; Andrew Neher, "Auditory Driving Observed with

External rhythms have a direct effect on both the psychology and the physiology of individuals. *Sonic body* refers to the body in its capacity to interact with sound; Man's body, it is said, is "a harp of a thousand strings."[1314] Each organ of the human body has its own acoustic properties including a particular, natural frequency at which that organ vibrates. This is called *resonance frequency*.

Rhythmic drumming is the most effective tool of *auditory driving*. Research has shown that the use of the rhythmic drumming in Shamanic and indigenous cultures in ritual and ceremony has specific neurophysiological effects and the ability to elicit temporary changes in brain wave activity, facilitating entry into altered states of consciousness. As Andrew Neher documented in 1962, "the behaviors observed in drum ceremonies and in the laboratory appear to have similar physiological and psychological characteristics which result from rhythmic stimulation" of the central nervous system.[1315] These drum-beat frequencies can entrain the entire body and synchronize the neural firing patterns of areas of the brain, thereby affecting sensory and motor areas which are connected to the areas being entrained. Vision, speech, etc. are all compartmentalized in the brain but music permeates the entire brain because drumming accesses the whole brain (both hemispheres). The sound of drumming generates dynamic neuronal connections in all parts of the brain, inducing synchronous brain activity.

II.   *The Neuroendocrinology of Music*

Music can also alter the electrochemical environment of the brain. Plant research indicates that music produces physiological effects in plants. Acoustic frequencies influence plant growth. As Anindita Roy Chowdhury and Anshu Gupta documented:

Scalp Electrodes in Normal Subjects," ***Electroenceph. clin. Neurophysiol.*** 13 (1961): 449-451.

[1314] Eva Augusta Vescelius, "Music and Health," ***The Musical Quarterly*** 4 (1918): 376-401 (378)

[1315] Andrew Neher, "A Physiological Explanation of Unusual Behavior in Ceremonies Involving Drums," ***Human Biology*** 34 (1962): 151-160.

Music is a harmonious and coherent blend of various frequencies and vibrations and has many different forms, qualities, and pitches. It is believed that loud and unharmonious sounds can ruin the mood and health of a plant and blossoms. Soft rhythmic music on the other hand is better for their growth and blossoms, and thus may increase plants rate of growth, their size and influence their overall health...soft rhythmic audible frequencies (that is music) expedites germination of seeds, growth and development of plants... Summing up all the experimental observations of various workers, it can be stated that specific audio frequencies in the form of music facilitated the germination and growth of plants, irrespective of the music genre... On the other hand noise which is a non-rhythmic and unharmonious superposition of various audio frequencies was observed to have a negative effect on the growth of plants." [1316]

Deepti Sharma et al. also documented the biochemical effects of rhythmic music on plants.

Music can cause drastic changes in plant metabolism...Results showed that music not only affects the plant growth, but it also affects the concentration of various metabolites. When the music was applied to the plants then there was increase in the concentration of total sugar and reducing sugar in treated plants as compare to the control one...When plants were exposed to the music, it affects the concentration of Phenols...Concentration of chlorophyll also increased in the plants which were treated with the music...[P]lants respond to sounds in profound ways which not only influence their overall health but also increase the speed of growth and the size of the plants. Science is now showing that soft sounds actually influences the growth of plants...Music therapy also increases the number of leaves and the number of flowers as compared to the plants which are not exposed with the music... Flowering was advanced and the flowers occurred one week earlier in treated set than the control one. Music was actually influencing the plant growth and in a similar manner, it was affecting the plants biochemically also. If plants were exposed to the music then there was also a change in the concentration of these metabolites...Chlorophyll is the most important green pigment

---

[1316] Anindita Roy Chowdhury and Anshu Gupta, "Effect of Music on Plants - An Overview," *International Journal of Integrative Sciences, Innovation and Technology (IJIIT)* 4 (2015): 30-34 (30, 33).

of the plants and music increases the amount of chlorophyll and starch content in the plants.[1317]

Humans are frequently identified as plants or the Tree of Life in religious myth and literature. We thus should not be surprised to learn that, as with actual plants, music has a biochemical effect in humans. Psycho-acoustic medicine uses sound and frequencies to impact the physical and emotional health of the body. Music therapy has been used to raise or lower blood

---

[1317] Deepti Sharma et al., "The Effect of Music on Physico-chemical Parameters of Selected Plants," **International Journal of Plant, Animal and Environment Sciences** 5 (2015): 282-287 (284, 286).

pressure, affect muscular energy, treat mental illness, change metabolism, and influence digestion.

Researchers believe that each brain center generates impulses at a specific frequency based on the predominant neurotransmitters it secrets, and thus different brainwave patterns are linked to the production in the brain of various neurochemicals. Certain frequencies are believed to catalyze the release of different brain hormones and by sonically manipulating brain wave patterns, production of these chemicals can be either stimulated or inhibited.[1318] Mona Lisa Chanda and Daniel J. Levitin speaks on the "neurochemistry of music":

> the reviewed evidence does provide preliminary support for the claim that neurochemical changes mediate the influence of music on health...Music listening reportedly lowers requirements for opiate drugs in postoperative pain, which suggests that *music may stimulate the release of endogenous opioid peptides within the brain.*[1319]

Listening to music can stimulate the release of the brain's opioids: the implications of this are profound. Dr. Robert C. Beck in 1983 predicted the direction of "neuro-electronics": "Tomorrow's alternative to drugs and surgery is coming from the new Electronic Medicine."[1320] Different forms music has been shown to have varying effects. Stimulating music, for example, increased plasma cortisol, ACTH, prolactin, growth hormone, and norepinephrine levels.[1321] As Abhishek Gangrade reports

> While the brain interprets music, successive biochemical reactions are induced within the body. Evidence indicates that music plays a role in activating pleasure-seeking areas of the brain that become stimulated by food, sex, and

---

[1318] Kathleen McAulife, "Brain Tuner," **OMNI** January 1983, 44-48,115-120.

[1319] Mona Lisa Chanda and Daniel J. Levitin, "The neurochemistry of music," **Trends in Cognitive Sciences** 17 (2013): 179-193 (179-180, 183).

[1320] Dr. Robert C. Beck, "Brain Turners, The EM Cure for Addiction," **Borderland Sciences Research Foundation** (1983): 1-6 (1).

[1321] Mona Lisa Chanda and Daniel J. Levitin, "The neurochemistry of music," **Trends in Cognitive Sciences** 17 (2013): 179-193 (186).

drugs...Listening to techno music was found to alter levels of ß-endorphin, adrenocorticotropic hormone (ACTH), norepinephrine, growth hormone, prolactin, and cortisol in healthy people...music influences production of steroids including cortisol, testosterone and estrogen as well as their receptor proteins, leading to neurogenesis and improvements in learning in the brain.[1322]

On the other hand, MM Moraes et al. report:

Listening to melodic music is regarded as a non-pharmacological intervention that ameliorates various disease symptoms, likely by changing the activity of brain monoaminergic systems...Our data indicate that auditory stimuli, such as exposure to melodic music, increase [dopamine] levels and the release of 5-HT [serotonin] in the [caudate-putamen] as well as DA turnover in the NAcc, suggesting that the music had a direct impact on monoamine activity in these brain areas.[1323]

Japanese scientists Hajime Fukui and colleagues from Nara University of Education, Japan, have demonstrated across several studies that "listening to music affects the steroid hormone cascade." In particular, music listening can decrease testosterone in men and increase cortisol and estrogen, and vis versa in women.[1324]

[1322] Abhishek Gangrade, "The Effect of Music on the Production of Neurotransmitters, Hormones, Cytokines, and Peptides: A Review," *Music and Medicine* 4 (2012): 40-43.

[1323] MM Moraes et al., "Auditory stimulation by exposure to melodic music increases dopamine and serotonin activities in rat forebrain areas linked to reward and motor control," *Neurosci Lett* 673 (2018): 73-78.

[1324] Hajime Fukui and Kumiko Toyoshima, "Chill-inducing music enhances altruism in humans," *frontiers in psychology* 5 (2014): 1-9; idem, "Influence of music on steroid hormones and the relationship between receptor polymorphisms and music ability: a pilot study," *frontiers in psychology* 4 (2013): 1-8; Hajime Fukui, A. Arai and Kumiko Toyoshima, "Efficacy of Music Therapy in Treatment for the Patients with Alzheimer's Disease," *International journal of Alzheimer's Disease* (2012): 1-6; Hajime Fukui and Kumiko Toyoshima, "Music and Steroids – Music Facilitates Steroid-Induced Synaptic Plasticity," *Steroids – Clinical Aspect*, ed. Hassan Abduljabbar (Rijeka, Croatia: InTech, 2011) 151-166; idem, "Music facilitate the neurogenesis, regeneration and repair of

Music influences the endocrine system to keep the body normal...auditory information passes through the limbic and paralimbic systems including the thalamus, the hypothalamus, and amygdala, to the neocortex, and influence the pituitary gland; as a result, various physiological effects are induced.[1325]

At this point, the effects of music on steroids are unclear, but music appears to be involved with steroid production via the pathway from the auditory system to the auditory area, particularly the neural pathway (emotion circuits) mediated by the cerebral limbic system (hypothalamic-pituitary-adrenal axis and amygdaloid complex).[1326]

---

neurons," *Medical Hypotheses* 71 (2008): 765-769; Hajime Fukui and Masako Yamashita, "The effects of music and visual stress on testosterone and cortisol in men and women," *Neuroendocrinology Letters* 24 (2003): 173-180; Hajime Fukui, "Music and Testosterone: A New Hypothesis for the Origin and Function of Music," *ANN NY Acad Sci* 930 (2001): 448-51.

[1325] Fukui and Toyoshima, "Music and Steroids," 152-153.

[1326] Fukui and Toyoshima, "Music facilitate the neurogenesis," 767.

Chapter Twenty-three

The Militarization of Music

Advances in technology have made possible devices that are now being employed both in war zones and in domestic crowd control contexts that employ sound, including music, to inflict pain and damage psychological health. We are already in the age of acoustic weapons, and will have to rethink many of our ideas about music and sound in light of that... Whereas previously medical language has been used to make a fuss and condemn music that has in fact no serious consequences for health, now we have a situation where music is being secretly used to inflict considerable long-term mental illness, based on actual scientific work.[1327]

Rap, metal, and even children's songs become repressive weapons, symbolizing the links between the entertainment industry and the military-industrial complex.[1328]

I.   Sonic Warfare

Between the world wars the U.S. Navy, the National Defense Research Council, and the Rockefeller Foundation collaborated to conduct acoustic war studies, the scientific studies in musical frequencies best suited for war making. The aim of these studies was to determine the musical factors capable of producing mass sociogenic illness: psychopathology, increased aggression, psychological agitation, and emotional distress. The ultimate objective was population control through sound control.

Considered from a military perspective, the ear is a vulnerable target: you can't close it, you can't choose what it hears, and the sounds that reach it can profoundly alter your psychological and physical state. The second half of the twentieth century saw

---

[1327] James Kennaway, *Bad Vibrations: The History of the Idea of Music as a Cause of Disease* (London and New York: Routledge, 2012) 132.
[1328] Juliette Volcler, *Extremely Loud: Sound as Weapon* (New York and London: The New Press, 2011)

the development of scientific research on the military and law enforcement uses of sound. The aim was no longer to use sound just to send out an alarm, intimidate the enemy, or rally the troops, but to exploit sound's biological effects, since sound waves-which are nothing more nor less than mechanical vibrations-can harm the ear and the entire body at certain frequencies and certain intensities. The advantage sound offers to those in power is that it produces the same results as other 'non-lethal' weapons, while defusing criticism and confusing debate.[1329]

These studies were aided by the field of behaviorism and the behavioral science of "herding" or herd behavior. Only a small percentage of the total population is required to be affected and to act at which point the momentum for change becomes unstoppable.[1330] This militarized music was intended to impose frequencies that herd populations into greater aggression, psychosocial agitation, and emotional distress, predisposing people to physical illnesses and generating mass sociogenic illness; generating maladies bioenergetically (musically/vibrationally).

These studies involved *acoustic energy research*: investigations into the psychological warfare application of *acoustic vibrations*. Sound waves traveling through a medium (e.g. air) produces pressure energy which is converted into electrical energy for the brain to translate into musical sounds. When sound waves reach the cochlea in the inner ear, they are translated into electrical impulses by the hair cells and these pulses travel along the auditory nerve into the brain. Thus, this is psychotronic warfare.

A leader of this research was Harold Burris-Meyer, the "magician of sound" of the 20th century. Burris-Meyer was a member of the War Department Planning Board during WWII, US Navy Commander in 1943, and consultant to the Defense Department during the Korean and Vietnam Wars. His was bioenergetic research in acoustic science aimed at emotional

---

[1329] Juliette Volcler, **Extremely Loud: Sound as Weapon** (New York and London: The New Press, 2011) 1.
[1330] Malcolm Gladwell, **The Tipping Point: How Little Things Can Make a Big Difference**

arousal and mass hysteria. His experiments analyzed and measured the influence of sound on behavior with a focus on the control of human emotion as a determinant of action. He found that "audio control of human emotions was possible for a large enough portion of an audience to provide effective crowd control". Burris-Meyer's work demonstrated the means to control emotion with sufficient precision to determine the action of from 2% to 8% of a given population, a small but decisive segment. He focused on engineering audio environments, sonic warfare and musical behaviorism.[1331]

II.   *Militarized Soundscapes and Urban Ecologies of Fear*

Since the 1990s, the US military and private companies researched infrasonic devices that could cause behavior changes at frequencies too low to be audible...infrasound is probably the hardest to weaponize.[1332]

Infrasound has been suggested as weaponry because it has potentially negative effects on people as it vibrates[1333]

The range of human hearing is generally considered to be between 20 Hz (hertz) and 20000 Hz. Low-frequency sound (LFS) is normally placed at 0-100 Hz. Infrasound is the inaudible frequency range below 20 Hz. Above 20 kHz (kilohertz) is ultrasound. The military has coveted weaponizing LFS and infrasound for a long time. LFS has been shown to

[1331] James Tobias, "Composing for the Media: Hanns Eisler and Rockefeller Foundation Projects in Film Music, Radio Listening, and theatrical Sound Design," **Rockefeller Archives**, 2009,
[1332] Nicole Chavez, "Using Sound to Attack: The diverse world of acoustic devices," *CNN* September 27, 2017.
[1333] Tim Radford, "Silent sounds hit emotional chords," *The Guardian* Mon 8 Sept 2003.

travel farther and trigger stronger stress responses and human exposure has been shown to cause emotional and psychological change. Infrasound as a military weapon has value because it is an incapacitating technology. Those frequencies can induce stress and a passive state within the targeted subject population and thus infrasound is deployed in crowd control and riot control situations. Areas exposed to constant LFS emissions feel like a "war zone" under "acoustic attack," according to a report in *The Atlantic*.[1334] LFS causes the adrenal glands to pump the stress hormone cortisol into the blood, raise blood pressure and heart rate, and slow down digestion. The emissions have been described as feeling like "an ice pick to the brain." They cause mounting anxiety and over a prolonged period can provoke people to murderous extremes. [1335]

> Experts say your body does not adapt to noise. Large-scale studies show that if the din [=low frequency noise emission] keeps up—over days, months, years—noise exposure increases your risk of high blood pressure, coronary heart disease, and heart attacks, as well as strokes, diabetes, dementia, and depression. Children suffer not only physically—18 months after a new airport opened in Munich, the blood pressure and stress-hormone levels of neighboring children soared—but also behaviorally and cognitively. A landmark study published in 1975 found that the reading scores of sixth graders whose classroom faced a clattering subway track lagged nearly a year behind those of students in quieter classrooms—a difference that disappeared once soundproofing materials were installed. Noise might also make us mean: A 1969 study suggested that test subjects exposed to noise, even the gentle fuzz of white noise, become more aggressive and more eager to zap fellow subjects with electric shocks. In the extreme, sound becomes a weapon.[1336]

[1334] Bianca Bosker, "Why Everything Is Getting Louder," *The Atlantic* November 2019.
[1335] Bosker, "Why Everything Is Getting Louder."
[1336] Bosker, "Why Everything Is Getting Louder."

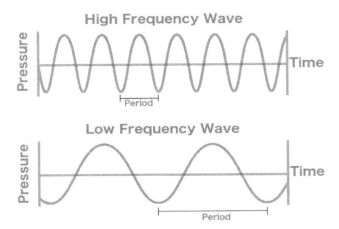

LFS and infrasound emissions in particular are concentrated in the urban city, which at least partly explains the high levels of aggression and violence that is the signature of urban areas.

> Low-frequency noise is common as background noise in urban environments, and as emissions from many artificial sources: road vehicles, aircraft, industrial machinery, artillery and mining explosions, and air movement machinery including wind turbines... Low-frequency noise (infrasound included) is the superpower of the frequency range...it is able to produce resonance in the human body.[1337]

The effect of infrasonic frequencies has been noted as a possible cause of city dwellers' stress. Even "city fatigue" may be attributable to low frequency or infrasound exposure. "The primary effect due to low frequency and infrasonic noise appears to be annoyance..."[1338] Because everyone in the city is annoyed and stressed, tensions stay high and violence is often only a small incident away. This concentration of environmental noise in the cities is one more illustration of *environmental racism*. "The largest sources of environmental noise are transportation and industrial activity...Industrial areas [are]

[1337] Birgitta Berglund, Peter Hassmen, and R.F. Soames Job, "Sources and effects of low-frequency noise," *J. Acoust. Soc.* 99 (1996): 2985-3002.
[1338] N. Broner, "The Effects of Low Frequency Noise on People-A Review," *Journal of Sound and Vibration* 58 (1978): 483-500 (483).

often designated for land close to the poorest nonwhite areas in a city..."[1339] As ***The Atlantic*** further reported recently.

> Not everyone bears the brunt of the din equally. Belying its dismissal as a country-club complaint, noise pollution in the U.S. tends to be most severe in poor communities, as well as in neighborhoods with more people of color. A 2017 paper found that urban noise levels were higher in areas with greater proportions of black, Asian, and Hispanic residents than in predominantly white neighborhoods. Urban areas where a majority of residents live below the poverty line were also subjected to significantly higher levels of nighttime noise, and the study's authors warned that their findings likely underestimated the differences, given that many wealthy homeowners invest in soundproofing.[1340]

III.   *The Haunted Hood*

And if all of that is not enough, "low-frequency sound can also, apparently, produce ghosts."[1341] It could thus be said, with only a touch of humor to it, that the hood is haunted. How many of us have had an experience in our life that you believe was a paranormal haunting experience? You were working late at the job one night or in your home office or you were home alone one summer night and all of a sudden you heard something and out of the corner of your eye you saw something: a grey or shadowy figure you believed was a ghost. You knew your mind wasn't playing tricks on you because you felt the presence: your body got cold shivers, you felt the hair stand on your neck and a chill go down your spine. Maybe you got a headache or felt nauseous. You had a real experience that wasn't your imagination. But the question is: what was the source of your experience?

It is now known that low frequency sound, specifically infrasound, causes haunting experiences: electromagnetic fields (EMFs) emitted by power lines and towers, clock radios and other electrical sources, and LFS waves both are sources of

---

[1339] Kate Wagner, "City Noise Might Be Making you Sick," ***The Atlantic*** February 20, 2018.
[1340] Bosker, "Why Everything Is Getting Louder."
[1341] Bosker, "Why Everything Is Getting Louder."

"apparitions."[1342] And because it is the inner cities across this country that are bombarded with EMFs and LFS waves, it is the Black and Brown people concentrated in these areas that are most exposed to these waves.

GIZMODO

LATEST   REVIEWS   SCIENCE   IO9   FIELD GUIDE   EARTHER   DESIGN   PALEOFUTURE | WHAT'S NEXT IN TEC

Some "Ghosts" May Be Sound Waves Just Below Human Hearing

Jennifer Ouellette
10/27/15 11:50am · Filed to: SCIENCE OF SOUND ∨

There are many possible explanations for hauntings, not least that humans are highly suggestible creatures, especially when we want to believe. But some ghost sightings might actually be the result of sounds — sound waves that vibrate just below our range of hearing, dubbed the "fear frequency."

[1342] Vic Tandy and Tony R. Lawrence, "The Ghost in the Machine," *Journal of the Society for Psychical Research* 62 (1998): Vic Tandy, "Something in the Cellar," *Journal of the Society for Psychical Research* 64 (2000): 129-140; ibid, "Ghost Story: Low Frequency Illusions Created By Standing Waves?" *ProSoundWeb* July 3, 2013 @https://www.prosoundweb.com/ghost-story-low-frequency-illusions-created-by-standing-waves/; Jonathan Amos, "Organ music 'instils religious feelings," *BBC News online* September 08, 2003; Adam Marcus, "Ghost Lusters: If You Want to See a Specter Badly Enough, Will You?" *Scientific American* October 27, 2008.

There is a certain frequency – around 18-19Hz – that, under certain conditions, can cause haunting effects by creating the sensory phenomena that are suggestive of a ghost or poltergeist event: the feeling of a presence, the cold shivers, the hair prickling on the back of the neck, etc. You even "see the ghost" with your own eyes because the eyeball vibrates at this same frequency of 18-19 Hz, and when the sound wave frequency syncs with your eyeball frequency, at that moment a shadowy or ghost-like apparition will appear in your eye. Scientists call this the "Ghost in the Machine" Effect and 18-19 Hz can be considered the "Ghost Frequency."[1343] So yes, there are "ghosts" haunting the hood. But this low frequency sound wave-soaked environment that we live in does more than just spook Black people by creating pseudo-poltergeist experiences: it makes us physically ill. It keeps the levels of our stress hormone cortisol chronically high, which produces aches and pain, high blood pressure, lowered immune function, and more.

Not only are urban Black populations constantly subject to a "Ghost Frequency" and its psychological and physiological effects, they are also subjected to a "Fear Frequency": the particular frequency that is believed to create a fearful brain state. Scientists have identified brainwave oscillations of a particular frequency – 4 Hz – that appears to regulate fear response and creates a "fearful" brain state, generating conditioned behaviors associated with fear. It is the generation of 4 Hz oscillations in the prefrontal-amygdala circuits that serves to regulate fear responses, according to new research.[1344] While 10 hz frequency has been shown to speed up production and turnover rate of serotonin,[1345] the "Fear Frequency" 4 Hz stimulates the production of catecholamine like noradrenalin.

British physiology researchers conducted very important research in 2003: the first controlled experiment of infrasound, an experiment to test the effects of infrasonic frequencies on the human brain and its ability to trigger

[1343] Tandy and Lawrence, "The Ghost in the Machine"; Tandy, "Something in the Cellar"; ibid, "Ghost Story: Low Frequency Illusions Created By Standing Waves?"
[1344] Nikolaos Karalis et al., "4 Hz oscillations synchronize prefrontal-amygdala circuits during fear behaviour," **Nat Neurosci** 19 (2016): 605-612.
[1345] Kathleen McAulife, "Brain Tuner," **OMNI** January 1983, 44-48,115-120.

sensations. The experiment was conducted during contemporary music concerts at the Purcell Room in central London and involved secretly exposing 700 concertgoers to musical pieces which were clandestinely, scientifically laced with a 17Hz frequency by physicists. The music with the silent notes caused 22% of the unwitting participants to report "unusual experiences" including a feeling of anxiety, extreme sorrow, chills and dread. As **The Guardian** reported:

> Scientists have found a way to add a spine-tingling dimension to modern music...sorrow, coldness, anxiety and shivers down the spine. They were playing with infrasound, the point at which an instrument resonates at an inaudible frequency...Infrasound has been suggested as weaponry because it has potentially negative effects on people as it vibrates...[1346]

Incidentally, it is *rap music* that is today characterized by LFS waves. In musical terms, low-frequency sound = bass. When you turn up the bass on your stereo, you are creating more low frequency sound. Rap contains a lot of low frequency sound (bass). In fact, LFS is pervasive in rap music. The iconic 808 drum machine (the Roland TR-808) became synonymous with Hip Hop itself and trap music is today based on 808 beats.[1347] As Future says in "Mask Off" (2016): "808, 8-o-fucking-8." The 808 provides very low frequency bass. It is said that most 808s are in the 40-60 Hz range.

The urban Black communities of America with their scientifically manufactured soundscapes of fear and dread are the products of *sonic warfare*. As Steve Goodman describes in his important book, **Sonic Warfare: Sound, Affect, and the Ecology of Fear**,

> Throughout history, often imperceptibly, the audiosphere has been subject to militarization...*Sonic warfare*...is the use of force (sound), *both seductive and violent, abstract and physical*, via a range of acoustic machines (biotechnical, social, cultural, artistic, conceptual), to modulate the physical, affective, and libidinal dynamics of populations, of bodies, of

---

[1346] Tim Radford, "Silent sounds hit emotional chords," **The Guardian** Mon 8 Sept 2003; "Sounds like terror in the air," **The Sydney Moring Herald** September 9, 2003.
[1347] Zainab Hasnain, "How the Rowland TR-808 revolutionized music," **The Verge** April 3, 2017.

crowds...Sound has a seductive power to caress the skin, to immerse, to sooth, beckon, and heal, to modulate brain waves and massage the release of certain hormones within the body.[1348]

Goodman rightly notes that, with the aid of "sonic warfare in ghetto musics," what has been produced is "urban dystopias, and their corollary ecologies of dread".[1349] What is Sonic Warfare? It is the use of sound and music to socially engineer urban dystopias with their ecologies of fear. What is an ecology of fear? It is an environment in which sound – unperceived LFS emissions or very perceived "ghetto musics (=rap)" – contribute to an immersive atmosphere of fear and dread. That is urban Black America.

IV.   *Musical Mind Control: Delgado's Dream Realized*

previous research has shown that low-frequency waves or beams can affect brain cells, alter psychological states and make it possible to transmit suggestions and commands directly into someone's thought processes.[1350]

The University of California at Berkeley psychologist and Lithuanian Jew Dr. David Krech (died 1977) predicted over forty years ago: "I foresee the day when we shall have the means, and therefore, inevitably, the temptation, to manipulate the behavior and intellectual functioning of all people through environmental and biochemical manipulation of the brain." On this, Bill Harris, the late founder of the Centerpoint Research Institute, remarked: "That day may very well be here now, and the gentle altering of brain wave patterns using sound may be *the easiest, most potent, and safest way to do it.*"[1351] Sound-

---

[1348] Steve Goodman, **Sonic Warfare: Sound, Affect, and the Ecology of Fear** (Cambridge, MA and London: The MIT Press, 2012) 10.

[1349] Steve Goodman, **Sonic Warfare: Sound, Affect, and the Ecology of Fear** (Cambridge, MA and London: The MIT Press, 2012) 3.

[1350] Christopher Leake and Will Stewart, "Putin targets foes with 'zombie' gun which attack victims' central nervous system," **Daily Mail** March 31, 2012.

[1351] Bill Harris, "The Science Behind Holosync and Other Neurotechnologies," Beaverton, Oregon: Centerpointe Research

manipulation as the "easiest, most potent, and safest way" to "manipulate the behavior and intellectual functioning of all people through environmental and biochemical manipulation of the brain." More effective even than the use of pharmaceuticals. As David Chagall pointed out already in 1983: "Music is used everywhere to condition the human mind. It can be just as powerful as a drug and much more dangerous, because nobody takes musical manipulation very seriously.[1352] As Dr. Leonard G. Horowitz explains as well: "people's bodies would bioenergetically entrain to the musical frequencies and electronically-engineered sound effects that would be most emotionally charged causing people to act in certain programmable ways."[1353]

Jose Delgado apparently envisioned the electronic remote control of people. According to a statement attributed to him he said:

> We must electrically control the brain. Someday armies and generals will be controlled by electric stimulation of the brain.

This would fall under the classification "neuro-electronics," which has been described as "tomorrow's alternative to drugs and surgery." Delgado's vision can be realized through weaponized music. Sound waves traveling through a medium (e.g. air) produces pressure energy which is converted into electrical energy for the brain to translate into musical sounds. When sound waves reach the cochlea in the inner ear, they are translated into electrical impulses by the hair cells, and these pulses travel along the auditory nerve into the brain. In addition, the microphone transduces sound waves into electromagnetic waves for amplification.

How is music weaponized as a mind control and behavior modification tool? By outfitting the music so as to surreptitiously "sink" the listener(s) into *theta state*. Neural

Institute,
http://www.centerpointe.com/about/articles_research.php. 1-13 (4)
[1352] David Chagall, "How Music Soothes, Stirs, and Slims You," *Family Weekly* January 30, 1983.
[1353] Dr. Leonard G. Horowitz, "Musical Cult Control: The Rockefeller Foundation's War on Consciousness through the Imposition of A=440Hz Standard Tuning," January 2011 @ https://www.bibliotecapleyades.net/ciencia/ciencia_consciousscience26.htm

activity produces brain waves that can occur at various frequencies, some faster, some slow.

Gamma 40Hz+ Rapid, rhythmic impulses generally associated with concentration
Beta   12Hz – 40Hz Generally associated with left-brain activity, "conscious mind."
Alpha 8Hz – 12Hz Generally associated with right-brain activity, "sub-conscious mind."
Theta 4Hz – 8Hz Right-brain. Deeper subconscious or superconscious. Associated with the hypnogonic state
Delta   0.5Hz – 4Hz Generally associated with no thinking.

Alpha and beta are our normal brain wave states. In beta we are alert and in alpha we are relaxed. Concentrated thinking produces rapid gamma waves. Theta state – where the brain synchronizes to theta waves - is the most conducive to hypnotic suggestion and is thus called the hypnogonic state or twilight state. Speech-Language pathologist Dr. Suzanne Evans Morris explains that the presence of theta patterns (4-7 Hz) in the brain has been associated with states of *increased receptivity* for learning and *reduced filtering* of information by the left hemisphere. Theta is associated with deep relaxation with a high receptivity for new experiences and learning.[1354]

The theta state also seems to be one where behavior and belief system changes can more easily be made.[1355] Neurotechnology and biofeedback researcher Thomas Budzynski (1981) described the theta state as a transition zone between wakefulness and sleep in which one can absorb new information in an uncritical, non-analytical fashion. Budzynski speculated that this allows new information to be considered by the right hemisphere – the subconscious mind - through bypassing the critical filters of the left hemisphere – the critical thinking brain. This can lead to an uncritical acceptance of verbal material or almost any material that it can process. Once

---

[1354] Suzanne Morris, "Music and Hemi-Sync in the Treatment of Children with Developmental Disabilities," **Open Ear** 2 (1996): 14-17 (15)
[1355] Bill Harris, "The Science Behind Holosync and Other Neurotechnologies," Beaverton, Oregon: Centerpointe Research Institute,
http://www.centerpointe.com/about/articles_research.php.

a theta state has been elicited in the brain, any auditory "change message" spoken to an individual during this "hypersuggestible state (theta)" is not subjected to the critical processing of the left hemisphere and is easily accepted and assimilated. Thus, information leading to a change in self-concept would become more available; modification of habitual behaviors or consideration of one's belief system could occur more easily *if alternatives were presented during a period of theta activity.*[1356] Theta is thus the *programming state* where verbal commands can be presented outside the awareness of the critical screening and defense mechanisms, which are inactivated.

Mind control and behavior modification is thus easiest to accomplish when the person or group has been sunk into theta state. How is that done? It can be done through music. Rhythmic drumming has a driving effect in the theta frequency range.[1357] In addition, in 1973 Gerald Oster published a game-changing paper.[1358] He had discovered the method to induce brain entrainment through music. The method is through the use of binaural beats. A binaural beat is an *auditory illusion* perceived when two different pure-tone waves, both with frequencies lower than 1500 Hz, with less than a 40 Hz difference between them, are presented to a listener dichotically (one through each ear). Through EEG monitoring the binaural beat or *difference tone* is identified by a change in the electrical pattern produced by the brain *in both hemispheres*. Under the influence of the binaural beat waveforms of both hemispheres exhibit identical frequencies, amplitude, phase, and coherence (synchronization).

1356 Morris, "Music and Hemi-Sync," 18 Thomas H. Budzynski, "Twilight Learning Revisited," *Biofeedback* 39 (2011): 155-166 156).
1357 Peggy A. Wright, "Rhythmic Drumming in Contemporary Shamanism and Its Relationship to Auditory Driving and Risk of Seizure Precipitation in Epileptics," *Anthropology of Consciousness* Winter (1991): 2-12; Melinda C. Maxfield, "Effects of Rhythmic Drumming on EEG and Subjective Experience." Unpublished doctoral dissertation. Menlo Park, CA: Institute of Transpersonal Psychology, 1990.
1358 Gerald Oster, "Auditory Beats in the Brain," *Scientific American* 229 (October 1973):94-102.

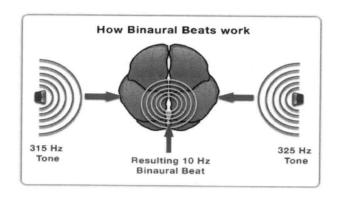

How Binaural Beats work

315 Hz Tone

Resulting 10 Hz Binaural Beat

325 Hz Tone

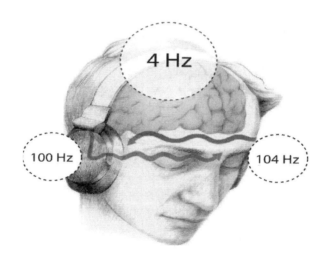

4 Hz

100 Hz

104 Hz

For example, if a 315 Hz pure <u>tone</u> is presented to a subject's left ear, while a 325 Hz pure tone is presented to the subject's right ear, the listener will perceive the auditory illusion of a third tone, in addition to the two pure-tones presented to each ear. The third or *phantom* sound is called a *binaural beat*, and in this example would have a perceived pitch correlating to a frequency of 10 Hz, that being the difference between the 325 Hz and 315 Hz pure tones presented to each ear. *The whole brain will then synchronize to 10 Hz*, both right and left hemispheres. This is thus called a *hemispheric synchronization* signal or a Hem-Sync signal. In this example the phantom 10 Hz signal that synchronizes the whole brain is the very frequency that quickens the stimulation and turnover of serotonin. [1359] On the other hand, a 100 Hz beat in the left ear and a 104 Hz beat in the right ear will result in a phantom beat of 4 Hz and thus synchronize the whole brain to the Fear Frequency, stimulating the release in catecholamines like serotonin's opposite, noradrenalin.

This is what Oster discovered. And the implications were clear from the beginning. As Bill Harris pointed out:

> Science ushered in a new era in our ability to learn, be creative, remember, control our moods, reduce stress, *resolve unwanted behavior patterns*, and a host of other desirable ends, with the appearance of a remarkable paper by Dr. Gerald Oster, of Mt. Sinai Medical Center, in the October 1973 issue of *Scientific American*.[1360]

Or stimulate a *desirable behavior pattern*; Behavior modification through binaural beats. Experiments with developmentally disabled children exposed to background music with and without lacing with Hem-Sync signals (binaural beats) have shown that permanent change in behavior occurred more quickly when exposed to the music laced with the Hem-Sync signals or binaural beats, which put the children's brain into theta state. As Morris explains:

[1359] Kathleen McAulife, "Brain Tuner," *OMNI* January 1983, 44-48,115-120.
[1360] Bill Harris, "The Science Behind Holosync and Other Neurotechnologies," Beaverton, Oregon: Centerpointe Research Institute,
http://www.centerpointe.com/about/articles_research.php.

Both clinical experience and preliminary research indicates that the addition of Hemi-Sync signals (containing frequencies which produce more theta patterns in the brain) to the background music increases the child's focus of attention and *creates a mental set of open receptivity*...more accepting of new possibilities.[1361]

This music containing Hemi-Sync signals is called "superlearning music" because it produced "open receptivity" in the children which resulted in changes in behaviors.[1362]

Using music laced with a Hem-Sync signal or binaural beat can put the listener in theta state. The lyrics of the music then can serve as "change messages" which sink into the listeners consciousness without any filtering by the critical apparatus of the left brain, producing permanent changes in behavior. Weaponized music is thus a "behavior modification protocol" which, compared to other methods (e.g. chemical) is "the easiest, most potent, and safest way," as Bill Harris pointed out.

How does this relate to The Weaponization of Hip Hop?

From the moment the Beats By Dre headphones hit the market they have been criticized for poor sound quality. What they do rather than provide clear sound quality is "jack up the bass to excessive levels," i.e. boost low frequency sounds waves!

much of Beats' engineered appeal is in its emphasis on low, bass-heavy frequencies of the 'Xxplosive' sort. It makes sense:

[1361] Suzanne Evans Morris, "Hemi-Sync and the Facilitation of Sensory Integration," **New Visions** (February 1998): 1-7 (3).
[1362] Suzanne Morris, "Music and Hemi-Sync in the Treatment of Children with Developmental Disabilities," **Open Ear** 2 (1996): 14-17 (15)

Rap music and hip hop are characterized by their heavy, booming bass lines.[1363]

Music is composed of sound waves at a variety of frequencies, from high to low, and <u>bass</u> is the lowest part of a song's range of noises. Think of the thumping bass drum in a rock song or a hip hop song's beat. A pair of headphones (or an audio system) can disproportionately represent some frequencies at the expense of others, and many audiophiles' problem with the (Beats by Dre) Studio headphones is that they jack up the bass to excessive levels, drowning out the other parts of the music.[1364]

In this way, Beats By Dre acts as portable subwoofers, which are speakers designed to amplify low frequency vibrations.[1365]

For the record, Beats by Dre was never Dr. Dre's intention. Based on advice from his lawyers, Dre entertained the thought of designing a sneaker line. But while Jimmy Iovine was in Malibu at the house of David Geffen, he ran into Dre at the beach and famously told him: "Fuck sneakers – let's make speakers."[1366] Iovine explains:

The whole headphones thing came to life on its own. Dre and I were out in Malibu, I know some of you think Dre lives in the hood, but he has a house in Malibu," said Iovine. "Anyway, we're on his terrace in Malibu, and he says, 'My lawyers want me to sell sneakers.' I look at him and I say, 'Fuck sneakers. Nobody cares what kind of sneakers you wear, but they would care about the speakers you use.' And speakers turned into headphones.[1367]

[1363] Katie Sharp, "What Beats By Dre Are Actually Doing to Your Ears," **Mic Daily** June 6, 2014.

[1364] Joseph Stromberg, "Sound experts agree: Beats by Dre aren't anything special," **VOX** May 29, 2014

[1365] Damon Krukowski, "Drop the Bass: A Case Against Subwoofers," **Pitchfork** June 17, 2015 @ https://pitchfork.com/features/oped/9667-drop-the-bass-a-case-against-subwoofers/

[1366] Matt Welty, "Dr. Dre Was Initially Encouraged to Design Sneakers, not Headphones," **Complex** August 18, 2015.

[1367]"Jimmy Iovine once detailed how Beats came about," **Capital Xtra** @ https://www.capitalxtra.com/artists/dr-dre/lists/facts/jimmy-lovine-creation-of-beats/

Who is David Geffen, and why should we be concerned about him "popping up" in the discussion about Beats By Dre?

Continue reading.

Part VI

The Queering of Hip Hop

"Hip Hop is at its queerest right now."
- ***Los Angeles Times***, July 31, 2019

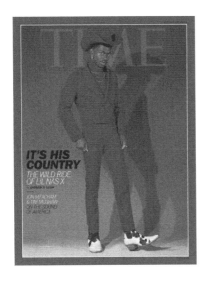

"Last year I was sleeping on my sister's floor, had no money, struggling to get plays on my music, suffering from daily headaches, now I'm gay." Lil Nas X, July 2019

"People judge me and people say I'm gay but it's like, at one point, I probably had more hoes... you know what I'm saying? It's serious. So if people think that I'm gay, they already misjudged me. I'm the straightest man in the world. I hate guys, like what? Fuck you talking about? I'm not even having no threesomes with no nigga." Young Thug, August 21, 2019

THE ARCHITECTURE OF "ILLUMINATI" INFLUENCE ON HIP HOP

By Dr. Wesley Muhammad © 2019

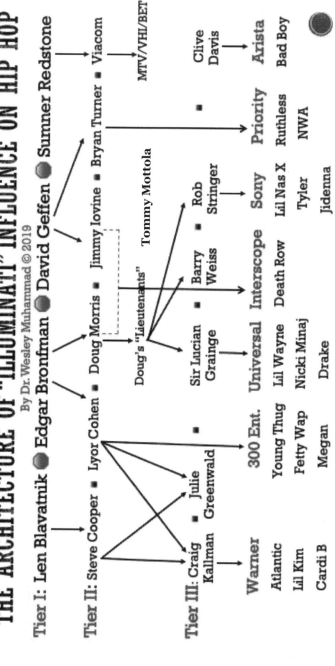

Tier I: Len Blavatnik ● Edgar Bronfman ● David Geffen ● Sumner Redstone → Viacom → MTV/VH1/BET

Tier II: Steve Cooper ■ Lyor Cohen ■ Doug Morris ■ Jimmy Iovine ■ Bryan Turner ■ Viacom

Doug's "Lieutenants"
Tommy Mottola

Sir Lucian Grainge → Barry Weiss ■ Rob Stringer

Tier III: Craig Kallman ■ Julie Greenwald

Warner
Atlantic
Lil Kim
Cardi B

300 Ent.
Young Thug
Fetty Wap
Megan

Universal
Lil Wayne
Nicki Minaj
Drake

Interscope
Death Row

Sony
Lil Nas X
Tyler
Jidenna

Priority
Ruthless
NWA

Clive Davis → Arista → Bad Boy

564

Chapter Twenty-four

The Gay Mafia and Hip Hop

Old white men is running this rap shit
Corporate force's running this rap shit
Some tall Israeli is running this rap shit
We poke out our asses for a chance to cash in
Cocaine, is running this rap shit
'Dro, 'yac and E-pills is running this rap shit...

MTV, is running this rap shit
Viacomm is running this rap shit
AOL and Time Warner running this rap shit
We poke out our asses for a chance to cash in
Cocaine, is running this rap shit
Hennessey, is running this rap shit
Quasi-homosexuals is running this rap shit

So goes the opening and the closing lyrics of Mos Def/Yasiin Bey's 2004 track "The Rape Over" which is all of a 90 second song. But it is possibly the most candid and most revealing song in the history of hip hop. The song itself also has a rather enigmatic history. The album *The New Danger* was released in October 2004. After an initial shipment of the album, Geffen Records (Mos Def/Yasiin Bey's label) printed and shipped 50,000 units of an alternative version of the album with the song "The Rape Over" removed. After repeated requests for an explanation, Jim Merlis, head of publicity for Geffen Records, sent a statement to the Jewish periodical **The Forward** claiming that the reason for the removal of the song was due to an uncleared sample used on the song.[1368] This is difficult to accept. Apparently The Doors sample was cleared within a few days. Why then was it necessary to print and ship 50,000 copies of a censored album? Geffen Records founder is, well, David Geffen, who is both Jewish and homosexual. Might this have something to do with the strange disappearance of "The Rape Over," the most precise and penetrating rap song ever made describing the forces behind Hip Hop?

[1368] Daniel Treiman, "Missing Rap Song Sparks Suspicious Musings," **Forward** December 10, 2004.

Geffen's influence in hip hop is palpable.

> David Geffen may not look like the usual Hip-Hop head, but the...mogul is *weaved into the fabric of the genre, for better or for worse*...[1369]

> Even though rap is a game with many non-Jewish artists, Jews do play a behind the scenes role in the music business. Individuals like Clive Davis (founder of J Records and Arista Records), David Geffen (head of Geffen Records), and Bryan Turner, creator of Priority Records, all pull the muscle strings that govern the biz.[1370]

> In addressing its misogyny problem, hip hop will have to question one overlooked but unavoidable fact. Hip Hop is owned by whites. The most powerful man in hip hop is not Puff Daddy; it is David Geffen...[1371]

I. *The Velvet Mafia is Real*

In 2012 Hollywood icon John Travolta was sued by a masseur who claimed the star attempted to coerce him into unwanted sexual acts in a California hotel. Travolta denied the allegations and the lawsuit was later dismissed by the court. But there is an interesting detail buried in the initial complaint for damages document filed with the United States District Court for the District of California:

> Defendant (Travolta) began screaming at Plaintiff, telling Plaintiff how selfish he was; that Defendant got to where he is now due to sexual favors he had performed when he was in his *Welcome Back, Kotter* days; and that *Hollywood is controlled by homosexual Jewish men* who expect favors in return for sexual activity. Defendant then went on to say how he had done things in his past that would make most people throw up.[1372]

[1369] "David Geffen Donates $100 Million, But There Was a Time When Money Couldn't Buy Love," **College HipHop** March 6, 2015 (updated April 5, 2017).

[1370] "Let Hip-Hop Lead the Way," **New Voices** January 20, 2010.

[1371] Ali Eteraz, "Dirty Hip Hop and Whether Blacks Need to Teach Whites Better," **HuffPost** April 12, 2007 (updated May 25, 2011).

[1372] Renee Ghert-Zand, "Travolta Sex Abuse Case Takes Anti-Semitic Turn," **The Schmooze** May 8, 2012; "Travolta Says Hollywood Run By Gay Jews Lawsuit Claims," **The Jewish Voice** May 16, 2012.

Charges of Anti-Semitism went flying in the press, of course, and Travolta did deny making such statements. But the claim of a Jewish homosexual cabal – a Jewish Gay Mafia, if you will - in Hollywood has deep resonance.

In 1992 Laureen Hobbs informs us in *Spy Magazine* of a "powerful gay tong" of Hollywood that included, among others, industry powerhouses Barry Diller, David Geffen, Sandy Gallin and Howard Rosenman.[1373] A "tong" is a Chinese concept that refers to a secret association, society, or sworn brotherhood that is frequently associated with criminal activity. The four

Adam Carolla: The Gay Mafia Is Real

members of this gay tong identified by Hobbs happened also to be Jewish. Writing for the *Baltimore Sun* in 1995 and attempting to dismiss the rumors of a "Velvet Mafia," a "nasty, vindictive, homosexual cabal that supposedly rules the entertainment world with an iron swish," Gabriel Rotello nevertheless correctly observed: "it hardly seems coincidental that most members of this latest alleged cabal are, in fact, both gay and Jewish."[1374] Celebrity crime investigative journalist and *New York Times* bestselling author Mark Ebner affirmed:

> Despite numerous denials, the Gay Mafia *does* exist, in hierarchical factions...Behind that [pink] curtain is a power so far-reaching it's mind-boggling (emphasis original).[1375]

Ebner identifies billionaire music and movie mogul David Geffen as the leader of the Gay Mafia ("sitting pretty at the helm"). "In the upper echelons of this 'family,' there exist

---

[1373] Laureen Habbs, "Diller's Crossing," *Spy Magazine* Vol. 6 May 1992, pp. 18-19.
[1374] Gabriel Rotello, "The velvet slur," *The Baltimore Sun* April 19, 1995.
[1375] Mark Ebner, "The Gay Mafia," *Spy Magazine* Vol. 9 May/June 1995, pp. 42-49.

men like David Geffen, who can end a career with a phone call."[1376] It is the case, according to Alan Citron, "Geffen is surrounded by a core group of high-powered friends with an almost familial loyalty."[1377] Comedian Andrew Dice Clay, who was signed to Geffen Records, said:

> I'd been around long enough to know that [Sandy] Gallin was part of what was known as the Gay Mafia. Along with his close friends David Geffen...and Barry Diller...he was part of an out-of-the-closet Hollywood powerhouse.[1378]

Reputed members of Hollywood's "Gay Mafia": Sandy Gallin, Calvin Klein, David Geffen (in jeans), Barry Diller, and unidentified friends.

In a very *mafioso* way the "best friends" Geffen, Diller, Gallin and Calvin Klein speak of their larger group as *family*, but in the "socialist state" type of way. As Matthew Trynauer writes in **Vanity Fair**:

> [Sandy] Gallin, it is very well known, has familial ties apart from the Queen of Country. He is a member of a group of people whose longtime association makes Bloomsbury look dull and unindustrious. "Barry Diller, Diane Von Furstenberg, Calvin and Kelly Klein, David Geffen, and Fran Lebowitz are like an extended family," Gallin acknowledges with a good deal of

---

[1376] Ebner, "Gay Mafia," 44.
[1377] Alan Citron, "David Geffen..." **Los Angeles Times** March 7, 1993.
[1378] Andrew Dice Clay with David Ritz, **The Filthy Truth** (New York: Touchstone, 2014) 174.

David Geffen

Sandy Gallin

pride. "There are a lot of other people in and out of the family, too . . . but over the last 20 years that's the core." This glamorous, *rich* crowd goes on vacations together, as they did last Christmas, to Harbour Island in the Bahamas. And everyone calls everyone else—especially Geffen, Diller, and Gallin, who are all Malibu neighbors—with great frequency. "Cradle to grave, just like a good socialist state" is how Barry Diller describes the loyalty and support of his group of close friends. Gallin confirms this: "Just like any family, [we] go through periods of fighting with each other, being disappointed with each other—and that's why it's like a family, because it has lasted for 20 to 30 years."[1379]

Gallin admits that keeping quiet about their dark activities is a code of this "family":

> Gallin admits that because of his place in this family he has been an eyewitness to some remarkable events in show-business and pop history. At one point he muses aloud about the bestseller he may write one day. "You're going to ask a question—why don't I write a book about all my friends and the things I've done? "My answer is: *Where would I live?*"[1380]

While he doesn't use any of the noted designations, the reality of the Velvet Underground or Gay Mafia was all but explicitly confirmed by one of the members of Laureen Hobbs' "Hollywood's powerful gay tong." In 2019, Howard Rosenman wrote a guest column for **Hollywood Reporter** entitled: "Why Being 'Gay in the '70s in New York and L.A. Was Magic' – and How Hollywood Has Changed." Rosenman was born in Brooklyn, New York to Ashkenazi Jews from Palestine. He fought for the Israeli Defense forces during the Six-Day War in 1967. In the column he recounts meeting that same year (1967) Barry Diller, David Geffen, and Sandy Gallin during a brunch in

---

[1379] Matthew Trynauer, "Sandy's Castle," **Vanity Fair** April 1996.
[1380] Matthew Trynauer, "Sandy's Castle," **Vanity Fair** April 1996.

New York, "I was the luckiest gay Jew in the world," Rosenman says. He goes on to describe Hollywood's gay tong:

The most wonderful thing about those days was that *the gay folks in power* lent a hand to young gay people trying to get a foothold in the business. There was *a powerful network* of older successful gay men ... who introduced younger gay men to successful showbiz types...You see, all the cognoscenti knew about each other and it wasn't secretive or shameful, *but there was a code that no one spoke publicly about it*. It wasn't being "out" as we know it today — *the press never wrote about it*. My very first feature film that I produced happened because of this gay network...If I wasn't gay, I never would have had the career that I have.[1381]

Why Being "Gay in the '70s in New York and L.A. Was Magic" — and How Hollywood Has Changed (Guest Column)

Rosenman (right) with David Geffen.

Names who have been associated with the "Gay Mafia" include but are not limited to: David Geffen, Barry Diller, Sandy Gallin, Howard Rosenman, Jeffrey Katzenberg, Calvin Klein, Steve Tisch, Steven Spielberg, Ray Stark, Aaron Spelling, etc.

[1381] Howard Rosenman, "Why Being 'Gay in the '70s in New York and L.A. Was Magic' – and How Hollywood Has Changed," **Hollywood Reporter** May 3, 2019.

1981 photograph of what *New York Magazine* (October 5, 2015) called "the Ultimate Power Nap" aboard the chartered yacht *Midnight Saga*: Barry Diller, then chairman of Paramount Pictures; Calvin Klein, fashion designer; David Geffen, music and movie mogul; and Sandy Gallin, Hollywood talent manager.

THE "EMPEROR"

"Hollywood is like the Balkans. 'There are duchesses and dukes and a court of sychophants'...And David [Geffen] is one of the emperors. There's Mike Ortiz and there's David. Two emperors."[1382]

And then there was one.

His mother would call him "King David" after the biblical prophet. "Geffen's parents, Abraham and Batya, were east European Jews who met in Palestine and immigrated to the United States."[1383] Geffen's "journey from middle-class Jewish

---

[1382] Bernard Weinraub, "David Geffen, Still Hungry," *The New York Times Magazine* May 2, 1993.
[1383] "David Geffen reinvented himself as a somebody," *CJ News* November 15, 2012.

boy from Brooklyn to masterful music and movie mogul,"[1384] was a journey filled with waging and wining wars against Geffen's rivals and enemies, real and perceived.

> Geffen wasn't tall or good-looking, and he certainly hadn't played football. Indeed, his fanatical drive to succeed was fueled by his considerable insecurities. With chutzpah, David figured he could beat just about anyone at the entertainment game. The key, though, was to earn the trust of an inner circle of artists and *then wage war on everybody else*..."That was the beginning of the end of the love groove in American music," [Paul] Rothchild says. "To me, that's the moment. When David Geffen enters the California waters as a manager, the sharks have entered the lagoon."[1385]

Before "King David" was the "King of Hollywood," that title was held by super-agent and Hollywood dealmaker Michael Ovitz, born of Romanian Jewish parents in Chicago. "Ovitz happens to be a close friend of the younger [Edgar] Bronfman."[1386] For 20 years through the 1980s and 1990s Ovitz was hailed as the "Most Powerful Man in Hollywood." By 2002 he was dethroned by David Geffen. In the August 2002 edition of *Vanity Fair*, an emotionally wrecked and thus candid Ovitz blamed his demise on a "shadowy Hollywood cabal" which he explicitly identifies as "The Gay Mafia."[1387] This Gay Mafia, led by David Geffen and his pal *New York Times* Los Angeles correspondent Bernard Weinraub, "stabbed him in his back" and engineered his downfall, according to Ovitz.[1388] As a result Hollywood had a new king: David Geffen. The ensuing controversy over his remarks forced Ovitz to later apologize for using the "stupid" and "offensive" language "gay mafia,"[1389] but

---

[1384] Danielle Berrin, "Deconstructing David Geffen," *Jewish Journal* September 11, 2012.
[1385] Barney Hoskyns, "Sex, drugs and the billion-dollar rise of David Geffen," *Independent* Friday 18, November 2005.
[1386] "Bronfman Clout Felt in L.a. by Movie and Jewish Worlds," *Jewish Telegraphic Agency* May 29, 1995.
[1387] Ryan Burrough, "Ovitz Agonistes," *Vanity Fair* August 2002.
[1388] Rick Lyman, "Ovitz Bitterly Bares Soul, and Film Industry Reacts," *The New York Times* July 3, 2002; Paul Tharp, "Ovitz: Felled By 'Gay Mafia,'" *New York Post* July 2, 2002.
[1389] Steven Gorman, "Ex-Hollywood Superagent OVITZ Regrets 'Gay Mafia' Remark," *Reuters* July 3, 2002; Rebecca Keegan, "Michael Ovitz Still Can't Help Himself," *Vanity Fair* October 5, 2018.

there can be no doubt that the "shadowy Hollywood cabal" of gay Jews that brought about his ruination was real.

Geffen has been described as "a ruthless schemer."[1390] Even one of Geffen's closest friends describes him thusly:

> And David sort of sits there in the darkness. Very quiet. You don't know what he's doing *except controlling and manipulating*. Sort of like the original-cast album cover of 'My Fair Lady.' That's David." [1391]

This is Geffen's *modus operandi*: he controls the people who control the people.

Geffen has been described in the press as "Hollywood's premier manipulator."[1392] "He's such a Machiavellian character," it is said. And his methods are ruthless.

1390 Barney Hoskyns, "Sex, drugs and the billion-dollar rise of David Geffen," **Independent** Friday 18, November 2005.

1391 Bernard Weinraub, "David Geffen, Still Hungry," **The New York Times Magazine** May 2, 1993.

1392 James Bates and Elaine Dutka, "Tom King, 39; Wall Street Journal Columnist Wrote Geffen Bestseller," **Los Angeles Times** April 15, 2003.

But David Geffen has trafficked in fictions all his life. The Operator (as he is called) could have easily been called The Liar...He'd advise clients to lie to get what they wanted; *he'd spread lies about people with whom he was feuding*...[1393]

Geffen seems at points to realize that his best traits are undermined by his worst traits—greed and *a vengeful spirit*—but seems at a loss to change his behavior...The richer Geffen became, the more good he did, but it is confounding that he hurt so many people in the process. Geffen's most disturbing trait as relayed in this book is *his willingness to sabotage the careers of others by manufacturing toxic and unfounded rumors.*[1394]

Before Geffen sank Ovitz, his subtle methods of vengeance such as rumors and press leaks hastened the downfall of his longtime nemesis CBS Records president Walter Yetnikoff in 1990, sending a clear message: "any of Geffen's other putative rivals might take a moment to reflect on the fact

---

[1393] David Handelman, "How David Geffen Got Ahead: Lies, Loot and a Little Luck," **Observer** March 13, 2000.
[1394] Tom King, **The Operator: David Geffen Builds, Buys, and Sells The New Hollywood** (New York: Broadway Books, 2000).

that the last person to take a shot publicly at David Geffen was Walter Yetnikoff. And nobody's quite sure what he's doing these days."[1395]   Geffen became "one of the most feared and loathed players in his field," "a slender man so puckish-looking that at 47 he could still be called the enfant terrible of the entertainment business."[1396]   But the enfant terrible is now "Hollywood Godfather,"[1397] "the industry godfather."[1398] "Geffen lives an awful lot like a sultan."[1399]

But both Yetnikoff and Orvitz got off easy compared to **Wall Street Journal** journalist Tom King, who wrote the only (originally authorized) biography about Geffen called **The Operator**. King was given by Geffen unique access to his life, including permission to interview many of Geffen's famous friends. King is gay like Geffen, who hoped King would immortalize him in print. However, the truthful portrait that was developing under King's pen was not to Geffen's liking. He felt King betrayed him. When the book was released in 2000 it is "said to have caused a panic not seen in America's entertainment capital since the revelations of the prostitute Heidi Fleiss."[1400]   The book infuriated Geffen. And then

> Typically, Geffen has vowed that King will come to regret his betrayal. At the very least, he has told friends, King will never write another book in this town again. That might be wishful thinking. Last week, before a single book appeared in stores, *The Operator* had already climbed to No. 20 on the Amazon list. King, who sets out on his book tour this week, is back to work at the *Journal,* writing a weekly column about Hollywood. *So far, being Geffen's No. 1 enemy hasn't hindered his job.* "If anything, I get my calls returned faster," he says. "At

---

[1395] Fred Goodman, "Who's the biggest Hollywood? Sizing Up David Geffen, the Toughest, Richest Impressario in show Business," **Spy Magazine** April 1997: 36-43 (42); Dannen, **Hit Men** 336-343.

[1396] Fred Goodman, "Who's the biggest Hollywood? Sizing Up David Geffen, the Toughest, Richest Impressario in show Business," **Spy Magazine** April 1997: 36-43 (37).

[1397] John Seabrook, "The many Lives of David Geffen," **The New Yorker** February 23, 1998.

[1398] Danielle Berrin, "Deconstructing David Geffen," **Jewish Journal** September 11, 2012.

[1399] Bernard Weinraub, "David Geffen, Still Hungry," **The New York Times Magazine** May 2, 1993.

[1400] "Hollywood mogul Geffen savaged in new biography," **The Guardian** February 25, 2000.

the end of the day," says one of King's colleagues, "Who cares what David Geffen thinks of him? He's a reporter at the *Wall Street Journal.* What's the worst thing that could happen to Tom? He won't get a contract at DreamWorks?"[1401]

This optimism in these words from Lisa DePaulo of **New York Magazine**, written in 2000, proved premature and tragic. Three years after the book's publication while on vacation the healthy, 39-year old King complained of a headache, collapsed on the floor and died of a brain hemorrhage. The managing editor of the **Wall Street Journal** Paul Steiger noted that King "was in apparently excellent health and fine spirits." Joanne Lipman, a deputy managing editor, said also: "He was in perfect physical health. He was always very boyish," she said. "Even though he was young, he looked even younger."[1402] The message that went throughout the industry was clear. When **The Daily Beast** reporter Nicole LaPorte asked one of Geffen's friends to speak on the record in 2010 (!), the friend replied: "The last person who wrote a book about David Geffen is dead! And he was young. And healthy. And now he's dead! Click."[1403] Geffen became "the most feared and powerful man in Hollywood."[1404] Tom King had been lauded: "He was courageous *to take on a sacred cow of the industry.*"[1405] But it cost him his life, according to the word on Hollywood's Palm tree lined streets. As Geffen's friend and fellow "Gay Mafia" member Howard Rosenman said: "David will do anything for you if you're his friend. But if you're his enemy, well, you might as well kill yourself."[1406]

[1401] Lisa DePaulo, "Whose Life Is It, Anyway?" **New York Magazine** March 13, 2000.

[1402] Nicole Laporte, "WSJ H'w'd columnist Tom King dies at 39 Journal staffers 'devasted and shocked'," **Variety** April 13, 2003.

[1403] Nicole LaPorte, "The Spectacular Rise and Fall of DreamWorks," **The Telegraph** June 9, 2010.

[1404] Lisa DePaulo, "Whose Life Is It, Anyway?" **New York Magazine** March 13, 2000.

[1405] James Bates and Elaine Dutka, "Tom King, 39; Wall Street Journal Columnist Wrote Geffen Bestseller," **Los Angeles Times** April 15, 2003.

[1406] Bernard Weinraub, "David Geffen, Still Hungry," **The New York Times Magazine** May 2, 1993.

By 2007, David Geffen had been crowned the most powerful gay man in America by **Out**.[1407] In 2016 he reportedly had a fortune of $6.5 billion.[1408] And he transparently had a "gay agenda." The **Los Angeles Times** described him as "a gay man with a liberal social agenda"[1409]

> Geffen's been a consistent support of progressive causes over the years. But the continuing battle over the gays in the military offers the best insights into *the behind-the-scenes manner* in which he now intends to use his considerable influence. [1410]

As a "movie-music kingpin,"[1411] Geffen is "the only man in the history of American cultural capitalism who has succeeded in three different industries-popular music, Broadway, and Hollywood."[1412] His fingerprint is all over the cultural industry.

> Geffen has played the architect, in his case refashioning the movie and music industries so substantially he's compared to Hollywood's founding fathers. As actor Tom Hanks plainly puts it... "He defined this culture. He built it.[1413]

II.   *The "Freaks of The Industry"*

But before there was David Geffen, there was Clive Davis.

Fredric Dannen, in his best-selling **Hit Men: Power Brokers and Fast Money Inside The Music Business** (1991), observed that "the record business...was culturally

---

[1407] "The Power 50," **OUT** April 3, 2007.
[1408] Laura M. Holson, "The Boy From Brooklyn: David Geffen Comes Home, With Cash to Spare," **The New York Times** February 20, 2016.
[1409] [1409] Alan Citron, "David Geffen..." **Los Angeles Times** March 7, 1993.
[1410] [1410] Alan Citron, "David Geffen..." **Los Angeles Times** March 7, 1993.
[1411] Paul Tharp, "Bronfman Adrift From Diller, Geffen," **New York Post** March 6, 2000.
[1412] John Seabrook, "The Many Lives of David Geffen," **The New Yorker** February 23, 1998.
[1413] Danielle Berrin, "Deconstructing David Geffen," **Jewish Journal** September 11, 2012.

Jewish" and that, during the 70s and 80s especially, "An outsized number of [record] label bosses were Jews from Brooklyn."[1414] One such Brooklyn Jew was Walter Yetnikoff, president of CBS Records (Columbia) and "the most powerful man in the music industry for much of the 80's".[1415]

CBS Records' Walter Yetnikoff and Michael Jackson

While Yetnikoff "wore his [Jewishness] like a gabardine," he was also "a philandering egomaniacal monster" who had a predilection for gentile women, which he amassed a stable of-his "*shiksa* farm," as it was refe rred to (the Yiddish *shiksa* is a derogatory Jewish term for a gentile woman).[1416] Yetnikoff's predecessor as president of CBS Records was his mentor and equally egomaniacal fellow Brooklyn Jew Clive Davis. In 1973 **Rolling Stone** could call Davis the "emperor" of the music industry.[1417] Both Yetnikoff and Davis were fully immersed in the hedonism that characterized the music industry then (and now), but they had different proclivities.

Made the undisputed head of CBS Records in 1967, the "emperor of the record industry" was abruptly and spectacularly fired in 1973. The Newark U.S. Attorney's Office Strike Force Against Organized Crime had launched an investigation and Davis and other Columbia executives faced a grand jury probe into interstate heroin trafficking and possible payola-by-drugs (drugola) at the record company. A bust of an international heroin smuggling ring

Clive Davis

[1414] Dannen, **Hit Men**, 22.

[1415] Lola Ogunnsike, "Sex, Drugs ad Ego: A Music Mogul's Swath of Destruction; A Deposed President of CBS Records Chronicles His Debauchery and Detox," **The New York Times** March 4, 2004; Fred Goodman, "The Rolling Stone Interview: Walter Yetnikoff," **Rolling Stone** December 15, 1988.

[1416] Dannen, **Hit Men**, 23; Johnny Davis, "Walter Yetnikoff: On the record," **Independent** February 29, 2004.

[1417] Robert Sam Anson, "Clive Davis Fights Back," **Vanity Fair** February 2000.

connected with the Mafia led right to CBS Records.[1418] One of those indicted on conspiracy and smuggling charges was Pasquale Falcone, who was associated with the Genovese crime family of New York and at the same time a manager of several Columbia artists, including Sly Stone as well as the country acts Lynn Anderson and Tommy Cash. But the connection with Clive Davis was closer than this. Falcone was a close associate of David Wynshaw, Vice President of Artist Relations at Columbia and Davis's closest aide, his "right-hand man."[1419] Falcone and Wynshaw together set up sham companies around New Jersey through which they funneled CBS Records money.[1420]

The New York Times coined the term *drugola* to describe the peculiar, *racialized* practice that Davis's CBS Records was allegedly engaged in. Wynshaw became a cooperating witness and reportedly told the grand jury about a $250,000 "hidden" budget that Columbia used to bribe specifically *black radio stations* into pushing records by Columbia's recently assembled group of Black artists (payola), while the Black artists themselves were apparently paid with drugs (drugola).

> The corporate corruption being investigated includes the old-fashioned payola-bribery to disk jockeys by record companies-*with a new, ethnic wrinkle.* One C.B.S. Records executive has recently reportedly told a grand jury that $250,000 in cash has been slipped to disk jockeys who direct their program to black audiences. But the return of payola, even on an unprecedented scale, is not the whole story: Federal investigators are looking into the use of hard drugs-cocaine and heroin-by the businessmen of music to bribe their distribution outlets, or to entertain their entertainers.[1421]

The word was that this was the operation of Clive Davis, the "most powerful man in the record industry," targeting black

---

[1418] Ben Fono-Torres, "Investigations, Rumors Mount In Columbia 'Drugola' Scandal," **Rolling Stone** July 18, 1973; Grace Lichtenstein, "Drug Charges Shake the Record Industry," **The New York Times** June 5, 1973; idem, "Columbia Payola Put At $250,000,"**The New York Times** June 6, 1973;

[1419] Geoffrey Stokes, "Clive's Comeback," **The New York Times** August 24, 1977.

[1420] Dannen, **Hit Men**, 92.

[1421] "The Drugola Scandal," **The New York Times** June 21, 1973.

radio stations with bribes but also targeting (Black) *artists with hard drugs*. I cannot help but think of the Clive Davis protégé of whom he is most proud: the tragic Whitney Houston, whom he signed when she was 19 years old.

It gets deeper. It is said also that Wynshaw handled the company's "Special Projects," such as providing the "entertainment" for Columbia executives and artists at CBS Records conventions. The insistent talk within the industry and within CBS Records was that the "drugola" operation investigated by the feds involved drugs (heroin and cocaine) *and prostitution*, and a once loyal executive assistant fingered Davis as the man who authorized it.[1422] Wynshaw was known as Columbia's "house pimp." As the ***Rolling Stone*** reported

> Whynshaw, it was said, was close to Clive Davis, and was variously known around the company and in the business as Davis' "royal procurer," or "Clive's pimp," or "the all-around Dr. Feelgood.[1423]

Armed with data provided by federal investigators, Arthur Taylor, president of CBS Inc (the parent corporation, of which CBS Records/Columbia was a subsidiary) fired Davis and had his memory "scrubbed" from the company. Kidder Meade, CBS's corporate press officer, reportedly leaked incriminating information to press, such as Davis being a "drug freak of some sort" and a homosexual,[1424] which was true. While Davis was never found legally guilty of payola, Taylor says Davis treated the record division as his personally owned and operated possession and he confirmed that the records division of CBS under Davis "had fun" at company conventions with drugs and prostitutes, *including young boys!*[1425]

> [Taylor] learned, for example, that one star had a standing arrangement: when he'd visit New York, 10 young women were made available to him. "There are a lot of whores hanging

---

[1422] Ben Fong-torres, "Clive Davis Ousted; Payola Coverup Charged," ***Rolling Stone*** July 5, 1973.
[1423] Ben Fong-torres, "Clive Davis Ousted; Payola Coverup Charged," ***Rolling Stone*** July 5, 1973.
[1424] Geoffrey Stokes, "Clive's Comeback," ***The New York Times*** August 24, 1977.
[1425] Ben Fong-torres, "Clive Davis Ousted; Payola Coverup Charged," ***Rolling Stone*** July 5, 1973.

around all the time," says Taylor. "In the building, out of the building." And not only there. Working girls (*and boys*) also entertained at Columbia conventions, where "aberration sex shows," in Taylor's words, were allegedly put on for top customers..." We had hookers and sex parties in Columbia Records forever, forever," says (an) executive.[1426]

This procuring of young girls *and boys* for sex company parties is of great importance. Clive Davis has confirmed that he is bisexual and was having sex with men in the 1970s.[1427] So the "emperor of the music industry" in the 1970s was a bisexual Brooklyn Jew who allegedly authorizes industry events that featured "sex parties" for which drugs, young girls *and boys were procured.*

Excursus: R. Kelly and the Real "Freaks of the Industry"

At best, the record industry consistently turned a blind eye to the charges swirling around [R] Kelly's private life. At worst, it enabled him. - **Chicago Tribune** *January 18, 2019.*

Let's talk about the music industry's seeming culpability. – **Rolling Stone** *June 5, 2019.*

[1426] Robert Sam Anson, "Clive Davis Fights Back," **Vanity Fair** February 2000.

[1427] Dan Gilmore, "Music Legend Clive Davis on Whitney Houston, Sexuality, and the Secret to His Success," **Vanity Fair** October 2, 2017; "Clive Davis Reveals Secrets About Legendary Artists and His Own Sexuality," **ABC News** February 2013; David Browne, "Six things You Didn't Know About clive Davis," **Rolling Stone** March 4, 2013

Since last year's airing of *Surviving R Kelly* and this week's airing of *Surviving R Kelly: Part II,* much talk has centered on R Kelly's aides and their complicity, and holding them accountable. This is appropriate talk, but the focus should not be on the low-level enablers who were small fish. Rather, the *real enablers* were the big shark higher-ups at Jive Records and RCA/Sony who can actually be described as *co-conspirators* in the reported predatory behavior directed at young, Black girls, at least they were wittingly complicit. In fact, the executives of Jive Records and associates not only helped create and foster the *industry culture* of sexually abusing young girls *and young*

boys, but Jive Records chief during the first round of the R. Kelly child pornography case, Barry Weiss, can be personally credited with playing a key role in making Black music, including Hip Hop, hypersexualized and exploitative of Black girls and women in particular.

Jive Records was founded in 1981 by Jewish South African émigré Clive Calder. In 1978 Calder met and entered into a partnership with the second of the two "Big Clives" of the music industry, Clive Davis, a fellow Jew from Brooklyn. Clive Davis had just founded Arista Records which became the first distributor for Jive Records. Five years prior in 1973, Clive Davis was "the most powerful man in the music industry" as president of CBS Records; until he got spectacularly fired for misappropriating company funds. According to what came out during a federal investigation and according to the man who fired Davis, CBS Inc. president Arthur Taylor, Davis oversaw an operation that involved having "aberrant" sex parties at the

Clive Calder

company office and at company conventions, and Davis's right-hand man (David Wynshaw) procured for these parties **young girls and boys**.[1428] Clive Davis is bisexual.[1429]

When Fredric Dannen, in his best-selling **Hit Men: Power Brokers and Fast Money Inside The Music Business** (1991), observed that "An outsized number of [record] label bosses were Jews from Brooklyn" and that, as a result, "the record business...was culturally Jewish,"[1430] it must be understood that this "Jewish culture" of the record business **involved the organized sexual exploitation of young girls and boys**. Fellow New York Jew (Long Island), Steve Rifkind who founded the Hip Hop label Loud Records in 1991 (Tha Alkaholiks, Wu Tang Clan, Mobb Deep, Akon, David Banner and Big Pun, among others) proudly confessed in 2015: "I wasn't into drugs, I was into pussy," and bragged that his Loud Records office "had orgies every Friday." "Loud got me laid," Rifkind fondly recalls.[1431] It was no doubt "Hip Hop Honeys" – i.e. mainly young Black girls - that were involved in these regularly scheduled weekly orgies at the label's office with the Jewish label head.

Steve Rifkind

Clive Davis of Arista and Clive Calder of Jive were partners. Barry Weiss, who confessed "I'm a Jew working in a black-Jewish environment,"[1432] joined Jive Records in 1982 becoming Manager of Artistic Development. Weiss pretty much always insisted on personally overseeing his artists "creative

---

[1428] Ben Fong-torres, "Clive Davis Ousted; Payola Coverup Charged," **Rolling Stone** July 5, 1973; Robert Sam Anson, "Clive Davis Fights Back," **Vanity Fair** February 2000.

[1429] Dan Gilmore, "Music Legend Clive Davis on Whitney Houston, Sexuality, and the Secret to His Success," **Vanity Fair** October 2, 2017; "Clive Davis Reveals Secrets About Legendary Artists and His Own Sexuality," **ABC News** February 2013; David Browne, "Six things You Didn't Know About clive Davis," **Rolling Stone** March 4, 2013

[1430] Dannen, **Hit Men**, 22.

[1431] Insanul Ahed, "Drop a Gen on 'Em: How Steve Rifkind Became One pf the Greatest Rap Execs Ever," **Complex** March 19, 2015.

[1432] Masha Leon, "Songwriter Denise Rich: 'Inside of Me Is a Black Woman'," **Forward** April 18, 2003.

decisions," i.e. Weiss was an A&R-type. Weiss became CEO of Jive in 1991 and, as ***Spin*** pointed out, led the label "through the singer's (R Kelly's) 2000s child pornography case before departing in 2011."[1433] Weiss credits the trajectory and success of his career to the two "Big Clives," Clive Calder and Clive Davis.[1434] R. Kelly, as we know him today, was a Clive Calder and Barry Weiss project. And we should not be surprised at what we see, because before there was Jive's R Kelly, there was Jive's Too $hort. That history is extremely important.

Barry Weiss called Too Short directly to sign him to Jive in 1988-1989. At first Too Short was a "Mack" with a social conscience and a social message (poverty, the effects of drug addiction, police brutality). The process by which Too Short the socially conscious Mack became Short Dogg the totally apolitical pervert, Mr. Freaky Tales, is instructive. In a 2012 interview with Hip Hop DX Too Short gives us

Barry Weiss

the background to the abrupt shift in the content of his songs in the mid-1990s to strictly sexual: Jive Records disallowed him from continuing to produce socially conscious music and pretty much coerced him into producing extreme, *hyper*sexual music.

> I'm rappin' this pimp image but I'm also – in all of my early albums with Jive [Records], they all had lots of songs that weren't about sex, that didn't have curse words in 'em, and I would pick subjects like crack cocaine, poverty and police harassment and rap about it...And, I'm not gonna blame this on anybody, ***but I was actually being pushed into a direction*** where I would talk to people at Jive [Records], I would go talk to the President, Barry Weiss, and he was like...I always wanted to do these [side] projects like the E-40 duet album, which was one they never would let me do. Jive would never let me and E-40 do an album together. They kept making excuses and so it never got done. I also wanted to do an album

---

[1433] Tosten Burks, "*Surviving R. Kelly* Producer Says Jive and BET Executives Declined Interviews, Too," ***Spin*** January 4, 2019.
[1434] Marids Fox, "The Music That Made Me: Barry Weiss, Chairman/CEO of Def Jam, Motown & Republic," ***billboard*** November 22, 2013.

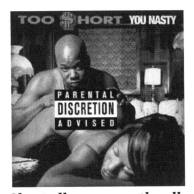

that was filled with songs like "The Ghetto," "Life Is...Too Short," "Money In The Ghetto," "I Want To Be Free." I wanted to do a whole album of positive Too Short songs, just to keep that balance. I had made a verbal deal with Barry Weiss, where he was like, "Right now would be the perfect time, *you should do like the raunchiest Too Short album ever – the album cover, the songs, just do a dirty fuckin' Too Short album."* This is the executive running the company advising mc to put out an entire album of just cursing and sex. So I'm like, "If I did that I'd have to then do the exact opposite and follow-up that with an album that's all positive." And so, I did the album for him, we did *You Nasty*. I thought it was a funny idea at first – we had like a porn star on the cover, I'm naked, the girls are naked and we really did a butt-naked photo shoot. And it got a gold album and all that stuff. *But when it came time to do the positive album, it was never a good idea. It never got the green light.* Once I did what they wanted, they would never let me do what I wanted. *I started noticing at that time in Hip Hop that the labels were actually signing the artists and promoting the artists who would bring in just the negative messages: let's have sex, drop ya booty.* We getting off into Crunk now, the bling bling is out there ... it's going down. It was a new swag...*So I'm just saying that at some point it wasn't that Hip Hop changed on its own, it had a little push. I'm a real conspiracy theorist,* and I just feel like there had to be a gathering of the major labels and somebody had to say like, "Look, we gotta keep this positive shit off the airwaves and let this booty-shaking shit take over. It's time." And after that it's like the floodgates just opened with sex and violence. And it was on the radio! You couldn't get Too Short songs on the radio back in the early days. But now I'm saying "Shake That Monkey" – the song is literally saying shake your vagina – and it gets played on the radio. C'mon man.[1435]

Enter R. Kelly.

[1435] Paul Arnold, "Too Short Says There Was An Industry-Wide Plot To Shut Down Conscious Hip Hop," *HipHopDX* February 29, 2012

Jive Records signed R Kelly in 1991 and he became their number one bread-winner instantly. His 1993 debut solo album

12 Play sold 6 million copies and over the decade R Kelly would make so much money for Jive Records that he helped Calder to become a billionaire in 2002. Kellz was Jive's gravy train. Barry Weiss, CEO of Jive from 1991 to 2011, was demonstrably disingenuous (even deceptive) when he claimed ignorance of his artist's (R Kelly) behavior in 2018. He told ***The Washington Post*** in 2018 that he *"never talked to Kelly about his behavior – it was none of his business."* Whoa. And Weiss blew off the matter: "I ran a record company, how was I supposed to know?" His claim that he was unaware of the lawsuits in which Jive was named is, of course, utterly ridiculous, as music journalist who first broke the R Kelly story Jim DeRogatis rightly points out:

> Well, you're being sued for $10 million, *that's how you know.* There's no way that didn't cross your desk. It's reprehensible, it's unconscionable [and] it's part of their corporate culture...Jive was a truly despicable company (emphasis added).[1436]

Weiss *did know.* As early as 1994 Clive Calder was warned that Jive's "meal-ticket" had a problem with young girls while on tour, and Calder now admits to having "missed something."[1437] What did he miss? He deliberately missed or, better said, *passed* on an opportunity to intervene to halt a situation that was consistent with the industry culture of sexual abuse *that Calder's peers were architects of.* Barry Weiss knew about the chargers of child pornography and in 2003 he admitted that it

---

[1436] Althea Legaspi, "R. Kelly Reporter Jim DeRogatis Talks Relentless Pursuit of 'Serial Sexual Predator'." ***Rolling Stone*** June 5, 2019.
[1437] George Edgers, "The star treatment," ***The Washington Post*** May 4, 2018.

was "a little bit scary" for him.[1438] What sacred you, exactly, Mr. Weiss? *The New York Times* reports:

> Mr. Kelly's career has flourished despite child pornography charges, but there is no saying what could happen if he were to be convicted. ("I try not to think about that stuff," Mr. Weiss said.)[1439]

What was scary to Weiss, Calder and the "corporate culture" of Jive Records and its parent, RCA/Sony, was the loss of this important "meal-ticket," or gravy train: "He's selling 100 million albums and nobody stops him, and instead thousands of people enable him…Jive Records [is] making almost a billion dollars on his record sales and of course never thinking to derail the gravy train," says DeRogatis.[1440]

Jive executives can be said to have conspired to cover it up. Jive Records helped to cover up R Kelly's relationship and illegal marriage to singer Aaliyah in 1994: when R Kelly and Aaliyah appeared on BET's "Video Soul" in the summer of 1994, Jive representatives instructed BET personnel not to inquire about Aaliyah's age or the relationship between the two. [1441] Even more incriminating is the testimony on *Surviving R Kelly: Part II* of Jimmy Maynes, former Senior Vice President Creative at Jive Records. He recounts being summoned to a late-night meeting with fellow executives and higher-ups in a conference room after the child pornography tape hit the streets in 2002.

> I remember being called to Jive late one night. We were brought into a conference room and they said, "Hey guys, we have a problem." During the time of the explosive tape, I remember them playing 15 or 20 seconds. At that point, *my bosses said*, "We've seen enough."… In a panic, they said to me and another executive, "You guys need to go to Chicago and you guys need to buy up all the tapes you can find." And we did.

[1438] Kelefa Sanneh, "Tarnished but Still Platinum; R. Kelly Is Popular Despite Pornography Charges,"*The New York Times* November 6, 2003.

[1439] Althea Legaspi, "R. Kelly Reporter Jim DeRogatis Talks Relentless Pursuit of 'Serial Sexual Predator'." *Rolling Stone* June 5, 2019.

[1440] Althea Legaspi, "R. Kelly Reporter Jim DeRogatis Talks Relentless Pursuit of 'Serial Sexual Predator'." *Rolling Stone* June 5, 2019.

[1441] George Edgers, "The star treatment," *The Washington Post* May 4, 2018.

Maynes adds,

> I remember one of my bosses telling me, "Jimmy, don't get caught up, because if Rob goes down, people are going to get fired." I was like, "Why? It's not our fault." He said, "Rob keeps the lights on around here."

And *that's* what it was all about. The possibly massive sexual exploitation and abuse of Black girls by a bread-winning artist was in *no way* offensive to Barry Weiss, Clive Calder or the other gate keepers of the music industry, because **the organized sexual exploitation and abuse of *young girls and boys was the industry culture*, a culture that Jive executives participated in, fostered and condoned fully**. Thus, when Weiss was asked in 2003 about R Kelly's continued sexually exploitative musical persona in the face of child pornography charges, his response was astounding, but revealing, as he appears to *justify his artist's predatory behavior*:

> Mr. Weiss quoted something he said the singer told him. "[R Kelly] said, 'I'm a lion in the jungle, and a lion's got to be a lion, otherwise he's going to get devoured,'" Mr. Weiss recalled. "For better or for worse, he's got to be true to his audience. R. Kelly's got to be R. Kelly."[1442]

I am not here arguing that R. Kelly should not be muted. I *am* arguing that, if we do so, by the same principle *we must* mute Barry Weiss, Clive Calder, Clive Davis, and *every contributing architect* of the music and movie industries' culture of organized and unorganized sexual exploitation and abuse of Black girls and women. We *must stop* unleashing all of our furry on low-ranking small fish who happened to be Black and continuously leave protected the high-ranking Great White Sharks.

[1442] Kelefa Sanneh, "Tarnished but Still Platinum; R. Kelly Is Popular Despite Pornography Charges,"*The New York Times* November 6, 2003.

Chapter Twenty-five

The Molly-fication of Hip Hop

"Get off drugs, xtasy is turning niggas into soft thugs." - Ice Cube of Westside Connection, "So Many Rappers in Love" (2003)

What connection can you the reader imagine between the irredeemably racist and genocidal regime of apartheid South Africa in the late 1980s and early 1990s, on the one hand, and American Hip Hop of the late 1990s and early 2000s, on the other? It seems unimaginable, doesn't it? These two phenomena are worlds apart temporally, geographically, culturally, politically, and *spiritually*. Yet, these two disparate and irreconcilable realities *can* be mentioned in the same breath *if* the discussion is about the recreational drug "Molly" or, to be exact, the militarized MDMA (3,4-Methylenedioxy methamphetamine), formerly known in Hip Hop as Xtasy (Ecstasy). Tracing this connection will, I believe, adequately introduce the subject of this Volume: the current scientific assault on Black America, including but not limited to the weaponization of marijuana and the weaponization of Hip Hop. Exploring this subject of "Molly" shines a *peaking* light on so many of the themes that we will elaborate on here.

I.   *Ecstasy to Quiet The Black Townships*

In the early 1980s, fears of a "black tidal wave" drove white scientists to try to develop a variety of means that could ensure the survival of white South Africa...[R]eportedly part of Project Coast was genetic engineering research, which was being conducted to produce a "black bomb," bacteria or other biological agents that would kill or weaken blacks not whites. The black bomb could be used to wipe out or incapacitate an entire area where an insurrection was taking place.[1443]

The Black Man and Woman in America who suffer under the scientific wickedness of the U.S. government should study closely the so-called "horrors of apartheid" that took place in South Africa during the 1980s and 1990s in particular, because America was South Africa's mentor and tutor in these horrors, and thus the mind, policies and practices at work in South Africa's apartheid reflects the mind, policies and practices at work in American white supremacy *and* Israeli colonialism. The US, Israel and apartheid South Africa worked closely together because they all shared the same problem: their most immediate enemy to be disposed of was not another nation-state threatening them from outside. Rather, in all three cases the real enemy threat came from *pockets of ethnic populations within their own borders*. The U.S. propped up the horrifically racist apartheid regime of South Africa (and Israel) for decades and the US helped repress the anti-apartheid movement in South Africa. In fact, it was the CIA who tipped off the apartheid government of the whereabouts of Nelson Mandela, leading to his capture in 1962. The US had pegged

---

[1443] Dr. Stephen Burgess and Dr. Helen Purkitt, *The Rollback of South Africa's Chemical and Biological Warfare Program* (Maxwell Air Force Base, Alabama: Air University, 2001) 21.

Mandela as "the world's most dangerous communist outside the Soviet Union."[1444]

Everything was fine in South Africa – from the Afrikaner rulers' point of view – until the Soweto Uprisings in 1976, which initiated unrest throughout the country. The eruptions in the Black townships of South Africa put the regime in the mind of "total war" and "total onslaught" against the Black South Africans: "it's now accepted that the 1976 Soweto uprising's (massive protests against the Apartheid regime) are what prompted the creation of the project [Coast], with the South African government hoping to develop methods of incapacitating or controlling large crowds."[1445]

In 1981 the regime initiated its chemical and biological weapons (CBW) program called Project Coast, headed by Dr. Wouter Basson, later known as "Dr. Death." Why the nickname? Because: "There are many people who think Basson was a war hero—because he killed the blacks big time,"[1446] in the words of Daan Goosen, Basson's subordinate in Project Coast. The South African CBW program was the protégé of the United States CBW establishment. During the 1940s and 1950s South African military officers were trained in CBW by the United States and the United Kingdom.[1447] As William Finnegan in *The New Yorker* observes: "According to Basson, Project Coast was *modelled on the American chemical-weapons program*, which he first managed to penetrate in the early nineteen-eighties."[1448] Basson received his training in CBW at Fort Detrick in Maryland and Porton Down in the U.K. From the U.S. he got knowledge, equipment, and viruses to weaponize. Basson

---

[1444] Ben Norton, "How the CIA helped apartheid South Africa imprison Nelson Mandela for 27 years – and is now facing lawsuits," *Salon* May 17, 2016.
[1445] Karl Kemp, "South Africa's 'Dr. Death' Was Accused of Selling Ravers Super-Strength MDMA," *VICE* November 4, 2014.
[1446] Boateng Osei, "Did This Man 'Kill Blacks Big Time'? (Special Report: south Africa)," *New African* November 2001.
[1447] Stephen Burgess and Helen Purkitt, "The Secret Program: South Africa's Chemical and Biological Weapons," in *War Next Time: Countering Rogue States and Terrorists Armed with Chemical and Biological Weapons* (USAF Counterproliferation Center, 2004) 27-66 (28); Jerome Amir Singh, "Project Coast: eugenics in apartheid South Africa," *Endeavour* 32 (2008): 5-9 (5).
[1448] William Finnegan, "The Poison Keeper," *The New Yorker* January 15, 2001: 58-74 (63).

himself would later confess: "I must confirm that the structure of the [CBW program] project was based on the U.S. system. That's where we learnt the most."[1449] Thus,

> The South African bioterrorist campaign depended upon very close relationships with U.S. scientists...From 1981 to 1993, the United States supported Wouter Bassoon's (sic) weaponization programs by financing close collaborations with U.S. scientists and by sponsoring Basson's sojourns to the United States for conferences education.[1450]

The U.S. supported the South African regime *and* the CBW program, tutoring the operatives in techniques and providing some chemical and biological weapons. The tactics used by the South African bioterrorists against Black people in Africa were also used by U.S. bioterrorists against Black people in America, and vice versa.

The chemical and biological programs of Project Coast were divided between two different facilities, and the programs had two specific operational objectives. Both programs aimed to undermine the health of the Black township communities, one through biological means the other through chemical.

- Roodeplaat Research Laboratory – the biological research, development and production facility located ten miles north of Pretoria. The aim of this program was a biological "Black Bomb" or *Kaffir-killer* and a sterilizing vaccine or agent. Later during our discussion on the weaponization of Black America's food, we will elaborate more fully on this program.

- Delta G Scientific - the chemical research, development and production facility located south of Pretoria. The aim was the development of incapacitating, crowd control chemical agents that could pacify the angry "insurrectionists" and quelle the townships: "chemical agents were being developed to make people passive".[1451]

[1449] Washington, ***Medical Apartheid***, 372.
[1450] Washington, ***Medical Apartheid***, 372.
[1451] Burgess and Purkitt, ***Rollback***, 28.

One of the chemical agents looked to "to make people passive" was MDMA. In 1999 the independent South African News organ ***Independent Online*** (***IOL***), under a headline that read "'Basson's men made ecstasy for warfare'," reported:

> The apartheid government manufactured ecstasy on a large scale in 1992 as a possible chemical weapon to incapacitate state enemies, a chemical scientist employed at Delta G at the time testified in the Pretoria High Court on Friday.[1452]

According to testimony and reports the Directorate of Covert Collections, a super-secret unit within the South African Defense Force (SADF), manufactured the weaponized MDMA for Dr. Wouter Basson. "Almost 100 percent pure ecstasy made from unique formula as part of a secret project to control crowds."[1453] The desire was for incapacitating agents which could affect the thinking and judgment capabilities of state enemies. MDMA was to be put in aerosols and sprayed over an angry crowd to "neutralize the offensive spirt."[1454] Dr. John Koekemoer, former head of chemical and biological research at Delta G, testified during the 1998 Truth and Reconciliation Commission trials that in the final days of apartheid the South African government ordered the Project Coast chemists to make one ton of ecstasy for riot control. Dr. Koekemoer acknowledged that ecstasy's effect was to enhance interpersonal relationships and make one "want to kiss [his] enemy." Therefore "Basson's production of ecstasy as a 'love drug' [was] aimed at pacifying unruly mobs".[1455] The ecstasy was

[1452] "'Basson's men made ecstasy for warfare'," ***IOL*** Friday October 29, 1999.

[1453] "Basson case: Ecstasy was made by experts," ***IOL*** Friday November 5, 1999.

[1454] William Finnegan, "The Poison Keeper," ***The New Yorker*** January 15, 2001: 58-74 (73).

[1455] "The deeds of Dr. Death," ***The Guardian*** October 4, 1999.

manufactured "in pure crystalline form" and delivered beginning in February 1992. As we shall see, 1992 was an important year in South Africa and in America.

Ecstasy was not the only incapacitating agent Delta G produced in order to pacify the Black townships. Mandrax (Quaaludes), LSD *and marijuana* were also weaponized for crowd control purposes. The plan was to extract the active ingredient (THC) from marijuana and insert it into crowd-control grenades.[1456] The overall aim of these efforts, some investigators suspect, was for the drugs to be "dumped into black areas to encourage addiction and sap the resolve to resist."[1457] According to Zhensile Kholsan, an investigator for the Truth and Reconciliation Commission, there are strong suggestions that "drugs were fed into communities that were political centers, to cause socioeconomic chaos."[1458] Also,

> The former head of police forensics in South Africa, Lothar Neethling, told the commission Mr Basson was briefed to produce riot-control equipment containing mood-altering drugs, and was therefore supplied with 200,000 mandrax tablets as well as LSD *and marijuana.* The TRC's legal officer, Hanif Valley, put it to Mr Neethling that the purpose of the research on drugs was to spread addiction among blacks, asking: "What better crowd control than to have an enslaved youth?" The scientist said the aim was to find non-lethal methods of crowd control."[1459]

"What better crowd control than to have an enslaved youth?" America would show the exact same mindset. In fact, while South Africa's Black townships were the primary destination for much or most of that "pure crystalline" ecstasy manufactured for Project Coast, at least some of it was reportedly intended for an international destination. One of the destinations, we now know, was Chicago, Illinois. Karl Kemp reported for **Vice**:

[1456] "Africa Apartheid government sought germs to kill blacks," **BBC News** June 12, 1998.

[1457] Dean E. Murphy, "Horrific Tales Emerge in Apartheid Hearings," **Los Angeles Times** June 19, 1998.

[1458] Alexander Cockburn, "South Africa's Dirty Secrets Have Echoes," **Los Angeles Times** June 21, 1998.

[1459] Raymond Whitaker, "SA planned chemical war on blacks," **Independent** June 13, 1998:

International concerns were raised when a drug bust (in Chicago) traced almost completely pure ecstasy all the way back to South Africa and the Delta G laboratories, which led to cooperation between American and South African intelligence.[1460]

What Kemp does not realize is that it was likely American and apartheid South African intelligence cooperation that brought the Delta G Ecstasy to Chicago *in the first place*. In fact, the evidence strongly points to South Africa having originally gotten their weaponized ecstasy from the U.S., who was the *first* to militarize the drug.

II.   *The U.S. Army Militarizes MDMA*

MDMA was first synthesized in 1912 by the German chemical company Merck and stayed shelved for fifty years. Then, the U.S. military and intelligence agencies got their hands on it and researched its weaponization. In 1953 the Army undertook studies to assess the toxicity of mescaline analogues, MDMA being the best-known member of the group.[1461] As Steven B. Karch relates in his "Historical Review of MDMA":

> Army researchers had hopes that MDMA could be used in its highly classified MK-ULTRA experimental program – an exercise in mind control. These experiments began in the 1950s and continued through the early 1960s. Military and intelligence interests were in MDMA as an interrogation and behavior manipulation tool. The experiments focused entirely on "weaponizing" MDMA.[1462]

The Army did human tests with mescaline analogues on patients at the New York State Psychiatric Institute (NYSPI); one died. Between 1953-1954 the US Army Chemical Center, Edgewood Arsenal funded University of Michigan scientists to study the Army's synthesis or form of MDMA - code named EA

[1460] Karl Kemp, "South Africa's 'Dr. Death' Was Accused of Selling Ravers Super-Strength MDMA," **VICE** November 4, 2014.
[1461] Steven B. Karch, "A Historical Review of MDMA," **The Open Forensic Science Journal** 4 (2011): 20-24;
[1462] Karch, "A Historical Review of MDMA," 20.

1475 - and other mescaline analogs.[1463] The scientists gave MDMA to guinea pigs, rats, mice, monkeys, and dogs in order to study its toxicity. This U of M study for the Army had an interest beyond MDMA as a chemical weapon, however. In a survey of researched substances conducted for the Army Medical Laboratories it was found: "of immediate interest: the mescaline series, the lysergic acid diethylamide (LSD) and the marijuana series."[1464] Mescaline (MDMA), LSD, and marijuana have been found together as chemical warfare interests of the military and intelligence organizations from the beginning, just as we found in South Africa. The U.S. Army Chemical Corps did its chemical warfare research at Edgewood Arsenal in Maryland, and therefore MDMA was called EA-1475, "EA" meaning both "Edgewood Arsenal" and "Experimental Agent."

III.   *The Godfather of Ecstasy: Dr. Alexander Shulgin*

The most important figure in the weaponization of MDMA is Dr. Alexander "Sasha" Shulgin, known popularly as "the Godfather of Ecstasy." For very good reason Shulgin, whose

---

[1463] Torsten Passie and Udo Benzenhöfer, "MDA, MDMA, and other "mescaline-like" substances in the US military's search for a truth drug (1940s to 1960s)," **Drug Test Anal.** 10 (2018): 72-80; Harold F. Hardman, Coryce O. Haavik and Maurice H. Seevers, "Relationship of the Structure of Mescaline and Seven Analogs to Toxicity and Behavior in Five Species of Laboratory Animals," **Toxicology and Applied Pharmacology** 25 (1973): 299-309.

[1464] Albarelli, **A Terrible Mistake**, 166-167; Passie and Benzenhöfer, "MDA, MDMA, and other "mescaline-like" substances," 76.

parents were Russian Jewish immigrants to the US in the early 1920s, is called a kind of "Einstein of pharmacology." At the beginning of the 20th century only two psychedelics were known to Western science: mescaline (the root of MDMA) and cannabis (the root of marijuana). By the year 2000, well over 200 psychedelic chemicals were known, most of which were created in the personal lab of Alexander Shulgin. Many of the Schedule 1 prohibited drugs are his creation. "[T]he Drug Enforcement Agency...believes the scientist (Shulgin) is largely responsible for creating drugs popular among today's club kids."[1465] Many of the party drugs, "such as ecstasy, STP, 2 CT 7, 2 CB and foxy methoxy – have slipped from his grasp and out to the street."[1466] In this way, Shulgin is said to have "influenced global youth culture more than any other in the last 30 years"[1467]

But here is the kicker: Shulgin created these sometimes outlawed youth drugs *while working for the government*! Indeed, "The DEA, having picked up a new substance on the streets, would often bring it Shulgin for analyses – and it would sometimes prove to be one of the 'materials' he had cooked up in his backyard."[1468] Shulgin worked for Dow Chemical, for whom he invented the world's first biodegradable pesticide. He left Dow in 1965 and worked in his home lab making psychedelics, all under the protection of the U.S. government. By the 1970s "Shulgin's establishment credentials were impeccable."[1469] He consulted for the National Institutes of Health and NASA and worked for decades as a Drug Enforcement Agency lecturer and adviser. As Dann Halem informs us:

[1465] Dann Halem, "Altered Statesman: Ecstasy Pioneer Alexander Shulgin Defends His Work; Making Mind-Bending Drugs Right Here in Contra Costa," *Time Out* (March 2002)

[1466] Mark Boal, "Blood, sweat and serotonin: The Master Chemist of the Psychedelic Movement and his 40-year Battle with the Government," *Playboy* March 2004.

[1467] Clive Martin, "The World Would Be So Much Worse without Ecstasy," *Vice* June 4, 2014.

[1468] Matthew Collin, *Altered State: The Story of Ecstasy Culture and Acid House* (1997), 24.

[1469] Mark Boal, "Blood, sweat and serotonin: The Master Chemist of the Psychedelic Movement and his 40-year Battle with the Government," *Playboy* March 2004.

For 30 years, while Shulgin was not-so-secretly inventing compounds and advocating drug legalization, he was also one of the DEA's leading consultants and expert witnesses at government drug trials. In the Shulgins' office, hidden behind a row of musty file cabinets, are two commendations from the U.S. Department of Justice's Bureau of Narcotics and Dangerous Drugs, a precursor to the DEA, presented in recognition of Shulgin's "significant personal efforts to help eliminate drug abuse".[1470]

Shulgin testified as an expert on both sides of drug trials. He gave expert testimony for the prosecution because "He didn't mind helping the government put amphetamine or cocaine dealers in jail."[1471] MDMA is an amphetamine. Shulgin even wrote the classic reference book on U.S. law and drugs, ***Controlled Substances: Chemical And Legal Guide To Federal Drug Laws***.[1472]

For over 20 years Shulgin "held a rare government license allowing him to study *and synthesize illegal drugs*."[1473] In other words, Shulgin was literally given license to create the illegal drugs that kept "appearing" on the streets. And if the DEA believed that Shulgin was "largely responsible for creating drugs popular among today's club kids," they *knew* this because Shulgin had such a close relationship with the DEA well beyond employment.

For a long time, though, Shulgin's most helpful relationship was with the D.E.A. itself. The head of the D.E.A.'s Western Laboratory, Bob Sager, *was one of his closest friends.* Sager officiated at the Shulgins' (Alexander and Ann Shulgin) wedding and, a year later, was married on Shulgin's lawn. Through Sager, the agency came to rely on Shulgin: he would give pharmacology talks to the agents, make drug samples for the forensic teams and serve as an expert witness -- though, he

---

[1470] Dann Halem, "Altered Statesman: Ecstasy Pioneer Alexander Shulgin Defends His Work; Making Mind-Bending Drugs Right Here in Contra Costa," ***Time Out*** (March 2002)

[1471] Mark Boal, "Blood, sweat and serotonin: The Master Chemist of the Psychedelic Movement and his 40-year Battle with the Government," ***Playboy*** March 2004.

[1472] Ros Davidson, "Archive, 1997: Interview with Alexander Shulgin, 'godfather of ecstasy'," ***The Guardian*** June 3, 2014.

[1473] Ros Davidson, "Archive, 1997: Interview with Alexander Shulgin, 'godfather of ecstasy'," ***The Guardian*** June 3, 2014.

is quick to point out, he appeared much more frequently for the defense. He even wrote the definitive law-enforcement desk-reference work on controlled substances. In his office, Shulgin has several plaques awarded to him by the agency for his service. (Shulgin denies that this had anything to do with his being given his Schedule I license.)[1474]

Shulgin in fact created these drugs in his home lab *protected by the government.*

Shulgin's lab is in the concrete-block foundation of what used to be a small cabin, set into a ridge a few dozen yards from his house along a narrow brick path. On the door is a laminated sign that reads, "This is a research facility that is known to and authorized by the Contra Costa County Sheriff's Office, all San Francisco D.E.A. Personnel and the State and Federal E.P.A. Authorities." Underneath are phone numbers for the relevant official at each agency. He posted it after the sheriff's department and the D.E.A. raided the farm a second time a few years ago. (They later apologized.)

And if this is not enough to certify his establishment credentials, Shulgin was also

a member of the Bohemian Club, one of America's most elite organizations. Every Republican president since Calvin Coolidge along with America's top CEOs and media moguls has been a member of the all-male fraternity, which meets once a year for a secretive two-week bacchanal in the California redwoods.[1475]

Yet, Shulgin is described as a "ghost of history," which is ironic given all of the press one can pull up about him today.

...Shulgin has created more than 100 molecules that produce altered states of consciousness, new ways of thinking, feeling and seeing-making him a kind of Einstein of pharmacology, if not one of the most influential scientists of his time. But even today his work is virtually unknown outside a select West Coast circle. At the age of 78 Shulgin is a ghost to history, mentioned

---

[1474] Drake Bennett, "Dr. Ecstasy," *The New York Times* January 30, 2005.
[1475] Mark Boal, "Blood, sweat and serotonin: The Master Chemist of the Psychedelic Movement and his 40-year Battle with the Government," *Playboy* March 2004.

only in passing in a few articles and missing from the scholarly drug books, the result of a careful, lifelong avoidance of the mainstream press as well as a dose of *government suppression* (emphasis added). [1476]

Playboy March 2004 depiction of Dr. Alexander Shulgin in his Bohemian Grove robe.

Dr. Alexander Shulgin is one of the 2,500 old white men (a pinch of token blacks has now been admitted) who constitute the "ultra-powerful" of the Bohemian Club, and this is the proper context to understand him *and his drug MDMA.*

The government on whose behalf Shulgin worked would be the "suppressor." What is a "ghost" to history is Shulgin's chemical warfare work. Shulgin worked with the Army to weaponize cannabis (THC). In fact, he was *the critical factor* in this process. He was also centrally involved with the government's operation to weaponize rock n' roll music against anti-war young White

Alexander Shulgin with Lt. Col. James Ketchum, former chief of clinical research at the U.S. Army's Edgewood Arsenal, where he conducted experiments on human guinea pigs of a host of prospective chemical warfare agents.

[1476] Mark Boal, "Blood, sweat and serotonin: The Master Chemist of the Psychedelic Movement and his 40-year Battle with the Government," ***Playboy*** March 2004.

rebels by using the Grateful Dead to spread LSD.

IV.   *Shulgin's "Love Drug" and the Revealing of Inner "Monsters"*

In the creation of Shulgin's new chemicals there was "a special emphasis on the sex-enhancing properties of psychedelics".[1477] This is especially true of his MDMA. Merck first synthesized MDMA in 1912, and the U.S. Army did its own synthesizing during the 1950s and 1960s, with Shulgin's help. In 1965, Shulgin came up with his own unique synthesis – easier and faster - and *his* synthesis will dominate the culture moving forward. This is why Shulgin is widely thought of as the "Father of MDMA," which, of course, is factually wrong. "Shulgin was not the first to synthesize MDMA, but he played an important role in its history."[1478] He *can* be considered the "Godfather of Ecstasy," because *his* MDMA gave birth to the "Ecstasy" culture.

In his first report on the human effects of the drug Shulgin and D.E. Nichols noted that MDMA produced "an easily controlled altered state of consciousness with emotional and sensual overtones."[1479] One source of this "sensuality" caused by MDMA is the triggering by the drug of the brain's release of the "hug hormone" oxytocin. Also relevant is Shulgin's focus on serotonin,[1480] an important brain chemical which we discussed in detail in our previous writing. This is what we documented in **Understanding The Assault Volume I** regarding serotonin:

[1477] Hamilton Morris, "The Last Interview With Alexander Shulgin," *Vice* May 1, 2010.

[1478] Torsten Passie and Udo Benzenhöfer,Rediscovering MDMA (ecstasy): the role of the American chemist Alexander T. Shulgin," *Addiction* 105 (2010): 1355-1361.

[1479] A.T. Shulgin and D.E. Nichols, "Characterization of three new psychotomimetics," in R.C. Stillman and R.E. Willette (edd.), *The Pharmacology of Hallucinogens* (New York: Pergamon, 1978) 74-82.

[1480] Alexander T. Shulgin, "The Background and Chemistry of MDMA," *Journal of Psychiatric Drugs* 18 (186): 291-304; idem, "History of MDMA," in *Ecstasy* ed. S.J. Peroutka (Kluwer Academic Publishers, 1990) 1-20.

What the UCLA scientists discovered was that serotonin was the "Rosetta Stone" for decoding the mysteries of aggression, violence and also social hierarchy, among other things. They found that high levels of serotonin were distinctly related to male social dominance and low levels of serotonin was associated with low social status or subordination... Serotonin is our brain's key modulator of several physiological processes, including our primitive drives and emotions. It is the brain's chemical *breaks*, our impulse inhibitor (it puts a lid on our impulsive behavior). High serotonin is required to rein in our basic drives – appetite, sex, aggression, etc. – and keep them from racing out of control. When serotonin is low, "all the basic drives that it regulates can burst out of control," because low serotonin results in loss of impulse control.

If serotonin is the brain's chemical breaks, noradrenalin is the chemical *accelerator*... Serotonin and noradrenalin are the two "brain buttons" that scientists discovered they can push and thereby determine a person's future, "two potent brain chemicals that researchers have successfully manipulated to make animals more violent or less violent," in the words of [**Chicago Tribune** writer Ronald] Kotulak. "[A]ggression can be controlled by manipulating brain levels of serotonin." By "twisting the architecture of the brain" scientists can "push noradrenalin production into overdrive and serotonin into low gear," thereby making an individual or group hyper-impulsive, hyper-aggressive and violent: "*the raging monster* was being forced into the open where scientists could begin to understand and tame it."

This metaphor of inner aggression as a *raging monster* that is unleashed by diminishing serotonin and increasing noradrenalin is important for our discussion of Shulgin's MDMA. His wife and scientific collaborator Ann Shulgin, a therapist, admitted that the *purpose* for the use of her husband's MDMA in therapy sessions was to unleash a person's "dark side," his "shadow," or "monster." This "monster" represents certain aspects of the personal psyche, "inacceptable" inner tendencies and fantasies which are usually suppressed in order to protect the conscious self. The Shulgins aim with their MDMA was to "help" a person release their "monster" and *become* their inner monster through the ingestion of MDMA.[1481]

[1481] Julie Holland, "The Godparents of MDMA: An Interview with Ann and Sasha Shulgin," in **Ecstasy: The Complete Guide**, ed. Julie

MDMA helps "release the monster" by diminishing brain serotonin and triggering the release of noradrenalin. While it is true that the drug stimulates an initial acute release of serotonin,

Studies investigating the long-term effects of MDMA on the serotonergic system in humans and animals have shown that MDMA can induce a lasting decrease in serotonin and 5-HIAA levels in the brain, a reduction in the activity of tryptophan hydroxylase, and a reduction in the density of the serotonin transporter. Decreased 5-HT (serotonin) levels have been associated with mood disorders, increased levels of impulsivity, hostility and aggression. Ecstasy's damaging effects on the serotonergic system thus can lead to heightened impulsivity, hostility and aggression.[1482]

In 1994 conclusive evidence of MDMA neurotoxicity in humans was reported. In controlled trials, McCann et al. found that the spinal fluid of test subjects exposed to MDMA had significantly lower 5-HIAA, the major serotonin metabolite, than did controls.[1483] This indicates MDMA diminishes serotonin.

Holland (Rochester, Vermont: Park Street Press, 2001): 58-65; Passie, "The early use of MDMA," 3.

[1482] The National Institute on Drug Abuse, *The Neurobiology of Ecstasy (MDMA)* (2007); Alinde E. Wallinga et al., "MDMA-induced serotonergic neurotoxicity enhances aggressiveness in low- but not high-aggressive rats," *European Journal of Pharmacology* 618 (2009): 22-27; Sarah M. Dickerson et al., "The Recreational Drug Ecstasy Disrupts the Hypothalamic-Pituitary-Gonadal Reproductive Axis in Adult Male Rats," *Neuroendocrinology* 88 (2008): 95-102.

[1483] U.D. McCann et al., "Serotonin neurotoxicity after (+/-)3,4-methylenedioxymethamphetamine (MDMA; "Ecstasy"): a controlled study in humans," *Neuropsychopharmacology* 2 (1994): 129-138.

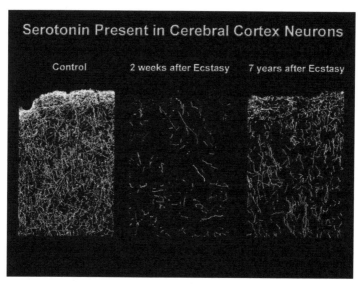

This image shows sections taken from the neocortex of monkeys that were given MDMA twice a day for 4 days and control monkeys that were given saline. The section on the left, taken from the brain of a control monkey, shows the presence of a lot of serotonin. The middle section shows a section from a monkey two weeks after receiving MDMA. Most of the serotonin is gone. The section on the right shows a monkey seven years after receiving MDMA. There has been some recovery of serotonin, but the brain still has not returned to normal.

The cumulative effect of long-term MDMA use is

- Depletion of serotonin
- Induction of the release of noradrenalin and the inhibiting of its uptake
- Increase in plasma cortisol
- Triggering of release of oxytocin (the "cuddle hormone")
- Lowering of sexual inhibition
- Suppression of serum testosterone

We have demonstrated that diminished brain serotonin and increased noradrenalin can lead to not only *hyper*sexuality but also *homo*sexuality.[1484] MDMA's increased stimulation of the "cuddle hormone" oxytocin also enhances homosexual inclinations. As ***IFL Science*** reported in 2015:

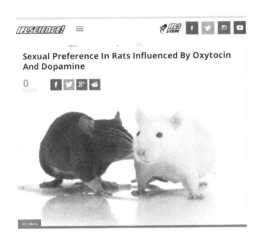

The basis for homosexual behavior has frequently—and often hotly—been debated. Is it nature? Nurture? A combination of both? Researchers from the Universidad Veracruzana, Mexico, have thrown their hat into the ring. They have been able to show that conditioned homosexual preference in male rats can be induced by oxytocin and the psychoactive drug quinpirole...

When sexually naive male rats were exposed to either the hormone oxytocin and/or quinpirole, and then made to cohabit with other sexually active males, they developed a social preference for the other males, even when the drugs were no longer present in their system. Interestingly, their preference wasn't just limited to that social situation. When given a choice days later between a male and a sexually receptive female, the treated rats displayed sexual preference not for the females, but again for the males... the study does suggest that it is possible for apparently heterosexual male rats to develop a conditioned homosexual social and sexual leaning, given the right conditions."[1485]

[1484] Wesley Muhammad, ***Understanding The Assault of the Black Man, Black Manhood and Black Masculinity***, **Volume I** (Atlanta: A-Team Publishing, 2017) 372-376.
[1485] Josh Davis, "Sexual Preference in Rats Influenced By Oxytocin and Dopamine," ***IFL Science*** April 23, 2015.

This, therefore is the scientific basis of MDMA's connection to homosexuality.

V.   *Shulgin's Double Life and His Bay Area Hub*

While Shulgin was working so closely with and for the government, even its CBW program, he was also guiding an *illegal underground drug culture and movement.*

> So talented a chemist is Shulgin, and so desperate was the government for his knowledge, that for 20 years he possessed a rare license to manufacture any illegal drug. But while working for the DEA and presenting himself as a friend of law enforcement, *he quietly carried on a double life, leading a tiny underground movement that continued the radical psychedelic research of the 1960s.* [1486]

The "underground movement" mentioned is the Psychedelic Therapy Underground, a secretive network of professional and lay therapists who "treat" patients with MDMA, LSD, and other (outlawed) psychedelics. Shulgin, with his "impeccable" establishment credentials, led this underground movement that spread his new drug across the country.

Shulgin's MDMA was first forensically detected on the streets of Chicago in 1970, five years after he synthesized it. This fact makes another fact even more interesting: that it was in Chicago that the nearly pure MDMA from the laboratory of Delta G Scientific, South Africa's chemical weapons facility, was found.[1487] South Africa's Delta G collaborated with U.S. CBW research front facilities. As a result, from 1970-1974 the Midwest was the first "hot region" of Shulgin-MDMA.[1488] This makes a lot of sense.

From 1976-1979 the "hot region" switched to California, Shulgin's home base. As NBC News reported, in "The story of

---

[1486] Mark Boal, "Blood, sweat and serotonin: The Master Chemist of the Psychedelic Movement and his 40-year Battle with the Government," ***Playboy*** March 2004.
[1487] Karl Kemp, "South Africa's 'Dr. Death' Was Accused of Selling Ravers Super-Strength MDMA," ***VICE*** November 4, 2014.
[1488] Torsten Passie and Udo Benzenhöfer, "The History of MDMA as an Underground Drug in the United States, 1960-1979," ***Journal of Psychoactive Drugs*** (2016): 1-9.

Alexander Shulgin" it's twists and turns "were all in the Bay Area, where the scientist was born, educated and did the majority of his work in Berkeley and surrounding environs."[1489] The Bay Area will thus become the hub of the underground movement of MDMA distribution. Sometime between 1974-1976 a lab was set up in Marin County, California, to manufacture MDMA which was active until the 1980s.[1490] By 1977 two labs capable of producing large amounts of MDMA were in operation in San Francisco and Redwood City, California. Even Timothy Leary, the CIA-planted guru of the 1960s LSD movement and friend of Shulgin, was conscripted to help widen distribution of MDMA through his personal connections.[1491] Specifically he was in Marin County propagating the new "wonder drug."[1492]

In 1976 Shulgin shared his new MDMA synthesis with his long-time friend Leo Zeff, a psychologist From Oakland, California. Like his friend Shulgin, Zeff was "an older Jewish

man from an Eastern European background,"[1493] and he once wrote about dancing with a Torah while tripping on LSD. With Shulgin's new MDMA formula, Zeff traveled the country introducing thousands of therapists to the drug, who in turn "treated" their patients with it. He is thus known as "the Johnny Appleseed of MDMA." He is also known as "The Secret Chief" of the psychedelic underground. He, along with the Shulgins, were the movement's leaders. It was Zeff who christened Shulgin's MDMA with its first street name, "Adam," the primal innocent,

---

[1489] "Berkeley Bredand Educated, MDMA's Major Figure Was Bay Area Man," *NBC Bay Area* June 2, 2014.

[1490] Passie and Udo Benzenhöfer, "The History of MDMA," 3.

[1491] Passie and Udo Benzenhöfer, "The History of MDMA," 5.

[1492] Bill Mandel, "The Yuppie Psychedelic," *San Francisco Chronicle* June 10, 1984.

[1493] Myron J. Stolaroff, *The Secret Chief Revealed: Conversations with Leo Zeff, pioneer in the underground psychiatric therapy movement* 139

"by which is meant not Adam as man, but rather Adam-and-Eve as androgynous ancestor."[1494] Indeed, as designed, "Ecstasy is the androgynising drug, melting psychic and bodily rigidities."[1495]

Soon after Leo Zeff was "activated" in 1976 the Bay Area, California "Group" – Shulgin's protégés - established a "Boston Group," the East Coast arm of the psychedelic underground set up to manufacture and distribute Shulgin's and Zeff's "Adam." The Boston Group consisted of tenured MIT and Harvard chemists, some of whom were connected to the MIT Artificial Intelligence Lab. [1496] What happens next is of extreme importance.

> The first mass-scale production of MDMA for recreational use in the United States came courtesy of the so-called Boston Group, a small contingent of chemists who were tenured professors at MIT and Harvard and who were colleagues of LSD guru Timothy Leary. The Boston Group *decided they wanted to conduct a social experiment*. First at Studio 54, then later at the legendary Paradise Garage, handpicked distributors in the New York area sold the drug as a healthier alternative to cocaine. Then they reported back to the Boston Group about the positive effects the drug was having on the dance floor. One of those distributors was David. Sitting in his Miami Beach apartment today, David is in his early 70s and still deejays, though he makes his real living running a small real estate company. Age hasn't dulled his vivid memories of the life-changing effects the first wave of recreational ecstasy use had on clubgoers at the time.

> "What happened was that these professors up in Boston, who had been using it for therapy for a long time, decided it would be a good idea for the world if MDMA became a social drug instead of cocaine and heroin and all the other bad drugs,"

[1494] Bruce Eisner, **Ecstasy: The MDMA Story**, Second Edition (1989) Chapter I. Introducing Adam; Margaret Katcher, "Can Underground Psychedelic Therapy Ever Go Mainstream? **Pacific Standard Magazine** October 19, 2017.

[1495] Simon Reynolds, "Wargasim: Militaristic imagery in popular culture," **National Network Opposing the Militarization of Youth** @ https://nnomy.org/en/content_page/item/517-wargasm-militaristic-imagery-in-popular-culture.html.

[1496] Torsten Passie, "The early use of MDMA ('Ecstasy') in psychotherapy (1977-1985)," **Drug Science, Policy and Law** 4 (2018):1-19 (2).

remembers David. "It was a relatively small circle of people on the club scene who were doing ecstasy back then, mainly artistic types. A lot of people wouldn't try it because they were scared of it. They didn't want to let their walls down, especially the straight boys, because the rumor was out that taking ecstasy *would turn you gay* (emphasis added – WM)."[1497]

This is a startling confession. It was decided among Shulgin's people in Boston to conduct a "social experiment" by making Shulgin's MDMA replace heroin and cocaine as a social drug. The small group of MIT and Harvard professors would employ select distributors at chosen nightclubs to introduce the new drug and then report back to the Group the effects observed. And the chosen night clubs to conduct this "experiment" were largely *gay black clubs* such as Paradise Garage in New York and the Warehouse in Chicago. This is why MDMA "exploded onto the gay club scene in the 1980s as 'Adam' and then quickly morphed into 'ecstasy,' 'E,' 'X,' or 'XTC,' in the 1990s." [1498] One of the "experimental" clubs, Chicago's Warehouse, was made "a centerpiece of the city's MDMA scene."[1499] As Max Daly writes:

> nightlife as we know it is owed to a dance revolution invented by gay black men in America. It was in venues such as the Warehouse in Chicago and the Paradise Garage in New York in the late 1970s and early 1980s where the cocktail of MDMA-enhanced house and garage music was first brewed.[1500]

Matthew Collin, in his book, ***Altered State: The Story of Ecstasy Culture and Acid House*** (1997), observed that through the 1970s, 80s, and 90s

> black and gay clubs consistently served as *breeding grounds* for new developments in popular culture, *laboratories* where

---

[1497] Frank Owen with Lera Gavin, "Chasing Molly," ***Playboy*** July 9, 2015.

[1498] James L. Kent, "The Truth About Molly," ***High Times*** August 05, 2014.

[1499] P. Nash Jenkins, "Electronic Dance Music's Love Affair With Ecstasy: A History," ***The Atlantic*** September 20, 2013.

[1500] Max Daly, "How Gay Clubs Changed the Way We Take Drugs," ***Vice*** April 12, 2017.

music, drugs, and sex are interbred to create stylistic innovations that slowly filter through to straight, white society.

In the 1980s the drug was widely distributed at "circuit parties," highly sexualized gay male dance events. In 1983, the southwest distributer of the Boston Group based in Texas (the Texas Group) launched the commercial operation, making Shulgin's MDMA officially a street drug. And then:

> [I]n 1990...the Boston Group closed shop. "Somebody drove out the chemists making ecstasy," says David. "They told me that some very dangerous people were threatening them. They had two days to get out of the country. They didn't use the word *mafia,* but that's the impression I got. They packed their bags and all moved to Belgium." Not coincidentally, over the next decade Belgium became a major center for ecstasy production."[1501]

By the turn of the millennium perhaps 80-90% of the world's MDMA was manufactured in Belgium and the Netherlands. It was likely not the Mafia who closed down the Boston Operation, but the underground movement's true puppeteer, the U.S. government, because quite possibly the "MDMA as social experiment" operation was moving into a Phase II.

VI.   *Molly Meets Rap*

Chris Lee says in his 2010 ***Los Angeles Times*** article "Hip Hop's chemical romance with Ecstasy"

> Ecstasy is reaching a kind of critical mass in hip hop...Time was when the drug of choice for rappers was either weed or booze (or, in certain cases down South, sippin' on "sizzurp"). And the notion of ingesting a powerful love drug – one known to overwhelm a person's inhibitions, eliciting bro hugs and feelings of cosmic interconnectivity that are distinctly at odds with rap's dog-eat-dog mentality – would have been as improbable as an MC wearing tight jeans.[1502]

[1501] Frank Owen with Lera Gavin, "Chasing Molly," ***Playboy*** July 9, 2015. See also Lauren Carter, "Molly Overtakes Weed in Music Culture," ***rap rehab*** May 17, 2013.

[1502] Chris Lee, "Hip Hop's chemical romance with Ecstasy," ***Los Angeles Times*** September 24, 2010

MOLLY OVERTAKES WEED IN MUSIC CULTURE

RAP ISN'T SINGLEHANDEDLY RESPONSIBLE FOR USHERING MOLLY FROM THE UNDERGROUND RAVE SCENE TO MAINSTREAM POP CULTURE AND RAPPERS AREN'T THE ONLY STARS PROMOTING THE DRUG

LAUREN CARTER – MAY 30, 2013   SHARE ON:

Georgia Chambers correctly describes MDMA as Hip Hop's "drug hype that no-one saw coming"[1503] because "hip-hop's love for MDMA simply wasn't reflected in black culture". This is because the "Mollyfication" of Hip Hop does not represent an organic growth out of the ground of Black culture but was fabricated by Hip Hop's external overlords who are distinctly *not* an indigenous part of Black culture, as we shall show later in this writing. I believe that it can be shown that the "Mollyfication" of Hip Hop began in 1996 and we are only today in 2019 witnessing its full effects. But why 1996? Why did this process of the "Mollyfication" of Hip Hop begin in *this* year? That is easy to answer. 1996 "happened" because 1992 (the Gang Truce and LA Riots) happened, and then 1995 (the Million Man March) happened, serving as pretext and *stimulants* for 1996, I am suggesting.

> Today [in 2013], it's rare to hear a rap song on mainstream radio that doesn't have at least one Molly reference. For example, Trinidad Jame\$, *"Popped a Molly, I'm sweatin' wooh!"* Kanye West, *"She gone off that Molly,"* and more. And what makes this even more ironic, is that in hip hop, it has never been cool to be a druggie. It was looked down upon to use any substances other than alcohol, weed, or lean (prescription cough syrup). In fact, most rap artists have talked about being on the other side of drug sales, as the dealer, taken advantage of the weaker consumer.[1504]

Diamond, Bermudez, and Schensul, in their article "What's the Rap About Ecstasy?" points out that *"Beginning in*

[1503] Georgia Chambers, "How MDMA Made White People Fall In Love With Hip Hop," *itchy silk* April 30, 2018 @ http://www.itchysilk.com/mdma-white-people-hip-hop/

[1504] Anthony "Cola" Mastrocola, "Don't Blame Hip Hop for Molly, We Got it from the Ravers," *Silicon Valley De-Bug* May 7, 2013.

1996, rap songs began to inform their listeners that ecstasy was *available* in urban settings and was being used outside of the context of raves (emphasis added – WM)."[1505] This is an important detail. *Out of nowhere* Ecstasy trended in rap between 1996 and 2003 because "a number of hit rap songs were released about ecstasy around the same time when ecstasy use began to spread into urban areas."[1506] The authors found that 69 rap songs released between 1996 and 2003 mentioned ecstasy. Between 2000 and 2002, the drug appeared in the title of five (plus one) popular rap songs.

Bone Thugs-N-Harmony, "Ecstasy" (2000)
Ja Rule, "Xtasy" (2000)
Big Tymers, "Hennessy & XTC" (2000)
Missy Elliot, "X-Tasy" (2001)
(D12 "Purple Pills" [2001])
Tech N9ne, "T9X" (2002)

According to the Monitoring the Future (MTF) survey in 1998 the rate of ecstasy use among Black 12th graders was 0.5%. By 2000 it had *tripled* to 1.3%. How did this happen? "[T]he emergence of rap songs about ecstasy coincided with the spread of ecstasy into the inner city," reports Diamond, Bermudez, and Schensul.[1507] They speculated that "rap music lyrics may be inadvertently helping to market the drug to urban minority youth."[1508] "Overall, the number of rap songs mentioning ecstasy increased each year from 1996 to 2001, paralleling the general increase in ecstasy use among high school youth reported in the Monitoring the Future survey."[1509] Amy Linden wrote 2002

[1505] Sarah Diamond, Rey Bermudez, and Jean Schensul, "What's the Rap About Ecstasy? Popular Music Lyrics and Drug Trends Among American Youth," *Journal of Adolescent Research* 21 (2006): 269-298 (291).
[1506] Diamond, Bermudez, and Schensul, "What's the Rap About Ecstasy?" 270.
[1507] Diamond, Bermudez, and Schensul, "What's the Rap About Ecstasy?" 282.
[1508] Diamond, Bermudez, and Schensul, "What's the Rap About Ecstasy?" 272-273.
[1509] Diamond, Bermudez, and Schensul, "What's the Rap About Ecstasy?" 283.

What is new is that Ecstasy, once an almost exclusive plaything of White subcultures, is being increasingly embraced by young African Americans. And heading up the X appreciation society are chart-toping platinum artists who have found in the drug a new lyrical obsession and de facto status symbol.[1510]

And Linden notes correctly: "when rappers talk, fans listen-and emulate."

This was confirmed in 2018 by the research led by Dr. Khary Rigg of the University of South Florida. The study determined that hip hop's lyrical glorification of MDMA has led to an increase in the number of new users that try the stimulant for the first time, and a shift in the demographic profile of MDMA users. The study suggests that MDMA messages in hip hop influence decisions to start using the drug.[1511] Four fifths (82%) of Black adults surveyed who used or tried the drug admitted that hip hop influenced their decision to try MDMA, confirming a link that has existed for decades. Participants in the study said they felt comfortable trying the drug only after the trendsetting rappers name-dropped it in their lyrics. Thus, **Daily Mail** announced, "Hip-hop stars Kanye West, Rick Ross and Jay-Z use their music to glorify MDMA, luring fans into trying the drug, claim academics."[1512] (Later, however, Jay Z actually said in his music he *does not* use Molly: *"I don't pop molly, I rock Tom Ford"* (Jay-Z, "Tom Ford").

The introduction of Shulgin's "Love Drug" resulted in Hip Hop's "hard-knock life (getting) soft around the edges,"[1513] writes Ethan Brown in **Vibe**.

> as long as E is involved, even the most hardened thugs will give more smiles than ice grills, more backrubs than beatdowns. "After they do ecstasy, brothers I know are much more hesitant

[1510] Amy Linden, "How high," **Honey Magazine** May 2002, pp. 97-99.

[1511] Khary K. Rigg and Anthony T, Estreet, "MDMA (ecstasy/molly) use among African Americans: The perceived influence of hip-hop/rap music," **Journey of Ethnicity in Substance Abuse** (2018) published online.

[1512] Stephen Matthews, "Hip-hop stars Kanye West, Rick Ross and Jay-Z use their music to glorify MDMA, luring fans into trying the drug, claim academics," **Daily Mail** February 13, 2018.

[1513] Ethan Brown, "The X Factor," **Vibe** September 2000, pp. 199-206.

about getting into a brawl, getting into a shoot-out," says Louie (a New York weed-turned-Ecstasy dealer). "Ecstasy is gonna make a lot of people who were violent, thugged-out, or whatever realize how foolish they were being."[1514]

As we saw, however, Shulgin's MDMA does *feminize*, but it actually *increases* violence in the process – subordinate male violence. We witness both trends in the very first hip hop song to name-drop the drug in the *title* and their song. Bone Thugs-N-Harmony released the first musical (rap) dedication to the drug, "Ecstasy," on their 2000 release **BTNHResurrection**. The song represents Ecstasy explicitly as a *new phenomenon* that should replace weed as hip hop's drug of choice. It is affirmed that "*this shit will have you on the level with your female*" (intro skit) and Flesh Bone, after poppin the pill, felt "too sexy" for his self, so he had to find his girl to sex her. Lazie Bone however, likewise made horny by the drug, was also compelled to tell "my niggas that I love 'em." Fish Bone's lyrics are revealing:

> *I feel so violent, violent fuckin with that ecstasy (come roll with me)...*
> *I thought the shit will have a nigga high and horny*
> *I'm high, but I'm too high. Wanna hurt somebody...*

This connection between MDMA use, hip hop and increased community violence will be discussed again below.

Shulgin's MDMA was associated not only with violent feminization in hip hop, but even *homosexualization* in hip pop. In this regard there is the extremely important interview that Ethan Brown of **Vibe** conducted with Bizzy Bone in 2000. Brown reported:

> Ironically, one of the most critical voices on the subject of ecstasy use is Bone Thugs-N-Harmony's Bizzy Bone, who says that he initially asked that his verse be removed from "Ecstasy" because, "I don't do that shit. Never tried it. I just thought I'd be sending a bad message." *Bizzy sees a sinister force behind the rise in ecstasy use*...Bizzy, who rhymes on "Ecstasy" about being "pilled out and movin' slow," also says he can't get down with the drug's lovey-dovey, nonassertive vibes. "That's some

---

[1514] Brown, "The X Factor," 206.

feminine-ass shit, make a motherfucker act all sweet," he says. "Anything that makes a man want to drop to his knees and give another man fellatio, something ain't right-unless he's already like that." He pauses and lets out a big, hearty laugh. "Black folks haven't seen shit like this before. They haven't experienced no euphoric-ass drugs like this."[1515]

There are several points here worth highlighting:

1. Bone-Thugs-N-Harmony were trend-setting pioneers in the "Mollyfication of Hip Hop" movement. The earliest song in Hip Hop dedicated to MDMA was their track from 2000 "Ecstasy," advocating the use of the drug. Yet not everyone rapping on that track used, tried or even supported the use of the drug, Bizzy Bone being an example.
2. Because he doesn't support the use of Ecstasy, Bizzy Bone wanted his pro-use lyrics removed from the song. They were *not* removed.
3. Bizzy, who with Bone-Thugs-N-Harmony was at the very center of the "Mollyfication of Hip Hop" phenomenon, had reason to believe that the phenomenon itself was the result of *a sinister force at work in Hip Hop!* (As it turns out, Bizzy Bone was correct.)
4. At least one of the causes of Bizzy's rejection of the drug Ecstasy was because he witnessed firsthand the drug's *feminizing* effects on Black men and its *homosexualizing effects.*
5. Bizzy Bone acknowledges that the use of such a drug as MDMA is a new thing among Black people, and there was a sinister force behind it.

In this Volume, we are identifying that *sinister force at work in Hip Hop.*

[1515] Brown, "The X Factor," 206.

VII. *The Wu, the Feds, and Molly*

Between 1990 and 2004 the FBI and the New York Police Department investigated the Wu-Tang Clan for a wide range of alleged federal crimes. Believing them to be engaged in drug running, gun running and executions, the FBI labeled the Wu a "major criminal organization" and devoted substantial resources to the inquiry in an effort to "take the Wu down."[1516] "Into this

Michael Caruso (left) and Tim Leary (right) and Limelight Night Club, 1992.

atmosphere of turmoil stepped Michael Caruso," writes journalist Frank Owen.[1517] Who is Michael Caruso? "Lord Michael" was the "Al Capone of Rave" who ran the first ecstasy empire in New York from 1991 to 1994, an empire backed by the Gambino crime family - but also by the Boston Group.

MDMA made its entrance into/onto the New York scene as part of the "social experiment" of the Boston Group to make the drug the new "social drug." In the late 1970s and early 1980s handpicked DJs and distributers at the famous Studio 54 and its less glitzy cousin Paradise Garage, a "utopia" for New York's Black and Hispanic gay communities,[1518] were supplied Shulgin's MDMA by the Boston Group. Shulgin's drug was "democratized" in New York by Michael Caruso.

> At that time, the drug was largely the preserve of trendy gay clubgoers and affluent New Age types. The proles hadn't yet

---

[1516] Jason Leopold, "A Close Look at the FBI's File on Wu-Tang Clan," *Vice* October 12, 2016.

[1517] Frank Owen, "Wu-Tang is Sumthing ta Fuck Wit," *The Village Voice* May 23, 2000.

[1518] On Paradise Garage see Ben Barna, "Memories of the Paradise Garage, From Those Who Danced There," *The New York Times Style Magazine* May 9, 2014.

turned it into a youth-culture phenomenon. Lord Michael spearheaded the democratization of E in New York."[1519]

According to Michele McPhee,

Lord Michael's crowd consisted of omni-sexual Ecstasy fiends, most dressed in drag, all with freak names like "Rah Shaky," "Loungin," "Vel," and "Ghost." If he wasn't hanging around gay cross-dressers, lord Michael preferred the company of black rappers, who often were members of violent members of their own street gangs.[1520]

Lord Michael pushed "huge quantities" of Ecstasy out of the New York nightclub Limelight. In 1992 Timothy Leary visited the club and he and Caruso did Ecstasy and tried out virtual-reality machines in the VIP section.[1521] The picture to the right shows Caruso (left) and Leary (right) at Limelight. The two were said to be "close friends," as Leary and Shulgin were close friends. According to former associate Frankie Bones, after that night meeting Leary in the club Caruso "really just flipped the scrip, he really wanted to be, like, *kingpin*".[1522] This makes sense. Recall that the Boston Group scientists were colleagues of Leary and that Leary was part of the underground psychedelic movement led by Shulgin and Zeff and on their behalf he promoted "Adam" in Marin County, California. Lord Michael's Ecstasy empire in the early 1990s in New York thus must be understood as a part of the Shulgin-led "social experiment" with MDMA.

But Caruso seems to have fallen out of favor and in 1997 he was arrested by the DEA for Ecstasy distribution. However, Caruso immediately began cooperating with the government against his former business partner and became a federal informant. In that role Caruso then reemerged as Cappedonna of Wu-Tang's personal manager. The next time we meet Caruso, he had rebranded himself as a Hip Hop impresario, having

---

[1519] Frank Owen, "The King of Ecstasy," *Village Voice* April 1, 1997, pp. 36-39 (38).
[1520] Michele McPhee, *A Mob Story* (New York: St. Martin's Press, 2002) 93.
[1521] Frank Owen, *Clubland: the fabulous rise and murderous fall of club culture* (New York: St. Martin's Press, 2004) 71-72.
[1522] Simon Reynolds, *generation ecstasy: into the world of techno and rave culture* (New York: Routledge, 1999) 147.

totally reinvented himself: from designer cloths and clean cut look to baggy jeans, cornrows and gold fronts; from Italian wannabe mafioso to a "white Negro"; "From downtown's version of Sammy 'the Bull' Gravano to Staten Island's answer to Vanilla Ice in one easy move-and all under the watchful eye of the feds."[1523] The new "hip" Caruso began traveling nationally with the Wu while reporting to his federal handlers, carrying weapons (and drawing them on people), and associating with people with criminal records (many in the Wu). All of this was in blatant violation of his government cooperation agreement which expressly forbid his leaving New York, possessing weapons or affiliating with felons.[1524] Caruso, till this day, has never served time in prison. Frank Owen believes that the best explanation is that "the federal government is aware of Caruso's breach of his cooperation agreement and is *simply looking the other way.*" Caruso's work with the Wu-Tang Clan while he was a government snitch clearly served the interest of the government, who was at that very time engaged in an effort to "take the Wu down." No charges were ever filed against the Wu, however. After Caruso was outed as a snitch by Frank Owen in the **Village Voice** it is reported that the Wu-Tang Clan fired him.

VIII. *Mac Dre and the Nation of Thizzlam*

This "social experiment" branded and rebranded Shulgin's MDMA at least three times, each time targeting a different subpopulation.

- In the late 1970s and early 1980s the name was "Adam" and the target group was gays, largely Black and Brown, in nightclubs.

- In the early 1990s the drug was rebranded as Ecstasy and the target population was ravers, most of whom

---

[1523] Frank Owen, "Wu-Tang is Sumthing ta Fuck Wit," **The Village Voice** May 23, 2000.
[1524] Frank Owen, "Wu-Tang is Sumthing ta Fuck Wit," **The Village Voice** May 23, 2000.

were young, white and suburban ("The majority of rave attendees in America were White, suburban youth."[1525]).

- In the late 1990s and early 2000s the chemical was rebranded "thizz" and the target population was the Hip Hop community and audience of the Bay Area in California.

The Bay Area was always the headquarters of the Psychedelic Therapy Underground which was since 1976 engaged in a "social experiment" to spread Shulgin's MDMA far and wide as a social drug. Shulgin is from the Bay (Berkeley) and his lab, wherein he cooked up all of his compounds, was there. Leo Zeff, "the Johnny Appleseed of MDMA," was there (Oakland), and the earliest documented laboratories for large scale manufacture were there (Marin County, San Francisco, and Redwood City). The Bay Area Group originated the Boston Group and is at the root of the Texas Group. And while the experiment seems to have initially targeted groups outside of California – Black and Brown gays and white youth in the Midwest and the East Coast, as well as Texas – it appears that the experiment came home to the Bay after 1995. We can provide a plausible explanation why it would return home and target the very population it targeted: the Bay Area Hip Hop community and its audience.

With the birth of the Black Panther Party in Oakland and the White youth rebellions in Berkeley (anti-war/Free-Speech Movement) and San Francisco (hippie movement), by the 1960s the Bay Area was seen as a breeding ground for revolution. The distinctive Bay Area hip hop scene has long had an activist impulse as well. Area Raptivists were important, for example, during the 1996-1997 grassroots Justice for Aaron Williams campaign and also the fight against the repressive 1998 Gang Violence and Juvenile Crime Prevention Act, better known as Prop 21, a vicious law that criminalizes Black and Brown youth. The statewide anti-Prop 21 efforts (the law was passed in 2000) produced a new youth movement in California, called by some a new civil rights movement, primarily led by youth of color and

---

[1525] Diamond, Bermudez, and Schensul, "What's the Rap About Ecstasy?" 272.

619

based to a great extent in Oakland and the Bay Area.[1526] And, as Elizabeth Martinez notes, "From the beginning, hip hop - youth's resistance culture – played a major, mobilizing role."[1527]

In the 1960s the CIA used Rock 'n' roll and the rock group the Grateful Dead to spread LSD to "rebellious" White youth in order to de-politicize them.[1528] If the Grateful Dead are the "primordial psychedelic rock band," it can be said that Mac Dre and his Nation of Thizzlam must be considered the "primordial psychedelic hip hop artists." The *sinister forces* that Bizzy Bone discerned were behind the "Mollyfication of Hip Hop" in the Midwest (Bone Thugs-N-Harmony are from Cleveland, Ohio) appear to have also sought to use Mac Dre and the Hyphy movement that he helped pioneer with Keak Da Sneak to spread Shulgin's MDMA among "rebellious" (= revolutionary) inner-city Black youth, particularly in Oakland and the Bay Area. As **High Times** reported:

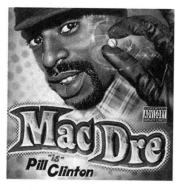

[MDMA] exploded onto the gay club scene in the 1980s as "Adam" and then quickly morphed into "ecstasy," "E," "X," or "XTC" in the '90s... At the turn of the century, the MDMA scene burned out — first in London, then in Boston, New York and Miami. It burned out hardest in San Francisco, where candy-colored rave kids rolled west with dreams of dot-com boom riches and nonstop Burning Man debauchery...Around this time in San Francisco, MDMA made its move into hip-hop under the name "thizz." Rapper Mac Dre's "Thizzle Dance" was an ode to the drug. *It remains unknown how Mac Dre was introduced to MDMA*, but it changed his life. After spending five years in jail for conspiracy to commit robbery, Dre reinvented himself in 1997, and by 1999 he was doing the Thizzle Dance with his own label, Thizz Entertainment, *becoming the first official MDMA rapper* and building the foundation for something called the "hyphy

---

[1526] Elizabeth Martinez, "The New Youth Movement in California," **Z Magazine** March 1, 2000; Andrea L.S. Moore, "Hyphy Sparked a Social Movement," **Ethnic Studies Review** 37 (2016): 45-62
[1527] Martinez, "New Youth Movement in California."
[1528] See below.

movement." He even had an alter ego called Thizelle Washington and *a fake religion called the Nation of Thizzlam*, and was reportedly rolling on thizzle every day all the way to the bank. Other influential rappers were introduced to E around 2000. Eminem rapped about it, Ja Rule was into it — but thizz, though it was definitely MDMA, was no longer the love drug of the candy-colored raver kids. Instead, it was a party drug to get you good and fucked up.[1529]

Mac Dre is a Bay Area Hip Hop legend. He was tragically gunned down in 2004 in a hit that occurred similar to the murders of Tupac and Biggie and, like their's, is still "unsolved." During the 1980s Dre did vintage Bay Area music with his Crest Side crew Romper Room Gang, some of whom were also into robbing banks. While Dre was apparently never involved in these crimes, the Vallejo Police Department developed a personal vendetta against the rapper. The FBI had Dre and his Romper Room Gang under surveillance and in 1991, with the help of an informant planted right in Dre's crew, Dre was arrested and charged with conspiracy to commit robbery. Sentenced to five years in 1992 because he refused to snitch on his homies, at the height of his rap career Dre was sent on March 12, 1993 to Lompoc Federal Penitentiary where he served four years and was released in 1997.

There is a common theme running through the remembrances of those who knew Mac Dre.

> That the man that emerged from prison differed from the one who had been put away was unsurprising, but what did surprise is the way in which Mac Dre's style changed. Rather than exploiting his gangster image, Dre instead began to pioneer a whole new movement known as "hyphy"... *Central to the hyphy movement was what Dre called "Thizz" or ecstasy*. Rarely the drug of choice among rappers, *Dre built a counterculture around the pill* in the same way weed rappers mixed blunts and beats...

> "Coming out hitting the ground running, I wasn't surprised," says [KMEL DJ] Davey D. "I think what kind of caught me was when he hit up on the Thizz and kind of really blew up and had a whole second coming. There's two Mac Dres. There's Mac Dre with the whole Thizz thing, and there's Mac Dre at the

---

[1529] James L. Kent, "The Truth About Molly," **High Times** August 5, 2014.

renaissance of the Bay Area, back in '91, '92. To me, he really is somebody who had a footprint in two different, in many ways, very distinct eras, and two distinct generations of people who really had gravitated towards him in those respected areas."[1530]

"Hyphy" was a distinctly Bay Area form of hip hop that developed around the late nineties and peaked around 2004-2006. While hyphy as a "movement" fizzled out by 2008-2009, it still has an influence on Bay Area hip hop till today.[1531] Differing from both the Bay Area's street or gangsta rap and it's conscious/politically oriented "back pack" hip hop, hyphy represented a hyperkinetic, party-centered culture.[1532] "Hyphy is energy," E-40 said;[1533] high energy. A signature of hyphy was "*Going dumb*," which suggests "losing all inhibition."[1534] A chief characteristic of Shulgin's chemical MDMA is to diminish the brain chemical serotine and trigger the release of noradrenalin, with the result of lowered or the loss of inhibition, sexual and otherwise. *Going Dumb* in the hyphy context was thus associated with the consumption of drugs, particularly ecstasy, rebranded here as *Thizz*.

"There's a flip-side to the whole hyphy movement," says Sean Kennedy, the proprietor of Moses Music, located on 90th Avenue and International Boulevard in deep East Oakland-the epicenter of hyphy culture. "This is a dance, but it's also a culture based around Ecstasy."[1535]

[1530] Dean Van Nguyen, "Vallejo rapper Mac Dre pioneered the hyphy movement," *Wax Poetics* Issue 53. Online @ https://www.waxpoetics.com/blog/features/articles/bay-area-boss-mac-dre/; Zack Ruskin, "Boss Tycoon: The Enduring Legacy of Mac Dre," *SF Weekly* August 9, 2019.
[1531] Steven J. Horowitz, "An Oral History of Hyphy: The story of the Bay Area's hyphy movement told by the people who built it," *Complex* June 13, 2016; Eric K. Arnold, "Dumbed Down," *Vibe* 14 (July 2006): 108-113; idem, "The Demise of Hyphy," *SF Weekly* August 10, 2019;
[1532] On which see Eric K. Arnold, "Backpack rappers embrace varied identities," *SF Gate* August 3, 2008; Amanda Maria Morrison, "Freaks of the Industry: Peculiarities of Place and Race in Bay Area Hip Hop," Ph.D. dissertation, the University of Texas at Austin, 2010.
[1533] Horowitz, "An Oral History of Hyphy."
[1534] Eric K. Arnold, "Dumbed Down," *Vibe* 14 (July 2006): 108-113
[1535] Arnold, "Dumbed Down," 112.

Fueled by cannabis, thizz pills, and top-shelf tequila, hyphy's uptempo, feverish sound put a psychedelic tint on turf rap.[1536]

The Bay's hyphy culture has always been more about partying than taking drugs, and *Hyphy* and *Thizzin* (taking *thizz* or MDMA pills) are not necessarily to be conflated with each other.[1537] Yet, *thizzin* will come to define the culture. Keak Da Sneak, who is credited with coining the term "hyphy" in 1994, would a decade later *define* hyphy as "thizzin, sniffing lines" ("Super Hyphy," **That's My Word** 2005), a reference to poppin MDMA pills and snorting cocaine.[1538]

MDMA had not been a "Black Thing" in the Bay Area. The Kansas City, Missouri rapper Tech N9ne, who has one of the first five songs released between 2000 and 2003 that name-dropped the drug in a songs title, remarked: "I think Mac Dre had a humungous impact on Hip Hop because when I was doing thizzels whatin' no Black people doin' it."[1539] Tech N9ne himself popped his first pill in 1998, "[b]efore it even hit the black community," and his supplier was a "white chick named Michele."[1540] So in terms of the Black community in the Bay Area, Mistah F.A.B., an artist from Thizz Entertainment, said it frankly: "Dre started that shit, man."[1541] But I am not convince that *it was Dre* who actually started it. And just as was the case with "Mollyfication of Hip Hop" pioneers Bone-Thugs-N-Harmony, not everyone at Thizz Entertainment who rapped about doing Thizz was actually doing Thizz. As Mistah F.A.B., once called by some "Hyphy's crown prince" and who is now a community leader and Black Liberation activist,[1542] acknowledged:

[1536] Arnold, "The Demise of Hyphy."

[1537] Eric K. Arnold, "Hyphy vs. thizzin'," **East Bay Express** November 2, 2005.

[1538] Roque Strew, "Wild Wild West," **Village Voice** April 18, 2006.

[1539] "Mac Dre – Legend of the Bay" 2015 Documentary.

[1540] Insanul Ahmed, "Interview: Tech N9ne Talks Ecstasy, G-Strings, & Smashing Fans," **Complex** June 3, 2011.

[1541] "Mac Dre – Ghost Ride The Whip," Bay Area Legends Documentary produced by DJ Vlad.

[1542] Nasita Voynovskaya, "Oakland Rap Legend Mistah F.A.B. Moves Past His Hyphy Legacy and Makes a Different, Lasting Impact on His Hometown," **East Bay Express** May 31, 2016.

And I be feeling bad cuz I make music like that (promoting MDMA use), you know what I'm sayin', our label *Thizz*! So, a lot of these kids be like, "Nigga, I'm thizzin off yo shit right now." And I'm like, "Man, *I don't Thizz. Don't Thizz!*"[1543]

James Kent in **High Times** makes the point: "It remains unknown how Mac Dre was introduced to MDMA."[1544] This is an important question. There are some very important facts to be considered when reflecting on this question. First, it is worth recalling again that Mac Dre's home in the Bay Area is the very headquarters of the Psychedelic Therapy *Underground* who were engaged in a social experiment to make a particular synthesis of MDMA the new social drug in America. The specific synthesis is that of Alexander Shulgin, who is a Bay Area son and whose lab was there. And the "Secret Chief" of this Underground and the "Johnny Appleseed of MDMA" himself, Leo Zeff, was from where Mac Dre was born, in Oakland. Shulgin and Zeff, the two leaders of this Bay Area-based Underground, were also Bay Area Jews. Why is this relevant?

Prior to going to prison Mac Dre and his crew did music under his label Romp Productions. In 1999, two years after his release from prison, Dre moved to Sacramento and inked a deal with Walter Zelnick to establish a new label, Thizz Entertainment. Zelnick (vice president of purchasing), along with Robin Cohn (president and CEO) ran City Hall Records in San Rafael, California, which was the distributer for Thizz Entertainment and Thizz Nation, an offshoot label. Both Zelnick and Cohn, along with Shulgin and Zeff, were members of the Bay Area Jewish community. The importance of this point will be developed more fully below. The label Mac Dre established with Zelnick and Cohn glorified and promoted *Thizz*, i.e. MDMA!

The spread of the hyphy movement and the growth of *thizzin*'s popularity coincided with the rise in ecstasy use by urban youth. "As hyphy caught on, local authorities began to notice a steady uptick in the drug's street-level sales," reports

---

[1543] "Mac Dre – Ghost Ride The Whip," Bay Area Legends Documentary produced by DJ Vlad. See also Arnold, "Dumbed Down," 113: "Although F.A.B. rhymes, 'thizz izz what it izz,' one can't overlook the fact that he's clean and sober and volunteers at the East Oakland community center Youth Uprising."

[1544] James L. Kent, "The Truth About Molly," **High Times** August 5, 2014.

NPR (National Public Radio).[1545] Due to its effects on serotonin and noradrenalin MDMA can make its user aggressive, even intensify violent impulses. Mac Dre associate and Thizz Entertainment rapper Dubee aka Sugawolf recounts poppin a pill for the first time: "I'm [became] like overly aggressive... Trippin... And I'm a cool dude. This shit had me ready to fight

At City Hall Records: (Top Row): Pete Magadini, Grace Cohn and Walter Zelnick. (Bottom Row): Robin Cohn

everybody for nothing...My first three pills nigga I had fights."[1546] With many in Oakland poppin' pills became a preparation – "get up the heart" - for committing a violent act: robbery, carjacking, revenge killing.[1547] Guns were going off at house parties because someone was "off a pill." During hyphy's height, the murder rate in Oakland soared to its highest level in ten years. Between 2004 and 2007 the Bay Area experienced an alarming spike in violent crimes; murder rates rose to levels rivaling those of the Crack 80s. In 2006 homicide victims under the age of 18 tripled compared to previous years.[1548] By 2007 Oakland had the 5th highest violent crime rate in the nation.[1549]

In 2008 former associate of Mac Dre and affiliate of Thizz Entertainment, PSD Tha Drivah, was caught at Sacramento International Airport trying to board a flight to Oklahoma with 6000 ecstasy pills and $5000 in cash on his

1545 Reyhan Harmanci and Shoshana Walter, "Federal Drug Case Ensnares The Home Of Hyphy"." *NPR. National Public Radio*. September 9, 2013.

1546 @ https://www.youtube.com/watch?v=HGeHoJTYRGI

1547 Sheerly Avni, "From Hug-Drug to Thug-Drug: Street Ecstasy and Violent Crime," *HuffPost* September 28, 2007.

1548 *2006 Homicide Report: An Analysis of Homicides in Oakland from January through December, 2006*. February 8, 2007.

1549 Source:http://www.fbi.gov/ucr/cius2007/.

person.[1550] PSD was with Dubee and with Mac Dre in a group called the Cutthroat Committee which released two albums. PSD was sentenced to 46 months and was released in 2010. In April 2012 the DEA and Vallejo Police Department raided Thizz Entertainment, alleging the label was engaged in a nationwide drug distribution network, primarily MDMA but also cocaine, heroin, marijuana, and codeine. During the raid 45,000 ecstasy pills were seized, as well as 4 pounds of crack cocaine and a half-pound of heroin. According to the DEA ecstasy pills were packaged in Mac Dre DVDs and Thizz label CDs and shipped from the Vallejo area to Oklahoma, New York, Atlanta and Miami.

Twenty-five persons were arrested and charged, only four of whom were artists with links to Thizz Entertainment. Among those four were artist and self-described Thizz Nation CEO Miami The Most (Michael Lott) and Dubee. According to the indictment Miami (Lott) supplied the marijuana for two Vallejo dispensaries.[1551] But as **NPR** reported: "But in the end, hundreds of pages of court records reveal that most of the people arrested in the operation had no connection to the label. A few were Thizz rappers and friends from the Crest. Michael Lott was not, in fact, CEO of the company". Dubee and Miami pleaded guilty to conspiracy to distribute or intent to distribute. According to Dubee, he possesses the paperwork showing that his former groupmate PSD Tha Drivah, after his arrest in 2008 at the airport, cooperated with the federal investigation as a confidential informant and his information led to the April 2012 raid and indictments. PSD has denied being a federal snitch. Mac Dre's mother Wanda Salvatto or "Mac Wanda," who assumed control of Thizz Entertainment after her son's murder, according to the **Mercury News**,

> acknowledged the term "thizz" is associated with the drug Ecstasy, but that her label has moved beyond that. "It may have

---

[1550] Henry K. Lee, "Rapper held on federal drug charge in airport ecstasy bust," **SF Gate** July 25, 2008.
[1551] Phillip Mlynar, "Thizzin' Sensation: DEA Calls Mac Dre's Label an Ecstasy Front, But Insiders Are Skeptical," **SFWeekly** May 9, 2012 ; Irma Widjojo, "Vallejo rappers tied to Mac Dre at core of drug trafficking ring, U.S. Authorities announce," **Times-Herald** April 24, 2012; Matthias Gafni, "Feds bust suspected Ecstasy drug ring centered around Bay Area rap label founded by Mac Dre," **The Mercury News** April 24, 2012.

had roots in drugs, but there are no drugs involved anymore. I have nothing to do with drugs," Salvatto said. "When he died he was on the right track. He was living a legitimate life."[1552]

I don't know how Mac Dre got introduced to MDMA or how he came to the decision to base his reinvented rap persona, *Thizzel Washington*, around the chemical. I don't know Walter Zelnick's or Robin Cohn's relationship with their Bay Area Jewish brothers Alexander Shulgin and Leo Zeff. I do not know if *anyone* affiliated with Thizz Entertainment or Thizz Nation was conscious of or wittingly involved in the social experiment that was being conducted with Shulgin's version of MDMA, that just happened to be the drug behind the name "thizz." We simply do not know *and I am **not** making a claim of witting complicity on the part of our Brother*. What I do know is this:

- This MDMA social experiment was headquartered in the very location (the Bay) where the anomalous "thizz (MDMA)" movement subsequently originated. As Margaret Katcher writes, "In California, *The Underground worked quietly to spread the use of MDMA*."[1553]
- The *underground* network (Psychedelic Therapy Underground) that conducted the social experiment was led by Bay Area Jews (Shulgin and Zeff), and the label behind the Thizz movement (City Hall Records) was also led by Bay Area Jews (Cohn and Zelnick).
- For over half a century the Bay Area has been the epicenter for resistive social movements that challenged the U.S. government and repressive social policies. In his interview with **East Bay Express** Mistah F.A.B. himself breaks it down perfectly:

  "The mecca of social consciousness was here, Oakland, California," [Mistah F.A.B.] began. "The Black Panthers started around the corner here, on 47th and West." He spoke of the arrival of crack cocaine in Oakland, and how it was brought to the Bay to "destroy Black identity, to destroy the minds of social consciousness."

[1552] Matthias Gafni, "Mac Dre's mother distances her son's label Thizz Entertainment from drug probe," **Mercury News** April 25, 2012.
[1553] Margaret Katcher, "Can Underground Psychedelic Therapy Ever Go Mainstream? **Pacific Standard Magazine** October 19, 2017.

He went on to detail how the inner-cities, from Oakland to Harlem, Los Angeles to Baltimore, were flooded with drugs. "It's no coincidence that these places were some of the biggest chapters of the Black Panthers," he said.

Mistah F.A.B.'s reading of the history is spot on. And the same government that used crack cocaine and other drugs "to destroy the minds of social consciousness" in the 1980s were also using MDMA to do the same in the late 1990s and 2000s. The Bay Area, Oakland in particular, had become by the late 90s the hub of a new "civil rights movement" composed of and led by Black and Brown *youth*. Then: Enter "thizz" (MDMA).

- After the introduction and popularity of ecstasy among Black youth in the Bay largely through the Thizz movement, an atmosphere of social consciousness was overcome by a drug-driven atmosphere of partying but also of drug-fueled aggression and violence.

THE NATION OF THIZZLAM

Wrote Zack Ruskin of the **SF Weekly**: "Ronald Dregan. Muhammad Al Boo Boo. Thizzle Washington. Andre Louis Hicks. Mac Dre was a rapper of many monikers."[1554] This is for me nothing more than a curiosity, but one that cannot go unmentioned. After connecting with Bay Area Jews Walter Zelnick and Robin Cohn and reinventing his post-prison

---

[1554] Ruskin, "Boss Tycoon."

persona as Thizzle Washington, becoming "the first official MDMA rapper," Mac Dre curiously also invented "a fake religion called the Nation of Thizzlam."[1555] One of his alter egos was named, offensively, Muhammad *Al Boo Boo*: "Yes, my name is Muhammad Al Boo Boo and I'm the genie of the lamp." (Mac Dre, "Genie of the Lamp," 2004). Dre coined the term *thizzlamic* (vs. *Islamic*) which is understood in popular culture thusly:

> **Thizzlamic** adj.- 1. To worship **thizz**, also known as ecstasy, in an extreme manner. Comparative to how Muslims worship **Muhammad**. v.- 2. To get so extremely high on ecstasy that you have no recognition of the night **prior**. (Urban Dictionary)

Another internet posting noted: "The Nation of Thizzlam's main export is ecstacy pills." It is unclear what our late Brother Mac Dre had in mind with this, nor will I venture to speculate on motive.

[1555] Kent, "Truth About Molly."

"Sometimes you have the trends that's not that cool. You may have certain artists portraying these trends [Molly] and don't really have that lifestyle and then it gives off the wrong thing. And it becomes kinda corny after awhile. It's really about keeping hip-hop original and pushing away the corniness in it...When everybody consciously now uses this term or this phrase [Molly] and putting it in lyrics, it waters the culture down. So it's really just time to move on." Kendrick Lamar to to MTV News correspondent Sway, 2013.

SALUT!

Part VII

The Final Chapter

"It was a pharmaceutical experiment on Michael Jackson. It was an obscene experiment in 2009..." – Prosecutor David Walgren, Dr. Conrad Murray trial

"Hollywood is murdering its movie stars." – Evi Quaid, 2010

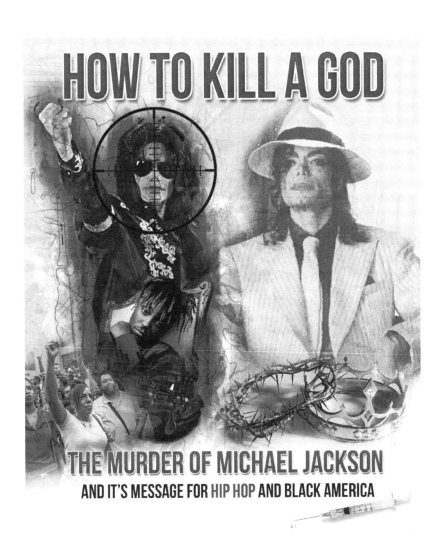

Chapter Twenty-six

HOW TO KILL A GOD

THE MURDER OF MICHAEL JACKSON
AND IT'S MESSAGE FOR HIP HOP AND BLACK AMERICA

How To Kill A God:
The Murder of Michael Jackson

I.   *"You aren't going to kill the artist, are you?"*

Despite a very rough week of being sick, emaciated, and suffering from alternating cold and hot spells such that he had to be sent home from rehearsal at the Staples Center on June 19th, on Michael Jackson's last night on earth Wednesday, June 24, 2009 during what would be his final rehearsal for his planned London concert run ("This Is It"), the King of Pop experienced a burst of energy and had his best performance in months, according to witnesses. "He came on stage, and he was electric. It was like he had been holding back and suddenly he was performing as one remembered him in the past," recalled lighting director Patrick Woodroffe.[1556] Michael might have found a reason to "just beam with gladness" as he did what he did best on that stage,[1557] but unbeknownst to him a darkness was playing out behind the scenes that night.

According to Michael Jackson's son Prince, while Michael was remarkably "bursting with enthusiasm" on stage at the Staples Center that night, Randy Phillips, CEO of the concert promoter AEG Live – who happens to be Jewish – was at Michael's Los Angeles home. Young Prince saw Phillips engaged in a "heated conversation" with Dr. Conrad Murray, the physician who would administer the drugs that would kill Michael Jackson by lunchtime the next day. According to Prince, the AEG Live executive "looked aggressive," even grabbing Murray's elbow. What were they arguing about? Why all of the aggression and, apparently, coercion? Was Phillips demanding something from Dr. Murray that evening which Dr. Murray was resisting? When Prince called his dad on the phone and informed him Phillips was there, Michael instructed his son

---

[1556] Anita Singh, "Video: Michael Jackson's weird and wonderful life," **Telegraph** June 26, 2009.
[1557] Chris Lee and Harriet Ryan, "Michael Jackson's last rehearsal: 'just beaming with gladness'," **Los Angeles Times** June 27, 2009.

to ask if Phillips wanted anything to eat or drink.[1558] A kind gesture, despite the fact that at times when Michael was home Prince often saw his father on the phone with AEG Live executives and witnessed conversations that frequently ended with Michael in tears; Prince would overhear Michael say after such calls: "They're going to kill me, they're going to kill me."[1559] On Michael's last night alive, sometime after Phillips' aggressive and heated conversation with Dr. Murray, who was *his* employee rather than Michael's,[1560] Dr. Murray began administering to Michael the fatal chemical cocktail that would hours later rob the world of much more than the "king" of popular music. Rather, what was murdered on June 25, 2009 was "the Archangel of sound, song, and dance" and a "herald of the Messiah," in the revealing words of Michael Jackson's close friend and confidant, The Honorable Minister Louis Farrakhan.[1561]

The words that Prince overheard from his father, "They're going to kill me, they're going to kill me," were neither rhetorical nor rare. The plot to kill Michael was a preoccupation of his. Following his death there was talk of "post-it notes" scattered around Michael's room. The L.A. detectives working on (*sic*) the case presented these notes as quite benign: "There were post-it notes, or pieces of paper taped all over the room and mirrors and doors with little slogans or phrases. I don't know if they were lyrics or thoughts. Some of them seemed like poems," claimed Detective Orlando Martinez.[1562] But motivating

---

[1558] Marc Hogan, "Michael Jackson Feared for His Life Before the End, Son Testifies," *Spin* June 27, 2013; " 'Sorry kids...Dad's dead': Prince Jackson reveals how Conrad Murray broke news of King of Pop's passing," *Daily Mail* June 26, 2013; "Michael Jackson's son Prince says father feared concert promoter," *India Today* June 27, 2013.

[1559] Marc Hogan, "Michael Jackson Feared for His Life Before the End, Son Testifies," *Spin* June 27, 2013.

[1560] Steve Knopper, "Why AEG Live Won the Michael Jackson Lawsuit," *Rolling Stone* October 4, 2013.

[1561] The Honorable Minister Farrakhan, "The Crucifixion of Michael Jackson and All Responsible Black Leadership," Mosque Maryam July 26, 2009 @ https://www.youtube.com/watch?v=JnoOa_A45dg; Richard Muhammad, "Farrakhan reveals truth about attacks on Michael Jackson, Black leadership," *The Final Call* July 28, 2009.

[1562] Tyler McDanold, "'Killing Michael Jackson' Reveals Scene Of Death Contained Pictures Of Babies And A Child's Doll," *The Inquisitr* June 20, 2019.

statements like "I am so grateful that I am a magnet for miracles," were accompanied by much darker notes with pleas like "help get these people out of my life" and warnings like "They are trying to murder me."[1563]

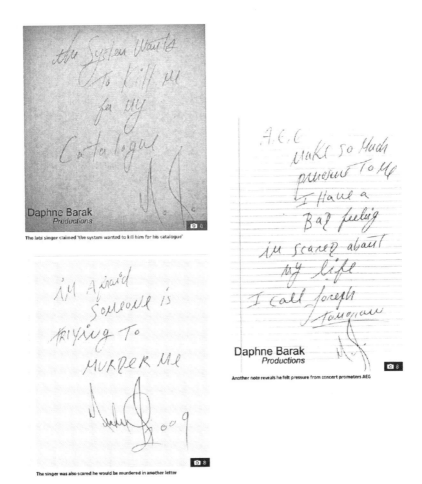

The late singer claimed 'the system wanted to kill him for his catalogue'

Another note reveals he felt pressure from concert promoters AEG

The singer was also scared he would be murdered in another letter

[1563] Sean Michaels, "Michael Jackson was murdered, says his sister La Toya," *The Guardian* June 23, 2011.

The nature of these notes was illustrated by the collection of letters and notes passed by Michael weeks before his death to German businessman and, reportedly, friend Michael Jacobshagen, who shared them with journalist Daphne Barak. The messages on these notes included: "the system wants to kill me for my catalogue"; "I'm scared about my life" because of AEG; "I'm afraid someone is trying to murder me."[1564] Journalist Ian Halperin reports that members of Michael Jackson's circle told him "[Michael] had nightmares about being murdered" and "when he did sleep, he had nightmares that he was going to be murdered...He said he thought he'd die before doing the London concerts."[1565] He did. According to emails revealed during the wrongful-death trial against AEG Live brought by mother Katherine Jackson and Michael's children, Michael even asked producers at one of the rehearsals, "You aren't going to kill the artist, are you?"[1566] This was June 19th, 6 days before the artist was indeed killed.

Michael's fears *before his death* are now *after his death* the conviction of those closest to him, his family in particular.

Jackson family patriarch Joe Jackson appeared on *Larry King Live* just hours after Dr. Conrad Murray was arraigned on involuntary manslaughter stemming from the death of Michael Jackson and revealed his belief that Murray was part of a conspiracy to murder the King of Pop — and that the real individuals responsible have yet to be charged. "To me, he's just a fall guy," Jackson said of Murray, according to CNN. "There's other people, I think, involved with this whole thing. But I think

[1564] James Beal, "Plot To Kill Jacko: Michael Jackson feared he would be murdered in notes written just weeks before his death," *The Sun* June 27, 2017; Jack Shepherd, "Michael Jackson predicted he would be murdered just before his death," *Independent* May 7, 2017.

[1565] Ian Halperin, " 'I'm better off dead. I'm done': Michael Jackson's fateful prediction just a week before his death," *Daily Mail* June 29 2009.

[1566] Nancy Dillion, "Michael Jackson feared for his safety during 'This Is It' tour, emails reveal," *New York Daily News* May 30, 2013. Dillion is wrong when she says: "[Jon] Hougdahl (who sent the email) said he assumed the comment was a passing reference to the pyrotechnics" that were a part of the show. In fact, Hougdahl says just *the opposite* of the that in his email, that Michael "didn't appear to be referring to the fireworks." "AEG Live CEO Randy Phillips Testifies About Emails on Michael Jackson's Condition," *Billboard* June 7, 2013.

that [if Murray's] interrogated — he would come clean and tell everything he knows."[1567]

Michael Jackson's sister La Toya has said there was a conspiracy to murder her brother. "People come into your life, wiggle their way in, control you, manipulate, control your funds, your finances, everything that you have," she told Piers Morgan on CNN this week. She said her brother knew he was going to be killed, and claimed he told her shortly before his death: "La Toya, I'm going to be murdered for my music publishing catalogue and my estate" ... "Michael told me that they were going to murder him," she told Morgan. "He was afraid. He was afraid for his life." She added: "I believe that when Michael walked in that house that night, whatever it was that greeted him, he knew that his end was upon him. And as soon as he had passed, some of the very people he had expressed suspicions about now controlled his estate" ... Although Michael's private physician, Conrad Murray, is due to stand trial for the singer's death, La Toya suggests he was far from the centre of the conspiracy. "I truly feel Dr Murray was simply the fall guy," she told the US TV show Extra. "I think it's too easy to blame him. I think the investigation needs to go ... further."[1568]

"[Dr. Conrad Murray] did not act alone. I, all feel, myself, Randy, LaToya, all of us feel that he's the fall guy. And knowing how this whole thing works and knowing it's higher up than just the doctor." - Jermaine Jackson with Larry King, *CNN* June 25, 2010.

Paris Jackson has claimed her father Michael Jackson was murdered and insisted everyone in her family is aware of it. The late singer's only daughter, who is now 18, suggested Jackson's death was a "set-up" and "all arrows" back up her belief that he was murdered. In her first ever in-depth interview, Paris said her father would hint people were after him and at one point even feared they might end up killing him. "He would drop hints about people being out to get him. And at some point he was like, 'They're gonna kill me one day'," she told *Rolling Stone*.

1567 Daniel Kreps, "Joe Jackson Hints at Michael Jackson Murder Conspiracy, Calls Murray 'Fall Guy,'" **Rolling Stone** February 9, 2010.
1568 Sean Michaels, "Michael Jackson was murdered, says his sister La Toya," **The Guardian** June 23, 2011; Katie Hodge, "Michael Jackson murdered for hit catalogue, claims LaToya," **Independent** June 24, 2010; Chris McGreal, "After the tributes, the twist: was Michael Jackson's death murder?" **The Guardian** July 15, 2009.

Paris said she was certain her father was murdered and argued it was "obvious". "All arrows point to that. It sounds like a total conspiracy theory and it sounds like bullshit, but all real fans and everybody in the family knows it. It was a setup. It was bullshit." When pressed about who would want the late singer dead, she said "a lot of people" but did not specify who. She said she was still seeking justice for the death. "It's a chess game. And I am trying to play the chess game the right way. And that's all I can say about that right now."[1569]

Michael not only knew that he would ultimately be murdered and why, but apparently, he knew (or had a premonition) of *how he would be murdered*. While on Oprah Winfrey's show in 2010 Michael's ex-wife Lisa Marie Presley revealed that during a conversation in 2005 Michael told her that he was afraid for his life: "The final part of the conversation was him telling me that he felt that someone was going to try to kill him to get a hold of his catalogue and his estate." According to Lisa Marie-Presley, Michael gave her names which she preferred not to disclose. But there is more: the day of Michael's death the daughter of Elvis Presley posted on MySpace:

Years ago Michael and I were having a deep conversation about life in general. I can't recall the exact subject matter but he may have been questioning me about the circumstances of my father's death.

At some point he paused, he stared at me very intensely and he stated with an almost calm certainty: "I am afraid that I am going to end up like him, the way he did". I promptly tried to deter him from the idea, at which point he just shrugged his shoulders and nodded, almost matter of fact, as if to let me know he knew what he knew and that was kind of that. Four years later I am sitting here watching on the news an ambulance leaving the driveway of his home, the big gates, the crowds outside the gates, the coverage, the crowds outside the hospital, *the cause of death* and *what may have led up to it* and the memory of this conversation hit me, as did the unstoppable tears. A predicted ending by him, by loved ones and by me, but

---

[1569] Maya Oppenheim, "Michael Jackson 'was murdered,' claim's singer's 18-year-old daughter Paris," *Independent* January 25, 2017; Brian Hiatt, "Paris Jackson: Life After Neverland," *Rolling Stone* January 26, 2017.

what I didn't predict was how much it was going to hurt when it finally happened.[1570]

If Michael "knew" he would "die like Elvis Presley," and according to Lisa-Marie Presley *he did die like Elvis*, how did Elvis Presley die?

II.   *"Die Like Elvis"*

The so-called "King of Rock n Roll" died of a drug overdose in his bathroom on August 16, 1977. There were signs that a cover-up immediately began. "The King's bedroom and bathroom were wiped clean of any drugs by his aunt and his staff before the police arrived."[1571] Elvis's "best friend" (sic) Joe Esposito admitted to finding Elvis's dead body in the bathroom and sanitizing the death scene by removing the rug and disposing of a bunch of pill bottles.[1572] Six hours after Elvis died the Memphis police closed the case. No real investigation into his death was conducted.[1573] The trauma team that worked on Elvis at the Baptist Memorial Hospital threw the stomach contents away before the autopsy and without being analyzed. "The medical examiner's notes, toxicology report, and photos, disappeared from official files."[1574]

Before an autopsy was even concluded the cause of death was officially announced as "fatal heart arrythmia" – a heart attack. The post-mortem report is secret until 2027. But independent tissue analysis showed something different which stunned the toxicologists. "Never before" had they "seen a more alarming case". They figured the yet unidentified subject they examined "must have been gobbling up prescription drugs like

---

[1570] "Michael Jackson feared he would die like Elvis Presley," **Telegraph** June 26, 2009.

[1571] Alice Vincent, "Touring, hamburgers and drugs that didn't work: the mystery of Elvis Presley's last days," **The Telegraph** April 11, 2018.

[1572] "What Really Killed Elvis? New Bombshell Discovery Exposes Truth Behind Singer's Death," **Radar Online** July 26, 2017.

[1573] Who killed Elvis Presley? A special investigation | 60 Minutes Australia,   1979   @ https://www.youtube.com/watch?v=8hOJFqawlPU&t=92s

[1574] David Comfort, "The King & the Cover-ups," **The Wrap** August 14, 2009.

a kid at a candy store".[1575] The independent toxicology reports that were released showed 14 different drugs in Elvis's system. The expert at the trial of his personal physician Dr. George Nichopoulos said that "he had never seen such a massive concentration of depressants."[1576] Elvis's was thus "death by polypharmacy."[1577] "Polypharmacy" refers to the combined reaction of several prescription drugs. The physician Dr. Nichopoulos was acquitted of charges he overprescribed Elvis. Of the 14 drugs in Elvis's system only 4 were Dr. Nichopoulos's prescriptions.

Dr. George Nichopoulos treated Elvis for insomnia[1578] (just as Dr. Conrad Murray treated Michael Jackson for insomnia). Among the drugs in Elvis's system was Demerol,[1579] as he had a Demerol addiction,[1580] (as *Michael Jackson had a Demerol addiction*). But the most toxic of this "chemical cocktail" was the codeine, which was present in Elvis's body *at 10 times the accepted level of toxicity*.[1581] Elvis surely would never have popped such a massive amount or *any amount* of codeine pills recreationally or medicinally because "he knew he was dangerously allergic" to the drug.[1582] Those around him knew it too. What or who is the source of all of the codeine found in Elvis's system *and how did it get there*?

The morning prior to his death Elvis visited his dentist Dr. Lester Hofman for a procedure. **Radar Online** announced that their investigation revealed that Elvis "was really killed by a fatal decision made by the dentist, who prescribed him prescription drugs in which he knew Elvis was allergic," i.e. the painkiller codeine, *even though the fact that Elvis was highly allergic was clearly marked on his medical charts and hospital*

[1575] James P. Cole and Charles C. Thompson, "The Death of Elvis," **Memphis Magazine** January 1991.

[1576] Pamela Murphy, "Fourteen different drugs –including 10 times the normal..." **UPI** October 19, 1981.

[1577] Cole and Thompson, "The Death of Elvis."

[1578] Adam Higginbotham, "Doctor Feelgood," **The Guardian** August 10, 2002.

[1579] Pamela Murphy, "Fourteen different drugs –including 10 times the normal..." **UPI** October 19, 1981.

[1580] Adam Higginbotham, "Doctor Feelgood," **The Guardian** August 10, 2002.

[1581] Murphy, "Fourteen different drugs."

[1582] David Comfort, "The King & the Cover-ups," **The Wrap** August 14, 2009.

records.[1583] The codeine prescription that Dr. Hofman wrote for Elvis was filled by one of his security personnel, presumably Ricky Stanley who was on duty that night and got Elvis's prescriptions filled at Baptist Memorial Hospital. Rickey Stanley had two brothers: David and Billy. The three of them are Elvis's stepbrothers who worked for him. David Stanley has been described as chief of security for Elvis.

On *Current Affair* in November of 1990 Dr. Nichopoulos revealed that someone close to Elvis confessed to several persons that he had killed the rock-n-roll singer.[1584] During the episode Dr. Nichopoulos said the name of the confessed killer a few times, but "for legal reasons" *Current Affair* bleeped the name out. However, from other interviews with Dr. Nichopoulos we learn the identity of the alleged confessor: David Stanley,[1585] Rickey's brother. According to Dr. Nichopoulos's account on national television, David Stanley confessed to having killed Elvis. How might that have happened? The "karate kick" theory is not convincing. On the other hand, David's brother Rickey was on duty at Graceland (the mansion of Elvis) that final night and, according to the account of Elvis's last hours as given by his fiancé Ginger Alden and by Rickey himself, it was Rickey who secured the drugs (went to the Baptist Memorial Hospital pharmacy and filled the prescriptions) that night for Elvis and handed them to him before Elvis went into the bathroom and was killed by a mysterious "polypharmacy of drugs," including the extreme amount of codeine, to which Elvis was highly allergic and thus would never have knowingly ingested it.[1586]

But who would have wanted Elvis dead? All three stepbrothers hated Elvis so they had their own personal motives, but there

---

[1583] "What Really Killed Elvis? New Bombshell Discovery Exposes Truth Behind Singer's Death," *Radar Online* July 26, 2017.

[1584] Elvis Was Murdered. Dr Nick. Current Affair November 11, 1990 @ https://www.youtube.com/watch?v=PTopxsWzX2w

[1585] "Dr. Nick talks to EIN about his new book and what really happened three decades ago! Interview by Nigel Patterson," *Elvis Information Network* Feb 2010 @ https://www.elvisinfonet.com/interview_drnick_2010.htm

[1586] Who killed Elvis Presley? A special investigation | 60 Minutes Australia, 1979 @ https://www.youtube.com/watch?v=8hOJFqawlPU&t=92s

was a bigger fish with a stronger reason to want Elvis Presley dead.

On August 16, 1977 – the very day of Elvis Presley's death – he and his father Vernon Presley were scheduled to appear in front of a grand jury to give evidence against the Italian Mafia as part of an extensive FBI investigation called Operation Fountain Pen. What most people don't know is this: Elvis Presley was a badge-carrying narc. On December 21, 1970 when Elvis Presley met with President Nixon in the Oval Office, Elvis pledged his help in fighting America's drug problem by infiltrating and influencing the hippie anti-war movement, the

SDS, and the Black Panthers.[1587] In return, Nixon gave Presley a Federal Bureau of Narcotics and Dangerous Drugs badge, credentialing him as a narc. Reportedly Elvis worked as an undercover agent and drug informant for the FBI while doing his tour in Las Vegas and while staying at Mafia-owned casinos. He provided cover as bass players and backup singers in his band for FBI agents investigating the Mob in Las Vegas. This can't be good. And then...

> On August 15 the FBI prepared arrest warrants for seven men in various cities around the world in connection with the Operation Fountain Pen scam. All of the men were located and were ready to be apprehended the following day when the unthinkable happened.

> Suddenly, on August 16th 1977, every television set around the world flashed the incredible news that Elvis Presley, the FBI's key witness, was mysteriously found dead. You would be the biggest fool in the world if you thought this was mere coincidence.[1588]

"The King" was dead. The Elvis "hit" was likely carried out via what is referred to by organized crime investigators as *a syringe job*: the victim was made to ingest a drug or drugs or the drug(s) was injected into the victim. There is considerable evidence that Michael Jackson's murder was contracted by the Mafia and, as we shall show, everything about his murder fits the profile of a syringe job as well.

Not only are there remarkable parallels (as we shall see) between the deaths of Elvis Presley and of Michael Jackson, but there are also *direct connections*. The co-CEO of AEG Live, whom Michael feared was trying to kill him, was Paul Gongaware. "Gongaware was specifically involved in AEG Live trying to secure Michael Jackson for the O2 shows." [1589]

[1587] Joanna Connors, "When Elvis Met Nixon: The true story behind the gun, the badge, and the movie," *Cleveland.com* Aril 2016; "Elvis Presley Died Working As A Federal Agent," *Radar Online* January 16, 2017.

[1588] Stephen B. Ubaney, *Who Murdered Elvis? 5thEdition* (Los Angeles: Writers Guild of America, West Inc., 2018).

[1589] Matt Richards and Mark Langthorne, *83 Minutes: The Doctor, The Damage, and the Shocking Death of Michael Jackson* (London: Blink Publishing, 2015) 120.

Gongaware's career as a concert promoter began with Elvis Presley's last tours. He worked advance promotion on Elvis Presley's tours under the direction of Colonel Tom Parker, Presley's tour manager.[1590] "In fact, Gongaware was working alongside Colonel Tom Parker, Presley's manager, when Elvis

Paul Gongaware

died in 1977 in a case coincidentally also related to prescription drugs, this time given to Presley by *his* doctor, Dr. Nick."[1591] It was Gongaware himself who confessed the direct connection between the two deaths that he was directly connected to. On July 5, 2009, two weeks after Michael's death, Gongaware emailed responses to condolence messages, stating: "I was working on the Elvis tour when he died so I kind of knew what to expect. Still quite a shock."[1592] *He expected Michael to die like Elvis.* Michael's fear that he would "die like Elvis" was thus not isolated. In fact, Gongaware was with Presley's manager Colonel Tom Parker when he first met Jackson in Las Vegas.[1593] This is extremely important because

> many suspicions were focused on Colonel Parker...Parker had a lot to gain from Elvis's death – only a day after the death, he had persuaded the singer's father to sign over to him 50 percent of The King's posthumous earnings.[1594]

Gongaware, as an understudy of Colonel Tom Park, therefore got good training, as we shall see.

[1590] Alan Duke, "What killed Elvis? It's a question at Michael Jackson's death trial," *CNN* June 2, 2013;

[1591] Matt Richards and Mark Langthorne, ***83 Minutes: The Doctor, The Damage, and the Shocking Death of Michael Jackson*** (London: Blink Publishing, 2015) 120.

[1592] Alan Duke, "What killed Elvis? It's a question at Michael Jackson's death trial," *CNN* June 2, 2013.

[1593] Alab Duke, "Promoter: 'I kind of knew what was going to happen' to Michael Jackson," *CNN* May 28, 2013.

[1594] Suzanna Leigh, "Why I'm convinced the Mob killed my soulmate Elvis," ***Daily Mail*** September 30, 2011.

Colonel Tom Park reportedly had many connections with the Mafia, connections which some investigators believe aided the plot to murder Elvis Presley. Michael Jackson apparently was very frightened because of his debt owed to Italian Mafia figures like Al Malnik (see below). Audio recordings from 2003 retrieved from the answering machine of associates of Michael attest to this fact.

The tapes reveal a man that was heavily paranoid and fearing for his life. He referred to the Italian mafia in the tapes and his fear that they would kill him. He also referred to being stalked on the tapes. On the tapes there are frequent requests for "150" to be placed into his account which meant $150,000.[1595]

In the first message he says: "It is Michael calling. It is very important, I want that 150 in that account for me, because... I am very concerned about my life." He then goes on to express fears that someone is trying to "sabotage" him and that he wants to be in a place where "they"- who he doesn't specify – can't find him. Then in a barely audible voice he repeats "help me" three times before ending: "We are brothers."

In another message left at 4.30am, Jackson returns, again in a slurring voice, to the theme of money. "I am very concerned. I don't trust that man. We think he's bad, we think he is Italian Mafia. Please... we must be smarter than him. So please, help me with this. I need to get that, those funds so I can do that, I wanna be away... I don't want to be in Neverland right now." The singer leaves a separate message saying he needs to talk about a "very top, top secret matter" and that he needs access to a German or Swiss bank. Shortly after he leaves another message using the words 'Sun Screen' which appears to be a code word, possibly relating to protection money. "I am very embarrassed. But, um, there should be that I have some finance that's coming up January, February 2nd, and um... that's why I, we need to have on Sun Screen to the account 150. Please don't be mad at me for ... [inaudible]."[1596]

[1595]Peter Kent, "Anthony Fiato Tapes Reveal Mafia Loan Debts Terrified Michael Jackson," *Constantine Report* July 12, 2010
[1596] Carol Driver, "'Top Secret' messages reveal Michael Jackson's troubled mind 'due to medication addiction' SIX years before he died," *Daily Mail* May 13, 2010;

In June of 2005 Michael Jackson was telling Dick Gregory "They're trying to kill me," and he would not eat because "They're trying to poison me."[1597]

The "they" involved in this conspiracy against Michael Jackson were not, according to him, just Italians. The conspiring "they" also included elements of the *Jewish* Mafia, as another set of recorded phone calls also from the year 2003 reveals. Michael describes a "conspiracy" of Jewish "leeches" that have conspired to leave him "penniless": "They suck. I'm so tired of it...It's a conspiracy. Jews do it on purpose."[1598]

We will document in this Report that the death of Michael Jackson was *not* an accident; that the guilty parties include Dr. Conrad Murray but go way beyond Murray. He was an employee; a patsy, if you will. The interests which converged resulting in the death of Michael Jackson on June 25, 2009 included AEG LIVE, Sony Music, the Italian Mafia, the Jewish Mafia, and a "Gay Mafia." Los Angeles law enforcement agencies and likely government agencies as well were involved, certainly at the level of the cover-up. This is not pure speculation. These charges are sustained by a tremendous amount of evidence, including most importantly the explosive testimony of a government witness who was a high-level investigator out of the State Attorney General's office as well as the detailed revelations of *a whistleblower – one involved in the plot who spilled a whole lot of beans!*

The Gay Mafia with its Hollywood pedophile ring *targeted Michael Jackson* with a slanderous media and legal campaign falsely charging him with *their own crime*: gay pedophilia. Michael Jackson was neither gay nor a child molester. Rather, he was vindictively framed by a circle of gay child molesters.

[1597] Claire Hoffman, "The Last Days of Michael Jackson," **Rolling Stone** August 4, 2009.

[1598] Gary Young, "Jackson in trouble after anti-semitic phone rant," **The Guardian** November 24, 2005; Nathan Guttman, "Michael Jackson calls Jews 'leeches'," **The Jerusalem Post** November 24, 2005.

III.   *Michael's Enemies*

The **New York Post** reported in 2003,

> [Steven] Spielberg and [David] Geffen were two of 25 people on
> [Michael] Jackson's "enemies list," [**Vanity Fair**] reported.[1599]
> Jackson reportedly hates Geffen for being a part of what he calls
> Hollywood's "Gay Mafia," which he believes sank his career.[1600]

According to Michael Jackson's former manager Dieter
Wiesner, Michael dictated to him a list of "enemies," persons
who sought to destroy Michael. This list was to be shared with
Michael's closest associates in order to "protect him."[1601] On the
list, according to Wiesner, were Israeli illusionist Uri Geller who
(fatefully) introduced Michael to Martin Bashir; Rabbi
Schmuley Boteach, Michael's one-time "spiritual advisor";
Feminist attorney Gloria Allred; Sony head Tommy Mottola;
Janet Arvizo, who falsely accused Michael of molesting her son;
as well as Santa Barbara, California, District Attorney Tom
Sneddon, who led the charge against Michael during the 1993
and 2005 child molestation cases.
    However, according to Maureen Orth of **Vanity Fair**,
Michael's Enemies List was topped by none other than music
and movie moguls David Geffen and Steven Spielberg.[1602] It was
this "Gay Mafia" that ruined Michael's career, he believed. He
wasn't wrong. In 1995, Michael was still proclaiming "My three
best friends are Jewish – David Geffen, Jeffrey Katzenberg and
Steven Spielberg."[1603] This was despite the fact that the three of
them had already turned against Michael. The evidence is clear
in hindsight. First, Spielberg dashed Michael's dreams when he
abruptly dropped the "Peter Pan" starring Michael Jackson
movie project in 1990 and replaced it with the "Hook" starring
Robin Williams project, released in 1991. It is reported that this

---

[1599] Maureen Orth, "Michael Jackson: You Cannot Make this Stuff Up.
New details on the boys, the business, the bizarre blood rituals,"
Vanity Fair April 2003.
[1600] Bill Hoffmann, "Jacko's Voodoo Curses," **New York Post** March
4, 2003.
[1601] "Uri Geller, Shmuley Boteach Are on Michael Jackson's 'List of
enemies'," **Haaretz** September 18, 2009.
[1602] Maureen Orth, "Losing His Grip," **Vanity Fair** April 1, 2003.
[1603] Bernard Weinraub, "In New Lyrics, Jackson Uses Slurs," **The
New York Times** June 15, 1995.

deeply hurt Michael. The betrayal continued when those three - Geffen, Katzenberg and Spielberg – formed DreamWorks in 1994 and not only locked Michael out of the deal that he was supposed to be a part of, *but they also reportedly stole his logo as well* (the boy on the moon). In addition, the tremendous controversy over Michael Jackson's "They Don't Care About Us" lyrics in 1995 was *all started* by a leak to and misrepresentation by Geffen's pal at ***The New York Times***, Bernard Weinraub.[1604] In 1995, Michael apparently didn't see what was going on with the people around him. Geffen, Katzenberg and Spielberg, while maybe "best friends" through the Eighties, had already morphed to "worst frenemies" by the Nineties. What happened? We may have at least part of an answer, and it's quite starling.

Michael was for a long time surrounded by "The Gay Mafia." It was David Geffen who introduced Gallin to Michael Jackson.[1605] Another important member of this extended family known as the (Jewish) Gay Mafia is Dr. Arnold Klein, "Dermatologists of the Stars" whose regular patients included, of course, Geffen, Gallin, and Diller, but also Michael Jackson.

> Jackson didn't become a Klein patient until his landmark appearance at the Pasadena Civic Auditorium, on the 25th anniversary of Motown, March 25, 1983, when he unleashed the Moonwalk. Among the cheering multitude in the audience was Arnie Klein. "I was blown away," he told me. "A week later *I was sitting in David Geffen's driveway and in comes Michael Jackson*. He is sitting in the back of a Lincoln Town Car and he looked very lonely. Within a week, *David brought Michael to me*.[1606]

As Michael met Sandy Gallin through Geffen, he also met Arnold Klein through Geffen. This is not an insignificant fact.

[1604] Bernard Weinraub, "In New Lyrics, Jackson Uses Slurs," ***The New York Times*** June 15, 1995. "Industry Standards," ***LA Magazine*** 49 (March 2004): 44-50 (48): "Some said he was way too close to Geffen and Walt Disney Motion Pictures chairman Joe Ruth."
[1605] Matthew Trynauer, "Sandy's Castle," ***Vanity Fair*** April 1996.
[1606] Mark Seal, "The Ugly world of Dr. Arnie Klein, Beverly Hills' King of Botox," ***Vanity Fair*** February 2, 2012.

Klein was Jewish, the son of a Rabbi. He liked to brag of his great, great uncle being Albert Einstein.[1607] Klein was a dermatology student of Dr. Albert Kligman – *connect the dots!*

"He was one of my best students and I truly think he deserves the fame," said Dr. Albert Kligman, who discovered the acne-treating substance Retin-A and was one of Klein's medical school professors. "He's very good with his hands and head. Dr. Klein is an intellectual and not just a technician, even though he chose to go out to California, the home of all the fruits and nuts in the world."[1608]

When he arrived in California Klein became "immensely wealthy and well connected."[1609] One of those connections was with David Geffen. "In 1984, in the living room of his Los Angeles home, Dr. Klein, along with David Geffen, Dr. Mathilde Krim, and others founded the American Foundation for AIDS Research (amfAR)."[1610] Klein became "an eminence in Los Angeles."

He demonstrated how willing he was to fight any accusations made against him during a lawsuit filed in 2004 by Irena

---

[1607] Mark Seal, "The Ugly world of Dr. Arnie Klein, Beverly Hills' King of Botox," *Vanity Fair* February 2, 2012.
[1608] Lisa Boren, "Kelin," (sic) *Los Angeles Business Journal* July 12, 1999.
[1609] Sullivan, *Untouchable*.
[1610] "Contributor: Dr. Arnold Klein," *HuffPost* @ https://www.huffpost.com/author/arnold-william-klein; Lisa Boren, "Kelin," (sic) *Los Angeles Business Journal* July 12, 1999.

Medavoy, wife of former TriStar Pictures chairman Morris Mike Medavoy, who accused the doctor of giving her Botox treatments that brought on crippling migraine headaches. Klein won the case even in the face of evidence that demonstrated how dependent his medical practice was on injection treatments, and that he had collected a good deal of money from Botox manufacturer Allergan. He was by then an eminence in Los Angeles, a confounder with his friend Rose Tarlow (LA's most prominent interior designer) of the Breast Cancer Foundation at UCLA and a philanthropist credited with raising more than $300 million for HIV research. He was among Southern California's leading art collectors and delighted in mentioning that one of his patients had offered to name a new building at UCLA's School of Medicine for him, but that he had modestly declined, accepting an Arnold Klein teaching chair instead.[1611]

Klein was Professor of Medicine and Dermatology at UCLA's David Geffen School of Medicine, so named after David Geffen donated $200 million in 2001 to UCLA's School of Medicine. In 2004, having been "a valuable member of the UCLA faculty for 25 years,"[1612] the UCLA Division of Dermatology at the David Geffen School of Medicine named an endowed chair to honor Klein: The Arnold Klein, MD Chair in Dermatology. This was five years before the murder of Michael Jackson.

With Geffen, Gallin, Diller, and Calvin Klein, among others, Arnold Klein was an eminent member of the Jewish Gay Mafia. He was part of a community of overweight gay men called "Bears," an assortment of gay men weighing 250-350-plus pounds.[1613] According to his former office manager Jason Pfeiffer in a lawsuit filed against him, Klein constantly prowled the internet and the streets for male sex partners, even homeless men.

In legal documents, Pfeiffer details the duties he says he agreed to perform for Klein: "Prepare him for sexual encounters with masseurs, paid escorts, and prostitutes [and] administer Klein's

---

[1611] Sullivan, **Untouchable**.

[1612] Rachel Champeau, "UCLA Announces New Endowed Chair: The Arnold Klein, M.D., Chair in Dermatology," **UCLA News** July 23, 2004.

[1613] Mark Seal, "The Ugly world of Dr. Arnie Klein, Beverly Hills' King of Botox," **Vanity Fair** February 2, 2012.

Cialis, Viagra, and similar prescription drugs. In Palm Springs, Klein dispatched Pfeiffer and another employee to find a man with whom Klein could have sex. Pfeiffer and the other employee returned with a large-bodied homeless man for Klein Dr. Klein repeatedly subjected Pfeiffer to unwelcomed, unwanted, offensive sexual conduct."[1614]

MICHAEL REBUFFS THE ADVANCE

While Dr. Conrad Murray *has* told lies regarding Michael Jackson, I do believe this part of his testimony.

[Michael Jackson] liked skinny brunettes. He told me his whole life gay men had tried it on with him. 'He was uncomfortable with a lot of it. He said it was part of being in showbusiness. I don't think he was homophobic but I know he'd had some terrible experiences.[1615]

One of those "terrible experiences" reportedly involved David Geffen.

Shana Mangatal was the receptionist for Gallin Morey Associates for 7 years during the time Sandy Gallin was managing Michael Jackson (1991-1997). Gallin is Geffen's close pal. Like Geffen, he is gay and a Jew from New York. It was Geffen who had Michael Jackson accept Gallin as his manager. Shana Mangatal was front and center at Gallin's office during these years and allegedly had some kind of relationship with Michael Jackson. Mangatal was friends with her boss Sandy Gallin while he was managing Michael and

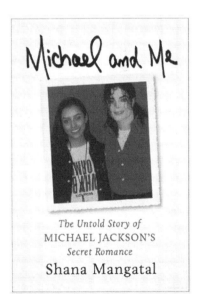

The Untold Story of
MICHAEL JACKSON'S
Secret Romance
Shana Mangatal

[1614] Mark Seal, "The Ugly world of Dr. Arnie Klein, Beverly Hills' King of Botox," **Vanity Fair** February 2, 2012.
[1615] Caroline Graham, "NO, I didn't kill Michael. He did it himself...with a massive overdose using his own stash," **Daily Mail** November 24, 2013.

she thus gives us something of an insider's view in her book, ***Michael and Me: The Untold Story of Michael Jackson's Secret Romance***.[1616] Mangatal shares with us a vitally important nugget and clue to understanding so many of the unfortunate events that had occurred in Michael's life. She relates:

> Gallin Morey Associates was one of the hottest music and talent management companies of the '90s. ... for seven years, I was front and center in this exclusive enclave of dream makers...

> Sandy Gallin was a flamboyant and charming Hollywood power player. His best friend was billionaire David Geffen. Together they knew everybody. They were a part of the so-called Velvet Mafia, which consisted of some of the most powerful gay executives in town...

> My desk was the calm in the middle of the storm and often I acted as a therapist, encouraging the assistants to hang in there. Some of those assistants were the young, gay, handsome boys Sandy met at his famous weekly pool parties, which were held at his sprawling mansion in Beverly Hills or his beach home in Malibu. Most of these boys were fresh off the bus from small towns across the country. They harbored dreams of becoming rich or famous – or both. I chuckled every time a new one stepped off the elevator for his first day on the job. They were so fresh-faced and eager. That excitement never lasted long...

> My first month on the job, I was invited to one of Sandy's famous parties. They were a thing of legend something you only read about in magazines. Think The Great Gatsby. This would be my first real Hollywood party...The bash was being thrown in honor of Sandy's boyfriend, Tom. It was his birthday...Sandy's best friend, David Geffen, was also there. At that moment, he was the richest, most powerful man in town...David and Sandy were both in their late forties but in incredible shape, able to attract any young, hot guy they desired. Everyone wanted to know David, and, at this time, Michael Jackson was no different. David and Michael had become fast friends, and David introduced Michael to Sandy. That's how Michael became Sandy's client...Years later, I asked Michael about David and why they were no longer close

---

[1616] Shana Mangatal, ***Michael and Me: The Untold Story of Michael Jackson's Secret Romance*** (Chicago: Chicago Review Press, Inc., 2016).

friends (Michael managed to fall out with most of his friends every few years). I don't know how true it is, because Michael was known to exaggerate on occasion, but he said that David had tried to seduce him, attempting to kiss him, and, according to Michael, he refused. Their friendship was strained after that.

David Geffen made a homosexual advance at Michael Jackson and he rebuffed it; he *rejected* Geffen's sexual advance. This is deep. According to Mangatal's recounting, Michael understood *this* moment as the moment he and Geffen's relationship "strained." Michael would come to know to what extent Geffen was insulted and how David Geffen handles being insulted.

IV. *Michael's False Accusers: Hollywood's Pedophile Ring*

Hollywood's Gay Mafia and its associates have been linked to what has been descried as "Hollywood's 'big secret'": it's "pedophilia crisis." In May of 2016 former child actor Elijah Wood ("Frodo Baggins" of *The Lord of the Rings*) told Britain's **Sunday Times** that "Hollywood is in the grip of a child sexual abuse epidemic, with rich and powerful industry figures abusing child actors with impunity."[1617] Wood descried the "darkness in the underbelly" of the industry as a "major," "organized" phenomenon in which "vipers" prey on young people and are protected by top

Elijah Wood Says Hollywood Has a Pedophilia Problem

By ALEX STEDMAN

[1617] Tom Sykes, "Elijah Wood Calls Out Hollywood's Pedophile Problem," **The Daily Beast** April 13, 2017.

Hollywood figures. According to Wood, Hollywood parties are the setting for this child abuse.

Wood is not alone. Former child actor Corey Feldman of the Eighties smashes *The Goonies* and *Stand By Me* "has made it his personal crusade to expose the ring of elite pedophiles" in Hollywood "that he says has been tormenting young actors for decades."[1618] Feldman, who was himself a victim, told ABC News in 2011:

> I can tell you that the No. 1 problem in Hollywood was and is and always will be pedophilia... I was surrounded by [pedophiles] when I was 14 years old... They were everywhere... There was a circle of older men... around this group of kids. And they all had either their own power or connections to great power in the entertainment industry... There are people... who have gotten away with it for so long that they feel they're above the law.

According to Feldman, this network of pedophiles is a circle of "some of the richest, most powerful people" in the business.[1619] "And all of these men were all friends."[1620] The "sick network targeted boys aged ten to 16, meeting them at awards shows and glitzy parties then *grooming them*." [1621] According to a number of lawsuits filed by alleged victims, Hollywood is in the grip of a cabal of predators who plie young boys and teens with hard drugs and alcohol before sexually assaulting them.[1622] A favorite

---

[1618] Yuliya Talmazan, "Corey Feldman Vows to Expose Hollywood Pedophile Ring," **NBC News** October 27, 2017.

[1619] **An Open Secret** 2014 Documentary by Amy Berg @ https://vimeo.com/142444429.

[1620] Grant Rollings, "The child sex scandal that could tear Hollywood apart: Lost Boys star Corey Feldman lifts lid on darkest movie secret," **The Sun** May 27, 2016.

[1621] Grant Rollings, "The child sex scandal that could tear Hollywood apart: Lost Boys star Corey Feldman lifts lid on darkest movie secret," **The Sun** May 27, 2016.

[1622] Michelle Malkin, "Hollywood's Sexual Predator Problem Explodes," **NewsBusters** May 6, 2014.

pastime of Hollywood's Gay Mafia is evidently throwing big orgy parties.

> It's this group of young, really good-looking guys that travel around everywhere, from coast to coast, and cater to the big orgy parties. They fly these guys out en masse, and they just party, party, party...so far out that no one would hear the screams.[1623]

David Geffen's biographer, Tom King, who was also gay, describes first meeting Geffen at such a party, "You know, one of these parties that are mobbed by the middle-aged – it's *charitable* to call them that – but the middle-aged moguls and the pretty mail-room boys who want to be producers."[1624] Some of these were reportedly "nude wrestling parties" involving underage boys.[1625] David Geffen's association with Digital Entertainment Network (DEN), an online video streaming service (pre-YouTube and Netflix), directly connects him with a notorious pedophile ring in Hollywood.

In 2014 award-winning and Oscar-nominated director Amy Berg premiered the documentary *An Open Secret* which exposes a child sex ring that was operating in the heart of Los Angeles in the late-Nineties. Because no distributer would touch the explosive film – "the film Hollywood doesn't want you to see," says film producer Gabe Hoffman – *An Open Secret* was released for free on Vimeo.[1626] The documentary centers on DEN, the 1998 precursor to modern streaming platforms. DEN provided original content staring child actors. But now we know that it was a front for a child abuse ring. DEN was founded by convicted child predator Marc Collins-Rector, his young victim/boyfriend Chad Shackley (Shackley was 15 and Collins-

---

[1623] Ebner, "Gay Mafia," 46.

[1624] Lisa DePaulo, "Whose Life Is I, Anyway?" *New York Magazine* March 13, 2000.

[1625] Howard Rosenman, "Why Being 'Gay in the '70s in New York and L.A. Was Magic' – and How Hollywood Has Changed," *Hollywood Reporter* May 3, 2019.

[1626] *An Open Secret* 2014 Documentary by Amy Berg @ https://vimeo.com/142444429; Jenna Marotta, "Hollywood's Underage Sexual Abuse Problem: 5 Shocking Injustices From 'An Open Secret', *Indie Wire* Oct 26, 2017.

Rector was 31 when their relationship began) and Brock Peirce, the former child actor from "Mighty Ducks" (1992).

Marc Collins-Rector, Chad Shackley and Brock Peirce

Collins-Rector's idea for DEN was to produce TV shows and movies for 14-to-24-year-olds *with an emphasis on stories for gay teens and distribute them online.*[1627] By 1999 DEN succeeded in raising $72 million in investment, before opening. And the list of investors is shocking. Except, it is not...not really.

> An SEC filing obtained by Hollywood periodical ***Radar Online*** reveals that DEN's investors included a shocking number of big name personalities such as media executives Garth Ancier and David Geffen, former Yahoo CEO Terry Semel, film producers Gary Goddard and Bryan Singer, Wall Street czar Mitchell Blutt, A&M Records head Gilbert Friesen (now deceased), former Disney executive David Neuman, manager and label executive Gary Gersh, investor Jeffrey Sachs, former Congressman Michael Huffington, actors Ben and Fred Savage, and tech companies such as Microsoft and Dell. *The lack of apparent revenue raises questions about what investors in DEN were expecting in return* (emphasis added – WM).[1628]

Collins-Rector and Shackley moved to Los Angeles in the mid-Nineties and chose as their residence the $4.2 million Spanish colonial mansion previously owned by Death Row Records C.E.O. Suge Knight. The digital pioneer and confessed

---

[1627] Alex French and Maximillian Potter, " 'Nobody Is Going to Believe You'," ***The Atlantic*** March 2019

[1628] Elizabeth Vos, "Tech Figure In Dot-Com Child Sex Scandal Was A Clinton Global Initiative Member," ***Disobedient Media*** January 25, 2017.

child molester Collins-Rector immediately got "well-connected" in L.A. "Among their new acquaintances in Los Angeles were such industry heavies as David Geffen, uber-manager Sandy Gallin, then–NBC Entertainment president Garth Ancier, and *Usual Suspects* director Bryan Singer."[1629] Bryan Singer invested $50,000 and David Geffen invested $250,000 in the company. In a letter written by Collins-Rector he speaks of "my *friend* Bryan Singer [who] introduced us to a young actor named Brock Pierce."[1630] In addition, "David Geffen...socializ[ed] at the estate with other investors".[1631]

The estate is the infamous palatial estate in Encino called the "M&C Estate" for "Marc & Chad." There, the three founders of DEN

> hosted lavish parties attended by Hollywood's gay A-list. Their guests included relative newcomer Bryan Singer, now the director of the *X-Men* movies, and legendary media mogul David Geffen, both of whom were investors in DEN. It was at those parties that Collins-Rector and others allegedly sexually assaulted half a dozen teenage boys, according to two sets of civil lawsuits...[1632]

The pool parties at the M&C Estate were all the rave in L.A. "The Encino mansion...was home to the wild gay sex parties where Hollywood bigwigs allegedly preyed on underage boys."[1633] According to reports, including lawsuits,

> Hollywood's rich and powerful men enjoyed a secret party [at the M&C Estate] that would go on late into the night. Behind its high walls were a group of young wannabes all desperate to make it in the movies. *They were all boys — no girls were allowed — carefully selected for the entertainment of the group*

[1629] John Gorenfeld and Patrick Runkle, "Fast Company: A high-flying Web start-up, DEN imploded among allegations of drug use, guns, and pedophilia," **Radar Magazine** November 5, 2007.

[1630] **An Open Secret** 2014 Documentary by Amy Berg @ https://vimeo.com/142444429.

[1631] Robert Kolker, "What Happens When You Accuse a Major Hollywood Director of Rape?" **Vulture** September 7, 2014.

[1632] Ellie Hall, Nicolás Medina Mora and David Noriega, "Found: The Elusive Man At The Heart Of The Hollywood Sex Abuse Scandal," **Buzzfeed** June 26, 2014.

[1633] Tracie Egan Morrissey, "Inside the Hollywood Sex Ring Mansion From the Bryan Singer Lawsuit," **Jezebel** April 25, 2014.

of predatory paedophiles. These wide-eyed hopefuls were plied with drugs and alcohol and told anyone using the hot tub had to strip naked.[1634]

According to online reports, the revelrous, sexually-fueled pool parties...are one of Hollywood's worst kept secrets, with a guest list often consisting of older show biz power brokers and youngish teenage boys culled from a time-tested selection process that starts on the nightclub circuit in West Hollywood and Hollywood each Thursday. At the 18-and-up parties, collaborators get the phone numbers of the youngish looking attendees, who are subsequently invited to weekend parties where <u>sex is common</u>, <u>behind closed doors</u> or in full display of the others.[1635]

The reckoning did come. Days before DEN's planned $75 million IPO (initial public offering) in October 1999 a young man filed a lawsuit claiming he'd been molested by Collins-Rector for three years, beginning when he was 13. Collins-Rector quickly paid a settlement. The IPO was withdrawn. A number of DEN employees eventually filed lawsuits alleging they were raped and/or sexually abused at the M&C Estate by the three cofounders and guests. Allegedly drugs were used to carry out the attacks:[1636] Valium, Vicodin, Xanax, Percocet, ecstasy, roofies, cocaine, marijuana. "Young actors who attended parties remember troves of prescription drugs and alcohol, plus Collins-Rector's gun collection. One man recalled when, as a minor, Collins-Rector threatened his career if he did not sleep in his bed. Although the actor refused and camped out on the couch, he nonetheless awoke in Collins-Rector's bed, convinced that a laced drink had led to abuse."[1637] The victims

---

[1634] Grant Rollings, "The child sex scandal that could tear Hollywood apart: Lost Boys star Corey Feldman lifts lid on darkest movie secret," **The Sun** May 27, 2016.

[1635] "Hollywood's Worst Kept Secret – 'Sexually-Fueled Pool Parties': The Latest Developments in Bryan Singer Teen Abuse Lawsuit," **Radar Online** April 18, 2014.

[1636] John Gorenfeld and Patrick Runkle, "Fast Company: A high-flying Web start-up, DEN imploded among allegations of drug use, guns, and pedophilia," **Radar Magazine** November 5, 2007.

[1637] Jenna Marotta, "Hollywood's Underage Sexual Abuse Problem: 5 Shocking Injustices From 'An Open Secret'," **Indie Wire** Oct 26, 2017.

claimed DEN was but "a front for a sex ring which operated in 1999."[1638]

> One early, senior-level DEN employee remembers asking why so many teenage boys were on the payroll and being told that they did computer work. The employee also recalls attending a company party and seeing teenage boys filing into a movie theater in the Encino mansion. The employee tried to go inside but was stopped by a bodyguard, who said: "Kids only." The employee asked a colleague what was going on. "[He] said that he had seen some of it, and that it was definitely porn ... [The kids] were all laughing and eating candy. But we were totally not allowed into that room.[1639]

But what about the "bigwig" investors in Collins-Rector's company? "Were Singer, Ancier, Goddard and Neuman really blind to where their money was going and what kind of behavior it was funding?" asked **Radar Online**.[1640] Daniel Cheren, the attorney who represented the DEN employees, says no, telling a reporter: "Some of these investors received in addition to their stock, *a piece of a male brothel for their money*"; "Anyone who had a dinner at that estate or went to a party there, had to know what was going on."[1641] **Radar Magazine** tells us that, in its heyday, "a Who's Who of gay Hollywood flocked to notorious all-night bashes at the M&C estate".[1642] Topping that "Who's Who" list were "the likes of record boss David Geffen, film producer Michael Huffington and X-Men director Bryan Singer.

[1638] Grant Rollings, "The child sex scandal that could tear Hollywood apart: Lost Boys star Corey Feldman lifts lid on darkest movie secret," **The Sun** May 27, 2016.

[1639] Alex French and Maximillian Potter, " 'Nobody Is Going to Believe You'," **The Atlantic** March 2019

[1640] "Bryan Singer & Other Hollywood Sex Ring Defendants Exposed As Investors in Shady Company Run By Pedophile," **Radar Online** April 24, 2014.

[1641] "Bryan Singer & Other Hollywood Sex Ring Defendants Exposed As Investors in Shady Company Run By Pedophile," **Radar Online** April 24, 2014.

[1642] John Gorenfeld and Patrick Runkle, "Fast Company: A high-flying Web start-up, DEN imploded among allegations of drug use, guns, and pedophilia," **Radar Magazine** November 5, 2007.

Those three men allegedly attended the parties..."[1643] According to his attorney, however "Geffen was not accused of any misconduct in the suits nor named as a defendant." [1644] The same could not be said of Geffen's protégé Bryan Singer, a fellow gay Jew who is from West Windsor, New Jersey.[1645]

"Singer and Collins-Rector were close friends, and according to at least five sources, Singer was a regular at the M&C Estate." [1646] It was Singer who introduced Collins-Rector to Brock Pierce, the third of the three founders of DEN. And even more than Collins-Rector, *Singer is known for his own Hollywood gay parties.*

> What is not in dispute is that, since launching his career with 1995's *The Usual Suspects* and becoming a blockbuster filmmaker with 2000's *X-Men*, Singer has been a fixture in the gay Hollywood party scene, hosting and attending gatherings at homes in Los Angeles that have drawn anywhere between a few dozen to 1,200 revelers, most of them very young men.[1647]

> By the late '90s, Singer also had a reputation on the gay Hollywood scene—in part for the pool parties he threw at a house he lived in on Butler Avenue, in the Mar Vista neighborhood. A friend of Singer's recalls attending one of these parties when he was in his early 20s (and Singer was in his early 30s) and being shocked by how young many of the guests looked. "It felt like a high-school party," the friend says. He remembers wondering: *How did all these boys get here? Where are their parents?* (emphasis original).[1648]

[1643] Grant Rollings, "The child sex scandal that could tear Hollywood apart: Lost Boys star Corey Feldman lifts lid on darkest movie secret," *The Sun* May 27, 2016.

[1644] Ellie Hall, Nicolás Medina Mora and David Noriega, "Found: The Elusive Man At The Heart Of The Hollywood Sex Abuse Scandal," *Buzzfeed* June 26, 2014.

[1645] Alex French and Maximillian Potter, " 'Nobody Is Going to Believe You'," *The Atlantic* March 2019

[1646] Alex French and Maximillian Potter, "'Nobody Is Going to Believe You'," *The Atlantic* March 2019

[1647] Adam B. Vary, "Inside Bryan Singer's Wild Hollywood World," *BuzzFeed* April 23, 2014.

[1648] Alex French and Maximillian Potter, " 'Nobody Is Going to Believe You'," *The Atlantic* March 2019

A-list Hollywood director Bryan Singer, friend of Marc Collins-Rector and protégé of David Geffen, pictured with one of his infamous "twinks." *Twink* is a gay slang term describing a young or young-looking slender male with little or no body hair or facial hair. In addition, "At its most pejorative, the term describes a uniquely disposable kind of young gay man: Hairless, guileless, witless. The term's namesake is Twinkie, a junk food containing shiny packaging, a sweet taste, and zero nutritional value." Scott Bixby, "Inside Hollywood's 'Twink' Pool Parties," **The Daily Beast** July 12, 2017.

The **American Psycho** author Brett Easton Ellis said he knew about Bryan Singer's "underage (sex) parties" where fake ID's were important because he dated two participants of those parties.[1649] Director Roland Emmerich (*Independence Day* and *2012*) co-hosted with Singer parties over Pride weekend at Emmerich's L.A. home, such as the one pictured below from June 15, 2009.[1650] Reportedly "the Hollywood Elite [flocked] to his parties," and these parties are said to be an entire production involving modeling agencies, club promoters, and studio

[1649] "Bryan Singer Sex Abuse Suit: Bret Easton Ellis Says He Dated Two People Who 'Went Through World of Underage Parties' (Audio)," **Hollywood Reporter** April 29, 2014.
[1650] "Friends In High Places: Bryan Singer and the Hollywood Elite Flocking to his Parties," **ONTD** October 31, 2017.

executives.[1651] The party drug Molly often fueled the gay bacchanals. [1652]

The Emmerich/Singer party on June 15, 2009

Singer's pool parties have been a topic of discussion in gay entertainment circles for years. Some parties, co-hosted with fellow out director Roland Emmerich, have featured more than a thousand celebrants. Emmerich told **The Advocate**, "when [Singer] makes a New Year's party, there's like 600, 700 twinks running around and he's hiding in his room. That's quite typical." Emmerich estimates that the last party they hosted, in 2009, drew 1,200 guests... "I don't recall anyone bringing a bathing suit," says [party attendant Jason] Dottley. "It was a healthy mixture of underwear and no underwear." He pauses. "Mostly no underwear, to be honest."[1653]

[1651] "Friends In High Places: Bryan Singer and the Hollywood Elite Flocking to his Parties," **ONTD** October 31, 2017 .
[1652] Alex French and Maximillian Potter, " 'Nobody Is Going to Believe You'," **The Atlantic** March 2019
[1653] Scott Bixby, "Inside Hollywood's 'Twink' Pool Parties," **The Daily Beast** July 12, 2017.

Singer was known for his own "Twink Parties" and he was also a fixture at the "pedophile sex den,"[1654] the "male brothel,"[1655] i.e. the M&C Estate of Collins-Rector. Subsequently, a number of lawsuits alleging rape and/or sexual abuse were directed at the bigwig investors and party-goers. The accusers "named prominent members of the gay Hollywood elite,"[1656] including Hollywood's A-list director Bryan Singer but also David Neuman (former Disney executive), Garth Ancier (president of NBC), and Hollywood producer Garry Goddard.

In 2019 after a 12-month investigation with over 50 sources spoken to *The Atlantic* published a blockbuster investigative report detailing decades of sexual abuse allegations against Bryan Singer.[1657]

Almost from the moment his star began to rise, Singer, who is now 53, has been trailed by allegations of sexual misconduct. These allegations were so well known that 4,000 students, faculty members, and alumni at the University of Southern California had signed a petition asking the school to take Singer's name off one of its

1654 Robert Kolker, "What Happens When You Accuse a Major Hollywood Director of Rape?" *Vulture* September 7, 2014.
1655 "Bryan Singer & Other Hollywood Sex Ring Defendants Exposed As Investors in Shady Company Run By Pedophile," *Radar Online* April 24, 2014.
1656 Robert Kolker, "What Happens When You Accuse a Major Hollywood Director of Rape?" *Vulture* September 7, 2014.
1657 Alex French and Maximillian Potter, "'Nobody Is Going to Believe You'," *The Atlantic* March 2019.

programs, the Bryan Singer Division of Cinema and Media Studies—which the school did immediately after Sanchez-Guzman filed his suit. As one prominent actor told us, "After the Harvey Weinstein news came out, everyone thought Bryan Singer would be next."[1658]

The Atlantic report built "a powerful case that friends, associates and ultimately his industry aided and abetted Singer."[1659] It was common knowledge in Hollywood

> the filmmaker's private world of gay Hollywood parties and the friends who scout young men to go to them... BuzzFeed has spoken with six people who have gone to them...These sources provided a stark portrait of an entrenched system, facilitated by these scouts, who bring Singer into regular orbit with 18- to 20-year-olds at parties sustained by large amounts of alcohol and drugs — edging precariously close to the line between legality and illegality...To scout for attractive young men to attend his parties, Singer has relied on a network of friends, according to multiple sources.[1660]

Some of the lawsuits against the Hollywood bigwigs began to unravel, no doubt due to the power of the Hollywood elite to fight and protect themselves.[1661] Nevertheless, Bryan Singer agreed to an out of court settlement,[1662] and others such as Garry Goddard soon faced further pedophilia charges.[1663]

[1658] Alex French and Maximillian Potter, "'Nobody Is Going to Believe You'," ***The Atlantic*** March 2019

[1659] Marina Hyde, "R Kelly, Michael Jackson and Bryan Singer. Who Knew? Everyone," ***The Guardian*** January 31, 2019.

[1660] Adam B. Vary, "Inside Bryan Singer's Wild Hollywood World," ***BuzzFeed*** April 23, 2014.

[1661] Alex French and Maximillian Potter, " 'Nobody Is Going to Believe You'," ***The Atlantic*** March 2019

[1662] Tim Teeman, "Bryan Singer Agreed to Settle Sex Abuse Lawsuit for $100,000, but Insists He's Innocent," ***The Daily Beast*** April 14, 2017; Becky Freeth, "Director Bryan Singer agrees to pay $150,000 to settle rape case," ***Metro*** Jun 13, 2019.

[1663] Gus Garcia-Roberts, "Hollywood producer Gary Goddard accused of sexual misconduct by 8 former child actors," ***Los Angeles Times*** December 20, 2017.

If Singer's alleged predatory behavior was able to continue unabated, it's because people in the industry protected him, and they did so because he made them lots and lots of money.[1664]

Reports are that Singer is David Geffen's acolyte, his "chosen replacement," and as such it is Geffen who has been Singer's "protector."[1665]

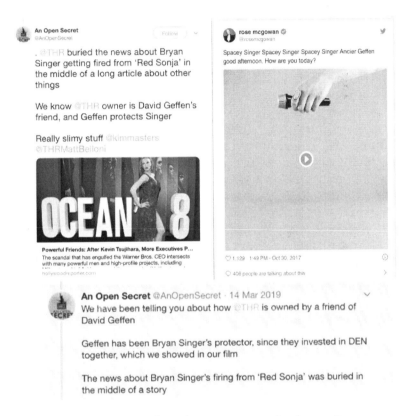

After *Star Treck: Discovery* star Anthony Rapp came out with an accusation against Kevin Spacey of sexual misconduct when Rapp was 14 years old – Spacey and Singer

---

[1664] Steven Blum, "Will the Industry Continue to Embrace Director Bryan Singer?" *Los Angeles Magazine* January 25, 2019.
[1665] codyave, "The Mogul, according to CDAN," *Medium* August 26, 2019.

are pals, by the way[1666] - Rose McGowan, one of the most outspoken accusers of Harvey Weinstein who accused him of raping her in 1997, offered her support in tweets that cryptically allude to David Geffen, Bryan Singer and the alleged Hollywood pedophile ring.[1667]

But Singer's sins seem to be surpassing even Geffen's protective shadow. 20th Century Fox fired Singer in December 2017, just two weeks before completion of the filming of Singer's blockbuster project *Bohemian Rhapsody*. Coincidently, also in December, news of another sexual abuse lawsuit against the director broke, a Seattle man charging Singer had raped him when he was 17. [1668] When the movie *Bohemian Rhapsody* won two Golden Globes in January 2019, Singer was conspicuously absent from the ceremony.

Shortly after the M&C Estate sexual assault allegations surfaced in 2000, Collins-Rector, Shackley and Pierce fled the country and lived undetected for two years in Spain before Interpol picked them up. Authorities discovered a cache of weapons and 8,000 images of child pornography in the villa where Collins-Rector's lived. In June 2004 Collins-Rector pled guilty to transporting minors across state lines for the purpose of sex. However, there is a deeper angel to this story.

According to court documents, Collins-Rector left the country, not because (or only because) of the charges that were filed against him. Rather, he fled *out of fear that David Geffen was out to destroy him*.[1669] In 2003 Brock Pierce testified under oath that Geffen, no longer satisfied with being a minority partner in DEN, tried multiple times to buy DEN outright from Collins-Rector. When Collins-Rector refused to sell, Geffen reportedly said, "I'm going to take your business, whether you

[1666] Rae Alexandra, "It's Not Hard to Connect the Dots in Hollywood's Culture of Abuse," **KQED** November 7, 2017.

[1667] Max Mundan, "Rose McGown Asks 'Are They Trying To Silence Me?' To News of Virginia Arrest Warrant," **Inquisitr** October 31, 2017.

[1668] Alex French and Maximillian Potter, " 'Nobody Is Going to Believe You'," **The Atlantic** March 2019

[1669] Deposition of Brock Pierce, October 21, 2003, Circuit Court of the Eleventh Judicial Circuit in and for Miami-Dade County, Florida, Case No. 02-3317 CA-20; Ellie Hall, Nicolás Medina Mora and David Noriega, "Found: The Elusive Man At The Heart Of The Hollywood Sex Abuse Scandal," **Buzzfeed** June 26, 2014.

like it or not."[1670] According to Pierce's testimony, Collins-Rector believed and feared that Geffen **and the "Gay Mafia"** *were intending to kill him*! These are the words found in the court records: Gay Mafia.[1671] Indeed, ultimately the Gay Mafia ran things at the M&C Estate. As John Connolly, former NYPD detective-turned-investigative reporter said in **An Open Secret**: "Hollywood is a company town. Marc Rector joined that company and that town. And they get away with murder, or in this case they get away with being pedophiles."[1672] As a company man you get away with murder and with pedophilia – until you run afoul with the company. According to one of the alleged victims of the M&C Estate sexual abuses, Bryan Singer told him, "We control Hollywood. We can eliminate you; we *will* eliminate you."[1673] That "we" is no doubt Hollywood's Gay Mafia. Collins-Rector knew their power. For this reason Collins-Rector, Shackley, and Peirce hastily charted a jet and flew to Spain where they hid from Geffen and the Gay Mafia for two years until Interpol caught up with Collins-Rector in Spain in 2002. This, according to testimony under oath.

Fear of David Geffen seems to be part of the very landscape of Hollywood. In 2015 a gay porn star and male prostitute, Justin Griggs, who appeared as a government witness in an extortion trial of a fellow porn actor and escort, told the court of his ties to David Geffen, and admitted that he feared disclosing the details of this relationship with the "very powerful" billionaire out of fear for his safety.[1674]

[1670] Hall, Mora and Noriega, "Found: The Elusive Man."

[1671] Deposition of Brock Pierce, October 21, 2003, Circuit Court of the Eleventh Judicial Circuit in and for Miami-Dade County, Florida, Case No. 02-3317 CA-20.

[1672] **An Open Secret** 2014 Documentary by Amy Berg @ https://vimeo.com/142444429.

[1673] "Bryan Singer's Accuser Claims He 'Was Like A Piece Of Meat' To The 'X-Men' Producer; Says Sex Ring Boasted 'We Control Hollywood...We Can Eliminate You'," **Radar Online** April 17, 2014; Tim Teeman, "'I Considered Suicide,' Alleged Sex Abuse Victim of Bryan Singer Tells The Daily Beast," **The Daily Beast** April 17, 2014.

[1674] Snejana Farberov, "Gay porn actor reveals his ties to David Geffen and says he 'fears for his safety' - as his male escort friend is found guilty of $1.4m extortion plot," **Daily Mail** July 10, 2015; "Male Escort Told FBI He Feared David Geffen," **the smoking gun** July 9, 2015.

A gay porn star who moonlighted as a paid escort recently told FBI agents that he did not want to discuss details of his relationship with David Geffen because the billionaire was very powerful, adding that his hesitance grew out of fear for his own safety, according to a court transcript.[1675]

Thus, Rea Alexandra wisely pointed out:

> If you spend even a small amount of time researching the rumors about and charges against Hollywood's pedophiles (both convicted and alleged), it doesn't take long to see the dots connecting and one large circle forming. As fresh tales of abuse continue to emerge over the next few weeks and months, that circle is bound to get larger. One can only guess at its final enormity.[1676]

[1675] Snejana Farberov, "Gay porn actor reveals his ties to David Geffen and says he 'fears for his safety' - as his male escort friend is found guilty of $1.4m extortion plot," **Daily Mail** July 10, 2015; "Male Escort Told FBI He Feared David Geffen," **the smoking gun** July 9, 2015.
[1676] Rae Alexandra, "It's Not Hard to Connect the Dots in Hollywood's Culture of Abuse," **KQED** November 7, 2017.

The dots certainly connect: David Geffen • Sandy Gallin • Bryan Singer • Marc Collins-Rector • The Gay Mafia • Jewish Hollywood • Edgar Bronfman Jr. • Michael Jackson's enemies

V.   *Deliberately Making Michael Jackson an Addict. 1993*

For Michael Jackson 1993 was a watershed year – a year of trauma and of conspiracy. In this year Michael was *made* into an addict and also this year Michael was first framed for a crime he never committed and for which he was never even indicted. Yet the false chargers changed the course of his career and likely of his life permanently.

After Michael's hair caught on fire during the filming of a Pepsi commercial in 1984, an accident that severely burned his scalp, the resulting surgeries introduced Michael to painkilling drugs. But by all accounts, Michael did not develop a dependency until the fateful year of 1993, and this dependency did not develop because Michael Jackson was a *drug seeker*. He was not. According to David Fournier, the certified nurse anesthetist who worked for Michael for 10 years (1993-2003), "Jackson never asked for specific drugs"[1677] and he "didn't exhibit any drug-seeking behavior or signs that he was doctor-shopping."[1678] Nor was Michael's drug dependency that did develop in 1993 the unfortunate but entirely conceivable consequence of all of the medical procedures he underwent during which anesthetics were required. Rather, Michael's first battle with drug addiction came as a consequence of an addiction that was *wholly unnecessary* and very likely *deliberately* induced in him by a yet unrecognized *frenemy* – unrecognized by Michael.

1993 was the year Michael Jackson became addicted to a specific drug: Demerol.[1679] Demerol is a synthetic (man-made) opioid, described as "the pharmacological equivalent of

---

[1677] Alan Duke, "Michael Jackson's drug use explored in trial," **CNN** July 26, 2013.
[1678] Associated Press, "Michael Jackson's Drug History Scrutinized in Court," **Billboard** July 26, 2013.
[1679] "'Michael Jackson was drug addict in 1993' – doctor," **Newshub** September 7, 2013.

heroin."[1680] Thus, Michael's 1997 song *Morphine* is a haunting reflection on addiction to Demerol. His friend and personal assistant Frank Cascio said that while Michael first encountered Demerol in 1984 after the hair fire, it was only in 1993 during the *Dangerous* tour that he first noticed Michael taking the drug.[1681] Cascio remembers being concerned later with the great amount of Demerol Michael was being given and voiced his concern. Michael then called the doctor that was injecting him with the drug and, on speaker phone, "asked him to verify that the quantity of Demerol he was taking was safe and appropriate."[1682] Who was this "Demerol Doctor"? It was Dr. Arnold Klein.

Dr. Stuart Finkelstein, the tour doctor who travelled with Michael Jackson during the *Dangerous* tour, recalled that in Thailand, before he could "administer pain relief to Jackson" Dr. Finkelstein called "the singer's Los Angeles doctor on the phone and agreed to give him pain medication to help the singer cope with a severe headache."[1683] Michael's Los Angeles doctor was Dr. Klein and the drug that Dr. Finkelstein went on to administer was Demerol. Reportedly, Michael was "given 'two to four' 10mg doses of Demerol *each day for the length of the tour.*"[1684] Dr. Klein was not on the tour, but on his behalf his nurse assistant since 1977 Debbi Rowe was. Karen Faye, Michael's make-up artist and hair-dresser, testified in 2013 that

> nurse Debbie Rowe, who would later become Jackson's second wife and the mother of his two oldest children, would travel with them on the "Dangerous" tour in 1992 with "a little bag" of medications.

> "Debbie Rowe asked me to learn how to give injections," [Karen Faye] said. "I thought about it and said 'No.' I am not qualified to handle any kind of medications."

[1680] Colin Vickery, "Michael Jackson should have died earlier, autopsy report reveals," **News Corp Australia** June 25, 2014.

[1681] The Associated Press, "Manager: Michael Jackson took drugs before performing," **Newsday** November 12, 2011.

[1682] Mark Seal, "The Doctor Will Sue You Now," **Vanity Fair** February 2, 2012

[1683] "'Michael Jackson was drug addict in 1993' – doctor," **Newshub** September 7, 2013.

[1684] Toyin Owoseje, "Michael Jackson Doctor: Star\'s Infected Buttocks Revealed Drug Addition," **IB Times** July 1, 2014.

When the tour was on its way to Bangkok, Thailand, Faye was asked to carry a package she was told contained medicine patches for Jackson's pain, she testified. She refused to travel with it, she said.

Faye testified that the tour doctor, Dr. Stuart Finkelstein, later told her "I'm glad you weren't carrying it. It has vials and syringes. If you had brought this in, you might not be here." The implication was she could have been arrested for smuggling drugs.

[Paul] Gongaware, now the Co-CEO of AEG Live, was in charge of logistics for the "Dangerous" tour and was involved in the incident, Faye said.[1685]

While Faye might have rejected Rowe's request that she help by learning herself how to administer the Demerol injections to Michael, according to Dr. Finkelstein Faye did give Michael two ampules of Demerol that were for Jackson's injections. Dr. Finkelstein also recalled Michael wearing a Duragesic patch, which contained another opiate which is absorbed through the skin.[1686]

Michael Jackson may even have been drugged against his will in order to *get him to Thailand*.[1687] On August 18, 1993 attorneys told Michael that a criminal investigation into child molestation allegations had begun. Michael was scheduled to fly to Bangkok in the next three days. The news killed Michael's spirit or desire to complete the tour. He "no longer felt like hitting the road."[1688] Sandy Gallin was Michael's manager at the time.

Bert Fields (Michael's lawyer), fearing Michael would be arrested, called Michael's manager Sandy Gallin and told him

---

[1685] Alan Duke, "Witness: Michael Jackson was paranoid, talking to himself in last days," *CNN* May 9, 2013
[1686] "'Michael Jackson was drug addict in 1993' – doctor," **Newshub** September 7, 2013.
[1687] Stefan Kyriazis, "Michael Jackson child abuse case: New shock revelations from his lawyer and manager," **Express** June 22, 2016.
[1688] Michael "may have been drugged to get him out of the country before the county police could arrest him in 1993": Stefan Kyriazis, "Michael Jackson child abuse allegations: His first lawyer believed he was Innocent," **Express** May 7, 2019.

they needed to get Michael out of the country as soon as possible. "Bert told me that if they didn't get him out of the country, Michael would be arrested," Gallin recalls. "And then the whole tour would have been cancelled at a huge financial loss...Michael did not want to go on the tour, but somehow, Anthony Pellicano got him on the plane. How, I don't know. He went to his apartment in Century City; he may have drugged him, tied him up, or talked him into going quietly."[1689]

Anthony Pellicano was Bert Fields' Private Investigator. The *Los Angeles Times* exposed Pellicano's Mafia ties in 1993.[1690]

Britain's *The Sun* (July 24, 2009) reported seeing proof that Michael Jackson's "first major battle with drug addiction occurred shortly after [Dr. Arnold Klein] treated him [in 1993] with *four times* the daily maximum recommended amount of the drug."[1691] Dr. Steven Hoefflin, Michael's long-time plastic surgeon, examined Michael's medical records in 1993 per Michael's request and discovered "the insane amount of Demerol" that Dr. Klein was *unnecessarily* administering to Michael for minor dermatological procedures. "The maximum amount you should give a patient of his weight and build in severe surgical pain is 200mg a day. Michael was being given 800mg a day," for minor procedures such as acne treatment.

> "I was shocked to see the huge amount of narcotics ... and other medications that both Dr. Klein and Debbie Rowe were injecting into Michael," Hoefflin states.

> For example, Klein and Rowe, who worked as a nurse for Klein, injected as much as 1,850 mg of Demerol into Jackson during a three-day period in August 1993, according to Hoefflin's declaration.[1692]

This is a massive and totally unnecessary amount. Dr. Hoefflin thus charged Dr. Klein: "You caused his Demerol and other prescription pain medicine addiction. You instructed Debbie

---

[1689] Stefan Kyriazis, "Michael Jackson child abuse allegations: His first lawyer believed he was Innocent," *Express* May 7, 2019.
[1690] Ken Auletta, "Hollywood Ending," *The New Yorker* July 17, 2006.
[1691] Mark Seal, "The Ugly world of Dr. Arnie Klein, Beverly Hills' King of Botox," *Vanity Fair* February 2, 2012
[1692] "Lawyers For 'Dermatologist' to the Stars' Argue Against Defamation Case," *Waven Newspapers* June 16, 2011.

Rowe to inject large quantities of Demerol while she was alone in his home."[1693] Debbie Rowe herself testified that Dr. Klein "regularly loaded up Jackson with Demerol and Percocet..."[1694] and, as his nurse assistant, she "provided the painkiller Demerol and Propofol for many of the hundreds of treatments Jackson received over 20 years."[1695] Dr. Klein himself admitted to Harvey Levin of TMZ Live in November 2009 that *Michael Jackson never requested Demerol* from him and *never wanted it!*[1696] Why, then, was Michael pumped with such an extreme amount of this "pharmacological equivalent of heroin"? Rowe reveals of Dr. Klein: he "*was not doing what was best for Michael.*"[1697] Then whose interests was he serving? If Michael Jackson's best interest *was not* Dr. Klein's concern, what was his objective in 1993 in treating Michael Jackson with *four times the daily maximum recommended amount of the drug*?

On November 11, 1993 the remainder of Michael Jackson's *Dangerous* tour was abruptly cancelled. According to Michael's attorney Bert Fields the cancellation was the consequence of a painkiller addiction which Michael developed "in recent weeks"[1698] - an addiction caused by Dr. Arnold Klein. This is why Dr. Hoefflin charged: "You [Dr. Klein] prevented [Michael] from continuing his Dangerous Tour."[1699] Michael was flown to England where he spent time in a drug

---

[1693] Mark Seal, "The Ugly world of Dr. Arnie Klein, Beverly Hills' King of Botox," *Vanity Fair* February 2, 2012
[1694] Richard Johnson, "They didn't care about him: Michael Jackson's ex-wife rips doctors in star's death," *New York Post* August 15, 2013
[1695] "Michael Jackson trial: Debbie Rowe cries during testimony," *ABC7* August 14, 2013.
[1696] November 5, 2009 Interview (90 minutes):

Harvey Levin	Did [Michael] ever ask you for Demerol?
Arnold Klein	No.
Harvey Levin	He never said, "I want Demerol"?
Arnold Klein	No, because I wouldn't give him what he wanted. You don't give a person what they want.

[1697] Jeff Gottlieb, "Debbie Rowe: Michael Jackson's doctors competed to give pain eds," *Los Angeles Times* August 14, 2013.
[1698] Jessica Seigel, "Ailing Michael Jackson Not 'hiding Out', His Lawyer Says," *Chicago Tribune* November 16, 1993.
[1699] Mark Seal, "The Ugly world of Dr. Arnie Klein, Beverly Hills' King of Botox," *Vanity Fair* February 2, 2012

rehabilitation program which, according to Dr. Klein's admission, was successful. Michael Jackson came home clean.[1700] He had won this first battle with drug addiction which was induced by one of the many enemies around him that posed as friends.

Excursus: How Michael Was Made White (And By Whom)

I'm a Black American. I am proud to be a Black American. I am proud of my race, and I am proud of who I am. I have a lot of pride and dignity of who I am. - Michael Jackson on Oprah Winfrey, 1993.

Dr. Steve Hoefflin informs us of another very important fact: "Dr. Klein is the one who made [Michael Jackson's] face white by using Benoquin, a permanent bleaching agent".[1701]

Michael had the skin condition called vitiligo which produces loss of skin color in blotches due to the death or dysfunction of pigment producing cells. Michael never wanted to go white. He first used a special make up to cover up (darken) the light blotches. Vitiligo can be treated with corticosteroids and oral medicine combined with ultraviolet light therapies to restore pigment to the skin. This available phototherapy treatment for vitiligo is called Narrowband UVB. I don't know if Michael ever tried this treatment (though Dr Klein below suggests that it may have been considered). However, Michael

---

[1700] Harvey Levin, TMZ Live Interview, November 5, 2009.
[1701] "Former Jackson Doctor Claims Michael 'Had Lethal Amounts of Demerol & Propofol'," **Access Hollywood** July 23, 2009.

did try to medically darken the blotches, i.e. *re*-pigmentize his skin. Dr. Richard Strick, one of the doctors appointed by the Santa Barbara District Attorney who performed the body search on Michael Jackson during the 1993 case reviewed Michael's medical records and testified:

> Michael had a disease vitiligo in which the pigment is lost and *attempts had been made to bring that pigment back* which had been unsuccessful so he tried to bleach it out so it would be one color.[1702]

But it categorically *was not* Michael Jackson who "tried to bleach it out."

> it was decided [in 1990] by his dermatologist, none other than Dr Arnold Klein, that the easiest way to treat the condition, rather than drugs and ultraviolet light treatments, was by using creams to make the darker spots fade so the pigments could be evened out across the body. The cream that Klein used on Jackson was Benoquin...[1703]

And as Dr. Klein admitted on Larry King Live, it was never Michael's decision to go white.

> KING: So let's clear up something. [Michael] was not someone desirous of being white?
>
> KLEIN: No. Michael was black. He was very proud of his black heritage. He changed the world for black people. We now have a black president.
>
> KING: So how do you treat vitiligo?
>
> KLEIN: Well, I mean there's certain treatments. *You have one choice where you can use certain drugs called* (INAUDIBLE) *and ultraviolet light treatments to try to make the white spots turn dark* or — his became so severe, that the easier way is to use certain creams that will make the dark spots turn light so you can even out the pigments totally.

[1702] https://www.youtube.com/watch?v=RTuvCalcgPw.
[1703] Matt Richards and Mark Langthorne, *83 Minutes: The Doctor, The Damage, and the Shocking Death of Michael Jackson* (London: Blink Publishing, 2015) 114.

KING: So *your* decision there was he would go light?

KLEIN: *Well, yes*, that's ultimately what the decision had to be, because there was too much vitiligo to deal with and...
.....

KING: How did you treat the vitiligo?

KLEIN: Well, we basically used creams that would even out the same color and *we destroyed the remaining pigment cells.*

KING: And did his color change a lot over the years?

KLEIN: No, because once we got — we got it more uniform, it remained stable. But you still had to treat it because once in a while — and he had to also be extraordinary careful with sun exposure because of a lot of things. And that's why he had the umbrellas all the time (INAUDIBLE) skin now.[1704]

Dr. Klein has been known to lie on Michael Jackson many times and even admitted to it (as we shall see), yet we unfortunately are forced to take his word here that Michael's vitiligo was so severe that the only real option was to go light rather than even out the dark skin. The "bleaching cream" that *Dr. Klein* put Michael on, Benoquin, not only lightens skin but *permanently removes pigment* and thus leaves the person "extremely sensitive to the sun."[1705] Thus Michael Jackson said in his 1996 VH1 interview: "I am totally completely allergic to the sun."[1706] A Black God *made* totally allergic to the sun?! Michael was *made allergic to the Life-Giving Sun by the same frenemy who drugged him unnecessarily and got him – no doubt deliberately – addicted.* If, as Debbie Rowe admitted, Dr. Klein "*was not* doing what was best for Michael" when he was drugging him, do we think Dr. Klein was doing what was best *for Michael* when he (Dr. Klein) was bleaching Michael white by *permanently destroying his pigment cells* (melanin = The Black God Molecule) and making Michael allergic to the sun? Hardly.

We have reason to believe that Michael Jackson regretted what was done to his appearance, including this skin

---

[1704] https://www.youtube.com/watch?v=2foESMQDBAY.
[1705] Madison Park, "In life of mysteries, Jackson's changed color baffled public," *CNN* July 8, 2009.
[1706] https://www.youtube.com/watch?v=E-YuS3UiDK4.

whitening.   Teddy Riley travelled with Michael on the *Dangerous* tour and said in **Rolling Stone** that during the *Dangerous* tour Michael spoke a lot about what was done to his face and his skin and Riley suggested that Michael indeed had regrets, saying: "I'm quite sure if Michael could have done it all over again, *he would not have done that.* But there's no turning back. Once you change your description, you can't turn back. You can't get your own face or your own skin back again."[1707]

VI.   *The Plot to Frame Michael Jackson. 1993*

In August 1993 while Michael Jackson was in London fighting his addiction to Dr. Klein's Demerol, back home in California the world woke up to *startling* news: an investigation has been launched of child molestation allegations against Michael Jackson. But the evidence is now clear and overwhelming that Michael Jackson was not guilty of those charges but was *framed* in 1993. Mary Fisher, senior writer at **GQ**, wrote a game-changing article in 1994 entitled, "Was Michael Jackson Framed?" She concludes

It is, of course, impossible to prove a negative—that is, prove that something didn't happen. But it is possible to take an in-depth look at the people who made the allegations against Jackson and thus gain insight into their character and motives. What emerges from such an examination, based on court documents, business records and scores of interviews, is a persuasive argument that Jackson molested no one and that he

---

[1707] Michael Goldberg, "Michael Jackson: The Making of 'The King of Pop'," **Rolling Stone** January 9, 1992.

himself may have been the victim of a well-conceived plan to extract money from him.[1708]

Who framed Michael Jackson? And *why*? We can actually go a long way in answering these critical questions.

THE PEDOPHILE AGENDA TARGETS MICHAEL JACKSON

Victor Gutierrez is a man who was *central* to the Set Up and Framing of Michael Jackson on bogus child molestation charges, both in 1993 and in 2005. Gutierrez is said to be the one man who has influenced the media reporting and probably

Victor Gutierrez

the formation of the allegations against Michael more than anyone else. According to anti-Michael Jackson journalist Maureen Orth of *Vanity Fair* the 2005 prosecution's case against Michael relied on Gutierrez's salacious and fraudulent 1996 book, *Michael Jackson Was My Lover: the secret diary of Jordy Chandler*. "Many of the witnesses who testified for the prosecution at Jackson's 2005 trial,

and on whom the prosecution's 'prior bad acts' case was mostly built, were people who had contact with Victor Gutierrez prior to selling their stories to the tabloids for money."[1709] Gutierrez features in almost every single allegation against Michael: "Every witness was through him, every victim was someone he had met at some point." Victor Gutierrez was deeply involved in crafting the pedophile narrative around Michael Jackson.

A free-lance journalist from Santiago, Chile, Gutierrez in his crusade against Michael Jackson actually served at least three different organizations who had targeted the singer: NAMBLA, the Los Angeles Police Department, and the F.B.I.

[1708] Mary A. Fisher, "Was Michael Jackson Framed: The Untold Story That Brought Down A Superstar" (The Original *GQ* Article) (2003) 1.
[1709] Linda-Raven woods, "The New Lynching of Michael Jackson: Dan Reed's *Leaving Neverland*, In Fact, Leave Blood on Many Hands," *Medium* February 27, 2019.

NAMBLA is the North American Man/Boy Association, a *pro-pedophilia* organization which "advocates sex between men and boys and cites ancient Greece to justify the practice."[1710] According to the F.B.I., at NAMBLA's "secret" conferences there takes place "networking for illicit activities" such as "trips abroad to abuse children."[1711] During November 7-9, 1986 NAMBLA held their conference (The 10th International Membership Conference) in Los Angeles. By Gutierrez's own admission he was in attendance.[1712]

According to Gutierrez it was at this 1986 NAMBLA conference that his mission came to him. He reports on discussions among the conference pedophiles about Michael Jackson. Michael's very public love of and surrounding by children, all very *innocent*, nevertheless gave those NAMBLA members hope *and an idea*: use a perverted caricature of Michael Jackson to *normalize their cause*. By "outing" Michael Jackson as, i.e. "converting" him into, a *pedophile* – a sexual lover of young boys – NAMBLA would have a celebrity poster-boy for their cause. "At the conference Gutierrez hears for the first time: 'Michael is one of us.' A pedophile. 'Jackson was treated like an idol there, as a hope for social acceptance.'"[1713] Gutierrez and his fellow pedophiles thought that, with the help of Michael Jackson's celebrity, "In a hundred years maybe such relationships will be socially accepted."

Gutierrez admits leaving that meeting with his mission clear: to "out" Michael Jackson as, not a "child molester" but a *pedophile* (pedophiles draw a strong distinction) like Gutierrez's fellow pedophiles at NAMBLA. For the next five years Gutierrez targeted Michael Jackson's Latin employees, ingratiating himself on them and planting seeds in their minds.

[1710] Onell R. Soto, "FBI Targets Pedophilia Advocates. Little-Known Group Promotes 'Benevolent' Sex," **San Diego Union-Tribune** February 18, 2005.

[1711] Onell R. Soto, "FBI Targets Pedophilia Advocates. Little-Known Group Promotes 'Benevolent' Sex," **San Diego Union-Tribune** February 18, 2005.

[1712] Robert Sandall, "Michael Jackson Was My Lover" **GQ Magazine** September 2006; Henning Kober, "Es war Liebe!" **Die Tageszeitung**, April 5, 2005 @ http://www.taz.de/1/archiv/?id=archivseite&dig=2005/04/05/a0170

[1713] Robert Sandall, "Michael Jackson Was My Lover" **GQ Magazine** September 2006.

He "Interviews" boys who had been around Michael. As is clear from his book, Gutierrez's modus operandi was to approach persons and *give them the idea* that Michael had these relations with boys and then invites the person to "add to" his information.

In this NAMBLA-inspired mission against Michael Jackson Gutierrez had some relationship with the LAPD as far back as 1986 and that relationship would be critical for the 1993 Set Up and "investigation" of the false charges. In his coverage of Victor Gutierrez for **GQ Magazine** in 2006 Robert Sandall makes the important revelation (mostly mis-read by Michael Jackson Fan commentators): "Gutierrez began his investigation [of Michael Jackson] in 1986 *when he went undercover with the LAPD.*"[1714] Gutierrez would thus send investigative reports to the LAPD, he admits.[1715] The LAPD would supply Gutierrez with legal documents, and the LAPD admitted to relying on Gutierrez's "original manuscript," which he sent them, after the Chandler allegations were publicized in 1993.[1716] This is why in his book, along with NAMBLA, Gutierrez thanks for their assistance "detectives of the Sheriff's Department of Santa Barbara" and "officials and detectives of the Child Abuse Unit of the LAPD." Gutierrez also thanked the F.B.I. How did they assist? Paulina Toro writing in the Spanish language periodical *El Universal* affirmed in 2005: "When no one imagined that Michael Jackson could have deviant sexual relations with boys, FBI agents gave journalist Victor Gutierrez a list of famous pedophiles in Los Angeles. Among them was Jackson's name."[1717] LAPD documents further suggest a relationship between the F.B.I. and Gutierrez. So these three institutions – NAMBLA, the LAPD and the FBI – all demonstrated an interest as far back as 1986 in (falsely) tagging Michael Jackson as a pedophile and they all relied upon this man Victor Gutierrez to deliver.

[1714] Robert Sandall, "Michael Jackson Was My Lover" *GQ Magazine* September 2006.

[1715] Robert Sandall, "Michael Jackson Was My Lover" *GQ Magazine* September 2006. He says he provided a copy of his book "after the first phase of his research."

[1716] Robert Sandall, "Michael Jackson Was My Lover" *GQ Magazine* September 2006.

[1717] Paulina Toro, "Victor Gutierrez, Bashir advisor," *El Universal* March 19, 2005.

We know that NAMBLA's interest was in using in their cause to normalize pedophilia a fabricated "pedophile Michael Jackson". Victor Gutierrez's book, *Michael Jackson Was My Lover*, presents the false sexual relationship between Michael Jackson and the first accuser, the 13-year old Jordan Chandler, as a consensual, loving, sexual relationship. And as Linda-Raven Woods writing for *Medium* pointed out:

> [The book] was, as it turned out, little more than a piece of NAMBLA propaganda, written with the intent of promoting man/boy love, with the added spice of throwing in the name Michael Jackson. What was even more disturbing was the fact that Gutierrez and the boy's father, Evan Chandler, obviously collaborated on the project...[1718]

In April 2005 Victor Gutierrez was interviewed by the German pro-pedophilia periodical *Tageszeitung*. The name of the article is "Es War Liebe!" "It Was Love!", referring to the alleged relationship between Michael Jackson and Jordan Chandler.[1719]

What was the LAPD and the FBI's interest in fabricating a pedophile Michael Jackson? We don't know, but we have good grounds to speculate: a fabricated and falsely charged "pedophile Michael Jackson" could be used to *distract attention from Hollywood's* **true pedophiles who were protected by the LAPD!** For example, Hollywood gay pornography figure-turned-celebrity sleuth who (like Victor Gutierrez) made money selling celebrity dirt to tabloids, Paul Barresi, once assisted the LAPD (as did Gutierrez) uncover a male prostitution ring. The investigation was derailed because, according to Barresi, "they [the LAPD] didn't want to touch [a high-ranking member of the Velvet Mafia, Hollywood's cadre of gay moguls]."[1720] That derailed investigation was likely the one that involved David Forest, a pal of David Geffen, who was arrested in November 1993 for running a male prostitution ring

---

[1718] Linda-Raven woods, "The New Lynching of Michael Jackson: Dan Reed's *Leaving Neverland*, In Fact, Leave Blood on Many Hands," *Medium* February 27, 2019.

[1719] Henning Kober, "Es war Liebe!" *Die Tageszeitung*, April 5, 2005 @ http://www.taz.de/1/archiv/?id=archivseite&dig=2005/04/05/a0170

[1720] Breitbart and Ebner, *Hollywood, Interrupted*, 172

in Los Angeles.[1721] According to Barresi – who assisted the LAPD in this case - Detective Keith Haight affirmed that Geffen's name was on the client list of Forest's escort service. Haight reportedly told Barresi that Geffen's name will not be used as evidence during any trial because "We don't wanna touch Geffen."[1722] According to Geffen's mysteriously deceased biographer Tom King, Geffen frequently engaged male prostitutes.[1723] Paul Barresi has been associated with John Travolta and David Geffen.[1724] According to Mark Ebner Barresi was once David Geffen's personal trainer.[1725] This male prostitution ring that was uncovered by the LAPD and was linked to David Geffen through his pal David Forest came to light in 1993 and was derailed. 1993 was the year the first false charges of child sexual abuse were leveled against Michael Jackson.

"LET'S GET RID OF MICHAEL JACKSON"

Chandler: "it could be a massacre if I don't get what I want...

"once I make that phone call, this guy's just going to destroy everybody in site in any devious,
nasty, cruel way that he can do it. And I've given him full authority to do that...

"If I go through with this, I win big time. There's no way that I lose. I've checked that out inside out...I will get everything I want, and they will be totally — they will be destroyed forever. They will be destroyed. June is gonna lose Jordy. She will have no right to ever see him again...Michael's career will be over.

[1721] See "David Forest Obituary" *Los Angeles Times* @ https://www.legacy.com/obituaries/latimes/obituary.aspx?n=david-forest&pid=175753794&fhid=20193.
[1722] See "David Forest Obituary" *Los Angeles Times* @ https://www.legacy.com/obituaries/latimes/obituary.aspx?n=david-forest&pid=175753794&fhid=20193.
[1723] Tom King, *The Operator: David Geffen Builds, Buys, and Sells The New Hollywood* (New York: Broadway Books, 2000) 321.
[1724] Andrew Breitbart and Mark Ebner, *Hollywood, Interrupted. Insanity Chic in Babylon-The Case Against Celebrity* (New Jersey: John Wiley & Sons, Inc., 2004) 170.
[1725] Ebner, "The Gay Mafia," 48.

Schwartz: "And does that help Jordy?"

Chandler: "It's irrelevant to me."
...

Chandler: "Michael Jackson — Michael Jackson's career, Dave. This man is gonna be humiliated beyond belief. You'll not believe it. He will not believe what's going to happen to him...Beyond his worst nightmares. [tape irregularity] not sell one more record..."

Schwartz: "I would do anything for Jordy. I would lose everything. I would die for Jordy. That's the bottom line.

Chandler: "Then why don't you just back me up right now and let's get rid of Michael Jackson."

These various excerpts are from three secretly taped phone calls between Evan Chandler, the father of the first Michael Jackson accuser in 1993, and David Schwartz, the accuser's stepfather. These calls were recorded on July 8, 1993. At this time the 13-year old accuser, Jordan Chandler, had denied that any sexual relationship existed between he and Michael Jackson and Evan Chandler himself in these very calls admits to having no knowledge of such abuse or activity.

> **Schwartz:** I mean, do you think that he's fucking him?
> **Chandler:** I don't know. I have no idea.

Why would this man want to "get rid of Michael Jackson" so much that he would frame him and set him up with false charges of molesting his son, while the potential damage that this could do (and did do) to his son was "irrelevant" to him? Two words: jealousy and money. And when you add to that the manipulations of Victor Gutierrez and the Pedophile Agenda, you have the recipe for one of the greatest social, legal, and cultural crimes of the century: the false child molestation allegations against Michael Jackson and his consequent cultural lynching or, better, crucifixion.

Evan Chandler was born Evan Robert Charmatz in the Bronx to Jewish parents. He changed his name from Charmatz to Chandler because he thought Charmatz was "too Jewish-sounding". He had been divorced from his son Jordan's mother,

June, since 1985 and she had remarried David Schwartz. In 1993, however, June and David were estranged and living separately. Evan and David seem to have had some sort of comradery at the time, even while Evan and June were in the middle of a bitter custody dispute over Jordan. By the time Michael entered their lives in May 1992 Evan owed June nearly $70,000 in back child support. And, reportedly, Evan was bipolar. Michael had no idea of the level of family and human dysfunction he was stepping into.

At first Evan was proud of his son's friendship with the biggest superstar on the planet, Michael Jackson. He bragged to his colleagues. But as the media got wind of Michael's new friends, trouble started. When the **National Enquirer** in May 1993 presented June, Jordan and David's daughter Lili as Michael Jackson's "secret family" and humiliated David, things changed. When Evan started "acting weird" and *entitled* to Michael, apparently Michael "fell back" from Evan Chandler and Evan clearly felt some type of way.

Chandler to Schwartz: "I had a good communication with Michael. We were friends. I liked him and I respected him and everything else for what he is. There was no reason why he had to stop calling me."

Add to this Evan's ambition and his expectations from his son's superstar friend. Evan Chandler was a Hollywood dentist with celebrity patients such a Carrie Fisher. He hated being a dentist, however, and had a big dream of being a Hollywood screenwriter. He expected Michael Jackson to finance his career as a Hollywood screenwriter. Michael Jackson had a film production company "Lost Boys Production" that Sony invested $40 million in. Evan Chandler, having known Michael himself for only a short while, expected Michael to make him a partner in the company, worth $20 million. As the *Los Angeles Times* reported: "Film industry sources have said that the boy's father sought a $20-million movie production and financing deal with Jackson."[1726] This is corroborated by painter David Nordahl, who revealed in his 2010 interview with Deborah L. Kunesh:

> I was working on sketches for his film production company, called "Lost Boys Productions"....Sony had given him (Michael) $40 million to start this production company and that little boy's dad (Evan Chandler), who considered himself to be show business material, because he had written part of a script....after that he considered himself a Hollywood screenwriter, and being friends with Michael and his son being friends with Michael, this guy had assumed that Michael was going to make him a partner in this film production company and that's where the $20 million figure came from. He wanted ½ of that Sony money. It was proven. It was an extortion.[1727]

[1726] Charles P. Wallace and Jim Newton, "Jackson Back n Stage; Inquiry Continues: Investigation: Singer resumes Bangkok concerts after two-day absence. Officials here are now looking into extortion claims," *Los Angeles Times* August 28, 1993.
[1727] Deborah L. Kunesh, "Friendship & A Paintbrush," (2010) http://www.reflectionsonthedance.com/interviewwithdavidnordahl.html

Evan Chandler and his attorney attempted to force Michael Jackson to set him up with four film projects, $5 million per year for four years or he will go public with child molestation allegations, even though "The boy repeatedly denied that anything had happened."[1728] When Michael's team refused, Evan Chandler was furious.

> Instead of making any report to the police for what supposedly happened to his son, [Evan Chandler] arranged a meeting with Michael and his attorneys to discuss movie deals. The father initially asked for funding for four movies, at $5 million each, a total of $20 million. This was refused by the Jackson camp and a counter-offer of $350,000 for one movie was made. After considering it, Chandler refused...According to [Private Investigator Anthony] Pellicano, the one picture deal was refused because it wasn't enough for Chandler to shut down his dental practice and focus on writing screenplays full time.[1729]

This is what Evan meant in his secretly recorded phone conversation with David Schwartz on July 8th: "it could be a massacre if I don't get *what I want*." But the plan to set up and frame Michael Jackson actually was *not Evan's*. He was a player, but he said: "I've been told what to do and I have to do it."

> **Chandler to Schwartz:** "There are other people involved that are waiting for my phone call that are intentionally going to be in certain positions – [tape irregularity]. I paid them to do it. They're doing their job. I gotta just go ahead and follow through on the time zone. I mean the time set out. Everything is going *according to a certain plan that isn't just mine. There's other people involved.*"

> "*My instructions* were to kill and destroy [tape irregularity], I'm telling you. I mean, and by killing and destroying, I'm going to torture them, Dave...

[1728] Mary A. Fisher, "Was Michael Jackson Framed: The Untold Story That Brought Down A Superstar" (The Original **GQ** Article) (2003) 13.
[1729] Campbell, **Michael Jackson**, 55.

"It's going to be bigger than all of us put together. The whole thing is going to crash down on everybody and destroy everybody in sight. It will be a massacre if I don't get what I want."

Clearly, by his own admission Evan Chandler's plot to frame and extort Michael Jackson involved other people higher up than him. Of course, a key figure here is the one whom Evan described as "the nastiest son of a bitch"; the guy who, on Evan's and the "other people's" behalf planned to "destroy everybody in site in any devious, nasty, cruel way that he can do it." That one is Attorney Barry K. Rothman. A New York Jew who graduated from UCLA and practiced entertainment law in Hollywood, there is no way this "nastiest so of a bitch" did not cross paths with David Geffen and his circle. Rothman had a buddy, a dental anesthesiologist named Mark Torbiner (= a Jewish surname). Rothman, who on at least eight occasions had been given a general anesthetic by Torbiner during hair-transplant procedures, introduced him to Evan Chandler in 1991.[1730] These three allegedly were the nucleus of the operationalization of the plot to frame Michael Jackson.

Barry Rothman   Evan Chandler   Mark Torbiner

[1730] Mary A. Fisher, "Was Michael Jackson Framed: The Untold Story That Brought Down A Superstar" (The Original *GQ* Article) (2003) 16.

During Rothman's involvement in the Chandler case Geraldine Hughes was Rothman's sole legal secretary. She literally was *witness* to the conspiracy as it unfolded *in her attorney's office*.[1731] She reports the attorney's *coaching* the 13-year old boy secretly in his office.

> I really believe that the whole thing was plotted and planned and the words were given to him [Jordan Chandler] to say because I actually witnessed the 13 year old in my attorney's office without any supervision of his parents and he was kind of snuck in there, it was like no one in the office knew he was in there. He was behind closed doors with my attorney for several hours, and I kind of believe that is where he was being told what to say... everything that they were doing was part of a plan. It was already mapped out, it was planned out. They even mapped out the part about how it was going to be reported...The way they plotted it was that he was supposed to go talk to a psychiatrist and that's where he would tell the psychiatrist the different things that he told him, and the psychiatrist would be the one that reported it because he's a credible cohort. He's somebody that nobody is going to question and he's a mandated reporter.

> I typed the letter to the father where the attorney was telling him how to report it using a third party. I remember typing the short letter. He typed him a letter and he sent him some information on child molestation being reported through a psychiatrist, so he was informing the father how to go about it and that was his plan. So he was literally just making him feel comfortable, making him so he felt okay with it, giving him some articles, we sent him some newspapers, something we sent along with it. But I remember when I typed that letter, I said, "Why are you writing him telling him?" I said if anybody has got a suspicion of child molestation, all he has to do is pick up the telephone. You

---

[1731] Geraldine Hughes, **Redemption: The Truth Behind the Michael Jackson Child Molestation Allegations** Radford, VA: Branch & Vine Publishers, LLC, 2004).

don't have to plot and plan and take him to a psychiatrist because nobody else has the credibility to report it.[1732]

"THERE'S OTHER PEOPLE INVOLVED": THE PEDOPHILES APPROACH

From the three secretly recorded calls between Evan Chandler and Dave Schwartz on July 8, 1993, it is clear that Evan chandler *had no suspicions whatsoever* regarding the (legal) appropriateness of Michael and Jordan's relationship. As he admitted, he had "no idea" of any sexual activity. June Chandler, who always accompanied Jordan and Michael, insisted there was nothing inappropriate taking place (until she later flipped for money). But there were *outside* people who, after the tabloids shinned a light on the family and their relationship to Michael Jackson, approached Evan and *convinced him* that there was something sexual going on in the Michael Jackson-Jordan Chandler relationship. Evan said he resisted their suggestions (because he knew better), but ultimately they "opened his eyes." These people planted seeds into Evan's already troubled mind about Michael and they manipulated his thinking about his son's relationship with the star.

> **Chandler:** Everybody agrees with that. I mean, they — *it's their opinions that have convinced me to not stay away.* You know, I'm not confrontational. I've got an [tape irregularity] inclination to do what you do, say, "Okay. Go fuck yourself. Go do what you want to do, and, you know, call me some day. I'll see you then. I got a [tape irregularity]," but I've been so convinced by professional opinions that I have been negligent in not stepping in sooner that now it's made me insane. Now I actually feel [tape irregularity] –
> ...

[1732] Deborah L. Kunesh, "A Witness To Extortion...: An Exclusive, In-Depth Interview with author Geraldine Hughes, sharing the truth behind the Michael Jackson 1993 Child Molestation Allegations," @ http://www.reflectionsonthedance.com/Interview-with-Geraldine-Hughes.html.

Chandler: In fact, in their opinion I have been negligent not to put a stop to [tape irregularity] opinion. *I happen to agree with them now. I didn't agree with them at first...I didn't even want to know about it...*I kept saying, "No, this is okay. There's nothing wrong. This is great." It took experts to convince me [tape irregularity] that by not taking action my son was going to be irreparably damaged for the rest of his life [tape irregularity]. That was what I heard.

Schwartz: Because his friend is older, or because of all the seduction?

Chandler: Well, you know, *age in and of itself is not a harmful thing.*

Schwartz: Yeah.

Chandler: But it could have been used to advantage, and in some ways Michael is using his age and experience and his money and his power to great advantage to Jordy. The problem is he's also harming him, greatly harming him, for his own selfish reasons. He's not the altruistic, kind human being that he appears to be...

Chandler: — and that's not my opinion. I mean, I happen to be believe it now because my eyes have been opened but I'm not the one that first [tape irregularity], so what I'm saying to you is that I'm acting because [tape irregularity] I'm going to cause him great harm, and you tell me if maybe it's gonna cause him harm right now. I think he'll be harmed much greater if I do nothing, and besides now I'm convinced that if I do nothing I'm going to be, from doing nothing, causing him harm, and I couldn't...I'm just trying to do what I have been led to believe is the right action to take so that he's not harmed.

Who are these people, these "professionals" and "experts" who opened Evan's eyes to the true nature of his 13-year old son's relationship with Michael Jackson? They certainly are not psychiatric professionals because, according to Evan's loyal brother Raymond Chandler in his book co-authored by Evan (***All That Glitters***) it is stated that, at this point Evan *had not* contacted any psychologist, psychiatrist or therapist. On the other hand, at least one of the "professionals" who approached Evan during this period was certainly Victor Gutierrez. And it was no doubt Gutierrez who planted the seed in Evan's mind of a "sexual relationship." Gutierrez admits that the Chandlers were given his attention when they began appearing in the media, around April and May 1993.

> It is known fact that Gutierrez actually knew and consulted with Evan Chandler, at just about the same time that Chandler was growing disgruntled with Jackson's lack of "cooperation" in funding his projects and had grown increasingly jealous of Jackson's relationship with his ex-wife June, son Jordan, and daughter Lily.[1733]

Evan's view was that his son's relationship with Michael "was great" and there was "nothing wrong." But we see in April the effects of the seeds that were dropped in Evan's mind even though he didn't meet Michael Jackson himself for the first time until May 20, 1993. Evan Chandler knew that one of his celebrity patients, Carrie Fisher ("Princess Leah" of *Star Wars*) was close friends with Dr. Arnold Klein. According to Evan Chandler on April 16, while he was giving Carrie Fisher a ride home Evan had her call Arnold Klein on his car phone and ask him about Michael Jackson's sexuality. Dr. Klein affirmed that Michael is "perfectly straight," "absolutely heterosexual."[1734] Dr. Klein and Victor Gutierrez had clearly not yet been in sync. Evan did not stop there, because I'm sure his "handlers" did not allow him to stop at Dr. Klein's testimony. So something very evil took place, as reported by both Randy/Evan Chandler and Victor Gutierrez.

Evan Chandler met Michael Jackson for the first time on May 20th. On May 21th he claims to have confronted Michael with the question: "Are you fucking my son in the ass?" Notice the wording?! Not, "are you sexually abusing my child?" Evan's

---

[1733] Linda-Raven woods, "The New Lynching of Michael Jackson: Dan Reed's *Leaving Neverland*, In Fact, Leave Blood on Many Hands," *Medium* February 27, 2019.
[1734] Diane Dimond, Be Careful Who You Love: Inside the Michael Jackson Case (New York: Atria, 2005) 51; J. Randy Taraborrelli, **Michael Jackson: The Magic, The Madness, The Whole Story, 1958-2009** (Grand Central Publishing, 2009) 465-467.

language reflects the perspective *of the pedophiles*! This is further confirmed by what allegedly happened next, on May 28th while Michael and Jordan were visiting Evan for Memorial Day weekend. Evan said to his son: "Hey Jordie, are you and Michael doin' it?" Jordan responded: "That's disgusting! I'm not into that!" To which Evan replied: "Just kidding."[1735] This is remarkable, if true. Again, Evan does not in any way frame his question in the context of sexual abuse, for example "Is Michael molesting you?!" or "Is Michael touching you?" etc. Rather, Evan's language reflects his thoughts of possible sexual relations between a grown man and his 13-year old son *as consensual*: "Are you and Michael doin' it?" Wow. This is *strong* evidence of the influence of the pedophile's perspective, like that of NAMBLA and Victor Gutierrez. According to Evan, Jordan was "repulsed" by his father's suggestion.

Still not satisfied, Evan Chandler takes his inquisition to a devilish low. The next day, May 29th, Michael complained about a headache. According to the account of Evan's brother Raymond, Evan

> called Mark Torbiner for advice. The anesthesiologist suggested an injection of Toradol, a non-narcotic equivalent to Demerol, and offered to pick some up at Evan's office and bring it to his house.

> Evan injected 30mg, half the maximum dose, *into Michael's gluteus*. But one hour later the star claimed he was still in a lot of pain, so Evan administered the remaining half and instructed him to lie down and try to relax.

> "Keep an eye on him," Evan told Jordie. "It'll take a few minutes to kick in. I'll be right back."

> "When I went back to check on him, maybe ten minutes later," Evan recalled, *"He was acting weird, babbling incoherently and slurring is speech.* Toradol is a pretty safe drug, and I thought that either he was having a rare reaction or had taken another drug and was having a combination reaction."

[1735] Raymond Chandler, **All That Glitters: The Crime and the Cover-Up** (Windsong Press, Ltd., 2004) 46.

Other than *the drunk-like symptoms*, Michael's pulse and respirations were normal and he appeared to be in no real danger. So Evan took no further action.

But Jordie was scared. He had seen his friend "acting strange" before, but never like this.

"Don't worry," Evan assured his son, "Right now Michael's the happiest person in the world. All we need to do is keep him awake and talking until the drug wears off."

Four hours and a serious case of cottonmouth later, Michael began to sober up. While Jordie was downstairs fetching water, *Evan decided to take advantage of Michael's still uninhibited but somewhat coherent condition.* "Hey, Mike, I was just wondering...I mean, I don't care either way, but I know some of your closest people are gay, and *I was wondering if you're gay too*?"

"You'd be surprised about a lot of people in this town," Michael mumbled, as he rattled off the names of a few prominent Hollywood players who were still in the closet.

Evan tried to get back on track before Jordie returned. *He stroked Michael's hair* and reassured him, "I don't care if you're gay, Mike. I just want you to know you can tell me if you are."

"Uh-uh", Michael slurred. "Not me."

Given Michael's willingness to talk openly about everyone else's sexuality, *his consistent denial about being gay reinforced Evan's belief that the singer was asexual.*[1736]

There is a lot here, even though the full account as presented by Raymond Chandler is disingenuous at parts. Because Michael, who has spent the night at Evan's house with Jordan, complains of a headache, Evan calls his and Barry Rothman's anesthesiologist friend Mark, who comes over and drugs

---

[1736] Raymond Chandler, ***All That Glitters*** 46-49.

Michael with an injection in his buttocks. Raymond claims the drug was Toradol, a non-steroid anti-inflammatory drug. But this can't be true. According to medical personnel Toradol does not produce the effects described: Michael babbled incoherently and had slurred speech, with drunk-like symptoms that lasted four hours. That was not Toradol. Evan all but admits this when he assures Jordan: "Don't worry, *right now Michael's the happiest person in the world.*" They doped Michael, clearly. The actress Carrie Fisher, Evan's celebrity patient, noted in her autobiography entitled **Shockaholic** that both Evan Chandler and Mark Torbiner were two shady Hollywood doctors who abused medications. At one time, according to journalist Mary Fischer, the U.S. Drug Enforcement Administration probed Torbiner's practice under the suspicion he inappropriately administered drugs during paid house calls.[1737]

Once Evan and Torbiner has Michael nice and doped up, they "take advantage of Michael's still uninhibited but somewhat coherent condition" by probing him about being gay. We can discern here the preoccupation of Victor Gutierrez and the Pedophile Agenda, because Evan presented himself as having a different personal viewpoint:

> **Chandler:** [tape irregularity] I mean, I'm young, I'm really liberal. As far as I'm concerned, anybody could do anything they want. That's my philosophy. You guys can do whatever you want. Just be happy. Don't get hurt. So...

But Michael clears that up: "Not me."

That was May 29th. By July 8th, the day of the three secretly recorded phone calls, we know that the "certain plan" by a group of people including Evan Chandler to "get rid of Michael Jackson" by "destroying" him, "humiliating him beyond his worst nightmare" was already operationalized to some extant: "**Chandler:** Because the thing's already — the thing has already been set in motion...it's out of my hands. I do nothing else again...I'm not even in contact anymore." And then July 16th happens. The boy Jordan and his father with Torbiner is drugged.

[1737] Fischer, **Was Michael Jackson Framed?** 18.

In the presence of Chandler and Mark Torbiner, a dental anesthesiologist, the boy [Jordan Chandler] was administered the controversial drug *sodium Amytal*—which some mistakenly believe is a truth serum. And it was after this session that the boy first made his charges against Jackson. A newsman at KCBS-TV, in L.A., reported on May 3 of this year [1994] that Chandler had used the drug on his son, but the dentist claimed he did so only to pull his son's tooth and that while under the drug's influence, the boy came out with allegations. Asked for this article about his use of the drug on the boy, Torbiner replied: "If I used it, it was for dental purposes."[1738]

Claiming he was sedating his son in order to pull a baby tooth, Evan injected Jordan with sodium amytal. Why is this significant?

"It's a psychiatric medication that cannot be relied on to produce fact," says Dr. Resnick, the Cleveland psychiatrist. "People are very suggestible under it. People will say things under sodium Amytal that are blatantly untrue." Sodium Amytal is a barbiturate, an invasive drug that puts people *in a hypnotic state when it's injected intravenously*...Scientific studies done in 1952 debunked the drug as a truth serum and instead demonstrated its risks: False memories can be easily implanted in those under its influence. "It is quite possible to implant an idea *through the mere asking of a question*," says Resnick. But its effects are apparently even more insidious: *"The idea can become their memory, and studies have shown that even when you tell them the truth, they will swear on a stack of Bibles that it happened,"* says Resnick.[1739]

Thus, Evan confesses that after he drugged his son with sodium amytal: "When Jordie came out of the sedation *I asked him to tell me about Michael and him.*"[1740] And Evan says to Jordan, oddly: "Look, Jordie, lots of famous

---

[1738] Mary A. Fisher, "Was Michael Jackson Framed: The Untold Story That Brought Down A Superstar" (The Original **GQ** Article) (2003) 16.
[1739] Mary A. Fisher, "Was Michael Jackson Framed: The Untold Story That Brought Down A Superstar" (The Original **GQ** Article) (2003) 16.
[1740] Diane Dimond, **Be Careful Who You Love**, 60.

people are bisexual and nobody gives a shit. They're not embarrassed. It's sorta cool, in a way." Huh? Evan is still presenting the idea of a sexual encounter between Michael Jackson and his 13-year old son as a simply matter of "bisexuality," which, he says, is sorta cool. These were apparently enough seeds planted for the drugged Jordan, who now for the first time "confesses" that Michael touched him sexually. Before this drugging, "The boy repeatedly denied that anything had happened."[1741] However, after being injected by his father with a drug that can induce false confessions by the mere asking of certain questions, Jordan for the first time allegedly confessed that Michael "touched" him, according to Raymond Chandler's account. Scott Lilienfeld writes in *Psychology Today*

> So what crucial fact has most of the press coverage omitted? It's that Jordan Chandler apparently never made any accusations against Jackson until his father, a registered dentist, gave him sodium amytal during a tooth extraction. Only then did Jackson's purported sexual abuse emerge; Jordan Chandler's reports became more elaborate and embellished during a later session with a psychiatrist.

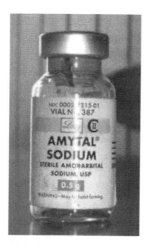

> Sodium amytal is a barbiturate and one of the most commonly used variants of what is popularly known as "truth serum," a spectacular misnomer. There's no scientific evidence that sodium amytal or other supposed truth serums increase the accuracy of memories. To the contrary, as psychiatrist August Piper has observed, there's good reason to believe that truth serums merely lower the threshold for reporting virtually all information, both true and false. As a consequence, like other suggestive therapeutic procedures, such as

[1741] Mary A. Fisher, "Was Michael Jackson Framed: The Untold Story That Brought Down A Superstar" (The Original *GQ* Article) (2003) 13.

guided imagery, repeated prompting, hypnosis, and journaling, truth serums can actually increase the risk of false memories—memories of events that never occurred, but are held with great conviction."[1742]

We know that subsequently Victor Gutierrez was personally meeting with Jordan Chandler, according to his admission.[1743] During the police investigation of the case, Gutierrez was one of the first people the LAPD "interviewed," and they did so for several hours over two days.

During the early stages of the Chandler investigation, Gutierrez "spoke to LAPD officers for two hours on Thursday and was interviewed again on Friday." "He would not disclose what transpired during those sessions, but he told The Times that he has interviewed for his book some of the same youngsters being sought for questioning by the LAPD."[1744]

In other words, Victor Gutierrez and the Pedophile Agenda's fingerprints are *all over this case.*

THE SHAM INVESTIGATION

The investigation of the Chandler case was launched in August and by November neither the Santa Barbara nor the Los Angeles police departments found *any corroborating evidence* to support Jordan Chandler's *drug-induced* allegation. This frustrated the authorities.

Police ended up confiscating a total of fifty boxes filled with photographs, notebooks, files, and documents and

[1742] Scott Lilienfeld, "Michael Jackson, Truth Serum, and False Memories," **Psychology Today** July 7, 2009.

[1743] Robert Sandall, "Michael Jackson Was My Lover" **GQ Magazine** September 2006:"Thanks to the intervention of someone he will only identify as 'a very good source within the house', Gutierrez was able to arrange meetings with Jordie while the terms of the legal settlement were being hammered out."

[1744] Charles P. Wallace and Jim Newton, "Jackson Back n Stage; Inquiry Continues: Investigation: Singer resumes Bangkok concerts after two-day absence. Officials here are now looking into extortion claims," **Los Angeles Times** Augus 28, 1993.

broke into a safe belonging to the star...*The police had reached a dead end in their investigation.* They had failed to turn up any evidence to corroborate Jordan Chandler's claims. [1745]

The smoking gun which the Santa Barbara D.A. Tom Sneddon desperately desired had eluded him. Then on November 19, 1993 it was delivered to him – or so he thought. And it was Dr. Arnold Klein who willingly handed it to him. On that day

Sergeant Deborah Linden of the Santa Barbara County Sheriff's Department tried to serve a search warrant on Dr. Klein's Beverly Hills office looking for Michael Jackson's medical records, which had been *removed from the premises* by Klein. Nevertheless, Sergeant Linden "spoke with Dr. Klein" and apparently Debbi Rowe, his nurse assistant.[1746] Dr. Klein offered Sergeant Linden some of Michael's medical information which Tom Sneddon and the Santa Barbara police used to make Michael Jackson endure "the most humiliating ordeal" of his life, a "horrifying nightmare":

Sergeant Deborah Linden

the shameful body search of December 20, 1993.

In the Spring (April or May) of 1993, Michael reportedly attempted to use the cream Benoquin on his scrotum and ended up causing some burning. Michael called Dr. Klein and told him, and Klein had Debbie Rowe tend to him.[1747] Klein shared this information with Sergeant Linden while she "spoke with" him on November 19, 1993 during the service of the search warrant.[1748] In addition, Debbie Rowe said that because she

---

[1745] Ian Halperin, **Unmasked: The Final Years of Michael Jackson**.

[1746] "Jackson Doc Hid Medical Records, Deputy Says," **TMZ** July 13, 2009.

[1747] J. Randy Taraborrelli, **Michael Jackson: The Magic, The Madness, The Whole Story, 1958-2009** XXX; Seal, "The Doctor Will Sue You Now."

[1748] Orth, **The Importance of Being Famous**: "according to the affidavit, in April or May 1993... 'Jackson told Dr. Klein that he had gotten Benoquin on his genitals and it burned. Dr. Klein told Jackson

gave Michael massages to help him sleep "she could identify any markings on his buttocks".[1749] The real reason Dr. Klein's nurse assistant could identify markings on Michael Jackson's buttocks is because, according to medical and police records, she gave Michael "repeated injections of Demerol" in his buttocks in 1993, creating the scars.[1750] These medical revelations were then put in a sworn affidavit signed by Sergeant Linden and known as the "Linden Affidavit." Interestingly, in this "Linden Affidavit" these medical revelations of Klein and Rowe appear with *alleged descriptions by Jordan Chandler of distinctive marks on Michael's genitals and buttocks!* However, Jordan specifically admitted to Private Investigator Anthony Pellicano on July 9, 1993 that *he never saw Michael's genital area or buttocks*:

> According to Pellicano, [Jordan] told him a lot in 45 minutes. "He's a very bright, articulate, intelligent, manipulative boy." Pellicano, who has fathered nine children by two wives, says he asked [Jordan] many sexually specific questions. "And I'm looking dead into his eyes. And I'm watching in his eyes for any sign of fear or anticipation—anything. And I see none," Pellicano says. "And I keep asking him, 'Did Michael ever touch you?' 'No.' *Did you ever see Michael nude?*' 'No.' He laughed about it. He giggled a lot, like it was a funny thing. *Michael would never be nude...* 'Did you and Michael ever masturbate?' 'No.' 'Did Michael ever masturbate in front of you?' 'No.' 'Did you guys ever talk about masturbation?' 'No.'

---

not to put Benoquin on his genitals." Emma Parry, "'He Did Not Deny It': Michael Jackson 'refused' to answer when asked: 'Are you f***ing my kid?' by first accuser Jordan Chandler's dad, police document reveals," **The Sun** February 15, 2019: "in an un-redacted section (of the affidavit), Jackson's doctors claim that the star suffered vitiligo, a disease which causes depigmentation of the skin, which gave him blotches and areas of discolouration on his body and legs. The same doctor - dermatologist Dr Arnold Klein also claimed that Jackson once put his vitiligo cream - which helps to even out the skin's colors - on his genitals, which "burned" them."

[1749] "Debbie Rowe Injected Jackson with Drugs," **TMZ** July 13, 2009.

[1750] Harvey Levin with Dr. Arnold Klein on TMZ Live, November 5, 2009.

"So you never saw Michael's body?" "One time, *he lifted up his shirt and he showed me those blotches.*"[1751]

Nevertheless, Tom Sneddon now had his "smoking gun" and the "Linden Affidavit" with its Klein and Rowe-derived information and its clearly manufactured or *coached* Jordan descriptions was the basis upon which court permission to "photograph Jackson's private parts" was secured.[1752] The result was a search warrant ordering officials to "search Jackson's body 'including his penis' – saying that the star had no 'right to refuse.'"[1753] That body search occurred on December 20, 1993.

Present during the profoundly intrusive procedure were police photographer Gary Spiegel, Michael's personal photographer Louis Swayne, the D.A.'s doctor Dr. Richard Strick, and Michael's dermatologist Dr. Arnold Klein. What is remarkable is that it *was Klein who gave Michael all of the instructions on behalf of the police department during this humiliating, nightmare procedure.* The D.A. photographer Gary Spiegel recalled in a declaration to the court:

> Dr. Klein made a statement [to Jackson] that we were interested in photographing Jackson's genital area *and directed Jackson* to stand and remove the robe he had on. Jackson protested, saying things like "What do I have to do that for?" and "Why are they doing this?" In my opinion, Jackson's demeanour was a combination of hostility and anger. Jackson complied with Dr. Klein's request...As Mr. Jackson was complying with Dr. Klein's request, Dr. Klein made the statement that others in the room should turn their heads so as not to view Jackson's genital area. At the time, I found this peculiar because the only persons in the room at the time were Mr. Jackson,

---

[1751] Mary A. Fisher, "Was Michael Jackson Framed: The Untold Story That Brought Down A Superstar" (The Original **GQ** Article) (2003) 13; Lisa D. Campbell, ***Michael Jackson: The King of Pop's Darkest Hour*** (Boston: Branden Publishing Company, Inc., 1194) 52; J. Randy Taraborrelli, ***Michael Jackson: The Magic, The Madness, The Whole Story, 1958-2009***.
[1752] "The Telltale 'Splotch,'" **the smoking gun** January 6, 2005.
[1753] Emma Parry, "'He Did Not Deny It': Michael Jackson 'refused' to answer when asked: 'Are you f***ing my kid?' by first accuser Jordan Chandler's dad, police document reveals," **The Sun** February 15, 2019.

the two doctors, me, and the other photographer. Dr. Klein also made a statement that he was not going to look. He said he had never seen Mr. Jackson's genital area and he was not going to do so at this time.[1754]

Klein's "peculiar" volunteering of the information that *he* never saw Michael's genital area seems to be a common theme of his during this case. During the grand jury that was impaneled in Santa Barbara he again voluntarily insisted "he had never seen" Michael's genital area.[1755] Such voluntary insistence is suspicious. We do know that it was Klein who gave the key information about genital discoloration in the Linden Affidavit which was the pretext for the humiliating body search. What's more, according to Santa Barbara Detective Russel Birchim's declaration to the court, at some point Michael Jackson struggled to leave the room where the body search was taking place *but Arnold Klein physically restrained him.* "Dr. Klein was successful in pulling Jackson back into the room and the door was once again closed,"[1756] so Michael Jackson's "horrifying nightmare" continued.

With all of this violation of Michael Jackson and the hope and excitement which DA Tom Sneddon placed in it, Sneddon *failed to get his smoking gun*! Why? Because as the **Los Angeles Times** reported Michael's appearance "does not match a description provided...by the alleged victim."[1757] In other words, with all of the assistance that Jordan Chandler had in describing Michael's private areas thanks to the tip that Arnold Klein offered, Jordan Chandler *still got it wrong.* For this reason, Tom Sneddon had no choice but to lobby for banning the body search photos from the trial.

With Tom Sneddon's "smoking gun" going up in smoke, the case had no foundation other than the uncorroborated word of a boy who first denied and then affirmed the allegations only *after being drugged.* Trial was scheduled to begin March 1994 and Michael Jackson no doubt would have won the case just as he did in 2005. However, Michael Jackson *was robbed* of his day in court. How? By his team of lawyers, who were friends

---

[1754] Dimond, **Be Careful Who You Love**, 14.

[1755] Taraborrelli, **Michael Jackson.**

[1756] Halperin, **Unmasked**, 72-73.

[1757] Jim Newton, "Grand Jury Calls Michael Jackson's Mother to Testify," **Los Angeles Times** March 16, 1994.

with his accusers' team of lawyers, settled the case with the Chandlers. It is reported that Michael never wanted to settle because he knew he could win in court, as he won in 2005.

By the time of the second child molestation case of 2005, during which Michael Jackson was *acquitted* and *exonerated*, Jordan Chandler had *confessed that he and his parents lied*. We learn this from Michael's 2005 attorney Thomas Mesereau, who spoke at Harvard on November 29, 2005 and revealed that, had the prosecution succeeded in forcing Jordan to testify in the new case, Mesereau had witnesses that were going to testify under oath that Jordan told them Michael Jackson *never* molested him. Mesereau said:

> Now the one you're talking about [Jordan Chandler] never showed up [to the 2005 case]. He's the one who got the settlement in the early 90s. And my understanding is prosecutors tried to get him to show up and he wouldn't. If he had, *I had witnesses who were going to come in and say he told them it never happened.* And that he would never talk to his parents again for what they made him say. And it turned out *he had gone into court and gotten legal emancipation from his parents.* His mother testified that she hadn't talked to him in 11 years.

One of Mesereau's listed potential witnesses was Josephine Zohny who attended New York University with Jordan Chandler. Zohny testifies that Jordan *openly* said Michael Jackson *was not capable of doing what his father (and later mother) accused him of*, and that his parents made him do things that he didn't want to do.[1758]

VII.   *Motive For Murder: The Billion Dollar Asset*

The Music Mafia is the tightknit group of predominantly Jewish and Italian New Yorkers who have controlled this business for decades. Some really are members of the official Mafia...Some are not. But in terms of running the music industry, these boys are a brethren. Outsiders (as well as women) aren't welcome in this clan...without a

---

[1758] "Square One: New Witness in Michael Jackson Case," 2019 Documentary   @
https://www.youtube.com/watch?v=ZxNDb2PVcoM.

fair understanding of Yiddish or Italian, there's no way to land a good job in music. The hit men who run the record labels, law firms, management companies and promotion agencies that steer the business may dislike -- even despise -- each other, but in the end they'd rather keep it all to themselves than allow access to newcomers.[1759]

In the 1980s Michael Jackson had an informal investment committee, a council of advisors, if you will, with which he met once every few months. The committee/council included music and movie mogul David Geffen, founder of **Ebony** John Johnson, and superlawyer John Branca, Michael's lawyer. "Had the organization been officially incorporated, it might have been called Michael Jackson, Inc."[1760] In 1985, against the objection of advisers such as David Geffen, Jackson instructed Branca to purchase ATV, the company which housed the prized music catalog of the Beatles. For $47.5 million Michael purchased ATV from Australian billionaire Robert Holmes à Court. This purchase made Michael Jackson one of the *best business minds in the industry.* By the time Michael Jackson died in 2009, the ATV catalog would be worth over $1 billion and some estimates have said $2 billion. Thus, this purchase *also* made Michael Jackson one of *the most marked men* in recent history.

The plot to separate Michael from this tremendously valuable asset started early. Mickey Schulhof, the CEO of Sony Corp. of America, had designs on the catalog. A brief visit once to Michael's Century City apartment — a fantasyland of overstuffed animals —convinced Schulhof that Sony's star singer someday would "spiral toward the poor house and be forced to sell everything," thereby allowing Sony to fully acquire Michael's catalog in the process.[1761]

That's always been Sony's dream scenario, full ownership. "But they don't want to do that [repossess

1759 Deborah Wilker, "Out From Under The Rock of the Music Business," **South Florida Sun-Sentinel** September 30, 1990.

1760 Zack O'Malley Greenburg, "Buying The Beatles: Inside Michael Jackson's Best Business Bet," **Forbes** June 2, 2014.

1761 Johnnie L. Roberts, "Fired, the Superlawyer Returns to Bail Jackson Out – for a Price," **The Wrap** December 8, 2010.

Michael's half of the catalog] as *they're afraid of a backlash from his fans.* Their nightmare is an organised "boycott Sony" movement worldwide, which could prove hugely costly. It is the only thing standing between Michael and bankruptcy."[1762]

If Michael's fan-base could be weakened – maybe by some widely publicized fabricated scandal, for example – Sony's fear of an organized "boycott Sony" movement could be allayed.

For years prior to the 1993 False Allegations Sony had been pressuring Michael to sell them his catalog but he refused. However, the False Allegations was the first step in helping Sony claw their way into full ownership. The consequences of the 1993 False Allegations put Michael in dire need of cash. He was making no money according to his lawyer John Branca.[1763] The child molestation scandal cost Michael $20 million (through his insurance company) in the private settlement. Michael owed promoters a fortune after having to suspend his world tour *due to his drugging by Dr. Arnold Klein.*[1764] So John Branca proposed his "brilliant idea" to Michael: sell half of your catalog to Sony through a merger and live off of the $150-million check. [1765] The circumstances forced Michael to sell half of his catalog *and take out loans.*

In August 1994 — five months after *Time* magazine reported Jackson had paid a multimillion-dollar settlement after a 14-year-old boy claimed he had molested him — the King of Pop signed loan papers with

---

[1762] Ian Halperin, " 'I'm better off dead. I'm done': Michael Jackson's fateful prediction just a week before his death," **Daily Mail** June 29 2009.

[1763] Pete Mills, "Sony exec claims Michael Jackson's 'image and likeness' worth less than a second-hand car," **Orchard Times** February 18, 2017.

[1764] Johnnie L. Roberts, "Fired, the Superlawyer Returns to Bail Jackson Out – for a Price," **The Wrap** December 8, 2010.

[1765] Johnnie L. Roberts, "Fired, the Superlawyer Returns to Bail Jackson Out – for a Price," **The Wrap** December 8, 2010; Pete Mills, "Sony exec claims Michael Jackson's 'image and likeness' worth less than a second-hand car," **Orchard Times** February 18, 2017.

Sony in which he used his catalog of songs to secure a loan. [1766]

But Sony would not stop there. The dream was for "full ownership" of Michael Jackson's most valuable asset. In 2002 Michael Jackson and Sony were embroiled in a nasty public dispute. Michael believed that Sony deliberately sabotaged the success of his **Invincible** album that was released in 2001. Sony *did* have something to gain by Michael's career failing: they hoped he would have to sell his share of the catalog and at a low price. During the height of the 2002 Michael Jackson vs. Sony standoff the press reported that Sony chief Tommy Mottola would *threaten to ruin Michael by destroying his career*: "I'll ruin you," he said to Michael on conference calls.[1767] As Roger Friedman of **Fox News** reported:

> The basis for all this (i.e., the threats)? "The Beatles catalog," says my source. "That's it in a nutshell. This has all been done by Tommy in an effort to squeeze Michael financially. Tommy wants the Beatles catalog."[1768]

It should also be noted that during the 1993 False Allegations a Mottola aide at the time recalled hearing Mottola bagger Michael: "I knew it was your problem. But you better @#%$ stop. You hear that Michael? You better @#%$ stop."[1769]

With Tommy Mottola threatening to ruin Michael Jackson on group conference calls, Michael began publicly exposing Mottola. At Al Sharpton's National Action Network in New York on June 2, 2002 Michael revealed Mottola's racism and called him "devilish." At a fan club event in London on June 15, 2002 however, Michael told the crowd, "Tommy Mottola is a devil." His larger remarks there are very revealing.

[1766] Roger Friedman, "Jackson May Claim 'Threats' by Mottola," **Fox News** July 12, 2002

[1767] Roger Friedman, "Jackson May Claim 'Threats' by Mottola," **Fox News** July 12, 2002

[1768] Roger Friedman, "Jackson May Claim 'Threats' by Mottola," **Fox News** July 12, 2002

[1769] Robert Sam Anson, "Tommy Boy," **Vanity Fair** November 1996.

And... Sony...Sony... Being the artist that I am, at Sony I've generated several billion dollars for Sony, several billon. They really thought that my mind is always on music and dancing. It usually is, *but they never thought that this performer — myself — would out think them*. So, we can't let them get away with what they're trying to do, because now I'm a free agent... I just owe Sony one more album. It's just a box set, really, with two new songs which I've written ages ago. Because for every album that I record, I write — literally, I'm telling you the truth — I write at least 120 songs every album I do. So I can do the box set, just giving them any two songs. So I'm leaving Sony, a free agent,... owning half of Sony! I own half of Sony's Publishing. I'm leaving them, and they're very angry at me, because I just did good business, you know. So the way they get revenge is to try and destroy my album! But I've always said, you know, art — good art — never dies. ...Thank you. *And Tommy Mottola is a devil!* I'm not supposed to say what I'm going to say right now, but I have let you know this. (Points to crowd). Please don't videotape what I am going to say, ok? Turn it off, please. Do it, do it, I don't mind! Tape it!

Mariah Carey, after divorcing Tommy, came to me crying. Crying. She was crying so badly I had to hold her. She said to me, "This is an evil man, and Michael, this man follows me." He taps her phones, and he's very, very evil. She doesn't trust him. *We have to continue our drive until he is terminated.* We can't allow him to do this to great artists, we just can't.

On January 9, 2003 – six months after Michael Jackson lead a *drive to terminate Tommy Mottola at Sony* - Mottola was "terminated," forced to resign as CEO of Sony. Michael Jackson won but he earned an enemy for life.

Who is Tommy Mottola?

"When Tommy has it in for somebody he can be unbelievably petty. He'll call maître d's to make sure people aren't given tables," says an acquaintance. Mottola's tactics were often brass-knuckle, but those who've known him for many years describe him as a gangster groupie who purposefully adopted the shiny-suited look of a Mafia lieutenant.[1770]

Tommy Mottola is an Italian who converted to Judaism in 1971 when he married the daughter of the Jewish "Music Mob" figure Sam Clark. Mottola had his own mob associations as well, including Jewish industry mobster Morris Levy, longtime associate of the Genovese crime family. Mottola also had a friendship with Father Louis Gigante, who was introduced to Mottola by his brother, Mob Boss Vinnie the Chin Gigante. Mottola showed up in a 1986 NBC report on the Mob infiltration of the music industry.[1771]

Geffen and Mottola

Equally important are Mottola's association with the reputed head of the "Gay Mafia". Roger Friedman of **Fox News** informs us: "David Geffen...is an ally of Tommy Mottola in the often brutal, warlike atmosphere of the record industry."[1772] In 2016 the **Observer** asked Mottola who he considered as the one person who *made* his career. His answer: David Geffen and Clive Davis.

> *If you could pick one person who you think gave you a leg up at a critical moment and made your career, who would you thank today?* Well, there are a couple of people. When I managed Hall & Oates in the late 70s and early 80s, I was very close to David Geffen, and he really taught me a lot. Clive Davis was an inspiration. But I used to look at him sort of on a pedestal cause the guy was sort of untouchable.[1773]

[1770] Phoebe Eaton, "Tommy Mottola Faces The Music," **New York Magazine** February 21, 2003.

[1771] Robert Sam Anson, "Tommy Boy," **Vanity Fair** November 1996.

[1772] Roger Friedman, "Jacko Will Get His Albums Back After All," **Fox News** July 19, 2002.

[1773] David Wallis, "Tommy Mottola: Strong Execs Need Someone to Say 'Shut the Fuck Up'," **Observer** December 12, 2016.

This makes sense as it was David Geffen who helped orchestrate the *coup* that removed Walter Yetnikof as chief of CBS in 1990. Mottola was Yetnikoff's number two man.

> Geffen staged a commando raid on Yetnikoff's own turf...Agreeing that Walter had gone off the rails, a loose-knit alliance of Geffen, [Allen] Grubman, Mottola, [Bruce] Springsteen manager Jon Landau and [Irving] Azoff staged a palace coup. Yetnikoff resigned in September 1990, a month after Mottola was honored at the annual City of Hope dinner on the Sony lot...[1774]

While Mottola was not immediately installed as Yetnikof's replacement, with Yetnikof out of the way eventually Mottola did assume the top spot. He owes much to David Geffen. Thus, two enemies of Michael Jackson – David Geffen ad Tommy Mottola – happened to be besties. This could not work out well for Michael.

THE PLOT TO FRAME MICHAEL JACKSON WITH GAY CHILD PORNOGRAPHY

[Michael Jackson] was very vulnerable to blackmail, having already paid out millions to settle one case. A gay pornographer had infiltrated his entourage with the possible goal of setting up the star and then blackmailing him.[1775]

After the 9/11 attacks in 2001 Michael Jackson organized the *What More Can I Give* charity single for the 9/11 victims. The contributors to the song were big: Beyonce, Ricky Martin, Mariah Carey, Carlos Santana, and others come contributed vocals. McDonalds agreed to a $20 million deal to sell the charity record. However, after the **New York Post** ran a story on the McDonalds deal on October 13 the white "American moms" complained, and McDonalds pulled out of the deal. Behind the scenes, though, an even bigger scandal was brewing.

[1774] "The Same Old Song, Part Three," **Daily Double** April 3, 2017; Dannen, **Hit Men**, 330ff.
[1775] Breitbart and Ebner, **Hollywood, Interrupted**, 174.

The executive producer of the song and its subsequent videos was Marc Schaffel. Michael, at that time, didn't really know who Schaffel was. But the celebrity sleuth Paul Barresi did. Because Barresi had been involved in Hollywood's gay pornography scene he knew Marc Fred Schaffel, who reportedly made gay porn with young boys imported from Eastern European countries like Hungary and the Czech Republic.[1776] According to Barresi, former Schaffel associate/employer David Aldorf in a taped interview on November 19, 2001 gave him some information: Schaffel shared with Aldorf a plan to blackmail Michael Jackson for $25 million by framing him "by planting kiddy porn on him."[1777] Aldorf also revealed that he possessed a video tape of Schaffel filming a gay porn video in Budapest with young Hungarian boys. Aldorf gave Barresi a copy of the video.[1778]

Barresi admits to trying to sell this information to Michael's personal accountant and business manager Barry Siegel. Barresi gave a copy of the video of Schaffel to the LAPD (whom he worked with in the past) and the FBI. Barresi also admits that he said to Eric Mason, a private investigator for Michael Jackson: "How much is it worth to save a pop star's ass?[1779]" Barresi claims Seigle and Mason refused to cooperate. However, John Branca received the video and set up a meeting with Michael to play the tape. Michael was angry and immediately fired Schaffel. "That same night, Jackson called Schaffel and told him he was off the charity project, acknowledged Schaffel..."[1780] Yet, for some reason some of Jackson's people *kept Schaffel around.*[1781]

Barresi then gave the info to the legal department of Sony and to Sony head Tommy Mottola (he would not be "terminated" until January, 2003). This potential scandal was to Sony's advantage because "The revelations could call into

[1776] Breitbart and Ebner, **Hollywood, Interrupted**, 175.
[1777] Breitbart and Ebner, **Hollywood, Interrupted**, 178.
[1778] "Jackson Kids In Danger? Debbie Rowe's New Fiancé Was Named As Co-Conspirator In MJ Child Molestation Indictment — PLUS His Secret Gay Porn Past Revealed!" **Radar Online** April 28, 2014.
[1779] Breitbart and Ebner, **Hollywood, Interrupted**, 182.
[1780] Tanya Caldwell, "Former Jackson Lawyer Testifies," **Los Angeles Times** July 11, 2006.
[1781] Tanya Caldwell, "Former Jackson Lawyer Testifies," **Los Angeles Times** July 11, 2006.

question [Michael's] credibility in the dispute with Sony."[1782] Right in the middle of Michael's dispute with Sony and a month after Michael called Mottola a devil in London, Barresi leaked the story to the *USA Today* which ran it on July 14, 2002. Barresi gave the video to NBC's *Dateline* and to Andrew Breitbart and Mark Ebner. The theme of the headlines went something like this: "Peter Pan had picked a [child] porn producer to be his private videographer in Neverland."[1783]

Michael reportedly accused Sony of blocking the release of the song as part of their ongoing dispute. "But," the *Los Angeles Times* says, "internal records and interviews indicate that it was Jackson's own advisers who quietly asked Sony to bury the charity project..."[1784] It is said that it was John Branca who pressed Sony to kill the *What More Can I Give?* project by refusing permission to stars scheduled to be own it. Barresi also desired to get the *What More Can I Give* project killed, which he ultimately did.[1785]

After being fired by Michael in 2001 Schaffel sued him for $3 million in November 2004. When the two legal teams met in London, Jackson made the statement about why he fired Schaffel: "I was shown a videotape by the lawyer [Branca] and I was shocked. He was *in that whole circle*, and I didn't know."[1786] "That whole circle" which Marc Schaffel was reputedly in was the Gay Pedophile circle! How did he infiltrate Michael Jackson's team? Through Arnold Klein.

Marc Schaffel was Dr. Arnold Klein's "friend and patient."[1787] It was coincidently (?) at an amfAR (American Foundation for AIDS Research) fundraiser – the foundation which Arnold Klein founded in his house with David Geffen and others[1788] – when Schaffel "ran into" Michael Jackson.

[1782] Chuck Philips, "Producers Porn Ties Said to Derail Jackson's Song," *Los Angeles Times* July 12, 2002.

[1783] Breitbart and Ebner, *Hollywood, Interrupted*.

[1784] Chuck Philips, "Producers Porn Ties Said to Derail Jackson's Song," *Los Angeles Times* July 12, 2002.

[1785] Breitbart and Ebner, *Hollywood, Interrupted*, 183.

[1786] Sullivan, *Untouchable*, 38.

[1787] Sullivan, *Untouchable*.

[1788] " 'Don't forget, I founded AmFAR in my house," [Klein] told me, referring to the American Foundation for AIDS Research, which he helped establish with Dr. Mathilde Krim, Elizabeth Taylor, and David Geffen in 1985": Mark Seal, "The Doctor Will Sue You Now," *Vanity Fair* February 2, 2012; "Jackson's Dermatologist Says Murray Fallout

However, "He and Jackson didn't have their first real conversations...until the year 2000, when they met at the home of the famous dermatologist they shared, Arnold Klein, a friend of Schaffel's..."[1789] In June 2001 Michael Jackson and Marc Schaffel met again at Klein's home. Evidently knowing Michael's film dreams Schaffel "Boast[ed] of his background in film production and flashing a bank account that approached eight figures, Schaffel pledged to organize Michael's various film and video projects through a company the two formed, called Neverland Entertainment. There was talk of building a movie studio at the ranch, of making short films, perhaps producing an animated television series."[1790] Schaffel was thus able to make himself – or someone made him – "the official videographer at Jackson's Neverland Ranch" and "despite Schaffel's total lack of music production experience, Jackson handed him the reins to oversee the recording of his 9/11 single "What More Can I Give," and its subsequent music video, later that year." [1791] Marc Schaffel the reputed gay pedophile pornographer who reportedly planned to frame Michael Jackson with "kiddy porn" in order to extort $25 million out of him did successfully infiltrate Michael's camp and it was Dr. Arnold Klein who introduced Schaffel to Michael in the first place.

In addition, according to Schaffel, Tommy Mottola had already known about his background: "Tommy Mottola knew [about my past] too. He brought Usher to the studio to sing on 'What More Can I Give?' and Tommy was sitting and joking with me about some girl in the porn business he knew, to see if I knew her too."[1792]

Hurts," *The Telegraph* October 15, 2011: "Klein teamed with other physicians, Taylor and Geffen to form the respected American Foundation for AIDS Research, AmFAR..."

[1789] Randall Sullivan, *Untouchable: The Strange Life and Tragic Death of Michael Jackson* (New York: Grove Press, 2012) 16.

[1790] Sullivan, *Untouchable*, 17.

[1791] "Jackson Kids In Danger? Debbie Rowe's New Fiancé Was Named As Co-Conspirator In MJ Child Molestation Indictment — PLUS His Secret Gay Porn Past Revealed!" *Radar Online* April 28, 2014.

[1792] Sullivan, *Untouchable*, 21.

BETRAYAL ON THE INSIDE:
THE INTERFOR REPORT

In 2003, Michael Jackson retained the services of Intefor Inc. to investigate the people in his inner circle. Intefor Inc. is a Manhattan-based corporate espionage and international investigative intelligence firm founded by Israeli-American security consultant Juval Aviv, a former major in Israel's Defense Force and former Mossad assassin. Aviv was retained by Pan Am in 1989 to investigate the bombed Pan Am flight 103, and his leaked report concluded that the Lockerbie Bombing was a CIA gun- and drug-smuggling operation gone wrong. The results of Aviv's investigation for Michael Jackson were shared in February and March and were compiled in a dossier known as the "Interfor Report," the final version of which is dated April 15, 2003 and was submitted to Michael as "Confidential." According to the Report the investigation found an insidious betrayal afoot within Michael's inner circle; specifically Aviv found a "tight business relationship between [Michael's lawyer] Branca and [Michael's enemy] Tommy Mottola, primarily in regard to the affairs of Jackson." The investigation uncovered evidence of "the flow of funds from Jackson through Mottola and Branca into offshore accounts in the Carribean (sic)," and "a scheme to defraud Jackson and his empire by Mottola and Branca diverting funds offshore." It is

> Additionally, Interfor's investigation found a tight business relationship between Branca and Tommy Mottola, primarily in regard to the affairs of Jackson. Interfor has begun investigating the flow of funds from Jackson through Mottola and Branca into offshore accounts in the Carribean. Interfor believes that, at this stage of the investigation, if we had additional time and a proper budget we could develop intelligence which would uncover a scheme to defraud Jackson and his empire by Mottola and Branca by diverting funds offshore.

reported that the results of this investigation prompted Michael to fire his attorney John Branca.[1793] According to Michael's manger Leonard Rowe, "The Interfor Report caused Michael Jackson great anguish and Michael demanded that Branca *was never to have anything to do with him, his business, his family,*

[1793] Johnnie L. Roberts, "The Secret Probe That Got Branca Fired," **The Wrap** December 5, 2010.

or his personal life again."[1794] Yet, a week before Michael Jackson was killed Branca pops back up and is later made executor of Michael's estate. It should be pointed out that Mottola abruptly resigned – was "terminated" - as CEO from Sony a month prior to the Interfor Report.

VIII.   *The Nation of Islam Pushes Back The Jewish Mafia*

Michael Jackson sitting with Al Malnik

In the year 2000 Michael Jackson developed a relationship with Florida attorney and businessman Al Malnik, son of Russian Jewish immigrants. Al Malnik was Mafia. He was an employee of Jewish Mobster Meyer Lansky and when Lansky died in 1983 at the age of 81 **Reader's Digest** named Malnik his "heir apparent." Between 2000 and 2002 Michael and Malnik developed a close relationship. Malnik is said to have loaned Michael up to $70 million, and he led a consortium that put together financial rescue plans to get Michael out of debt. However, by 2003 Michael ended his relationship with the Jewish Mobster because he came to believe that Malnik, whom he found out had Mafia associations, was conspiring with Sony's Tommy Mottola and film director Brett Ratner to wrangle the catalog from him. John Branca and Al Malnik were longtime

[1794] Leonard Rowe, **What _Really_ Happened to Michael Jackson The King of Pop: The Evil Side of the Entertainment Industry** (n.p: Linell-Diamond Enterprises, LLC, 2010) 238.

friends as well. In 2005 Michael hired an investigator to verify his suspicions, Gordon Novel. Novel worked in the Lyndon Johnson administration and spent years as an investigator for former U.S. Attorney General Ramsey Clark. Before that, he assisted former New Orleans District Attorney Jim Garrison investigate the J.F.K. assassination. Michael believed this conspiracy was behind the 2005 child molestation charges, which Michael was ultimately acquitted and exonerated of. As Maureen Orth detailed in 2009:

> According to Novel, the Jacksons believed that it was all a grand conspiracy, that the accuser's mother was being paid by Jackson's enemies, who wanted to take control of his major economic asset, the Sony/ATV Music catalogue, which holds publishing rights to 251 Beatles songs and works by scores of other pop artists. Jackson claimed that the main conspirators were Sony Records; its former president, Tommy Mottola; and Santa Barbara County district attorney Tom Sneddon, the prosecutor, who also investigated Jackson in 1993. The catalogue is held jointly by Jackson and Sony, and Jackson's share is mortgaged for more than $200 million. If Jackson defaults, Sony has first chance to buy his half as early as this coming December. (A Sony spokesperson said, "We are not going to comment on any aspect of this.")

> Jackson explained to Novel that the conspirators had introduced him to Al Malnik, a wealthy Miami attorney who had once represented Meyer Lansky...According to Novel, Jackson said he was lured to Malnik's house in Miami Beach by film director Brett Ratner to see a house so beautiful it would make him catatonic. He said that once he was there, however, Malnik, who Jackson claimed had Mafia ties, wanted to put his fingers in the singer's business. Jackson also said he received a call from Tommy Mottola while he was there, which aroused his suspicion, but he did not tell Novel that he later put Malnik on the board of the Sony/ATV Music partnership. (Reached by telephone, Malnik scoffed at the idea of a conspiracy or of his having any Mafia ties. He said, "It does not make any sense." Ratner confirmed that he took Jackson to Malnik's house and that he considers Malnik a father figure.)

716

Jackson and Mottola have been at odds for years. In New York in July 2002, Jackson staged a public protest against Mottola with the Reverend Al Sharpton, calling him a racist and "very, very devilish." He called for a boycott of Sony, which is believed to have contributed to Mottola's ouster from the company six months later. Jackson is reportedly so frightened of Mottola that one of the reasons he surrounded himself with Nation of Islam guards in 2003 was that he thought Mottola could put out a hit on him. (Mottola could not be reached for comment.)

Jackson wanted Novel to find the links among these characters. Novel told me in March that "he believes he'll get convicted.[1795]

Bob Norman who interviewed Novel says further:

"The whole thing centered on Tommy Mottola setting him up," Novel told me. "Mottola and him were at odds, and Jackson's information was that Mottola and Malnik got together to fuck him. He said he believed Malnik was representing the Mob."

I asked Novel if he believed Jackson's theory about the conspiracy against him. He said that he thought Jackson was not guilty of the criminal charges and that he was probably set up, but he had no idea if Mottola was involved.

"He thought that Mottola was Mob-connected and that Malnik was representing the Mob, but I can't vouch for any of that shit," Novel said. "I don't have anything against Tommy Mottola and don't know if what he thought was true or not. *I don't want to get on Mottola's bad side.* My sources in New York say he's a dangerous guy."[1796]

[1795] Maureen Orth, "C.S.I. Neverland," ***Vanity Fair*** July 2005.
[1796] Bob Norman, "The Malnik Family's Michael Jackson Photo Dump," ***Broward Palm Beach New Times*** June 29, 2009.

It was around this time that Michael Jackson surrounded himself with the Nation of Islam. The Nation not only provided soldiers as a security detail for Michael but also lent him the Chief-of-Staff of the Nation, Leonard Farrakhan, to help with Michael's business and legal affairs, the reports say. According to *The New York Times* "Officials from the Nation of Islam...have moved in with Michael Jackson and are asserting control over the singer's business affairs, friends, employees and business

The Honorable Minister Farrakhan and Michael Jackson

associates of Mr. Jackson said."[1797] I'm sure this is an overstatement. But the word went out: "Farrakhan and the Nation of Islam; those people are very protective of Michael."[1798] At this point, the presence of the Nation of Islam in Michael Jackson's world was now so palpable that Michael's official spokesman, Stuart Backerman, resigned claiming, "I quit because the Nation of Islam had infiltrated Michael's world."[1799] Others followed. "Michael LePerruque, Jackson's chief of security, and other top advisers, were soon gone. *Malnik was done.*"[1800] This strong presence of the Nation around Michael removed the immediate threat from Michael's world.

More costly [in terms of Michael's affiliation with the Nation of Islam] in the short term, ...was that Muhammad and his henchmen were destroying Jackson's

---

[1797] Sharon Waxman, "Dispute on Michael Jackson Camp Over Role of the Nation of Islam," *The New York Times* December 30, 2003.
[1798] Roger Friedman, "Claim: Jacko's Rep Threatened Harm From Nation of Islam," *Fox News* March 24, 2009.
[1799] "Michael Jackson's aide 'quit due to Nation of Islam," *Telegraph* July 7, 2009.
[1800] Gerald Posner, "Michael's Missing millions," *The Daily Beast* August 2, 2009.

relationships with almost everyone who had done anything to help him (*sic!*) in recent years. The most expensive exclusions were those of *Marc Schaffel...and Al Malnik...*"I told Michael that it was the worst mistake of his life when he allowed the Nation of Islam to come in and convince him to stop speaking to Al Malnik," Schaffel said. With Leonard Farrakhan and associates whispering in Michael's ear, *the relationship with Malnik deteriorated far beyond the point of not talking to one another.* By the spring of 2004, Jackson...was convinced that Malnik was part of a conspiracy against him that included Sony, Bank of America, and Tom Sneddon and that all of them were after the Beatles songs.[1801]

Not only did Al Malnik and Marc Schaffel disappear from Michael's circle around 2003, so too did Dr. Arnold Klein. He told TMZ's Harvey Levin in 2009:

Levin   Well, you know, but you were in contact with him at that time (2005).
Klein   Not at that time. Not during the whole second trial. I was not.
Levin   You never talked to him?
Klein   Not during that trial.
Levin   You had a falling out?
Klein   No, it wasn't a falling out but he was up there in that trial and I never talked to him during that trial whatsoever. There were periods of time, vast periods of time, from 2003 to now that I never spoke to him. You know that. I hadn't spoken to him since 2003...[1802]

IX.   *AEG Live: Setting The Stage For Murder*

His aides weren't the only ones who recognised that a 50-concert run was foolhardy. In May, Jackson himself reportedly addressed fans as he left his Burbank rehearsal studio. "Thank you for your love and support," he told them. "I want you guys to know I love you very much. "I don't know how I'm going to do 50 shows. I'm not a big

---

[1801] Sullivan, **Untouchable**,
[1802] November 5, 2009 Harvey Levin Interview.

eater. I need to put some weight on. I'm really angry with them booking me up to do 50 shows. I only wanted to do ten."...Whatever the final autopsy results reveal, it was greed that killed Michael Jackson. Had he not been driven – by a cabal of bankers, agents, doctors and advisers – to commit to the gruelling 50 concerts in London's O2 Arena, I believe he would still be alive today.[1803]

After his exoneration during the 2005 False Allegations Michael Jackson spent eleven months in Bahrain as a guest of the royal family. Upon his return to the U.S. Michael took up residence in Las Vegas. He had not performed for four years when, in January 2009 he was approached by representatives from AEG Live about a string of concerts to take place at the new O2 arena in London. Reportedly, Michael or his team twice rebuffed Randy Phillips, CEO of AEG Live, and his concert proposal.[1804] As is clear from internal emails that surfaced during the 2013 trial, AEG Live executives had a disdain for Michael Jackson the *person*: while trying to "hook" him they were yet referring to him as a "creepy" "freak,"[1805] and they disrespectfully among themselves called him "Mikey."[1806] They were also deceiving him from the very beginning by deliberately presenting an exaggerated earning potential and deceptively downplaying the labor on Jackson's part involved. "AEG tried to mislead Michael Jackson about how hard his concert tour would be, e-mails imply...Greedy concert promoters tricked...Michael Jackson into signing up for his grueling final concert."[1807] Michael signed the contract. The deception didn't stop there. Michael Jackson agreed to a 10-concert deal. That is

---

[1803] Ian Halperin, " 'I'm better off dead. I'm done': Michael Jackson's fateful prediction just a week before his death," **Daily Mail** June 29 2009.

[1804] Ian Halperin, " 'I'm better off dead. I'm done': Michael Jackson's fateful prediction just a week before his death," **Daily Mail** June 29 2009.

[1805] On January 28, 2009 AEG Live Senior VP and General Counsel Shawn Trell to his boss Ted Fikre, AEG's chief legal officer. Alan Duke, "AEG exec called Michael Jackson 'freak' before signing concert contract," **CNN** May 23, 2013.

[1806] Alan Duke, "AEG drops Michael Jackson insurance claim," **CNN** September 10, 2012.

[1807] Richard Johnson, "Concert promoters pulled fast one on Jackson, emails imply," **New York Post** May 29, 2013.

what in January 2009 Michael was confident he could pull off. However,

> Before long...ten concerts had turned into 50 and the potential revenues had skyrocketed. The vultures who were pulling his strings somehow managed to put this concert extravaganza together *behind his back*, then presented it to him as a fait accompli,' said one aide... "We knew it was a disaster waiting to happen," said one aide. "I don't think anybody predicted it would actually kill him but nobody believed he would end up performing."[1808]

It is extremely important to point out that, in January 2009, *"Michael Jackson was not abusing pain medication in years leading up to comeback tour deal with AEG Live*, says doctor"[1809] As the **New York Daily News** reported in 2013

> "Michael Jackson apparently *was clean and not abusing pain medication* in the years leading up to his comeback tour deal with concert promoter AEG Live, a Connecticut doctor testified Wednesday.
>
> Dr. Sidney Schnoll based his opinion on medical records stating the King of Pop only needed 100 milligrams of the narcotic pain medication Demerol to knock him out for a dermatology procedure in late 2008.
>
> Schnoll said Jackson would have built up too much tolerance for that dose to work if he frequently abused opioids during the era of his 2005 molestation trial and subsequent travels abroad.

[1808] Ian Halperin, " 'I'm better off dead. I'm done': Michael Jackson's fateful prediction just a week before his death," **Daily Mail** June 29 2009.

[1809] Nancy Dillion, "Michael Jackson was not abusing pain medication in years leading up to comeback tour deal with AEG Live, says doctor," **New York Daily News** July 3, 2013.

"He would have to take a much higher dose of Demerol to get the (necessary) effect for the surgery," Schnoll told jurors." [1810]

This is because Michael fought this addiction and apparently won. To help him battle the Demerol addiction which doctors such as – and reportedly *primarily* – Arnold Klein *created*, Michael Jackson was in 2003 fitted with a "secret medical implant" called the Narcan Implant which stopped its user from getting enjoyment from opiates, effectively making drug-taking pointless. The Narcan Implant releases into the patient doses of Narcan (Naloxone) which blocks pleasure receptors in the brain. According to court papers in the 2013 Katherine Jackson v. AEG Live case the implant was discovered in Michael's body after his death.[1811] So Michael Jackson *could not have been* a Demerol addict; he got no pleasure from Demerol. Rather, Michael Jackson would be *deliberately drugged with Demerol (and other drugs)* by AEG Live employees.

Thus, at the start of Michael's relationship with AEG Live in 2009 he was *a healthy, non-drug addict*. This is confirmed by the physical exam conducted on February 4, 2009 by the London insurance company Lloyd's of London. AEG Live was seeking insurance for the (at first) ten shows in London which covered cancellation or postponement of the shows or illness of the singer *or death of the singer*.[1812] Remarkably, the insurance policy AEG Live was seeking included a *drug overdose* provision as well! Before Lloyd's of London would approve such policy they required Dr. David Slavit from New York to conduct a physical examination of Michael Jackson in his Los Angeles home. Blood samples were drawn which, upon examination by Westcliff Medical Laboratories, resulted *in normal and consistent findings*! Dr. Slavit found Michael

---

[1810] Nancy Dillion, "Michael Jackson was not abusing pain medication in years leading up to comeback tour deal with AEG Live, says doctor," **New York Daily News** July 3, 2013.

[1811] "Michael Jackson 'had secret implant to prevent him getting enjoyment form opiates', court papers reveal," **Daily Beast** April 11, 2013.

[1812] "Michael Jackson's estate, Lloyd's of London settle insurance dispute," **Reuters** January 15, 2004; "AEG boss: Jackson insurance covers overdose," **Today** July 2, 2009.

Jackson to be in excellent condition and notified AEG Live that he "passed with flying colors". The insurance policy for ten shows was thus completed in April 2009.[1813]

Michael Jackson was a *healthy, non-drug abuser* at the start of this process with AEG Live in January and February, until in March *Dr. Arnold Klein was brought back into Michael's life after being absent for years.*[1814] The pretext or pretense was that Klein would "rebuild" Michael's face for the "This Is It" tour. As an employee of AEG Live Klein *immediately* began pumping Michael with "insane" amounts of Demerol, just as he did in 1993. For example, over a three-day period in May Klein pumped Michael with *900 milligrams of Demerol* and according to the medical testimony during the Dr. Conrad Murray trial these "stiff doses" of Demerol *were not* required for the Botox and Restylane treatments that were listed in the medical records.[1815] "Dr. Robert Waldman, an addiction specialist, was of the opinion that Jackson had exhibited signs of developing tolerance to Demerol by late April and by early May he believed the singer was dependent on Demerol and possibly addicted to opioids."[1816] Klein's medical documents reveal he injected Michael with Demerol *51 times* in three months, mostly for minor procedures like acne treatments, lip treatments and Botox.[1817]

In a highly unusual and unorthodox protocol—in fact, a number of medical professionals consulted with for this

---

[1813] Matt Richards and Mark Langthorne, *83 Minutes: The Doctor, The Damage, and the Shocking Death of Michael Jackson* (London: Blink Publishing, 2015) 111-112.

[1814] Klein claims that in October 2008 Michael Jackson first contacted him after five years requesting a doctor's note to get out of a court appearance. Mark Seal, "The Ugly world of Dr. Arnie Klein, Beverly Hills' King of Botox," *Vanity Fair* February 2, 2012; "Lawsuit Accuses Doctor Arnie Klein of Fueling Michael's Jackson's Drug Addiction," *TMZ* August 4, 2011. This does not imply, however, that Michael became a patient of Klein's again. That would not happen until March 2009.

[1815] Matthew Perpetua, "Doctor: Michael Jackson Was Dependent on Demerol," *Rolling Stone* October 28, 2011.

[1816] Matt Richards and Mark Langthorne, *83 Minutes: The Doctor, The Damage, and the Shocking Death of Michael Jackson* (London: Blink Publishing, 2015) 119.

[1817] "MJ and Klein – Affection for Injections," *TMZ* October 28, 2009.

piece had never heard of such a thing before—Klein administered 100mg to 200mg of the highly addictive painkiller Demerol to Jackson when he was getting injections of the cosmetic fillers Botox and Restylane, according to medical records. Setting aside that Botox and Restylane are supposed to last for at least two months and no one this writer or any dermatologist consulted knows has ever received anything but "numbing cream" (or in one instance a half a Vicodin) for the same treatment, according to medical documents Arnie Klein gave Restylane and Botox to Jackson almost every other day accompanied by a total of 2,475 mg of Demerol in April 2009 and in a two-week period in May, more than 1,400 mg of Demerol. This has led some medical professionals familiar with the records to wonder if some of the Botox and Restylane injections listed on the medical billings were simply "cover."[1818]

Dr. Arnold Klein reportedly made Michael Jackson a Demerol addict in 1993, which Michael successfully overcame; and Klein made Michael a Demerol addict again in 2009! In the three months that Klein worked to "rebuild" Michael's face Klein injected 6,500 milligrams of Demerol into Michael. [1819] And during these three months (March 23-June 22) of injecting Michael with medically non-warranted amounts of Demerol Klein submitted his invoice totaling $48,000 to AEG.[1820] As he admitted: "AEG and not the Jackson Estate was to pay me"[1821]

And *then* came Conrad Murray. On May 8, 2009 AEG Live co-CEO Paul Gongaware called Dr. Murray to officially retain his services. Like Dr. Klein, Dr. Murray was AEG Live's employee, not Michael Jackson's employee. He was to be paid

[1818] Amy Ephron, "Conrad Murray Michael Jackson Trial: The Evidence the Public Won't Hear," *The Daily Beast* September 29, 2011.

[1819] Alan Duke, "'Perfect storm' of drugs killed Michael Jackson, sleep expert says," *CNN* October 14, 2011.

[1820] Roger Friedman, "DEA 'Inspected' Office of Michael Jackson's Dr. Klein Last Week: Exclusive," *Showbiz 411* June 30, 2010.

[1821] Initially on his web page @ http://www.arnoldwklein.com/?p=2128
But that's now removed. The post can be currently found here: https://www.michaeljacksonhoaxforum.com/forums/index.php?topic=23648.0

not from Michael Jackson's advanced budget but from AEG Live's own budget.[1822] On May 12, Dr. Murray ordered the drug Propofol which was to be used on Michael Jackson. Propofol is an intravenously administered *hypnotic drug*. While AEG Live was paying (in theory) Dr. Arnold Klein, who was loading Michael Jackson with Demerol, AEG Live was also paying (in theory) Dr. Conrad Murray who was pumping Michael with Propofol as well as a "cocktail" of other drugs, which we will discuss below.

Michael Jackson was a healthy, non-drug abusing man in January. By May, under the "medical care" of AEG Live's two employees Dr. Conrad Murray and Dr. Arnold Klein, Michael Jackson was suffering the effects of drug abuse.

> In May and June, Michael Jackson was confused, easily frightened, unable to remember, obsessive, and disoriented. He had impaired memory, loss of appetite, and absence of energy. He was cold and shivering during summer rehearsals for his show, and as shown in photographs and motion pictures of him, he uncharacteristically wore heavy clothing during the rehearsals, while other dancers wore scant clothing and were perspiring from the heat.[1823]

While leaving his Burbank rehearsing studio in May Michael addressed some of his fans and one of his employees at the time recalled to Ian Halperin of *Daily Mail*:

[1822] "AEG Live controller Julie Hollander ... her testimony about the company's budgeting, which she acknowledged included $1.5 million approved to pay Dr. Murray. The doctor's costs were listed as production costs — expenses that AEG is responsible for paying — and not as an advance, which Jackson would ultimately be responsible for giving back to the company, she testified. The controller's testimony appears to contradict the argument AEG lead lawyer Marvin Putnam made in a CNN interview days before the trial began (that Murray was an employee of Michael Jackson rather than of AEG Live)." "AEG files claim for losses from Michael Jackson's death the day he died," *Fox* * May 20, 2013.

[1823] Superior Court of California, County of Los Angeles, Joseph Jackson v. Conrad Murray et al. Case No. BC450393, 30 November 2010, pg. 12.

"The way he was talking, it's like he's not in control over his own life anymore," she told me earlier this month. "It sounds like somebody else is pulling his strings and telling him what to do. Someone wants him dead. They keep feeding him pills like candy. They are trying to push him over the edge. He needs serious help. The people around him will kill him."[1824]

Why would AEG Live take a healthy Michael Jackson, sign a contract with him for a series of *50 concerts* at *their* newly renovated arena in London and then deliberately drug him to the point of incapacitation? The answer is a simple, two-part answer.

The Plan was clearly to drug Michael Jackson and then take advantage of his reduced mental capacity. The incapacitation made Michael incompetent to make rational decisions, and this served AEG Live's interests. Michael was indeed *chemically controlled*. As the 2013 complaint stated:

> AEG's control of Jackson's person was further extended by the drugs being administered by Murray, which weakened Jackson's physical and mental health, rendering him vulnerable, confused, *and subject to direction*.[1825]

Family friend Terry Harvey describes the effects of this intentional *drugging* of Michael Jackson:

> [Michael] had a sharp mind, but he was deluded, hampered by the drugs. He didn't know what he was saying to people. To make his life easy *he would just say 'yes'*. He was walking around in a daze like a zombie."
> Another friend said: "He shouted out, 'They are punishing

[1824] Ian Halperin, " 'I'm better off dead. I'm done': Michael Jackson's fateful prediction just a week before his death," **Daily Mail** June 29 2009.
[1825] Superior Court of California, County of Los Angeles Katherine Jackson v. AEG Live LLC et al., Case No. BC445597 September 15, 2010, 10-11.

me and I can't take it anymore. They are gonna kill me."[1826]

It appears that Michael was chemically maintained in a state of continuous confusion and compliance. Detectives Orlando Martinez, Dan Meyers and Scott Smith said in the 2019 documentary **Killing Michael Jackson** that Murray "purposefully kept [Michael Jackson] under the influence."[1827] Then he did so on AEG orders, no doubt. By the time of his death on June 25th Michael had already been suffering from chronic pneumonia, chronic respiratory bronchitis, anemia, and brain swelling.[1828] The respiratory problems could have been caused by his severely damaged lungs (the autopsy revealed there was widespread inflammation and extensive scarring), which damage could be due to Michael's noted discoid lupus or it could have been caused by his Demerol drugging.[1829]

The days before Michael was killed his mental incapacitation was clear to everyone. He was described by the show director on June 19 as a "basket case," who was "trembling, rambling, obsessive," and the stage manager said "My layman's degree tells me [Michael] needs a shrink"[1830] He was disoriented and Karen Faye testified that "He kept repeating, 'why can't I choose.'"[1831] According to other testimony Michael told Kenny Ortega the show director, "God keeps talking to me."[1832] This latter "uttering," however, just may have been true.

[1826] "'Drugged, exhausted' MJ 'could barley walk' during This Is It rehearsals," **Thaindian News** October 31, 2009.

[1827] Adam Starkey, "Michael Jackson's doctor waited 25 minutes to call police after finding singer's body, claims new documentary," **Metro** June 21, 2019.

[1828] Superior Court of California, County of Los Angeles, Joseph Jackson v. Conrad Murray et al. Case No. BC450393, 30 November 2010, 12.

[1829] Colin Vickery, "Michael Jackson should have died earlier, autopsy report reveals," **News Corp Australia** June 25, 2014.

[1830] "AEG Live CEO Randy Phillips Testifies About Emails on Michael Jackson's Condition," **Billboard** June 7, 2013.

[1831] Alan Duke, "Witness: Michael Jackson was paranoid, talking to himself in last days," **CNN** May 9, 2013

[1832] Alan Duke, "Witness: Michael Jackson was paranoid, talking to himself in last days," **CNN** May 9, 2013

A most illuminating illustration of AEG taking advantage of Michael Jackson's mental incapacitation occurred within days prior to Michael's death. Remember the Interfor Report of April 15, 2003 showed Michael's attorney John Branca had been colluding with Michael's enemy Tommy Mottola to rob Michael. Michael thus fired Branca and according to Michael's manger Leonard Rowe, "Michael demanded that Branca *was never to have anything to do with him, his business, his family, or his personal life again.*"[1833] But on the eve of Michael's death, while he was drugged, mentally incapacitated, zombified and chemically controlled by Randy Phillips and his team, an treacherous event occurred:

> At around 7 o'clock one evening during the third week of June 2009, John Branca arrived in Michael Jackson's dressing room at L.A.'s Fabulous Forum, where rehearsals were under way for the performer's "This Is It" concert.
>
> It was their first meeting in three years. They immediately hugged, before *Branca handed Jackson a letter to be signed, formally rehiring the superlawyer.*
>
> It was an abrupt reunion after a bitter split — and *just days before the show business legend died.*
>
> "They hadn't really spoken since 2006," says CEO Randy Phillips of AEG Live, the promoter of Jackson's "This Is It" concert series.
>
> So how did Branca's and Jackson's epic relation come full circle, as if according to a Hollywood script?
>
> In fact, Branca had begun to seek a return to the fold no sooner than Jackson wrapped up the press conference unveiling "This Is It" in early March 2009. The lawyer phoned Phillips. "'I'd do anything in the world to be involved,'" Phillips remembers Branca saying. The AEG executive was noncommittal then.

[1833] Leonard Rowe, **What *Really* Happened to Michael Jackson The King of Pop: The Evil Side of the Entertainment Industry** (n.p: Linell-Diamond Enterprises, LLC, 2010) 238.

Later, however, Phillips and Frank DiLeo, Jackson's manager from the 1980s glory days, phoned Branca. *DiLeo himself had only recently been invited back onto the brain trust, exactly two decades after Jackson fired him in 1989*, a year before Branca was booted for the first time.

...

After the dressing-room meeting, Jackson headed off apparently to his intravenous Propafol drip and Branca to a Mexican vacation, where a few days later, on June 25, his phone rang with (fellow attorney Joel) Katz on the line. Jackson had just died after Dr. Conrad Murray, his private physician, administered the drug.

"Does anyone have a will," Katz wondered?

"I have one," he says Branca answered. "If it's valid."

It was, in fact, the will that installed Branca, along with longtime Jackson family friend John McClain, as co-executor of the Jackson estate.[1834]

As Johnnie L. Roberts writes: "in June 2009, within a week of Jackson's death, Branca...returned to the fold after a three-year break-up. Six days after Jackson's drug-fueled death – having spoken to [Branca] only once in three years – he, along with longtime Jackson family friend John McClain, emerged as co-executor of the tragic icon's extraordinary holdings."[1835]

The Plan was also *to make Michael Jackson physically incapable of performing.*

The AEG-JACKSON AGREEMENT provided that AEG would have the exclusive right to manufacture and sell Michael Jackson merchandise associated with the Tour. In exchange for these and other revenues associated with

---

[1834] Johnnie L. Roberts, "A Superlawyer Return, A Pop Icon Dies – a Will is Discovered," *The Wrap* December 9, 2010.
[1835] Johnnie L. Roberts, "How Michael Jackson Nearly Lost his Prized Music Catalog," *The Wrap* December 5, 2010.

the Tour, as well as for the prestige associated with sponsoring the This Is It Tour, AEG advanced Michael Jackson substantial sums of money, which it was to recoup through revenue from the Tour. *If, however, Jackson failed to perform,* or failed to generate the revenue to cover the advances, then AEG would have the right to collect the advance against security provided by Michael Jackson and his company, Michael Jackson LLC. *The assets from which AEG could seize from Michael Jackson include the Sony/ATV song catalogue owned by Jackson...his* assets stood security if he failed to perform.[1836]

Randy Phillips and his fellow AEG Live collaborators can be said to have deliberately made Michael Jackson physically unable to rehearse for the show, and then used his absence from rehearsal as the pre-text for "pulling the plug" or cancelling the tour, thereby seizing Michael's assets as collateral.

AEG threatened that if Jackson missed any further rehearsals, they were going to "pull the plug" on the show, Jackson's house, the doctor, and all the expenses for which they paid. If AEG called off the Tour, Jackson would be required to repay AEG for its advances to him. If he could not repay AEG, AEG would be entitled to collect the collateral Jackson had put up to secure his obligation to perform.[1837]

But co-CEO Paul Gongaware admitted in court that, per the contract between AEG Live and Michael Jackson, Michael *was NOT obligated to attend ANY rehearsals.*

Gongaware explained MJ didn't have to attend rehearsals, since it was not part of his deal. He said they never required an artist to rehearse. "I didn't have any expectation", Gongaware said regarding MJ

[1836] Superior Court of California, County of Los Angeles Katherine Jackson v. AEG Live LLC et al., Case No. BC445597 September 15, 2010, 4-5.
[1837] Superior Court of California, County of Los Angeles Katherine Jackson v. AEG Live LLC et al., Case No. BC445597 September 15, 2010, 4-5.

rehearsing. He said that during the HIStory tour, MJ didn't rehearse, nailed it.[1838]

So the "rehearsal mandate" was a false pretext. In fact, the insistence by Randy Phillips was tantamount to nothing short of *weaponizing the rehearsals* against Michael. The concurrent drugging of Michael Jackson with Demerol by Klein and Propofol by Murray as well as with the other drugs made Michael progressively unable to physically rehearse. On June 2, 2009 Randy Phillips and Frank DiLeo confronted Michael Jackson at his home about missing rehearsals and Michael

> attended the meeting wearing a surgical mask and layers of clothing as he was complaining about feeling very hot, then extremely cold. These are classic withdrawal symptoms of an addict coming down from Demerol and it's possibly no coincidence that Jackson visited Dr Klein twice in the first week of June and received two injections, totally 400mg of Demerol. [1839]

Nevertheless, Michael's AEG Live handlers showed him no sympathy at all.

> [Michael's chef] Kai Chase suggested that Jackson was an emotional wreck at the time; that he was scared, fearful and anxious about the meeting. She had to go in an out of the room refilling beverage glasses but didn't overhear anything while she was briefly in the room but did, however, hear raised voices when she had left. On one occasion when she returned to fill the glasses she noticed a vase was lying on the floor and it wasn't long after that Dr Murray stormed into the kitchen having escaped the meeting and exclaimed: "I can't handle this shit!" before leaving via the back door.[1840]

[1838] Testimony during Katherine Jackson et al. v. AEG Live, Monday June 3, 2013. DAY 22.

[1839] Matt Richards and Mark Langthorne, *83 Minutes: The Doctor, The Damage, and the Shocking Death of Michael Jackson* (London: Blink Publishing, 2015) 135

[1840] Matt Richards and Mark Langthorne, *83 Minutes: The Doctor, The Damage, and the Shocking Death of Michael Jackson* (London: Blink Publishing, 2015) 135

June 19, 2009 can be considered the day the die was set. That date marked the beginning of the end for Michael Jackson. Battling the devastating effects of the forced drug abuse, Michael showed up at the Staples Center for rehearsal at 9:30 p.m. and in bad condition: "trembling, rambling and obsessive." The show director Kenny Ortega sent Michael home without setting foot on stage. Stage manager John Houghdahl emailed Phillips and Gongaware informing them that Michael was sent home from rehearsal and also candidly stating: "I have watched [Michael] *deteriorate in front of my eyes over the last 8 weeks.* He was able to do multiple 360 spins back in April. He'd fall on his ass if he tried it now."[1841] Michael could do 360 spins eight weeks prior because, before he fell into the clutches of AEG Live's drug pushers Klein and Murray, Michael was healthy. In eight weeks, Michael did not deteriorate on his own; he was chemically assaulted.

Hougdahl also revealed that earlier that night after watching a pyrotechnics demonstration, Michael said, "You aren't going to kill the artist, are you?" Hougdahl wrote to Phillips that Michael, whose scalp was badly burned while shooting a Pepsi commercial in 1984, *"didn't appear to be referring to the fireworks."*[1842] Associate producer Alif Sankey after the rehearsal called Kenny Ortega: "I kept saying that 'Michael is dying, he's dying, he's leaving us, he needs to be put in a hospital...Please do something. Please, please.' I kept saying that. I asked [Ortega] why no one had seen what I had seen. He said he didn't know."[1843] What Ortega *did* know on that day is that they were "pulling the plug" on Michael Jackson: "The situation came to a head after the June 19, 2009, rehearsal, when Ortega sent an email to Phillips saying that they should consider 'pulling the plug' on the upcoming concert dates."[1844]

[1841] Hannington Dia, "Katherine Jackson Leaves Court In Tears During M.J. Civil Trial," **News One** May 24, 2013.
[1842] "AEG Live CEO Randy Phillips Testifies About Emails on Michael Jackson's Condition," **Billboard** June 7, 2013.
[1843] Alan Duke, "Witness: 'Everybody was lying' after Michael Jackson died," **CNN** May 13, 2013.
[1844] Kimberly Potts and Tim Kenneally, "Michael Jackson Producer Wanted to Pull Plug on Concert Tour," **The Wrap** October 25, 2011. "Kenny Ortega feared Michael Jackson's tour would fail days before death," **Our Weekly** July 11, 2013: "Ortega said: 'On the 19th, I had more than a serious concern. I didn't think it was going to go on.'"

In fact, according to Karen Faye's text messages that were read to the court on September 9, 2013 Ortega and Randy Philips that night "told [Michael] they will PULL THE PLUG IF HE DOESN'T GET HIS SHIT TOGETHER. IF HE DOESN'T DO THIS, HE LOSES EVERYTHING, **PROBABLY EVEN HIS KIDS**."

The AEG Live executives showed *zero* sympathy for Michael Jackson's rapidly deteriorating physical and mental condition. They threatened even to take his children away. The next day on June 20th Phillips and Ortega confronted a physically and mentally suffering Michael Jackson at his home during a so-called "crisis meeting" and verbally and mentally assaulted him further. During the meeting AEG Live threatened to "pull the plug."[1845] Murray, who was present, recounts details from the meeting during a November 2011 interview:

> The producer Kenny Ortega made several statements. He was going to quit; this could not go on if Michael was not going to do what he was expected to do they cannot have a show. And they could not get Michael to conform to what they wanted. Michael on the other hand was saying they were working him too much. He was ...He did not want to be worked as a machine. He felt like a machine...

> That's when I got the shock. Randy Phillips asked that they just step out of the living room when the meeting had ended. This is him, grinding his teeth. "He does not have a fucking cent, a fucking cent. What's this bullshit all about? Listen, this guy is next to the skid row, he's going to be homeless, the fucking pop sickles that his children are sucking on... Look, those kids...what's that all about? Nine security guards, why does he need that? I'm paying for that shit. I'm paying for the toilet paper he wipes his ass with. He has never a fucking cent. And if he don't get his show done, *he's over*. This is it. This is the last chance

---

1845 Richard Johnson, "Michael Jackson cut off financially by promoters in final days because he was missing rehearsal," **New York Post** June 7, 2013.

that he has to earn any kind of money. He is ruined. Financially he has *nothing. Zero.*[1846]

And then the move was made: the plug was officially pulled.

> Michael Jackson was cut off financially by promoters of his last concert tour days before he died (June 20th) and told he couldn't have another advance of $1 million because he was missing rehearsals, according to testimony today. Five days before Jackson died in 2009 of an anesthetic overdose, AEG was threatening to 'pull the plug' on his 50-concert tour, *and cut him off,* testimony and e-mails revealed in court.[1847]

The reference is to the request sent to Randy Phillips by Michael's lawyer Michael Kane on June 19th for a $1 million advance so Michael could pay staff. For the first time, Phillips refused the request, announcing in his response email to Kane: "it is impossible to advance any $$$. He may, unfortunately, be in *anticipatory breach* at *this point.*"

> AEG Live executives feared Michael Jackson would sabotage his comeback concerts five days before his death, the company's CEO testified Thursday. Randy Phillips refused to advance money to help Jackson pay his staff because he believed the singer was "in an anticipatory breach" of his contract because he had missed rehearsals, he testified.[1848]

An anticipatory breach refers to an action that shows a party's *intention to fail* to perform or fulfill its contractual obligations to another party. An anticipatory breach negates the counterparty's responsibility to perform its requirements under the contract. Phillips is here claiming that, because the

---

[1846] See also Caroline Graham, "NO, I didn't kill Michael. He did it himself...with a massive overdose using his own stash," **Daily Mail** November 24, 2013.

[1847] Richard Johnson, "Michael Jackson cut off financially by promoters in final days because he was missing rehearsal," **New York Post** June 7, 2013.

[1848] Alan Duke, "AEG exec feared Michael Jackson would sabotage his comeback tour," **CNN** June 7, 2013.

physically incapacitated Michael Jackson was missing some rehearsals *which he was NOT contractually mandated to attend*, Michael showed *intent* to fail to honor the terms of his contract!!!!

> the chief executive of AEG LIVE thought Jackson might be preparing to breach his contract by not rehearsing...Phillips said he thought Jackson might be preparing to break his contract by not showing up for rehearsals. "You felt Mr. Jackson's not going to rehearsal...may have placed him in breach of the contact. That's why you wouldn't advance him any more money?" [Jackson attorney Brian] Panish asked. "Yes," replied Phillips.[1849]

But this was all a big ruse. As Alan Duke of **CNN** pointed out:

> Phillips' testimony that he believed Jackson was contractually obligated to attend rehearsals contradicted AEG Live Co-CEO Paul Gongware's previous testimony that Jackson *was not required to rehearse*.[1850]

On June 20, 2009 the plug was officially pulled on Michael Jackson. And as Karen Faye noted in a September 26, 2013 tweet: "When [Randy Phillips] threatened to 'pull the plug' it meant a lot more than stop the show." That morning Randy Phillips spoke to Dr. Murray on the phone. In Phillip's video deposition that was shown to the jury in 2013 he claimed that the conversation lasted only three minutes. However, he was shown phone records that showed it lasted 25 minutes. Phillips was caught in a lie. When he was then asked what he and Murray discussed on that 25- minute call the morning of June 20th, he claimed that "he did not recall."[1851] Of course not. However, in an email he sent to Ortega that afternoon he hints: "I had a lengthy conversation with Dr. Murray, who I am

---

[1849] Jeff Gottlieb, "Michael Jackson was 'trembling, rambling,' director said," *Los Angeles Times* June 7, 2013.

[1850] Alan Duke, "AEG exec feared Michael Jackson would sabotage his comeback tour," *CNN* June 7, 2013.

[1851] Jeff Gottlieb, "Michael Jackson case: AEG exec admits Murray characterizations wrong," *Los Angeles Times* June 10, 2013.

gaining immense respect for as I get to deal with him more".[1852] Whatever conversation transpired on that call, it endeared Murray to Phillips.

On June 23rd – two days before Michael Jackson was killed by drugs delivered to him by AEG Live employees - AEG Live moved to finalize the new insurance policy on Michael Jackson's life.[1853] While the first policy was approved in April, it only covered the original ten shows. When AEG Live expanded the run to 50 shows, Lloyd's of London the insurance company required Michael Jackson to undergo a second medical exam, four hours that involved three doctors, heart-monitoring and blood work. [1854] AEG Live did everything they could to avoid that second physical, because they *knew* that the newly "drug-addled" Michael would *never* have passed that second physical exam. And a lot was at stake. While the original policy that covered 10 shows had the potential to net AEG Live $17 million, a successful claim on the expanded policy covering the 50 shows may have netted AEG Live 300 million euros, according to ***The Guardian***.[1855] Murray was called in to assist AEG Live lie to the insurance company about Michael Jackson's health. [1856]

AEG's insurance broker tried to persuade Lloyd's to drop the physical, according to the email discussions. AEG suggested that Jackson's physician, Dr. Conrad Murray, could give an oral recitation of Jackson's recent medical history instead, the Times reported. Lloyd's refused.

[1852] Jeff Gottlieb, "Michael Jackson case: AEG exec admits Murray characterizations wrong," ***Los Angeles Times*** June 10, 2013.

[1853] Corina Knoll, "AEG sought life insurance on 'basket case' Michael Jackson," ***Los Angeles Times*** May 21, 2013: "In days before Michael Jackson's death, AEG executives were still attempting to secure a life insurance policy on the performer who had been acting erratically at rehearsals for his comeback tour, according to testimony and emails..."

[1854] Steve Starr, "Promoter emails say Michael Jackson was out of shape, consumed with doubt," ***Today*** September 2, 2012.

[1855] Sean Michaels, "Michael Jackson concert insurer refuses $17.5m payout," ***The Guardian*** June 8, 2011.

[1856] Andrew Gumbel, "Conrad Murray – the man who supplied Michael Jackson's lethal dose of propofol," ***The Guardian*** November 7, 2011.

A Lloyd's underwriter wrote that repeated requests for written records and details about Jackson's daily fitness program were met "always with no response."

Murray responded to the last of the requests June 25 at Jackson's Southern California home, according to emails presented at the doctor's criminal trial. He wrote that he had talked to Jackson and "Authorization was denied."

Jackson died less than an hour later, according to a timeline Murray gave investigators.[1857]

Indeed, less than an hour later Michael Jackson was dead by the hand of AEG Live's hired doctor Conrad Murray. And only hours after that *AEG LIVE filed their insurance claim to collect the payout!*

AEG Live filed an insurance claim to recover losses from Michael Jackson's death the same day he died, according to a lawyer for Jackson's family...AEG's insurance claim...was filed with Lloyds of London on June 25, 2009 — hours after Jackson was pronounced dead at UCLA Medical Center.[1858]

The insurance policy was taken out to cover the cancellation or postponement of the London concerts in the case of the death, accident or illness of Jackson.[1859]

TODAY

POP CULTURE

AEG boss: Jackson insurance covers overdose

July 2, 2009, 7:49 PM CDT / Source: The Associated Press

Concert promoter AEG Live's chief executive says insurance will help cover any losses on the now-canceled Michael Jackson concert series if the pop star died accidentally, including of a drug overdose, but not if he died of natural causes.

[1857] Steve Starr, "Promoter emails say Michael Jackson was out of shape, consumed with doubt," *Today* September 2, 2012.

[1858] "AEG files claim for losses from Michael Jackson's death the day he died," *Fox* * May 20, 2013.

[1859] "Michael Jackson's estate, Lloyd's of London settle insurance dispute," *Reuters* January 15, 2004.

Concert promoter AEG Live's chief executive says insurance will help cover any losses on the now-cancelled Michael Jackson concert series if the pop star died accidentally, ***including of a drug overdoes***, but not if he died of natural causes.[1860]

A most revealing detail was reported on June 26th by Katherine Blackler on the U.K. insurance page ***Insurance Post***: according to sources within Lloyd's of London the much resisted second physical exam on Michael – which he was sure to fail – *was scheduled for June 26th*, the very day after Michael Jackson was killed by AEG Live's hired doctors![1861] In other words, Michael Jackson was killed the day before his scheduled physical exam that most certainly would have blown AEG Live's chance of *any* insurance payout! Who is naïve enough to believe this is a mere coincidence? Just as thinking Elvis Presley being killed by a mysterious drug overdose the day before he was schedule to testify against the Mafia is a mere coincidence is naïve. Incidentally, two weeks after Michael was killed, on July 5, 2009 Paul Gongaware who was a part of Elvis Presley's tours when he was likely killed by a Mafia "syringe job" wrote in emails: "I was on the Elvis tour when he died so I kind of knew what to expect [with Michael Jackson]."[1862] Indeed, he did know what to expect. In some ways the murder of Elvis Presley was the prototype of the murder of Michael Jackson.

Former X Factor judge Sharon Osbourne revealed on The Talk what she was told by AEG Live people:

There were people at the company who knew he was not well but didn't care. *Whether he performed or not, they'd still make money.* I had conversations with people

---

[1860] "AEG boss: Jackson insurance covers overdose," ***Today*** July 2, 2009,

[1861] Katherine Blackler, "Claims for cancelled UK Michael Jackson concerts could cost industry up to £300million," ***Insurance Post*** June 26, 2009 @ https://www.postonline.co.uk/reinsurance/1406311/claims-for-cancelled-uk-michael-jackson-concerts-could-cost-industry-up-to-ps300million.

[1862] Matt Richards and Mark Langthorne, ***83 Minutes: The Doctor, The Damage, and the Shocking Death of Michael Jackson*** (London: Blink Publishing, 2015) 120.

who said exactly that. I will tell people who said it (if subpoenaed).[1863]

By August 2009 Randy Phillips would be bragging in an email: "Michael's death is a terrible tragedy, but life must go on. *AEG will make a fortune from merch sales, ticket retention, the touring exhibition and the film/dvd.*" [1864] In addition, "The promoter (AEG)...said at the time that it was reimbursed by Jackson's estate for its concert-related losses."[1865] Randy Phillips did not lie about the fortune that Michael Jackson's death meant for them. On June 21 2010, a year after Michael was killed, it was reported that

> since the singer's death a year ago, the King of Pop's assets have grossed more than $1 billion, **Billboard** reports, thanks largely to a new record contract *with Sony*, renewed interest in his catalog and *the concert rehearsal documentary* This Is It, already the most successful film of its kind in history.[1866]

Michael's estate and legacy – and thus his fortune – was of course hijacked. Why did Randy Phillips bring Michael's enemy John Branca back into Michael's camp while Michael was drugged? A fraudulent will.

On the day the will was brought and shown to Katherine Jackson, the signature page was not presented. It was missing. When the will was supposedly signed in Los Angeles by Michael Jackson, *the singer was provably thousands of miles away* – protesting in New York against his perceived mistreatment at the hands of Sony

---

[1863] " ' They knew he was not well and didn't care': Sharon Osbourne reveals she will testify in Michael Jackson wrongful death trial," **Daily Mail** April 6, 2013.

[1864] "Tour Executive's E-Mail After Michael Jackson Died: We're Going To Make A Fortune From Merchandise Sales," **Radaronline** June 11, 2013: "Michael Jackson's death was seen as an opportunity to make a fortune off the singer, according to an email from the CEO of the company promoting his tour."

[1865] "Michael Jackson's estate, Lloyd's of London settle insurance dispute," **Reuters** January 15, 2004.

[1866] Daniel Kreps, "Michael Jackson Estate Earned $1 Billion Since Death," **Rolling Stone** June 21, 2010.

Music. Following his ex-client's death, John Branca is on record as stating, "I am Michael Jackson now".[1867]

In 2012 Michael's siblings (Jermaine, Janet, Randy, Tito, Rebbie) sent a letter to Branca and John McClain demanding their resignation as executors of the Michael Jackson estate for, among other things, *using a fraudulent will with a forged signature* to secure their position over the estate. In the letter they state:

> We know there is most certainly a conspiracy surrounding our brother's death and now coarse manipulation and fear are being used to cover it up...THIS HAS TO STOP NOW: NO MORE!! You will not succeed. John Branca, after our brother passed, you said to our mother: "I AM MICHAEL JACKSON NOW". How dare you. Make no mistake, Mr. Branca, before we hit the stage, we were a family and still to this day we are a family. We're not going to let anyone abuse our mother, nor will we tolerate any further attempts to divide us.[1868]

X.   The Cause of Death?

As Michael Jackson's life slipped away, his personal physician delayed calling 911, hid evidence of his medical treatment, misled paramedics and doctors, and then abruptly left the hospital before police could question him, prosecutors and the pop star's employees said in court Tuesday...[Dr. Conrad] Murray initially did not return police calls, but two days after Jackson's death he met with police...[Before calling 911] Murray ordered another security guard, Alberto Alvarez, to help collect pill bottles and medical paraphernalia in a bag.[1869]

[1867] Pete Mills, "Sony exec claims Michael Jackson's 'image and likeness' worth less than a second-hand car," **Orchard Times** February 18, 2017.

[1868] "Michael Jackson's Family Demands Executors of Estate Resign: Report," **ABC News Radio** July 18, 2012; "THIS HAS TO STOP NOW": Michael Jackson's family claim singer's will was forged," **FACT Magazine** July 19, 2012

[1869] Harriet Ryan and Victoria Kim, "Michael Jackson's doctor frantically tried to cover up singer's treatment," **Los Angeles Times** January 5, 2011.

Detectives Orlando Martinez, Dan Meyers and Scott Smith in the 2019 documentary *Killing Michael Jackson* claim that

> Murray spent 25 minutes clearing away medical supplies, making phone calls, and sending emails before assisting Jackson with CPR and calling the police. 'Mr Murray started cleaning up the mess that he had left, covering up the medical treatment that he was giving,' Martinez said. 'He put that away, called for help from security, and directed them to call 911 while he gave ineffective, one-handed CPR.' Detective Martinez argues Murray attempted to cover up Jackson's death by hiding receipts worth up to the value of five gallons of propofol at his girlfriend's apartment, saying that 'at that point we knew this was not an honest mistake, but that this was on purpose, bad medicine'.[1870]

The Coroner's Office conducted an autopsy on Michael on June 26, 2009 but did not release its final conclusions until September 18, 2009. There is good reason to believe that the results that were ultimately published in September are not completely consistent with what was discovered during the autopsy on June 26. "Acute propofol intoxication with a contributory benzodiazepine effect" is the established cause of death. This means that Michael died from an overdose of the drug propofol combined with other drugs of the benzodiazepine class. This is the September 18th conclusion. Propofol was the primary killer and Dr. Conrad Murray was the sole administrator. However, almost every bit of the early press focused on a different drug and a different doctor – Demerol and Arnold Klein.

[1870] Adam Starkey, "Michael Jackson's doctor waited 25 minutes to call police after finding singer's body, claims new documentary," *Metro* June 21, 2019.

"Jackson Family: Demerol Shot Caused Death," *TMZ* June 26, 2009:

> A close member of Michael Jackson's family has told us Jackson received a daily injection of a synthetic narcotic similar to morphine — Demerol — and yesterday he received a shot at 11:30 AM. Family members are saying the dosage was "too much" and that's what caused his death.

"Michael Jackson Death Caused By A Demerol Shot?," *The Examiner* June 26, 2009:

> New reports are in that say Michael Jackson may have died from a Demerol overdose. Many news agencies and websites are reporting that Michael Jackson died from

receiving an overdose of Demerol. Toxicology results will take 4 to 6 weeks to confirm cause of death. *The Sun* reports an Emergency Room source at UCLA hospital said Jackson aides told medics he had collapsed after an injection of potent Demerol. A Michael Jackson source said: "Shortly after taking the Demerol he started to experience slow shallow breathing. His breathing gradually got slower and slower until it stopped…Shortly after the Demerol shot was given 911 was called.

Susan Donaldson James, "Friend Says Michael Jackson Battled Demerol Addiction," *ABC News* June 26, 2009:

The Los Angeles police were told that Jackson received a Demerol injection one hour before his death, according to a senior law enforcement official. Paramedics at the Los Angeles hospital where Jackson died Thursday, according to the British tabloid the Sun, said the star's breathing got 'slower and slower until it stopped.'

Anita Singh, "Video: Michael Jackson's weird and wonderful life," *Telegraph* June 26, 2009.

He last performed on Wednesday night, 12 hours before the emergency services were called to his Los Angeles home. Following that performance he reportedly took a painkilling injection of Demerol, a commercial name for the morphine-based drug pethidine. Pethidine is known to have dangerous side effects including cardiac arrest if used wrongly.

Fox News,[1871] ***ABC News***,[1872] and ***The Sun***,[1873] all reported that by July 15 police have confirmed that Demerol was one of the many drugs found in Michael's home, thus giving credence to the "Death by Demerol" reports. Propofol was found as well and an early theory developed of the relation between the two drugs in the death of Michael Jackson.

> Both of pop superstar Michael Jackson's arms were scarred with track marks, investigators probing his death say, and the marks are consistent with the finding of the potent sedative propofol (trade name Diprivan) in his home -- a drug that is increasingly at the center of their probe into what caused Jackson's death, ABC News has learned...

> Medical experts point out that the abuse of Demerol could have set the stage for cardiac arrest, by increasing Jackson's risk.
> One pharmacologist blogged about Propofol this week and explained in his science blog how Demerol abuse could have caused cardiac problems and could have increased his risk for heart rhythm disturbances from the Propofol: "As I wrote last week in my blog post on Demerol ® (meperidine), Jackson's reported long-term use of this analgesic for back pain may have already primed him for cardiac problems due to the accumulation of a toxic metabolite, normeperidine," Dr. David Kroll

---

[1871] Jana Winter, "At Least Nine Doctors Who Treated Michael Jackson Under investigation," ***Fox News*** July 15, 2009: "Law enforcement sources confirmed to FOXNews.com that Demerol, propofol (Diprivan) alprazolam (Xanax), Percocet and antibiotics were found in Jackson's rented Holmby Hills mansion after he died."
[1872] Russell Goldman, "The Accident that Sparked Jackson's Addiction," ***ABC News*** July 15, 2009: "Police investigating Jackson's June 25 death have confirmed that his home was filled with powerful prescription drugs including the painkillers Oxycontin and Demerol and the hospital-grade anesthetic Diprivan..."
[1873] As reported in Vic Walter and Richard Esposito, "Michael Jackson's Arm's Marred by Track Marks Consistent with Potent Sedative Use," ***ABC News*** July 1, 2009: "The Sun has reported there were at least 20 drugs found in Jackson's home, and many of these can be injected, including Methadone, Fentanyl, Demerol, Versed, and Lidocaine."

said. "However, most relevant to the Jackson case is that propofol can cause cardiac tachyarrhythmias (rhythmic disturbances at high heart rate), especially in people predisposed to cardiac problems." ...

The Sun has reported there were at least 20 drugs found in Jackson's home, and many of these can be injected, including Methadone, Fentanyl, Demerol, Versed, and Lidocaine.[1874]

It was reported that Michael's mother Katherine Jackson and other members of Michael Jackson's family gave the LAPD a list of doctors whom they believed misprescribed drugs to Michael and Dr. Conrad Murray and Dr. Arnold Klein topped the list. [1875] Dr. Steven Hoefflin announced on July 22nd:

"Over the last few days I have been with the family when the police were present and obtaining their information from the family about Michael. The evidence, as it is mounting, is horrifying." Dr Hoefflin said Mrs Jackson believes two doctors are responsible for her son's death and up to eight more could have their medical licenses reviewed.

"In my understanding of this case, from being present when police talk to the family, there are two, who if found guilty of the acts suspected of them, could go to jail...It is my professional opinion that - although there are successful and much safer ways of treating these problems - some of his doctors chose to use large doses of Demerol for his pain and administer Propofol to induce sleep." [1876]

Dr. Hoefflin was a Government Witness working with the State Attorney General's Office in the Investigation of Michael

---

[1874] Vic Walter and Richard Esposito, "Michael Jackson's Arm's Marred by Track Marks Consistent with Potent Sedative Use," *ABC News* July 1, 2009.

[1875] "Jackson Family Gave LAPD Doctor List," *TMZ* July 8, 2009.

[1876] "Michael Jackson 'left to die on drugs drip after a doctor fell asleep', his plastic surgeon claims," *Daily Mail* July 23, 2009.

Jackson's death.[1877] On July 23 he spoke to *Access Hollywood*:

> Dr. Steven Hoefflin, a longtime friend and doctor of Michael Jackson, has claimed that the King of Pop "had lethal amounts of Demerol and Propofol in his body" at the time of his death...Hoefflin claimed to *Access* that according to a reliable source of his, Jackson's toxicology report indicated Michael "had lethal amounts of Demerol and Propofol in his body" when he died on June 25. Results from the LA Coroner's official autopsy of Jackson have yet to be publicly released...Hoefflin claimed that the Demerol came from Dr. Arnold Klein – Michael's dermatologist – and the Propofol came from Dr. Conrad Murray, Jackson's personal physician in the weeks before his death.[1878]

On June 30 *TMZ* reported: "We've learned that the LAPD wants to talk to Michael Jackson's longtime dermatologist Arnold Klein about drugs he may have prescribed or given Michael Jackson. We're told Klein has already gotten a lawyer but as far as we know the LAPD has not spoken with him."[1879] On July 2 the Coroner's Office requested medical records from Klein's office and on July 10 the Coroner's office subpoenaed Klein's records.[1880] On July 15, 2009 *The Sun* reported:

> Michael Jackson's skin doctor is under investigation over the singer's death, it was announced yesterday. Assistant Chief Coroner Ed Winter barged into Dr Arnold Klein's office to seize medical records - as the doc told of "rebuilding" the star's face. Cops will probe the dermatologist's prescription practices with regard to the vast amount of drugs [Michael Jackson] was taking. They will investigate whether medication was given to aliases. Dr Klein admitted "occasionally" giving him the sedative

---

[1877] See below.

[1878] "Former Jackson Doctor Claims Michael 'Had Lethal Amounts of Demerol & Propofol'," *Access Hollywood* July 23, 2009.

[1879] "Cops Interested in Another Michael Jackson Doc," *TMZ* June 30, 2009

[1880] "Jackson Doc Did Not Fully Cooperate," *TMZ* July 14, 2009.

Demerol, but said: "That was the strongest medication I ever used."

Of course, it is demonstrable that Klein is not being forthright here, as we will show.

But Dr. Arnold Klein was an "eminence in Los Angeles" and well-connected as a member of Hollywood's Gay Mafia. So he was protected – at first. When the Coroner's Report was released on September 18, 2009 *there was no mention of Demerol as a contributing factor to Michael's death*, only propofol and the contributory benzodiazepines. This is no doubt because if *Klein* is connected to Michael Jackson's death through his Demerol injections then *David Geffen* and other members of the Gay Mafia might be brought into view as well. So Klein's Demerol legally disappears.

Dr. Conrad Murray was charged with involuntary manslaughter for the death of Michael Jackson in February 2010. As part of his defense Murray contended that while he was giving Michael propofol for his insomnia Klein was (allegedly unbeknownst to Murray) at the same time giving Michael Demerol; that Klein made Michael dependent on Demerol and *caused* Michael's insomnia with the Demerol; and that Klein should be a co-defendant with him as he is at least partly to blame for Michael's death as well.[1881]

But Dr. Conrad Murray was never able to make that case in court. Why?

The judge in the forthcoming trial of Michael Jackson's doctor Conrad Murray has barred the singer's dermatologist from giving evidence. Dr Murray's lawyers had wanted to argue that Arnold Klein injected Jackson with the painkiller demerol "for no valid medical purpose"

[1881] Matthew Perpetua, "Doctor: Michael Jackson Was Dependent on Demerol," *Rolling Stone* October 28, 2011; Alice Gomstyn and Chris Connelly, "Michael Jackson's Secret World: Willing Doctors, Hospital-Grade Sedatives," *ABC News* November 4, 2011; Alan Duke, "'Perfect storm' of drugs killed Michael Jackson, sleep expert says," *CNN* October 14, 2011; Caroline Graham, "NO, I didn't kill Michael. He did it himself...with a massive overdose using his own stash," *Daily Mail* November 24, 2013; "Dr. Murray Targets Arnie Klein in MJ Death," *TMZ* September 5, 2010.

and that the star became addicted to the drug. The judge said it was "not relevant".[1882]

Indeed, Judge Michael Pastor "dealt a crushing blow" to Murray's defense by disallowing Klein to be called to testify. The justification that Klein's testimony "isn't relevant to the case, and that it could confuse the jury,"[1883] is of course ridiculous.

> lead defense attorney Ed Chernoff invoked Klein's name seven times during his opening statement and has referred to the dermatologist repeatedly throughout the trial. The defense, which is expected to begin presenting its side next week, sought to call Klein as a witness but was blocked by Los Angeles Superior Court Judge Michael Pastor, who ruled Klein's testimony was not relevant to the case. [1884]

At this time Klein was still protected. His emotions, his hubris, and his mouth will cost him this protection, however, and his life.

 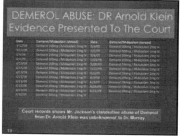

[1882] "Michael Jackson judge bars skin doctor from testifying," **BBC News** August 30, 2011.
[1883] Jen Heger, "Dr. Conrad Murray Dealt Crushing Blow In Upcoming Michael Jackson Trial," **Radar Online** August 29, 2011.
[1884] "Jackson's Dermatologist Says Murray Fallout Hurts," **The Telegraph** October 15, 2011.

XI.   Death By Polypharmacy

"It was a pharmaceutical experiment on Michael Jackson. It was an obscene experiment in 2009..." - Prosecutor David Walgren

The toxicology report that was finally released revealed that "there was a bewildering number of drugs coursing through his veins at the time of his death."[1885] And while Demerol mysteriously "disappeared" from the conversation as totally as did the second shooter who was apprehended during the Malcom X assassination, propofol became known as *the killer* of Michael Jackson. But the toxicology report reveals *a*

billboard

Doctor: Drug 'Cocktail' Killed Michael Jackson

Dr. Conrad Murray's use of a cocktail of drugs on Michael Jackson as he struggled to fall asleep on the day he died was a "recipe for disaster" and ultimately caused his death, a UCLA sleep therapy expert testified Thursday.

much darker picture of what was being done to Michael Jackson. It might even be said in fact that propofol, like Conrad Murray who wielded it, was but the fall guy for a much more complex conspiracy.

Like Elvis Presley "Michael Jackson had a 'polypharmacy' of drugs in his system."[1886] In addition to propofol the examiner also found traces of **lorazepam** (a benzodiazepine drug, also called Atvian); **midazolam** (another benzodiazepine, also called Versed); **lidocaine** (a local anesthetic often included with propofol to relieve injection pain); **diazepam** (a benzodiazepine to treat anxiety, insomnia and alcohol withdrawal, also called Valium); and **nordiazepam** (a benzodiazepine-derived sedative, often used

---

[1885] Colin Vickery, "Michael Jackson should have died earlier, autopsy report reveals," ***News Corp Australia*** June 25, 2014.

[1886] Superior Court of California, County of Los Angeles, Joseph Jackson v. Conrad Murray et al. Case No. BC450393, 30 November 2010, pg. 12; Jeff Gottlieb, "Michael Jackson had several drugs in his system when he died," ***Los Angeles Times*** May 7, 2013; "The drugs found in Michael Jackson's body after he died," ***BBC Newsbeat*** November 8, 2011.

to treat anxiety) in Michael's bloodstream. It was AEG Live's hiree Dr. Conrad Murray who administered this fatal polypharmacy to Michael Jackson.

On June 22, 2009, three days before Michael died, Dr. Murray gave him a 25mg dosage of propofol, along with ativan (=lorazepam) and versed (=midazolam). The next night, on June 23, 2009, Murray gave him ativan and versed. And on that fateful mourning of mornings, Dr. Murray gave Michael a 10mg tab of valium [1] at the wee time of 1:30 in the morning. Then, a half hour later (2:00 am), he gave him a 2mg IV of Ativan [2]. Then, just an hour later (3:00 am), he gave him a 2mg IV of versed [3]. Another two hours later (5:00 am), he gave him yet another 2mg IV of ativan. Then, two and a half hours later (7:30 am), he gave him still another 2mg IV of versed. Now, you don't have to be a medical professional to know, as one medical expert said, that **this much dosage "is enough to put an elephant down"**!"[1887]

And the frail, emaciated Michael Jackson was the furthest thing from a bull elephant. This combination of drugs administered to Michael Jackson which was so strong it "could bring down several people," it "'was the perfect storm' that killed him."[1888] Dr. Nader Kamanger, a UCLA sleep therapy expert and prosecution witness, said it was the "cocktail of drugs" - diazepam (Valium), lorazepam (Ativan) and midazolam (Versed) and propofol – that was the "recipe for disaster" and "ultimately caused [Michael Jackson's] death."[1889] Longtime friend Frank Cascio said Michael once confided in him that he feared he would die from a gunshot. But, Cascio said, "no one would have ever thought that a shot of a prescription drug would claim Jackson's life so prematurely." [1890] But death by

---

[1887] Dr. Firpo W. Carr, "The Drug-Induced Death of Michael Jackson," *Los Angeles Sentinel* August 27, 2009.

[1888] Alan Duke, "'Perfect storm' of drugs killed Michael Jackson, sleep expert says," *CNN* October 14, 2011.

[1889] Anthony McCartney, "Doctor: Drug 'cocktail' killed Michael Jackson," *Associated Press* October 13, 2011.

[1890] Alice Gomstyn and Chris Connelly, "Michael Jackson's Secret World: Willing Doctors, Hospital-Grade Sedatives," *ABC News* November 4, 2011.

gunshot is only *one* method of a Mafia hit. Another is the so-called *syringe job* – death by drugs. Just like Elvis Presley's death, Michael's has all of the earmarks of a syringe job. Family friend Terry Harvey gave an interview to the **News of the World** on July 19, 2009 and said "Michael was poisoned," a position Michael's brother Jermaine Jackson expressed as well:

Terry Harvey: "Michael was poisoned"

Monday,   20/07/2009
11:14 AM (GMT +7)

NME

Music Film TV Video The Gig Guide Shop Radio Discount Codes NME AAA

Jermaine Jackson: 'Michael was toxically poisoned'

Sibling says he noticed a dramatic change during late singer's final days

NME ⏱ 16th September 2017   ⟨ Share   f   ⅏

According to the News of the World, the autopsy report shows that Michael was murdered.

Police told Michael's family that their investigation will focus on one or several people who took care of Michael's treatment in his final days. In the near future a criminal trial will be open to hear who is responsible for Michael's death.

This means the doctor who was treating and caring for Michael will be included in the list for the investigation. Police are conducting an investigation in order to quickly find the guys who injected high doses of pain medication into Michael's body.

Last week, La Toya Jackson – Michael's sister said to the News of the World that she knows who killed her brother. And the amazing thing is yesterday, 19/7, Terry Harvey – a longtime friend of the Jackson family also gave an exclusive interview to the News of the World.

Terry said: "According to the survey results Michael died from an overdose of painkiller Diprivan and many other poisonous drugs. The investigators found very much of the drug in his stomach. The body of Michael had a lot of scars from injections ".

It should be pointed out that Conrad Murray's claim that he was injecting Michael with Propofol every night for two months in order to "treat insomnia" is medically dubious. "Propofol is an intravenously administered *hypnotic drug*."[1891] Beverly Phillip, professor of anesthesia at Harvard Medical School, says Propofol is "not a sleeping aid at all. What it is is a general anesthetic (i.e. it numbs pain)...So the use as a sleep aid is way off the mark...Everyone has been saying, 'Michael Jackson wanted to sleep.' No one talked about relaxing drugs. With this drug in unskilled hands, this sleep is permanent. It induces general anesthesia, which is not like a night's sleep."[1892]

But there is one drug within this deadly cocktail that was administered to Michael Jackson which hints at an experimental poisoning operation originating from a source much higher than Dr. Conrad Murray and even higher than AEG: the drug Midazolam (Versed).

Recall that, according to his own accounting (which, giving how many times Murray has lied and changed his story,[1893] must be assumed to *not* give the full story) on the night that Murray killed Michael Jackson, the polypharmacy Murray administered included 10mg of Valium, 4mg of Atvian and 4mg of Versed, along with 25mg of propofol. We learn also that Murray administered this "polypharmacy of drugs" to Michael over *several weeks*, not just on that fateful night.[1894] The presence of Versed/Midazolam in this cocktail is quite alarming.

[1891] Superior Court of California, County of Los Angeles Katherine Jackson v. AEG Live LLC et al., Case No. BC445597 September 15, 2010, pg. 6.

[1892] Katherine Harmon, "What is Propofol—and How Could It Have Killed Michel Jackson?" *Scientific American* October 3, 2011.

[1893] Superior Court of California, County of Los Angeles, Joseph Jackson v. Conrad Murray et al. Case No. BC450393, 30 November 2010.

[1894] Superior Court of California, County of Los Angeles Katherine Jackson v. AEG Live LLC et al., Case No. BC445597 September 15, 2010, pg. 6, 8: "The 'cocktail' Murray provided was similar to the medicaitons he had given Jackson for the prior five (5) weeks".

Versed is the most commonly used drug in a group of drugs called benzodiazepines...This class of drugs is designed to provide for sedation, *hypnosis-like compliance*, relieve anxiety, muscle relaxation, and anticonvulsant activity. The "side effect" that medical professionals most like about these drugs is that they generally induce *anterograde amnesia* (prevent memory by blocking the acquisition and encoding of new information). In other words, medical professionals like these drugs because most people *will not remember what happens to them while under their effect even though they are "awake."*

In medical terms, this is called conscious sedation. While under the influence of these drugs, patients ... will therefore *be very compliant* with medical professionals (they will not advocate for themselves), and they will most likely not remember anything about what happened. It is these last two consequences that most appeal to the healthcare industry. If you're given Versed prior to being brought into the Operating Room, you will likely not remember who is in the room, being placed on the OR table or being prepared for anesthesia. Further, once surgery is over, you will likely be give a few more doses of Versed, again that means you will likely not remember being in the PACU... Keep this in mind: Versed or similar sedative drug legally invalidates any patient testimony regarding their treatment...Also note that Versed is also known as a date-rape drug. Versed is perfect for predators because *it makes the recipient completely compliant* and generally induces memory loss of traumatic events.[1895]

Versed/Midazolam has the ability to bend the mind of the patient and make him obedient and compliant. It is thus used as a "patient control drug." Patients have testified that Versed/Midazolam turned them into "compliant zombies" with no will of their own.[1896] Dr. Conrad Murray injected Michael Jackson with this drug on a regular basis. Recall that Terry

---

[1895] "Sedation, *Versed*, and Your Procedure," **Medical Patient Modesty** @ http://patientmodesty.org/versed.aspx.
[1896] http://versedbusters.blogspot.com/2005/12/introduction.html

Harvey described Michael in his final days under the influence of the drugs as "walking around in a daze like a zombie," and simply telling people "yes" to their demands – being compliant.[1897] By June during rehearsals Michael appeared "very stoic."[1898] Recall also that, according to Karen Faye Michael stoically kept repeating, "why can't I choose,"[1899] but he offered no resistance.

Versed/Midazolam as a "patient control drug" due to its ability to bend the mind into compliance or as a "date-rape" drug due to its amnesia effect are only two of the drug's scary characteristics.[1900] The drug is also used "as part of a cocktail of chemicals for executions,"[1901] in certain jurisdictions in the U.S. Usually, it is part of a three-drug protocol during execution by lethal injection, also including an opioid. Experts say "the drug in effect paralyzes the brain."[1902] Versed/Midazolam acts as a sedative to render the condemned prisoner unconscious, at which time the vecuronium bromide and potassium chloride are administered, stopping the prisoner's breathing and heart, respectively.[1903]

[1897] "'Drugged, exhausted' MJ 'could barley walk' during This Is It rehearsals," *Thaindian News* October 31, 2009.
[1898] Colin Bertram, "The Final Days of Michael Jackson," *Biography* June 24, 2019 @ HTTPS://WWW.BIOGRAPHY.COM/NEWS/MICHAEL-JACKSON-FINAL-DAYS.
[1899] Alan Duke, "Witness: Michael Jackson was paranoid, talking to himself in last days," *CNN* May 9, 2013
[1900] "New date rape drug hits Sydney nightclubs," *The Sydney Morning Herald* February 2, 2003.
[1901] Tom Porter, "What Is Midazolam and Why Do Protesters Claim Its Use in Executions Is Cruel," *Newsweek* July 26, 2017.
[1902] Tom Porter, "What Is Midazolam and Why Do Protesters Claim Its Use in Executions Is Cruel," *Newsweek* July 26, 2017.
[1903] Ben Bryant, "Life and Death row: How the lethal injection kills," *BBC* March 5, 2018.

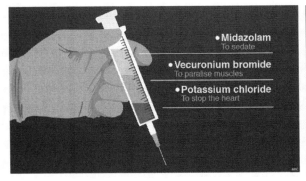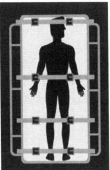

• Midazolam
To sedate

• Vecuronium bromide
To paralise muscles

• Potassium chloride
To stop the heart

The drug midazolam – a sedative used by several states to cause unconsciousness – has proved so controversial that, in 2017, Alabama inmate Thomas D Arthur asked to be executed by firing squad. Arthur lodged an appeal with the Supreme Court to postpone his execution on the basis that midazolam, one of the drugs in Alabama's three-drug lethal injection combination, could contribute to 'prolonged torture'. The Supreme Court denied the appeal, and Arthur was executed (by lethal injection) in May 2017.[1904]

Dr. Conrad Murray delivered a three-drug cocktail to Michael Jackson the night of June 24th: Valium, Atvian and Versed/Midazolam. He then likely delivered an opioid, Demerol, which we believe he later injected into Michael, adding to this three-drug cocktail. There occurred a "reaction" that succeeded in killing Michael. We will consider that below.

During Conrad Murray's manslaughter trial in 2011 the prosecutor David Walgren in his closing argument described Murray's polypharmacy administration to Michael Jackson as an "obscene" "pharmaceutical experiment on Michael Jackson."[1905] There are strong grounds for believing that this choice of language is appropriate…and revealing.

[1904] Ben Bryant, "Life and Death row: How the lethal injection kills," *BBC* March 5, 2018.
[1905] Alice Gomstyn and Chris Connelly, "Michael Jackson's Secret World: Willing Doctors, Hospital-Grade Sedatives," *ABC News* November 4, 2011.

After the 9/11 attacks in 2001 in New York, so-called terrorism suspects that were detained in U.S.-controlled facilities were subject to a U.S. "torture program." Part of that program was spearheaded by the C.I.A.'s Office of Medical Services (OMS). OMS conducted a drug-research program called "Project Medication," in which the detainees were chemically experimented on. Project Medication lasted "officially" from 2001 to 2003 (though we have reason to believe it had a longer "unofficial" existence). Project Medication was heir to the CIA's MK-Ultra program of the 1960s and the Soviet experimental program of the 1950s, both of which were studied by the Project Medication researchers. OMS chose a specific drug to experiment with on prisoners during Project Medication: Versed/Midazolam.[1906]

One of the purposes of Project Medication was to test the CIA's theory of "learned helplessness."[1907] *Learned helplessness* is a condition in which a person suffers from a sense of *powerlessness* arising from a traumatic event or *persistent failure* to succeed. It is thought to be one of the underlying causes of depression, resulting from a real or perceived *absence of control* over the outcome of a situation. The C.IA. spent $81 million investigating learned helplessness as "a technique of stripping someone of their will" by exposing people to aversive events which they cannot control.[1908] The scientific aim is to *induce the apathetic attitude that one's actions do not have the power to affect one's situation.* "But it's also more than that. Learned helplessness occurs when a subject is so broken he will not even attempt escape if the opportunity presents

---

[1906] Eli Rosenberg, "The CIA explored using a 'truth-serum' on terrorism detainees after 9/11, newly released report shows," *The Washington Post* November 13, 2018; Dror Ladin, "Secret CIA Document Shows Plan to Test Drugs on Prisoners," *ACLU* November 13, 2018 @ https://www.aclu.org/blog/national-security/torture/secret-cia-document-shows-plan-test-drugs-prisoners.

[1907] "CIA considered potential truth serum to force suspects to talk," *CBS News* November 13, 2018.

[1908] Terrence McCoy, " 'Learned helplessness': The chilling psychological concept behind the CIA's interrogation methods," *The Washington Post* December 11, 2014.

itself," **The Washington Post** reports.[1909] The C.I.A.'s experimentally induced "learned helplessness" on terrorist detainees such as Abu Zubaydah successfully produced "compliance":

When the interrogator "raised his eyebrow," without instructions, Abu Zabaydah "slowly walked on his own to the water table and sat down," one account said. "... When the interrogator snapped his fingers twice, Abu Zabaydah would lie flat on the waterboard"... He had been trained. Like one of [the laboratory] dogs."[1910]

Through their "learned helplessness" techniques the C.I.A. successfully trained Abu Zubaydah "Like one of [the laboratory] dogs."

One of the apparent aims of Project Medication was to experiment with Versed/Midazolam, "the preferred drug," in the production of the C.I.A.'s "learned helplessness." Project Medication's "preferred drug" was also one of the drugs that Dr. Conrad Murray, as a part of his work for the Jew Randal Phillips and AEG Live, regularly injected into Michael Jackson. The result: Michael's *learned helplessness.*

AEG's control of Jackson's person was further extended by the drugs being administered by Murray, which weakened Jackson's physical and mental health, rendering him vulnerable, confused, *and subject to direction.*[1911]

In May and June, Michael Jackson was confused, easily frightened, *unable to remember*, obsessive, and

---

[1909] Terrence McCoy, " 'Learned helplessness': The chilling psychological concept behind the CIA's interrogation methods," **The Washington Post** December 11, 2014.
[1910] Terrence McCoy, " 'Learned helplessness': The chilling psychological concept behind the CIA's interrogation methods," **The Washington Post** December 11, 2014.
[1911] Superior Court of California, County of Los Angeles Katherine Jackson v. AEG Live LLC et al., Case No. BC445597 September 15, 2010, 10-11.

disoriented. He had *impaired memory*, loss of appetite, and absence of energy.[1912]

"The way he was talking, it's like *he's not in control over his own life any*more," she told me earlier this month. "It *sounds like somebody else is pulling his strings and telling him what to do.* Someone wants him dead. They keep feeding him pills like candy...The people around him will kill him."[1913]

[Michael] had a sharp mind, but he was deluded, hampered by the drugs. He didn't know what he was saying to people. To make his life easy *he would just say 'yes'.* He was walking around in a daze *like a zombie."* Another friend said: "He shouted out, 'They are punishing me and I can't take it anymore. They are gonna kill me.'"[1914]

Emotionally frail and physically thin, Jackson was described by *This Is It* makeup and hair artist Karen Faye as paranoid, shivering from chills and repeating himself during his last days...He was "very upbeat, but he was on the thin side," Faye said of an earlier, April 2009 meeting with Jackson. Come June, everything had changed. "He was not the man I knew," Faye testified. "He was acting like a person I didn't recognize"...Jackson appeared "*very stoic*" but "frightened"..."He kept repeating, '*why can't I choose,*' it was one of the things he repeated over and over again," Faye said...[1915]

[1912] Superior Court of California, County of Los Angeles, Joseph Jackson v. Conrad Murray et al. Case No. BC450393, 30 November 2010, pg. 12.

[1913] Ian Halperin, " 'I'm better off dead. I'm done': Michael Jackson's fateful prediction just a week before his death," **Daily Mail** June 29 2009.

[1914] "'Drugged, exhausted' MJ 'could barley walk' during This Is It rehearsals," **Thaindian News** October 31, 2009.

[1915] Colin Bertram, "The Final Days of Michael Jackson," **Biography** June 24, 2019 @ HTTPS://WWW.BIOGRAPHY.COM/NEWS/MICHAEL-JACKSON-FINAL-DAYS.

By June 2009 Michael Jackson was *clearly* put in a state of *learned helplessness* which was chemically induced, and one of the main chemicals used is the very "preferred drug" of the C.I.A.'s Project Medication: Versed/Midazolam. Michael was chemically controlled by being chemically maintained in a state of continuous confusion and compliance. And then, he was killed – the day before he was scheduled for a physical examine that would have killed AEG Live's insurance application hopes, costing them a potential 300 million euros.

Murray had been administering this drug cocktail to Michael Jackson for several weeks before the night of June 24, 2009. This is no doubt how Michael was chemically controlled and manipulated during the months of May and June. But something specific happened on the morning of June 25, 2009 that caused Michael's *death*. Murray injected Michael with something that morning. After Michael was found dead, according to the testimony of Michael Jackson's personal assistant Michael Amir Williams, Murray called him and said Michael Jackson "had a bad reaction."[1916] If Murray only injected Michael Jackson with 25mg of propofol, it is hard to see how such a fatal "bad reaction" could have all of a sudden occurred. It should be pointed out that the combination of propofol and Versed/Midazolam helped with sedation and even has a synergistic effect: "Clinical and animal studies indicate that the combinations of propofol and midazolam...have a synergistic interaction with respect to their ability to *produce hypnosis*."[1917] The combination of Midazolam and propofol thus increases the *hypnotic effect*!

[1916] Harriet Ryan and Victoria Kim, "Michael Jackson's doctor frantically tried to cover up singer's treatment," **Los Angeles Times** January 5, 2011;

[1917] David C. Oxorn et. Al, "The Effects of Midazolam on Propofol-Induced Anesthesia: Propofol Dose Requirements, Mood Profiles, and Perioperative Dreams," **Anesth Analg** 85 (1997): 553-559 (554); S. McClune et al., "Synergistic interaction between midazolam and propofol," **Br J Anaesth** 69 (1992): 240-5; T.G. Short and P.T. Chui, "Propofol and midazolam act synergistically in combination," **Br J Anaesth** 67 (1991): 530-545; T.G. Short, J.L. Plummer and P.T. Chui, "Hypnotic and anaesthetic interactions between midazolam, propofol and alfentanil," **Br J Anaesth** 69 (1992):162-7; E. Taylor, A.F. Ghouri and P.F. White, "Midazolam in combination with propofol for sedation during local anesthesia," **J Clin Anesth** 4 (1992): 213-6.

On the other hand, the combination of Versed/Midazolam and Demerol *can be deadly.*

> Using meperidine (Demerol) together with midazolam may increase side effects such as drowsiness, dizziness, lightheadedness, *confusion, depression,* low blood pressure, *slow or shallow breathing,* and *impairment in thinking, judgment,* and motor coordination. Occasionally, *severe reactions may result in coma and even death.*[1918]

This perfectly describes Michael Jackson's state and condition in his final days as well as the moments of his death as we are told.

> **The Sun** reports an Emergency Room source at UCLA hospital said Jackson aides told medics he had collapsed after an injection of potent Demerol. A Michael Jackson source said: "Shortly after taking the Demerol he started to *experience slow shallow breathing. His breathing gradually got slower and slower until it stopped...*Shortly after the Demerol shot was given 911 was called.[1919]

It is very conceivable that the "bad reaction" that Conrad Murray informed Michael Amir Williams about was caused by an injection of Demerol at 11:30 A.M. as has been claimed which then interacted with the Versed/Midazolam which Murray had already injected Michael with at 3:00 A.M and again at 7:30 A.M.

XII.   *Whodunit?*

We know that Dr. Conrad Murray was convicted of involuntary manslaughter on November 7, 2011. Mother Katherine Jackson demanded that the charge of manslaughter

---

[1918] "Drug Interactions between Demerol and Versed," **Drugs.com** @ https://www.drugs.com/drug-interactions/demerol-with-versed-1557-939-1628-3562.html.
[1919] "Michael Jackson Death Caused By A Demerol Shot?" **The Examiner** June 26, 2009.

be upgraded to second degree murder.[1920] "Second degree murder requires malice aforethought, which can be implied by the conduct of the defendant" in interrupting CPR on Michael Jackson in order to conceal drug evidence, said attorney Adam Streisand. This is most appropriate. Conrad Murray's actions throughout the months of May and June 2009 and culminating with his deeds on June 25th surely meet the requirements of the State of California's Depraved Heart Murder crime. Joe Jackson, LaToya Jackson and Jermaine Jackson have gone on record with their belief that Dr. Murray's role in the death of Michael Jackson was a part of a larger conspiracy in which Murray was but the fall guy, the patsy.[1921] Much evidence strongly supports – even vindicates – their belief. Who else was involved in the conspiracy to *murder* Michael Jackson?

MAFIA CONFESSIONS

- *"Hollywood is murdering its movie stars"*

Randy Quaid is an Oscar-nominated and Golden Glove winning Hollywood veteran and his wife Evi Quaid is a former model and one-time Hollywood "It Girl." Today, however, they are both fugitives from the law in Canada, having once sought asylum in Vancouver, to which they fled in October 2010.

[Quaid's] fleeing prosecution in California and seeking refugee status north of the border because he and Evi, 47,

---

[1920] Nancy Dillon, "Katherine Jackson demands upgraded charge of second-degree murder against son's doctor Conrad Murray," **Daily News** March 23, 2010.

[1921] Daniel Kreps, "Joe Jackson Hints at Michael Jackson Murder Conspiracy, Calls Murray 'Fall Guy,'" **Rolling Stone** February 9, 2010; Sean Michaels, "Michael Jackson was murdered, says his sister La Toya," **The Guardian** June 23, 2011; Katie Hodge, "Michael Jackson murdered for hit catalogue, claims LaToya," **Independent** June 24, 2010; Chris McGreal, "After the tributes, the twist: was Michael Jackson's death murder?" **The Guardian** July 15, 2009; Jermaine Jackson with Larry King, **CNN** June 25, 2010.

believe they are being hunted by Hollywood "star whackers," the same mysterious "they" who *offed Michael Jackson* and Heath Ledger and David Carradine.[1922]

According to the Quaids, Hollywood is home to a "celebrity-killing cult,"[1923] a shadowy cabal of what they called "Star Whackers" who "whack[ed] celebrities for their money."[1924] The Quaids believed that the group had killed several of their personal friends including Heath Ledger and David Carradine and were now targeting Randy. Before Canada's Immigration and Refugee Board in Vancouver, British Columbia they said they were seeking refuge in Canada "because they are afraid of a shadowy group responsible for killing their Hollywood friends."[1925] Evi Quaid told the board hearing, "We feel our lives are in danger." In a Vancouver interview Randy Quaid said:

TODAY

SHARE 5625 · f 𝕏 ✉ ...

NEWS

Randy Quaid, wife flee 'Hollywood 'star whackers' '

Oct. 22, 2010, 3:46 PM CDT / Source: msnbc.com news services

Get the latest from TODAY

Sign up for our newsletter

SUBSCRIBE

Actor Randy Quaid and his wife told Canada's immigration board Friday they are seeking refuge in Canada because they are afraid of a shadowy group responsible for killing their Hollywood friends.

Quaid, 60, and his wife, Evi, were released on cash bonds of $10,000 each after they appeared before an Immigration and Refugee Board hearing in Vancouver, British Columbia.

They were arrested Thursday afternoon in a shopping area of an affluent Vancouver neighborhood on U.S. warrants related to vandalism charges.

The pair told an adjudicator that the actor has had eight close friends murdered in recent years and fear they could be next.

"We feel our lives are in danger," Evi Quaid told the board hearing.

We believe there to be a malignant tumor of star whackers in Hollywood. It's possible for people to gain control of every facet of your life. We're not faking it. I am being embezzled by a monstrous ring of accountants, estate planners and lawyers who are mercilessly slandering me and trying to kill my career and, I believe, murder me in order to gain control of my royalties.

[1922] Nancy Hass, "The Deeply Strange Saga of the Quazy Quaids," **GQ** December 1, 2010.

[1923] "What Happened to Randy Quaid?" **The Week** November 3, 2010.

[1924] Philip Sherwell, "Why actor Randy Quaid and wife Evi Fled the Hollywood 'star whackers' to Canada," **Telegraph** November 6, 2010.

[1925] "Randy Quaid, Wife flee 'Hollywood 'star whackers'," **Today** October 22, 2010.

His wife added: "We are refugees. Hollywood refugees. I genuinely feel these people are trying to kill us. They are businessmen. It's the mafia, it's organised crime."[1926] "Hollywood is murdering its movie stars."[1927] The Quaids believe they are running from a Mob hit; that a former business manager took out a million-dollar life-insurance policy on Randy and hired the Mafia to kill both Quaids, making it look like a murder-suicide.[1928] According to them, this group has done that before:

"They"—the aforementioned Hollywood Star Whackers—"decide, O.K., if we knock off David [Carradine], then what we can do is simply collect the insurance covering his participation in the television show he was working on overseas," Evi said. "It's almost moronic, it's so simple." She said she also suspected Jeremy Piven's falling ill from mercury poisoning was another sign of a dastardly plot by the Broadway producers of *Speed-the-Plow* to collect insurance money. "It was an orchestrated hit," she said. "They could have put mescaline in his water bottle." Jeffrey Richards, one of the producers of the play, declined to comment.[1929]

The Quaids are convinced that their friends Heath Ledger and David Carradine were victims,[1930] but also that "the web of intrigue...somehow involved the death of Michael Jackson and the 'framing' of Mel Gibson."[1931] Michael Jackson was "set up" and murdered by the Star Whackers, they allege.

[1926] Philip Sherwell, "Why actor Randy Quaid and wife Evi Fled the Hollywood 'star whackers' to Canada," **Telegraph** November 6, 2010.

[1927] Mike Von Fremd and Sarah Netter, "Randy Quaid, Wife Seek Asylum in Canada, Saying They Fear for Their Lives," **ABC News** October 20, 2010.

[1928] Diane Dimond, "Hollywood's Nightmare Couple," **The Daily Beast** September 28, 2009.

[1929] Nancy Jo Sales, "The Quaid Conspiracy," **Vanity Fair** December 1, 2010.

[1930] Moriah Gill, "Randy Quaid Claims Hollywood Star Whackers Killed Heath Ledger," **Rare** September 11, 2019.

[1931] Nancy Jo Sales, "The Quaid Conspiracy," **Vanity Fair** December 1, 2010.

"'It's a conspiracy with the police in Santa Barbara,' Evi insisted... '[Santa Barbara Detective Ron] Forney was heavily involved in the Michael Jackson setup,' Evi alleged."[1932] It was in fact shortly after the death of Michael Jackson in June 2009 that the Quiads trouble with the law first occured. The Quaids have a very interesting connection to Michael Jackson. According to Becky Altringer, a private investigator hired by the Quaids, Evi, who reportedly heavily used Demerol, shared doctors with Michael Jackson – *Dr. Conrad Murray! She got her Demerol from Dr. Murray.* "[Evi Quaid] told me she and Michael Jackson had the same doctors."[1933] This "bizarre connection between the couple and Michael Jackson"[1934] means that there is only "one degree of separation between...Evi Quaid and Michael Jackson: Dr. Conrad Murray and His Magical Prescription Pad."[1935]

Another interesting connection with Michael Jackson may be through the Gay Mafia. It seems that at least some of the Quaids' troubles in Hollywood may have begun with a neighborly dispute – with the Gay Mafia. Sandy Gallin was their Beverly Hills neighbor in the mid-2000s. The Quaids believe Gallin was part of a plot to financially scam Randy, and some time in 2006 when Gallin threw one of his famous star-studded parties, the Quaids deliberately tried to sabotage it with music from *Home on the Range* blasted from speakers lodged in trees.[1936] They laughed about what they did that night, but a year later Randy Quaid was permanently expelled from Actor's Equity Association, Hollywood's union.

[1932] Nancy Jo Sales, "The Quaid Conspiracy," **Vanity Fair** December 1, 2010.
[1933] "P.I. Says Evi Quid & Michael Jackson Had Drug Connection: Conrad Murray," **Radar Online** September 27, 2009.
[1934] "P.I. Says Evi Quid & Michael Jackson Had Drug Connection.".
[1935] "Evi Quaid used Michael Jackson's doctor, Conrad Murray, to get Demerol and other drugs," **Starcasm** September 27, 2009.
[1936] Nancy Jo Sales, "The Quaid Conspiracy," **Vanity Fair** December 1, 2010.

Susan Donaldson James for ***ABC News*** makes the ominous observation that, like Michael Jackson "Both rock icon Elvis Presley and movie star Heath Ledger died of combination overdoses."[1937]

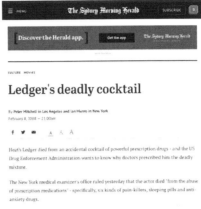

Elvis Presley's was no doubt a Mob Hit via "Death by Polypharmacy" (a syringe job). A New York medical examiner ruled that a cocktail of six different painkillers, sleeping pills and anti-anxiety drugs killed Heath Ledger as well in 2008, just as a similar cocktail killed Michael Jackson in 2009. According to the information the Quaids are attempting to spread, both Ledger and Michael Jackson were killed by the Hollywood Mafia of "Star Whackers." There is strong, additional support to the claim of the Quaids.

- *Frank DiLeo and the Mafia Hit*

All of the suspicious activities that had transpired months and weeks prior to his death played out in my mind over and over again. People that Michael vowed to never do business with again such as John Branca and Frank DiLeo had suddenly been brought back into his life by Randy Phillips of AEG. Michael and I could never figure out why...Michael Jackson, The King of Pop, in my opinion was murdered, and his words still haunt me to this day: "They want my catalogue (music publishing rights) Rowe and they will kill me for it." – Leonard Rowe, Michael Jackson manager

Leonard Rowe, who was close to Joe Jackson, was retained by Michael Jackson in March 2009 to oversee Michael's financial and business affairs and to keep an eye on

---

[1937] Susan Donaldson James, "Friend Says Michael Jackson Battled Demerol Addiction," ***ABC News*** June 26, 2009.

AEG, who had just backdoored Michael with a 50-show tour.[1938] Rowe says that Randy Phillips refused to work with him and instead brought back Frank DiLeo, whom Michael fired years earlier, and then Phi llips practically blackmailed Michael Jackson into accepting DiLeo over Rowe by threatening to "pull the plug" on the London shows and demand all of the advances back if Michael didn't give in.

Leonard Rowe

Randy Phillips knew he had to do something about me, when Michael asked me to come and work with him and to watch over his financials and other business affairs. This also included the shows th at were scheduled for London. Michael told me that Randy Phillips had said to him that he refused to work with Leonard Rowe, and that he was calling in Frank DiLeo to manage him. If he didn't

Frank DiLeo

accept this, then he was going to pull the plug on everything. He knew he had Michael trapped. From that point on, Michael and I began speaking a lot less often. I received a phone call from Michael a day or so later and he said to me, "I want you to meet and work with Frank DiLeo...Randy Phillips and Frank DiLeo claim that Michael had hired Frank DiLeo to be his manager and he was to replace me. I never heard any of this from Michael. When it came to Michael Jackson it appeared that Randy Phillips had a tendency to make things like he wanted them to be without having a signed agreement or a contract in place. I have asked numerous times where is Frank DiLeo's management contract signed by Michael. They surely would have one if

[1938] Leonard Rowe, *What __Really__ Happened to Michael Jackson The King of Pop: The Evil Side of the Entertainment Industry* (n.p.: Linell-Diamond Enterprises, LLC, 2010) 125.

that was Michael's wish, but it wasn't. In my opinion, this was an act forced on Michael by Randy Phillips. Michael told me himself that he would never hire Frank DiLeo again. He could have hired Frank DiLeo before he signed an agreement with me but he didn't. In my opinion, and the words of Michael, this was a move being forced on him by Randy Phillips in an effort to get rid of me.[1939]

So, right before the murder of Michael Jackson, Randy Phillips brought back both John Branca and Frank DiLeo, both of whom were fired years ago by Michael Jackson and whom Michael said he would never heir again. At least in the case of Branca, he was declared an enemy by Michael. No, it is not a coincidence.

Frank DiLeo shared his bosses' Randy Phillips' and Paul Gongaware's disdain toward Michael and total indifference to his heath degeneration. Karen Faye testified in 2013 that during Michael's final days she tried to warn DiLeo about the singer's health *on that fateful night of June 19th*, but his response was cold.

> "Frank was saying pretty much, 'I got it under control, don't worry about it,' " Faye testified Friday.
> "I said, 'But he's losing weight rapidly.' ... I said, 'Why don't you ask [costume designer] Michael Bush to verify taking in his pants and how much weight he's actually losing?'"
>
> Faye said DiLeo went to speak to Bush and she overheard the manager say, "Get him a bucket of chicken." "It was such a cold response," she said. "I mean, it broke my heart."[1940]

Terry Harvey says that he also tried to get through to Frank DiLeo: "I told Frank, '[Michael] needs to get clean first', but

---

[1939] Rowe, *What **Really** Happened to Michael Jackson The King of Pop*, 144-147
[1940] Corina Knoll, "Jackson witness: Answer to health was 'Get him a bucket of chicken'," *Los Angeles Times* May 10, 2013.

[DiLeo] didn't want to know." Terry says he specifically told DiLeo: "You are going to kill Michael." [1941]

Yet, *DiLeo gave Dr. Murray instructions regarding Michael's "medical care"!* This was made evident by a voice mail message DiLeo left Dr. Murray on June 20th, instructing Dr. Murray to get a blood test on Michael.

> I'm sure you're aware he had an episode last night. He's sick. Today's Saturday. Tomorrow, I'm on my way back. I'm not going to continue my trip. I think you need to get a blood test on him. I – I – we gotta see what he's doing. All right. Thank you.

Katherine Jackson's lawyer during the 2013 AEG Live lawsuit, Brian Panish, believed that DiLeo spoke with an AEG executive just prior to making the phone call.[1942] This call was made the day after DiLeo mocked Michael's physical condition with "Give him a bucket of chicken"; the call was made the day after that fateful June 19th day when Randy Phillips and AEG Live decided to "pull the plug" on Michael Jackson. This call was made five days before Michael Jackson was murdered via a chemical cocktail.

On August 24, 2011 Frank DiLeo died, two years after Michael Jackson's murder. DiLeo's cause of death was reported as complications following heart surgery – a surgery he had six months prior. At the time of his death, DiLeo was reportedly *feuding with the executors of the hijacked Michael Jackson estate* – John Branca and John McClain, whom DiLeo *helped with the hijacking.* But a falling out had apparently occurred, such that reportedly DiLeo's last days were "darkened" by his disenchantment with and feuds with Branca and McClain. One reason given for the feud is that DiLeo felt his power and his

---

[1941] James Desborough and Christopher Bucktin, "Michael Jackson could not sing and dance live at the same time, claim emails to be presented in court," **Mirror** May 13 2013.

[1942] Alan Duke, "Michael Jackson manger's e-mails found, could be key in AEG trial," **CNN** May 19, 2013; "Frank's Phonecall," **The Michael Jackson World Network** May 5th, 2013.

money were being cut, and he protested it.[1943] And then he was dead.

There is another reason to be suspicious of DiLeo's reported cause of death. Before he died DiLeo let it slip out that he prepared a manuscript, a "tell-all" book.

DiLeo reportedly declared before he died: "The truth has to be told. *I'm going to set the record straight once and for all.*"[1944] "Frank knew where all the bodies were buried," said an insider.[1945] What sort of bodies might be revealed by this "tell-all"? Mark Lamica, DiLeo's long time business partner, manager and producer, who is in possession of the manuscript, says that DiLeo told him to publish it "if anything happened to him."[1946] Something did happen to him and Lamica is trying to put that book out: ***DiLeo: I Am Going To Set the Record Straight***. Lamica says

> This book...promises to name and shame all of *those who ripped off and used Michael*, including some big names in the music business. It will include details of his dealings with his record label, his Neverland Ranch deal with Colony Capital, *plus a shocking mob hit on Michael* that was stopped by DiLeo. It will also *lift the lid on* the deal

---

[1943] Gatecrasher, "Frank Dileo, Michael Jackson's former manager, fed up with pop star's estate before death: source," **New York Daily News** August 25, 2011.

[1944] "Jackson trial breakthrough," **Page Six** July 8, 2013.

[1945] "Jackson trial breakthrough," **Page Six** July 8, 2013.

[1946] Emily Smith, "MJ had plastic surgery to not look like 'abusive' dad," **New York Post** February 7, 2015.

for his "This Is It" tour and *the final difficult months of Michael's life* (emphasis added – WM).[1947]

This of course implies that there is something hidden under the lid over the AEG deal. According to Lamica, DiLeo shared with him that there was a ***"planned Mafia contract to kill Michael Jackson"***.[1948] Allegedly, DiLeo "managed to stop it from happening." "The Mafia planned to carry out a contract killing on Michael."[1949] The claim is that "DiLeo used his influence to call off the hit."

Whoa. This is an extremely important confession: *there was a Mafia contract out on Michael Jackson!* This of course agrees with Randy and Evi Quaid's claim that Michael Jackson was in fact killed by the Mafia "Star Whackers" of Hollywood. The only difference is that, according to Lamica, DiLeo allegedly got the Mafia hit "called off" while the Quaids say the Mafia Star Whackers actually succeeded in "whacking" Michael Jackson for his money (=catalog). Lamica probably has good reason to add that embellishing (and likely fabricated) detail to the story, that DiLeo called off the Mod contract kill on Michael Jackson: Lamica is probably aware that DiLeo himself was likely killed after threatening to tell "where all the bodies are buried." DiLeo will be the first potential whistleblower who is killed, but he is not the last. Lamica no doubt read the handwriting on the wall and provided some "cover" for himself.

SOUNDING THE ALARM ON THE CONSPIRACY

Dr. Steven Hoefflin at one time was known as "the favorite plastic surgeon of Hollywood celebrities."[1950] This past President of the Los Angeles Society of Plastic Surgeons was Michael Jackson's surgeon for 25 years since 1979 when he performed Michael's first rhinoplasty after the singer broke his

---

[1947] Emily Smith, "MJ had plastic surgery to not look like 'abusive' dad," **New York Post** February 7, 2015.

[1948] Jenn Selby, "Mafia planned to murder Michael Jackson, Goodfellas star Frank DiLeo reportedly claimed," **Independent** February 9, 2015.

[1949] Paul Thomson, "Mafia planned to kill Michael Jackson in mob hit reveals Goodfellas star," **Mirror** February 8, 2015.

[1950] Michael Sheldon, "The man who made Michael Jackson," **The Telegraph** April 2, 2001.

nose while rehearsing a dance routine. It was Hoefflin who performed the skin graft to Michael's scalp after the 1984 burning during the shooting of the Pepsi commercial.

But Hoefflin has another side as well. This UCLA-educated doctor with a genius IQ  worked as a witness for the FBI, DEA, CIA, and the Secret Service. Beginning at least in June of 2008 Hoefflin began exposing corruption within the LAPD. On June 13, 2008 he sent an email to the LAPD leadership warning about *organized crime's infiltration* of the LAPD, LAX Police, and the Sheriff's Department.[1951] According to Hoefflin, while working on "undercover cases" he discovered the problem of "dirty cops" in Los Angeles. He went to California Governor Arnold Schwarzenegger and Daniel McMullen, the Special Agent in Charge of the L.A. office of the FBI. Hoefflin had in the past "work[ed] with the FBI on several investigations..." However, the California "establishment" had now iced Hoefflin: he clearly crossed a line attempting to expose the corruption of Los Angeles law enforcement and its relationship with the Mafia. Less than a week after Hoefflin communicated what he knew to the LAPD leadership in an email, the department's special Threat Assessment Unit was in Hoefflin's neighborhood, officers allegedly confronting Hoefflin up in a tree yelling at them about a conspiracy to assassinate him.

But Hoefflin ultimately proved to be too well-connected to be taken down. As an "established Government Witness" Dr. Hoefflin assisted the State Attorney General's Office of Jerry Brown as a "primary witness" in their Michael Jackson Death Investigation. Hoefflin interviewed 100 persons and examined medical records. He threatened to make public "all of the credible evidence in my possession on *the corruption in Los Angeles Law Enforcement pertaining to the Michael Jackson Investigation*," and to expose members of law enforcement,

[1951] Diane Dimond, "Its Getting Even Weirder," **Daily Beast** August 5, 2009.

claiming to possess "abundant incriminating evidence that is going to put a lot of people in prison."[1952] Claiming to have evidence that various agencies and interests in Los Angeles were colluding to obstruct the Michael Jackson Death Investigation, Hoefflin demanded a cessation of the threats to him and his family. Hoefflin was so sure of his findings that he reached out to his "friend" former Secretary of State Colin Powell asking him to engage a congressional investigation into the LAPD and the Los Angeles Sheriff's Department and the corruption that is taking place in the Michael Jackson and other investigations.[1953]

Dr. Hoefflin's Findings

- Michael Jackson's death was the result of a "large conspiracy"
- Dr. Arnold Klein was part of this "large conspiracy"
- Corrupt elements within Los Angeles law enforcement obstructed the investigation into Jackson's death

---

According to Hoefflin's revelations, he not only possessed the evidence of the role of the corrupt/organized crime elements within Los Angeles law enforcement in obstructing the investigation into Michael Jackson's death, he

---

[1952] Klein v. Hoefflin, Decided April 3, 2012" @https://casetext.com/case/klein-v-hoefflin.
[1953] "Michael Jackson's Doctor Says He Has Evidence to Put People in Prison," *Radar-Online* September 17, 2009.

also possessed the incriminating evidence against Dr. Arnold Klein and his role in the "larger conspiracy" that resulted in Michael Jackson's death itself. [1954] On July 22, 2009 Dr. Hoefflin sent an email to Dr. Klein charging:

Dr. Klein: Prior to his death, Michael Jackson asked you to send me a copy of his medical records. Those records were reviewed and *are now in the hands of the Los Angeles Police Department.*

In your own writing and in your own public statements, is found evidence that you:

(a) Ruined Michael's health.
(b) Ruined his appearance.
(c) Ruined him emotionally.
(d) You caused his Demerol and other prescription pain medicine addiction.
(e) You instructed Debbie Rowe to inject large quantities of Demerol while she was alone in his home.
(f) You prevented him from entering a drug rehabilitation program.
(g) You prevented him from continuing his Dangerous Tour.
(h) You administered IV Diprivan [a brand name for propofol] to him in your own office.
(i) You instructed others to unsafely administer IV Diprivan
(m) You are definitely not the father of his two older children and are making fraudulent claims that you are.
(n) You contributed to the death of Michael Jackson.[1955]

On that day Hoefflin aired his explosive charges in an interview with ***Access Hollywood***:

Dr. Steve Hoefflin, a longtime friend and doctor of Michael Jackson, has claimed that the King of Pop "had lethal amounts of Demerol and Propofol in his body" at

---

[1954] "Plastic surgeon airs conspiracy theory for Jackson's death," ***Mirror*** September 18, 2009.
[1955] Mark Seal, "The Ugly world of Dr. Arnie Klein, Beverly Hills' King of Botox," ***Vanity Fair*** February 2, 2012.

the time of his death...Hoefflin claimed to *Access* that according to a reliable source of his, Jackson's toxicology report indicated Michael "had lethal amounts of Demerol and Propofol in his body" when he died on June 25. Results from the LA Coroner's official autopsy of Jackson have yet to be publicly released...

Hoefflin claimed that the Demerol came from Dr. Arnold Klein – Michael's dermatologist – and the Propofol came from Dr. Conrad Murray, Jackson's personal physician in the weeks before his death. Further, Hoefflin claimed it was Jackson himself who told him about his heavy drug intake — at the time of his intervention. "Michael told me Dr. Klein was injecting him with massive amounts of Demerol" in 2002, Hoefflin claimed...

"Dr. Klein is the one who made his face white by using Benoquin, a permanent bleaching agent," Hoefflin claimed. "[Michael] had Lupus and it was made worse by Dr. Klein's massive injections of collagen. Patients who have lupus should not have collagen... For many years, Dr. Klein was using the very powerful cortisone Celestine to inject into the deep pimples on Michael's face and nose – cortisone injections can thin out tissue in the face. I told him that he should not have any further injections... as it was thinning out his face and nose... [And Klein] was prescribing him narcotics under an alias name, Omar Arnold." ...

Denying the gay allegation, Hoefflin, who Michael lived with the doctor during the time surrounding his 1987 album "Bad," also said he previously took the singer to the Playboy mansion.

"All the time, Michael was commenting on the beautiful women," he said. [1956]

[1956] "Former Jackson Doctor Claims Michael 'Had Lethal Amounts of Demerol & Propofol'," **Access Hollywood** July 23, 2009; "Former Jackson Doctor Claims Michael 'Had Lethal Amounts of Demerol & Propofol'," **KNBC-TV** July 23, 2009.

On July 24 Dr. Klein's attorney Bradley P. Boyer sent Dr. Hoefflin an email demanding that he "immediately agree to retract all false information which you have disseminated about Dr. Klein and not to publish any further such false statements.'" Hoefflin responded by suggesting to Klein's attorney that he and Klein sit down and Klein be "interviewed openly covering his medical records and other materials in my possession"[1957]: "On July 24th, 2009...I invited Dr. Klein and Mr. Boyer to sit down with me and go over all of the evidence that I had on Dr. Klein's criminal activities and that I would delete anything that they proved to be false. I never heard back from them."

Note also that Debbie Rowe, Dr. Klein's long-time nurse assistant, also accused Klein and contributing to Michael's death.

> Michael Jackson's ex-wife Debbie Rowe blamed his former doctor, Arnold Klein, for his death when she first heard about it...She then called him, saying: "What the f**k did you give him? He's dead and *it's your fault.*'"[1958]

On August 26, 2009 Dr. Hoefflin was interviewed by reporter David Willets of *The Sun* and was told that, on the day of Michael's death Dr. Murray called Dr. Klein.[1959] According to phone records, between the time that Dr. Murray initially said he found Michael Jackson not breathing (10:52 a.m.) and the time the Los Angeles Fire Department recorded the 911 telephone call (12:22 p.m.), Murray spent 47 mins on three phone calls – two in-state calls and one out-of-state call. Three journalists and the editor of *The Sun* told Dr. Hoefflin:

> that there were phone records in their possession indicating that Dr. Murray had called Dr. Klein on June 25, 2009 *prior* [to] Michael's Death. I was also told that Dr. Klein was one of the doctors who showed Dr. Murray how to administer Propofol. I had no reason to doubt the

---

[1957] "Klein v. Hoefflin, Decided April 3, 2012" @https://casetext.com/case/klein-v-hoefflin.

[1958] "Arnold Klein blamed for Jackson death," **Contactmusic** July 26, 2013

[1959] David Willetts, "Jacko 'dead 47 mins' as doc made 3 calls," **The Sun** Aug 26 2009; "Lawyers For 'Dermatologist' to the Stars' Argue Against Defamation Case," **Waven Newspapers** June 16, 2011.

veracity of what they said especially in light of the ongoing investigation of Dr. Klein by the Los Angel[e]s Police Dept. I was further advised that they had turned over this information to the police.[1960]

Of course, Dr. Klein and his office personnel (who had now gone into "protection mode" for Klein[1961]) denied talking to Dr. Murray on the day of Michael Jackson's death.

According to Klein, on the day Jackson died, Klein was working with patients. He received no telephone calls from Murray or anyone claiming to act on his behalf. His office manager, Jason Pfeiffer (Pfeiffer) was fielding all his telephone calls, and Pfeiffer was the one who told him about Jackson after a patient called the office with the news.

Pfeiffer explained in his declaration that Klein's office switchboard did not refer incoming calls to Klein but the calls went first to Pfeiffer. When Klein was working, Pfeiffer answered calls on Klein's cell phone. Pfeiffer never received a call from Murray or anyone claiming to be from Murray's office. "More specifically, any statement that Conrad Murray or anyone claiming to be calling on behalf of Conrad Murray spoke to, or called, Dr. KLEIN on the morning that Michael Jackson died is false. I received no such calls and I have personal knowledge that Dr. KLEIN, who spent the entire morning with patients, took no such calls.[1962]

But Hoefflin doubled down. In a sworn declaration Hoefflin claimed that *The Sun* reporters told him that Dr.

[1960]   Klein   v.   Hoefflin,   Decided   April   3,   2012" @https://casetext.com/case/klein-v-hoefflin.
[1961] Mark Seal, "The Ugly world of Dr. Arnie Klein, Beverly Hills' King of Botox," *Vanity Fair* February 2, 2012: ""According to Khilji, Klein's office staff went into protection mode to keep the doctor away from the press. "He really wanted to take the opportunity to go to the media and exploit it," said Khilji. "Our plan was to try to tell him this was not a good idea."
[1962]   Klein   v.   Hoefflin,   Decided   April   3,   2012" @https://casetext.com/case/klein-v-hoefflin.

Klein showed Murray how to administer propofol.[1963] According to Hoefflin, "They [*The Sun*] check their facts with an electronic microscope. There is factual evidence that the statements that I made are true. They have in their possession phone records, recordings, documents and other evidence that confirms facts in their stories before they're published."[1964] Hoefflin thus declared: "I know that one of those individuals that Dr. Murray called during those 47 minutes was indeed Dr. Klein."[1965] Hoefflin said he expected Klein to be "arrested and indicted for contributing to Michael's death"[1966]

Jackson's King of Collagen: I Didn't Help Kill Michael

Dr. Hoefflin presented the allegedly incriminating evidence against Dr. Klein to the executors of the Jackson estate, Howard Weitzman and John Branca, and both stated that "he and Mr. Branca did not condone me providing evidence to the public about Dr. Klein's criminal activities, that may have actually contributed to Michael's death, the very person who's estate they now represent." Hoefflin will later reveal that Weitzman and Branca colluded with Klein's attorneys to protect Klein. At this point – September 2009 – Klein is still a protected "eminence" in Los Angeles and member of the Gay Mafia of Hollywood. Dr. Hoefflin thus got no assistance from the hijackers of Michael Jackson's estate in exposing the conspiracy behind Michael Jackson's death and Dr. Arnold Klein's alleged role in it.

On September 14, 2009 Dr. Klein filed a complaint against Hoefflin alleging causes of action for slander,

---

[1963] "Lawyers For 'Dermatologist' to the Stars' Argue Against Defamation Case," *Waven Newspapers* June 16, 2011.

[1964] "Michael Jackson Doc Sues," *TMZ* September 15, 2009.

[1965] Klein v. Hoefflin, Decided April 3, 2012" @https://casetext.com/case/klein-v-hoefflin.

[1966] Klein v. Hoefflin, Decided April 3, 2012" @https://casetext.com/case/klein-v-hoefflin.

defamation, etc.[1967] In his defense, Dr. Klein through his attorneys told a demonstrable lie:

> "Dr. Klein and Conrad Murray have never met, spoken, nor communicated with each other," read a statement from Klein's attorneys, Richard L. Charnley and Bradley P. Boyer. "Indeed, Dr. Klein did not know that Conrad Murray even existed until his name came out in the press. Further, Dr. Klein did not provide Propofol to Conrad Murray and obviously did not teach him how to administer it."[1968]

Dr. Klein stated in his declaration that "he had never met or spoken to Murray."[1969] As we shall show below, this claim that Klein never met or spoke to Dr. Murray and didn't even know of his existence until his name appeared in the press is wrong, which makes one wonder what the *point* of the lie was.

Responding to the lawsuit filed against him, Hoefflin published a long and very revealing Statement on September 16, 2009. *Mirror* reported that Dr. Hoefflin has made a "series of damning conspiracy-like allegations" that "the King of Pop's death was part of a larger conspiracy."[1970] Below is his full statement.

Statement from Steven M. Hoefflin, M.D., F.I.C.S., F.A.C.S.[1971]

> I am personally going to put a stop to all of the threats on my life and the threats against my family.
> I am now bringing out to the public *all of the credible evidence in my possession on the corruption in Los Angeles Law Enforcement pertaining to the Michael Jackson Investigation.*

[1967] "Michael Jackson Doc Sues," *TMZ* September 15, 2009.
[1968] Josh Grossberg and Claudia Rosenbaum, "Jackson's King of Collagen: I Didn't Help Kill Michael," *E News* September 15, 2009.
[1969] Klein v. Hoefflin,Decided April 3, 2012" @https://casetext.com/case/klein-v-hoefflin.
[1970] "Plastic surgeon airs conspiracy theory for Jackson's death," *Mirror* September 18, 2009.
[1971] See "Michael Jackson's Doctor Says He Has Evidence to Put People in Prison," *Radar-Online* September 17, 2009.

I am going to personally stop all of the threats from the LAPD on my life and the threats against my family. These are occurring because *those members of law enforcement know that I possess abundant incriminating evidence that is going to put a lot of people in prison.*

I am not going to allow and will expose those people who are colluding together, such as Diane Dimond of Entertainment Tonight, with the police to use false documents to threaten me, obstruct my independent investigation into Michael's death and to stop me from providing evidence to the proper authorities.

All of the people that have been threatening my family and I that I have incriminating evidence on are going to be exposed with this evidence in the public eye so they will stop their attempts on my life that I have been experiencing for too long. For me to wait for the slow wheels of government investigations to catch on and bring these people to justice is no longer feasible.

Colin Powell is a friend of mine. I have already called his house and left a message for him. *I am asking him to engage a congressional investigation into all of the LAPD and Los Angeles Sherriff Department Law Enforcement Corruption in Los Angeles that is taking place in the Michael Jackson and other important investigations* that is ruining our city. I want a Congressional Committee to subpoena these people, put them under oath, gather credible evidence for a good District Attorney, and bring them to proper justice. I have already asked Bob Woodward to report on this matter in the Washington Post.

I am going to put an end to these threats now. I owe it to my family. I owe it to myself. But, most of all, I owe it to the public who always wants to know the truth and especially the truth about what happened to Michael Jackson. In reference to yesterday's lawsuit filed against me by Dr. Arnold Klein, *I am established Government Witness in the Michael Jackson Death Investigation.* It is my clear opinion that Dr. Arnold Klein and his attorneys are attempting to prevent me from discussing incriminating evidence that I possess on Dr. Klein.

They know that I have provided this evidence to the authorities. They also know that credible, incriminating evidence is going to be *shortly released in my book.* In my opinion and that of others, they desperately want me to stop any further investigation and to stop providing the public and the authorities the evidence that I acquire. It is my opinion that

Dr. Klein is using a letter with falsified information sent to him by Howard Weitzman, Esq. In July 2009, I was asked to have a privileged meeting with Mr. Weitzman and another attorney.

I shared incriminating evidence that I possessed on Dr. Klein and that he was under investigation by multiple agencies of the Department of Justice. Mr. Weitzman told me that he would neither talk with Dr. Klein, would not provide him any defense, nor would he assist his defense attorneys. On August 1st, 2009, after that privileged legal meeting, Mr. Weitzman prepared a letter with false information to Dr. Klein's defense attorney, Mr. Charnley, in an attempt to discredit me. The false information in his letter was known to be false by both he and Mr. John Branca.

Mr. Weitzman had told me he had discussed it with Mr. Branca. Mr. Weitzman falsely stated that I had no permission nor right to talk about Michael or his mother. He also stated that *he and Mr. Branca did not condone me providing evidence to the public about Dr. Klein's criminal activities, that may have actually contributed to Michael's death, the very person who's estate they now represent.* Shortly after the publication of his letter containing false information, I had left Katherine Jackson's home, and Mr. Weitzman, my wife and I had a telephone conversation.

We requested that he provide a corrected letter to Mr. Charnley, to the media who requested a correction, and to send a copy to me. He already had the hand-written and signed consents from both Michael Jackson in March 1999 giving me permission to publicly discuss his medical records and from Katherine and Rebbie Jackson from July 18, 2009 giving me permission to talk with the media about Michael. He told me that he had discussed the issue with Mr. Branca and that both of them agreed to provide me, Mr. Charnley and the media with a corrected letter. Both of them failed to do this despite having documents proving the information in Mr. Weitzman's letter was false.

On July 24th, 2009, [I] had corresponded about the issue of slander and defamation with one of Dr. Klein's lawyers, Mr. Boyer. I invited Dr. Klein and Mr. Boyer to sit down with me and go over all of the evidence that I had on Dr. Klein's criminal activities and that I would delete anything that they proved to be false. I never heard back from them. His client, Dr. Klein, also had knowledge of my being given consents by Michael Jackson and by Katherine and Rebbie Jackson to discuss

Michael and his medical records. Dr. Klein, all of his attorneys Richard Charnley, Bradley Boyer, Susan Wootton and the firm "Ropers, Majestic, Kohn, and Bentley" together with Howard Weitzman and now apparently John Branca knew of the falsity of Weitzman's letter, yet are attempting to use it in their attempts to bring a frivolous lawsuit against me, obstruct my testimony, and to discredit me.

With this evidence, I have contacted the Attorney General of California, Jerry Brown. I expect that he will put a stay on this lawsuit because he would never allow a court to proceed in an action that would obstruct one of *their primary witnesses (myself) in a federal investigation.* In addition, I expect that he will now open an additional investigation into probable felonies that all of these individuals have committed in attempting to obstruct justice, intimidating a government witness with a document that is known to be false, and possibly other crimes. I believe that with this evidence, I now have a legal standing to bring a lawsuit against all of them, which I certainly will, for possible felonies committed against me.

I am going to start providing the media and Michael Jackson's fans all of the evidence that I have involving *the Michael Jackson Death Investigation, the Corrupt Los Angeles Law Enforcement, and others colluding together to obstruct Justice.* If anyone wants to file another slander and defamation suit, I suggest that they send a copy directly to the Attorney General of California Jerry Brown. Those trying to hurt my family and I should stop because all of the evidence that we possess will not be with us but with the public.

Steven M. Hoefflin, M.D., F.I.C.S., F.A.C.S.
Sincerely,
Steven M. Hoefflin, MD, FACS
Immediate Past President
Los Angeles Society of Plastic Surgeons

THE WHISTLEBLOWER AND HIS DEMISE

Frank DiLeo threatened to "blow the lid" off of the conspiracy against Michael Jackson but he was dead before he could do any blowing (2011), 2 years after Michael's death. Dr. Arnold Klein lasted longer, but his death in 2015 was much more ignominious than DiLeo's. This is no doubt because, before his death, Klein *did a lot of whistleblowing.*

Klein fell hard and fell far from his position of eminence in Hollywood. Once a protected member of Hollywood's Gay Mafia, he fell so hard that even David Geffen could not halt it, even though he offered a lame and transparently disingenuous show of public support during Klein's darkest hour. I think it can be confidently said that Klein's tremendous fall was precipitated by three factors: his emotionalism, his hubris, and his big mouth that came with no filter.

In November of 2009 Klein was still a member of the Gay Mafia in good standing. Certainly, at that time he was still helping to carry out the agenda of the Gay Mafia against Michael Jackson. Part of that agenda was to make Michael "gay" in the public view. This of course was part of the Pedophile's Agenda against Michael. On August 14, 2009, less than two months after his "friend's" death Klein and his office manager Jason Pfeiffer sold a salacious story to the Australian tabloid **Women's Day** claiming that Michael Jackson was gay and he and Jason were lovers.[1972] Klein publicly supported this lie until April of 2011 when he confessed that "Allegations about...Jason being Michael Jackson's lover are ridiculous. *That story was made up...*"[1973] However, up until November 2009 Klein was still peddling that "ridiculous...made up" story about Michael Jackson.

November 5, 2009 I think must be considered the day Arnold Klein crossed the Rubicon River. He spoke for 90 minutes to TMZ's Harvey Levin and there was no way his life

---

[1972] "Clinic worker claims to have had homosexual love affair with Michael Jackson," **The Telegraph** August 21, 2009. Mark Seal, "The Ugly world of Dr. Arnie Klein, Beverly Hills' King of Botox," **Vanity Fair** February 2, 2012: "On April 30, 2010, Klein told the Web site TMZ that Michael Jackson was a homosexual and that Klein's office manager, Jason Pfeiffer, had had an affair with him. Pfeiffer was "the love of [Jackson's] life," Klein said. The television show *Extra* had just aired an interview with Pfeiffer, who declared, "I was Michael Jackson's boyfriend He was very passionate, he was very sexual." On May 1, 2010 Klein called in to Harvey Levin on TMZ Live to support the Pffeifer lie.

[1973] Arnold Klein, "TMZ Torture" Facebook post dated April 18, 2011; "Arnie Klein -- My Buddy Was Not Michael's Lover," **TMZ** April 22, 2011; Mark Seal, "The Ugly world of Dr. Arnie Klein, Beverly Hills' King of Botox," **Vanity Fair** February 2, 2012

could have been the same afterwards. No doubt wounded in some ways by his feud with Dr. Hoefflin and the latter's exposure of him, Klein's emotionalism got the best of him and during that hour and a half that he sat with Levin Klein dug his grave with his mouth. He does lie throughout the interview, mainly to protect himself by obfuscating his crimes; but he drops bombs on others, such that at one point in the interview he knows he has crossed the line and he thinks out loud, "I'll probably get shot on the way out." Here are examples of Klein's lying during the interview:

Levin   Did you know Murray?
Klein   No, I never met him. *I didn't know he existed.*
Levin   Ever talk to him on the phone?
Klein   No. I only knew he existed from Michael telling me he'd met him in Las Vegas...
Levin   And he was treating his kids?
Klein   Yeah, he primarily told me...he wanted to know, very strangely...he called me up and he said what I thought of Afro-American black doctors and I said I don't really judge doctors by color, and he said, "What do you think? Are they good doctors"? I said anyone could be a good doctor. The great doctors are black doctors. I mean, orange doctors, yellow doctors, white doctors. I mean, it doesn't matter the colour, it matters the quality of the doctor. Is he a good doctor? And he said, "He's a cardiologist" he tells me. He was a heart doctor. I said, "Are you sure that he's a good doctor?" He said, "Well, I think he's a great doctor." I said, "Fine, then he's a good doctor" and that's the last we ever discussed Dr Murray until I read his name in the newspaper when everyone knew about him...

Of course, this is just a repeat of what Klein through his lawyers proclaimed in 2009 in response to Hoefflin's charges: "[Dr. Klein] had never met or spoken to Murray." However, in 2015 when the charade was long over Klein admits to having met Dr. Murray in 2007 and throwing him out of Michael's room! Speaking of himself in the third person he says:

Klein went to see Michael In Vegas in 2007 and met Dr. Conrad Murray who Michael said was incompetent. Klein asked Murray to leave and had a long talk with Michael about Propofol.[1974]

Michael had first met [Dr. Conrad Murray] in 2006 and *I threw him out of Michael's room at the Mirage.*[1975]

Klein was thus lying when he and his lawyers publicly proclaimed that he never met or knew Conrad Murray. Also, Levin asks Klein about propofol, which has by this time replaced Demerol in the press as the cause of Michael's death.

> **Levin**   Okay. Did you ever administer propofol to Michael Jackson?
> **Klein**   *Never.*
> **Levin**   Did he ever ask you for propofol?
> **Klein**   Yes. He called me one weekend and he asked me if I would administer propofol and I told him he was absolutely out of his mind.

We know from his nurse assistant since 1977 Debbie Rowe that this is not true. In her testimony during the 2013 AEG Live trial she testified under oath that Klein gave Jackson propofol: "Rowe was a nurse assistant to dermatologist Arnold Klein, who she said provided the painkiller Demerol and Propofol for many of the hundreds of treatments Jackson received over 20 years...[1976]

A final, quite hilarious example of Klein getting tangled up in his lie is this: that he nor his nurse ever injected Michael Jackson with Demerol for minor procedures such as acne in his office:

[1974] Arnold Klein, "Michael Jackson and Arnold Klein," June 21, 2015 @ https://awkleinmd.wordpress.com/2015/06/21/470/

[1975] Arnold Klein, "What Happened to Michael? Live From Los Angeles," October 23, 2015 @ http://mjhoaxlive.blogspot.com/2013/09/it-wasnt-michael-jackson-they-wanted-it.html.

[1976] "Michael Jackson trial: Debbie Rowe cries during testimony," *ABC7* August 14, 2013; Jeff Gottlieb, "Debbie Rowe: Michael Jackson's doctors competed to give pain eds," *Los Angeles Times* August 14, 2013.

Klein   Debbie Rowe treated Michael at Neverland.

Levin   Well, she treated... Debbie Rowe treated Michael Jackson in your office in 1993 and gave him repeated injections of Demerol.

Klein   I don't know if I was even there. You have to understand this is according to records of Steve Hoefflin's trying to say...

Levin   No, no, no, no, no, I can tell you that that's not true. *This is according to records from the Santa Barbara County Sheriff's Department investigation* where Debbie Rowe is quoted by one of the officers, because I've seen the report, and the report talks about Debbie Rowe repeatedly injecting Michael Jackson in the buttocks, *in your office...*

Klein   Okay, I have to tell you one thing...

Levin   *...for acne treatments.*

Klein   No, we don't give...***I don't give Demerol for acne, ever***. She could have done it. You want to know why? Because she treated Michael at different times. Don't forget she posed for...

Levin   She said acne by the way.

So, Klein first tries to deny that he, through his nurse assistant, ever injected Michael with Demerol for acne. Then Levin reveals that Santa Barbara County Sheriff's Department records prove that it *was done* and in *his office*, not at Neverland. Then Klein tries to distance himself personally from the act by declaring: "I don't give Demerol for acne, *ever.*" But then, *this happens.*

Levin   The LAPD has some of the records...

Klein   Yes.

Levin   ...that the Coroner took from the office. At least one of the records involves...it talks about *you filling acne scars and putting him under with Demerol.*

Klein   **Yeah**. *You know how many acne scars he had*? You know how terrible his acne was, that he wouldn't go to school?

So now, the truth comes out! Klein is forced to *admit that he DID* inject Michael Jackson with Demerol for acne – *you know how many acne scars he had?!*

So much for "ever."

But of course, it was not Klein's lies to Harvey Levin that got him into so much trouble: it was his truthful disclosures, surely made in a period of frustration. The two biggest disclosures – at this point more Freudian slips than whistleblowing – have to do with AEG's complicity in the death of Michael and with the three phone calls made by Dr. Murray during the 47 minutes that Michael Jackson lay dead or dying.

> **Klein** I think if we just sit here and we talk about the drugs, it's a terrible thing. I think the horror of this whole thing is that AEG hired Murray, and we will agree with that, will we not?

> **Levin** Well, what do you know about that? I mean...

> **Klein** It was...I read the article in People magazine that AEG hired Murray and I think that if I would hire a doctor for a very famous person I would make sure that the doctor was qualified to be the physician to this patient...

> **Klein** ...I think what we have here though is a situation where this Dr Murray existed and I feel this man is responsible for his death...AEG hired Murray.

> **Levin** Do you think Dr Murray should be prosecuted?

> **Klein** Of course he should be prosecuted I feel, but I think also...*I think the people responsible for hiring him are culpable also because I think they didn't do a background check to know enough...*

> **Klein** ...And then when AEG has every satellite truck around the place, rented, every satellite space rented and then wants to charge us, the City of Los Angeles, it's totally ridiculous. Then AEG films the funeral and they feed it to CNN, don't you begin to think about how much AEG was involved in this? ***I'll probably get shot on the way out but***, I mean, how much is their money involved in this whole thing. And then they own the movie, which they released through John Branca.

Levin　　You're not suggesting there was foul play here?

Klein　　*No, I don't think there's foul play* but I think they're making a lot of money there and I don't think they should have the City of Los Angeles pay for the funeral. That's what I'm saying. Why should we pay nickels and dollars for the funeral when AEG's making money off of this whole thing and rented out the satellite spaces all around the Staples Centre when they filmed this. So I don't think there's anything here but I think they're culpable in this because they should have known the background of Dr Murray when they hired him.

This is pretty stunning. Klein must have developed some frustration with AEG executives, as Frank DiLeo would as well, and this frustration hindered Klein's filter. We do know that Klein was still trying to get not only the $48,000 invoice to AEG Live paid, but he claimed that AEG Live owed him over $100,000 for the work he did on Michael Jackson for them.[1977] So here we have Klein totally impeaching AEG Live's legal covering in the case of the death of Michael Jackson. AEG was claiming that it has no culpability in the death because Dr. Conrad Murray, who killed Michael, was *an employee of Michael Jackson and NOT an employee of AEG Live.* Klein is here saying on national television that it was *AEG* who hired Murray and *shares culpability in Michael's death*, and then made money off of the death! Klein seems to instantly realize that he has messed up: ***I'll probably get shot on the way out but***... He then tries to pull back by saying that there was no foul play. However, once Klein goes *full* whistleblower, he will explicitly reveal the foul play.

And then, the whopper:

[1977] Arnold Klein, "What Happened to Michael? Live From Los Angeles," October 23, 2015 @ http://mjhoaxlive.blogspot.com/2013/09/it-wasnt-michael-jackson-they-wanted-it.html.

Levin ...about a phone call that came to your office during the emergency when Michael Jackson was taken to the hospital, by one of Michael Jackson's people.

Klein Yes. *Frank DiLeo called the office.* Now here's the question that always remains. *Who was called by Dr Murray?* We know I wasn't called, contrary to what a certain doctor said. Again, this lovely doctor said I was called. But who was called? And, I mean, is it public who was called? Do people publicly know who was called?

Levin No.

Klein Okay. But there's been conjecture about many people who's been called.

Levin Right.

Klein And one was a conjecture was that *the head of AEG was called.* That's a conjecture. *One was Frank DiLeo*, who used to be his manager, was called and whoever the third call was, was supposedly a patient who was suing Dr Murray. Okay? That was supposedly what the third call was about and *that's my knowledge.* I can't say for a fact and it maybe a big lie but *that's what I was told.*

I was told one call went to a patient who was suing Dr Murray – that's the first person he talks to after his patient has died, *next thing went to the head of AEG, then* **they talked** *to Frank DiLeo* and those were the three calls. And I know fairly well, *I was assured yesterday* that the first call was to this patient who was very angry. So I don't know where these calls...

Levin What happened when Frank DiLeo called to your office?

Klein Well, he was telling us that it didn't look very good. Now I didn't take the call. I mean, Jason, who's my office manager, took the call.

Levin And what did he say.

Klein   He said that it didn't look very well, it didn't look very good.

Levin   *Did it...my understand is there was something said about what caused Michael Jackson to have an emergency.*
Klein   Yeah, and I mean you have to repeat it...I mean, I wish Jason was around to repeat it but he's not here right now to repeat it...

Levin   Okay, fair enough.

Two extremely important revelations here. The first is that Arnold Klein doesn't conjecture but *was told* and was *assured* of the identity of those whom Dr. Murray called after he killed Michael Jackson with his cocktail of drugs, **before he called 911**: the first call was to an as yet unidentified "patient" of Dr. Murray who was suing Murray at the time. Who was he and *why was he the first call* after Murray killed Michael? The second call after Michael was killed was to Randy Phillips of AEG Live! The third call was from both Murray *and Phillips* to Frank DiLeo, who later revealed his closeness to a Mafia contract hit on Michael Jackson! There is here the *strong* impression that, after killing Michael Jackson Murray called his bosses to tell them: mission accomplished! Only then, after cleaning up the crime scene, did Murray have 911 called. And then we learn that Frank DiLeo *called Arnold Klein!* Thus,

> Murray kills Michael Jackson
> Murray calls Randy Phillips of AEG Live
> Murray and Randy Phillips call Frank DiLeo
> Frank DiLeo calls Arnold Klein

When Klein insists that he wasn't one of the three calls made after the death of Michael, he no doubt is correct and this does not contradict the records in the possession of **The Sun** because their records actually showed, reportedly, "that Dr. Murray had called Dr. Klein on June 25, 2009 **prior** [to] Michael's Death."[1978] This would mean that sometime in the

---

[1978] Klein v. Hoefflin, Decided April 3, 2012" @https://casetext.com/case/klein-v-hoefflin.

morning of June 25, 2009 Dr. Murray called Dr. Klein. At around 11:30 a.m. Murray likely administered to Michael a fatal injection of Demerol or propofol or maybe both, which may have reacted negatively to midazolam already in Michael's system. It is possible that such a reaction caused Michael's death. At this point, Dr. Murray does *not* call 911 but instead calls the "patient" that is suing him, then Randy Phillips, then he and Phillips call Frank DiLeo. Later, Frank DiLeo calls Arnold Klein. It is interesting how Klein shuts down the question above about Frank DiLeo's call, and Harvey Levin seems happy to oblige him.

It was not long before the "powers that be" started responding to Klein's "loose lips." That next month on December 18, 2009 Dr. Klein's former office employee Bruce Ayers, "Dr. Klein's research assistant and confidant," was found dead on a sidewalk. Klein claims he fired Ayers in February 2009,[1979] but he also suspected that Ayers was murdered by his own enemies.[1980] On June 30 2010 the DEA conducted an Administrative Inspection Warrant on Klein's Beverly Hills office, "a rather stringent regulatory examination" in which they "went through all his logs, and did extensive checking to make sure what drugs are being administered to which patients."[1981]

It was 2011 when Dr. Arnold Klein became a full-fledged whistleblower, and the circumstances are pretty transparent. Like Randy Quaid before him, after that 2009 interview Klein claimed to be the victim of a financial conspiracy that forced him to file bankruptcy in January of that year.[1982] While Klein is having a public meltdown, he is spilling all of the beans in the process. In a September 22, 2011 interview with the **Associated Press** Dr. Klein announced he is writing a book

---

[1979] "Michael Jackson's Doc—Ex-Employee Dies," *TMZ* December 30, 2009.

[1980] Diane Dimond, "Doctor Demerol: Michael Jackson Dermatologist Arnold Klein Under Investigation," *Daily Beast* December 5, 2011.

[1981] Roger Friedman, "DEA 'Inspected' Office of Michael Jackson's Dr. Klein Last Week: Exclusive," *Showbiz 411* June 30, 2010.

[1982] "EXCLUSIVE DOCUMENTS: Michael Jackson Doctor Arnold Klein Files For Bankruptcy; Owes Creditors $3.5M -- Read His Petition," *Radar Online* January 25, 2011; Klein v. Khilji, United States Bankruptcy Court Central District of California Los Angeles Division, November 4, 2015 CV15-8713-JAK.

about Michael.[1983] This book "will expose the people whose greed killed Michael" and "even if no one reads this book in this generation I have to leave behind the truth," Klein said. On October 14, 2011 David Geffen breaks his silence regarding his friend's troubles, but says really *nothing*:

> Dear Arnie, in light of all that is being said about you in the press I feel compelled to add my truths. I have never known a doctor who tries to know and learn everything as completely as you do, a doctor who has always been there for me.[1984]

And those were apparently the only "truths" Geffen was prepared to share publicly about Klein, and they do not speak to or even help Klein's current situation. On December 5, 2011 the Medical Board of California subpoenaed Klein, "reportedly for pumping the singer full of prescription painkillers," and his lawyer Herbert L. Weinberg resigned.[1985] Klein's former ally in the press Diane Dimond is now calling him "Doctor Demerol."[1986]

And so, he lashes out with details. Mark Seal, who covered Klein's fall for **Vanity Fair**, reported:

> In his phone call with me, Klein insisted that he's not the villain but the victim of a vast conspiracy. "*If you don't think everything's interconnected—it is*," he said. He implied that the powers behind Jackson's comeback were engaged in dark maneuvers. "A.E.G. was behind the whole thing," he said. [1987]

[1983] "Jackson's Dermatologist Says Murray Fallout Hurts," **The Telegraph** October 15, 2011

[1984] "Jackson's Dermatologist Says Murray Fallout Hurts," **The Telegraph** October 15, 2011.

[1985] "MJ's Skin Doc: The Med Board Is On My Ass...And My Lawyer Just Quit," **TMZ** December 5, 2011.

[1986] Diane Dimond, "Doctor Demerol: Michael Jackson Dermatologist Arnold Klein Under Investigation," **Daily Beast** December 5, 2011; Diane Dimond, "Dr. Arnold Klein, Michael Jackson's Longtime Physician, Courts Substance-Abuse Allegations," **Daily Beast** August 25, 2011.

[1987] Mark Seal, "The Ugly world of Dr. Arnie Klein, Beverly Hills' King of Botox," **Vanity Fair** February 2, 2012.

Klein now comes clean, announcing "I am very much aware of the events surrounding Mr Jackson's death"[1988] and "The Death of Michael Jackson was not accidental...Michael Jackson's death was caused by a group of people or an investment consortium who were more interested in Michael's Immense Music Catalogue than his survival"[1989]; "Michael Jackson's death was caused by a group of people who were more interested in Michael's Immense Music Catalogue than his survival"[1990]; "Michael Jackson's death was about money not him as a performer."[1991] According to Klein, Michael Jackson was "murdered...by an incompetent physician who was nothing short of *a hired hit man* employed by a Rich Entertainment Conglomerate. They only wanted his music Catalogue."[1992]

Klein names names. "Phillip Anscutz is an evil man who was deeply involved in the death of Michael Jackson."[1993] Who is Phillip Anscutz? He is the Jewish billionaire head of AEG, the parent company of AEG Live. According to Klein's revelations, Anschutz was good friends with Tom Barrack (Lebanese Christian parents) who owned Colony Capital, Inc. In 2008 Barrack bought the $23 million loan on Michael Jackson's Neverland Ranch, thus saving it from foreclosure. The terms of

---

[1988] Arnold W. Klein, M.D., "Corrupt Officials Exposed: $30 Million Embezzlement Cover-up Surrounding the Death of Michael Jackson" www.arnoldwklein.com February 28, 2013.

[1989] Arnold Klein, "The truth about Jackson's death, the 2003 Will," June 22, 2015 @ https://awkleinmd.wordpress.com/2015/06/22/the-truth-about-jacksons-death-the-2003-will/

[1990] Arnold Klein, "Michael Jackson and Arnold Klein," June 21, 2015 @ https://awkleinmd.wordpress.com/2015/06/21/470/

[1991] Arnold Klein, "The Destruction and Death of Michael Jackson, the Theft of His Catalogue and Attempted Destruction and Resurrection of Dr. Klein," February 3, 2015 @ https://awkleinmd.wordpress.com/2015/02/03/the-destruction-and-death-of-michael-jackson-the-theft-of-his-catalogue-and-attempted-destruction-and-resurrection-of-dr-klein/

[1992] Arnold Klein, "What Happened to Michael? Live From Los Angeles," October 23, 2015 @ http://mjhoaxlive.blogspot.com/2013/09/it-wasnt-michael-jackson-they-wanted-it.html.

[1993] Arnold Klein, "What really happened to Michael (there is much more)." February 2013 post @ https://www.michaeljacksonhoaxforum.com/forums/index.php?topic=23648.0.

Barrack's rescue of Michael was this: Barrack's Colony Capital agreed to bail Michael out and in return Michael had to agree to allow Barrack's friend, Phillip Anscutz and his AEG, to stage Michael's comeback.[1994] AEG had just completed renovations on their O2 Arena in London and they wanted to open with a series of Michael Jackson concerts. While Michael was not eager to tour again, the terms of Barrack's/Colony Capital's bail out put a lot of pressure on him to agree to the concerts.

Tom Barrack was also co-owner with William Bone of Sunrise Colony, who owned the mortgage on Conrad Murray's $1.2 million mansion in the Red Rock Section of Las Vegas.[1995] Barrack and Sunrise Colony were foreclosing on the property, as Dr. Murray had fallen $100,000 behind in mortgage payments. Murray was indebted to Barrack, and thus beholden to Barrack. So according to Klein, "That is how they found the incompetent Murray to care for Michael"[1996]; "Murray was totally incompetent and hired by Tom Barrack because Barrack was foreclosing on his home in the Red Rock Section of Las Vegas and Murray was up to his neck in debt and had to take the Job. Barrack hired him for Phillip Anschutz of AEG."[1997]

The conspiracy gets deeper, according to Klein's revelations. While the terms of Barrack's bail out of Michael's Neverland Ranch stipulated that Michael agree to allow Anschutz's AEG to stage Michael's comeback with a series of planned concerts, according to Klein *The plan was never*

[1994] Arnold Klein, "What really happened to Michael (there is much more)." February 2013 post @ https://www.michaeljacksonhoaxforum.com/forums/index.php?topic=23648.0.

[1995] Langthorne, *83 Minutes*, 100.

[1996] Arnold Klein, "What really happened to Michael (there is much more)." February 2013 post @ https://www.michaeljacksonhoaxforum.com/forums/index.php?topic=23648.0.

[1997] Arnold Klein, "who killed Michael Jackson?" November 8, 2014 @ https://awkleinmd.wordpress.com/2014/11/08/howard-weitzman-and-the-first-molestation-why-did-you-; Arnold Klein, "The truth about Jackson's death, the 2003 Will," June 22, 2015 @ https://awkleinmd.wordpress.com/2015/06/22/the-truth-about-jacksons-death-the-2003-will/.

for the concerts it was for the catalogue."[1998] Klein exposes:

> Murray was not licensed in England because England was never in their plan.[1999]

> Murray was not Licensed in England? England was never a part of their plan...[They] killed Michael for his Catalogue...[2000]

> They want the Catalogue and [the] person Michael was not totally necessary. The Catalogue was their main interest...The death of Michael Jackson rests on whoever allowed Murray to care for him. He was not licensed in California. For this reason alone Anschutz, Barack, Phillips and Tome Tome should be on trial for Michael Jackson's death as accomplices because commonly criminal offences involve individuals who act at a distance, providing information, transportation, and supplying the Propofol. They all knew what Murray was doing up there for that is the reason the long-standing Nanny Grace quit.[2001]

Actually going to London was "never in the plans." Wow. We said above:

> Why would AEG Live take a healthy Michael Jackson, sign a contract with him for a series of *50 concerts* at *their* newly built arena in London and then deliberately drug

---

[1998] Arnold Klein, "What Happened to Michael? Live From Los Angeles," October 23, 2015 @ http://mjhoaxlive.blogspot.com/2013/09/it-wasnt-michael-jackson-they-wanted-it.html.

[1999] Arnold Klein, "The truth about Jackson's death, the 2003 Will," June 22, 2015 @ https://awkleinmd.wordpress.com/2015/06/22/the-truth-about-jacksons-death-the-2003-will/

[2000] Arnold Klein, "Michael Jackson and Arnold Klein," June 21, 2015 @ https://awkleinmd.wordpress.com/2015/06/21/470/

[2001] Arnold Klein, "What Happened to Michael? Live From Los Angeles," October 23, 2015 @ http://mjhoaxlive.blogspot.com/2013/09/it-wasnt-michael-jackson-they-wanted-it.html.

him to the point of incapacitation? ... The Plan was clearly to drug Michael Jackson and then take advantage of his reduced [mental] capacity. The incapacitation made Michael incompetent to make rational decisions, and this served AEG Live's interests. Michael was indeed *chemically controlled*...A most illuminating illustration of AEG taking advantage of Michael Jackson's mental incapacitation occurred within days prior to Michael's death [- the re-signing of his enemy John Branca].

Klein's revelations confirm our suspicions and gives details. He says:

Additionally, Michael's resigning with Branca makes no sense in that He hated Branca and Sony as I, Lisa Marie Presley and everyone close to him knew. However during the last week of his life Murray had taken to skin popping him with Propofol (which means giving him little or large shots under the skin.) This would make Michael incompetent to make any rational decision. Through these illegal acts, Anschutz, Branca and Weitzman now own Michael Jackson and his catalogue. John Branca was very close to Sony. Sony recently bought Epic so with the amount held by the Prince of Bahrain Michael's Legacy is the property of Anschutz, Branca and Weitzman.[2002]

(Michael) called Branca a Monster a month before he died.[2003]

Now remember Branca=Sony. You know how Michael hated Sony! He was drugged from shots of Propofol by Murray into his muscles. That's the reason he re-signed with Branca. Levin, Philips, Branca, Weitzman did not

[2002] Arnold Klein, "What really happened to Michael (there is much more)." February 2013 post @ https://www.michaeljacksonhoaxforum.com/forums/index.php?topic=23648.0.
[2003] Arnold Klein, "What Happened to Michael? Live From Los Angeles," October 23, 2015 @ http://mjhoaxlive.blogspot.com/2013/09/it-wasnt-michael-jackson-they-wanted-it.html.

care if they got his rights dead or alive. Who bought the drugs [?] AEG. Tell everyone this will is a total fraud.[2004]

Michael's resigning with Branca makes no sense...However during the last week of his life Murray had taken to skin popping him with Benzodiazpines (which
explains the body marks.) This would make Michael incompetent to make any rational decision. [2005]

Thus, Klein declares that Michael Jackson was **"murdered...by an incompetent physician who was nothing short of *a hired hit man* employed by a Rich Entertainment Conglomerate. They only wanted his music Catalogue."**[2006] Klein said the Conrad Murray manslaughter trial in 2011 "was an absolute hoax."[2007]

By 2012, the press was officially declaring of the "dermatologist of the stars" that his own "star has faded"[2008] and they began eulogizing his "dramatic" and even "astonishing fall from grace."[2009] "Everything unraveled for Klein when Michael died" and his "life went into a tailspin and he ended in financial ruin."[2010] Once a very wealthy, powerful "eminence in Los

---

[2004] Facebook comment date June 12, 2011.

[2005] Arnold Klein, "What Happened to Michael? Live From Los Angeles," October 23, 2015 @ http://mjhoaxlive.blogspot.com/2013/09/it-wasnt-michael-jackson-they-wanted-it.html.

[2006] Arnold Klein, "What Happened to Michael? Live From Los Angeles," October 23, 2015 @ http://mjhoaxlive.blogspot.com/2013/09/it-wasnt-michael-jackson-they-wanted-it.html.

[2007] Mark Seal, "The Ugly world of Dr. Arnie Klein, Beverly Hills' King of Botox," **Vanity Fair** February 2, 2012.

[2008] Harriet Ryan, "A-List doctor's star has faded." **Los Angeles Times** January 1, 2012.

[2009] "From chauffeured Bentleys and mansions to foreclosure and insolvency: The dramatic fall of Jacko's dermatologist," **Daily Mail** January 3 2012; "Dr. Klein Michael Jackson's Physician & Friend Dies," **TMZ** October 23, 2015.

[2010] "Dr. Klein Michael Jackson's Physician & Friend Dies," **TMZ** October 23, 2015.

Angeles" with an endowed chair named after him in UCLA's medical school,

> The perfect face Klein long presented to the world is now sagging. The man once touted as the "dermatologist to the stars" is bankrupt. Palatial homes where he entertained celebrity clients are in foreclosure. Mementos bestowed by grateful Hollywood friends are to be auctioned off to pay bills... "The assets that Dr. Klein worked long and hard to build have been decimated"...[2011]

But the financial ruination of Dr. Arnold Klein The Whistleblower was only the opening act.

The four days between Monday October 19 and Thursday October 22 2015 Klein reportedly suffered severe abdominal pains. Finally on Thursday he called 911 himself and was taken to a Palm Springs hospital. However, he had to waite for a bed to become available to him, and while waiting he had a heart attack and died at 7:50 p.m. October 22. The coroner issued a brief press release which failed to mention a cause of death and no investigation was listed.[2012] According to an autopsy report obtained by **Radar Online** Klein died after "suffering in excruciating pain" from a "mysterious" "cocktail of medications" found in his system.[2013] How ironic. According to **Radar Online**, "Eight meds over the three or four his doctor prescribed were found in his system". Further irony: one of the drugs found in Klein's system was midazolam. There was a hole in Klein's bowel, "a side-effect of multiple drug interactions which caused excrement to seep into his stomach." What is the source of these extraneous medications that were interacting in Klein's system? There is a remarkable detail cited in the Coroner's Report:

> On 10/23/15 coroner personnel received disturbing information from Arnold's husband, Shaun Anderson, that he had concerns regarding an incident that occurred

---

[2011] Harriet Ryan, "A-List doctor's star has faded." **Los Angeles Times** January 1, 2012.

[2012] "Michael Jackson's dermatologist Dr. Arnold Klein dies," **CBS News** October 23, 2015.

[2013] " 'Slow Suicide'? Alleged Biological Father of Michael Jackson's Kids Died an Excruciating Death," **Radar Online** April 13, 2016.

in 2014 involving Arnold's caregiver was mixing Arnold's medications. The Palm Springs Police Department interviewed Shaun on 11/28/14. The investigative report was written and was documented as "Information Only."[2014]

Klein had himself claimed to have been poisoned through the unauthorized "mixing" his medications in an attempted homicide. He claimed to have discovered that a potentially fatal dose of the antipsychotic drug Moban was daily hidden in his lunchtime medications by an office worker.[2015] **Radar Online** quotes some interesting reflections of "an insider":

> Now, the insider is demanding answers to what really was happening behind the scene's during Klein's final hours. "Was there no one there to say look you're in such excruciating pain we need to call an ambulance? No. He suffered for four days in excruciating pain so finally 911 was called — and who called? He was the one!" blasted the insider. "Where are these people [who were supposed to care about Dr. Klein] when this guy was suffering for four days?"

> Tragically, Klein died after he had a heart attack while waiting for help in a Palm Springs medical facility. "By the time he got to the hospital he didn't even make it to the bed," said the insider. "The responsibility falls on whoever was closest to him. The [coroner] ruled it a natural death but I think it was a slow suicide." [2016]

Or, a slow homicide.

Nobody claimed Klein's body – no family or friends. For two weeks it remained on ice in the morgue and when the body

---

[2014] Riverside Counter Sheriff – Coroner Division. Coroner Investigation Case # 201510769 November 30, 2015.
[2015] Arnold Klein, "Elder Abuse And Money Laundering Penal Code Section 186.9-186.10," October 28, 2014 @ https://ebolausadotme.wordpress.com/2014/10/28/145/.
[2016] " 'Slow Suicide'? Alleged Biological Father of Michael Jackson's Kids Died an Excruciating Death," **Radar Online** April 13, 2016.

was finally released to a funeral service for burial no burial plans information was given.[2017]

The words of friend and patient of Dr. Klein, Sandy Gallin, regarding the Gay Mafia's "code of silence" comes to mind:

> Gallin admits that because of his place in this family he has been an eyewitness to some remarkable events in show-business and pop history. At one point he muses aloud about the bestseller he may write one day. "You're going to ask a question—why don't I write a book about all my friends and the things I've done? "My answer is: *Where would I live?*""[2018]

That was a code that, ultimately, Arnold Klein couldn't keep and he apparently paid a very steep price for it. However, partly because of Klein's leaky mouth, we know what happened to Michael Jackson.

XIII. *Conclusion: Message For Hip Hop and Black America*

[2017] Regina F. Graham, "The body of Michael Jackson's doctor Arnold Klein remains on ice at the coroner's office," **Daily Mail** October 28, 2015; "Arnold Klein's Body Released for Private Burial," **Extra** November 2, 2015.

[2018] Matthew Trynauer, "Sandy's Castle," **Vanity Fair** April 1996.

The world of Hip Hop was stunned when on December 8, 2019 it was announced that Chicago rapper Juice WRLD died after suffering a seizure at Midway Airport. The seizure was reportedly caused by an accidental Oxycodone and codeine overdose; reportedly he had swallowed several Percocets just before. The autopsy report revealed that Juice WRLD "had several drugs in his blood," including Promethazine and Naloxone.[2019] Juice WRLD's therefore was a "death by polypharmacy." This current generation of rappers is dying young, and mainly by two causes: murder or drug-combination overdose. XXXTentacian was stalked and killed outside a Florida motorcycle dealership in 2018 and Nipsey Hussel was murdered outside his Los Angeles clothing store in March 2019. The Hip Hop trend now is "death by polypharmacy." Before Juice WRLD there was Mack Miller (2018) who died from a "mixed drug toxicity" and Lil Peep (2017), whose fentanyl and Xanax combo put him to sleep and he never woke up. More recently, there was Lexii Alijai (January 1, 2020) who

died of a combination of fentanyl and ethanol. Of course, DJ Screw (2000) died of codeine overdose in addition to "mixed drug intoxication" and 'Ol Dirty Bastard (2004) was likewise killed by "a lethal mixture of cocaine and the prescription painkiller Tramadol."[2020]

Dr. Denise Herd from the University of California Berkley, School of Public Health, studied the changing portrayal of alcohol, drug use, and violence in popular rap songs between 1979-1997.[2021] She documented how "Rap music went from an

---

[2019] *TMZ* January 23, 2020.

[2020] Zoe Zorka, "Hip Hop and Drugs: How Prominent Rappers Lose Their Lives For The High," *Source* December 10, 2019.

[2021] Denise Herd, "Changing images of violence in Rap music lyrics: 1979–1997," *Journal of Public Health Policy* 30 (2009): 395-406; Denise Herd, "Changes in drug use prevalence in rap music songs, 1979-1997," ***Addiction Research & Theory*** 16 (2008): 167-180 (168); Denise A. Herd, "The Politics of Representation: Marketing

art form that warned against the dangers of drug abuse to one that glorifies illegal drug use."[2022] "Despite the trends in contemporary rap music, some writers have pointed out that the widespread focus on recreational drug use in rap music *is a relatively new phenomenon.*"[2023] Calvin John Smiley, writing in **The Journal of Hip Hop Studies**, has coined the term "Addict Rap" and documented a "cultural shift" in Hip Hop wherein the focus has gone from glamorizing the "Drug Distributer" (D-Boy, Trapper) to glamorizing the "Drug Consumer" (the addict)."[2024] Commercial rap now widely distributes a script that *normalizes drug abuse.* There is also a shift in the *types* of drugs glamorized within Hip Hop.

Hip Hop is seeing a shift in the types of drugs used to authenticate the culture, ranging from marijuana and alcohol consumption to pharmaceutical drugs and "purple drank." In addition, the point of view is shifting from the third person narrative to a first-hand account of drug use... Beginning in the early 2000s, a cultural shift occurred in Hip Hop music. In particular, the types of drugs being discussed and the perspective of the user transformed. Songs about substances such as codeine and prescription medicines began to emerge: "Sippin on Some Sizzurp" by Three 6 Mafia (2000), "Purple Pills" by D12 (2001) and "I Feel like Dying" by Lil Wayne (2007). Rappers began to overtly talk about using and abusing pharmaceutical drugs and codeine in their lyrics. While the trope of being a drug dealer remains prominent in Hip Hop music, some rappers have placed themselves at the center, the consumer, of drug substances, whereas in previous decades, drug use in songs was always about the "other." The consumer is no longer an unfamiliar face that is indistinguishable from the next, nor is it the third person narrative. Rather the dialogue has been reinvented (remixed) so that the drug user is from the first-person perspective.[2025]

Alcohol through Rap Music," in **Constructing the New Consumer Society**, ed. Pekka Sulkunen et al. (New York: St. Martin's Press, 2007) 134-151 (139-140).

[2022] "Rap music didn't start glorifying drug use," **UPI** April 2, 2008.

[2023] Denise Herd, "Changes in drug use prevalence in rap music songs, 1979-1997," **Addiction Research & Theory** 16 (2008): 167-180 (168).

[2024] Calvin John Smiley, "Addict Rap?: The Shift from Drug Distributer to Drug Consumer in Hip Hop," **The Journal of Hip Hop Studies** 4 (2017): 94-117.

[2025] Smiley, "Addict Rap?" 100.

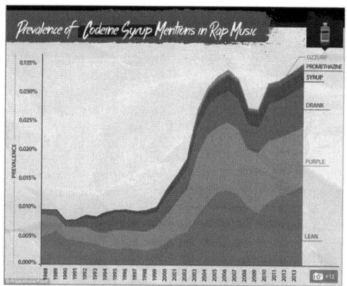

Prevalence of Codeine Syrup Mentions in Rap Music

The charts also reveal that the year 2000 marked the beginning of a steep rise in codeine syrup's inclusion in rap songs. The prescription-strength cough syrup is also known as purple drank. Despite a brief dip in the mention of the drug around 2008, recent lyrics have shown an increased use of the syrup mixed with alcohol, soda, juice, or, as in the case of 'sizzurp,' Jolly Ranchers. Its sale and use has reportedly led to an escalation in crime and pharmacy robberies, added the researchers

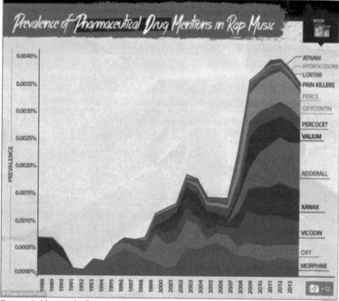

Prevalence of Pharmaceutical Drug Mentions in Rap Music

Pharmaceutical drugs were hardly mentioned in rap songs during the 1990s but over the past 20 years - and in particular since 2007 - their prevalence has soared. Morphine and oxy were the main pharmaceutical drugs mentioned in rap music prior to the mid-1990s. Since then, other prescription medications have become notorious for appearing in hip-hop songs including Adderall and Xanax

Indeed, "Aside from the occasional reference to 'woo blunts' (marijuana laced in cocaine that is then sealed into a blunt wrap), use of drugs other than weed seemed to be something that was not largely accepted until the 2000s."[2026] Codeine entered Hip-Hop largely through Lean in the early 2000s. But since 2007 Hip Hop "has entered its psychedelic age," and references to pharmaceuticals like Molly, Xanax, and even Adderall began to skyrocket.[2027] Compounding the problem is that artists are extolling in their lyrics "mixed drug toxicities." Soulja Boy has two songs, "Zan with That Lean" (2014) and "Molly with That Lean" (2012). Lil Wayne let us know, "And I got Xanax, Percocet, promethazine with codeine" ("Rich as Fuck," 2013). Of course, the most successful – and the most haunting – of drug combo songs is Future's 2017 smash "Mask Off." The hypnotic hook, "Percocet, Molly, Percocet," can "really only be taken as an endorsement of mixing the two drugs which, by themselves already have a high potential for lethal overdose."[2028] Hip Hop producer James Duval noted: "That's a horrible combination of drugs. The whole hook is you having a fucking heart attack."[2029]

A 2015 study published in *The Journal of General Internal Medicine* found that "taking benzodiazepines on top of the narcotics (specifically opioids)" is a particularly dangerous "cocktail" and it multiplies the risk of overdose *eightfold!*[2030] Why is this important for our discussion of Hip

---

[2026] Shaka Shaw, "The Evolution of Drugs in Hip-Hop," *Ebony* September 11, 2013.
[2027] Victoria Woollaston, "How rap reveals trends in DRUGS: Graphs show how hip-hop lyrics plot the rise of illegal substances," *Daily Mail* May 9, 2014; A-Trak, "License To Pill," *HuffPost* May 20, 2013; Adrienne Black, "From Weed to Adderall: New Study Shows Shift in Drug References Throughout Rap History," *Pigeons and Planes* May 13, 2014.
[2028] Sammy Bhatia, "Hip hop culture perpetuates dangerous drug use," *The Johns Hopkins News-Letter* October 12, 2017.
[2029] Sirin Kale, " 'It's a war zone': why is a generation of rappers dying young?" *The Guardian* January 31, 2020.
[2030] Barbara J. Turner and Yuanyuan Liang , "Drug Overdose in a Retrospective Cohort with Non-Cancer Pain Treated with Opioids, Antidepressants, and/or Sedative-Hypnotics: Interactions with Mental Health Disorders," *The Journal of General Internal Medicine* 30 (2015): 1081–1096.

Hop and Addict Rap? When Soulja Boy raps about "Zan with That Lean" he is extolling this toxic cocktail: Xanax is a powerful benzodiazepine and Lean's key ingredient is the opioid codeine. It was this combination that killed Lil Peep: Xanax (benzodiazepine) and fentanyl (synthetic opioid). And, it was likely this very combination that Michael Jackson was *murdered* with: Midazolam (benzodiazepine)

and Demerol (synthetic opioid). Donny Morrison wrote about "Hip-hop's relationship with drugs that make you sleep" and, after noting Lil Peep's case of dying of the overdose in his sleep, admonished: "at the end of the day, loving drugs that make you sleep is only fun if you actually wake up in the morning."[2031]

The very means by which Michael Jackson was chemically controlled so that he can be robbed and the means by which he was murdered – death by polypharmacy - is now the *trendy* social practice in hip hop. And now a whole generation of you rappers – young gods – are being killed the same way – death by polypharmacy. Commercial rap now widely distributes a script that not only normalizes drug abuse but *normalizes the murder weapon that was used against Michael Jackson.* This is not an accident. The same crowd who circled around Michael Jackson is also in control of hip hop.

[2031] Donny Morrison, "The accidental overdose: Hip-hop's relationship with drugs that make you sleep," *Daily Emerald* April 8, 2019.